OXFORD HISTORICAL MONOGRAPHS

Calvinism on the Frontier
1600–1660

International Calvinism and the Reformed Church in Hungary and Transylvania

GRAEME MURDOCK

CLARENDON PRESS · OXFORD

OXFORD

UNIVERSITY PRESS

Great Clarendon Street, Oxford OX2 6DP

Oxford University Press is a department of the University of Oxford
and furthers the University's aim of excellence in research, scholarship,
and education by publishing worldwide in

Oxford New York

Athens Auckland Bangkok Bogotá Buenos Aires Calcutta
Cape Town Chennai Dar es Salaam Delhi Florence Hong Kong Istanbul
Karachi Kuala Lumpur Madrid Melbourne Mexico City Mumbai
Nairobi Paris São Paulo Singapore Taipei Tokyo Toronto Warsaw

with associated companies in Berlin Ibadan

Oxford is a trade mark of Oxford University Press
in the UK and in certain other countries

Published in the United States
by Oxford University Press Inc., New York

British Library Cataloguing in Publication Data

Data available

Library of Congress Cataloging in Publication Data
Murdock, Graeme.
Calvinism on the frontier, 1600–1660: international Calvinism and the
Reformed Church in Hungary and Transylvania / Graeme Murdock.
p. cm.—(Oxford historical monographs)
Includes bibliographical references.
1. Magyarországi Református Egyház—History—17th century.
2. Calvinism—Hungary—History—17th century. 3. Hungary—Church
history—17th century. 4. Calvinism—Romania—Transylvania—History—
17th century. 5. Transylvania (Romania)—Church history—17th century.
I. Title. II. Series.
BX9444.2 M87 2000   284'.2439—dc21   00-022950

ISBN 0-19-820859-6

1 3 5 7 9 10 8 6 4 2

Typeset in Ehrhardt MT
by Alliance Phototypesetters, Pondicherry, India
Printed in Great Britain
on acid-free paper by
Biddles Ltd,
Guildford and King's Lynn

To MUM *and* DAD

ACKNOWLEDGEMENTS

The history of Hungary, and indeed of all eastern Europe, has for too long been unjustly neglected by western writers. Political divisions in the twentieth century restricted Europeans' vision of the breadth of their own continent but, as I hope this book shows, it has not always been so. Venturing far on a road 'less travelled by' has certainly made all the difference to me, and I want here to acknowledge all the support which has made the completion of this project possible.

I want particularly to thank the rector, staff, and students at the Kolozsvár Protestant Theological Institute of the Transylvanian Reformed church who warmly welcomed a stranger within their gates in 1991, and were patient with my faltering steps to learn the dreaded Magyar tongue. From my return to Brasenose College, Oxford, in 1992 I have been especially fortunate to receive wise guidance from Robert Evans, whom I thank for all his encouragement and direction, and for taking the trouble to comment on different drafts of this text. I gladly acknowledge the help which I received as a graduate student from the Department of Education for Northern Ireland. I also want to thank the examiners of my thesis, Gillian Lewis and Katalin Péter. I have gained valuable assistance from many librarians and archivists in Hungary and Romania, and thanks are owed especially to staff in archives and libraries in Budapest, Pápa, Sárospatak, Debrecen, Kolozsvár, and Marosvásárhely. Many thanks also to Juliet Vale and the editorial staff at OUP for their help in the production of this book. The map appears by permission of Robert Evans and OUP from M. Prestwich (ed.), *International Calvinism, 1541–1715* (Oxford, 1985), 168.

This book could not have been completed without the support of many friends from Belfast to Budapest (especially the book-finder general Ružica Maraš and Froukje de Hoop). Most of all I want to thank my family for everything, and this book is dedicated to my parents with much love. Hungarian Reformed ministers chose many different Bible passages to commit their books to God, and I hope they might have approved of my choice: 'For the foolishness of God is wiser than man's wisdom, and the weakness of God is stronger than man's strength' (1 Cor. 1: 25).

CONTENTS

MAP

TABLE

NOTE ON FAMILY NAMES AND PLACE-NAMES

Some Hungarian family names from the early modern period often appear with a variety of spellings. I have followed my preferred choices throughout. All family names will be placed after Christian names, for example Gábor Bethlen rather than Bethlen Gábor as in customary Hungarian usage. Many individuals also have two given names, one of which often refers to a place of origin, as in János Tolnai Dali or Péter Szathmári Baka. I have followed contemporary Reformed writers' usage and employed Hungarian names for most towns in the region, occasionally using German names where appropriate. However, cities and towns were, and are, known to the different linguistic communities of this region by different names, the most important of which appear in the list below.

PLACE-NAMES

Hungarian	German	Romanian	Slovak/Ukranian/Croatian
Brassó	Kronstadt	Braşov	
Dés	Desch	Dej	
Déva	Diemrich	Deva	
Fogaras	Fogarasch	Făgăraş	
Gyulafehérvár	Weissenburg	Alba Iulia	
Karánsebes	Karansebesch	Caransebeş	
Kolozsvár	Klausenburg	Cluj-Napoca	
Lugos	Lugosch	Lugoj	
Marosvásárhely	Neumarkt	Tîrgu Mureş	
Nagybánya	Frauenbach	Baia Mare	
Nagyenyed	Strassburg	Aiud	
Nagyszeben	Hermannstadt	Sibiu	
Nagyvárad	Grosswardein	Oradea	
Segesvár	Schässburg	Sighişoara	
Szászváros	Broos	Orăştie	
Szatmár	Sathmar	Satu Mare	
Székelykeresztúr	Kreutz	Cristuru Secuiesc	
Székelyudvarhely	Hofmarkt	Odorheiu Secuiesc	

Torda	Thorenburg	Turda	
Bártfa	Bartfeld		Bardejov
Eperjes	Preschau		Prešov
Érsekújvár	Neuhäusel		Nové Zámky
Kassa	Kaschau		Košice
Komárom	Komorn		Komárno
Lőcse	Leutschau		Levoča
Nagyszombat	Tyrnau		Trnava
Németújvár	Güssing		
Pozsony	Pressburg		Bratislava
Munkács			Mukačevo
Ungvár			Užhorod
Eszék			Osijek

LIST OF TRANSYLVANIA'S PRINCES

1604–6	István Bocskai
1606–8	Zsigmond Rákóczi
1608–13	Gábor Báthori
1613–29	Gábor Bethlen
1629–30	Catherine of Brandenburg
1630	István Bethlen
1630–48	György I Rákóczi
1648–57/60	György II Rákóczi
1657–8	Ferenc Rhédei
1658–60	Ákos Barcsai
1661–2	János Kemény
1661–90	Mihály Apafi

LIST OF LEADING REFORMED SUPERINTENDENTS, CLERGY, AND TEACHERS

Johann Heinrich Alsted (Gyulafehérvár Academy, 1629–38)
Isaac Basire (Gyulafehérvár Academy, 1655–8)
Johann Heinrich Bisterfeld (Gyulafehérvár Academy, 1629–55)
Jan Comenius (Sárospatak College, 1650–4)
György Csulai (Transylvanian superintendent, 1650–60)
István Geleji Katona (Transylvanian superintendent, 1633–49)
Lukács Hodászi (Eastern Tisza superintendent, 1604–13)
János Kanizsai Pálfi (Western Danubian superintendent, 1629–41)
István Keresszegi Herman (Eastern Tisza superintendent, 1629–41)
János Keserüi Dajka (Transylvanian superintendent, 1618–33)

Pál Medgyesi (Rákóczi family chaplain, 1638–48)
István Miskolczi Csulyak (Zemplén archdeacon, 1629–45)
István Pathai (Western Danubian superintendent, 1612–28)
János Samarjai (Upper Danubian superintendent, 1622–52)
Mihály Tasnádi Ruber (Transylvanian superintendent, 1605–18)
János Tolnai Dali (Zsigmond Rákóczi's chaplain, 1646–1649)

ABBREVIATIONS

DREL	Dunántúl Reformed Church Province Archives (Pápa)
EPK	*Erdélyi Protestáns Közlöny*
ETA	*Erdélyi Történelmi Adattár*
ÉTTK	*Értekezések a Történelmi Tudományok Köréből*
Hartl.	Hartlib Papers, Sheffield University Library
ITK	*Irodalomtörténeti Közlemények*
MOL	Hungarian National Archives (Budapest)
MPEA	*Magyar Protestáns Egyháztörténeti Adattár*
MPEF	*Magyar Protestáns Egyházi és Iskolai Figyelő*
MPEIF	*Magyar Protestáns Egyházi és Iskolai Figyelmező*
PEIL	*Protestáns Egyházi és Iskolai Lap*
RMK	*Régi Magyar Könyvtár*
SNK	Tiszáninnen Reformed Church Province Library Manuscript Collection (Sárospatak)
TT	*Történelmi Tár*
ZEP	Zempléni Egyházmegye Protocolluma (Hungarian National Archives)

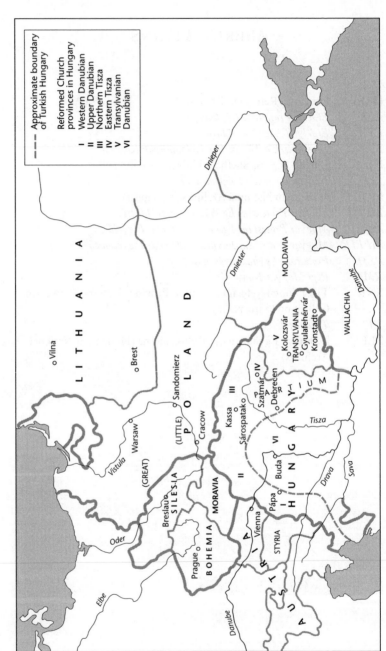

Hungary and her Neighbours, c.1600

Introduction:
International Calvinism

The second wind of Protestant religious reform blew across the Continent from Geneva to France, the Netherlands, the British Isles, Germany, and to central and eastern Europe. Calvinism proved to be an international form of Protestantism, and unlike Lutheranism its origins were not so deeply rooted within a single social and cultural milieu to confine its later expansion. French refugee ministers mostly led the reform of religion in Geneva, and by 1560 the city also had considerable numbers of resident Dutch, German, British, and Italian exiles. The perspective of these refugees naturally extended beyond the Genevan church to their own homelands, and their presence in the city did much to promote a cosmopolitan outlook and culture within Calvinism. Calvinist communities emerged across the Continent during the 1550s and 1560s, adapting to some unpromising surroundings from the Highlands of Scotland to the Transylvanian principality, on the frontier of Christian Europe. Reformed churches in France and the Netherlands had to survive in adverse and threatened circumstances, but proved resilient in resisting the malign intentions of political and confessional opponents. As Reformed churches became more securely established in some German territories and also in the Dutch Republic, Geneva's role within the Calvinist world steadily diminished. After Calvin's death in 1564, and even more so after Theodore Beza's partial retirement in 1580, the international authority of the Genevan Company of Pastors waned. However, Geneva retained a powerful symbolic role as the founding citadel of Reformed religion, and Calvinists across the Continent anxiously took up collections to aid the defence of the city from Savoyard aggression towards the end of the sixteenth century.[1]

Calvin alone among Reformed theologians proved to have a sufficiently broad international appeal and reputation to become an alternative Protestant focus to Luther during the second half of the sixteenth century. Nevertheless, the Reformed tradition resulted from a *rapprochement*

[1] M. Prestwich (ed.), *International Calvinism, 1541–1715* (Oxford, 1985); A. Pettegree, A. C. Duke, and G. Lewis (eds.), *Calvinism in Europe, 1540–1610. A Collection of Documents* (Manchester, 1992); A. Pettegree, A. C. Duke, and G. Lewis (eds.), *Calvinism in Europe, 1540–1620* (Cambridge, 1994).

between Calvinists and Zwinglians after the Zurich Consensus of 1549, and the credentials of Reformed churches across the Continent certainly cannot be judged on the degree to which they faithfully and exactly copied the model provided by the Genevan church. Despite some theological diversity and differences between the structures and practices adopted by urban and territorial churches, a sufficiently coherent core of shared doctrine and patterns of organization was retained to sustain sentiment among Calvinists of belonging to an identifiably international cause. The 1566 Second Helvetic Confession, drawn up by Zurich's Heinrich Bullinger, was eventually recognized by Reformed churches in France, Scotland, the Netherlands, Poland, and Hungary. The 1563 Heidelberg Catechism was also widely accepted by Reformed churches across the Continent, including by the constituting synod of the Dutch Reformed church at Emden in 1571. In 1583 a national synod of the French Reformed church at Vitré marked 'sweet union' with the Dutch church by subscribing to its 1561 Belgic confession, and the French even suggested that the two churches should share clergy as need arose. The appearance of such uniformity amongst Reformed churches in fact had a strong ideological appeal for Calvinists, since it offered justification to claims that their theological insights and doctrinal statements represented universal truths.[2]

A strong sense of unity among Calvinists was established by this mutual recognition of doctrinal confessions, and was sustained by a broad range of contacts which developed between Reformed churches across the Continent. Geneva had been ideally stationed at a crucial crossroads of western Europe to begin such a network of connections along trading routes which serviced the city's developing role as a printing centre. International associations generated by Calvinist merchant families indeed proved important in supporting these trans-territorial linkages. Reformed clergy were also involved, and the Genevan Academy became a destination for student ministers from across the Calvinist world after 1559. A network of Calvinist ministers, teachers, and students built up in contact and communication with one another initially after periods of study together in Geneva, and then later at cosmopolitan universities such as Heidelberg and Leiden.

Fraternal relations between Calvinists were also fostered by a shared experience of the threat, or reality, of physical persecution. Calvinists' experience of persecution and exile intensified a sense of belonging to an

---

[2] Pettegree, Duke, and Lewis (eds.), *Calvinism in Europe, 1540–1610. A Collection of Documents*, 209–10; B. J. Kaplan, 'Dutch Particularism and the Calvinist Quest for "Holy Uniformity"', *Archiv für Reformationsgeschichte*, 82 (1991), 239–56; *The Reformed Confessions of the 16th Century*, ed. A. C. Cochrane (London, 1966).

international fellowship of co-religionists, as more secure Reformed congregations and churches frequently extended spiritual solidarity and generous financial support to suffering co-religionists and displaced refugees. Calvinists also often proved to be temperamentally suited to minority status, with persecution and even martyrdom widely interpreted as a vindication of their faith. The forced exile of Antwerp Calvinists in 1567 only acted to strengthen the development of committed Reformed congregations 'under the cross' in London, Emden, the lower Rhineland, and in the Palatinate. Calvinists could meanwhile become somewhat uncomfortable in the face of success, and Reformed churches made uncertain steps towards adapting to the demands of becoming the public church and dominant confession within some territories.[3]

This international network of professors, ministers, churches, communities, and refugees extended to include princes as well. Calvin's extensive correspondence with royal courts, princes, and nobles across the Continent marked how important he believed international political linkages were to the success of the Reformed cause. Reformed princes were encouraged by their clergy both to champion religious reformation at home and to develop diplomatic policies of international Protestant co-operation. These appeals were often couched in providential and apocalyptic language, as when George Abbot, archbishop of Canterbury, looked forward in 1618 to a Protestant alliance from Scotland to Transylvania so that 'by piece and piece, the kings of the earth that gave their power unto the Beast shall now tear the whore and make her desolate'.[4] This notion of a Protestant cause in international politics was sustained from the French Wars of Religion and the Dutch revolt through to the Thirty Years War. Widespread belief in the papal inspiration of a conspiracy to subvert true religion on occasions led to concerted Protestant diplomatic action mainly against the Habsburgs, who were perceived to be the prime agents of the Catholic church.

The possibility of extending diplomatic and military assistance to beleaguered colleagues was a constant theme of discussions between Calvinist princes. Some historians have been convinced of 'the existence of a

---

3 R. M. Kingdon, 'International Calvinism', in J. D. Tracey, T. A. Brady, and H. A. Oberman (eds.), *Handbook of European History, 1400–1600. Late Middle Ages, Renaissance and Reformation, 2: Visions, Programs and Outcomes* (Leiden, 1995), 229–47; A. C. Duke, 'Perspectives on European Calvinism', in A. Pettegree, A. C. Duke, and G. Lewis (eds.) *Calvinism in Europe, 1540–1620* (Cambridge, 1994), 1–20; H. A. Oberman, '*Europa afflicta*: The Reformation of the Refugees', *Archiv für Reformationsgeschichte*, 85 (1992), 91–111.

4 Quoted in S. L. Adams, 'Foreign Policy and the Parliaments of 1621 and 1624', in K. Sharpe (ed.), *Faction and Parliament. Essays on Early Stuart History* (Oxford, 1978), 147.

political Calvinism, revolving around the organizing power of the Palatinate'. However, there was also much internal argument and prevarication among Calvinist rulers, especially over financing forces to defend the common cause of religion, leaving one historian to write in scathing tones of a Calvinist 'correspondence club of incompetent aristocrats' and raising questions about the real degree of political harmony and unity among Calvinists.[5] Diplomatic and military plans for an anti-Catholic league within the Empire before the Thirty Years War were indeed repeatedly thwarted by the withdrawals of some German princes, and more seriously by the failure of the English, French, or Dutch to live up to expectations and support grandiose plans to challenge Habsburg power, but solidarity between Calvinist princes nevertheless remained more than a product of contemporary propaganda or merely a figment of Catholic imagination.[6]

From the perspective of Reformed churches as well as princes, tensions could exist between the demands of constructing a 'Calvinist International' or concentrating on the development of 'Calvinism in one country'. From Europe's British periphery, it is clear that Calvinists in Scotland held a compelling vision of the unrivalled perfection commonly ascribed by Scots to the progress of reform in their own kirk, which could on occasions overtake ideas about an international Calvinist brotherhood. These two notions did not, however, have to be mutually exclusive, and Highland Scots ministers could think of themselves as both firmly rooted in local Gaelic culture and also proud members of the brotherhood of international Calvinism.[7] In England, James I offered support in 1614 for proposals put before the French synod at Tonneins for a permanent association between all Europe's Reformed churches. Many English divines also established very close contact with continental Reformed churches and universities, and English representatives at the 1618 Dort synod joined in the international defence of Calvinist orthodoxy from Arminian infection.

5 See for example J. Bahlcke, 'Calvinism and Estate Liberation Movements in Bohemia and Hungary (1570–1620)', in K. Maag (ed.), *The Reformation in Eastern and Central Europe* (Aldershot, 1997), 74. Scepticism is expressed by H. G. Koenigsberger, *The Habsburgs and Europe, 1516–1660* (Cornell, 1971), 233.

6 S. L. Adams, 'The Union, the League and the Politics of Europe', in G. Parker (ed.), *The Thirty Years War* (London, 1984), 25–38; J. Raitt, 'Elizabeth of England, John Casimir, and the Protestant League', in D. Visser (ed.), *Controversy and Conciliation. The Reformation and the Palatinate, 1559–1583* (Allison Park, Pa., 1984), 117–45; A. Pettegree, A. C. Duke, and G. Lewis (eds.), *Calvinism in Europe, 1540–1610. A Collection of Documents* (Manchester, 1992), 230–4.

7 J. Dawson, 'Calvinism and the Gaidhealtachd in Scotland', in A. Pettegree, A. C. Duke, and G. Lewis (eds.), *Calvinism in Europe, 1540–1620* (Cambridge, 1994), 253; M. Lynch, 'Calvinism in Scotland, 1559–1638', in M. Prestwich (ed.), *International Calvinism, 1541–1715* (Oxford, 1985), 225–57.

However, relations between the English church and its continental Reformed partners always remained somewhat insecure, perhaps, it has been suggested, since 'religiously inspired nationalism, and ethnocentric enthusiasm, were never entirely absent when English Calvinists contemplated their Reformed neighbours, even if such sentiments were not necessarily directly in conflict with Calvinist internationalism'.[8]

The international perspective of urban, regional, or national Reformed churches could at times be obscured by domestic preoccupations. Calvinist churches were, however, never merely concerned with narrow, parochial affairs, partly because of Calvinism's international origins and ongoing cosmopolitan linkages, and partly because the character of Calvinist religion across the Continent was shaped by an expansive common ideology. Calvinists agreed that their church alone was the true inheritor of the traditions of the early church, and that they held a monopoly on doctrinal truth. Proponents of further Calvinist reformation asserted that the work of the first Lutheran reformation had not yet been brought to completion. This perspective was promoted for example by Abraham Scultetus, court preacher to Johann Sigismund, the Hohenzollern Calvinist convert from Lutheranism. On the prince's conversion to the Reformed cause, Scultetus starkly declared that in Brandenburg 'the leftover papal dung is now to be swept completely out of Christ's stable'.[9]

This work of ongoing reformation by Calvinist churches was marked by a determination to wage war on idolatry and superstition, to become detached from sacramental Lutheran theology, and to advance a strident anti-Catholicism. From adopting a Calvinistic confession, to making changes to church ritual and liturgy, to the introduction of structures to monitor congregational discipline, the building-up of Reformed churches across Europe was also marked by intensive efforts to impose high standards of theological orthodoxy and moral discipline upon society. Calvinist reformers stressed the need both to complete the reformation of Christian theology and worship, and to effect a 'reformation of life' through the exercise of church and community discipline. Calvinist discipline was

---

[8] A. Milton, *Catholic and Reformed. The Roman and Protestant Churches in English Protestant Thought, 1600–1640* (Cambridge, 1995), 410. See also P. Collinson, 'English and International Calvinism, 1558–1640', in M. Prestwich (ed.), *International Calvinism, 1541–1715* (Oxford, 1985), 198–216; P. Lake, 'Calvinism and the English Church, 1570–1635', *Past and Present*, 114 (1987), 32–76; W. B. Patterson, 'James I and the Huguenot Synod of Tonneins of 1614', *Harvard Theological Review*, 65 (1972), 241–70.

[9] H. J. Cohn, 'The Territorial Princes in Germany's Second Reformation, 1559–1622', in M. Prestwich (ed.), *International Calvinism, 1541–1715* (Oxford, 1985), 135–65; B. Nischan, 'The Second Reformation in Brandenburg: Aims and Goals', *Sixteenth Century Journal*, 14 (1983), 173–87.

applied in particular to efforts to reform personal piety, family life, sexual morality, and violent or scandalous public conduct, particularly on the Sabbath and religious festivals. Reformed churches were also distinctive in highlighting the role which local congregational bodies, variously called 'consistories', 'kirk-sessions', or 'presbyteries', could play in achieving these goals.

Reformed religion stressed the importance of uniformity, order, and discipline, but ideas about renewal and regeneration were also central to early modern Calvinism. This was made manifest in such guises as puritanism, attachment among some intellectuals to alchemical projects, and even interest in the supposed 'brothers of the rosy cross', but most prominently in apocalyptic and millenarian expectancy. Calvinists' perception of the satanic nature of the Roman church and expectation of impending divine judgement sustained interest about the apocalypse in many Reformed communities, and especially among refugees. There was a broadly held conviction of the imminence of 'the last days', and of a final judgement which the godly could look forward to. Some theologians even tried to work out the exact date of the end of the world, despite the explicit biblical proscription against such efforts. Contemporary events were routinely seen by Calvinists from an apocalyptic perspective, often tinged by a millenarian optimism which looked for gradual improvements in the state of society towards the end of the world, through increasing revelations of knowledge and potential victories over satanic powers which required political and military activism. Calvinist princes, too, played their apocalyptic role, commonly depicted as Old Testament kings of Israel who would defend the true church in battle until the long-awaited apocalyptic age, when human and divine powers would work in concert towards achieving the ultimate renewal of the church and the world.[10]

So far as the social and political impact of this agenda of religious reform is concerned, Calvinists were not alone in wishing to impose standards of orthodox belief and upright behaviour on reticent and often-unwilling adherents. The Calvinist reformation, together with the late sixteenth-century consolidation of Lutheran churches and the counter-reformation of the Catholic church, have indeed been seen by some historians as part of a single disciplinary process in early modern Europe in three parallel, although distinct, confessional guises. The churches' formation of tighter

---

[10] K. R. Firth, *The Apocalyptic Tradition in Reformation Britain, 1565–1645* (Oxford, 1979); B. W. Ball, *A Great Expectation: Eschatological Thought in English Protestantism to 1660* (Leiden, 1975); G. Murdock, 'The Importance of Being Josiah: An Image of Calvinist Identity', *Sixteenth Century Journal*, 29 (1998), 1,043–59.

regulations on doctrine and discipline mostly ran alongside the centralizing tendencies of the civil authorities of early modern states, and harness-
ing state power often proved essential in the cause of renovating and
directing religious life.[11] This pattern certainly applied to many Reformed
churches, where clergy often acted as partners with state officials in enforcing moral and social controls. Reformed ministers emerged as a well-
educated, and often inbred, professional preaching élite, only too well
aware of the challenges to their 'reformation of life' from competing confessions, passive magistrates, and indifference amongst the general popu-
lace. Such resistance has led some historians to doubt the social impact of
the whole Calvinist reform effort, and suggest that this 'abstract, intellectual religion of the elite' in the end had to be imposed upon the vast majority of the people.[12]

Reformed churches certainly worked wherever possible in alliance with
urban and territorial authorities, a buttress to civil power rather than a
challenge to it. Brandenburg's Calvinists supported their prince's efforts
to impose reform on their overwhelmingly Lutheran nobility, and Calvinism was espoused at the courts of other German princes, attracted both
by its internationalism and by the emphasis on strong discipline. Calvinists
in some circumstances, however, opposed princely authority in favour of
civic constitutionalism, and on rare occasions Calvinists even supported
the extension of political power to nobles in theories of rights of resistance
to monarchical authority. In the Emden 'mother church' of the Dutch
Reformed movement, Calvinist opposition to the Lutheran lords of East
Friesland was complemented by their defence of Emden's civic liberties.
The famous Huguenot monarchomachist writers of the 1570s provided
justification for Calvinist nobles and assemblies in France to oppose the
rule of Catholic monarchs. Alongside such theories on rights of political
resistance to tyrants, Reformed structures of governing lay presbyteries
and clergy synods might lead us to think that Calvinists were in some way
democratic or modern spirits, the kind of radicals who, as their opponents

---

[11] H. Schilling, 'The Second Reformation: Problems and Issues', in his *Religion, Political
Culture and the Emergence of Early Modern Society. Essays in German and Dutch History* (Leiden, 1992), 205–301; H. Schilling, 'Die Konfessionalisierung im Reich: Religiöser und
gesellschaftlicher Wandel in Deutschland zwischen 1555 und 1620', *Historische Zeitschrift*,
246 (1988), 1–45; H. Schilling, 'Confessional Europe', in J. D. Tracey, T. A. Brady, and H. A.
Oberman (eds.), *Handbook of European History, 1400–1600, Late Middle Ages, Renaissance
and Reformation, 2: Visions, Programs, and Outcomes* (Leiden, 1995), 641–81.

[12] R. Po-Chia Hsia, *Social Discipline in the Reformation: Central Europe, 1550–1750* (London, 1989), 154; A. Pettegree, 'The Clergy and the Reformation: From "Devilish Priesthood" to New Professional Elite', in A. Pettegree (ed.), *The Reformation of the Parishes*
(Manchester, 1993), 1–22.

depicted them, could sanguinely contemplate regicide. Calvinists were, however, only induced to consider actively challenging lawfully established authorities when faced with violent persecution, and many Reformed churches in fact exercised hierarchical controls through provincial superintendents. Calvinist churches were able to survive in such a wide variety of political and social environments across Europe by adapting their strategy for implementing core ideas about religious reform to suit differing local circumstances. Viewed from an international perspective, the impact of Calvinism cannot therefore be linked with exclusively moulding either rebellious individualists or conformist absolutists.[13]

Inclusion of the Hungarian Reformed church in analysis of this international Calvinist movement has hitherto mostly been lacking, even among historians concerned to redress the common concentration on Reformed Protestantism in western Europe.[14] The Hungarian church remains the most significant missing piece in our appreciation of centres of Reformed religion. The following chapters seek to establish Hungary's place within the Calvinist world, emphasizing the role played by Hungarians and Transylvanians in international connections which underpinned the development of the Calvinist community. Hundreds of Hungarian student ministers attended western Reformed universities, and Transylvania's princes became engaged in efforts to co-ordinate Protestant powers behind confessional diplomatic policies. Since the notion of international Calvinism was partly sustained by the contacts established between Reformed courts, universities, ministers, and students, Hungary's neglected contribution to this international network urgently needs to be highlighted. The physical distance between the Hungarian church and Calvinist centres in western Europe should reveal much about the strength of Calvinist cohesiveness when it was stretched to the maximum geographical extent. This examination of Hungary's role within the international Calvinist world will also raise further major questions. To what degree, if

[13] B. Nischan, *Prince, People and Confession. The Second Reformation in Brandenburg* (Philadelphia, 1994); H. Schilling, *Civic Calvinism in Northwestern Germany and the Netherlands. Sixteenth to Nineteenth Centuries* (Sixteenth Century Essays and Studies 17; Kirksville, Mo., 1991); R. M. Kingdon, 'Calvinism and Resistance Theory, 1550–1580', in J. H. Burns (ed.), *The Cambridge History of Political Thought, 1450–1700* (Cambridge, 1991), 193–219; M. van Gelderen, *The Political Thought of the Dutch Revolt, 1555–1590* (Cambridge, 1992).

[14] 'When we think of European Calvinism in the early seventeenth century, we tend to limit our sights to Western Europe—the French Huguenots, the Flemish and Dutch Protestants, the Scottish Presbyterians, or the English Puritans. Yet there was also an important strand of German Calvinism.' M. Greengrass, 'Samuel Hartlib and International Calvinism', *Proceedings of the Huguenot Society*, 25 (1993), 464–75.

at all, did reformers in Hungary think of their church as a frontier outpost of a Genevan mission? How important was Calvin's theology in inspiring Hungarian Reformed confessional statements? If Geneva's importance within the Reformed world was already in decline before 1600, which Reformed centres became most influential for Hungarian clergy during the early seventeenth century?

The first chapter will trace the development of Reformed religion in Hungary and Transylvania from the reformation period up to the mid-seventeenth century. The Hungarian Reformed church faced the determined opposition of Habsburg monarchs and an uncertain world bordering on the Ottoman empire. Calvinism survived in the region largely thanks to support from many native nobles and a series of Transylvanian princes. Church patrons and leading clergy worked together to improve the education available for student ministers at western universities and local academies (Chapters 2 and 3), and to bolster the position of the Reformed church against local confessional rivals (Chapter 4). This relationship between sovereign princes, noble patrons, and clergy was at times strained by competing claims for authority within the Reformed church. This tension emerged over the need perceived by some ministers for further reforms to patterns of worship (Chapter 5), over the impact of puritanism and presbyterianism (Chapter 6), over efforts by the clergy to impose moral and social discipline (Chapters 7 and 8), and over the interpretation of prophetic insight about the apocalypse (Chapter 9). This analysis of Reformed religion in Hungary and Transylvania aims throughout to reveal important comparisons and contrasts with the priorities and activities of other Reformed churches across the Continent. Calvinism also played a crucial role in shaping Hungarian politics and society during the early modern period, and Calvinism's impact upon Hungary and Transylvania will be discussed here from a variety of perspectives.

Invasions and revolutions have taken a heavy toll on historical records in Hungary and Transylvania. There are almost no surviving parish records from this period, and detailed consideration of Reformed moral discipline relies heavily on the partial records which remain for only one Hungarian county, Zemplén. Such limitations make the reconstruction of Reformed religion in towns, and especially among nobles and in the countryside, extremely difficult. Whilst gaps in our knowledge will always remain, I hope that it has still proved possible to bring the Hungarian Reformed church out of the shadows and into its rightful place within the community of international Calvinism.

I

The Hungarian Reformation

The success of the reformation in sixteenth-century Hungary was primarily linked to the perceived attractions within Hungarian society of ideas about religious renewal, but was also closely connected with significant political changes of the period, above all the catastrophic collapse of the Hungarian kingdom and dramatic expansion of Ottoman power in the northern Balkans. The triumphant progress of Suleiman the Magnificent's army of 15,000 janizaries and 50,000 sipahi cavalry continued unchecked from the capture of Belgrade in 1521 to the fall of Buda and Esztergom in 1541, until the peace of Adrianople finally brought war to an end in 1568. Among a series of disastrous Hungarian defeats, the battle of Mohács on 29 August 1526 stands out as the day when Hungary lost its last Jagiellonian monarch, Lajos II, many leading nobles, both archbishops of Esztergom and Kalocsa, five bishops, and more than three-quarters of its army. In the aftermath of this unmitigated calamity, two rival kings were elected to succeed Lajos and try to reverse Hungary's fortunes; János Zápolyai, from 1510 governor of Transylvania, and the Habsburg archduke, Ferdinand, who claimed succession through his marriage to Lajos's sister and his sister's marriage to Lajos. In the remaining parts of Hungary not occupied by the Ottomans, surviving Hungarian nobles were largely left to maintain order, grabbing vacated ecclesiastical lands without censure from either of the rival monarchs, both of whom were anxious to garner their support. Hungary was then divided into three parts, with southern and central counties under Ottoman occupation, a 'western kingdom' under Habsburg control extending in an arc running from the Croatian coast to the mountains of Upper Hungary, and the 'eastern kingdom' under Zápolyai, incorporating Transylvania (*partes transilvanicae regni Hungariae*) and eight counties to the east of the Tisza River on the Hungarian plain, known as the Partium (*partium regni Hungariae*).[1]

---

[1] Á. R. Várkonyi (ed.), *Magyarország története* [gen. ed. P. Zs. Pach, 10 vols.], *iii pts 1–2 (1526–1686)* (Budapest, 1987) (hereafter *Magyarország története*); B. Hóman and Gy. Szekfű, *Magyar történet* (5 vols.; Budapest, 1935–6), iii–iv; K. Benda (ed.), *Magyarország történeti kronológiája, 2 (1526–1848)* (Budapest, 1989); P. F. Sugar, *Southeastern Europe under Ottoman rule, 1354–1804* (A History of East Central Europe, 5; London, 1977), 142–67.

There had been some humanist activity and Lutheran influences at the Hungarian court of the early 1520s, and the Hungarian diet was sufficiently concerned about clergy connections with German academic centres to pass measures to punish heretics in 1523. Religious as well as political division swiftly followed in the wake of military defeat, with support for religious reform often driven by a desire to purify the Catholic church, whose spiritual power was badly discredited by the Ottoman invasion. Catholic church structures were in any case badly disrupted in war-affected areas, where there was little institutional resistance to the spread of reform. Initially, Protestant ideas of roughly Lutheran origin made an impact in Hungary, with reform-minded clergy often influenced by study at Cracow and at German universities, including Wittenberg. German-speaking towns were the first to be infected with Protestantism, as itinerant preaching clergy and merchants moved between the towns of Upper Hungary and Transylvania during the 1530s and 1540s. Local ministers who became disaffected with Catholic theology and traditional ritual received a sympathetic hearing almost everywhere from urban magistrates. The German towns of Upper Hungary had already adopted a variant of the Lutheran Augsburg Confession by 1544, a position which they then anxiously defended against the 1548 Hungarian diet's clear denunciation of 'sacramentarian' views of the Eucharist as a mere memorial of Christ's death. Meanwhile in Transylvania, Johannes Honter, who had studied and worked at Cracow, Vienna, and Basel, introduced Lutheran liturgical changes at Kronstadt which were quickly copied in Transylvania's other German 'Saxon' towns.[2]

Communication barriers delayed the spread of ideas about religious reform to non-Germans in Hungary and Transylvania, which meant that Magyars were mostly exposed to heterodox ideas when southern German and Swiss cities were the most dynamic continental centres of Protestant reform. Thus, whilst Lutheran influences were strong amongst early Hungarian reformers, parish clergy who abandoned the Catholic church during the middle decades of the sixteenth century were on the whole drawn towards Reformed religion. Differences between German and Hungarian reformers in the region were accentuated by Lutheran towns' anxiety to avoid being linked with Hungarian Protestants, and thereby risk being tainted by association with outlawed sacramentarian views on

---

[2] M. Bucsay, *Der Protestantismus in Ungarn, 1521–1798. Ungarns Reformationskirchen in Geschichte und Gegenwart, 1. Im Zeitalter der Reformation, Gegenreformation und katholischen Reform* (Vienna, 1977); D. P. Daniel, 'Hungary', in A. Pettegree (ed.), *The Early Reformation in Europe* (Cambridge, 1992), 49–69.

communion. A Hungarian Reformed church gradually emerged from the late 1550s, distinctive primarily through its adherence to Calvinist explanations of the sacraments, and particularly by denying that Christ's body and blood were really present in the bread and wine which rather provided 'signs and tokens' of Christ's sacrifice and of the forgiveness of sins. However, contact between Hungary and Geneva remained irregular, and when synods of Hungarian ministers agreed on confessional statements in the 1560s they proved to be rather eclectic mixtures of Calvinist, Bezan, Zwinglian, and some Melanchthonian ideas.[3]

Hungarian reformers were not as reliant as their German colleagues upon the support of urban magistrates, looking instead to great noble families for patronage. There were large numbers of legally privileged landowners in Hungary, forming over 5 per cent of the population. Among the ranks of these nobles, a small number of significant magnate families dominated Hungarian county society.[4] Reformers gained support from some of these powerful lords. In western Hungary, Mihály Sztárai received protection from the Török family, whilst Mátyás Dévai Biró was backed by Tamás Nádasdy. Magnates in eastern Hungary such as the Thurzós, Péter Perényi, Gáspár Drágfi, György Ecsedi Báthori, and Péter Petrovics also aided reform-minded preachers including István Szegedi Kis, Márton Kálmáncsehi, and Péter Méliusz Juhász.

Whilst some individual nobles undoubtedly became convinced about the need for religious renewal, broad support from the Hungarian nobility for Protestant reform also reflected continued insecurity about Ottoman power in the region and discontent with Habsburg rule. Nobles were anxious to defend their corporate privileges against the growing claims of crown sovereignty, and this concern found new focus from the middle decades of the century on the need to defend rights of religious liberty. Reformed religion also gained strong support in the market towns of the Partium, particularly at Debrecen during the 1550s under the leadership of Márton Kálmáncsehi. The mass desertion of ordinary clergy and their parishioners from the Catholic church in this area was marked by enthusiasm for a religion purified of idolatry, as a response to the perception

---

3 J. Zoványi, *A reformáczió magyarországon 1565-ig* (Budapest, 1921); R. J. W. Evans, 'Calvinism in East Central Europe: Hungary and Her Neighbours', in M. Prestwich (ed.), *International Calvinism, 1541–1715* (Oxford, 1985), 167–96; K. Péter, 'Hungary', in R. Scribner, R. Porter, and M. Teich (eds.), *The Reformation in National Context* (Cambridge, 1994), 155–68; W. Toth, 'Highlights of the Hungarian Reformation', *Church History*, 9 (1940), 141–56.

4 O. Subtelny, *Domination of Eastern Europe. Native Nobilities and Foreign Absolutism* (Gloucester, 1986); R. Kann and Z. David, *The Peoples of the Eastern Habsburg Lands, 1526–1918* (A History of East Central Europe, 6; London, 1984).

of divine judgement in the Turkish invasion and ongoing occupation of Hungary. Reformed ministers, meeting at Debrecen in 1567, described Catholics as having abandoned God's ways for their own traditions and superstitions, and preachers proclaimed the imminent destruction of the papal Antichrist. One popular prophet even raised a holy army in 1570, which marched out from Debrecen to its destruction at the hands of the nearby Ottoman garrison at Törökszentmiklós.[5]

The Habsburgs attempted to reunite the Christian parts of Hungary under their rule from the 1520s onwards, but were repeatedly thwarted. The 1538 Nagyvárad treaty contained the provision that after János Zápolyai died, his eastern kingdom would return to Ferdinand's control. However, when János died in 1539 only months after marrying Isabella, daughter of the Polish king, this treaty was ignored. Ottoman intervention supported Isabella's determined defence of her infant son's rights, and agreement was only finally reached in 1570 between Emperor Maximilian II and the childless János Zsigmond Zápolyai on the future relationship between their two territories. Maximilian accepted János Zsigmond's authority as prince over Transylvania and the Partium (he was styled *Dei gratia Transylvaniae princeps, partium regni Hungariae dominus, Siculorum comes*), and in return János Zsigmond abandoned all claims to kingship over the whole Hungarian kingdom and recognized Habsburg suzerainty over his principality.

When János Zsigmond died in 1571 the Transylvanian diet again overlooked Habsburg claims of succession, and instead elected István Báthori as their new prince (Báthori was also elected king of Poland in 1576). The diet accepted Ottoman suzerainty over the principality, and agreed to pay annual tribute to the Porte of some 10,000 ducats. The division between Habsburg Royal Hungary and the Transylvanian principality began to solidify after 1570, and from the late sixteenth century the writ of Transylvania's princes ran over around 1 million people from the eastern Carpathian mountains to the plains and semi-independent market towns of the Partium, and into periodic control of contested counties in Upper Hungary. Despite being lodged somewhat precariously between the Habsburg monarchy and Ottoman-dominated territories in southern Hungary, Moldavia, and Wallachia, the principality retained its semi-autonomous status under loose Ottoman overlordship until the end of the seventeenth century.[6]

---

5 Gáspár Heltai, *Két könyv minden országoknak és királyoknak jó és gonosz szerencséjeknek okairól* (Debrecen, 1563); I. Révész, 'Debrecen lelki válsága 1561–1571', in *ÉTTK* 25/6 (Budapest, 1936).

6 The Transylvanian principality had seven counties (Hunyad, Fehér, Torda, Küküllő, Kolozs, Doboka, and Belső-Szolnok) with a population of 450,000, along with 150,000 people

During the latter part of the sixteenth century the Hungarian Reformed church developed according to the different circumstances prevailing within the Transylvanian principality and Habsburg Royal Hungary, and each of these areas will now be considered in turn. Transylvania had acted as the eastern defence buffer of the medieval Hungarian kingdom, governed by a royal officer, or voivode. Transylvania's princes retained many of the powers of these previous voivodes, for example to select and dismiss members of their council. Princes also had the right to choose county sheriffs, except in the Saxon lands, and received support from a normally pliant diet. Selected 'regalist' nobles, princely officials, and representatives from towns and border forts were joined in this single chamber diet by delegates from the three constituent 'nations' of Transylvania. The role of these political nations dated from the 1437 union of Transylvania's Hungarian nobility, Saxon towns, and Szekler people, with Szeklers gaining their constitutional privileges in return for military service. These three nations represented in the diet adopted varying paths towards religious reform, although confessional loyalty did not by any means become entirely consistently divided between the various political, ethnic, and linguistic groups of the principality.[7]

The institutional and economic power of the Catholic church in Transylvania was not dismantled so much by Ottoman invasion as in parts of Hungary, but instead by the Catholic princes and the diet. The Transylvanian diet agreed in 1556 that all church property within the bishoprics of Nagyvárad and Gyulafehérvár be brought under the control of the prince. This acquisition of church lands bolstered princely power, but maintaining internal stability still required that the princes accept demands within the diet for the legal recognition of Protestant churches. The Saxon towns received sanction for the free practice of Lutheran religion in 1557, and the Transylvanian Lutheran church remained dominated by Germans, although not to the complete exclusion of others. Although the diet outlawed sacramentarian views on communion in 1558, support for Reformed ideas about the sacraments was advocated by Hungarian clergy in a series of

in the nine Szekler districts in the east and 80,000 German Saxons in eleven districts mainly in the south. There was a further independent manor in southern Transylvania of Fogarasföld. In addition, princes controlled a further 350,000 people in the Partium of Máramaros, Közép-Szolnok, Kraszna, Bihar, Zaránd, Arad, Temes, and Krassó counties, and in the early seventeenth century for some time gained seven north-eastern Hungarian counties of Szabolcs, Szatmár, Bereg, Ungvár, Zemplén, Borsod, and Abaújvár.

7 L. Makkai, *Histoire de Transylvanie* (Paris, 1946); G. Barta, 'Az erdélyi fejedelemség első korszaka (1526–1606)', in B. Köpeczi (ed.), *Erdély története* (3 vols.; Budapest, 1988), (hereafter *Erdély története*), i, 409–521; I. Imreh, *Székelyek a múló időben* (Budapest, 1987).

doctrinal debates against local Lutherans. In 1559 Hungarian ministers from Transylvania, the Partium, and Upper Hungary met in a joint synod at Marosvásárhely and agreed upon a statement drawn up by Péter Méliusz Juhász that communion services should be held as memorials of Christ's death. The Reformed credentials of these ministers were more firmly established in 1567 when a synod at Debrecen agreed to the *Confessio Catholica*, or Debrecen Confession, published in 1562 by Méliusz and Gergely Szegedi. The synod also subscribed to Bullinger's Second Helvetic Confession, and the Reformed church was thereafter sometimes described as the church of the Helvetic Confession.[8]

Péter Méliusz Juhász was again involved in a synod of reform-minded ministers which met at Torda in 1563, and in 1564 the Transylvanian diet demanded that Saxon and Hungarian clergy try to resolve contested points of theology. However, when the two sides completely failed to agree, the diet recognized the existence of two distinct Protestant churches in Transylvania, one for Saxons and another for Hungarians. The diet also proclaimed that parish ministers should preach according to the wishes of their local congregations, leaving remaining Catholic clergy mostly to retreat to the lands of sympathetic Hungarian nobles or Szekler lords. The Calvinist church in Transylvania proved to be almost entirely a Magyar affair, although some leading reformers were Saxon by origin, including Gáspár Heltai and Ferenc Dávid, and not all Hungarian-speakers in Transylvania became Calvinists, with others Lutheran, remaining Catholic, or turning in the 1560s to anti-Trinitarianism.[9]

Protestant religion in Transylvania indeed splintered again in the 1560s when a faction of Hungarian preachers raised doubts over the doctrine of the Trinity. After 1565 this group was led by Ferenc Dávid, then superintendent of the Hungarian church. The anti-Trinitarian challenge,

---

[8] [Magyar], *A xvi. században tartott magyar református zsinatok végzései*, ed. Á. Kiss (Budapest, 1881) (hereafter *Zsinatok végzései*, ed. Kiss), 611–12; E. Tóth, 'A második helvét hitvallás története magyarországon', in T. Barth (ed.), *Tánulmányok és okmányok a magyarországi református egyház történetéből. Studia et acta ecclesiastica, 2. A második helvét hitvallás magyarországon és Méliusz életművei* (Budapest, 1967) (hereafter Barth (ed.), *Tánulmányok, 2*) 11–53.

[9] I. Révész (ed.), *A magyar református egyház története* (Budapest, 1949), 25–176; J. Zoványi, *A magyarországi protestántizmus 1565-től* (Budapest, 1977); Pál Debreceni Ember, *Historia Ecclesiae Reformatae, in Hungaria et Transylvania* (Utrecht, 1728), 51–558; Péter Bod, *Historia Hungarorum Ecclesiastica* (3 vols.; Leiden, 1888–9), bks. 2–3; Péter Bod, *Magyar Athenas avagy az erdélyben és magyarországon élt tudós emberek* [1766], in I. Torda (ed.), *Bod Péter válogatott művei* (Budapest, 1982), 237–459; *Zsinatok végzései*, ed. Kiss; D. P. Daniel, 'Calvinism in Hungary: The Theological and Ecclesiastical Transition to the Reformed Faith', in A. Pettegree, A.C. Duke, and G. Lewis (eds.), *Calvinism in Europe, 1540–1620*, (Cambridge, 1994), 205–30.

influenced by Italian and Polish humanist intellectuals, also gained some endorsement from Prince János Zsigmond before his death in 1571. Support for anti-Trinitarian preachers' insistence that there were not three gods came particularly from amongst the Szeklers of eastern counties, and also from Transylvania's Hungarian-speaking towns. In June 1568 the diet met at Torda and responded to this further confessional division by recognizing the constitutional validity of four 'received religions' in Transylvania, and giving ministers the right to teach Christianity according to their understanding of it. Legal status was offered to the Roman Catholic, Lutheran, Reformed, and anti-Trinitarian churches, and freedom of worship granted to their supporters. This Torda agreement was a product of the relative weakness of central political authority in Transylvania and intended to balance the interests of the three nations represented in the diet. Given Transylvania's precarious international position, it was hoped that acceptance of religious division would prevent the implosion of the fledgling state under confessional conflict. In 1572 the diet, led by the new prince, István Báthori, tried to prevent the emergence of any further religious groups in the principality by introducing a decree outlawing any theological innovation among ministers of the four received religions.[10]

Although political calculations were probably decisive in establishing a wide degree of religious toleration in Transylvania, there was also long experience within the principality of managing peaceful co-existence between different ethnic and religious groups. Before the reformation the confessional allegiance of Transylvanians was already divided between the Catholic and Orthodox churches. Although Transylvania's Romanians were not represented as a political nation in the diet, free practice of their Orthodox religion was granted as a privilege by the princes. Whilst some clergy entered into heated arguments about doctrine and liturgy, the legal acceptance of a remarkable plurality of confessions in Transylvania after 1568 fostered local traditions of successfully accommodating religious differences within regional communities, towns, neighbourhoods, and even amongst families. The 1568 Torda diet had described faith as a gift from God which could not be compelled, and religious persecution proved to be minimal in Transylvania. Forced conversions were in any case prohibited by law, and denominational disputes were only very rarely characterized by violence. In 1564 the diet tried to avoid any potential conflicts over the

---

[10] *Erdélyi országgyűlési emlékek. Monumenta comitialia regni Transylvaniae.* ed. S. Szilágyi (21 vols.; Budapest, 1875–98), ii, 374; G. H. Williams, *The Radical Reformation* (Philadelphia, Pa., 1962); M. Balázs, *Az erdélyi antitrinitarizmus az 1560-as évek végén* (Budapest, 1988); Ferenc Dávid and Georgio Blandrata, *Catechismus Ecclesiaru[m] Dei* (Kolozsvár, 1566).

contentious issue of ownership of church buildings, by deciding that churches belonged to the confessional group with majority support (*maior pars*) in each parish. New occupants of churches were supposed to provide an alternative place of worship for any displaced minority. Even landowners with rights to select parish ministers were forbidden to introduce clergy of a different religion from that of the local community. The diet's support for popular involvement in the appointment of ministers helped to sustain the tradition in some areas of annual re-selection of the clergy by their congregations. However, in practice patterns of religious loyalty tended largely to be determined by the rights of patronage and social power of the privileged élite, whether Hungarian nobles, Saxon burghers, or Szekler lords.[11]

Once synods of ministers in Transylvania and the Partium had agreed on formal statements of their Reformed beliefs, they moved to establish regulations on the appearance of church buildings and conduct of services. Articles agreed at Debrecen in 1567 and at Nagyvárad in 1577, and a revision of canons for the Transylvanian church completed in 1606, set out this new pattern of Reformed religiosity which was slowly spreading into the localities. Decoration in churches was condemned in these articles as a cause of idolatry, and images, statues, ornamental windows, organs, candles, and altars were ordered to be removed. There is only very limited evidence of isolated instances of iconoclasm in the region, and the ordered removal of decoration from churches instead took place under the supervision of clergy and church patrons. Some sources do however speak of the 'destruction' of church buildings by Calvinists in Transylvania at Marosvásárhely and Kolozsvár around the turn of the century.[12]

Reformed articles also drew up a new pattern for church services, with an obligation placed upon ministers to introduce vernacular readings from the Bible, and then to preach clear explanations of scripture passages. Reformed clergy were compelled to possess a Bible from the 1570s, and the 1567 Debrecen synod required that ministers introduce regular catechism classes for their congregations. Whilst there was a sharp rise in the production of vernacular books by Protestants from the 1570s, low rates of literacy ensured that preaching and oral instruction rather than books and popular

---

[11] K. Péter, 'Tolerance and Intolerance in Sixteenth-Century Hungary', in O. P. Grell and R. Scribner (eds.), *Tolerance and Intolerance in the European Reformation* (Cambridge, 1996), 249–61; L. Rácz, 'Vallási türelem erdély- és magyarországon', *Protestáns Szemle* (1934), 198–204; Á. R. Várkonyi, 'Pro quite regni; az ország nyugalmáért', *Protestáns Szemle* (1993), 260–77.

[12] Ferenc Nagy Szabó, 'Marosvásárhely Memorial', in *ETA*, i (Kolozsvár, 1855), 71–2; Bálint Segesvári, 'Kronika, 1606–1654', in *ETA*, iv (Kolozsvár, 1862), 190.

pamphlets remained the prime means of transmitting ideas to local communities. The liturgy and ceremony of church services were also altered, particularly the conduct of sacraments. Ordinary water was used for infant baptism, and wafers were replaced by bread and wine in communion services held by Reformed clergy only seven times a year. Liturgical songs were abandoned and vernacular singing of the psalms and traditional hymns introduced, with any references to offensive theological ideas carefully removed. Reformed synods were anxious to establish a clear divide between their services and Catholic rites, extending from the 'scandal' of Protestant burial alongside Catholics in 'Popish, enchanted ground' to drastic simplifications to the way in which religious holidays were celebrated. There is limited evidence on the varying speed and enthusiasm with which local communities adopted these changes, but whilst some ministers complained bitterly about the persistent survival of Catholic abuses, as has already been noted there were clear signs of popular enthusiasm for a purified, reformed religion in some Hungarian towns.[13]

Clergy synods during the 1560s also established the pattern of administration for the Hungarian Reformed church, which retained a hierarchical form of government. Whilst Reformed church government in Hungary certainly developed a very different regime from that in Geneva, it was similar to the organization of other Reformed churches in central Europe. All-clergy synods elected superintendents for each of seven church regions or provinces (egyházkerületek) across Hungary and Transylvania, and archdeacons or seniors (esperesek) were elected for local church districts (egyházmegyék). The Transylvanian Reformed province contained around 450 congregations organized into nine districts, whilst the eastern Tisza church province (Tiszántúl) of the Partium had around 670 churches by the early seventeenth century divided into fourteen districts.[14]

---

[13] Zsinatok végzései, ed. Kiss, 146, 153–7, 189, 196–7, 236–7, 240, 554–5, 574, 586–7, 591–2, 690–5: 'Az erdélyi anyaszentegyház közzsinatainak végzései kivonatban', ed. I. Szilágyi, MPEIF 3 (1872), 1–9, 77–84, 473–479; K. Péter, 'A bibliaolvasás mindenkinek szóló programja magyarországon a 16. században', Századok, 119 (1985), 1006–28; K. Péter, 'A reformáció és a művelődés a 16. században', in Magyarorszag története, iii pt 1, 475–604.

[14] These were the Transylvanian districts of Vajdahunyad, Gyulafehérvár, Nagyenyed (Küküllő), Kolozskalota, Dés (Szék), Maros, Udvarhely, Háromszék, and Fogaras, and the Eastern Tisza districts of Bihar, Közép Szolnok, Szabolcs, Szatmár, Máramaros, Ugocsa, Bereg, Érmellék, Békés, Debrecen, Szilágy, Zaránd, Nagybánya, and Nagykunság. J. Zoványi (ed.), Magyarországi protestáns egyháztörténeti lexikon (3rd edn., ed. S. Ladányi; Budapest, 1977); J. Pokoly, Az erdélyi református egyház története (5 vols.; Budapest, 1904); J. Zoványi, A tiszántúli református egyházkerület története (Debrecen, 1939); J. Barcsa, A tiszántuli év. ref. egyházkerület történelme (Debrecen, 1906), 1–110; K. Kiss, A szatmári református egyházmegye története (Kecskemét, 1878); J. Soltész, A nagybányai reformált egyházmegye története (Nagybánya, 1902).

The Transylvanian prince held powers to confirm selections made by all the Protestant denominations for the office of superintendent, and also granted rights to conduct ordinations and parish visitations. There was some debate within the Reformed church over the exact status of superintendents and archdeacons, and whether they formed a different order of clergy from the ranks of ordinary ministers. The results of some synods in the 1560s looked for superintendents to be appointed as representatives to speak for the church, not leaders who ruled over the clergy. The 1567 Debrecen articles, however, described superintendents and archdeacons not only as the heads of the church, but also as the heads of individual ministers, and over time the status and authority of Reformed superintendents was steadily to increase. Reformed articles also set out the duties and responsibilities of superintendents. The 1562 Debrecen Confession charged superintendents to lead the church in teaching and preaching, and to defend the church against its confessional opponents. Superintendents presided over provincial synods, which alone held powers to alter church canons and ordain new ministers, and were also empowered to call together archdeacons in their province as a clergy presbytery, or *senatus ecclesiasticus*. Superintendents were supposed to maintain discipline amongst the clergy, although various church articles emphasized that they should not act on their own initiative but first consult with archdeacons and other senior clergy. Archdeacons meanwhile organized regular district synods, where financial or other complaints of local clergy were discussed and reports heard from parish visitations. Archdeacons were also responsible for monitoring standards amongst the clergy, and the Debrecen articles recommended that parish visitations should take place twice or three times a year, and such occasions indeed became regular inquisitions into local religious life.[15]

The Reformed church carried widespread support in Transylvania, and especially in the Partium, but could not count upon the active patronage of ruling princes during the sixteenth century. With the backing of co-religionist princes from the beginning of the seventeenth century, the Reformed church could then move to marginalize its confessional rivals. The legal recognition of four received religions in the principality remained in place, however, throughout this period. Enthusiasm waned within the Reformed church for this legal protection of alternative faiths, but a codification of Transylvanian state laws in 1653 again confirmed the 1568 Torda

---

[15] *Zsinatok végzései*, ed. Kiss, 73–285, 563–613, 691–695, 709–22; Ö. Miklós, *A magyar protestáns egyházalkotmány kialakulása a reformáció századában* (Pápa, 1942); Péter Bod, *Smirnai szent polikárpus... erdélyi református püspököknek historiájuk* (Nagyenyed, 1766), 55–95.

agreement, forbade any imposition of religion on the common peasantry, and repeated the *maior pars* laws deciding ownership of church buildings.

Of the other churches, Transylvania's Romanians remained mostly loyal to Eastern Orthodoxy, although there were attempts to stimulate reform among Orthodox clergy, and some Romanian churches were brought under the authority of a Romanian Protestant bishop from the 1560s.[16] The Lutheran church remained secure but largely isolated among the Saxon community, with the Lutheran superintendent's powers confined to Saxon counties. Support for anti-Trinitarianism peaked in the 1570s and internal disputes then weakened the church's position. A radical wing of anti-Trinitarian clergy, known as Sabbatarians, denied the divinity of Christ and began to adopt Mosaic laws. Ferenc Dávid, who led the anti-Trinitarian church, was himself arrested on suspicion of Sabbatarianism, accused of breaking the 1572 law which prevented further religious innovation, and subsequently died whilst imprisoned within Déva castle in 1579. The anti-Trinitarian church was also affected by the diet's decision in 1576 to limit their superintendent's powers of visitation to the areas of Kolozsvár and Torda, leaving anti-Trinitarians elsewhere under the aegis of the Reformed superintendent. Anti-Trinitarianism retained significant support among Hungarian nobles in Transylvania until the turn of the century, when Mózes Székely led many to bloody defeat in the turmoil of the Fifteen Years War. This defeat was soon followed by the triumph of armies under the Reformed noble István Bocskai, who was then able to establish himself as the first Reformed prince of Transylvania in 1604.[17]

The Catholic church in Transylvania only partially managed to recover from its loss of land, church buildings, and so many of its clergy during the mid-sixteenth century, and Catholics remained few in number at the beginning of the seventeenth century. Whilst all the Protestant churches in Transylvania were led by superintendents, the Catholic church had no bishop after 1542 because of disagreement between the Papacy and Habsburgs on rights of confirmation of new appointments. The secularization of church land also gave the princes and many nobles a direct interest in limiting any Catholic revival, with even the palace of the former bishop of Gyulafehérvár converted for use as the main princely residence. Restrictions were placed on the movements and activities of Catholic priests in the

---

[16] K. Zach, *Orthodoxe Kirche und Romänisches Volksbewusstsein im 15. bis 18. Jahrhundert* (Wiesbaden, 1977).

[17] A. Pirnát, *Die Ideologie der Siebenbürger Antitrinitarier in den 1570er Jahren* (Budapest, 1961); S. Kohn, *A szombatosok: történetük, dogmatikájuk és irodalmuk* (Budapest, 1890); M. Balázs, *Ungarländische Antitrinitarier. Bibliotheca Dissidentium, 12. Répertoire des non-conformistes religieux des seizième et dix-septième siècles* (Baden-Baden, 1990), 7–16.

principality until 1581. The diet then offered the church a foothold outside the lands of Catholic nobles, by permitting priests to be selected to serve in towns and villages if they could attract majority support in the locality. In 1579 István Báthori had invited Jesuits to set up schools at Gyulafehérvár, Kolozsvár, and Nagyvárad; nevertheless, although the Jesuits were not permitted to become involved in missionary work, pressure from the diet still forced their exclusion from the principality in 1588. Jesuits were re-admitted but then expelled twice more before 1606, further disrupting the halting progress of the counter-reformation within Transylvania. The lack of leadership for Transylvanian Catholics was partly remedied from the 1610s, when Gábor Bethlen nominated an administrator to oversee the Catholic church, but even then the prince only acted to forestall any Habsburg interference in the principality's religious affairs.[18]

In Royal Hungary, Habsburg kings claimed that they ruled over around 2.5 million people by hereditary right, and incumbent monarchs worked to gain prior acceptance by the diet of successors to the throne. The Hungarian nobility, however, maintained that their monarchy was determined by election in the diet, a principle only finally relinquished in 1687. Nobles clung to the 1514 codification of their privileges compiled by István Werbőczi, who asserted that nobles were 'members' of the holy crown of St István, which alone conferred authority upon those crowned to rule over Hungary. Hungary's kings were supposed to put forward four candidates from which the diet selected a palatine (*nádor*) to mediate between the nobility and their king, to act as Hungary's chief justice and as president of the council. After 1562 Habsburg government operated instead through a carefully controlled regency council at the capital, Pozsony, and the repeated failure to allow for the election of a palatine was a major source of resentment among nobles. Noble indignation could be expressed within the Hungarian diet, where leading magnates had rights of individual representation in the Upper Chamber (*felső tábla*) of the diet, alongside a bench of archbishops and bishops. Gentry representatives from the counties sat in the Lower Chamber (*alsó tábla*), vastly outnumbering delegates from royal free towns and mining towns. The main function of the diet was to grant requests for taxation, and after the two chambers had heard royal proposals, the estates were permitted to respond with their own petitions.

[18] The pre-reformation church had two bishoprics in the region at Gyulafehérvár and Nagyvárad, with the Saxons having autonomous control over their church's affairs. V. Biró, *Bethlen Gábor és az erdélyi katholicizmus* (Kolozsvár, 1929); A. Jakab, 'Az erdélyi római katolikus püspöki szék betöltésének vitája a xvii. században', *Erdélyi Múzeum*, 49 (1944), 5–20; Révész, *A magyar református egyház története*, 81–5. On the Jesuits, see A. Meszlényi, *A magyar jezsuiták a xvi. században* (Budapest, 1931).

The ranks of magnates and nobles who dominated the diet also commanded Hungarian society, with a dozen major magnate families holding vast estates across the countryside. These magnates directed local government through powerful county courts and assemblies. In each court four judges were headed by a crown nominee, the high sheriff (*főispán*), and by the deputy sheriff (*alispán*) who was chosen by the county assembly. Only royal free towns were exempt from the jurisdiction of county courts, whilst the councils of market and mining towns exercised varying degrees of judicial and administrative competence. County assemblies organized contributions for the defence of the kingdom and were responsible for tax collection from the peasantry. Along with the burden of royal taxes, the tithe, and seigneurial dues paid in cash and kind, peasants owed labour dues to their lords which increased during the sixteenth century from one day a week to two or even three days a week.[19]

By the latter decades of the sixteenth century confessional division in Royal Hungary was a social reality, and the vast majority of Hungarians remained loyal to one of the Protestant churches over the next half-century. Unlike the Transylvanian principality, in Royal Hungary the diet was slow to grant legal freedoms to Protestants. Lutherans in royal free towns were offered rights to practise their religion, but royal decrees continued to be promulgated against Calvinists in the 1560s and 1570s. This failure to offer legal status to Protestantism in the sixteenth century obscured and delayed the development of distinct Lutheran and Calvinist churches. Whilst accurate estimates on the exact breakdown of confessional strength are therefore impossible to provide, broadly speaking the royal towns and Protestant nobles of western Hungarian counties were by 1570 mostly Lutheran, whilst Calvinism had gained widespread support from the nobles, gentry, and market towns of eastern counties. Reformed ministers were entirely dependent upon noble protection but, since increasing numbers of nobles were converting to Protestantism from the 1570s, most ministers could easily find local patrons. The Catholic church, although losing support across Hungarian society, remained a much more significant institutional force in Royal Hungary than in Transylvania through episcopal representation in the Upper Chamber of the diet and because the Hungarian chancellor was always drawn from the ranks of bishops and archbishops. Significant efforts were also made to train a new generation of Catholic

[19] R. J. W. Evans, *The Making of the Habsburg Monarchy, 1550–1700* (Oxford, 1979); Kann and David, *The Peoples of the Eastern Habsburg Lands, 1526–1918*, 55–71, 135–52; L. Makkai, 'The Crown and the Diets of Hungary and Transylvania in the Sixteenth Century', in R. J. W. Evans and T. V. Thomas (eds.), *Crown, Church and Estates. Central European Politics in the Sixteenth and Seventeenth Centuries* (London, 1991), 80–91.

priests to replace those lost to the Protestant churches. In 1580 the Collegium Germanicum-Hungaricum was founded in Rome, a new seminary was opened at Nagyszombat in 1590, and Jesuit houses were set up in western Hungary with the aim of re-catholicizing the Hungarian nobility.[20]

Reformed church organization in Royal Hungary developed the same hierarchical structure as in Transylvania, but with weaker centres of power, and based on more scattered congregations than those of the consistent parochial system in the east. Even in the northern Tisza province (Tiszáninnen) of Upper Hungary, where there was strong support for the Reformed church in around 400 congregations, there was a more decentralized system of church government and no provincial superintendent. Reformed clergy in the four county districts of Borsod, Abaújvár, Zemplén, and Ungvár instead only elected archdeacons, who were assisted in their responsibilities by strong clergy presbyteries.[21] The Protestant churches of western Hungarian counties were the last to split into distinct Evangelical and Reformed branches. In the upper Danubian province (Felsődunamellék) of north-western Hungary a separate Reformed church administration only appeared after the Galánta synod of 1592. The western Danubian church province (Dunántúl) of some 130 to 150 churches emerged after the 1591 Csepreg colloquy, called by Protestant patron Ferenc Nádasdy, failed to resolve differences between Protestant ministers supporting Lutheran and Reformed views of communion theology. A Reformed superintendent was finally appointed in 1612 by ministers meeting at Köveskút, who also selected area archdeacons and adopted canons for the western Danubian church. These Köveskút canons asserted the superintendent's authority to call bi-annual synods, conduct visitations, and to discipline disobedient ministers, but only if the superintendent acted with the advice and approval of his archdeacons.[22]

The organization of the Reformed church in Ottoman-occupied Hungary meanwhile made uncertain progress, with strict controls imposed

---

[20] M. Zsilinszky, *A magyar országgyűlések vallásügyi tárgyalásai a reformátiotól kezdve* (Budapest, 1880); I. Bitskey, 'The *Collegium Germanicum Hungaricum* in Rome and the Beginning of Counter-Reformation in Hungary', in R. J. W. Evans and T. V. Thomas (eds.), *Crown, Church and Estates: Central European Politics in the Sixteenth and Seventeenth Centuries* (London, 1991), 110–22.

[21] *Zsinatok végzései*, ed. Kiss, 710–22.

[22] These were the western Danubian districts of Vép, Körmend, Németújvár, Vízlendva, Pápa, Veszprém and Kiskomárom, and upper Danubian districts of Bars, Csallóköz, Komját, Komárom and Drégelypalánk. Zoványi, *Magyarországi protestáns egyháztörténeti lexikon*; [Dunántúl], *A dunántúli református egyházkerület története*, ed. E. Thury (Pápa, 1908). Köveskút canons are to be found in [Dunántúl], 'Adatok a dunántúl és felsődunamellék kerületekről', ed., E. Thury, in *MPEA* 7 (1908), 127–40.

upon Catholic and Protestant churches alike, including some anti-Trinitarians in the region. Letters of approval were required from the Turkish authorities to guarantee the undisturbed practice of Christian religion, limits were placed on the construction and renovation of church buildings, and official sanction was required before any church could hold a synod. Opinions differed widely on the impact upon Protestants of Turkish rule. In 1549 Imre Eszéki from Tolna claimed that the Buda pasha allowed Lutheran preaching without any hindrance because the pasha himself believed in the truth of the Gospel! Gál Huszár also wrote to Bullinger in 1557 that the Turks favoured Protestants in Hungary, in many places even taking part in church services. However, Pál Thúri Farkas wrote in the mid-1550s that the Turks could not be trusted under any circumstances, and that their strategy was at first to allow Christians to maintain their religion but ultimately aimed to convert them all to Islam, by force if necessary. Thúri wrote that Ottoman officials were already questioning locals in Tolna as to whether they believed in the truth of Mohammed the Prophet. Thúri maintained that the only answer which avoided punishment was to claim ignorance, adding that dire consequences would follow if the Turks ever found out that they already had Latin translations of the Koran. Thúri pointed to the experience of other areas to the south under longer Ottoman occupation as an indicator of what Hungary could soon expect, with ever-higher taxes, unfair administration, the collapse of Christian religion, and children stolen away for military training.[23]

Despite such stark warnings, a synod of Reformed ministers was able to meet at Hercegszőllős in 1576 to adopt a hierarchical order for the Reformed church in Ottoman Hungary. Synods were called by superintendents whenever possible in lower Danubian counties (Baranya province), and with more regularity in the Danubian province (Dunamellék) of around 160 churches. In 1623 a synod at Komját formulated canons which ratified the role of superintendents and archdeacons in the Danubian province. These canons also established powers for archdeacons to visit parish churches and investigate local standards, but the agreement of local Ottoman officials was still needed before archdeacons could exercise this duty.[24]

[23] M. Bucsay, 'Eszéki Imre levele Flaciushoz' and 'Thúri Farkas Pál körlevele', both in T. Barth (ed.), *Tánulmányok és szövegek a magyarországi református egyház xvi. századi történetéből. Studia et acta ecclesiastica, 3* (Budapest, 1973) (hereafter Barth (ed.), *Tánulmányok, 3*), 903–20; E. Zsindely, 'Bullinger Henrik magyar kapcsolatai', in T. Barth (ed.), *Tánulmányok 2*, 74.

[24] These Danubian districts were Tolna, Vértesalja, Pest, Solt, Kecskemét and Külső-Somogy. Dunamellék Reformed Church Province Archives (Ráday College, Budapest), Gyöngyös református község levéltárából, nos. 19, 26; Hungarian National Archives [MOL],

Around the turn of the century more than three-quarters of over 5,000 parishes across Hungary and Transylvania were Protestant. A majority of these Protestant parishes were held by the Reformed church, with approximately 1,150 Reformed parishes in Transylvania and the Partium, a further 650 in Royal Hungary, and perhaps 250 in Ottoman Hungary. Since urban churches were overwhelmingly Protestant, it seems that around 80 per cent of the population attended Protestant services, although this figure is somewhat misleading given the role of lay patrons in deciding local church affiliation. However, Robert Evans has commented that 'sixteenth-century Calvinism thus made gains in east-central Europe which were comparatively bloodless, but which by the same token we might equally call anaemic'.[25] Reformed Protestant growth was certainly soon severely tested by counter-reformation pressure from the Catholic hierarchy and Habsburg dynasty, and by the disruption of renewed war against the Ottomans.

The Reformed church in many ways seemed ill prepared for Catholic revival. Protestant Hungary could not boast any outstanding native theologians, nor its own university, although some grammar schools had been founded at Debrecen and Sárospatak. Urban centres' economic and cultural significance remained relatively limited. The largest town in Hungary was Debrecen, with between 15,000 and 20,000 inhabitants when swelled by refugees from Ottoman-occupied areas, whilst in Transylvania neither the largest German town of Kronstadt nor the Hungarian town of Kolozsvár contained more than 10,000 people. The Hungarian church could not call upon the enthusiasm and cohesive organization provided by colonies of religious refugees which bolstered Reformed churches elsewhere, although eastern Hungarian towns were certainly alive to the threat of social dislocation through further Ottoman encroachment. Calvinism

box 1890, Simandianum (Mihály Simándi) Protocollum (1629–1731); Pál Thuri, *Idea Christianorum ungarorum sub tyrannide Turcica* (Oppenheim, 1616); *A herczegszöllösi kánonok más egyházi kánonokkal egybevétve*, ed. Gy. Mokos (Budapest, 1901); *Canones ecclesiastici in quinque classes distributi* [1623 Komját canons] (Pápa, 1625); A. Földváry, *Adalékok a dunamelléki év. ref. egyházkerület történetéhez* (Budapest, 1898); G. Kathona, *Fejezetek a török hódoltsági reformáció történetéből* (Budapest, 1974), 58–70; A. Földváry, *A magyar református egyház és a török uralom* (Budapest, 1940); M. Fábién, *A dunamelléki egyházkerület története* (Sárospatak, 1867).

[25] Evans, 'Calvinism in East Central Europe', 177–9. Kálmán Benda suggested that, in 1600, 50 per cent of Hungarian society was Reformed, with 25 per cent Lutheran, and the remainder Unitarian, Catholic, or Orthodox: K. Benda, 'La réforme en Hongrie', *Bulletin de la Société de l'histoire du Protestantisme Français*, 122 (1976), 30–53. Katalin Péter agrees that 75–80 per cent of Hungarians were Protestant between 1570 and 1620: K. Péter, *Papok és nemesek. Magyar művelődéstörténeti tanulmányok a reformációval kezdődő másfél évszázadból* (Budapest, 1995), 10. See also J. Zoványi, *Kisebb dolgozatok a magyar protestantismus történetének köréből* (Sárospatak, 1910), 97–100.

was also strongly supported by peasants and soldiers displaced during the Ottoman wars from southern Hungary to the eastern plain, where they formed irregular mercenary bands of Hajducks (*hajdúk*).[26]

The decision to become Protestant in sixteenth-century Hungary and Transylvania had certainly not been determined by ethnicity or language amongst those with the ability or legal right to make a personal choice. Undoubtedly a mixture of geography and communication networks, pre-reformation patterns of religiosity and ecclesiastical organization, and feudal, regional, local, and family loyalties largely decided emerging patterns of religious adherence. However, ethnic cohesiveness cannot be discounted entirely in reinforcing attachment to a particular religion, and Calvinism in particular certainly became effectively bound to converted Magyar communities. Above all it is the political circumstances of sixteenth-century Hungary which explain the dramatic rise in support for Protestantism. The noble élite adopted Reformed or Lutheran religion both from sincerely held convictions, and also in order to bolster their political ambitions for greater autonomy from monarchical power. Nobles were anxious to establish a balance between their corporate privileges and monarchical sovereignty over religious affairs, as over other spheres of public life. Protestant strength in Hungary was therefore intimately linked with the political fortunes of the diet, and the depth of loyalty among noble converts to their religion would prove crucial to the later fortunes of the Protestant churches. This pattern of largely Protestant estates clashing with the ruling Catholic dynasty was repeated across the Habsburg monarchy, but the Hungarian nobility was in a particularly strong bargaining position, since in return for religious freedoms they could offer not only royal solvency and political loyalty in local administration but also military co-operation against the Ottomans. The Turkish threat certainly constrained the Habsburgs' ability to act against Protestants in Hungary, but their enduring determination to promote the interests of the Catholic church also weakened any plans to challenge Ottoman power, as the Fifteen Years War demonstrated.[27]

Skirmishes along the borders of Ottoman-occupied Hungary flared up in the early 1590s, and hostilities culminated in the first major attempt to push back Ottoman forces since the early 1540s. A joint Habsburg and Transylvanian army took the field, only to be defeated at the battle of Mezőkeresztes in 1596, with mostly indecisive encounters continuing until

---

[26] For more on the Hajducks' role, see I. Rácz, *A hajdúk a xvii. században* (Debrecen, 1969).
[27] Evans and Thomas (eds.), *Crown, Church and Estates*, p. xx, 'Introduction', by R. J. W. Evans; J. T. McNeill, *The History and Character of Calvinism* (New York, 1954), 288.

the end of the Fifteen Years War in 1606. The Transylvanian prince, Zsigmond Báthori, who had renounced Ottoman suzerainty to join Emperor Rudolf II in the 1596 campaign, then resigned the principality to Rudolf in 1598. Báthori soon returned to power in Transylvania but then resigned again, this time in favour of András Báthori. This confusion encouraged invasions of Transylvania, first by the Wallachian Prince Mihai 'the Brave' and then by a Habsburg army in 1603 under General Giorgio Basta. Transylvanian nobles led by Mózes Székely were left to seek Ottoman support to repel these attacks, but after Székely was defeated near Kronstadt in battle against the Wallachian prince in 1603, Basta's bloody occupation of Transylvania could be completed. István Bocskai, a leading Reformed noble from the Partium, had initially supported the anti-Ottoman alliance between Zsigmond Báthori and Rudolf. After these years of turmoil in Transylvania, Bocskai concluded in 1604 that Habsburg control of the principality posed a greater threat to domestic stability, noble privileges, and religious freedom than Ottoman suzerainty had done. Bocskai sought backing from the Porte to challenge this extension of Habsburg power, and joined with other dissident nobles, including Gábor Bethlen, who had already declared themselves opponents of Habsburg rule and were taking shelter from Basta in the Romanian principalities.[28]

Among nobles in Royal Hungary, anti-Habsburg sentiment was also being fuelled by resentment at the inconclusive war against the Turks, and by fears about Habsburg intentions behind the replacement of Hungarian soldiers with around 12,000 foreign troops in the ninety or so fortified towns along the southern border zone. Nobles were also indignant at Rudolf's heavy-handed attempts to reassert Habsburg sovereignty over all non-Ottoman Hungary for both his dynasty and the Catholic church. Basta's vicious rule in Transylvania was ably complemented by General Jacob Belgiojoso in Upper Hungary, with Protestants expelled from some towns, the leading Protestant noble István Illésházy put on trial for sedition, and royal agents confiscating Protestant nobles' lands. The town of Kassa became a particular flashpoint when in January 1604 the local Catholic bishop used imperial troops to occupy the central Lutheran church and to evict Lutheran ministers from the town. When complaints were raised about events in Kassa at the Hungarian diet in February 1604, Archduke Matthias, acting for Rudolf, responded by asserting that anyone who raised religious issues before the diet was guilty of treason.

[28] G. Barta, 'Az erdélyi fejedelemség első korszaka (1526–1606)', in *Erdély története*, i, 522–41; L. Makkai, 'A Bocskai felkelés', in *Magyarország története*, iii pt 1, 709–74; K. M. Setton, *Venice, Austria and the Turks in the Seventeenth Century* (Philadelphia, Pa., 1991).

The response of the Hungarian estates to this potent cocktail of military, political, and religious grievances amounted to a crisis of confidence in Habsburg authority to rule Hungary, and resulted in a rebellious assertion of local corporate rights. István Bocskai's call to arms met with an impressive response both from nobles in Hungary and Transylvania and from Hajduck mercenaries, drawn from displaced peasants from Ottoman-occupied territory. Bocskai was at first supported by free Hajducks from the eastern plain operating under their own elected captains, then also by Hajducks nominally in the pay of the Habsburgs. Support for Bocskai's revolt quickly grew in Upper Hungary and, despite stiff resistance from Belgiojoso, Bocskai was able to enter Kassa in triumph in November 1604. In December 1604 Bocskai called upon the Transylvanian estates to revolt, and by February 1605 he had been elected prince by the diet. Bocskai's soldiers then successfully resisted a new imperial army in 1605 and had advanced by April to the capital of Royal Hungary at Pozsony, whilst Hajduck bands backed by Ottoman forces reached as far as Lower Austria.[29]

In April 1605 the Hungarian diet meeting at Szerencs elected Bocskai as prince-protector over Hungary, or 'Moses of the Hungarians'. This Old Testament imagery indeed reflected how Reformed ministers had consistently idealized Bocskai as a defender of religious liberty, and as a divinely appointed liberator of Hungary from the tyrannical government of Habsburg monarchs. Bocskai himself declared in an *Apology* that his aims in the revolt were 'the maintenance of ourselves, our nation's life and, further, of our religion, liberty, and property'. Such notions indicate that Bocskai's revolt against the rule of a lawful monarch was being justified to some extent by resorting to Calvinist theories of rights of resistance against sinning higher authorities.[30] However, this seems to amount only to a rather muted Hungarian echo of Huguenot monarchomachist responses to French royal persecution of the early 1570s. Unlike French rebels, Bocskai was anxious that his appeal for resistance extend not only to Reformed co-religionists but also to Lutheran towns and nobles, whose support was crucial for the success of his revolt. Even if Bocskai had wished to quote Calvin's views on civil government to support rebellion in his *Apology*, he would have had to

---

[29] L. Makkai, 'István Bocskai's Insurrectionary Army', in J. M. Bák and B. K. Király (eds.), *From Hunyadi to Rákóczi. War and Society in Late Medieval and Early Modern Hungary* (Brooklyn, Mass., 1982), 275–97; D. P. Daniel, 'The Fifteen Years War and the Protestant Response to Habsburg Absolutism in Hungary', *East Central Europe*, 8 (1981), 38–51; István Szamosközy, *Erdély története (1598–9, 1603)* (Budapest, 1981).

[30] K. Révész, 'Bocskay István apologiája', *Protestáns Szemle*, 18 (1906), 304–12; Nagy Szabó, 'Marosvásárhely Memorial', 100; Ferenc Pápai Páriz, *Romlott fal felépítése (Rudus Redivivum)* [1685]', in *MPEA* 5 (1906), 129–73; *Bocskai István levelek*, ed. K. Benda (Budapest, 1992). All translations from Hungarian are my own.

overlook long passages in which Calvin insisted upon the need to obey divinely appointed magistrates, before reaching his brief and rather vague discussion of potential contemporary equivalents of Spartan ephors.[31] It is hardly surprising that Bocskai and his supporters instead cited the thirty-first article of the 1222 Golden Bull of András II, which supported the right of Hungarian nobles to resist any ruler who ignored noble rights and privileges. Whilst Bocskai's rebellion was not therefore an immediate consequence of Calvinist influence over Hungarian politics, Reformed clergy were only too pleased to chime in with spiritual sanction for noble aspirations to prevent the centralization of power in Hungary in the hands of the Habsburgs and the Catholic hierarchy.[32]

Bocskai was content to relinquish his claim to the Hungarian crown, once Rudolf was prepared to negotiate with Bocskai and accept his rule as prince over Transylvania. The terms of the Vienna peace agreed between Bocskai and Rudolf in June 1606 also dealt with the grievances of the Hungarian nobility and finally acknowledged the reality of confessional division in Royal Hungary. The treaty extended the free exercise of religion to the nobility, royal towns, and military garrisons of Hungary and established the rights of both Lutheran and Reformed churches to regulate freely their own affairs. The Fifteen Years War was also soon concluded by the Zsitvatorok peace of October 1606, which confirmed some territorial gains made by the Ottomans. The balance between the two great powers of the region was nevertheless largely re-established along pre-war lines, with the Sultan acknowledging Rudolf as Emperor and king of Hungary. Both sides accepted the integrity of Transylvania's borders and the right of princes to determine the territory's internal affairs. The end of the war also saw the Hajducks emerge as free peasants in a new warrior estate, exempt from taxes but owing military service to the Transylvanian prince, and some Hajducks were granted lands for settlement around Debrecen on the eastern Hungarian plain.

---

[31] Calvin, 'On Civil Government', in *Institutio Christianae Religionis* (Geneva, 1559), bk. 4, ch. 20, para. 31; Kingdon, 'Calvinism and Resistance Theory, 1550–1580', 193–219.

[32] K. Benda, 'Le calvinisme et le droit de résistance des ordres hongrois au commencement du xviie siècle', in *Études Européennes. Mélanges offerts à Victor-Lucien Tapié* (Publications de la Sorbonne, 6; Paris, 1973), 235–43; K. Benda, 'Le droit de résistance de la Bulle d'Or hongroise et le calvinisme', in B. Köpeczi and É. Balázs (eds.), *Noblesse Française, Noblesse Hongroise xvie–xixe siècles* (Budapest–Paris, 1981), 155–63; K. Benda, 'A kálvini tanok hatása a magyar rendi ellenállás ideológiájára', *Helikon*, 17 (1971), 322–30; L. Makkai, 'Nemesi köztársaság és kálvinista teokrácia a 16. századi Lengyelországban és Magyarországon', *Ráday Gyűjtemény Évkönyve*, 3 (1983), 17–29; K. Benda, 'Habsburg Absolutism and the Resistance of the Hungarian Estates in the Sixteenth and Seventeenth Centuries', in R. J. W. Evans and T. V. Thomas (eds.), *Crown, Church and Estates: Central European Politics in the Sixteenth and Seventeenth Centuries* (London, 1991), 123–8.

The gains made by Protestants in Hungary through the peace of Vienna still remained to be ratified by the diet, thanks to Rudolf's delaying tactics. In 1608 Protestant nobles were able to take advantage of the struggle between Rudolf and Matthias for control of Bohemia and Hungary to force Matthias to endorse the Vienna peace in return for supporting him against Rudolf. Matthias also agreed to nominate candidates for the office of palatine, and the Lutheran noble István Illésházy was chosen by the diet. The diet then approved the religious clauses of the Vienna settlement, which effectively devolved absolute rights of religious patronage over local churches to the Hungarian nobility. The diet's articles also contained an implicit suggestion that peasants across Hungary would gain religious liberties. Protestant nobles indeed supported the extension of freedom of worship to peasants, in so far as it permitted peasants who lived on the lands of Catholic nobles to become Protestant, an advantage calculated as outweighing the risk of losing peasants on Protestants' lands to the Catholic church.[33]

Protestants' confidence about the future soon proved to be largely unwarranted. From the 1610s a stream of noble converts to the Catholic church, especially in western and north-western counties of Royal Hungary, reclaimed church buildings for use by Catholics, expelled Protestant ministers and teachers from their lands, and disregarded any suggestion of peasant religious freedoms. Faced with this vulnerable and weakening position, Protestant nobles in Hungary began to argue that the religious liberty established by the 1608 diet could only have practical meaning if it was understood to include access to a place of worship. This argument was placed before the 1619 diet at Pozsony, by which time Catholics formed a majority in the Upper Chamber, with fifteen Catholic prelates sitting alongside sixty-six Catholic magnates and only sixty-one Protestant magnates. The complaints of Protestants in both chambers about Catholic interference with Protestant freedoms, and especially over restricted access to church buildings, also received support from the Transylvanian prince, Gábor Bethlen. The palatine, Zsigmond Forgách, responded to this concerted pressure by drawing up a confirmation of the Vienna peace which acknowledged that there was disagreement on whether freedom of religion in Hungary was *una cum templis*, that is, entailing free use of churches, church bells, and graveyards. This statement recognized that there were also differences of opinion in the diet as to whether the rights of landowners as

33 Zsilinszky, *A magyar országgyűlések vallásügyi tárgyalásai*, 358–9; K. Péter, 'Az 1608 évi vallásügyi törvény és a jobbágyok vallásszabadsága', *Századok*, 111 (1977), 93–113; I. Szabó, *Tanulmányok a magyar parasztság történetéből* (Budapest, 1948), 203–63.

church patrons, or the rights of a majority within local communities, took precedence in determining parishes' confessional allegiance.[34]

The example provided by the Hungarian estates' resistance to monarchical centralization and counter-reformation was not lost upon Protestant nobles in Poland, Bohemia, Moravia, and Austria. In Poland, Protestant nobles had gained guarantees of free practice of their religion by the 1573 Warsaw confederation, with Calvinists, Bohemian Brethren, and Lutherans in Poland joined together by mutual recognition of the 1570 *Consensus Sendomirensis*. In 1606 many Protestant and some Catholic nobles responded to royal demands for taxation and diet reform by forming a league of Sandomierz, only for their revolt to be crushed by the king and Catholic magnates. In 1608 the estates of Moravia, Upper Austria, and Lower Austria combined with the Hungarian diet to exact declarations of religious freedom from Archduke Matthias. The Bohemian estates, meanwhile, saw their loyalty to Rudolf repaid by the 1609 Letter of Majesty which offered religious liberty to nobles and towns, and granted legal recognition to Protestant churches in loose association under the 1575 *Confessio Bohemica*. However, once the crisis within the ruling dynasty was resolved, pressure was soon renewed upon Protestant estates across the Habsburg monarchy. In 1618 the estates of Bohemia and Upper Austria rebelled against Ferdinand II, in defence of noble privileges and Protestant freedoms. In turn the estates of Lower Austria, Silesia, Lusatia, and Moravia refused to accept Ferdinand's rule, and in August 1619 this new defiance of Habsburg authority spread to Hungary when the Transylvanian prince, Gábor Bethlen, advanced his army into Royal Hungary as far as Pozsony.[35]

---

[34] This May 1618 proclamation is in Tiszáninnen Church Province Archives (Sárospatak), Zsoldos Benő-féle időrendes sorozat, A.II.72, 1–2. For a Reformed view, see Máté Sepsi Laczkó, 'Krónika, 1521–1624', in *ETA*, iii (Kolozsvár, 1858), 119–246.

[35] R. R. Betts, 'Poland, Hungary and Bohemia: The Reformation in Difficulties', in G. R. Elton (ed.), *The New Cambridge Modern History, 2. The Reformation, 1520–59* (7th edn., Cambridge, 1987), 186–209; F. Kavka, 'Bohemia', in R. Scribner, R. Porter, and M. Teich (eds.), *The Reformation in National Context* (Cambridge, 1994), 131–54; W. Eberhard, 'Reformation and Counterreformation in East Central Europe', in J. D. Tracey, T. A. Brady, and H. A. Oberman (eds.), *Handbook of European History, 1400–1600. Late Middle Ages, Renaissance and Reformation, 2: Visions, Programs and Outcomes* (Leiden, 1995), 552–84; W. Eberhard, 'Bohemia, Moravia and Austria', in A. Pettegree (ed.), *The Early Reformation in Europe* (Cambridge, 1992), 47; A. Pettegree and K. Maag, 'The Reformation in Eastern and Central Europe', in K. Maag (ed.), *The Reformation in Eastern and Central Europe* (Aldershot, 1997), 1–18; O. Odlozilík, 'A Church in a Hostile State: The Unity of Czech Brethren', *Central European History*, 6 (1973), 111–27; D. P. Daniel, 'Ecumenicity or Orthodoxy: The Dilemma of the Protestants in the Lands of the Austrian Habsburgs', *Church History*, 49 (1980), 387–400; K. J. MacHardy, 'The Rise of Absolutism and Noble Rebellion in Early Modern Habsburg Austria, 1570–1620', *Comparative Studies in Society and History*, 34 (1992), 407–38;

Bocskai's revolt had supplied the Transylvanian state with a clear sense of Protestant mission to oppose Habsburg claims of sovereignty over Hungary and efforts to impose counter-reform measures, and Bethlen's 1619 attack on Royal Hungary revived and strengthened this perception of the principality's role. When Bocskai died in December 1606, the diet had elected Zsigmond Rákóczi to replace him. In 1608 Rákóczi resigned in favour of Gábor Báthori, whose family had ruled Transylvania before the Fifteen Years War. Báthori forged an alliance with the Hajducks, promising that he would remain faithful to the Calvinist cause, but also offered his loyalty to the Catholic primate of Esztergom. Báthori's attempts to play the different parties off against one another soon backfired, and he was opposed first by some Catholic nobles in Transylvania, and then by the Saxon towns. In 1613 Gábor Bethlen, another old ally of Bocskai, gained sanction from the Porte to remove Báthori and become prince, on condition he concede two border fortresses at Lippa and Jenő. As an Ottoman army marched towards Transylvania's south-western borders in support of Bethlen, he was elected prince by the diet in October 1613. Four days after this election, Gábor Báthori was assassinated at Nagyvárad by the men of András Ghyczy, one of his former councillors, and the prince's body was thrown into a stream. After further negotiations Bethlen eventually handed Lippa over to the Ottomans in 1616, which gave new life to Catholic accusations of far too cosy a relationship between Reformed princes in Transylvania and the Ottomans.[36]

By 1620 Bethlen, supported by many Hungarian nobles, had conquered most of Royal Hungary. Bethlen was offered the Hungarian crown when the diet met at Besztercebánya in August 1620. Bethlen refused to be crowned, perhaps wishing to receive the Apostolic crown with greater ceremony after his power had been consolidated, certainly unwilling to become the figurehead of the diet's vision of limited monarchy, and also concerned about the potentially hostile reaction at the Porte to his spectacular success. Bethlen's caution proved astute, since the triumph of the confederation of Protestant estates in central Europe was to be short lived. Bohemian defeat at the White Mountain in November 1620, despite the

J. Bahlcke, 'Calvinism and Estate Liberation Movements in Bohemia and Hungary (1570–1620)', in K. Maag (ed.), *The Reformation in Eastern and Central Europe* (Aldershot, 1997), 72–91.

36 Z. Hangay, *Erdély választott fejedelme* (Budapest, 1987); L. Demény, *Bethlen Gábor és kora* (Bucharest, 1982); Gy. Szekfű, *Bethlen Gábor* (Budapest, 1929); K. Kovács (ed.), *Bethlen Gábor állama és kora. Bethlen-bibliográfia, 1613–1980* (Budapest, 1980); B. Köpeczi et al., 'Bethlen Gábor és állama', *Századok*, 115 (1981), 659–750.

presence of 8,000 troops sent by Bethlen, struck a severe blow against the pretensions of Protestant estates in the region. Left largely bereft of allies, Bethlen agreed to the Nikolsburg peace treaty with Ferdinand in December 1621. By the terms of this peace Bethlen renounced his claim to the Hungarian crown, and in return gained the imperial lands of Ratibor and Oppeln in Silesia and control over seven counties in Upper Hungary for his lifetime. Although Bethlen conducted two subsequent campaigns against the Habsburgs in the 1620s, both ended in stalemate and further peace treaties in 1624 and 1626 which mostly confirmed what had already been agreed at Nikolsburg.[37]

After the collapse of Bohemian resistance in 1620, Ferdinand was able to crush the power of estates outside Hungary and, equating Protestantism with disloyalty, destroyed religious freedoms across much of his monarchy. By 1625 Protestant worship had ceased in Bohemia, and only the Catholic church received recognition from the renewed constitution of 1627. Protestant clergy were also forced out of Upper and Lower Austria in the 1620s, and Protestant nobles forced to convert or leave Moravia, Upper and Inner Austria.[38] The Protestant challenge to Habsburg attempts to enforce counter-reformation in the first two decades of the seventeenth century had certainly not been a popular movement, with the partial exception of the Hajducks. The acquisition and defence of Protestant freedoms in east-central Europe instead had relied very heavily upon noble estates. The Hungarian diet alone proved able to preserve the concessions wrung out of Rudolf at Vienna in 1606. Hungarian Protestants held the advantage over co-religionists elsewhere that they did not have to rely exclusively upon the diet to defend their liberties, since the military strength of Transylvania's princes could place additional limits upon Habsburg power in Hungary. Hungarian Protestants indeed became increasingly dependent upon Transylvanian intervention, and with both Bocskai and Bethlen directly backed by the Ottomans, Catholics in Hungary could make claims with some justification of a Protestant–Turkish pact.

---

[37] Ratibor and Oppeln were held by Bethlen until 1623. The seven counties of north-eastern Hungary were Abaúj, Zemplén, Borsod, Bereg, Szabolcs, Szatmár, and Ugocsa. I. Lukinich, *Erdély területi változásai a török hódítás korában, 1541–1711* (Budapest, 1918), 199–335; L. Makkai, 'Az ellenreformáció és a harmincéves háború. Az erdélyi fejedelmek Habsburg-ellenes küzdelmei', in *Magyarország története*, iii pt 1, 777–936; K. Péter, 'A fejedelemség virágkora', in *Erdély története*, ii, 656–86; [Bethlen, Gábor], 'Adalékok Bethlen Gábor szövetkezéseinek történetéhez', ed. S. Szilágyi, in *ÉTTK* 2/8 (Budapest, 1873), 78–93.
[38] J. Lecler, *Toleration and the Reformation* (2 vols.; London, 1960), i, 397–423; R. Bireley, *Religion and Politics in the Age of the Counterreformation. Emperor Ferdinand II, William Lamormaini S.J., and the Formation of Imperial Policy* (Chapel Hill, NC, 1981).

The leading Catholic propagandist of this period was Péter Pázmány, primate of Hungary from 1616 and a cardinal from 1629. Pázmány was responsible for much of the recovery in Catholic support among Hungarian nobles, and he worked hard to improve the quality of Catholic clergy. In 1623 the Jesuit Collegium Pazmaneum opened in Vienna to train middle-ranking clergy, a further college opened at Pozsony in 1626, and the college at Nagyszombat was declared a university in 1635. Some measure of the extent of this Catholic recovery can be judged from the dwindling numbers of Protestant magnates in the Upper Chamber of the diet to a mere handful by the 1640s. Many of Hungary's most prominent families converted back to the Catholic church during this period, including the Batthyánys, Nádasdys, Thurzós, and Illésházys. Some nobles undoubtedly converted after a sincere change in their private beliefs, whilst others acted out of loyalty to the Habsburgs and with hopes of office and advancement. Protestant gentry continued to be strongly represented in the Lower Chamber of the diet but faced the combined force of the crown, magnates, and Catholic hierarchy, and in the 1630s and 1640s Protestants fought a long and ultimately unsuccessful battle to maintain their hard-won privileges.[39]

At the 1634 Hungarian diet at Sopron the Reformed church presented a catalogue of complaints of mistreatment, alleging that Catholic landowners had occupied dozens of church buildings, prevented church services from taking place, and expelled Reformed ministers from their lands. These grievances received no remedy from the diet until 1644 when the Transylvanian prince György I Rákóczi invaded Royal Hungary. Backed by France and Sweden, Rákóczi launched a successful attack against Ferdinand III, hoping to join up with the Swedish army in Moravia. Ferdinand was only too anxious to bring peace negotiations held with Rákóczi at Linz in 1645 to a successful conclusion. To get agreement, Ferdinand had to concede a re-definition of the meaning of Protestant religious liberty to include rights of access to church buildings, graveyards, and the use of church bells. Protracted negotiations then followed at the 1646 Pozsony diet on how to interpret this Linz treaty. Protestants claimed that 300 churches had been illegally seized by Catholics and ought to be returned, but could only in fact name some 146 confiscated churches. Many Catholic nobles were also anxious to settle the matter in the diet and avoid the decision on religious rights being left to a royal decree. After churches built by Catholic patrons and those on the estates of Catholics were omitted from

39 L. Makkai, 'Művelődés a 17. században', in *Magyarország története* iii, 1,461–576; *Pázmány Péter művei*, ed. M. Tarnoc (Budapest, 1983); I. Bitskey, *Pázmány Péter* (Budapest, 1986); Biró, *Bethlen Gábor és az erdélyi katholicizmus*.

the list, the diet agreed in 1647 that 90 church buildings seized by Catholics must be returned to the control of the Lutheran and Reformed churches.[40] These concessions did not long survive the waning of Transylvanian military influence, and Catholic nobles soon steadily reimposed restrictions on the free practice of Protestantism in Royal Hungary. After 1648 Protestants turned to the Hungarian diet for redress of their grievances entirely in vain. Ministers were expelled from their parishes, churches and schools either closed to Protestants or destroyed altogether, books confiscated, Protestants forced to recognize Catholic holidays, blocks placed in the way of Protestant guild membership, Protestants were forced to make payments demanded by Catholic priests and were unable to marry or have relatives buried without declarations of support for the Catholic church, all of which rendered the terms of the 1606 Vienna peace entirely meaningless. By the 1650s even Reformed ministers in Ottoman Hungary were in some respects in a more secure position than many of their colleagues in Habsburg Hungary. At the 1662 Hungarian diet, Protestants' complaints that hundreds of churches had been illegally taken over by Catholic landowners were ignored. More severe persecution was still to follow, when in January 1674 a special court set up at Pozsony under Archbishop György Szelepcsényi impeached over 700 Protestant ministers and teachers. Found guilty of preaching against Mary and the saints, and of being in alliance with the Turks, these ministers were sentenced to death. Many converted, renounced their offices, or went into exile in the ensuing months, but over forty ministers who refused to recant were sent on a forced march through Italy in 1675, with thirty survivors then sold on as galley-slaves to the Spanish fleet.[41]

The fortunes of the Hungarian Reformed church became increasingly reliant upon the political support and patronage of Transylvania's princes during the early seventeenth century, both within the principality itself and in Royal Hungary. Transylvanian princes had to offer oaths of loyalty to the Sultan on their election and paid annual tribute to the Porte. Incumbent princes and the diet attempted as far as possible to promote one

---

[40] Szabó, *Tanulmányok a magyar parasztság történetéből*, 203–63; M. Zsilinszky, *A linczi békekötés és az 1647-ki vallásügyi törvényczikkek története* (Budapest, 1890); M. Zsilinszky, *A magyar országgyűlések vallásügyi tárgyalásai a reformátiotól kezdve* (Budapest, 1880), 358–9; K. Péter, 'The Struggle for Protestant Religious Liberty at the 1646–47 Diet in Hungary', in R. J. W. Evans and T. V. Thomas (eds.), *Crown, Church and Estates: Central European Politics in the Sixteenth and Seventeenth Centuries* (London, 1991), 261–8.

[41] Révész, *A magyar református egyház története*, 107–20; *A Short Memorial of the Most Grievous Sufferings of the Ministers of the Protestant Churches in Hungary by the Instigation of the Popish Clergy there* [trans. from Dutch] (London, 1676).

outstanding candidate to succeed as prince, so that Ottoman interference could be kept to a minimum. In 1626 the diet accepted the nomination by Gábor Bethlen of his second wife Catherine, daughter of the Brandenburg elector, as his successor. On Bethlen's death in 1629, Catherine ruled in his place and was persuaded to attempt to place Transylvania under Habsburg rule. However, György Rákóczi, son of the former prince Zsigmond Rákóczi, and the most extensive landowner in north-eastern Hungary, was able to build a coalition of nobles and Hajducks to support his challenge to become prince. Catherine resigned in September 1630 in favour of István Bethlen, Gábor's younger brother, but Rákóczi continued his advance towards Transylvania and in December 1630 won election in the diet.

Rákóczi then had to withstand several challenges to his position, first from Catherine, who was still intent on handing over at least Gábor Bethlen's estates in north-eastern Hungary to the Habsburgs. Soldiers were mobilized to the area by both sides, and fears raised of an imminent campaign of forced re-catholicization. The northern Tisza region was further destabilized in 1631 by a major revolt of peasants and the residents of small towns in the area. This revolt was also sparked by the growing demands of powerful lords, such as Rákóczi, for greater labour service from peasants and for restrictions to be placed on the economic rights of local towns involved in wine production. The rebels, including some landless petty nobles resident in these towns, declared that they aimed to defend traditional local rights, prevent destruction and looting by soldiers, and uphold the 'true faith'. A peasant army, at first marshalled by Péter Császár, of between 5,000 and 10,000 men, looked in vain for help from the Hajducks or from Transylvania. The peasants also sought support from local Reformed clergy but, with very few exceptions, ministers advised the rebels to make their peace with the authorities. The revolt was finally crushed by Rákóczi and local nobles at Nyírbátor in 1632.[42] Rákóczi only managed conclusively to secure his position as Transylvanian prince in 1636 after his decisive victory at Szalonta over István Bethlen, despite Bethlen having the support of some Turkish forces. Once Rákóczi had gained acceptance from the Porte for his rule, he could consolidate his power through control not only of his vast family estates but also of princely estates in Transylvania. The Rákóczi family soon added to their wealth by the marriage of the prince's eldest son, György, to the Báthori heiress, Zsófia. In 1642 the diet accepted Rákóczi's nomination of György as his successor, and after György II Rákóczi became prince in 1648 the diet also agreed that his son Ferenc would in turn succeed him as prince.

[42] L. Makkai, *A felső tiszavidéki parasztfelkelés, 1631–1632* (Budapest, 1954).

Gábor Bethlen and the Rákóczi princes consolidated the centralized feudal structure of their principality during the early seventeenth century, and constructed an effective state, if one with limited resources. Princes by force of their personalities, private wealth, and patronage dominated the diet and council which decided financial, political, and military affairs. Princes confirmed the corporate liberties and local privileges of the diet's three nations, but also organized their own competent central institutions. Once Transylvania's Hungarian nobility saw one of their own elected to office, they remained seemingly content to let princes mostly have their way, and the absence of religious conflict in the principality promoted still further this centralization of power.[43]

The Transylvanian diet began to meet less frequently during the early seventeenth century, normally only sitting annually after 1622, when previously it had met twice a year. Whilst thirty-four diets were held during the 1610s, twenty-three were held in the 1630s and only thirteen in the 1620s and 1640s. When diets were called, nobles in public offices, unlimited numbers of nominated 'regalist' nobles, as well as delegates from the three nations were all commanded by the prince to attend. The diet could present grievances to the prince, but only after the prince's taxation requests and other proposals had been answered. The diet usually agreed to demands for taxation in order to pay annual tribute to the Porte, and to meet the costs of maintaining the court and border castles, although the diet was not involved in deciding how the money they voted was actually used. Gábor Bethlen augmented his finances by establishing monopolies on foreign trade in cattle, salt, iron, mercury, and wax, and by the 1620s ordinary taxation only provided around a tenth of state revenues. After Bethlen died, the diet overturned some of these monopolies, but by 1631 György I Rákóczi had recovered the sole right to benefit from customs on external trade in a range of goods. Initiative at the diet therefore clearly lay with the princes, once securely in power and in control of sufficient patronage to ensure the support of 'regalist' nobles, and the diet was mostly restricted during this period to raising detailed points with the prince or to general grumbling.[44]

---

43 R. J. W. Evans, 'Introduction', in Evans and Thomas (eds.), *Crown, church and estates*, pp. xxii–xxiii: 'The material resources at the disposal of the ruler, and the absence of any entrenched estates organisation, or of religious confrontation between estates and government, favoured the development of a precocious absolutism.' For the oath made by Bethlen before the diet on his accession, see *Erdélyi országgyűlési emlékek*, ed. Szilágyi, vi, 368.

44 Zs. Trócsányi, *Erdélyi központi kormányzata, 1540–1690* (Budapest, 1980), 210–50; Zs. Trócsányi, *Az erdélyi fejedelemség korának országgyűlései* (Budapest, 1976); V. Biró, *Az erdélyi fejedelmi hatalom fejlődése* (Kolozsvár, 1917); Zs. Trócsányi, 'Bethlen Gábor erdélyi állama',

Gábor Bethlen and his Rákóczi successors proved capable of exercising real authority over the government of their principality. Princes were advised by a council, dominated by Hungarian nobles, which debated matters under consideration at the diet, and served by a treasury and chancery at the capital, Gyulafehérvár. The treasury administered revenue from taxes, tithe collection, and mining and trade monopolies, and both the treasury and the various departments of the chancery seem to have become more efficient in their administrative practices during this period. Princes also raised and commanded the army of around 10,000–12,000 men formed from Hajduck soldiers, about 7,000 Szeklers, and from mercenaries paid for out of the princes' income or sometimes from the subsidies of foreign allies. Much expense and organizational effort was also dedicated to sustaining a ring of defensive castles and forts along the principality's frontiers. Princes directed diplomatic and foreign policy through the chancery, but approval was needed from the Porte before the army could become involved in any international conflict. Whilst both Gábor Bethlen and György I Rákóczi showed willingness to act within this restraint, Transylvania nevertheless became engaged in ever-closer contacts with foreign Protestant powers. Bethlen intervened three times in the Thirty Years War, with his distant allies eager to open an eastern front and tie down Habsburg forces. In November 1626 a Westminster treaty of mutual co-operation was signed between Transylvania and England, later ratified by England's Dutch and Danish allies. During the 1630s lengthy negotiations were held between György I Rákóczi, the French, and Swedes, which eventually led to an anti-Habsburg alliance in 1643. In February 1644 Rákóczi finally attacked Royal Hungary but then quickly concluded a peace treaty with Ferdinand at Linz in 1645 by which he regained control over the seven counties in north-eastern Hungary previously held by Bethlen.[45]

During the early seventeenth century the princely government of Transylvania moved towards efficient control of financial, administrative, and

Jogtudományi Közlöny (1980), 617–22; L. Rácz, 'I. Rákóczi György erdélyi állama', *Jogtudományi Közlöny* (1981), 495–502; L. Rácz, 'Főhatalom a xvi.–xvii. századi erdélyben', *Jogtudományi Közlöny* (1981), 857–64.

45 Rákóczi gained Abaújvár, Zemplén, Borsod, Bereg, Szabolcs, Szatmár, and Ugocsa counties in 1645, and after 1648 György II Rákóczi retained Szatmár and Szabolcs. Lukinich, *Erdély területi változásai a török hódítás korában, 1541–1711*, 199–335; 'I. Rákóczi György összeköttetése francziaországgal', ed. S. Gergely, *TT* (1889), 686–7, 692–4; [Rákóczi György I], *Okirattár Strassburg Pál 1631–1633-iki követsége és I. Rákóczi György elsö diplomacziai összeköttetései történetéhez*, ed. S. Szilágyi (Budapest, 1882) (hereafter [Rákóczi György I], *I. Rákóczi György elsö diplomacziai összeköttetései töurténetéhez*); [Rákóczi György I], *Okmánytár I. Rákóczi György svéd és franczia szövetkezéseinek történetéhez*, ed. S. Szilágyi (Budapest, 1873), pp. xviii, xxiii, xliv.

military affairs. The Fifteen Years War had demonstrated the potentially disastrous results of a power vacuum in the principality, and the continued primacy of defending Transylvania's territory in precarious international circumstances certainly galvanized the central administration, favoured compliance with princely rule, and fostered acceptance of social discipline. Transylvania's Calvinist princes found willing partners to support their efforts to bring order to Transylvanian society from the clergy of the Reformed church. Whilst Hungarian Protestantism had initially relied upon noble support, and at the turn of the century Reformed ministers had enthusiastically backed the cause of noble rebellion against monarchical authority, during the early seventeenth century the Reformed church in Transylvania became closely allied with princely authority and power.

The Reformed church acquired the status of public orthodoxy in Transylvania during the period of Calvinist princely rule, although princes were careful never to equate allegiance to the Reformed church with political loyalty. Formal connections between church and state were limited, with no clergy on the prince's council nor any formal representation for the churches in the diet, although the Reformed and Lutheran superintendents were usually in attendance. More significant, however, was the informal influence exerted on princes and their families by court chaplains, Reformed superintendents, archdeacons, and other leading clergy. Certainly princely commitment to the Reformed church was no public façade merely constructed for political advantage, with György I Rákóczi and his wife Zsuzsanna Lórántffy notably pious in their private devotions, and Bethlen too, although perhaps more calculating, at least widely believed to be

a zealous Calvinist, seldome going without a Latin Testament in his pocket . . . [who] takes the right course to advance religion; to encourage, countenance, and promote learning, etc. to do that in beating down heresie by the word, which the laws of his nation forbid him to do by the sword.[46]

The princes certainly derived great advantages from their close relationship with the Reformed church, since Reformed preachers portrayed their rule as being divinely appointed and sanctified princes as godly magistrates who guaranteed the survival of the principality. Transylvanian successes in battles against the Habsburgs reinforced the impression among Reformed ministers that Transylvania had become a resting place of divine favour

---

[46] Péter Maksai Őse in Giovanni Botero, *The World; or, An historicall description of the most famous kingdomes and commonweals therein* (1630); I. Gál, 'Maksai Péter angol nyelvű Bethlen Gábor életrajza 1629-ből', *ITK* 80 (1976), 223–38.

and that their princes were comparable to the faithful biblical kings of the Old Testament. A powerful concentration in fact developed during this period among Transylvanian Calvinists on the motif of biblical Israel, as a way of describing Transylvania's position as a lone Reformed outpost in eastern Europe, stoutly defended by godly princes against surrounding, demonically inspired Habsburg and Ottoman powers.[47]

Transylvania's Calvinist princes in turn resolutely promoted the interests of the Reformed church and its clergy. In July 1605 all Transylvanian ministers' widowed or orphaned families were exempted from taxes and from any feudal services, to relieve suffering endured because of the Fifteen Years War. In 1619 a Reformed district synod in Transylvania asked Bethlen to introduce tougher regulations to uphold moral standards in private behaviour and public life. Bethlen swiftly responded to their request and proposed articles at the next diet which prohibited work and travel on Sundays, placed restrictions on the sale of alcohol, and imposed the death penalty for murderers, thieves, and adulterers.[48] In 1629 Bethlen offered clergy in the Transylvanian principality collective ennoblement, with privileges and exemptions from feudal service extending to ministers' sons and daughters, and their descendants. This privilege brought tremendous practical advantages for Reformed clergy, and Bethlen acted out of particular concern to protect ministers in the counties of north-eastern Hungary which were due to return to Habsburg rule on his death.[49]

Bethlen and the Rákóczi princes were also generous in offering financial support for the education of Reformed student ministers. Bursaries were given for students to travel to western universities, and princes paid for the development of local Reformed academies, schools, and printing-presses. Princes also responded to Reformed demands for action to extirpate heresy in their territory, with laws after 1610 against Sabbatarianism, and in 1638 somewhat crude controls even placed over mainstream anti-Trinitarians in the Unitarian church. In disputes between the Reformed church and other

47 János Redmeczi, *Az felséges Bethlen Gábornak öt rendbeli Isten anyaszentegyházával cselekedett jótéteményéről* (Kassa, 1622); I. Révész, 'Bethlen Gábor, a kálvinista fejedelem', *Protestáns Szemle*, 26 (1914), 339–58; M. Tarnóc, *Erdély művelődése Bethlen Gábor és a két Rákóczi György korában* (Budapest, 1978); J. Barcza, *Bethlen Gábor, a református fejedelem* (Budapest, 1980); J. Pokoly, 'Az erdélyi fejedelemek viszonya a protestáns egyházakhoz', *Protestáns Szemle*, 8 (1896), 546–61, 608–24.

48 [Küküllővári], 'Az 1619. évi küküllővári zsinat felterjesztése Bethlen Gábor fejedelemhez', ed. G. Illyés, *Református Szemle* (1934), 501–5; 'Articuli Bethleniani, Illustrissimi Gabrielis Bethlen, ad ecclesiam Dei pertinenti', are to be found in E. Illyés, *Egyházfegyelem a magyar református egyházban* (Debrecen, 1941), 95.

49 MOL box 2177, Tiszántúli református egyházkerület levéltárának . . . válogatott iratai, no. 1; I. Kiss Rugonfalvi, *Az egyházi rend közjogi helyzete erdélyben és Bethlen Gábor armalisa* (Debrecen, 1936).

'received religions' to establish the majority in a parish who could take possession of church buildings, Reformed supporters could often count upon
princely interference in their interests. Anti-Trinitarians and Catholics
consistently lost out during this period to the combined authority of
princes and Reformed nobles in towns and villages across the region, and
the Reformed church's rivals were left mostly confined to eastern Szekler
and southern Saxon counties.[50]

The Reformed church thus benefited hugely from close connections
established by leading clergy with princes at the Transylvanian court. The
important role played by superintendents, archdeacons, and court chaplains in co-operating with princes, encouraged still further the accretion of
powers within the church to this clergy élite. The pattern of Reformed
church government in Transylvania steadily shifted from one based upon
clergy synods, to one dominated by superintendents and archdeacons. In
1606 the Transylvanian synod stated that those ministers raised above
others by the grade of their office or knowledge deserved the respect of
clergy underneath their personal authority. Canons agreed the same year
allowed greater freedom of independent action for the superintendent than
ever before. Superintendents were released from the obligation to seek
prior agreement for their decisions from the provinces' archdeacons, except on the most important or contentious matters. In 1639 the synod even
decided that superintendents should have the right to sanction the
appointment of newly elected archdeacons.[51]

In June 1646 the Transylvanian superintendent, István Geleji Katona,
convened an extraordinary national synod at Szatmár attended by over one
hundred clergy from all of the church provinces. This synod, conducted in
the presence of György I Rákóczi, confirmed again the governing authority
of superintendents and archdeacons in the church, and Geleji was asked to
draw up new canons to reflect the synod's decisions. Geleji's canons
affirmed the 'aristocratic–democratic' balance of Hungarian Reformed
church government and set out the major responsibilities allotted to superintendents, referred to in the canons as bishops (*episcopi provinciarum*),
including powers to suspend or remove disobedient ministers. Geleji's 1649

[50] I. Juhász, *A székelyföldi református egyházmegyék* (Kolozsvár, 1947), 39; S. Szilágyi,
'Egyháztörténelmi adatok', *Keresztény Magvető*, 11 (1876), 62–4. S. Szilágyi and B. Orbán,
'Az unitáriusok 1638-diki üldöztetéseinek s a deési complanatiónak történetéhez', *Keresztény
Magvető*, 9 (1874), 150–62; Segesvári Bálint, 'Krónikája, 1606–1654', 157–218.

[51] György Gönci, *De disciplina ecclesiastica; seu, Gubernationis ecclesiasticae legitima forma,
in Ungarica natione Cis Tibiscus* (Debrecen, 1613); 'Az erdélyi kőzzsinatainak végzései', ed.
Szilágyi, 1–9, 77–84, 473–79; Miklós, *A magyar protestáns egyházalkotmány kialakulása a reformáció századában*; G. Nagy, *Fejezetek a magyar református egyház 17. századi történetéből*
(Budapest, 1985).

canons also strengthened the powers held by archdeacons, who were instructed to approve the appointment of all new parish clergy and to ensure that a uniform pattern of church services was maintained in their districts.[52]

György I Rákóczi used the opportunity of the Szatmár national synod to demand that the northern Tisza province elect a superintendent for the first time. The four northern Tisza archdeacons, however, proved tenacious in resisting this pressure, claiming in August 1646 that each archdeacon in their province had the authority equivalent to a superintendent, able to call synods, ordain ministers, and conduct visitations. Nevertheless in 1648 the archdeacons did agree to co-operate more closely on matters of common interest and created a rotating office with the responsibility to intervene across the province to prevent any doctrinal innovation.[53] Some ministers had travelled from western Hungary to attend the Szatmár synod, and they too subscribed to the synod's declarations on the form of church government. Reformed superintendents in the western Danubian province, however, faced altogether different circumstances from their counterparts in Transylvania and the Partium. In 1628 Sámuel Pathai was forced to resign as superintendent and leave his province after threats were made by local Catholics against him. Pathai's successor, János Kanizsai Pálfi, was excluded from his own church at Pápa, after the Catholic Eszterházy and Csáky families gained control over the town. The western Danubian synod then tried to deflect attention away from their beleaguered superintendents by adopting a less centralized structure of authority, and by developing the role of clergy councils to assist with the general supervision of local clergy, and to aid archdeacons during their parish visitations.[54]

Catholic persecution of Reformed ministers in Royal Hungary also encouraged greater lay participation in running local congregations. In 1616 János Kanizsai Pálfi had been given permission to appoint lay 'church councillors' from among his Pápa congregation, and at the 1630 Pápa synod Kanizsai recommended the setting up of 'governing congregational

---

52 Tiszáninnen Reformed Church Province Library MS Collection (Sárospatak), István Szilágyi Benjámin, 'Acta synodi nationalis Hungaricae... 1646', vol. 21 (hereafter 'Acta synodi nationalis'); *Egyházi kánonok- Geleji Katona István 1649 és a Szatmárnémetiben 1646 évben tartott zsinat végzései*, ed. Á. Kiss (Kecskemét, 1875) (hereafter *Egyházi kánonok*, ed. Kiss), 81–98; I. Révész, *A szatmárnémeti nemzeti zsinat és az első magyar református ébredés* (Budapest, 1947).

53 A superintendent was not appointed in the northern Tisza province until 1734. MOL boxes 1907–8 (Hungarian National Archives), ZEP (1638–51), 159–60. 'Magyar protestáns egyháztörténeti kútfők', ed. P. Finkei, *Sárospataki Füzetek*, 1 (1857–8), 471–3; L. Hegedüs, 'A tiszáninneni egyházmegyék kormányzata a Carolina resolutio kiadása elött', *Sárospataki Füzetek*, 3 (1859) 475–83.

54 Thury, *A dunántúli református egyházkerület*; [Dunantúl], 'Adatok a dunántúli ref. egyházkerület történetéhez', ed. E. Thury, in *MPEA* 8 (1909), 1–101, and 9 (1910), 1–113.

presbyteries' throughout the western Danubian province. Kanizsai had picked up ideas about the practical assistance which lay elders could provide to ministers from time spent studying at Heidelberg. The elders appointed at Pápa were made responsible for order and discipline in the town and could also call the minister to account over his behaviour or his standard of preaching. Many ministers from Transylvania and the Partium who had also studied in Germany and in the Dutch Republic were equally keenly aware of the potential benefits for parish life of appointing elders. From the later 1630s critical voices began to be raised in Transylvania about the dangers and limitations of the hardening clergy hierarchy. Reform-minded ministers proposed the introduction of presbyteries in each parish, at least to complement the regime of superintendents and archdeacons, or perhaps even entirely replacing existing church structures. In 1646 the Transylvanian synod assented to the piecemeal introduction of parish presbyteries, where approval to appoint elders was forthcoming from local church patrons. This resolution was repeated by the national synod at Szatmár, which the clergy hierarchy and György I Rákóczi intended should conclude all debate among Reformed ministers on the issue.[55]

From the late 1640s some patrons encouraged ministers to form parish presbyteries, including most notably Zsuzsanna Lórántffy, György I Rákóczi's widow, who supported lay presbyteries in the 1650s around Sárospatak in the northern Tisza province and at Fogaras in Transylvania.[56] However, any further consideration of devolving powers from the clergy hierarchy to individual ministers, supported by local lay presbyteries, was curtailed in 1653 by new Transylvanian state laws. These laws made any unauthorized effort to change either Reformed doctrine or church government a civil offence, and reform-minded ministers who continued to be defiant were demoted, and some were even imprisoned. When, during the latter decades of the seventeenth century the authority of the Reformed clergy hierarchy gave way, it was not in favour of congregational

55 Dunántúl Reformed Church Province Archives, A pápai református egyházközség levéltára Liskay-féle besorolás, no. 29. Dunántúl Reformed Church Province Library MS Collection (Pápa), Veszprémi ref. egyházmegye protokolluma, o.969, ff. 114–22. MOL boxes 1882, A. 1525, A kiskomáromi ref. egyházközségi legrégébbi anyakönyve, 1624–1732; J. Pokoly, 'Az első magyar ref. presbyterium keletkezése és szervezete', *Protestáns Szemle*, 2 (1890), 202–20; Thury, *A dunántúli egyházkerülete*, 246–53; E. Tóth, *A pápai református egyház története* (Pápa, 1941); K. Révész, 'A presbyterium legelső nyomai hazai református egyházunkban', *Protestáns Szemle*, 4 (1892), 419–46; *Egyházi kánonok*, ed. Kiss, canon 99.

56 'A fogarasi egyházközség levéltárából', ed. J. Pokoly, in *MPEA* 8 (1909), 120–5; B. Csernák, *A református egyház Nagyváradon, 1557–1660* (Nagyvárad, 1934), 125–263; G. Komjáthy, *Adalékok az ungvári ev. ref. egyház történetéhez* (Ungvár, 1906), 12; G. Illyés, 'Az Apafiak szerepe a küküllői református egyházmegye történetében', *Református Szemle* (1930), 468–72, 482–6.

presbyteries but rather to Transylvania's princes and Reformed noble patrons. The prince called an ecclesiastical council of ten invited lay and clergy leaders to meet in parallel with the provincial synod, and from 1671 this council played an increasingly important role in directing church affairs in Transylvania towards the end of the century.[57]

The Transylvanian court and most leading clergy of the 1640s and 1650s remained trenchantly opposed to any fundamental changes of the hierarchical church order, concerned that any weakening of the authority of superintendents would lead to widespread doctrinal innovation. István Geleji Katona suspected that dissident clergy who favoured presbyteries also wanted to change existing patterns of liturgy and ceremony. Geleji feared the growth of a clergy faction within the church inspired by foreign Calvinist sectarians, variously labelled as Arminians, puritans, and Independents. During the 1650s György II Rákóczi even perceived some sort of radical clergy faction who, following the example of English extremists, might try to challenge political as well as ecclesiastical authority in Transylvania.

Some Hungarian Reformed ministers certainly became attached to a puritan agenda from the late 1630s, enthusiastic to introduce further reform of church practices and to implement a reformation of life in the Hungarian countryside. Informed by contacts and connections with Protestants in the Dutch Republic and England, Hungarian puritan clergy advocated tighter moral discipline in Reformed congregations, greater personal piety among ordinary believers, the extension of educational opportunities, reforms of liturgical and sacramental practices to rid them of any semblance of surviving Catholic influence, and institutional reform of the church to ease the implementation of this programme. There was broad acceptance among Reformed clergy and patrons of the need to impose higher standards of moral discipline within the church. The suggestion that this required changes to be made to the pattern of church government, however, led to reforming ministers being stigmatized as puritan troublemakers and separatists. International links with western Calvinists encouraged some ministers to persist in questioning the increasingly hierarchical church order during the 1640s and 1650s, jolting the established matrix of princely, noble, and clerical power which dominated the church. Puritan clergy received some wider popular support, most notably at Nagyvárad near the Ottoman border, but were hardly political radicals

57 Nagy, *Fejezetek a magyar református egyház 17. századi történetéből*, 201–37; I. Révész (ed.), *A magyar református egyház története*, 132–42; Pokoly, *Erdélyi református egyház története*, iv, 179–213.

and worked to implement reforms with such godly magistrates as Zsuzsanna Lórántffy and her younger son Zsigmond Rákóczi.[58]

Support for the Hungarian puritan project dissipated during the early 1660s following the deaths of the leading reformers Pál Medgyesi and János Tolnai Dali, and also of their patron Zsuzsanna Lórántffy. The Reformed church indeed could no longer afford the luxury of internal debate and disruption as it faced the changed political realities in the region following György II Rákóczi's disastrous campaign in Poland in 1657. Rákóczi had invaded Poland in alliance with Sweden, the Cossacks, and Romanian princes, but once Charles X withdrew from Poland to face an attack by the Danes, Rákóczi was forced to surrender and retreat. Rákóczi had not attempted to gain permission from the Porte for his Polish campaign, and the Ottoman response was to launch a devastating invasion of Transylvania in 1658, ransacking the capital. Rákóczi attempted to rally support but was killed from injuries sustained in a battle at Gyalu near Kolozsvár in May 1660. The principality slid into internal division, eventually losing one-fifth of its territory to Ottoman control, including the godly citadel of Nagyvárad. During the latter decades of the century Transylvania's Prince Mihály Apafi was compelled to become more pliant to Ottoman demands, and was unable to lead the army outside Transylvania's borders except on the express orders of the Porte.[59]

The progress of the reformation in Hungary and Transylvania was profoundly affected by Ottoman involvement in Hungarian politics. The military catastrophe at Mohács in 1526 had opened up possibilities for the spread of Protestant ideas in the region, but the Ottoman response after 1657 to Rákóczi's Polish adventure gravely weakened Protestant Transylvania. The fortunes of the Hungarian Reformed church suffered as Transylvania declined from a golden age of independence. Catholic persecution of Protestants in Royal Hungary increased, and there were further conversions to Catholicism among noble families, including the Rákóczis. Contact between Hungarian clergy and western co-religionists became more restricted during the latter decades of the century, lowering the church's international perspective, as attention focused instead upon a grim defence of local Reformed privileges, churches, and schools.

---

[58] J. Zoványi, *Puritánus mozgalmak a magyar református egyházban* (Budapest, 1911); L. Makkai, *A magyar puritánusok harca a feudálizmus ellen* (Budapest, 1952); L. Makkai, 'The Hungarian Puritans and the English Revolution', *Acta Historica*, 5 (1958), 13–45; I. Révész, 'Szempontok a magyar kalvinizmus eredetéhez', *Századok*, 68 (1934), 257–75.

[59] *Szalárdi János és siralmas magyar krónikája*, ed. F. Szakaly (Budapest, 1980); Á. R. Várkonyi, 'Válság Erdélyben', in *Magyarország története*, iii, 1,068–90; K. Péter, 'A fejedelemség virágkora', in *Erdély története*, ii, 711–25.

2

Hungarian Reformed Clergy and International Calvinism

The international character of Calvinism was sustained by close contact between Reformed activists across the Continent. International Calvinism was fashioned and strengthened above all at academic centres where Reformed theologians, ministers, and students gathered together, and where the bonds forged between Calvinists reinforced a sense of belonging to an international brotherhood of true believers. This chapter will trace the developing intellectual communication between east-central European Calvinists and western Calvinism, establishing how student ministers from the Hungarian Reformed church participated in the international Calvinist community. The Reformed church in Hungary and Transylvania became increasingly involved during the early seventeenth century in international connections between Calvinist pastors, professors, and students. Hungary and Transylvania could not boast a Protestant university of its own and so, whilst local academies were being developed, student ministers were supported to travel to universities abroad. By the early seventeenth century hundreds of Hungarian students were involved in a major peregrination to western Europe. This *peregrinatio academica* was supported by the patronage of Transylvania's princes, Hungarian nobles, and town councils. It was hoped that the expense of sending student ministers to be educated abroad would soon be repaid on their return home through their service to the Reformed church in local colleges and schools, and in parishes across the region.

Western Calvinist centres had in fact long provided important support for the Hungarian church. There had been contact with Swiss Reformed leaders from the mid-sixteenth century, and Theodore Beza and Heinrich Bullinger corresponded with Hungarian reformers Péter Méliusz Juhász, Gál Huszár, Gergely Belényesi, and István Szegedi Kis, and with the nobleman Miklós Thelegdi. In 1559 Protestant ministers in Kolozsvár, including Gáspár Heltai, published a letter which they had received from Bullinger explaining his views on communion theology. Other Swiss leaders were also in contact with Hungarians, including Wolfgang Musculus at

Berne who replied to one unknown writer in 1550 that just as doors were then closing to the Gospel in Germany, so God had provided the Turkish invasion as an instrument to open the way for Protestant preaching in Hungary. However, the extent of these connections hardly amounted to decisive Swiss direction of the spread of Reformed ideas in Hungary and Transylvania, but rather encouragement and support for a process already underway.[1]

This association between the emerging Hungarian Reformed church and western co-religionists was bolstered from the 1560s by Hungarian students who visited Zurich and Geneva, including Mihály Paksi, Mátyás Thuri, and Mátyás Skaricza. Bálint Szikszai Hellopoeus visited Geneva for six months during 1566, and before his early death in 1575 completed a work on the sacraments which Beza had published in Geneva in 1585. Szikszai dedicated the book to Beza, writing that he wanted to show how the ripened fruit of Beza's 'planting' was returning from the furthest regions of the Continent. In 1569 Péter Méliusz Juhász wrote to Bullinger requesting the publication in Zurich of his work refuting anti-Trinitarian opinions. Bullinger and Beza discussed the project, but Beza wrote back to Méliusz in 1570 that because of difficulties in deciphering his manuscript they could not publish it.[2]

During the latter decades of the sixteenth century rather than study at Geneva, where the Academy's reputation was in decline, Reformed student ministers from Hungary and Transylvania instead tended to follow Lutheran colleagues to Wittenberg University. Towards the end of the sixteenth century Melanchthonian theology was being steadily replaced by doctrinaire Lutheranism in Saxony, and the imposition of strict Lutheran formulas for prospective students at Wittenberg from 1592 forced

---

[1] *Correspondance de Théodore de Bèze*, ed. H. Meylan et al. (eds.) (16 vols.; Geneva, 1978–93), ix, 234–9; x, 185–6; xi, 83, 186–7; xiv, 25–7, 74–9, 169–71; xvi, 33–6; C. d'Eszlary, 'Jean Calvin, Théodore de Bèze et leurs amis hongrois', *Bulletin de la Société de l'histoire du Protestantisme Français*, 110 (1964), 74–99; B. Vogler, 'Europe as Seen through the Correspondence of Theodore Beza', in E. I. Kouri and T. Scott (eds.), *Politics and Society in Reformation Europe* (London, 1987), 252–66; I. Schlegl, 'Die Beziehungen Heinrich Bullinger zu Ungarn', *Zwingliana. Beiträge zur Geschichte Zwinglis, der Reformation und des Protestantismus in der Schweiz* 12 (1966), 330–70; Heinrich Bullinger, *Libellus epistolaris . . . pressis et afflictiss[imis] ecclesiis in Hungaria, earu[n]demq[ue] pastoribus et ministris transmissus* (Kolozsvár, 1559); Gy. Ráth, 'Bullinger Henrik és a magyar reformáczió', *ITK* 6 (1896), 42–58.

[2] B. S. Nagy and M. Szentimray, 'Szikszai Hellopoeus Bálint kátéja', in Barth (ed.), *Tanulmányok, 3,* 727–69; E. Zsindely, 'Svájci levelesláda a reformáció korából', ibid. 929–1,001; Zsindely, 'Bullinger Henrik magyar kapcsolatai', in Barth (ed.), *Tánulmányok, 2,* 55–86; H. A. Oberman, '*Europa afflicta*: The Reformation of the Refugees', *Archiv für Reformationsgeschichte*, 83 (1992), 91–111. A donation was sent from Transylvania for the defence of Geneva in the 1590s: E. W. Monter, *Calvin's Geneva* (New York, 1967), 234.

Hungarian Calvinists to look elsewhere. Hungarian students started to attend various German Reformed academic centres such as Marburg in Hesse and Herborn in Nassau. Hungarian students travelled in greatest numbers to Heidelberg University in the Palatinate, with twenty Hungarian Calvinists at Heidelberg in the 1580s, fifty-two in the 1590s, and thirty-seven in the 1600s. There had been contacts with Heidelberg from 1565, when ministers at Kolozsvár received encouragement from Heidelberg university teachers to stand by Reformed understanding of the sacraments. From the 1580s Hungarian student ministers added to Heidelberg's cosmopolitan atmosphere, and between 1610 and 1615 over one-third of non-German students attending the university were from eastern and central Europe including Hungarians and Transylvanians, as well as Poles, Bohemians, Moravians, and Silesians.[3]

The division between Lutheran and Calvinist educational institutions in Germany continued to solidify during the early seventeenth century. Whilst Hungarian Lutheran students travelled to Wittenberg, Altdorf, or to Königsberg in Prussia, these universities were only very rarely visited by Hungarian Calvinists. When Heidelberg fell to Catholic forces in 1622, Reformed students switched instead to the university at Frankfurt an der Oder in Brandenburg, or to the college at Bremen, and began for the first time to attend universities in the Dutch Republic. Johann Sigismund had established Calvinist dominance at the university of Frankfurt in the 1610s and, despite floods and outbreaks of plague, Frankfurt became an important staging post for Hungarian students in the 1620s until it was stormed by the Swedish army in 1631.[4]

The disruption which this caused to Hungarian students was short lived, and from the 1630s they travelled in ever greater numbers via Cracow to Danzig, before venturing onwards to Franeker, Leiden, Utrecht, and

---

3 K. Maag, *Seminary or University? The Genevan Academy and Reformed Higher Education, 1560–1620* (Aldershot, 1995); G. Lewis, 'The Genevan Academy', in A. Pettegree, A. C. Duke, G. Lewis (eds.), *Calvinism in Europe, 1540–1620* (Cambridge, 1994), 35–63; G. Szabó, *Geschichte des Ungarischen Coetus an der Universität Wittenberg, 1555–1613* (Halle, 1941), 105–23; 'Epistola professorum theologiae inclytae academiae Heydelbergensis: Ministris ecclesiae Claudiopolitanae et coniunctarum transmissa: Negocium controversiae de coena dominij concernens', printed in T. Barth (ed.), *Der Heidelberger Katechismus in Ungarn* (Budapest, 1967), 387–91; C. P. Clasen, *The Palatinate in European History, 1559–1660* (Oxford, 1963), 36.

4 B. Nischan, 'The Schools of Brandenburg and the "Second Reformation": Centers of Calvinist Learning and Propaganda', in R. V. Schnucker (ed.), *Calviniana. Ideas and Influence of Jean Calvin* (Sixteenth Century Essays and Studies, 10; Kirksville, Mo., 1988), 215–33; [Königsberg], *Die Matrikel der Albertus-Universität zu Königsberg, 1544–1829*, ed. G. Erler (3 vols.; Leipzig, 1910–17); A. Varga, 'Az altdorfi egyetem magyar diákjai (1583–1718)', *Lymbus. Művelődéstörténeti Tár*, 5 (Szeged, 1994).

Groningen. The Dutch Reformed church was by then seen as a bastion of orthodoxy in the Calvinist world, after theologians at the 1619 Dort synod had excluded Remonstrants from the Dutch church and universities. The largest university in the Republic was at Leiden, which had been at the centre of the Remonstrant controversy. Of the other universities, Franeker in Friesland was the oldest, with the university at Groningen founded in 1614, Utrecht University established in 1636, and that at Harderwijk in 1646. Elsewhere in the Republic high schools flourished, with the school at Deventer attracting some Hungarian students in the 1640s. All these Dutch academic centres drew teachers and students from across the Calvinist world. Around half of the students at Franeker in the second quarter of the seventeenth century came from outside the Republic. Leiden had more foreign than Dutch students during the same period, with Hungarians accounting for one in twenty of some 5,500 foreign students.[5]

The overall numbers of Hungarian Calvinist students attending or registering at continental universities reached its peak during the 1640s. As the Table shows, Hungarians mostly attended Heidelberg University in the 1610s, then moving to Frankfurt an der Oder, Franeker, and Leiden in the 1620s and 1630s. The vast majority of Hungarian students who studied in the Dutch Republic visited more than one university, but registration records still indicate that by the 1640s Franeker had become the most popular destination, only to be surpassed by Utrecht in the 1650s, with a fall in those choosing to study at Leiden. A small number of Hungarian Reformed student ministers also travelled to study in France, Switzerland, and Italy during the early seventeenth century, helping to bring a wide range of theological learning and literature back to Hungary and Transylvania.[6]

Some Reformed students who reached the Dutch Republic were emboldened to risk a further voyage from the Dutch coast to England, mostly living in London and visiting Oxford or Cambridge, although at least one student travelled on to Scotland. Contact between student ministers from the Hungarian Reformed church and Protestants in England expanded from sporadic visits during the late sixteenth century and early decades of the seventeenth century, with the road to London and the English

---

5 Ö. Miklós, *Magyar diákok a leideni staten collegeben* (Debrecen, 1928); J. Israel, *The Dutch Republic. Its Rise, Greatness, and Fall, 1477–1806* (Oxford, 1995), 565–94, 899–902; T. H. Lunsingh Scheurleer and G. H. M. Posthumus Meyjes (eds.), *Leiden University in the Seventeenth Century. An Exchange of Learning* (Leiden, 1975).

6 E. Veress, *Olasz egyetemeken járt magyarországi tanulók anyakönyvei és iratai* (Budapest, 1941); M. Szabó, 'Erdélyi diákok külföldi egyetemjárása a xvi.-xviii. században', in Zs. Jakó, S. Tonk, and E. Csetri (eds.), *Művelődéstörténeti tanulmányok* (Bucharest, 1980), 152–68.

TABLE: Registrations and attendance of Hungarian and Transylvanian Reformed students at western European universities, 1610–1659

	1610–19	1620–9	1630–9	1640–9	1650–9	Total
Heidelberg	91	17	0	0	3	111
Wittenberg	4	0	0	0	0	4
Herborn	4	0	0	0	0	4
Marburg	24	0	0	0	0	24
Frankfurt an der Oder	0	98	5	1	6	110
Bremen	1	25	10	0	0	36
Basel	3	12	2	0	1	18
Geneva	0	0	0	0	2	2
Leiden	0	52	93	96	38	279
Utrecht	0	0	0	61	124	185
Franeker	0	66	74	127	97	364
Groningen	0	0	9	38	58	105
Deventer	0	0	0	36	0	36
Harderwijk	0	0	0	3	1	4
Total	127	270	193	362	330	–

Sources: 'A heidelbergben tanult magyarok névsora', ed. J. Szeremlei, *Sárospataki Füzetek*, 5 (1861), 452–71, 556–7; 6 (1862), 559–67; [Heidelberg], 'Adatok a heidelbergi egyetem magyarországi hallgatóinak névsorához', ed. J. Zoványi, *Protestáns Szemle*, 16 (1904), 111–14; 'A wittenbergi egyetem magyarországi hallgatóinak névsora 1601–1812', ed. M. Asztalos, in *MPEA* 14 (1930), 111–74; Á. Hellebrant, 'Adalék a külföldi iskolazás történetéhez a xvii. században' [Herborn], *Századok*, 17 (1883), 154–5; [Bázel], 'A bázeli egyetem anyakönyvéből', ed. I. Zsindely, *Sárospataki Füzetek*, 4 (1860), 161–5; [Genfi], 'A magyarhoni egyházra vonatkozó egyes adatok a genfi papi testület jegyzőkönyvből', ed. K. Szél, *Sárospataki Füzetek*, 6 (1862), 922–9; 'A genfi akadémia magyar diákjai (1566–1772)', ed. B. S. Nagy, *ITK* 87 (1983), 388; J. Zoványi, 'A marburgi egyetem magyarországi hallgatói 1859-ig', *Irodalomtörténet*, 37 (1955); [Frankfurt an der Oder], 'A magyarországi ifjak az odera melletti Frankfurt egyetemében', ed. J. Zoványi, *Protestáns Szemle*, 1 (1889), 178–202; 'A brémai főiskola magyar diákjai (1618–1750)', ed. I. Czegle, *ITK* 78 (1974), 88. Some students returned to study at one of the Dutch universities more than once, and the number of registrations is therefore larger than the number of Hungarian students who visited the Dutch Republic. [Leiden], 'Die Studierenden aus Ungarn und Siebenbürgen an der Universität Leiden 1575–1875', ed. F. Teutsch, *Archiv des Vereins für Siebenbürgische Landeskunde*, 16 (1881), 204–26; G. Antal, 'Az utrechti és leideni egyetemeken járt magyar ifjak névjegyzéke', *PEIL* 31 (1888), 278–9, 409–12, 437–41; 'Verzeichnis der Studenten aus Ungarn und Siebenbürgen an der Universität Utrecht in den Jahren 1643–1885', *Archiv des Vereins für Siebenbürgische Landeskunde*, 22 (1889), 79–92; L. Segesváry, *Magyar református ifjak az utrechti egyetemen 1636–1686* (Debrecen, 1935); 'A franekeri egyetemen tanúlt magyarok', ed. Á. Hellebrant, *TT* (1886), 599–608, 792–800; 'A groningeni egyetemén tanult magyarok névsora', ed. Ö. Miklós, *Dunántuli Protestáns Lap* (1917), 194–7, 202–7; 'A deventeri athenaeumon tanult magyarok 1644–9', ed. L. Segesváry, *Századok*, 71 (1937), 506–8; 'A harderwijki egyetem magyarországi hallgatói', ed. J. Zoványi, *ITK* 1 (1891), 433–6.

universities more regularly used by Hungarians from the 1620s. The presence of Hungarian and Transylvanian students in England was indeed noted in 1644 by John Milton: 'not for nothing . . . the grave and frugal

Transylvanian, sends out yearly from as far as the mountainous borders of Russia and beyond the Hercynian wilderness, not their youth, but their stay'd men to learn our language, and our theologic arts'.[7] The exact number of student ministers who spent part of their peregrination to western Europe in England is difficult to ascertain. Evidence that Hungarian students were in England during this period comes from a variety of sources, such as gaps in registrations at Dutch universities, records from Oxford and Cambridge, students' albums, book dedications, and from travel passes issued during the Commonwealth. These sources suggest that over one hundred Hungarian students were in England between 1600 and 1660, which indicates that at least one in eight of those students who travelled to the Dutch Republic are also known to have visited England.[8]

Turning to examine the impact of this peregrination by Hungarian student ministers to Germany, the Dutch Republic, and England, travel to western Protestant centres on the whole served to reinforce Hungarian student ministers' familiarity with, and commitment to, orthodox Calvinist theology. Hungarian students were widely encouraged to study polemic theology at western universities in order to enable them to criticize the beliefs of other rival confessions. Nevertheless, leaders of the Hungarian church were anxious to monitor the effect on student ministers of periods of study abroad. Fears were aroused amongst senior clergy that foreign influences might have the potential to undermine good order in the Hungarian church. On their return home, some students indeed raised questions about the hierarchical pattern of local church government, and also about differences between western and Hungarian forms of worship and discipline. Some returning students also began to place a distinctive emphasis on issues of personal piety and morality, leading to concern that a disruptive puritan infection was spreading to the Hungarian church. Student ministers were soon discouraged from visiting England and compelled to agree to a range of conditions before they were allowed to travel abroad. This chapter will assess how justified these concerns were,

---

7 John Milton, *Areopagitica*, ed. J. W. Hales (Oxford, 1898), 45.
8 B. Trócsányi, 'Református theológusok Angliában a xvi. és xvii. században', *Angol Filológiai Tanulmányok*, 6 (1944), 115–46; J. Pongrácz, *Magyar diákok angliában* (Pápa, 1914); G. Kathona, 'Pótlások az 1711-ig angliában tanult magyar diákok névsorához', *ITK* 80 (1976), 92–8; G. Gömöri, *Erdélyiek és angolok* (Budapest, 1991), 20–37; G. Gömöri, 'Magyar látogatók a Cromwell-kori angliában', and 'Magyar peregrinusok a xvii. századi Cambridge-ben', in G. Gömöri, *Angol-Magyar kapcsolatok a xvi.–xvii. században. Irodalomtörténeti Füzetek* (Budapest, 1989); B. Pettkó, 'Külföldi alumnusok levelei', *TT* (1885), 179–84; *Calendar of State Papers (Domestic)* SP16: (1627–8), 92/26; (1651–2), 31/22; (1655), 8/587; (1656), 76/544, 112/213, 76/601, and 77/233; L. Kropf, 'Egy ismeretlen magyar költő skócziában, 1628', *ITK* 24 (1914), 19.

highlighting university teachers who were particularly influential among Hungarian students, the subjects which Hungarians tended to study at western universities, and the broader pattern of contacts which Hungarians established in Germany, the Dutch Republic, and England.

GERMANY

Hungarian Reformed patrons supported students so that they could attend foreign universities in a deliberate effort to create a well-educated clergy élite to lead the Hungarian church. The success of these efforts can be judged from the eleven future superintendents and twenty-nine future regional archdeacons who all studied at Heidelberg before 1622. This list includes such figures as István Geleji Katona, György Csulai, János Kanizsai Pálfi, János Keserüi Dajka, János Samarjai, Mihály Simándi, and István Tolnai. Gábor Bethlen sponsored students at Heidelberg from 1614, and the Bethlen family supported over twenty students who studied there before 1622. The Rákóczi family and other nobles also gave financial backing to student ministers to cover the expenses of their peregrination, as did the councils and leading families of large towns such as Kassa, Nagyszombat, Sárospatak, Debrecen, and Szatmár. Gábor Bethlen also financed the study abroad of both his nephews, István and Péter, and the prince took a personal interest in their progress. Bethlen gave instructions to those accompanying Péter in 1625 that he was not to be allowed to speak Hungarian whilst abroad and ordered strict controls over Péter's behaviour and application to his studies.[9]

Hungarian Calvinist students in Germany generally kept their patrons well informed of their progress. In 1613 Gáspár Komáromi wrote to his Rákóczi patrons of his safe arrival at Marburg, but expressed his disappointment at spending the whole winter there without being able to study theology. Komáromi informed his patrons that he had decided to move on to Heidelberg, commenting that whilst many of his Hungarian colleagues were dabbling in all sorts of subjects without mastering any of them, he firmly wished to concentrate his efforts on studying the Bible.

---

9 I. Lukinich, *A Bethlen-fiúk külföldi iskoláztatása 1619–1628* (Budapest, 1926); S. Gergely, 'Bethlen Péter utazása történetéhez', *TT* 1884, 590–2; *Magyar utazási irodalom a 15–18. században*, ed. I. S. Kovács and I. Monok (Budapest, 1990), 34–8; János Redmeczi, 'Az felséges Bethlen Gábornak öt rendbeli isten anyaszentegyházával cselekedett jótéteményéről', ed. Makkai, 24–46; Zoványi, *Magyarországi protestáns egyháztörténeti lexikon*; J. Heltai, *Alvinczi Péter és a heidelbergi peregrinusok* (Budapest, 1994), 45; J. Heltai, 'Adattár a heidelbergi egyetemen 1595–1621 között tanult magyarországi diákokról és pártfogóikról', *Országos Széchenyi Könyvtár Évkönyve* (1980), 243–345.

Students also wrote home from Germany to request more funds, a slow process since letters could take many weeks to get back to Hungary and Transylvania. The diary of István Miskolczi Csulyak, later archdeacon of Zemplén, recorded his travels from 1601 to Poland, Prague, and Wittenberg, and his stay at Heidelberg for almost four years until 1607. Miskolczi's plans to proceed from Heidelberg to France and England were only thwarted when news reached him that his patron had died, and Miskolczi was then forced to return home.[10]

Hungarians who studied for several years at Heidelberg such as István Miskolczi Csulyak and Péter Alvinczi were instrumental in establishing a network of contacts for other Hungarian students who followed them to Germany. Albert Szenczi Molnár was perhaps even more important in establishing links between the Hungarian church and German Calvinists. In the 1590s Molnár studied at Wittenberg, Heidelberg, and Strasburg when still in his teens, then travelling to Italy and to Geneva where he met Beza in 1596. Molnár later referred to Beza as his father in Christ, and demonstrated his enthusiasm for the international Calvinist community by adapting a verse by Beza which eulogized Calvinists from every corner of the Continent. After 1600 Molnár returned to Germany and worked at Heidelberg, Herborn, Altdorf, and Marburg. Molnár's extensive connections at these German universities and academies proved valuable to other Hungarian students. In August 1623 Imre Pataki, for example, was able to write to his patron Kata Kisvárdai about letters of introduction which he had gained from Molnár, which opened possibilities for him to further his studies in Germany.[11]

Molnár became a well-known figure in Reformed German academic circles, corresponding with Johann Heinrich Alsted at Herborn, and with Bartholomaeus Keckermann at Danzig. Molnár also made connections at German princely courts, in contact with both Maurice of Hesse and Frederick V of the Palatinate. Molnár even went on a boat trip with Maurice, and in 1607 wrote to a former teacher at Basel of Maurice's efforts to learn Hungarian.[12] Molnár also established important links with refugee

[10] S. Szilágyi, 'Egyházi férfiak levelei', *EPK* (1875), 69–70; 'Thállyai János Cambridge-i tanuló levele', ed. L. Kemény, *ITK* 19 (1909), 484–5; *Magyar utazási irodalom*, ed. Kovács and Monok, 301–13; Zs. Jakó, 'Miskolci Csulyak István peregrinációs albuma', in B. Keserű (ed.), *Acta Historiae Litterarum Hungaricarum, 10–11* (Szeged, 1971), 59–71.

[11] 'Adatok angliában járt magyar deákokról és egyéb angol emlékek', in B. Keserű (ed.), *Adattár 3. Művelődési törekvések a század második felében* (Szeged, 1971), 419–41.

[12] *Szenci Molnár válogatott művei*, ed. J. Vásárhelyi and G. Tolnai (Budapest, 1976), 469–551, 575–8; *Szenczi Molnár Albert naplója, levelezése és irományai*, ed. L. Dézsi (Budapest, 1898); B. Varga, *Szenci Molnár Albert. A magyar zsoltáréneskszerző élete és írói működése* (Budapest, 1932), 37.

Calvinists in Germany and gained financial support and practical assistance from both French and Flemish congregations. Clemens Dubois, minister to the French community at Frankfurt am Main, offered Molnár
free use of his library, and Molnár was also warmly received at Frankfurt by
the Flemish minister, Isaac Genius. Genius was in contact with Jean Boil-
blanc, a French minister at Heidelberg who later wrote to Molnár from
Sedan. In 1607 Molnár received a further letter from another contact at
Sedan, Jean Combillon, who sought news through Molnár of Clemens
Dubois.[13]

There was evidently a strong sense of empathy between Molnár, far
from his distant homeland, and various refugee communities in Germany
who were deeply committed to the international Calvinist cause. In 1600
Molnár had translated a prayer-book of Daniel Toussain, a minister from
Orléans who had been forced into exile after the St Bartholomew's day
massacre. Toussain had been invited by Frederick III to Heidelberg, where
he served as a court preacher and also taught at the university until his
death in 1602. Molnár's 1608 revised publication of Gáspár Károlyi's Hungarian Bible was assisted by a donation from the widow of an exiled mathe-
matician from Ghent, and the introduction to Molnár's translation of
Calvin's *Institutes* in 1624 remembered assistance given to him by our
'French and Flemish twin churches'.[14] Molnár also dedicated a work about
Hungarian Protestants living under Turkish occupation to the ministers
and congregations of French and Flemish Protestants at Hanau and
Frankfurt, writing that the situation of Reformed exiles in Germany was
still happier than that of some Hungarians in their own land. Molnár, however, wrote that: 'our Bibles, which through the support and efforts of your
people, have been published in the past years . . . and which have been sent
to Hungary in great numbers, show the providential results of the afflictions and exile of the French and Flemish'.[15]

The impact of Hungarian student peregrination to Reformed Germany
was indeed not limited to the students themselves. Albert Szenczi Molnár
and other students were able to publish works which they thought would be
useful in building up the church at home, and many more students brought

---

[13] *Szenci Molnár művei*, ed. Vásárhelyi and Tolnai, 205–17, 224–6, 469–551.

[14] Albert Szenczi Molnár, *A keresztyéni religióra és igaz hitre való tanítás* (Hanau, 1624),
Consecratio Templi Novi (Kassa, 1625), and *Imádságos könyvecske* (Heidelberg, 1621) are all
printed in *Szenci Molnár művei*, ed. Vásárhelyi and Tolnai, 331–68; J. Vásárhelyi, *Eszmei
áramlatok és politika Szenci Molnár Albert életművében* (Budapest, 1985), 1–20.

[15] Pál Thuri, *Idea Christianorum Ungarorum sub tyrannide Turcica* (Oppenheim, 1616), in
Szenci Molnár művei, ed. Vásárhely and Tolnai 285–8 (quotation at 285); *Szent Biblia*, published by Szenczi Molnár (Hanau, 1608).

western theological texts back with them on their return to Hungary and Transylvania. One of the most impressive book collectors was István Geleji Katona, later superintendent of the church in Transylvania. Whilst Geleji studied at Heidelberg he acquired a copy of Calvin's *Institutes*, along with works by Beza, William Perkins, Keckermann, and David Pareus.[16] István Miskolczi Csulyak similarly brought many books back with him to Hungary including classical texts, biblical commentaries by Calvin, and works by Beza, Bullinger, Pareus, Johannes Piscator, and Alsted.[17] Reformed students frequently donated books which they brought back from Germany to their patrons or to local schools. Through students and other means, the Rákóczi family acquired a wide collection of books by western Calvinist authors during these decades, and the library at their Sárospatak College quickly gained a stock of around 2,000 books. In Transylvania, the library of the princely academy at Gyulafehérvár also accumulated many recent Reformed theological and philosophical texts among around 5,000 volumes held there during the early seventeenth century.[18]

These collections of books confirm the importance among Hungarian clergy and students of certain key theologians of the period. Amongst German Calvinists perhaps most notable was David Pareus, the sometime rector and professor of New Testament theology at Heidelberg University. Pareus had many personal connections with the Hungarian church and corresponded with Gábor Bethlen. Pareus sent Bethlen a copy of his celebrated 1614 work, *Irenicum, sive De Unione et Synodo Evangelicorum Concilianda Liber Votivus*, in which he advocated that Calvinists and Lutherans should work together against their common Catholic enemies. Pareus suggested a conference of Calvinist and Lutheran rulers and theologians to seek out common ground and to move towards a unified Protestant church. In January 1617 Bethlen wrote back to Pareus with thanks for this gift, and in return sent a picture of himself as a New Year's present. Bethlen also recommended two new students, Gáspár Bojti and Márton Szilvási, to Pareus'

---

[16] J. Koncz, 'Geleji Katona István könyveinek lajstroma', *Magyar Könyvszemle*, 24 (1899), 270–6.

[17] *Adattár 13. Magyarországi magánkönyvtárak, 1533–1657, 1*, ed. A. Varga (Szeged—Budapest, 1986), nos. 30, 47, 57, 68, 69. A 1657 inventory of Zemplén minister András Demétei is printed in J. Zoványi, 'Egy református pap könyvtára a xvii.-ik században', *Magyar Könyvszemle*, 32 (1907), 381.

[18] I. Harsányi, 'A Rákóczi könyvtár és katalogusa', *Magyar Könyvszemle*, 38 (1913), 17–28, 136–47, 232–40, 341–4; Tiszáninnen Church Province Library MS Collection (Sárospatak), Rakocziana, vol. 1,113; *Adattár 14. Partiumi könyvesházak, 1623–1730*, ed. B. Keserű (Szeged, 1988); *Adattár 15. Kassa város olvasmányai, 1562–1731*, ed. B. Keserű and I. Monok (Szeged, 1990); Zs. Jakó, 'A nagyenyedi Bethlen kollégium könyvtárának kezdetei és első korszaka (1622–1658)', in *Írás, könyv, értelmiség* (Bucharest, 1976), 199–209.

care at Heidelberg. Pareus maintained contacts with other Hungarian students, writing to both István Miskolczi Csulyak and Albert Szenczi Molnár, who in turn invited Pareus to his wedding. In 1618 Pareus wrote again to Bethlen, praising Bojti and Szilvási, and commenting on his pleasure at the improving situation for the Reformed community in Transylvania, with 'the raising up of the true church, and the spreading of good schools, which are the kitchen gardens of every virtue and piety'.[19] Another influential figure for Hungarian students in Germany was Abraham Scultetus, who taught at Wittenberg and Heidelberg, before becoming court preacher to Frederick V in 1615. Molnár translated a number of Scultetus' sermons, including those which Scultetus had given at the Reformation jubilee of 1617. Molnár added his own tracts to this collection on the importance of combating Jesuit schools and described his horrified reaction to the Catholic idolatry which he claimed to have witnessed when he visited Loreto in Italy.[20]

When Hungarian students reached Heidelberg University they were able to follow a course on Reformed dogmatics organized by David Pareus and his colleagues. Lectures were offered on all the major areas of theology, and academic debates held regularly under the presidency of resident professors. Very few Hungarians worked towards gaining a degree, and so the public defence of theological theses in these debates was their most significant contribution to the academic life of Heidelberg and other German universities which they attended. The defence of a thesis did not necessarily mark any independent contribution by a student to theological study on that subject, but these debates provided valuable opportunities for Hungarian and other student ministers to rehearse key aspects of Reformed theology. Debates frequently focused on areas of dispute with theological rivals, and thus acted to buttress students' orthodoxy on contentious issues. A total of 125 of these theological disputations are known to have been conducted by Hungarians at Heidelberg between the beginning of the seventeenth century and the early 1620s. Pareus noted the involvement of Hungarians in his introduction to a 1611 volume of Heidelberg

[19] Pápai Páriz, 'Romlott fal felépítése (Rudus Redivivum)', 129–73; J. Heltai, 'David Pareus magyar kapcsolatai', in J. Herner (ed.), *Adattár 23. Tudóslevelek: Művelődésünk külföldi kapcsolataihoz 1577–1797* (Szeged, 1989), 13–77; P. Uray, 'Az irénizmus magyarországon a 16–17. század fordulóján', in B. Varjas (ed.), *Irodalom és ideológia a 16–17. században. Memoria Saeculorum Hungariae, 5* (Budapest, 1987), 187–207.

[20] Albert Szenczi Molnár, *Postilla Scultetica: az egész esztendő által való vasárnapokra és fő innepekre rendeltetett evangeliomi textusoknak magyarázatja* (Oppenheim, 1617); Albert Szenczi Molnár, 'De idolo Lauretano et horribili papatus Rom. idolomania et tyrannide', printed in *Secularis concio evangelica; azaz, Jubileus esztendei prédikáció Abraham Scultetus után* (Oppenheim, 1618), 75–94.

disputations, which contained contributions by 43 Hungarian students out of a total of 127 disputants. Hungarian students' disputations often articulated a strident anti-Catholicism, and a 1620 volume of Heidelberg disputations which challenged the opinions of the Catholic theologian Robert Bellarmine had 71 'ex natione Ungarica et Transylvania' out of 109 respondents. This volume was dedicated to the Transylvanian Bishop János Keserüi Dajka, another former Heidelberg student with whom Pareus was in regular contact.[21]

The extent of Pareus' influence over many of the Hungarian students who visited Heidelberg is apparent from some of the subjects taken up in their public disputations. Whilst the primary purpose of disputations was to instruct students on Reformed dogma, some Hungarian students nevertheless advanced ideas about the essential unity of the Protestant interest and mirrored Pareus' irenic appeals for inter-Protestant co-operation against the Catholic church. András Prágai's 1617 disputation, for example, argued that the use of the terms 'Lutheran' and 'Calvinist' was misleading and divisive, and that only their opponents promoted the label 'Calvinist' in an effort to impute schism amongst those who were in fact defending early church traditions.[22] Disputations by István Velich, András Prágai, and Pál Kévi stressed the similarities between Reformed and Lutheran communion theology, the issue which had proved the major stumbling-block preventing any *rapprochement* between the two churches. János Samarjai, later a superintendent in western Hungary, advanced commonly held Protestant objections to the perceived Catholic idolatry of the host in his disputation. While Samarjai stopped short of accepting the Lutheran view on the real presence of Christ in the sacrament, he argued that Calvinists believed that the elements of bread and wine in the communion service were more than merely empty signs commemorating Christ's death. It might be argued that these disputations only signified Hungarian students' ability to repeat politely what Pareus wanted to hear, but in fact some former Heidelberg students continued to promote ideas on Protestant union and tried to build closer relations with Lutherans

[21] See David Pareus, *Collegiorum theologicorum pars prima* (Heidelberg, 1611), for surviving introduction and index. See also David Pareus, *Collegiorum theologicorum quibus universa theologica orthodoxa, et omnes prope theologorum huius temporis controversae perspicue et varie explicantur, pars altera* (Heidelberg, 1620); Heltai, 'Adattár a heidelbergi egyetemen 1595–1621 között tanult magyarországi diákokról', 243–345; H. Hotson, 'Irenicism and Dogmatics in the Confessional Age: Pareus and Comenius in Heidelberg, 1614', *Journal of Ecclesiastical History*, 46 (1995), 432–53.

[22] András Prágai, *An Calviniani, quos vocant, Fundamentum Fidei Sartum, Tectum retineant?* (Heidelberg, 1617). See also Ferenc Széki, *De orthodoxa Antiquitate et Heterodoxa Novitate* (Utrecht, 1656).

when they returned home, a theme which will be discussed again in Chapter 4.[23]

(II) THE DUTCH REPUBLIC

Hungarian students converged on the Dutch Republic from the 1620s, and most left deeply affected by their experience of Dutch university life. Márton Szepsi Csombor wrote in awe-struck tones about his impression of the grand buildings of Leiden University and was especially inspired by an academic procession which he saw before a lecture given by the university rector.[24] The noble Gábor Haller was only seventeen when he began to study at Franeker and Leiden Universities in the 1630s, taking a wide range of classes in logic, mathematics, geography, and rhetoric, and also attending dancing lessons from 1632. Haller was at one stage forced to borrow money from fellow Hungarian students, but in 1633 recorded a different problem in his diary, when he had behaved badly after drinking, promising himself not to drink any more wine for a month.[25] Not all Hungarian students were able to enjoy life in the Dutch Republic as much as Haller, and some constantly struggled with financial problems. László Gyöngyösi complained bitterly about his 'lamentable fate' of spending three years as a student at Dutch universities in utter poverty, and 'a wretched and sickly state'.[26]

Sharing the difficulties of travel and offering mutual support when in hardship often helped to engender camaraderie amongst the so-called 'academic ministers' who attended western universities. Hungarian students already knew many of their colleagues at Dutch universities, since 578 of some 959 students who studied in the Dutch Republic between 1623 and 1711 had previously gone to school at either Debrecen or Sárospatak.[27] Further evidence of an *esprit de corps* among Hungarian students comes from their travel albums, which are filled with signatures and inscriptions from friends and teachers. Pál Kismarjai Veszelin's album shows that he studied under Johannes Cocceius at Leiden, Samuel Maresius at Groningen, and Nicholas Arnold at Franeker during 1653 and 1654. The album contains inscriptions in Hebrew, Greek, Latin, and Aramaic from teachers

---

[23] Pareus, *Collegiorum theologicorum . . . pars altera*, 326–30, 342–4, 515–25.
[24] Márton Szepsi Csombor, *Europica Varietas* [1620], ed. S. Kovács and P. Kulcsár (Budapest, 1979), 171.
[25] Gábor Haller, 'Naplója, 1629–1644', in *ETA 4* (Kolozsvár, 1862), 1–103.
[26] László Gyöngyösi, *A keresztyeni vallasnak fundamentumi* (Utrecht, 1657), Introd.
[27] G. Kathona, 'A debreceni és sárospataki tanulók részvétele a hollandiai és angliai peregrinációban 1623-tól 1711-ig', *Theológiai Szemle*, 22 (1979), 89–94; Zoványi, *Magyarországi protestáns egyháztörténeti lexikon*.

and fellow students, both Hungarians and others, welcoming Kismarjai into the academic brotherhood. Kismarjai's album even includes an inscription in the ancient runic script of Transylvania's Szeklers, and István Bányai added his inscription of February 1654 in English: 'Prayer is like Jonathon's bowe, which sent out the arrowes, but faith is like Jonathon's boy, which fetcht backe the arrowes.'[28]

Most Hungarians studied at more than one university in the Dutch Republic. Among leading ministers, Pál Medgyesi studied at Frankfurt an der Oder, Leiden, and in England from 1628 until 1631; János Tolnai Dali studied from 1632 until 1639 at Leiden, Franeker, Groningen, and in England; István Szilágyi Benjámin moved between Frankfurt, Franeker, and Utrecht between 1639 and 1641; János Apáczai Csere studied at Leiden, Franeker, Utrecht, and Harderwijk in the 1640s; whilst András Váczi studied at Franeker, Deventer, Leiden, Groningen, Utrecht, and in England during the 1640s. Partly because they preferred to move from university to university, only a few Hungarians studied for formal degrees. However, in the 1650s György Komáromi Csipkés, Sámuel Enyedi, and János Pósaházi were all awarded doctorates at Utrecht, as was György Mártonfalvi at Franeker, and János Apáczai Csere at Harderwijk. Most Hungarian students did participate in public theological debates, used at Dutch universities, as at Heidelberg, to aid the study of Reformed dogmatics and to rehearse polemic theological arguments. Students at Franeker defended theses on Wednesdays and Saturdays, with lectures given by professors on other working days. Visiting students also had access to university libraries, with Leiden's library open on Wednesday and Saturday afternoons, again when there were no lectures at the university.[29]

More Hungarian students were attracted to Franeker than any other Dutch university during this period. It was there in the 1620s that Hungarians encountered William Ames, who was to prove one of the most influential foreign theologians in the Hungarian church. Ames had fallen out of favour with the Anglican establishment and was suspended from Cambridge University, before leaving England for exile in the Dutch Republic in 1611, and was appointed to teach theology at Franeker in 1622. Along

---

[28] Tiszántúl Reformed Church Province Library MS Collection (Debrecen) R. 692, Kismarjai Veszelin Pál peregrinációs albuma 1653–1654, 275.

[29] 'Az utrechti és leideni egyetemeken járt magyar ifjak névjegyzéke', ed. G. Antal, *PEIL* 31 (1888), 278–9, 409–12, 437–41; L. Segesváry, *Magyar református ifjak az utrechti egyetemen, 1636–1686* (Debrecen, 1935); 'A franekeri egyetemén tanúlt magyarok', ed. Á. Hellebrant, *TT* (1886), 599–608, 792–800; 'A groningeni egyetem tanult magyarok névsora', ed. Ö. Miklós, *Dunántuli Protestáns Lap* (1917), 194–7, 202–7; Tiszántúl Reformed Church Province Archives (Debrecen), Egyházkerületi iratai, 1/J, D67c, D67e/2, D69c.

with previous proponents of practical divinity in England, most notably William Perkins, Ames stressed the need to make theology more applicable to everyday life, and he advocated methodically organizing theological inquiry into one essential system, or 'marrow'. For Ames, the study of theology provided an ordered structure for personal salvation, moving from predestination to sanctification and eventual glorification. Within this scheme of salvation, Ames set out to provide practical advice on the art of 'living well' and tried to put his ideas into practice by promoting personal godliness and strict Sabbatarianism among his students at Franeker. Ames also held distinctive views on church government, believing that each particular church was a visible church in its own right, while maintaining that congregations should not remain entirely independent from one another but send representatives to synods where matters of common interest could be discussed and decided.[30]

Ames presided over many academic debates at Franeker in which Hungarian student ministers gave disputations. A 1625 collection of anti-Catholic disputations included 103 disputations under Ames's presidency by twenty-six different Hungarian students. The influence which Ames exerted over the Hungarian church soon extended beyond the dozens of Hungarian students at Franeker, with former students adopting Ames's methods of teaching theology in Hungarian schools, which will be examined in more detail in Chapter 3.[31] Ames's books also featured prominently in the literature which was brought home by student ministers from the Dutch Republic and England. Catalogues from the school libraries at Szatmár and Nagybánya contain many more works connected with Dutch and English Protestantism than earlier catalogues at other schools. By the 1630s, the Szatmár library had acquired many books by Pareus and Keckermann

---

[30] William Ames, *The Marrow of Sacred Divinity* (London, 1643); K. L. Sprunger, 'Technometria: A Prologue to Puritan Theology', *Journal of the History of Ideas*, 29 (1968), 115–22; K. L. Sprunger, *The Learned Doctor William Ames* (Chicago, 1972); R. T. Kendall, *Calvin and English Calvinism to 1649* (Oxford, 1979), 151–64; G. T. Jensma, F. R. H. Smit, and F. Westra (eds.), *Universiteit te Franeker 1585–1811* (Leeuwarden, 1985), 264–75; P. Berg, *Angol hatások tizenhetedik századi irodalmunkban* (Budapest, 1946).

[31] William Ames, *Bellarminus Ennervatus; vel, Disputationes anti-Bellarminae in Illustri Frisiorum Academia, quae est Franekerae, publice habitae, a Guilielmo Amesio, theologiae doctore* (Franeker, 1625); Tiszántúl Reformed Church Province Archives (Debrecen), Egyházkerületi iratai, 1/J, D67a; F. Postma, *Disputationes Exercitii Gratia: Een inventarisatie van disputaties verdedigd onder Sibrandus Lubbertus Prof. Theol. te Franeker, 1585–1625* (Amsterdam, 1985); I. Czegle, 'Amesius korai magyar tanítványai', in *Acta Historiae Litterarum Hungaricorum, 10–11*, ed. B. Keserű (Szeged, 1971); J. Barcza, 'A puritanizmus kutatásának ujább eredményei', *Theologiai Szemle*, 19 (1976), 333–6; K. Koltay, 'Perkins és Ames recepciója magyarországon 1660-ig', in A. Tamás and I. Bitskey (eds.), *Studia Litteraria. Tanulmányok a xvi.–xvii. századi magyar irodalomból* (Budapest, 1991), 99–109.

and also works by William Perkins and Ames. The school library at Kolozsvár held commentaries in the 1660s by most of the period's major Reformed authors, with works by Ames, Alsted, and Pareus, and also a
considerable selection of theological texts in English.[32]

The pattern of Hungarian peregrination changed again during the
1650s as more Hungarian students chose to study at Utrecht than at any
other Dutch university. The leading theology professor there was Gisbert
Voetius, an enthusiastic moralist and leading advocate of practical theology
within the Dutch church. Voetius championed efforts to reform Dutch society further by stimulating greater piety in Reformed congregations. In
response to criticism about his concentration on a strict code of personal
religiosity and morality, Voetius argued that only the 'pontifical religion . . .
tries to vilify the true Reformed faith, by the hated name of puritan'.
Voetius also became a standard-bearer of Calvinist orthodoxy who, along
with allies Johannes Teellinck and Johannes Hoornbeeck, rejected the
more liberal theology of Johannes Cocceius. Cocceius argued that theologians needed to re-examine dogma in the light of close analysis of biblical
texts, and was more open than many of his colleagues within the Dutch
church to the results of Cartesian philosophical inquiry. Cocceius was certainly well known to Hungarian students from his years at Bremen College
in the early 1630s and from his period teaching at Franeker. In 1650 Cocceius moved to Leiden, but the numbers of Hungarian students there fell
significantly during the 1650s.[33] Although arguments about Cocceian theology were to cause divisions in the Hungarian church during the latter
decades of the century, Voetius' strident moralism had the greater influence over Hungarian students in the Dutch Republic. Many Hungarian
ministers later attempted to stimulate practical divinity and higher standards of personal morality within their own church. A number of piety
tracts were translated and published by former students at Dutch universities, and the impact in Hungary of these works on practical theology will
be considered in Chapter 5.

[32] K. Koltay, 'Two Hundred Years of English Puritan Books in Hungary', *Angol Filológiai
Tanulmányok*, 20 (1989), 53–64; M. Hazagh, 'Amesius és a magyar puritanizmus', *Angol
Filológiai Tanulmányok*, 4 (1942), 94–112; *Adattár 14. Partiumi könyvesházak*, ed. Keserű, 56,
328, 330, 356–63, 377; *Adattár 16. Erdélyi könyvesházak*, ed. B. Keserű (Szeged, 1991),
49–65, 90; G. Sipos, *Olvasmánytörténeti dolgozatok, 1. A kolozsvári református kollégium
könyvtára a xvii. században* (Szeged, 1991).

[33] G. Gömöri, 'A fiatal Coccejus magyar barátai és tanítványai', in *Acta Historiae Litteraum
Hungaricarum*, 25 (Szeged, 1988), 189–96; J. Koltay-Kastner, 'Tótfalusi Kis Miklós cocce-
jánizmusa', *ITK* 58 (1954), 284–99; J. Zoványi, 'Coccejus és theológiai rendszere', *Protestáns
Szemle*, 2 (1890), 78–104, 241–66; Israel, *The Dutch Republic*, 585–9, 889–99.

A second major focus of Reformed Hungarians' study at Dutch universities was attacking anti-Trinitarian ideas. The Dutch church was itself engaged in a campaign against the perceived dangers of anti-Trinitarian and Socinian theology, and Reformed synods repeatedly pressed the States General for action against anti-Trinitarians from the late 1620s. Some local authorities seized and destroyed anti-Trinitarian books, and in 1639 Socinians were prevented from entering the Republic. Given this atmosphere, it is hardly surprising that visiting Hungarian students were instructed to observe strict Calvinist orthodoxy and strident polemic theology, or that many of the public disputations given by Hungarian student ministers at Dutch universities were concerned with attacks against anti-Trinitarianism. Hungarian Calvinists may have been anxious to dispel any doubts about their own orthodox credentials by condemning anti-Trinitarian ideas. Certainly Hungarians' and especially Transylvanians' experience of Unitarianism was greatly valued in the west, and theology professors were anxious that Hungarians and Transylvanians should be familiar with arguments refuting anti-Trinitarianism before they returned home.[34]

Disputations by Hungarian students against anti-Trinitarian beliefs poured out of all the Dutch universities. A collection of forty-eight anti-Socinian disputations was published by Johannes Polyander at Leiden in 1640, ten of which were by Hungarian Reformed students. Most of these disputations either directly attacked anti-Trinitarian writers, or detailed Reformed understanding of the role of Christ in salvation. This collection of disputations was dedicated by Polyander to György I Rákóczi, and Polyander expressed his wish that the Hungarian church continue to flourish under Rákóczi's leadership. Polyander also recognized the valuable contribution of students from Transylvania who, he claimed, had come to the Dutch Republic to defend Reformed orthodoxy, and to share their knowledge of anti-Trinitarianism with the Dutch church.[35] In 1640 Nicholas Vedelius also published a *Collegium Hungaricarum* of twenty-six Franeker students who provided fifty-four disputations, almost all directed against Socinian and anti-Trinitarian opinions, although some highlighted Arminian and Anabaptist errors as well.[36]

34 E. M. Wilbur, *A History of Unitarianism. Socinianism and Its Antecedents* (Cambridge, Mass., 1946), 553; E. M. Wilbur, *A History of Unitarianism in Transylvania, England and America* (Cambridge, Mass., 1952).

35 Johannes Polyander, *Prima concertatio anti-Sociniana disputationibus XLVIII in Acad. Leydensi* (Amsterdam, 1640), nos. 3–5, 7, 9, 13, 15, 28, 30, 48 (disputations by Hungarians); I. Monok, 'Johannes Polyander magyar kapcsolataihoz', in J. Herner (ed.), *Adattár 23. Tudóslevelek; Művelődésünk külföldi kapcsolataihoz, 1577–1797* (Szeged, 1989), 89–115.

36 Nicholas Vedelius, *Opuscula Theologica Nova Nicolai Vedelii SS. Theologiae Doctoris ac Professoris in Academia Franecquerana* (Franeker, 1651); iii, *Collegium Hungaricarum, in quo*

From the late 1640s pressure intensified from the Dutch Reformed church to have anti-Trinitarian worship prohibited in the Republic. Leading Calvinist figures including Nicholas Arnold, Johannes Hoornbeeck, and Samuel Maresius, all published attempts to discredit Socinian ideas. Gisbert Voetius, too, denied that Socinians, anti-Trinitarians of any kind, deists, or atheists should be tolerated within a Christian society. Voetius also remained highly suspicious of other dissenting groups such as Remonstrants, since he believed that they might well harbour anti-Trinitarians within their midst. Although Johannes Cocceius was often in disagreement with Voetius, he was equally hostile to anti-Trinitarianism, and a 1653 report by Leiden university theologians concluded that Socinianism was hardly different from paganism. After receiving this report, the States of Holland issued a ban on Socinian meetings and forbade the import, printing, sale, or circulation of anti-Trinitarian and Socinian books, although the church often found it difficult to persuade magistrates in many towns to apply such laws.[37] This crusade against anti-Trinitarianism continued to affect the education of Hungarian student ministers at Dutch universities. Voetius published a collection of disputations in 1648 which included the views of Hungarian students on whether Socinians should properly be called Christians. A 1650 volume of Groningen disputations under the Huguenot professor, Samuel Maresius, included nineteen disputations by Hungarian Calvinists mostly directed against anti-Trinitarianism, although some students also considered questions relating to practical theology.[38]

Hungarian students also attacked the beliefs and practices of other rival churches in theological debates at Dutch universities. A 1652 collection of disputations published by Frederick Spanheim, a Palatine exile who had first worked at Geneva before moving to Leiden in 1624, included twelve disputations in which Hungarian students identified the errors of anti-Trinitarians, Anabaptists, and Catholics.[39] There was much less reticence

Disputationis LI. Controversiae Theologicae quae nobis cum omnibus adversariis intercedunt, sunt propositae (Franeker, 1640), of which the only surviving copy is to be found in the Teleki Library, Marosvásárhely.

37 Israel, *The Dutch Republic*, 909–16; Wilbur, *A History of Unitarianism. Socinianism and Its Antecedents*, 555–8.

38 Gisbert Voetius, *Selectarum Disputationum Theologicarum pars prima* (Utrecht, 1648), 434–41, 1,118–37; Samuel Maresius, *Xenia Academica; sive, 1. Disputatio Theologica de Personalitate adeoque Divinitate Spiritus Sancti contra Socinianos* (Groningen, 1650); Pál Jászberényi, *Examen doctrinae ariano-socinianae* (London, 1662).

39 Frederick Spanheim, *Disputationum Theologicarum Syntagma (Miscellanearum pars prima) (pars secunda . . . Anti-Anabaptisticas controversias complectitur)* (Geneva, 1652); J. J. Woltjer, 'Foreign Professors', in T. H. Lunsingh Scheurleer and G. H. M. Posthumus Meyjes (eds.), *Leiden University in the Seventeenth Century. An Exchange of Learning* (Leiden, 1975), 461–6.

to criticize Lutherans at Dutch universities than there had been at Heidelberg, and a 1654 volume of forty anti-Lutheran disputations given under the Pole Nicholas Arnold at Franeker included eleven studies by Hungarians. In the dedication to this volume addressed to the Friesland stadholder William Frederick, Arnold wrote that these disputations were by 'the most learned young men of Hungary, who for many years past have been frequenting our academy'.[40] Many disputations also continued to be directed by student ministers against the Catholic church, with one Hungarian at Utrecht rehearsing the common argument that Catholics could not be good citizens of any state since their first loyalty lay with Rome. A second volume of Utrecht disputations published by Voetius in 1655 also included eight anti-Catholic disputations by Hungarians, which considered the case for the Pope as Antichrist. One Hungarian student was even anxious to gain Voetius' approval for his denial of the spiritual powers of Hungarian Catholic clergy, after well-publicized claims were made that priests at Pozsony had successfully exorcized a ghost which had been tormenting a young woman.[41]

(III) ENGLAND

The most distant destination for Hungarian Reformed students was England, and the journey from Hungary to England could involve enormous personal sacrifices. Mátyás Rudabányai worked for almost a decade to collect sufficient money to study abroad. Rudabányai eventually set off from Hungary, travelling by ship for England in the mid-1650s, but fell foul of Barbary pirates and was carried off to prison at Tunis. Rudabányai turned to his former colleagues to try to pay the ransom for his release, and a collection was taken up at Sárospatak, but it seems that sufficient money could not be raised. Rudabányai died in his Tunis gaol some time after 1678, proof of the not inconsiderable sense of adventure and physical courage required of Hungary's Reformed students.[42] The distance between Hungary and England also caused problems when students needed to contact their patrons at home. In 1641 Péter Szerencsi needed more money from his

---

[40] Nicholas Arnold, *Heinrici Echardi, Lutherani, Scopae Dissolutae seu Fasciculus ejus controversiarum succincte refutatus et quadraginta publicis disputationibus in Academia Franekerana dissolutus a Nicolao Arnoldo* (Franeker, 1654).

[41] Gisbert Voetius, *Theologiae in acad. Ultrajectina professoris, selectarum disputationum theologicarum pars secunda* (Utrecht, 1655), 1,138–9; Melchior Baczoni, *De fide Papistarum, salutari an damnabili?* (Utrecht, 1648).

[42] E. Tanka, 'Rudabányai A. Mátyás levele tuniszból 1678 Dec. 1', *Lymbus Füzetei*, 6 (1989).

patron to support his study at Cambridge, but students who were supposed to carry money for him were robbed at Cracow. Szerencsi was then forced to appeal to William Sancroft at Emmanuel College for financial assistance until he could get more help from home.[43]

Some students also displayed general ignorance about England, with Márton Szepsi Csombor failing in his effort to visit an English university, when he confused Canterbury for Cambridge (*Cantabrigae*).[44] Such *naïveté* was soon overcome as Hungarian students established a network of supporters, mostly in London, who could provide them with information and practical assistance. Hungarian Reformed students began to visit the English universities, more frequently travelling to Cambridge than to Oxford. Very few Hungarians appear to have studied for a degree in England, although in the 1650s Gáspár Tiszabécsi, his brother Tamás, and István Budai all received degrees at Oxford.[45]

Many Hungarian students spent a considerable part of their time in England in the capital and found a warm welcome there from foreign Calvinist congregations. This was no doubt a product of natural sympathy between exiles and foreign students, and an extension of established links between Hungarians and refugee congregations on the Continent. These congregations of foreigners in England came under sustained attack during the 1630s from Archbishop William Laud, who considered such churches as schismatic nests of Calvinist radicalism. In 1632 Laud drew the attention of the Privy Council to foreign Reformed churches as 'nurseries of ill-minded persons to the Church of England'. Laud aimed to root out links between strangers' churches and native puritans, and in 1634 launched an investigation of the liturgy used by French and Dutch congregations in England. In 1635, injunctions demanded that the strangers' churches use translated versions of the Anglican liturgy and compelled attendance at parish churches from all but foreign-born members of strangers' churches and first-generation immigrants. As one of the charges against Laud at his trial in 1645 claimed, the archbishop had 'endeavoured to cause division and discord between the Church of England, and other reformed Churches; and to that end hath suppressed and abrogated the privileges and immunities . . . granted to the French and Dutch churches in this Kingdom'.[46]

---

43 Gömöri, 'Magyar látogatók a Cromwell-kori angliában'; Gömöri, 'Magyar peregrinusok a xvii. századi Cambridge-ben'.
44 Szepsi Csombor, *Europica Varietas*, 183–93.
45 'Adatok angliában járt magyar deákokról és egyéb angol emlékek', 419–41.
46 M. Greengrass, 'Samuel Hartlib and International Calvinism', *Proceedings of the Huguenot Society*, 25/5 (1993), 464–75. See also J. Lindeboom, *Austin Friars. History of the*

Hungarian students in London became associated both with threatened strangers' churches and with other divines in the capital with links to those churches, such as John Stoughton, minister at St Mary's, Aldermanbury. Stoughton worked in close co-operation with the Dutch congregation at Austin Friars to aid refugee continental Calvinists. St Mary's indeed produced the greatest sum of any London parish for the 1628 royal collection for the Palatinate, which was administered by the Austin Friars' consistory. While Laud opposed closer integration between Anglicans and continental Calvinists, these collections gave an opportunity for Stoughton and others to affirm cords of solidarity which they felt with Reformed churches across Europe. Stoughton was brought before the High Commission in 1635 for resisting Laudian reforms but continued to offer assistance to continental Calvinist ministers and students in London. Stoughton was inspired by meeting Hungarian students to write a millenarian tract in 1638 about the progress of the church in Transylvania, published after Stoughton's death in 1640 by Samuel Hartlib. This open letter from Stoughton was addressed to János Tolnai Dali, then resident in London, and was dedicated by Hartlib to György I Rákóczi. Stoughton wrote that Rákóczi's patronage of school reforms and support for the Reformed cause was making Transylvania into a strong bastion in the international battle against Rome.[47]

Another contact for Hungarians in London from the 1620s was János Bánfihunyadi, a Transylvanian alchemist experimenting at Gresham's College. Bánfihunyadi was in touch with Pál Keresztúri and Pál Medgyesi, and probably assisted other Hungarian student ministers establish connections with London congregations who were sympathetic towards

Dutch Reformed Church in London, 1550–1950 (The Hague, 1950), 117–49; O. P. Grell, 'The French and Dutch Congregations in London in the Early Seventeenth Century', *Proceedings of the Huguenot Society*, 24/5 (1987), 362–77; P. Collinson, 'The Elizabethan Puritans and the Foreign Reformed Churches in London', *Proceedings of the Huguenot Society*, 20/5 (1962–3), 528–55; S. L. Adams, 'The Protestant Cause: Religious Alliance with the West European Calvinist Communities as a Political Issue in England, 1585–1630', D.Phil. thesis (Oxford, 1973); O. P. Grell, *Dutch Calvinists in Early Stuart London* (Leiden, 1989); H. Trevor-Roper, *Archbishop Laud, 1573–1645* (London, 1962), 197–8; B. Cottret, *The Huguenots in London. Immigration and Settlement, c.1550–1700* (Cambridge, 1991), 98–117; *Ecclesiae Londino-Batavae archivum epistulae et tractatae formationis historiam illustrantos*, ed. J. Hessels (Cambridge, 1897), vol. 3, nos. 3,124, 3,494; W. J. C. Moens (ed.), *The Walloons and Their Church at Norwich: Their History and Registers* (Huguenot Society of London, 1; 1887–8), 90.

47 John Stoughton, *Felicitas ultimi saeculi* (London, 1640); J. C. Whitebrook, 'Dr J. Stoughton the Elder', *Transactions of the Congregational Historical Society*, 6 (1913–15), 89–107, 177–84; G. Gömöri, 'Két levél a xvii. századból Tolnai D. János levelezéséből', in B. Keserű (ed.), *Adattár 10. Collectanea Tibortiana* (Szeged, 1990), 331–7; C. Webster, *The Great Instauration. Science, Medicine and Reform, 1626–1660* (London, 1975), 32–7; Milton, *Catholic and Reformed*, 434; T. Liu, *Puritan London. A study of Religion and Society in the City Parishes* (Newark, NJ., 1986), 187.

wandering foreign Calvinists. Bánfihunyadi, known to many as 'Hunniades', was in contact with Samuel Hartlib, and Hartlib's notes contain references to Hunniades' knowledge of artificial gems and his work on the
magnetic properties of load-stone.[48] Hartlib, an exile from Elbing, possibly
attended services at Austin Friars although he was not a member of the
congregation. Hartlib certainly had strong ties with the Dutch Reformed
community in London and was involved in collections for the Palatinate,
working alongside refugee ministers such as Theodore Haak and John
Rulice.[49] Hartlib opened his home to a number of foreign Protestant visitors, and was in contact with Hungarian students in London, most notably
with János Tolnai Dali. Hartlib wrote in a memorandum how

the Prince of Transylvania hath ever since sent his stipendate schollars to learn the
language and converse with our ministers, to bee trained up in our way for a seminary to his Churches so that by this wee may see how soone a Correspondencie for
the things of Christ's kingdome may bee settled, with those that are thus convinced
of our partaking of the truth of the Gospell.[50]

Hungarian Reformed student ministers arriving in England from the
1620s were received in the capital by those such as Hartlib and Stoughton
who were actively interested in developing links with continental Calvinists. Many of those known to be in contact with Hungarian students in
London also supported reforms of Anglican ceremony and church government, were advocates of practical divinity, and would have commonly been
described as puritans. When the Hungarian church became divided over
charges of puritanism against some ministers, and over calls for changes to
church government, contemporaries almost uniformly blamed these problems on the deleterious effects of student ministers' contact with religious
radicals in England.[51] There had always been some concern within the
church hierarchy to control students' peregrination, and to monitor the
influence of foreign Calvinist universities and theologians on the Hungarian church. A synod held at Keresztúr in eastern Hungary in 1593 decided

---

[48] Hartl., 'Ephemerides' 1639, 31; 'Notes on Natural Philosophie', Hartl. 31/23, f. 1929;
44/1, ff. 1a, 2a, 6a, 16a, 19a, 20a; M. Rady, 'A Transylvanian Alchemist in Seventeenth-
Century London', Slavonic and Eastern European Review, 72 (1994), 140–51; Gy. Orient,
Erdélyi alchimisták. Bethlen Gábor fejedelem alchimiája (Kolozsvár, 1927); L. Szathmáry,
Magyar alkémisták (Budapest, 1986); [Comenius], Korrespondence Jana Amosa Komenského,
ed. J. V. Kvacsala (Prague, 1897), p. xlvi, 37–41.

[49] O. P. Grell, Calvinist Exiles in Tudor and Stuart England (Aldershot, 1996), 76–7; Grell,
Dutch Calvinists in Early Stuart London, 209–10, 245; Greengrass, 'Samuel Hartlib and International Calvinism', 464–75.

[50] Hartl. 6/7, f. 1a.

[51] Zoványi, Puritánus mozgalmak a magyar református egyházban; Makkai, A magyar
puritánusok harca a feudálizmus ellen.

to write to the university authorities at Heidelberg and Wittenberg asking
that no more loans be given to Hungarian students, and denouncing students in Germany who had, the synod claimed, brought the name of the
Hungarian church into disrepute. An eastern Tisza synod meeting in September 1631 at Nyirbátor warned of the danger of Arminianism infiltrat-
ing into Hungary from the west, and wanted students to subscribe to
conditions dedicating themselves to Reformed orthodoxy before going
abroad. The synod also required that students only visit England if they
had received express permission from their patrons to do so.[52]

Fears that connections with English Protestants might lead to demands
for radical reform within the Hungarian church were raised again after the
so-called 'League of Piety' was signed by ten Hungarian students in London on 9 February 1638. These students, led by János Tolnai Dali, bound
themselves in a pact to restore purity to the Hungarian church by bringing
to an end all hierarchical authority among ministers and by replacing some
traditional church ceremonies. One of the signatories, Miklós Kecskeméti,
handed a copy of this statement over to the eastern Tisza provincial superintendent, István Keresszegi Herman. The matter was then raised in September 1638 at a joint synod of the northern and eastern Tisza provinces at
Debrecen. The synod resolved that any complaints about church practices
must proceed through the proper channels. The Debrecen synod also decided not to receive any more 'anglo-academic ministers' into any position
within the church until they had given absolute assurances of their orthodoxy and promised to acquiesce in the traditional pattern of Hungarian
church government. The clergy synod was also concerned to prevent any
infiltration of Arminianism and other 'exotic dangers' into Hungary and
set out seven conditions to which all students had to subscribe before permission would be granted for them to travel to foreign universities. These
conditions concentrated on the need for students' patrons to sanction
every part of any academic peregrination, and students were particularly
warned to avoid consorting with puritans or Arminians. In February 1646
the northern Tisza church forced students to swear allegiance to the Heidelberg Catechism and Second Helvetic Confession before they could
travel to western universities. The national church synod held at Szatmár
in June 1646 agreed that all returning students should be asked to subscribe
to the Heidelberg Catechism and Helvetic Confession before they could
take up any church office. Students also had to promise not to propagate
puritanism, Anabaptism, Socinianism, or Arminianism, nor privately to

---

[52] Tiszántúl Reformed Church Province Archives (Debrecen), Egyházkerületi iratai,
1/J, D1, Catalogus studiosorum beneficiariorum ad academias extera.

promote any innovation to the normal ceremonies and festivals of the Hungarian church.[53]

The Hungarian clergy hierarchy feared that imported heterodox opinions were gaining support among its clergy during the 1640s. Ministers who had visited England indeed translated many piety tracts and some put forward presbyterian proposals, which will be examined in detail in Chapter 6. However, the precise activities of most Hungarian students once in England, both before and during the Interregnum, remain rather uncertain. The fleeting nature of most recorded contacts between Hungarians and English divines presents some difficulty in reconstructing the mechanics of English puritan and presbyterian influence on Hungarian students. Some light can be shed on the developing pattern of connections between Reformed students and networks of godly English clergy by examining the travel album of Péter Körmendi, which provides details about Körmendi's life in England between 1660 and 1663.[54]

Péter Körmendi embarked for western Europe in 1660, studying for a short period at Franeker before moving on to London. Körmendi then spent several months in the capital, where he could count on the support of at least seven fellow Hungarians. These included Mátyás Harsányi, who wrote in Körmendi's inscription book that 'A friend loveth at all times, and a brother is born for adversity'.[55] With his knowledge of English presumably steadily advancing, Körmendi moved to live in Somerset, where he remained from the spring of 1661 until April 1662. Körmendi's album contains inscriptions from the ministers of villages in northern Somerset on the edge of the Mendip Hills. William Gregory, rector at Chelvey, wrote that the Hungarian 'had come . . . to Somerset to teach, devote himself to reading, writing, and discussion, and to dedicate himself to become a model of learning amongst ministers of the Gospel'. In the summer and autumn months of 1661 Körmendi evidently became well acquainted with the clergy of these Somerset communities. His album records inscriptions

---

53 'Acta Synodi Nationalis'; Makkai, *A magyar puritánusok harca a feudálizmus ellen.*

54 Dunamellék Reformed Church Province Manuscript Collection (Ráday college, Budapest), K-1. 461, 'Körmendi Péter peregrinációs albuma 1662 [sic!] -1663' (hereafter 'Körmendi Péter albuma'); G. Murdock, 'The Experience of Péter Körmendi. Foreign Calvinist Students' Contact with Presbyterians and Puritans in England', in M. Balázs et al. (eds.), *Adattár 35. Művelődési törekvések a korai újkorban. Tanulmányok Keserű Bálint tiszteletére* (Szeged, 1997), 433–52; G. Gömöri, 'Some Hungarian *alba amicorum* from the Seventeenth Century', in J. Fechner (ed.), *Stammbücher als kulturhistorische Quellen* (Wolfenbütteler Forschungen 2; Munich, 1981), 97–109, with thanks to Mr Gömöri for drawing this to my attention. Miklós Bethlen also described his 1660s studies in the west in *Bethlen Miklós önéletírásai*, ed. E. Windisch (Budapest, 1955), chaps. 13–16.

55 'Körmendi Péter albuma', ff. 54, 83, 106, 110, 117–121, 125–6.

from Samuel Westoby, the minister at Blagdon, and William Thomas, rector at neighbouring Ubley, with further entries from ministers at Wrington
and Cheddar.[56] Körmendi also became acquainted with Thomas Baynard,
the squire at Blagdon, and on Körmendi's departure from Somerset Baynard offered a demonstration of the strength of local good will towards him
in a moving tribute:

'As the mountaynes are around about Jerusalem, so the Lord is round about His
people from henceforth even for ever. God is good to us; when He sends evill; because He sends evill for our good'. Mr Peter Keörmendi having sojournd in Somer-
set-shire about the space of a yeare, hath so demeand himselfe, during his residence
here, That I esteeme him worthy of this deserved Testimony and encomium: That
he is a man of singular piety, learning, and candour; whose patience under the hard-
ships of his peregrination is exemplary, and whose prayers for, and longings after
his owne country (now almost ruinated by the barbarous Turks) are incessant, to
whome I wish divine protection in his travells by Land and Sea, and all prosperity
in his own Country, when God shall please to returne him in health, safety, and
comfort thither. Better a man's owne works praise him than anothers' words Apr. 1
1662.[57]

The villages known to Körmendi to the north of the Mendips had
formed one of two distinct pockets of resistance in Somerset to Laudian reforms during the 1630s. William Thomas was suspended twice from the
ministry before the Civil War and then moved to St Pancras, Soper Lane, in
London to work alongside other determined presbyterian ministers in the
capital.[58] By 1648 Thomas had moved back to Ubley and joined with
Samuel Westoby, the ministers at Wrington and Blagdon, and sixty-seven
other Somerset clergy in signing a 'Testimony to the Truth'. This 'Testimony' supported by around nine hundred clergy across England offered
devoted adherence to the Solemn League and Covenant, asserting that
'Presbyteriall Government is that Government which is most agreeable to
the minde of Jesus Christ, revealed in Scripture' and that '[we] sadly
lament England's generall backwardnesse to embrace, yea forwardnesse to
oppose this Government'. When presbyterian pleas were finally answered,
Thomas Baynard became an elder in his Somerset class district. Baynard
had solidly supported the parliamentary cause during the Civil War and

---

[56] Ibid. ff. 84–5, 116, 122–4, 128.

[57] Ibid. ff. 89–90.

[58] D. Underdown, *Somerset in the Civil War and Interregnum* (Newton Abbot, 1973); T. G.
Barnes, *Somerset, 1625–1640. A County's Government during the 'Personal Rule'* (Oxford,
1961); M. Stieg, *Laud's Laboratory. The Diocese of Bath and Wells in the Early Seventeenth
Century* (London, 1982).

was one of the few minor gentry in Somerset who continued to be involved in local government during the Cromwellian Protectorate.[59]

Péter Körmendi therefore chose to spend over a year in a locality of Somerset which had long demonstrated allegiance to a puritan agenda of religious reform, and in the company of clergymen and gentry who backed presbyterian government, some of whom were old enough to have bitter memories of the impositions of pre-war episcopal authority. Körmendi's stay in Somerset during 1661 and 1662 came at a crucial time for these ministers. Samuel Westoby and William Thomas were among over thirty Somerset ministers deprived of their livings following the 1662 Act of Uniformity, which demanded that clergy renounce the Solemn League and Covenant and declare their support for the Book of Common Prayer. Thomas Baynard, too, was unable to hold his place under the restored Stuart monarchy, replaced in a clear-out of county officers in April 1666 from his post as Hospitals' Treasurer.[60]

In 1662 Körmendi returned to London where he contacted the London strangers' churches, with an inscription in his album from Cesar Calandrini, one of the three ministers at Austin Friars. From a prominent Lucchese family and resident in England from 1619, Calandrini had been friends from the early 1630s with John Stoughton and Herbert Palmer. Palmer was yet another link in the chain of contacts between native clergy, strangers' churches, and foreign Calvinists visiting England. Palmer occasionally preached alongside John Bulteel at the Walloon congregation in Canterbury and, based at Queen's College, Cambridge, liberally assisted visiting students from Germany and Hungary. There are also inscriptions in Körmendi's album from Louis Hérault, one of the ministers of the French church at Threadneedle Street, and from Jacques Le Franc, minister of the Walloon church at Norwich.[61]

[59] J. Batten, 'Somersetshire Sequestrations during the Civil War', *Somersetshire Archaeological and Natural History Society Proceedings*, 4 (1853), 60–77; 16 (1870), 13–34; Underdown, *Somerset in the Civil War and Interregnum*, 126–7.

[60] *Calamy Revised. Being a Revision of Edmund Calamy's Account of the Ministers and Others Ejected and Silenced, 1660–2*, ed. A. G. Matthews (Oxford, 1934), pp. xi–xiii, 522, 556–7; Underdown, *Somerset in the Civil War and Interregnum*, 126–7, 180.

[61] 'Körmendi Péter albuma', ff. 55, 58, 67; Grell, *Dutch Calvinists in Early Stuart London*; Grell, *Calvinist Exiles in Tudor and Stuart England*, 87, 102–8; Lindeboom, *Austin Friars*, 162–3; O. P. Grell, 'Merchants and Ministers: The Foundations of International Calvinism', in A. Pettegree, A. C. Duke, and G. Lewis (eds.), *Calvinism in Europe, 1540–1620* (Cambridge, 1994), 259–67; *Letters of Denization and Acts of Naturalization for Aliens in England and Ireland, 1603–1700*, ed. W. A. Shaw (Huguenot Society of London, 18; London, 1911), 26; W. A. Shaw, *A History of the English Church during the Civil Wars and under the Commonwealth, 1640–1660* (2 vols.; London, 1900), ii, 373, 403; *A Calendar of the Letter Books of the French Church of London from the Civil War to the Restoration, 1643–1659*, ed. R. D. Gwynn

In 1662 Körmendi wrote an appeal for financial assistance to John Cosin, bishop of Durham, with Körmendi's hopes for a generous response probably connected with Isaac Basire, recently appointed as archdeacon of Northumberland under Cosin. Basire had returned to England in 1661 from Transylvania, where he had worked for six years at the princely academy at Gyulafehérvár.[62] By August 1662 Körmendi had managed to collect sufficient funds to travel to Utrecht where he encountered Gisbert Voetius, then to Amsterdam in September where he met Jan Amos Comenius. Körmendi also studied at Groningen and in February 1663 responded to a public disputation on providence under Samuel Maresius. Körmendi then moved on to Leiden, where he took part in disputations under both Johannes Cocceius and Johannes Hoornbeeck. All these performances were published, with the last dedicated by Körmendi to three of his English benefactors, Edward Reynolds, bishop of Norwich, George Morley, bishop of Winchester, and Isaac Basire.[63]

In the spring of 1663 Körmendi moved back to England once again. Körmendi visited Cambridge, encountering some leading churchmen and academics who were known to support foreign Protestants and needy students. Körmendi also met Benjamin Calamy, a student at Catherine Hall, and Calamy wrote with personal warmth to 'his friend' Körmendi of his affection and goodwill towards the 'learned and talented' Hungarian. Calamy was the second son of a prominent clergy dynasty of Huguenot extraction, with his father Edmund becoming minister at St Mary's, Aldermanbury, after John Stoughton died in 1639. Edmund Calamy also signed an entry in Körmendi's album from London, again with a testimony to his affection for the 'most learned' Körmendi, whilst Edmund Calamy junior too expressed his respect for Körmendi in the album and wished him every happiness. Edmund Calamy had commanded great prestige in London during the Interregnum, as one of the authors of the 1641 Smectymnuan tracts which articulated presbyterian solutions to demands for the reform of Anglican church government, and Calamy's home became a centre of discussion and planning for London's presbyterians. Another inscription in Körmendi's album was provided by Lazarus Seaman, one of Calamy's presbyterian colleagues who had acted as moderator of the provincial assembly of London during the 1640s. Calamy's participation in the 1661

(Huguenot Society of London, 54; 1979), 4–18, 35; C. M. Vane, 'The Walloon Community in Norwich: The First Hundred Years', *Proceedings of the Huguenot Society*, 24/2 (1984), 129–40.

[62] 'Körmendi Péter albuma', f. 125; Durham University Library, Cosin letter-book, 1A, f. 84.

[63] 'Körmendi Péter albuma', ff. 27, 44, 69, 71, 75, 81, 86, 88, 91, 100, 103.

Savoy Conference between episcopalians and presbyterians led to hopes that he would conform to the restored Anglican church and even accept a bishopric himself. However, both Calamy and his eldest son were eventually ejected from the ministry as nonconformists under the 1662 Act of Uniformity.[64]

Péter Körmendi finally set off for home in the autumn of 1663, via Rotterdam and Germany, and was received at Hamburg in October 1663 by Andreas de la Fontaine, minister of the local French and Walloon congregation. On his return to Hungary, Körmendi was soon promoted to become archdeacon of the Közép-Szolnok district, and in 1686 Körmendi was chosen as the new superintendent of the eastern Tisza province, an office which he held until his death in March 1691.[65] Körmendi's travel album reveals much about the experience of Hungarian students in England up to the early 1660s. The most striking aspect of Körmendi's period of study in England was his time spent in Somerset. There is an indication in Körmendi's album that he may have spent some of these months working as a teacher to the children of Dutch spinners at Bradford-upon-Avon. This would still have allowed him to go sermon-gadding in the neighbourhood, and to pursue other interests in the area with contacts of his London friends. It would seem likely that these friends, perhaps from Austin Friars or at St Mary's, Aldermanbury, had suggested that Körmendi move to Somerset. Edmund Calamy, who directed Körmendi to meet his son at Cambridge, might well have recommended that the young Hungarian leave the capital in 1661 for Blagdon. There Körmendi could strive to 'become a model of learning amongst ministers of the Gospel', including William Thomas, Calamy's former presbyterian colleague in London.[66]

The connections which Péter Körmendi made with a group of English clergy in London, Cambridge, and Somerset represented a pattern of significant influence beyond fleeting visits, chance encounters, pleas for financial aid, or autograph-hunting. Körmendi apparently chose to spend much of his time in England with earnest puritans and convinced presbyterians, and sought contact with those in the English church dedicated to the pursuit of practical theology, to the practice of puritan piety, and to presbyterian church government. This evidence from Körmendi's inscription album strongly supports the impression that, whilst Hungarian students

[64] Ibid. ff. 56–7, 120. I. M. Green, *The Re-Establishment of the Church of England, 1660–1663* (Oxford, 1978); C. Cross, *Church and People, 1450–1660* (Oxford, 1976), 199–242.
[65] 'Körmendi Péter albuma', ff. 93, 97, 117; Keserű (ed.), *Adattár 3*, 406–7.
[66] 'Körmendi Péter albuma', ff. 84–5; K. G. Ponting, *The Woollen Industry of South-West England* (Bath, 1971), 30–4.

who visited England from the 1630s established connections with a varied assortment of divines, an important network of contacts had been built up with strangers' congregations and with puritans.

Calvinists across Europe shared a belief in the existence of a universal true church, a belief which was partly sustained by personal experience of contact with co-religionists from different parts of the Continent. The peregrination of student ministers from the Hungarian Reformed church to Protestant universities in western Europe advertised the fact that the international Calvinist movement encompassed communities from eastern and central Europe. Beyond the lecture halls of Heidelberg, Franeker, Leiden, and Utrecht, Hungarian students were particularly warmly received in the west by refugee communities and exiles, who were often strongly committed to Calvinism as a trans-national movement. By the early seventeenth century this international Reformed world was no longer centred on Geneva, nor exclusively on Calvin, with teaching at universities and colleges in Germany and the Dutch Republic relying on leading theologians' interpretations of the cumulative insights of a range of sixteenth-century reformers.

Several prominent themes emerged for the Hungarian church from the expansion of connections with western co-religionists during the early seventeenth century. The later careers of many Hungarian ministers demonstrated the significant influence of their exposure to the universities, theological teaching, literature, and church life of western Europe. Travel across a confessionally divided continent seems in many ways not to have broadened the minds, but rather to have narrowed the intellectual horizons, of Hungarian student ministers concerning the acceptable limits of belief in a Christian society. The access of Reformed student ministers to western universities stiffened their resolve to defend Reformed orthodoxy and fostered growing animosity towards the Unitarian church in particular. Many student ministers were also drawn to support a more practical Reformed theology and to promote personal piety within their congregations. When Hungarians began to visit England, links were mostly established with Anglicans whose commitment to the Reformed world was one of the factors which brought them into dispute with their own church hierarchy before the Civil War. Tales about radical London Protestants, and about the content of some theology teaching in the Dutch Republic, provoked the Transylvanian Reformed church leadership to act first in a misdirected fashion against possible Arminian infiltrators, and then more accurately against puritan influences.

Despite apparently causing some disruption to the good order of the Hungarian church, links with western co-religionists remained highly valued by the Hungarian Reformed leadership. The Hungarian church's goal of playing its full part in the Calvinist International was never replaced by an aim of merely defending Calvinism in one country. Concern to protect domestic harmony led to suggestions that the extent of contacts with other Calvinist churches should be controlled, but not abandoned. This meant that, at least until the early 1660s, England continued to offer wandering students from Hungary and Transylvania the possibility of contact with a group of clergy and godly gentlemen who closely identified with international Calvinism, who were enthusiastic to welcome foreign Reformed students, and who were associated with puritanism and from the 1640s with presbyterianism. Such contacts were maintained despite the restrictions placed upon Hungarian students from consorting with puritans whilst abroad and the legal proscription against advancing any changes to the hierarchical structure of the Reformed church in Hungary and Transylvania on their return home.

As we shall see, western Calvinist influences within the Hungarian church affected the development of local colleges and schools, relations with other churches, styles of church ceremony, forms of church government, and the exercise of moral discipline. However, there were discernible limits to the impact on Hungarian clergy of exposure to foreign Calvinist churches. Hungarian student ministers travelling to western universities were hardly empty vessels waiting to be filled by the ideas of whichever wing of the Calvinist community they first came into contact with in Germany, the Dutch Republic, or in England. Some students who visited England remained implacably opposed to practical theology, and returned home to battle against puritan clergy. Other students, although linked with puritans and presbyterians whilst abroad, showed little sign on their return home of any commitment to implement changes to patterns of religiosity or church government. What after all would William Thomas, Samuel Westoby, and the Calamys have made of the 'singular piety, learning, and candour' of superintendent Péter Körmendi? It is almost certainly unfair to conclude that Körmendi and others were consummate trimmers who ditched puritan and presbyterian opinions once they had arrived home to further their careers. Körmendi's experience rather points to a developing maturity among Hungarian clergy which enabled them to take advantage of the education and opportunities available in western Europe and adapt knowledge gained of western churches to suit local circumstances. Many Hungarian puritan clergy and supporters of presbyteries pressed their case before 1660 but, in the unstable decades which followed for the church, tended rather to relegate opinions about church reform to the private sphere. Attention by then was instead increasingly directed to the more immediate need for unity, if the Reformed church in Hungary and Transylvania was to survive the twin threats posed by Ottoman invasions and Catholic persecution.

3
Reforming Hungarian Education

A central aim of the Hungarian reformation was to improve standards of education. In articles drawn up by the Debrecen synod of 1567, Hungarian reformers identified better education as an important means both of raising standards among the clergy and of promoting public morality.[1] The previous chapter charted one part of this project, with hundreds of student ministers travelling abroad to study at western universities, and this chapter will examine the developing network of domestic Protestant schools and colleges. Leading clergy in the Reformed church worked together with noble patrons and town authorities in determined efforts to improve local educational facilities. This process was significantly influenced by the presence of foreign Calvinist teachers, who attempted to bring about a further reformation of Hungarian society by renovating patterns of schooling in the region.

Intellectual communication between Hungarian Calvinists and their western co-religionists was therefore not solely dependent upon the presence of Hungarian students in Germany, the Dutch Republic, and England. Whilst student ministers were sent westward to study at Reformed academic centres, a series of prominent Protestants moved eastward to teach at new Reformed schools in Hungary and Transylvania. Three foreigners in particular, Johann Heinrich Alsted, Johann Heinrich Bisterfeld, and Jan Amos Comenius, sponsored attempts to develop Protestant colleges at Gyulafehérvár and Sárospatak. These three teachers and theologians were dedicated to the task of reforming education and to finding means by which to expand knowledge and understanding about God and His world. They planned reforms to the structure of schools, textbooks, and teaching methods, within a philosophy which stressed the importance of education in achieving broader purposes of religious reform and social renewal. All three were also dedicated to international Protestant co-operation, and held grand expectations of imminent victories over political and confessional enemies, as well as over darkness, confusion, and ignorance in schools and society. Their anticipation of universal regeneration helped to intensify eschatological enthusiasm in Protestant Hungary, a theme which will be considered in Chapter 9.

[1] *Zsinatok végzései*, ed. Kiss, 602.

Alsted, Bisterfeld, and Comenius were not alone in trying to implement proposals for the reorganization of Hungarian Protestant schools, with native Reformed clergy also committed to the renovation of their church and society through educational reform. Some ministers who had studied at western universities championed plans for school reform, most notably János Tolnai Dali at Sárospatak, and János Apáczai Csere at Kolozsvár. Ideas on how to improve the syllabus used in Hungarian schools, and on the need to change methods of teaching and learning, were however to prove highly controversial among Reformed ministers during this period. Some of the leading advocates of reform clashed over their different proposals, and school reform became especially contentious when intertwined with perceived challenges to the authority of the Reformed church hierarchy. This chapter will assess the sometimes disjointed and localized progress of Hungarian school reform during the early seventeenth century, first outlining the emerging network of Reformed schools and considering early attempts to improve standards of teaching, then secondly focusing on the educational philosophy promoted by Alsted, Bisterfeld, and Comenius, before finally looking at the implementation of school reforms by these three foreigners and by some Hungarian ministers and teachers.

(I) HUNGARIAN REFORMED SCHOOLS

The patronage of Transylvania's princes, some Hungarian nobles, and town councils was largely responsible for the early seventeenth-century development of Reformed colleges, schools, libraries, and printing-presses. This concerted financial support of local educational facilities improved the training available to Reformed student ministers, offered access to Protestant schooling for noble families, and broadened the provision of basic learning throughout Hungary and Transylvania. The emerging network of Reformed schools centred on a number of colleges at Gyulafehérvár, Debrecen, Sárospatak, and Pápa. These colleges, or grammar schools, drew in students from so-called 'particular' schools of towns in surrounding areas, although the numbers of these satellite schools and other village schools varied considerably across the region.

Around Debrecen in the Partium about half of all congregations could boast an active school, whilst in central Transylvania perhaps only one-fifth to one-third of parishes had a working school. In 1649 revised canons for the Transylvanian province suggested that a better network of vernacular schools ought to be established across the principality in which boys and girls might be able to learn to read, and perhaps also to write, and

Transylvanian state laws from 1653 repeated this need for more local schools. Meanwhile, in the northern Hungarian county of Zemplén around Sárospatak, almost all parishes had a village school which provided some basic instruction for local pupils. Regulations for Zemplén in 1648 structured rough divisions between four levels of schools from village schools teaching some elementary Latin grammar, to schools in small towns teaching Latin, basic Greek, poetry, and rhetoric, to somewhat larger schools where some logic was also taught, and finally to the 'particular' schools serving Sárospatak College where students could learn some basic theology. Complaints were frequently aired about the erratic standard of teaching available at schools in villages and small towns, and it was left to the Reformed church authorities to investigate and monitor the standards of schoolmasters during parish visitations. Teachers were often drawn from the ranks of former students at larger colleges, allowing improvements made at such centres during this period to percolate down at least to some extent to schools in smaller market towns and larger villages.[2]

In 1622 Gábor Bethlen established an academy in Transylvania to provide a new centre-piece for Reformed education in the principality, and to compete with schools being established by the Jesuits in Royal Hungary. After some debate over the best site for the academy, officials from the prince's council began supervision of plans to found a college at the capital Gyulafehérvár. In 1622 'Instructions' were drawn up to regulate the administrative structure of the academy, the teaching programme, and the behaviour expected of staff and students, with the state council appointing officials to take care of the academy's finances. Teaching at Hungarian schools was mostly undertaken by student ministers for one or two years before their ordination, but Bethlen looked abroad to obtain dedicated and proficient teachers for his new academy. Bethlen was first able to gain teachers by using connections with Silesia, where he held the territories of Oppeln and Ratibor after the 1621 Nikolsburg treaty, and in 1622 the poet Martin Opitz, Friedrich Pauli, and Jakob Kopisch arrived at Gyulafehérvár. Opitz taught Latin at the academy until the summer of 1623, when

---

[2] MOL box 1884, Tiszántúli református egyházkerület; debreceni egyházmegye jegyzőkönyvei, vol. 1 (1615–55), 'Reditus Ecclesiasticus dioecesis Debreczinensis' (1621), 414–26; Bod, *Historia Hungarorum Ecclesiastica*, iii, 399–457; I. Mészáros, *Az iskolaügy története Magyarországon, 996–1777 között* (Budapest, 1981), 368–406; E. Thury, *Iskolatörténeti adattár* (Pápa, 1906); K. Sebestyén, 'A kolozs-kalotai (kalotaszegi) református egyházmegye népoktatásának adattára a xv. századtól 1900-ig', in *MPEA* 17 (Budapest, 1993); J. Lugossy, 'Nagybányai, máskép aranyasmeggyesi egyházvidék személyzete a xvii. században', *Protestáns Szemle*, 6 (1847), 186–91; I. Magyarósi, *A zilahi ev. ref. anyaszentegyház története* (Kolozsvár, 1880); J. Barcsa, *A debreceni kollégium és partikulái* (Debrecen, 1905), 5–36; *Egyházi kánonok*, ed. Kiss, 1649 canons, nos. 94–7.

he was succeeded by Johann Schwarzenbach from Zurich, who taught Greek there until 1625.[3] Bethlen maintained a close interest in the progress of his college, taking the title of 'chief warden', and offering bursaries to dozens of students. In 1624 Bethlen also sponsored a measure through the diet which threatened fines against landowners who prevented the free access of their peasants' children to schooling. In 1628 Bethlen could write to Péter Alvinczi of his pleasure at how the academy was thriving, with a growing library and a new printing-press also established at his capital.[4]

Gáspár Bojti was sent by Bethlen to Germany in 1628 to secure new teachers for the Gyulafehérvár Academy. Bojti was already familiar with the universities and academies of Reformed Germany, having studied under Pareus at Heidelberg from 1617. Bojti's mission had a successful outcome when Johann Heinrich Alsted, Johann Heinrich Bisterfeld, and Ludwig Piscator agreed to move to Transylvania from the Herborn Academy in war-torn Nassau. Alsted's services were secured despite competition from both Leiden and Franeker Universities. Contacts with Bojti and other Hungarian student ministers, including Albert Szenczi Molnár, may well have encouraged Alsted to agree to move to Transylvania. Alsted, Bisterfeld, and Piscator arrived in the principality just before Bethlen's death in 1629, and verses which they composed were read out at his funeral. Bethlen made extensive provision in his will to support the Gyulafehérvár Academy, with an annual grant of 20,000 forints for building and maintenance costs provided through revenue from some Tokaj vineyards and from taxes levied on Debrecen. However, this legacy became a source of dispute in the 1630s when György I Rákóczi borrowed money from this fund to help finance his battle against István Bethlen for control of the principality.[5]

Bethlen's untimely death did not deter the three new German teachers, and in 1630 they expanded upon Bethlen's 1622 'Instructions', drawing up

3 B. Jakab, *Opitz Márton a gyulafehérvári Bethlen-iskolánál* (Pécs, 1909); I. Komor, 'Tanulmányok a xvii. századi magyar-német kulturális érintkezések köréből. Martin Opitz gyulafehérvári tanársága', *Filológiai Közlöny*, 1 (1955), 534–44; Tiszántúl Church Province Library Manuscript Collection (Debrecen), Lugossy József oklevél gyűjtemény 1281–1854, R. 111, no. 68, for a 1625 letter of safe passage to Schwarzenbach.

4 I. Juhász and Zs. Jakó (eds.), *Nagyenyedi diákok, 1662–1848* (Bucharest, 1979), 5–46; F. Varó, *Bethlen Gábor kollégiuma* (Nagyenyed, 1903); K. P. Szathmáry, *A gyulafehérvárinagyenyedi Bethlen-főtanoda története* (Nagyenyed, 1868); A. Ballági, *A magyar nyomdászat történelmi fejlődése, 1472–1877* (Budapest, 1878).

5 *Szenczi Molnár levelezése és irományai*, ed. L. Dézsi, 109, 167, 187–8, 316–17, 332–4, 433–4; G. Menk, 'Das Restitutionsedikt und kalvinistische Wissenschaft. Die Berufung Johann Heinrich Alsteds, Philipp Ludwig Piscators und Johann Heinrich Bisterfelds nach Siebenbürgen', *Jahrbuch der Hessischen Kirchengeschichtlichen Vereinigung*, 31 (1980), 29–63; 'Bethlen Gábor levele Alvinczi Péterhez', ed. S. Szilágyi, *EPK* (1879), 26–7; Gy. Kristóf, 'Zsidó, görög és latin gyászversek Bethlen Gábor temetésére', *Erdélyi Múzeum*, 36 (1931), 90–7; Demény, *Bethlen Gábor és kora*, 196–211.

new school regulations (*leges illustris scholae Transylvaniae*) which copied laws used at Herborn and Heidelberg. These regulations set a clear goal for the academy to match the standards of the best schools in Germany and France and outlined the duties of the academy's director, school council, teachers, and of student officers in charge of discipline. Students at the academy were mostly destined for the Reformed ministry, although some were also from noble families, and separate classes were set up by 1640 for noble and non-noble students. Some foreign students were also attracted to study at the academy, including visiting Dutch and German students, and students from Poland and Bohemia.[6]

The three foreign teachers were paid very generously by local standards, with Alsted receiving 900 forints in 1630, which was some nine times the salary for local schoolmasters, whilst Bisterfeld and Piscator each received 630 forints. Such treatment ensured that the academy was successful in retaining the services of their illustrious foreign teachers. Alsted remained in Transylvania until his death in 1638, and although Piscator returned to Germany in 1647, Bisterfeld married into a family from Hermannstadt and continued to work for Transylvania's princes until his death in 1655. In 1643 János Veresegyházi Szentyel visited Jan Amos Comenius with an invitation from György I Rákóczi to take up a post at Gyulafehérvár to replace Alsted, but instead another Moravian exile, Johann Crispinus, taught at the academy from 1647 until 1655. In 1653 state laws appointed an inspector of the academy answerable to the prince, and in 1655 György II Rákóczi invited Isaac Basire, an exiled Anglican priest then serving French Protestants at Pera near Constantinople, to lead the Gyulafehérvár Academy. Basire renewed the academy's regulations in 1656, renaming it a 'school university', and a new coat of arms was chosen by the school council.[7]

Reformed schools also flourished elsewhere in Transylvania, most notably at Kolozsvár, which had been initially considered as a potential site for the new princely academy. Bethlen and the Rákóczi princes consistently supported the development of the Reformed community and school in

---

[6] K. Szabó, 'A gyulafehérvári Bethlen féle főtanoda szervezeti szabályzata', *TT* (1879), 797–805; Juhász and Jakó (eds.), *Nagyenyedi diákok, 1662–1848*, 5–46; J. Herepei, 'Magyarországi iskolákban tanult külföldi ifjak', in B. Keserű (ed.), *Adattár I* (Budapest–Szeged), 539–43; *De Domini Nostro Jesu Christo . . . Petrus Mylius, Polonus* and *De Divina Scripturae Sacrae Eminentia . . . Samuel Decanus, Bohemus* (Gyulafehérvár, 1641).

[7] Isaac Basire, *Correspondence*, ed. W. N. Darnell (London, 1831), 127; Durham Cathedral Library, MS Hunter, 10/22, *Codices Manuscriptae Ecclesiae Cathedralis Dunelmensis* ed. T. Rud; *A gyulafehérvári főiskola 1657-iki szabályzata*, ed. Z. Vargha (Budapest, 1907); [Rákóczi György II], 'II. Rákóczy György ismeretlen iskolatörvénye', ed. P. Török, *Erdélyi Irodalmi Szemle*, 4 (1927), 118–24.

Unitarian-dominated Kolozsvár. When Albert Szenczi Molnár returned from his extensive period of study abroad in 1624, he was overlooked for a post at Gyulafehérvár, perhaps because he had not gained a degree at any of the German universities he visited. Instead, Molnár began to teach at Kolozsvár, where he could consider implementing some of his ideas on educational methods which he had published in 1621 as *Syllecta Scholastica*. These included arguments favouring schooling for girls and greater use of the vernacular in teaching. The school at Kolozsvár moved to new buildings in 1644, but these were destroyed by fire in 1655. The school was then rebuilt under the leadership of János Apáczai Csere, and new regulations were laid down in 1656 which mostly copied the example of the Gyulafehérvár Academy.[8] Other large Reformed schools in Transylvania at Marosvásárhely, Dés, and Broos also received patronage from ruling princes during this period, and from 1657 György I Rákóczi's widow, Zsuzsanna Lórántffy, also supported a new Romanian school at Fogaras in southern Transylvania.[9]

The Rákóczi family also gave financial assistance to Reformed schools in eastern Hungary, and György I Rákóczi supported schools at Kassa and Nagyvárad. Rákóczi paid for a Venetian called Marcus Antonius to teach at Nagyvárad in the 1630s, and made provision for a second teacher to be employed there from 1636.[10] The Rákóczis concentrated primarily on developing the college at Sárospatak at the centre of their north-eastern Hungarian estates. A school had operated in Sárospatak from the sixteenth century, but its growing aspirations during the early seventeenth century were marked by a series of new regulations issued in 1618, 1621, and 1648. The 1621 laws restructured the school and student body, drawing on Palatinate school laws to set out rules on teaching and discipline. From the 1620s the Rákóczi family financed new school buildings at Sárospatak, with a college library founded in 1641 and a printing-press also established in 1650. The college statutes charged the director to lead teaching in theology,

---

[8] Albert Szenczi Molnár, *Syllecta Scholastica. Lexicon Latino-Graeco-Ungaricum* (Heidelberg, 1621); J. Herepei, 'Szenci Molnár Albert tragédiája', *ITK* 70 (1966), 160–5; Debreceni Ember, *Historia ecclesiae reformatae*, 744–5.

[9] 'A marosvásárhelyi református iskola xvii. századi törvényei', ed. R. Békéfi, in *ÉTTK* 18/8, 26–37; J. Koncz, *A marosvásárhelyi evang. reform. kollégium története* (Marosvásárhely, 1896); D. Dósa, *A szászvárosi ev. ref. Kún-kollégium története* (Szászváros, 1897), 1–20; Z. Náhlik, 'Lórántffy Zsuzsanna fogarasi román iskolája', in I. Mészáros (ed.), *Tanulmányok a magyar nevelésügy xvii.–xx. századi történetéből* (Budapest, 1980), 17–29.

[10] Csernák, *A református egyház Nagyváradon*, 125–263; L. Naményi, 'A nagyváradi nyomdászat története', *Magyar Könyvszemle*, 16 (1901), 280–91; J. Herepei, 'Adatok a Rákócziak váradi kollégiumának történetéhez', in B. Keserű (ed.), *Adattár 2. Apáczai és kortársai* (Budapest–Szeged, 1966), 118.

philosophy, Latin, some Greek and Hebrew, poetry, and rhetoric, and determined that the Heidelberg Catechism should be taught every Wednesday and Saturday morning. Students at Sárospatak were again mostly
studying for the ministry, and an experiment to develop a separate class for
noble students proved a failure.[11]

The Rákóczis also looked abroad for suitable teachers to lead their college, as Bethlen had done for his Transylvanian academy. During the late
1630s David Valerius, a Spanish Jew converted to Christianity by Alsted,
taught theology at Sárospatak. However, by far the most important foreign
recruit to the teaching staff at Sárospatak was Jan Amos Comenius. Educated at Herborn under Alsted and then at Heidelberg, Comenius was
from 1648 the senior superintendent of the Unity of Bohemian Brethren.
Comenius had lived in exile since 1628, first in Poland, where he taught at
Leszno from 1632, then visiting London in 1641, before moving back to Elbing in Polish Prussia. In May 1650 Comenius came to northern Hungary
to visit exiled members of his Brethren church in the area. Whilst at
Sárospatak, Comenius wrote a draft programme of potential reforms for
the local college, and was invited by Zsigmond Rákóczi and Zsuzsanna
Lórántffy to return there to implement his plans. After travelling back to
Poland to gain approval from his church council for the move, Comenius
returned to begin work at Sárospatak in October 1650, accompanied by his
son-in-law Peter Figulus[12]

The Reformed schools at Sárospatak and Debrecen admitted approximately sixty students to follow theology classes each year between 1620 and
1660. Between twenty and thirty new students arrived each year at the
school in Debrecen, making it one of the most important training grounds
for Reformed ministers during this period. A school had been established
at Debrecen during the 1530s, and the town council elected its director and
was mostly responsible for its financial support and development, although
the school also received a grant in Gábor Bethlen's will. The role of local
councils and churches was also crucial in supporting schools elsewhere

---

[11] MOL box 1903, Nomina Studiosorum Illustris Scholae Saros Patachinae, 1–35;
L. Makkai, 'A kollégium története alapításától 1650-ig', in *A sárospataki református kollégium*
(Budapest, 1981), 17–59; J. Gulyás, *A sárospataki ref. főiskola rövid története* (Sárospatak,
1931), 1–20; J. Marton, *A sárospataki református főiskola története 1621-ig* (Sárospatak, 1931),
129–56; J. Román, *A sárospataki kollégium* (Budapest, 1956); R. Békéfi, 'A sárospataki református főiskola 1621-iki törvényei', in *ÉTTK* 18/3 (Budapest, 1899), 44–73.

[12] A. Ötvös, 'Geleji Katona István élete és levelei I. Rákóczi Györgyhöz', *Új Magyar
Múzeum*, 10 (1859), 199–233; Keserű (ed.), *Adattár 1*, 239–77; [Rákóczi György I],
'I. Rákóczi György fejedelem levelezése Tolnai István sárospataki pappal', ed. S. Szilágyi,
PEIL 18 (1875), 802–5; M. Spinka, *John Amos Comenius. That Incomparable Moravian*
(Chicago, 1943).

in the Partium, and the council at Nagybánya for example was responsible for appointing a director and donating new buildings for its school in 1657.[13]

Some directors tried to get approval from councils to introduce changes to teaching methods and improve the general standards of their schools. Imre Szilvásújfalvi Anderkó, school director at Debrecen between 1596 and 1599, published his *Suggestions on Plans for Learning and Teaching* in 1597 which detailed his perception of current failures in Hungarian schools. Szilvásújfalvi, who had studied at Wittenberg and in England, advocated that more Hungarian students should attend foreign universities. He recommended that students at local schools be divided into classes according to aptitude, and that traditional student-led private study groups and practices of dividing students by the payment of fees and other non-academic criteria should be abandoned. Szilvásújfalvi also proposed that Debrecen should develop three graded classes to teach Latin grammar and instruct pupils in Reformed theology.[14] His proposals met with little immediate response and, although the council faced repeated student disturbances over a variety of grievances, it took until 1657 for new regulations finally to introduce six graded classes and to divide the school year into two terms.[15]

Reformed education in Royal Hungary made more uncertain progress during this period, especially after the conversion of many former noble patrons to Catholicism. Nobles who left the Reformed church sent their children to the growing numbers of Catholic schools, whilst the largest

[13] Tiszántúl Church Province Library Manuscript Collection (Debrecen), Series Studiosorum in Schola Debrecina, sign. R. 495; F. Zsigmond, *A debreceni református kollégium története, 1538–1938* (Debrecen, 1938), 31–73; K. Irinyi and K. Benda (eds.), *A négyszáz éves debreceni nyomda (1561–1961)* (Budapest, 1961), 7–59, 313–408; R. Békéfi, *A debreczeni református főiskola xvii. és xviii. századi törvényei* (Budapest, 1899), 79–117; I. Révész, 'A debreceni főiskoláról' *MPEIF* 1 (1870), 275–90, 391–427; F. Thurzó, *A Nagybányai ev. ref. főiskola (schola Rivulina) története, 1547–1755* (Nagybánya, 1905), 41–7; I. Szilágyi, 'A máramarossziget református tanoda történeteinek rövid vázlata', *Sárospataki Füzetek,* 1 (1857–8), 957–71.

[14] Imre Szilvásújfalvi Anderkó, *Admonitiones de ratione discendi, atque docendi* (Debrecen, 1597). B. K. Nagy, 'Szilvásújfalvi Imre pedagógiai intelmei', in *Studia et Acta Ecclesiastica, 3* (Budapest, 1955), 879–87; B. Keserű, 'Ujfalvi Imre és a magyar későreneszánz', in *Acta Historiae Litterarum Hungaricarum,* viii, 3–16; ix, 3–47 (Szeged, 1968).

[15] Zsigmond, *A debreceni református kollégium története, 1538–1938,* 31–73; 'A debreceni tanács által alkőtőtt rendszabályok a debreceni főiskolára vonatkozólag, 1657-ből', *MPEIF* 5 (1874), 395–7; Révész, 'A debreceni főiskoláról', 275–90, 391–427; S. Nagy, *A debreceni kollégium* (Debrecen, 1940), 21–108; J. Barcza, *A debreceni református kollégium története* (Budapest, 1988), 5–43; É. S. Kiss, 'Diákzendülések a debreceni kollégiumban', in I. Mészáros (ed.), *Tanulmányok a magyar nevelésügy xvii–xx. századi történetéből* (Budapest, 1980), 31–9.

Reformed school in Royal Hungary at Pápa came increasingly under the supervision of the Reformed superintendent. Although a library was established at Pápa during the 1630s, student numbers fluctuated, and in 1651 the deputy regional governor, Ferenc Bottka, wrote to András Klobusiczky, administrator of the Rákóczi estates at Sárospatak, claiming that 'although in times past our school at Pápa was filled with intelligent and knowledgeable men, it has become so wasted that it is almost completely destroyed'.[16] Whilst in the earlier part of the century the political strength of the Transylvanian principality was able to check Catholic persecution of Reformed and Lutheran communities across Royal Hungary to some degree, from the late 1640s their position steadily deteriorated with the confiscation of Protestant church property. Protestants in Pozsony wrote to Zsuzsanna Lórántffy in 1656 that there was quite simply nowhere left for their children to go to school in the area and asked her to support their faltering efforts to build a new school. Meanwhile, in Ottoman-occupied Hungary some Reformed schools were maintained along border areas and under more benevolent local pashas. Students from the largest school at Tolna occasionally reached western universities, but many children were lost to the church if taken away by the Ottoman authorities for instruction, a fate which nearly befell the Transylvanian superintendent, István Geleji Katona.[17]

After György II Rákóczi's disastrous adventure into Poland in 1657, the security of Reformed colleges in the Transylvanian principality also came under threat. The Gyulafehévár Academy was irreparably damaged and its library destroyed by an invading Tartar army in 1658, and the school at Nagyvárad was lost after a Turkish siege in 1660. After György II Rákóczi's death in 1660, his widow Zsófia Báthori, only ever a reluctant convert to the Reformed church at her 1643 wedding, reconverted to Catholicism with her young son Ferenc. In 1671 Báthori deprived Sárospatak College of financial support and expelled its teachers and remaining students from the town. This severe contraction in the provision of Protestant education highlighted the dependence of Reformed schools upon the support of princes, nobles, and local authorities. The only major centres of Reformed education in the region which survived into the later seventeenth century

---

[16] L. Ruzsás, *A pápai kollégium története* (Budapest, 1981), 7–40; G. Lamperth, *A pápai református főiskola története, 1531–1931* (Pápa, 1931), 21–35; E. Kis, *A dunántúli ev. ref. egyházkerület pápai főiskolájának története, 1531–1895* (Pápa, 1896), 9–48; [Ferenc Bottka], 'Ferenc Bottka kéri Klobusiczky Andrást pápai iskola számára', ed. B. Szilágyi, *MPEIF* 7 (1876), 43–4.

[17] 'Pozsony városának elöljárói főiskola épitéséhez fogvan, kérnek Lórántfi Zsuzsanna fejedelemnőtől', ed. S. Szilágyi, *MPEIF* 6 (1875), 153–4.

were at Debrecen, Kolozsvár, Marosvásárhely, and at Nagyenyed, where Mihály Apafi refounded the princely academy in 1662.[18]

(II) THREE FOREIGNERS

Johann Heinrich Alsted, Johann Heinrich Bisterfeld, and Jan Amos Comenius made the most systematic and significant attempts to shape the philosophy of learning and styles of teaching used in Hungarian Reformed schools during the early seventeenth century. Whilst these three did not entirely agree upon the educational reforms which they wanted Hungarian schools to adopt, their ideas and proposals emerged from a similar intellectual background and outlook, and were supported by the same group of international Protestant theologians and activists. This section will first outline the ideas which Alsted developed on methods of learning, then examine the connections between Alsted, Bisterfeld, and Comenius, before considering Comenius' own plans to re-order education and teaching.

The educational philosophy advanced by Alsted and Bisterfeld emerged from Reformed German universities and academies in the latter decades of the sixteenth century. At Herborn, where Alsted, Bisterfeld, and Piscator worked prior to moving to Transylvania, methods were employed to try to simplify processes of learning from the 1580s. Teachers at Herborn and other German academies utilized techniques on the teaching of logic devised by the Huguenot, Petrus Ramus. Ramus, who perished in the 1572 massacres in France, had tried to sweep away some of the complications of Aristotelian science, which applied strict processes of logical deduction to derive truthful statements about any body of information. This accepted pattern of learning was challenged by Ramus' technique of classifying and sub-dividing branches of knowledge to reveal a unified, schematized system which could be committed to memory. Whilst a version of Ramism sometimes known as Philippo-Ramism was accepted and used at the Herborn Academy, elsewhere Reformed theologians, including David Pareus, rejected Ramism's simplified methods of logic as unsuitable for application to complex areas of study at universities. However, when Bartholomaeus Keckermann, who worked at Heidelberg and Danzig before his death in 1609, constructed a new systematized Aristotelian logic which adopted a Ramist form of classification, this 'methodical peripateticism' was warmly embraced by Pareus and others who had earlier refused to accept Ramism.[19]

---

[18] G. Várkonyi, *II. Rákóczy György esküvője* (Budapest, 1990), 13–45; 'Egyháztörténelmi adatok', ed. S. Szilágyi, *EPK* (1880), 344–5.

[19] W. J. Ong, *Ramus: Method and the Decay of Dialogue* (Cambridge, Mass., 1958); G. A. Benrath, 'Die Theologische Fakultät der Hohen Schule Herborn im Zeitalter der

These developments formed the backdrop to Alsted's own attempts to reform logic as an academic discipline. Alsted was convinced that knowledge must be approached and treated as one universal system, with an essential unity, order, and harmony. Alsted assumed that when all categories of knowledge were properly arranged these essential characteristics would be revealed. To achieve this, Alsted extended Keckermann's application of systematic methods to logic to cover all branches of knowledge. However, Alsted's preoccupation with philosophical harmony led him to attempt to draw together various other revisions of Aristotelian logic including Ramism, and also to use insights gained from mystics who had tried to expand the potential of human understanding. Alsted became particularly interested in memory arts, which relied on images and numbers to aid the retention of information. Among eight published works between 1609 and 1612 on encyclopaedic systems of knowledge, memory arts, and on the ideas of the early fourteenth-century numerologist and mystic Ramon Lull, Alsted published his *Philosophical Panacea* in 1610 on his perception of harmony between the logic of Aristotle, Ramus, and Lull. Alsted was also interested in incorporating into his system of knowledge the ideas of Giordano Bruno, who in the sixteenth century had envisaged a magical reform of society based on developing combinations of numbers which could reveal keys to higher truths and harmony in nature. Bisterfeld, too, became interested in Lull's ideas, and when he moved to Transylvania acquired something of a reputation as a practitioner of magical arts.[20]

Alsted was concerned to make practical use of his developing ideas on methods of learning, and above all to provide teachers and schools with more effective means of studying core subjects such as grammar and rhetoric, and then to expand teaching over an enormous range of subjects including theology, law, medicine, metallurgy, agriculture, and alchemy. Alsted worked to accumulate and classify information within his reordered logic which, he believed, made the subject matter more productive of

Reformierten Orthodoxie (1584–1634)', *Jahrbuch der Hessischen Kirchengeschichtlichen Vereinigung*, 36 (1985), 1–17; I. Czegle, 'Rámista volt-e Szenczi Molnár Albert', in B. Keserű (ed.), *Adattár 4. Szenci Molnár Albert és a magyar késő reneszánsz* (Szeged, 1978), 43–8; Israel, *The Dutch Republic*, 589–91.

[20] H. Hotson, 'Johann Heinrich Alsted', D.Phil. thesis (Oxford, 1994); H. Hotson, 'Philosophical Pedagogy in Reformed Central Europe between Ramus and Comenius: A Survey of the Continental Background of the "Three Foreigners"', in M. Greengrass, M. Leslie, and T. Raylor (eds.), *Samuel Hartlib and Universal Reformation. Studies in Intellectual Communication* (Cambridge, 1994), 29–50; H. Hotson, 'Johann Heinrich Alsted's Relations with Silesia, Bohemia and Moravia: Patronage, Piety and Pansophia', *Acta Comeniana*, 12 (1997), 13–35; Hartl. 'Ephemerides' 1648, f. 14. For Bisterfeld's 'magic-books', see Ferenc Benkő, *Parnassusi időtöltés 7. Enyedi ritkaságok* (Nagyenyed, 1796), 10, 29.

meaning and understanding. In 1629 Alsted was finally able to publish his *Encyclopaedia of all Knowledge* encompassing thirty-four disciplines and subjects, through which he was convinced that the interrelatedness and harmony of universal knowledge could be fully revealed. Alsted envisaged his *Encyclopaedia* being used as a stepping-stone in order to advance beyond the bounds of hitherto understood knowledge towards the ultimate goal of recovering the perfection lost since the fall of Adam. Alsted believed that this project would not only improve standards of learning and education, but also in turn lead to the progress of religious and moral reformation. This expectancy was part of the broader eschatological framework of his ideas, and in 1627 Alsted predicted that a millennial age of renewal would begin before 1694.[21]

Alsted's efforts to realize these ambitious proposals for 'Christian encyclopaedism' continued to develop after his arrival in Transylvania. In 1637 he proposed to recast his entire *Encyclopaedia* using mnemonic systems of combinatory and numerological logic. Alsted seemed to be aware that this work was on the fringe of what was publicly acceptable in Reformed academic circles. In a letter written in December 1638 shortly after Alsted's death, the Transylvanian superintendent István Geleji Katona revealed to György I Rákóczi that Alsted had declared his later writings to be 'sub anathemate' and ordered them to be burned. Geleji refused to cooperate, and so Alsted, although close to death, cut up his papers 'with a great bodily effort' and threw the papers into an outside privy. The faithful Geleji got a local beggar to recover what was salvageable from the mess, despite opposition from Alsted's wife. Geleji kept the papers until Bisterfeld, then on diplomatic mission for the Transylvanian prince, returned home, when they were entrusted to him.[22]

News of Alsted's continued work at Gyulafehérvár on his *Encyclopaedia* caused great interest among his friends and contacts across the Continent. These included Samuel Hartlib and John Dury, who both had a range of close connections with central Europe. Hartlib was the son of a merchant from Elbing, whilst Dury's father was an exiled Scottish minister at Elbing, and Dury himself served as minister to the English merchant company at

---

[21] R. J. W. Evans, 'Alsted és Erdély', *Korunk*, 32 (1973); P. Cole, *A Neglected Educator: Johann Heinrich Alsted* (Sydney, 1910); J. V. Kvacsala, 'Johann Heinrich Alstedt', *Ungarische Revue*, 9 (1889), 628–42; L. E. Loemker, *Struggle for Synthesis: The Seventeenth Century Background of Leibniz's Synthesis* (Cambridge, Mass., 1972), 46–8, 189–93.

[22] 'Geleji Katona István levelei Rákóczyhoz', ed. A. Beke, *ITK* 4 (1894), 336–46: 'utolsó szavaiban és cselekedetiben meg, hogy a manuscriptomit sub anathemate hagyé, hogy megégessük, de mi mondánk: távol legyen az mi tölünk, s mi onnan eljövén, elöl vétette és egynéhány részre metszette egy itt való nagy testes munkáját, és tisztességgel legyen írva, az árnyék székben vettette.'

Danzig during the 1620s. Hartlib was the conduit for much communication between widely dispersed adherents of a variety of projects on educational, religious, and political reform. Partly thanks to Hartlib, reformers, theologians, and activists were linked in a chain of Reformed intellectual communication which stretched right across the Continent. It reached even Constantinople where Thomas Roe, the English ambassador at the Porte, was a patron and supporter of Dury and in contact with Hartlib during the 1630s.

Roe was also in correspondence with Transylvania's princes, but news was brought to Hartlib of Alsted's work in Transylvania by another route, through an exiled Silesian called Cyprian Kinner. Kinner had studied at Brieg with Hartlib and had been supported by the Dutch church in London around 1630. He became acquainted with Alsted and Bisterfeld from visits to Gyulafehérvár in 1635 and was later to collaborate with Comenius. Alsted and Kinner conferred on the writings of a Silesian astrologer, and Kinner was able to report to Hartlib in 1636 on the contents of a letter which he claimed to have received from Alsted, which hinted at how Alsted may have been working towards revealing secrets of knowledge. Hartlib and his associates were certainly very anxious to get hold of Alsted's revised 'Encyclopaedia', and both Hartlib and Dury remained in contact with Bisterfeld, who had studied in England during the 1620s. In 1648 Hartlib received word that Alsted's son had a copy of the revised 'Encyclopaedia' at Herborn, but the work seemingly remained undiscovered and was certainly never published. Hartlib's interest in Transylvania was also sustained at this time by John Stoughton, whose tract on the progress of the Hungarian church Hartlib had published in 1640 with a dedication to György I Rákóczi. Stoughton had particularly praised Rákóczi's patronage of school reforms in this work and suggested that Hartlib, Dury, and Comenius would prove to be the agents of great reforms which would ultimately lead to the defeat of the confusion of Babylon.[23]

Exchanges of information flowed between the various members of Hartlib's circle of correspondents on a diverse range of subjects, with a shared millenarian vision of expected future improvements in learning, religion, and politics. In March 1642 Hartlib joined with Dury and Comenius to sign a fraternal covenant in London which advertised their interests

[23] Hartl. 1/33, ff. 16–17, 39*a*, 102*a*; 4/5, f. 4*a*; 9/1, f. 95*b*; 46/6, f. 35*a*; 'Ephemerides' 1638/34*b*; 35*b*, f. 18. Cyprian Kinner, *A Continuation of Mr. John-Amos-Comenius School-Endeavours; or, A summary delineation of Dr Cyprian Kinner Silesian his thoughts concerning education* (London, 1648) [pub. by Hartlib]; Stoughton, *Felicitas ultimi saeculi*; *The Negotiations of Sir Thomas Roe in His Embassy to the Ottoman Porte from 1621 to 1628*, ed. S. Richardson (London, 1740); Greengrass, 'Samuel Hartlib and International Calvinism', 464–75.

in educational reform and in promoting harmony among Protestants. This pact between these 'three foreigners' in England supported Hartlib's initiatives to establish a state agency, or 'Office of public addresses', to coordinate advances in learning and science and to assist the progress of a true reformation of religion and society. Hartlib's ideas indeed gained some official backing in England, but although he received financial aid from Interregnum regimes, Hartlib was to remain disappointed by the limited action taken to fulfil his ambitions. Meanwhile, Dury was interested in ideas about philosophies of knowledge, commenting in the 1640s, 'make use of Keckermann so farre as hee hath written; and what he hath not written of, you will find done by Alstedius'. Dury also tried to develop a magical language which would reveal the secrets of nature, firmly believing that improvements in standards of education and knowledge would lead to greater piety and understanding of religion. However, Dury mostly concentrated on the task of promoting peace and unity among Protestants across the Continent, and from the 1620s undertook a series of voyages to advance this cause in Sweden, the Dutch Republic, Germany, and Switzerland. Dury also addressed the Transylvanian church in 1634 with his plans for Protestant union, which will be considered in more detail in Chapter 4.[24]

Comenius brought his proposals for a practical philosophy to guide school reform to the 1642 London pact. Comenius' ideas were grounded in his belief in the harmony, order, and unity of universal truth and knowledge. Comenius was convinced that it should prove possible to proceed 'to the utmost degree of knowledge' in the short period which he conceived remained before an imminent apocalypse. Comenius proposed that all knowledge about religion, science, philosophy, and politics could be drawn together into 'a store-house of universal learning', 'to be termed pansophy, a universal harmony'. Comenius proposed that this 'pansophia', or Christian pansophic learning, would be the sum total of previous bodies of wisdom and encyclopaedias. Pansophic learning for Comenius was the key to unlocking the mysteries of nature and the Scriptures. He believed that improving standards of education and learning would awaken men and

[24] Hartl. 68/4. H. Trevor-Roper, 'Three Foreigners: The Philosophers of the Puritan Revolution', in H. Trevor-Roper (ed.), *Religion, the Reformation and Social Change* (London, 1972), 237–93; J. M. Batten, *John Dury: Advocate of Christian Reunion* (Chicago, 1944); G. H. Turnbull, *Hartlib, Dury and Comenius* (London, 1947); G. H. Turnbull, *Samuel Hartlib. A Sketch of His Life and His Relations to Comenius* (Oxford, 1920); C. Webster, *Samuel Hartlib and the Advancement of Learning* (Cambridge, 1970); Webster, *The Great Instauration*; M. Greengrass, M. Leslie, and T. Raylor (eds.), *Samuel Hartlib and Universal Reformation* (Cambridge, 1994); S. Mandelbrote, 'John Dury and the Practice of Irenicism', in N. Aston (ed.), *Religious Change in Europe, 1650–1914. Essays for John McManners* (Oxford, 1997), 41–59; Greengrass, 'Samuel Hartlib and International Calvinism', 464–75.

women to the centrality of God in the world and recover something of the divine image in man. Comenius proposed that advances in learning should be co-ordinated by a central universal college, and then dispersed through schools and books, which all used uniform principles of learning, and a new, universal language which Comenius dubbed 'panglottia'.[25] Comenius claimed that such methods would facilitate 'the multiplication of learned men in precisely the same way that the discovery of printing had facilitated the multiplication of books' and 'increase the sum of Christian wisdom, and sow the seeds of piety, of learning, and of morality'.[26] Comenius also saw pansophic learning as the basis for 'the quick and complete overthrow of the great Babylon of our confusions and the establishment of God's Zion in its sublime light for the nations of the world'. This vision of an approaching time of general restoration also extended beyond education into ideas for world bodies to oversee international politics and to regulate the administration of justice.[27]

In 1642 Hartlib was able to have two of Comenius' treatises published as *A Reformation of Schooles*, and through this text and other works Comenius set out in detail his ideas on methods of teaching practical and useful knowledge, some of which he later revised after his experience at Sárospatak College. Comenius identified three aspects of the process of education which in his view were in greatest need of reform: the organization of schools, the quality of school-books, and standards of teaching. On the structure of schools, Comenius argued that there should be four phases to education, beginning with the 'school of infancy' at home from when children were born until they were six years old, to be followed by vernacular schooling until children were aged twelve, then Latin schooling until eighteen, with university to follow until students were twenty-four years old. Comenius described these six-class schools as 'fortresses of light', and he particularly emphasized the importance of using the vernacular as a necessary base for further progress in education. Comenius also argued that education should be made equally available to both women and men,

[25] J. E. Sadler, *J. A. Comenius and the Concept of Universal Education* (London, 1966); D. Murphy, *Comenius. A Critical Reassessment of His Life and Work* (Dublin, 1995); Jan Amos Comenius, *A Patterne of Universall Knowledge* (London, 1651), 3–4, 42, 55; M. Spinka, 'Comenian Pansophic Principles', *Church History*, 22 (1953), 155–65.

[26] Jan Amos Comenius, *Didactica Magna* [pub. in Czech, 1632; in Latin, 1657], ed. M. W. Keatinge (New York, 1910), 293–4.

[27] Jan Amos Comenius, *Panglottia; or, Universal language*, ed. A. M. O. Dobbie (Warwick, 1989); Jan Amos Comenius, *Panorthosia; or, Universal reform*, ed. A. M. O. Dobbie (Sheffield, 1995) (both tracts are taken from *De rerum humanarum emendatione consultationes catholicae* (Amsterdam, 1657); I. Komor, 'A Comenius utópia alkotmánya', *Pedagógiai Szemle*, 20 (1970), 916–22.

and to both rich and poor, since he argued that all had an equal capacity for learning. Comenius then turned his attention to the graded textbooks, or 'funnels of wisdom', to be used in his schools. In the 1630s Comenius produced textbooks for the first three years of his Latin school, beginning with the *Janua linguarum reserata* (*The Gateway to Languages Unlocked*), followed by the *Vestibula* (*Entrance*) and *Atrium* (*Hallway* [*to Learning Latin*]). In addition to these books, Comenius stressed the importance of using realistic examples, visual images, plays, and drama to assist students learn Latin grammar and vocabulary. Comenius identified the abilities of teachers as the third key element of education. He described the task of teachers to 'plant and water the tender grafts of paradise', by connecting abstract knowledge with the practical experiences of their pupils and ordering subject matter so that it could be easily understood. Comenius intended that his methods of instruction would mean that 'teachers may teach less, but learners may learn more'.[28]

Unlike the three foreigners in England joined by their 1642 pact, Alsted, Bisterfeld, and Comenius were not bound by any common formula of action in Transylvania. Comenius had been a student under Alsted at Herborn and mostly agreed with Alsted's approach to teaching and learning and on the wider consequences of educational reform for society. Nevertheless, some points of disagreement were later to emerge between Comenius and Bisterfeld, after Bisterfeld took on the leadership of the Gyulafehérvár Academy after Alsted's death in 1638. When Hartlib sent a copy of tracts by Comenius on pansophic learning to Transylvania, Bisterfeld responded with criticisms of Comenius' ideas. Bisterfeld argued that Comenius' plans to attain universal knowledge were flawed because of his neglect of metaphysics, which Bisterfeld thought was key to the right ordering of all knowledge. Bisterfeld stressed that any encyclopaedia must be 'solid' and ordered by metaphysics, otherwise the essential unity between academic disciplines would be lost. Bisterfeld described a true encyclopaedia as nothing other than 'the proportions of nature, or a picture of truth', and in his *First Nursery of Philosophy* Bisterfeld stressed again the importance of metaphysics and logical order to establish the harmony of knowledge. This 1641 work was later to influence Leibniz, who adapted some of Bisterfeld's ideas within his own plans to write an encyclopaedia in 1671. Despite these disagreements between Bisterfeld and Comenius, the two men corresponded in 1643 on reforms to patterns of learning, and

---

[28] Works written by Comenius in Hungary were in his *Opera Didactica Omnia* (Amsterdam, 1657), pt 3. See also Jan Amos Comenius, *A Reformation of Schooles* (London, 1642); Comenius, *Didactica Magna*, ed. Keatinge.

Comenius even at one point described Bisterfeld as a vehement pansophist. In 1647 Bisterfeld certainly wrote to Hartlib restating his belief in the fundamental unity of knowledge and the possibility of developing schools and textbooks which would allow a return to a Genesis state of complete knowledge. Bisterfeld also expressed strong support for the development of pansophic methods in schools to advance the prospect of this universal knowledge.[29]

Alsted, Bisterfeld, and Comenius were among a group of early seventeenth-century Protestant intellectuals who looked to simplify processes of learning with a view to achieving universal knowledge. Their ideas for practical changes to schools and teaching were coupled with a strong mysticism, and sometimes with wild expectations about the extensive benefits which would accrue from reordering patterns of learning. Whilst there were some issues about the means to achieve these visionary objectives on which they were divided, and on occasion personal tension between Bisterfeld and Comenius after 1650, all three were committed to a programme of practical educational reform in Hungary and Transylvania as part of the renewal of the church and of society at large, and their impact upon Reformed colleges and the Hungarian church will now be examined.

(III) REFORMING HUNGARIAN EDUCATION

The arrival of Alsted, Bisterfeld, and Piscator at the Gyulafehérvár Academy in 1629 did not mark the development from scratch of changes to traditional methods of teaching in Hungarian Reformed schools. The attempts made by Imre Szilvásújfalvi Anderkó and Albert Szenczi Molnár to stimulate reform in Hungarian schools have already been briefly considered. Other student ministers returning from western universities to work in local colleges also suggested improvements to the provision of teaching. Alsted and his colleagues were none the less responsible for almost entirely re-shaping teaching at the Gyulafehérvár Academy according to their agenda of encyclopaedic learning, a goal of providing an all-encompassing knowledge later taken up by Comenius at Sárospatak. Alsted, Bisterfeld,

---

[29] Hartl. 7/107, f. 1a; 7/63; L. E. Loemker, 'Leibniz and the Herborn Encyclopedists', *Journal of the History of Ideas*, 22 (1961), 323–38. Daniel Jablonski, Comenius' grandson, also had personal links with Leibniz: Loemker, *The Seventeenth Century Background of Leibniz's Synthesis*. In the 1710s Leibniz offered himself as a suitable candidate to lead the Transylvanian chancery: Evans, *The Making of the Habsburg Monarchy*, 288–9. [Comenius], *Korrespondence*, ed. Kvacsala, 37–41; [Rákóczi Zsigmond], 'Herczeg Rákóczy Zsigmond levelezése', ed. S. Szilágyi, *TT* (1888), 108–10; J. V. Kvacsala, 'Bisterfeld János Henrik élete', *Századok*, 25 (1891), 552.

and Comenius reorganized school classes, expanded the number of subjects taught, and used a simplified logic to clarify the unity which they saw
between all academic disciplines. All three made a significant impression
on Reformed clergy training in Hungary and Transylvania both as teachers
and as authors of school textbooks, and their influence spread out from
Gyulafehérvár and Sárospatak to other larger schools at Debrecen,
Kolozsvár, Szatmár, and Nagyvárad.

In 1630 Alsted and his colleagues drew up new regulations for the Gyulafehérvár Academy, which set out a highly structured timetable of five
graded classes to teach students Latin, Greek, Hebrew, rhetoric, poetry,
philosophy, the natural sciences, and theology and stressed the importance
of the vernacular in assisting students to learn languages. The school rules
also set out the disciplinary regime for students, but only allowed for corporal punishment if students had committed very serious moral offences.
This proved not entirely to the satisfaction of the Transylvanian superintendent István Geleji Katona, who wrote to György I Rákóczi in 1640 of
disciplinary problems at the college, which he felt had not been dealt with
satisfactorily by Bisterfeld and Piscator. Geleji wanted to appoint a 'hard,
authoritarian Hungarian master' to exercise discipline over the students,
but thought that the pre-eminence which the German teachers had
achieved would prevent any Hungarian from establishing sufficient authority at the college.[30]

Teaching duties at Gyulafehérvár were initially divided between the
Herborn teachers, with all three involved in language teaching, and in addition Alsted was responsible for teaching philosophy, Piscator took classes
in theology, and Bisterfeld taught the natural sciences. Public disputations
by students to rehearse and defend arguments became an important part of
the pattern of teaching at Gyulafehérvár and, in the foreword to the first of
these debates published in March 1630, Alsted committed himself and his
colleagues to raise standards at the academy and to prepare a three-year
course in philosophy and theology.[31] The three teachers soon became an
integral part of life in the Transylvanian capital, frequently dining at court
and involved in the education of György I Rákóczi's two sons, György and

[30] Juhász and Jakó, Nagyenyedi diákok, 1662–1848, 5–46; Ötvös, 'Geleji Katona levelei
I. Rákóczi Györgyhöz', 199–233; Kvacsala, 'Bisterfeld János Henrik élete', 447–78, 545–77.

[31] Disputatio Philosophica (Gyulafehérvár, 1630) was held by the Academy Library, Buda-
pest, but has been lost. Disputatio theologica de Deo (Gyulafehérvár, 1630), has a foreword by
Alsted, but this volume was among those stolen from Sárospatak by the Soviet army. Beata
Beatae Virginis Ars; seu, Regia genuini Scripturae Sacrae sensus omnigeniq usus inveniendi via
(Gyulafehérvár, 1651), includes twenty-two students' disputations. Gladii Spiritus Ignei . . .
seu, Scripturae Sacrae Divina eminentia et efficientia (1653) is only to be found in the Teleki
Library, Marosvásárhely.

Zsigmond. After Alsted's death in 1638, direction of the Gyulafehérvár Academy became increasingly dependent on Bisterfeld. Bisterfeld was sometimes absent from the academy during the late 1630s on diplomatic missions to western Europe, but he remained at Gyulafehérvár during the 1640s, refusing offers to move to Leiden University in 1649 and 1650.[32]

Alongside their re-organization of teaching at the academy, Alsted and his colleagues devised new textbooks for the classes which they had established. Improvements to the Gyulafehérvár printing-press allowed Alsted to publish texts on Hebrew and Greek in 1635, as well as on Latin grammar, whilst Piscator provided texts on rhetoric, oratory, and poetry in the 1630s and 1640s, and Bisterfeld published books on Latin and elementary logic. In 1636 Alsted also supervised the production of a Latin–Hungarian, shortened Heidelberg Catechism for use at Gyulafehérvár, and this appeared in five editions at the capital alone before 1660.[33] Miklós Bethlen recorded in his autobiography that the syllabus at Gyulafehérvár continued to be heavily reliant on these school-books during the 1650s. A new curriculum from 1657 advised using sections of Alsted's *Encyclopaedia* alongside the textbooks published by Alsted at Gyulafehérvár on Greek, Hebrew, and physics, as well as Piscator's text on rhetoric.[34] Through these textbooks the Herborn teachers' influence extended from Gyulafehérvár into other schools across the region, and Alsted's texts were, for example, used to teach Latin at Nagybánya. Former students at Gyulafehérvár also used the academy's syllabus when they taught at other schools, such as András

---

[32] *Schola Triumphata per illustrem et Magnificum Dominum, D. Georgium Rakoci, Filium Illustrissimi Transylvaniae Principis* (Gyulafehérvár, 1638), foreword by Alsted; Pál Keresztúri, *Csecsemő keresztyén, mellyet ... Rakoczi György és Sigmond ... igaz vallásokban való szép épületekröl abban az probában bizonságot tennének* (Gyulafehérvár, 1638); *Pallas Dacica, quam ... Sigismundus Rakoci ... auditorum corona praestitit ... praecinenta schola aulica, applaudentibus omnibus* (Gyulafehérvár, 1640), Foreword by Bisterfeld; György I Rákóczi, *Instructio, quam tradidit Georgio Rakoci, filio suo* (Gyulafehérvár, 1638); György I Rákóczi, *Instructio, quam tradidit Sigismundo, filio suo* (Gyulafehérvár, 1640); F. W. Cuno, 'Bisterfeld János Henrik', *MPEF* 4 (1882), 295–304.

[33] Johann Heinrich Alsted, *Rudimenta Linguae Graecae* (Gyulafehérvár, 1634); and his *Rudimenta Linguae Latinae* (Gyulafehérvár, 1634; also pub. 1635, 1640); *Rudimenta Linguae Hebraicae* (1635); *Latinus in nuce* (Gyulafehérvár, 1635; also pub. 1648); *Grammatica Latina* (Gyulafehérvár, 1635; also pub. 1642); *Catechismus religionis Christianae- Catechismus; azaz, A keresztyéni vallásnak és hütnek rövid kerdesekben és feleletekben foglaltatott* (Gyulafehérvár, 1636). Ludwig Piscator, *Rudimenta Rhetorica* (Gyulafehérvár, 1635; also pub. 1644, 1649); and his *Ars Poetica* (Gyulafehérvár, 1642); *Rudimenta Oratoricae* (Gyulafehérvár, 1645; also pub. 1649); Johann Heinrich Bisterfeld, *Elementa Logica* (Gyulafehérvár, 1635; also edns. in 1641, 1645, 1649); and his *Medulla Priscae Puraeque Latinitatis* (1646). J. V. Ecsedy, 'A gyulafehérvári fejedelmi nyomda második korszaka (1637–58) és utóélete', *Országos Széchényi Könyvtár Évkönyve* (1978), 291–341.

[34] *Bethlen Miklós önéletirásai*, ed. Windisch, chs. 8–9; 'Schema primum generale sive forma studiorum Albensium', in *A gyulafehérvári föiskola 1657-iki szabályzata*, ed. Vargha.

Porcsalmi, a student at Gyulafehérvár in the late 1630s who then taught at Kolozsvár from 1642 until 1666. Porcsalmi copied out lectures given by Bisterfeld at Gyulafehérvár on philosophy, and large sections of Alsted's *Encyclopaedia*, and later used these notes as the basis for his own teaching at Kolozsvár.[35]

These efforts to construct a new expanded syllabus and to provide effective teaching materials at the Gyulafehérvár Academy were enthusiastically supported by the Transylvanian court. Reformed princes in Germany had proved equally supportive of reforms at academies such as Herborn and sanctioned projects to improve standards of education and moral discipline. Such attempts at further reformation in Germany were in fact largely implemented by leading Reformed ministers and theologians with the active support of princes. This pattern, of a Reformed clergy hierarchy, academics, and princes combining to try to effect a reformation of clergy education and public morality from above, was mirrored by the development of educational facilities in the Transylvanian principality, and especially at Gyulafehérvár. However, initiative for further reforms in the Hungarian church did not solely come from above, and the church authorities and court responded anxiously to the reforms of teaching methods and the syllabus undertaken at Sárospatak College by János Tolnai Dali from the late 1630s.

In 1638 Reformed inspectors described the standard of teaching at Sárospatak College as poor and reported that the study of 'logic, rhetoric, and philosophical and theological debate . . . have died at Sárospatak'. The Zemplén synod also complained that holidays at Sárospatak were too long, that the school buildings were in poor condition, and that the students' food was bad.[36] The need for change was made clear to the college's patron, György I Rákóczi, and when János Tolnai Dali returned to Hungary in 1639 after studying for seven years in western Europe he was appointed by Rákóczi as the new director to revive Sárospatak College. Tolnai had been taught by Bisterfeld at Gyulafehérvár, before leaving for Franeker University to study under William Ames. Tolnai then spent several years resident in London, where he had established contact with Samuel Hartlib among others. Whilst Tolnai's lengthy exposure to English religion and support for the 'League of Piety', signed in London in February 1638, unsettled some of the Zemplén church leadership, his appointment at Sárospatak

---

35　I. Török, *A kolozsvári év. ref. collégium története* (Kolozsvár, 1905); Thurzó, *A nagybányai főiskola története, 1547–1755.*

36　'Miskolczi Csulyak István zempléni ref. esperes (1629–45) egyházlátogatási jegyzőkönyvei', ed. J. Zoványi, *TT* 7 (1906), 292–5.

was eventually, if reluctantly, accepted. However, Tolnai soon justified the worst fears of local traditionalists, as his reforms of the syllabus at Sárospatak brought years of turbulence to the Reformed church in northern Hungary.[37]

The syllabus at Sárospatak during the early 1630s had been dominated by language instruction, by the study of Bartholomaeus Keckermann's works on logic and rhetoric, and by Alsted's works on metaphysics.[38] János Tolnai Dali wanted to introduce to Sárospatak the tradition of interpreting Ramism which he had encountered at Dutch universities, and especially its use by William Ames at Franeker. Supported by colleagues Dániel Kolosi and János Bényei, Tolnai acted quickly to change the syllabus, replacing the core textbooks by Keckermann and stopping the teaching of metaphysics altogether. Instead, Tolnai began to teach from Ramus' *Dialectics* and used only works by Ames to teach theology. István Geleji Katona responded to Tolnai's reforms in a letter to Rákóczi in October 1640, refuting Tolnai's right to bring about such changes to a school syllabus on his own authority. Geleji also defended Keckermann's *Logic* as a textbook unsurpassed by other available texts on logic, and indeed the previous year the Transylvanian synod under Geleji's leadership had recommended Keckermann's *Logic* for use in the principality's schools.[39] Geleji also wrote to the prince that his personal experience of studying at Heidelberg University suggested that Keckermann's works were fundamental to developing an understanding of theology and helped to structure polemic defences of orthodox religion. Geleji claimed support for his stance from Bisterfeld, who was reported as saying that he would rather 'his own logic book were burned, than see it replace Keckermann's work'.[40]

Whilst an inspection of Sárospatak College in 1641 proceeded relatively smoothly, by 1642 new assistant teachers had been appointed who were unsympathetic to Tolnai's reforms. During that year's visitation by the regional church authorities some students began to complain that logic, philosophy, metaphysics, and polemic theology had been thrown out of the curriculum, and that there had been no examination of grammar in four

---

[37] L. Makkai, 'Tolnai Dali János harca a haladó magyar kultúráért', *ITK* 57 (1953), 236–49; Zoványi, *Puritánus mozgalmak a magyar református egyházban*, 37–85.
[38] 'Acta Synodi Nationalis', ff. 50–2; J. Szombathi, *A sárospataki főiskola története*, ed. J. Gulyás and G. Szinyei (Sárospatak, 1919); L. Szimonidesz, 'A sárospataki ref. főiskolában és sárospatak környéke iskolaiban használt, ismert és ismeretlen tankönyvek', *Magyar Könyvszemle*, 58 (1942), 410–13.
[39] Szilágyi, 'Az erdélyi anyaszentegyház közzsinatainak végzései kivonatban', 1–9, 77–84, 473–9.
[40] MOL box 1907, Liber Reditum Ecclesiasticum Comitatus Zempleniensis 1623, 466–70; 'Geleji István levele', ed. J. Erdélyi, *Sárospataki Füzetek*, 1 (1857–8), 177–80.

years. The inspectors' report found that Tolnai's syllabus, 'of no use to the students', was solely based on the study of Ramus and Ames, and that Tolnai had only taught from the first twenty-six chapters of Ames' *Technometria* between 1640 and 1642. The church inspectors complained that Tolnai had 'exterminated peripatetic logic' at Sárospatak and had acted against school regulations. István Miskolczi Csulyak, the archdeacon in Zemplén, wrote to the prince in April and again in November 1642 with news of the perceived deterioration in standards at Sárospatak. According to Miskolczi, this had been caused by the removal of proper logic teaching and by the failure of Tolnai to heed the advice and warnings of the inspectors. By the end of 1642 Tolnai's position at Sárospatak became untenable, with opposition to his changes growing on all sides, threats from students to move to Jesuit schools, complaints from neighbouring schools, and most importantly the withdrawal of Rákóczi's support.[41]

Tolnai resigned, and was then brought before the Zemplén synod, accused of causing disruption at Sárospatak in both the college and the local church over a number of issues. His responsibility for causing these scandals was eventually investigated by a national synod of all the Reformed church provinces which met at Szatmár in 1646 under the presidency of the prince. The resolutions of this national synod included recommendations for future patterns of education in Reformed colleges and schools. The synod required that school directors recognize they could not introduce major changes to teaching without seeking the prior approval of school patrons and the proper church authorities. Teachers were ordered to offer instruction in true piety, fine Latin drawn from classical authors, 'pure' theology, and 'temperate' philosophy. In the wake of this Szatmár national synod, István Geleji Katona completed new canons for the Transylvanian church in 1649 which stipulated that 'school teachers should not teach any new opinions or ceremonies in schools, especially concerning religion'. The canons also warned that 'those who try to bring in new opinions are causing the ruination of youth, and if they do not stop after repeated warnings from their superiors, then their membership of the body of the church will end, and they will be thrown out of the church'.[42]

As outlined in the previous chapter, the Szatmár synod also agreed that all student ministers returning from western universities should be asked to subscribe to the Heidelberg Catechism and the Second Helvetic

---

[41] Tiszáainnen Church Province Library Manuscript Collection, vols. 16–18, also to be found in MOL boxes 1907–8, ZEP (1629–45), ff. 384–5, 398–9, 424–6; 'Miskolczi Csulyak jegyzőkőnyvei', ed. Zoványi, 389–96; 'Miskolczi István és Görgei János esperesek levelei I. Rákóczi Györgyhez', ed. S. Szilágyi, *EPK* (1875), 267–9.

[42] *Egyházi kánonok*, ed. Kiss, 1646 resolutions, nos. 26, 27.

Confession and to promise not to promote any innovations to traditional church practices. Whilst a strong commitment endured in the Hungarian church to send students to western Calvinist academies, the attempts by Tolnai and his supporters to reform the syllabus at Sárospatak were opposed, partly because they were associated with foreign radicals, particularly English puritans and those in Dutch universities, such as Ames, who tended to oppose hierarchical forms of church government. Tolnai was suspected of trying to challenge the established order of the Reformed church and was accused of introducing puritanism to Hungary, a charge which will be examined in greater depth in Chapter 6.

The Reformed church leadership gained the support of György I Rákóczi, and after 1648 of György II Rákóczi, for their efforts to impose controls on the content and direction of teaching at Hungarian colleges and schools. On the death of her husband in 1648, the dowager princess, Zsuzsanna Lórántffy, moved away from the Transylvanian court and took up residence with her younger son Zsigmond at Sárospatak. Lórántffy had retained faith in János Tolnai Dali and in 1649 asked him to return to lead Sárospatak College. Lórántffy's patronage of Tolnai ensured that the ability of the clergy hierarchy to control the direction of school reforms, or to obtain complete respect for the established pattern of church government from all ministers, remained incomplete. During the 1650s critical concerns continued to be voiced on the unsatisfactory pace and extent of educational reforms in Hungary and Transylvania, and on the impact that this supposed lack of progress was having upon the church and society.

Tolnai was still teaching at Sárospatak in 1650, when Comenius arrived to take over the leadership of the college. In a letter requesting that Comenius come to Hungary, Lórántffy stressed that, whilst Tolnai had been able to make some improvements to methods of teaching at Sárospatak, she hoped that Comenius would be able to push on even further with this work. Tolnai also wrote to Comenius, offering his assessment that progress could be made at Sárospatak towards realizing his goal of pansophic learning.[43] In the opening speech which Comenius gave to the assembled college at Sárospatak in November 1650, he outlined his plans for the renewal of society through a thoroughgoing reformation of schools and teaching methods. This speech, entitled 'On the Cultivation of the Intellect', enabled Comenius to explain his views on the moral potential of education to enable men correctly to perceive good and evil in the world. Comenius then turned his attention to the particular problems of Hungary. Comenius

---

43 G. Szinyei, 'A sárospataki főiskola Comenius előtt és Comenius idejében', *Sárospataki Lapok* (1898), 294–7, 325–7, 359–63, 385–8, 454–60.

argued that cultural stagnation in Hungary was not caused by any lack of schools, teachers, or willing pupils. Comenius instead suggested that Hungarian culture remained at an intermediate stage because of the poor quality of Latin teaching, and the lack of effective training in medicine, philosophy, law, and theology. Comenius continued:

If you, my Huns, will be able to make use of your spiritual possibilities, then you will not stand behind any people in Europe for culture.

. . . there is not only gold in your mines, but your souls are also deep in wisdom. If there remains any remnant of your Scythian past, then wipe it out completely, so that you may shine in your full splendour.44

Comenius' ideas met with an enthusiastic reception from his new patrons, Zsuzsanna Lórántffy and Zsigmond Rákóczi. Zsigmond wrote to his elder brother, György, of Comenius' impeccable behaviour at Sárospatak and forwarded to the prince the programme of reforms which Comenius had submitted. In early December 1650 Zsigmond also wrote to András Klobusiczky, who together with János Tolnai Dali and Ferenc Veréczi helped to implement Comenius' plans at Sárospatak, of his pleasure at Comenius' skill in leading his students. Particularly warm relations evidently developed between Comenius and Zsigmond. Comenius helped Zsigmond acquire a telescope from the Danzig astronomer, Johannes Hevelius, and Zsigmond asked Comenius to officiate at his 1651 wedding to Maria Henrietta, daughter of Frederick V of the Palatinate.45 Later in 1651 Comenius addressed Zsigmond in a 'Secret sermon of Nathan to David', which suggested that Zsigmond would lead Hungary out of the 'labyrinth of confusion' in politics, religion, and education, by supporting the systematic ordering of universal knowledge at Sárospatak College. Comenius then claimed that extravagant benefits would flow from these reforms, as Zsigmond would become the liberator of central Europe and Hungary act as a beacon of light to the rest of central Europe, saving the region from the twin Antichrists of Rome and Constantinople.46

44 Jan Amos Comenius, 'De cultura ingeniorum oratio', in *Primitiae laborum scholasticorum in illustri Patakino gymnasio* (Sárospatak, 1652); Tiszáninnen Reformed Church Province Archives (Sárospatak), A/II/105.1, Zsoldos Benő-féle időrendes sorozat; [Jan Amos Comenius], 'Comenius sárospataki beköszöntője', ed. L. Stromp, *Protestáns Szemle*, 12 (1900), 560–83.

45 [Rákóczi Zsigmond], 'Herczeg Rákóczy Zsigmond levelezése', ed. Szilágyi, 603–4, 612–13; L. Rácz, *Comenius Sárospatakon* (Budapest, 1931), 106–7.

46 'Sermo secretus Nathanis ad Davidem', in [Jan Amos Comenius], 'Comenius irata Rákóczi Zsigmondhoz', ed. J. V. Kvacsala, in *MPEA* 4 (1905), 128–43; J. Polišenský, 'Comenius, magyarország és az európai politika a xvii. században', *Magyar Pedagógia*, 72 (1972), 179–84.

Whether or not Zsigmond was convinced by Comenius' prophetic voice, Comenius was allowed to implement his ideas for a pansophic college at Sárospatak.[47] Comenius had provided an 'Outline of a Pansophic School', dedicated to Zsigmond, which developed his three major areas in need of reform: the structure of classes, the quality of textbooks, and teaching methods. Comenius set out a curriculum and timetable for seven classes in the school, progressing from the first three classes, devoted to learning Latin, to the four remaining classes dedicated to philosophy, logic, politics, and theology. In February 1651 the first ('vestibular') Latin class opened with over one hundred pupils, and Comenius delivered a 'Panegyric on True Methods' to celebrate the occasion. In March 1651 Tolnai sent his warm regards to Hartlib and Dury and was able to report on Comenius' success in developing 'pansophic studies' at Sárospatak. A second ('janual') Latin class indeed opened in March 1651, and the third ('atrial') class followed in January 1652.[48]

In November 1651 Comenius gave another speech on 'Books as the Chief Instruments of Culture', establishing his concern that appropriate textbooks be made available to his students. By 1652 the books which Comenius had devised for the first three Latin classes had already been published at Sárospatak.[49] Comenius also supervised the work of János Tolnai Dali, János Szőlősi, and István Szilágyi Benjamin as they began a vernacular class to prepare students to learn Latin in the 'vestibular' class.[50] This was part of Comenius' attempt to assist his students to express themselves naturally in Latin, not merely to learn abstract explanations of grammar. Comenius also enthusiastically supported the use of visual images and

---

[47] M. Blekastad, *Comenius. Versuch eines Umrisses von Leben, Werk, und Schicksal des Jan Amos Komensky* (Oslo, 1969), 467–525; E. Földes and I. Mészáros (eds.), *Comenius and Hungary* (Budapest, 1973); [Jan Amos Comenius], *Comenius Magyarországon. Comenius Sárospatakon írt műveiből* ed. E. Kovács (Budapest, 1970); C. Csorba, F. Földy, and J. Ködöböcz (eds.), *Comenius és Magyarország* (Sárospatak, 1990); Á. R. Várkonyi, 'Comenius éjszakái', *Liget* (1993), 46–57; I. Bán, 'Comenius és a magyar szellemi élet', *Pedagógiai Szemle*, 8 (1958), 928–36.

[48] Comenius, 'Scholae latinae delineatio ad Sigismund Rakoci', and 'Laborum scholasticorum in illustri Patakino gymnasio continuatio', in *Primitiae laborum scholasticorum*; Comenius, *Didactica Magna*, ed. Keatinge, 138–47; Hartl. 49/43, f. 1; 15/3, f. 5*a*: 'I read over with great delight mr Tolnay his letter, and am glad to understand that the learned Comenius hath resolved speedily to devote him self studijs Pansophicis.'

[49] Jan Amos Comenius, *Eruditionis scholasticae pars prima, Vestibulum; Pars secunda, Janua; Pars tertia, Atrium* (Sárospatak, 1652). There were also Hungarian versions of *Vestibulum* and *Janua* (Nagyvárad, 1634; Bártfa, 1643; Lőcse, 1649). Comenius, 'De primario ingenia colendi instrumento, solerter versando, libris', in *Primitiae laborum Scholasticorum*.

[50] I. Mészáros, 'Comenius és a sárospataki kollégium anyanyelvi osztálya', *Magyar Pedagógia*, 72 (1972), 185–97; J. Bakos, 'Comenius az anyanyelvről és az anyanyelvi oktatás jelentőségéről', *Pedagógiai Szemle*, 20 (1970), 998–1,007.

drama as aids to memory and learning. Comenius intended that the words and texts of his Latin school-books be accompanied by numbered pictures from an 'Encyclopaedia of the Senses', which he completed in 1653, but no engraver competent to produce the necessary illustrations could be found at Sárospatak. An illustrated version of Comenius' textbook for his second ('janual') Latin class was only eventually published at Nuremberg in 1658 as *Orbis Pictus*, or *The World in Pictures*. This acclaimed work became an extraordinary success in teaching children Latin and ran to countless editions across the Continent.[51] Comenius also oversaw the production of educational plays to accompany the 'janual' class at Sárospatak from his *Schola Ludus*, which he described as a 'living encyclopaedia'. If Comenius is to be believed, these plays using basic Latin vocabulary received an ecstatic reception at Sárospatak. Comenius claimed that his fellow teachers, otherwise somewhat suspicious of the changes which he had introduced at the college, after these plays joyously recognized the value of his textbooks and acknowledged the dramatic improvements in their pupils' knowledge of Latin.[52]

In 1652 Comenius outlined the major remaining obstacle which he perceived to be blocking the establishment of a new order at the Sárospatak College in the lack of permanent teachers dedicated to the profession and the continued use of older students as class teachers. Comenius complained that some of the teachers at Sárospatak were lazy, measured their authority in how little their pupils spoke, and were too critical of students when they failed in some exercises, preferring to be feared than loved. Comenius responded by publishing his version of an advice-book on how teachers, students, and those in charge of schools could best go about their work. Comenius indeed wrote that his experiences of seeing unskilful teaching at Sárospatak had helped him to understand what the true connection between a teacher and a student should be.[53]

Comenius also devoted himself to questions of student discipline at Sárospatak, stressing that students should aim to be honest, humble, and ready to take correction. Comenius recommended that students get up early in the morning, and then use their time wisely and avoid taking afternoon naps. Boys were encouraged to run and jump about during breaks from their classes in the playground to allow their minds to rest. Comenius

51 G. H. Turnbull, 'An Incomplete *Orbis Pictus* of Comenius Printed in 1653', *Acta Comeniana*, 16 (1957), 35–40.

52 Jan Amos Comenius, *Schola Ludus; seu, Encyclopaedia vive . . . janua linguarum praxis comica* (Sárospatak, 1656); I. Komor, 'Schola ludus', *Pedagógiai Szemle*, 8 (1958), 975–90.

53 Jan Amos Comenius, *Fortius Redivivus* (Sárospatak, 1652), from Joachimus Fortius Ringelbergius, *De ratione studii liber vere aureaus* (Sárospatak, 1652).

also outlined examples to be followed on appropriate dress, posture, speech, and manners for students both at school and in church. Comenius set out advice for students on correct behaviour in extraordinary detail, and his rules on manners whilst eating forbade students from leaning on the table, from taking food out of their mouths, gnawing on bones, handing half-eaten food to others, picking their teeth, or drinking when their mouths were full of food.[54]

Comenius was able to make very considerable progress towards testing the practicality of his ideas on pansophic learning during his years at Sárospatak College. Despite his undoubted achievements, Comenius became frustrated by ongoing problems at the college, with some local opposition to his plans, and he eventually departed for Poland in 1654. Indeed, only Comenius' belief in the accuracy of the prophecies of his countryman and childhood friend, Mikuláš Drabík, about the future role for Transylvania and the Rákóczi princes, had ensured that he remained in Sárospatak during 1653. In 1654 Comenius reported to Hartlib of his relief at being 'freed' from Hungary, mixed with disappointment at the Rákóczi family's stubborn failure to trust in Drabík's predictions.[55] Comenius later reflected on his disappointment at the lukewarm reception given in Hungary to Drabík's visions:

> To the Hungarians. To them too, it was necessary . . . that I went to them (in 1650) as Paul went to Rome, for the same goal, but although the devil had not prevented my coming, he prevented any success of it, . . . with you [Hungarians] God awakened the gift of prophecy (although not through one of yourselves, but one of those whom God deemed to be your guests), but nevertheless there was no success in it.[56]

In a speech entitled 'On the happiness of People', given on his departure from Sárospatak, Comenius had tried to rouse prince Rákóczi to act on the international stage as a political messiah, and the political response to

---

54 Jan Amos Comenius, *Praecepta Morum, in usum juventutis collecta* (Nagyvárad, 1658); I. Komor, 'Comenius a pataki ifjúság iskolánkivüli neveléséről', *Pedagógiai Szemle*, 10 (1960), 888–98. Cf. Márton Szepsi Csombor, *Udvari Schola, melyben . . . minden szép erkölcsökre . . . oktatja* (Bártfa, 1623).

55 Hartl. 7/72: 'verifaci in me, quod D. Bisterfeldius dicere solet: Eniditor, vel Artifices in Hungariam vocatos ad perpetuor vocari carceres.' [Comenius], *Korrespondence*, ed. Kvacsala, 187; J. V. Kvacsala, 'Comenius és a Rákóczyak', *Budapesti Szemle* (1889), 113–51; Drabík's prophecies were published in *Lux in Tenebris* (1657).

56 J. V. Polišenský, 'Comenius, Hungary, and European Politics in the Seventeenth Century', in E. Földes and I. Mészáros (eds.), *Comenius and Hungary* (Budapest, 1973), 19. See also J. V. Kvacsala, 'Egy álpróféta a xvii-ik században', *Századok* 23 (1889), 745–66; J. V. Kvacsala, 'A xvii. századbeli chiliasmus történetéhez', *Protestáns Szemle*, 2 (1890), 428–50; N. Mout, 'Chiliastic Prophecy and Revolt in the Habsburg Monarchy during the Seventeenth Century', in M. Wilks (ed.), *Prophecy and Eschatology*. (Studies in Church History. Subsidia. 10; Oxford, 1994), 93–109; K. Péter, 'Drabik Miklós, a lehoktai próféta', *Világosság*, 18 (1977), 36–41.

Comenius' support for Drabík's prophecies will be examined in more depth in Chapter 9. Comenius also used this occasion to repeat his demand that Rákóczi tackle the academic backwardness and moral weakness which he perceived in Hungary and Transylvania. Comenius identified ignorance as the main cause of Hungary's political, economic, and moral problems. He advised that greater attention should urgently be paid to the study of religion, to the establishment of more vernacular schools, and to the development of teaching in the liberal arts, philosophy, and medicine, if Hungary was to make progress.[57]

The clearest Hungarian response to Comenius' various proposals for reform came from János Apáczai Csere. Apáczai had studied at Dutch universities during the 1640s, at Utrecht from 1648 and then at Harderwijk where he was awarded a doctorate in 1651. In 1650 he published a *Shorter Catechism* at Amsterdam, based on the Heidelberg Catechism, and in the introduction attacked the lamentable ignorance of his nation. Apáczai linked this 'backwardness' to the condition of many ordinary people, arguing that 'if the body has no freedom, how can the spirit have freedom?'[58] Apáczai stated that he wanted to 'raise the flag of the freedom of truth' before his fellow countrymen, by devising an *Encyclopaedia* in the Hungarian language 'on the basis of famous authors, containing those things which are the most necessary and useful for a man to know . . . so that for students there will be at least one book in our mother tongue, from which they can unravel the threads of the fabric of all civilization'.[59] Apáczai's *Encyclopaedia* was published at Utrecht in 1653, dedicated amongst others to Bisterfeld. Apáczai compiled his *Encyclopaedia* by translating a range of works by Descartes, Ames, Ramus, Alsted, Henri Regius, and Johann Althusius on a diverse range of subjects including philosophy, logic, mathematics, astronomy, physics, music, medicine, history, ethics, politics, law, and theology. Apáczai had already copied out sections of Alsted's *Encyclopaedia* whilst a student at Gyulafehérvár and then, in the Dutch Republic, compiled further material which could provide a basis for widening the range of subjects

57 [Jan Amos Comenius], 'Comenius irata II. Rákóczi Györgyhöz', ed. J. V. Kvacsala, in *MPEA* 4 (1905), 144–68; L. Makkai, 'Gentis Felicitas', *Pedagógiai Szemle*, 8 (1958), 964–72; W. Rood, *Comenius and the Low Countries* (Prague, 1970); J. Herepei, 'Az öreg Comenius néhány magyar híve', in B. Keserű (ed.), *Adattár 3* (Szeged, 1971), 394–418.

58 János Apáczai Csere, *A keresztyéni vallasra rövid kérdésekben és feleletekben tanito Catechesis* (Amsterdam, 1650); I. Bán, *Apáczai Csere János* (Budapest, 1958); Cs. Fekete et al. (eds.), *Apáczai Csere János, 1625–1659* (Budapest, 1975); I. Komor, 'Comenius in Sárospatak; Apáczai in Gyulafehérvár', in *Acta Litteraria Academiae Scientiarum Hungaricae* (1960), 191–204; I. Schneller, 'Comenius és Apáczai', *Protestáns Szemle*, 30 (1918), 27–39.

59 János Apáczai Csere, *Magyar Encyclopaedia; az az, Minden igaz es hasznos böltségnek szep rendbe foglalása és magyar nyelven világra botsátása* (Utrecht, 1653), Introd.

studied in Transylvania's schools. The most original chapter of Apáczai's *Encyclopaedia* was his own summary of traditional Hungarian beliefs on health, medicine, and the weather.[60]

On Apáczai's return to Transylvania he consistently promoted ideas for school reform, most notably in a speech given when he was appointed to teach at Gyulafehérvár in November 1653. Apáczai argued that, despite the efforts of Alsted and Bisterfeld, poor teaching standards were still to blame for backwardness in Transylvanian society. Apáczai suggested that the Gyulafehérvár Academy should copy reform measures undertaken at Sárospatak College and at schools in Nagyvárad and Nagybánya. Apáczai professed himself shocked at the defective methods of learning still commonly used in Transylvanian schools and published a translation of a work on logic by Ramus in an attempt to remedy the situation. A growing attachment to Ramism in some Hungarian schools was indeed to prove enduring. It was sustained in part by György Martonfalvi's production of a version of Ramus' *Dialectics* in 1658, and a predilection for using Ramist styles of logic continued in Hungarian Protestant schools into the eighteenth century when it had long since died out in the west.[61] In his 1653 speech to the Gyulafehérvár Academy, Apáczai also proposed that reading and writing should be first taught in the vernacular. Although the use of Hungarian had increased in schools during the early seventeenth century, Latin remained the predominant language in higher levels of education. Apáczai suggested that only once students had learned Hungarian should they then be taught Latin, Greek, and Hebrew, to be followed by study of the wide range of subjects encompassed in his *Encyclopaedia*.[62]

Apáczai was unable to implement these proposals, as he was soon forced to leave the Gyulafehérvár Academy in disgrace. Apáczai's dismissal followed his participation in a controversial debate held before György II

---

[60] Apáczai Csere, *Magyar Encyclopaedia*; *Apáczai Csere János válogatott pedagógiai művei*, ed. L. Orosz (Budapest, 1956), 59–88; I. Bán, 'Apáczai Csere János magyar enciklopédiája', *Irodalomtörténet*, 35 (1953), 146–66; V. Laurentzy, 'Apáczai Csere János calendarium perpetuuma', *Debreceni Szemle*, 7 (1933), 257–66.

[61] Petrus Ramus, *Dialecticae libri duo* (Nagyvárad, 1653), includes William Ames's 'Technometria', 'Demonstratio Logicae Verae', 'Theses Logicae', 'Disputatio Theologica adversus metaphysicam', and 'Disputatio Theologica de perfectione S. S. Scripturae'. [Petrus Ramus], *Petri Rami dialecticae libri duo . . . ungarico idiomate resoluti et illustrati*, ed. György Martonfalvi (Utrecht, 1658); György Martonfalvi and György Komáromi Csipkes, *Ars concianandi Amesiana* (Debrecen, 1666); B. Tóth, 'Ramus hatása Debrecenben', *Könyv és Könyvtár*, 17 (1979), 85–107.

[62] 'Oratio de studio sapientiae', in *Apáczai Csere János*, ed. Orosz, 102–47; *Apáczai Csere János beszéde 'a bölcsesség tanulásáról'*, ed. I. Bán (Debrecen, 1955); János Apáczai Csere, *Magyar Logikácska* (Gyulafehérvár, 1654); János Apáczai Csere, *Tanács, mellyet Joachymus Fortius ad Apáczai János által egy tanulásba élesüggedt ifjúnak* (Gyulafehérvár, 1654).

Rákóczi at Marosvásárhely in September 1655. Apáczai argued in support of presbyterian church government against the recently arrived episcopalian Isaac Basire, who implied that dire political consequences would follow from any introduction of presbyteries in Transylvania. Rákóczi then blocked an attempt by Zsuzsanna Lórántffy to appoint Apáczai at Sárospatak, and he was only able to teach at the smaller school in Kolozsvár from 1656. Seemingly undeterred by this opposition, Apáczai returned to his themes of Hungarian backwardness and the need for improvements to standards of local education in his opening speech to the Kolozsvár school in November 1656. This speech drew on similar messages delivered by Comenius at Sárospatak, concentrating on the need for better teaching in vernacular village schools to allow more students to proceed on to study at larger Latin schools. Apáczai argued that schools were dominated by townsmen, to the exclusion of peasants and nobles, and that some students were in any case insufficiently committed to education, using it rather only to escape feudal service. Apáczai also complained about the lack of a centre in Transylvania capable of adequately completing a student's education, and that the established colleges taught only theology and Latin, not the natural sciences or mathematics, nor many of the other subjects which Apáczai had included in his *Encyclopaedia*. This meant that Hungarians had to revert to foreign universities and academies to study these subjects, and Apáczai's experiences in the west led him to think that Hungarians were treated as if they were ignorant when they went abroad.[63]

In Apáczai's eyes the lack of a true Transylvanian academy was also having disastrous consequences for the church and state, arguing that 'it is certainly not to be wondered at, that Hungary and Dacia are so full of the denial of God, injustice, intemperance, and inconstancy'. Apáczai compared the situation in Hungary with the Dutch Republic which, he claimed, had gained its political freedom and cultural strength by developing strong colleges and academies. Hungary and Transylvania, Apáczai argued, still had cruel lords, faithless servants, corrupt judges, unfair tax officers, and devastated farms, houses, and towns, all because there was nowhere properly to learn the sciences, philosophy, and morality. Patrons, teachers, and students needed to be roused to further efforts, since Apáczai believed that even the natives of the Dutch East Indies had already overtaken Hungary in their dispersal of barbarism: 'It is time then to awake, you sleepy, drunken, dim Hungarian people! Finally, finally, wake up from your dreams, awaken, and found village schools'.[64]

---

[63] 'De summa scholarum necessitate', in *Apáczai Csere János*, ed. Orosz, 167–91.
[64] Ibid. 167–91.

György II Rákóczi, having dismissed Apáczai from his academy, was hardly willing to permit this assessment of the progress of educational standards in Transylvania to go unanswered. New regulations for Transylvanian schools were published only three days after Apáczai's speech at Kolozsvár in November 1656. These regulations marked a determined effort by Rákóczi and the new director of the Gyulafehérvár Academy, Isaac Basire, to limit Apáczai's scope to change the syllabus at Kolozsvár. It seems clear that Rákóczi wanted to stifle any challenge to the dominance of the academy at Gyulafehérvár and to prevent an apparent drift of students away from Gyulafehérvár to follow Apáczai to Kolozsvár.[65] Despite these legal restrictions, Apáczai tried to expand on the basis of the previous efforts made by András Porcsalmi at the Kolozsvár school and restructured the school into six graded classes. Apáczai's efforts seem to have met with some success, and Miklós Bethlen recalled in his autobiography being taught by Apáczai at Kolozsvár from texts by Ames, Descartes, and Regius, and 'in privata' from Ramus.[66]

The 1656 Transylvanian school regulations marked the culmination of Basire's own proposals for school reform, referring to Gyulafehérvár as a school–university at a time when Apáczai denied there was even a decent college in Transylvania. Basire offered suggestions to put the buildings at Gyulafehérvár to better use, set tougher conditions for entry to the academy, and made efforts to find better-qualified teachers. Basire was also not immune from Apáczai's demands to widen the syllabus at Gyulafehérvár, and he suggested introducing a more open course for noble students.[67] In 1657 Basire formulated another reform plan based upon the regulations devised by Alsted, Bisterfeld, and Piscator in 1630. Basire set out a detailed description of the daily routine of classes and worship for students, with a revised timetable allowing only one subject to be studied each day so that it could be examined in sufficient depth.[68]

Following György II Rákóczi's disastrous invasion of Poland in the spring of 1657, in October 1658 the Transylvanian diet elected the former

[65] 'II. Rákóczi György ismeretlen iskolatörvénye', ed. Török, *Erdélyi Irodalmi Szemle*, 4 (1927), 118–24; L. Orosz, 'Apáczai kolozsvári helyezése és az 1656-i erdélyi iskolatörvény', *Pedagógiai Szemle*, 10 (1960), 162–9.

[66] *Bethlen Miklós önéletírása*, ed. Windisch 552; Török, *A kolozsvári ev. ref. collégium története*.

[67] A damaged copy of this proposal is in Durham Cathedral Library, MS Hunter 10/33. C. Brennen, 'The Life and Times of Isaac Basire', Ph.D thesis (Durham, 1987); L. Kropf, 'Basirius Izsák életrajzához', *TT* (1889), 491–502; D. N. Griffiths, 'Isaac Basire, 1607–1676', *Proceedings of the Huguenot Society*, 17 (1986), 303–16.

[68] Isaac Basire, *Schema primum generale sive forma studiorum Albensium* (Gyulafehérvár, 1657); I. Domján, 'A gyulafehérvári akadémia 1657 tanrendje', *Erdélyi Múzeum*, 13 (1896), 481–4; *A gyulafehérvári főiskola 1657-iki szabályzata*, ed. Vargha.

president of Rákóczi's council, Ákos Barcsai, to replace him as prince. Apáczai wasted no time in putting his proposals for the development of Transylvania's schools to the new prince. Apáczai wrote to Barcsai claiming that the restrictions imposed by the 1656 school regulations had rendered teaching at Kolozsvár inappropriate, ineffective, and a source of ridicule. Apáczai asked that more money be given to appoint better teachers, if only to prevent Reformed children moving to Catholic schools.[69] Apáczai wrote that previous mistakes made at the Gyulafehérvár Academy included the slavish overpaying of foreign teachers, money which Apáczai suggested would have been better distributed among local teachers. Apáczai thought 'that since two theology professors are needed, one should be Hungarian and the other Scot, or from some other nation that would come for little money[!]'. Apáczai recalled advice which Gisbert Voetius had offered him at Utrecht, that a foreigner should only work in Transylvania alongside a native, so that Hungarians might learn from this co-operation. Embittered by his treatment under Basire and sensitive to any perceived slight, Apáczai compared this approach to that of the Rákóczi regime, where only foreigners taught the higher sciences and Hungarians were left to teach only grammar, rhetoric, and poetry. Apáczai also presented formal plans to Barcsai for a new academic complex including a college, library, printing-press, and 'academic garden' containing rare plants for use in medicine, to provide a 'true crown' for Protestant education in Transylvania. However, Barcsai and his successors proved understandably more concerned to defend the weakened position of existing Reformed schools from further Ottoman attacks and Catholic persecution, rather than attempt to realize Apáczai's grandiose schemes.[70]

Any assessment of the progress of Reformed education in Hungary and Transylvania during the early seventeenth century must balance the criticisms made by Apáczai and others against their very high expectations of what could be achieved in local schools. The foundation and improvement of Reformed schools had increased access to basic education and enabled hundreds of student ministers to move on to study at western universities. Leading local colleges at Sárospatak and Gyulafehérvár were hardly backwaters using outdated teaching practices, as they had been directed by some of the leading educationalists of the period who tried to implement plans for encyclopaedic or pansophic learning. Transylvania's princes and

---

[69] [János Apáczai Csere], 'Apáczai Jánosnak egy eddig ismeretlen levele Barcsai Ákos fejedelemhez', ed. G. Herepei, *EPK* (1879), 492–3.

[70] 'A magyar nemzetben immár elvégtére egy academia felállításának módja és formája', in *Apáczai Csere János*, ed. Orosz, 198–211; Ö. Miklós, 'Apáczai Cseri János utrechtbe történt meghivásáról', *Dunántuli Protestáns Lap* (1917), 178–81, 186–9.

the church hierarchy proved to be much more comfortable with this agenda of further school reform when it was firmly located within support for the established church order, and when advanced by illustrious foreign intellectuals. This respect for the authority of foreign educators seems to have been a particular source of frustration for János Apáczai Csere, who expressed his resentment as defensive localism. Certainly, Apáczai and János Tolnai Dali received an altogether more nervous reception when they suggested changes to the pattern of teaching in local colleges, or stressed the importance of spreading vernacular learning throughout society. This hostility was also partly caused by the perception that Apáczai and Tolnai showed little or no respect for the authority of the clergy hierarchy. Despite such disquiet about the agenda of some reformers, enthusiasm was largely retained within the Hungarian church and at the Transylvanian court to improve standards of education, both as a crucial part of the whole project of religious reform and to strengthen the Reformed church against its confessional rivals.

4

Constitutional Toleration and
Confessional Rivalry

The impact of religious reform and the breakdown of confessional uniformity during the sixteenth century forced states across the Continent to choose between either attempting to reimpose the orthodoxy of a single church or accepting a variety of religions and negotiating some accommodation between them. The Transylvanian diet which met at Torda in June 1568 faced up to this problem and resolved to offer legal status to the Reformed, Lutheran, Catholic, and anti-Trinitarian churches. This settlement offered freedom of conscience and rights to public worship to supporters of all four religions. Transylvania's Romanians were not represented in the diet, but freedom to worship was also extended to their Orthodox church as a privilege granted by the prince. The Torda diet proclaimed that:

Ministers should everywhere preach and proclaim [the Gospel] according to their understanding of it, and if their community is willing to accept this, good; if not, however, no one should be compelled by force if their spirit is not at peace, but a minister retained whose teaching is pleasing to the community. Therefore, no one should harm any superintendent or minister, nor abuse anyone on account of their religion . . . and no one is permitted to threaten to imprison or banish anyone because of their teaching, because faith is a gift from God.[1]

The diet had already decreed in 1564 that church buildings should be occupied by whichever confession held majority support in the locality. The new occupants of the church were then supposed to provide an alternative place of worship for any displaced minority. Whilst local patterns of religious adherence continued to be dominated by the rights of patronage of the privileged élite, whether Hungarian nobles, Saxon burghers, or Szekler

---

[1] *Erdélyi Országgyűlési Emlékek*, ed. Szilágyi, ii, 374: 'minden helyökön az prédikátorok az evangéliumot prédikálják, hirdessék, kiki az ő értelme szerént, és az község ha venni akarja jó, ha nem penig senki kénszerítéssel ne kénszerítse az ű lelke azon meg nem nyugodván, de oly prédikátort tarthasson, az kinek tanítása ő nekic tetszik. Ezért penig senki az superintendensek közül, se egyebek az prédikátorokat meg ne bánthassa, ne szidalmaztassék senki az religióért senkitől . . . és nem engedtetik ez senkinek, hogy senkit fogsággal, avagy helyéről való priválással fenyögessön az tanításért, mert az hit Istennek ajándéka.'

lords, landowners were forbidden from introducing a priest of a religion different from that of the local community. A clear limit on the extent of this practical toleration of a multiplicity of confessions was established in 1572, when the diet placed a firm restriction on any doctrinal innovation among followers of the four 'received religions', stifling further threatened divisions amongst the established confessions.

Opinions among historians have differed as to whether this pattern of confessional relations in early modern Transylvania was shaped mostly by a native spirit of tolerance or rather by the political weakness of the principality's central administration. Whilst many Transylvanians exhibited fierce loyalty to their own churches, confessional disputes were very mild by contemporary standards and only rarely characterized by violence. Transylvanians had been accustomed to some accommodation between the pre-reformation Catholic and Orthodox communities, and this may have offered precedents for the local arrangements which needed to be made after 1568. The existence of a range of legal churches within Transylvanian society by the late sixteenth century also saw acceptance of mixed marriages, where sons usually followed the religion of their father and daughters attended the church of their mother. In some families things proved more complicated still, such as the family of Kozma Petrityvity, an early seventeenth-century chronicler. Petrityvity's grandfather converted from Unitarianism to his wife's Catholic religion, and Petrityvity's mother was raised in this Catholic family, although one brother later converted to Calvinism. Petrityvity's mother then married a Unitarian, who raised the chronicler and his brothers as Unitarians whilst his sisters went to the Catholic church with their mother.[2]

Inter-confessional arrangements in early modern Europe were only partly the result of convictions about the nature of religious faith, or of the ability of any society to cope with a range of legal churches, but were also determined by domestic political imperatives and by diplomatic considerations. During the 1560s the Transylvanian prince and diet had been forced to balance the disruptive consequences of denying Protestant churches constitutional status against the potential for instability caused by legalizing four churches. It was hoped that giving four churches constitutional status would hold together the three nations represented at the diet and prevent the fledgling principality from falling apart. Whilst the Transylvanian diet's apparent expression of support for the toleration of a variety of churches was largely the product of this political necessity, the

---

[2] Kozma Petrityvity-Horváth, 'Önéletirása, 1634–1660', in G. Daniel, *Történelmi kalászok, 1603–1711* (Pest, 1862), 5.

effect of Transylvania's constitution over time was to foster traditions of accommodating religious differences within regional communities, towns, neighbourhoods, and even families.3

In Royal Hungary the social reality of religious division was not recognized by the state until the Vienna peace of 1606 between István Bocskai and Rudolf II. When this treaty was ratified by the diet in 1608, the Lutheran and Reformed churches across Hungary were finally conceded legal equality with the Catholic church. The Vienna peace extended the free exercise of religion to the noble orders, royal towns, and military garrisons. At the diet there was some suggestion that peasants across Hungary would also gain religious liberties, but in practice powers of noble patronage over local churches prevailed. As the numbers of Protestant magnates in the Upper House of the diet dwindled to only a handful by the 1640s, Protestants were often denied access to places of worship. Remaining Protestant gentry were only able to gain some redress for their mounting grievances thanks to the intervention of György I Rákóczi. After the 1645 Linz peace treaty between Rákóczi and Ferdinand III, the 1647 diet agreed that ninety churches should be returned to Protestants out of around three hundred claimed to have been seized illegally by Catholics. After 1648 the pleas of Protestants in Royal Hungary against the forcible expulsion of their ministers and outright destruction of their churches and schools were rejected by the diet, rendering the terms of the Vienna peace almost meaningless.4

In Transylvania the 1568 constitutional settlement remained intact, and in 1653 state laws confirmed again the position of all four received religions within the principality and renewed the prohibition on imposing religion by force. During the 1620s Gábor Bethlen had in fact extended the range of religious communities in Transylvania still further, introducing a

---

3 O. P. Grell and R. Scribner (eds.), *Tolerance and Intolerance in the European Reformation* (Cambridge, 1996), 32–47, 182–98; Rácz, 'Vallási türelem erdély- és magyarországon', 198–204; Várkonyi, 'Pro quite regni; az ország nyugalmáért', 260–77; G. Barta, 'A tolerancia társadalmi gyökerei; erdély a 16. században', in A. Miskolczy (ed.), *Europa. Balcanica-Danubiana-Carpathica*. (Annales, 2A; Budapest, 1995), 102–11.

4 Zsilinszky, *A magyar országgyűlések vallásügyi tárgyalásai a reformátiotól kezdve*, 358–9; Péter, 'Tolerance and Intolerance in Sixteenth-Century Hungary', 249–61; Péter, 'Az 1608 évi vallásügyi törvény és a jobbágyok vallásszabadsága', 93–113; Szabó, *Tanulmányok a magyar parasztság történetéből*, 203–63; Zsilinszky, *A linczi békekötés és az 1647–ki vallásügyi törvényczikkek története*. Cf. M. G. Müller, 'Protestant Confessionalisation in the Towns of Royal Prussia and the Practice of Religious Toleration in Poland–Lithuania', and J. Pánek, 'The Question of Toleration in Bohemia and Moravia in the Age of the Reformation', both in O. P. Grell and R. Scribner (eds.), *Tolerance and Intolerance in the European Reformation* (Cambridge, 1996), 231–49, 262–81; E. Opalinski, 'The Local Diets and Religious Tolerance in the Polish Commonwealth (1587–1648)', *Acta Poloniae Historica*, 68 (1993), 43–57.

settlement of Anabaptists in 1621 which later expanded under György I Rákóczi. Bethlen also permitted a colony of Jews to move from Ottoman territory to Transylvania in 1623, even allowing the settlers to wear Christian clothes to prevent them being marked out and insulted. However, patterns of toleration in Transylvania were strained during the early seventeenth century, not so much by popular animosity towards the provisions of the Torda settlement, but rather by the determination of the Reformed ecclesiastical and secular élite to exploit their commanding position, just as Catholic élites were doing elsewhere in central Europe. The resolve of Hungarian Reformed clergy to combat their confessional opponents with increasing vigour and determination strengthened as student ministers returned from western universities having gained a thorough grounding in Calvinist dogmatics and polemic theology. Transylvania's princes remained aware of the importance of stable relations between the various confessional communities, and Gábor Bethlen's will contained a pious plea for the churches not to argue with each other nor attempt to persecute one another. However, by consistently promoting the interests of their Reformed co-religionists, princes and nobles placed increasing pressure upon local patterns of co-existence across the principality.[5]

This chapter will examine relations between the Reformed church and its rivals within this context of Calvinist dominance of Transylvania and growing Catholic power in Royal Hungary. Reformed relations with the other churches will be examined in turn, first with the Catholic church, which was perceived not only as a domestic opponent but also as a demonic international enemy. Closer connections with western Protestants brought a noticeable hardening of Reformed attitudes towards the Unitarian church, increasingly seen by Hungarian Calvinists as something of an international embarrassment. Meanwhile, a more complicated relationship developed with local Lutherans, with some irenic appeals made to Lutherans for Protestant unity alongside continuing inter-confessional rivalry and doctrinal disputes. While contact with foreign Calvinists mostly contributed to the hardening of confessional boundaries in Hungary and Transylvania, it also encouraged some Reformed ministers to consider the

---

5 E. Jakab, 'Erdély és az anabaptisták a xvii.-xviii. században', *Keresztény Magvető*, 11 (1876), 1–14; *Erdélyi Országgyűlési Emlékek*, ed. Szilágyi, viii, 143–5: 'Engedtessék meg nekik, hogy a keresztyének ruházatával éljenek . . . nehogy sérelmekkel illettessenek, vagy bármiféle illetlen megjelöléssel.'; 'Approbatae Constitutiones (Pars 1/1/8)', *Magyar törvénytár. 1540–1848 évi erdélyi törvények*, ed. D. Márkus (Budapest, 1900); J. Barcza, 'A vallási türelem elvi alapjai a xvii. század magyar protestáns teológiájában', *Theológiai Szemle*, 21 (1978), 282–91; Pokoly, 'Az erdélyi fejedelmek viszonya a protestáns egyházakhoz', 546–61, 608–24.

possibility of a pan-Protestant, anti-papal front. The Reformed church's missionary efforts to Orthodox and Muslim communities will also be considered, particularly highlighting attempts to sponsor reform among Orthodox priests.

(I) INTERNATIONAL OPPONENTS: CATHOLICS

During the early seventeenth century the Catholic church in Hungary was able to recover support among the nobility, but this revival in the church's fortunes began from a very low starting-point. In 1644 Ferdinand III received a report from György Lippai, archbishop of Esztergom, on the number of churches held by Catholics and Protestants across Hungary. Whilst this report deliberately underestimated Catholic strength, it suggested that Catholics held a majority of churches in only one Hungarian county, and in over thirty Hungarian counties Lippai listed a total of 743 Catholic churches, against 4,402 Lutheran and Calvinist churches. Lippai claimed that Catholics did not have a significant presence in most Hungarian towns and that, whilst in the west there was some balance between the confessions, in the counties of eastern Hungary the Catholic church was still practically non-existent.[6]

In Transylvania, Catholic support was strongest in the eastern Szekler region, and public worship continued elsewhere only on the lands of sympathetic nobles. Despite the constitutional status of the Catholic church, only a handful of Jesuits were allowed residence in the principality. The Catholic church was also the only religion in Transylvania without a bishop, because the Papacy and Habsburgs failed to resolve differences on how to appoint candidates and because disputes remained unresolved over episcopal lands which had been appropriated by the prince and many nobles.[7] In 1640 Transylvania's Catholics made a formal appeal to the prince for redress of their many grievances, asking for restrictions on rights of church visitation to be removed and for guarantees to worship freely in those areas where Catholics were in a minority. The appeal argued that whilst 'the Catholic church, as a received religion, has no bishop, nor any leader with full authority to inspect the church, even the Romanians have a bishop, who is able to visit and correct the churches under his control'.[8]

The attitudes of Hungarian Reformed clergy towards the Catholic church were largely strident and confrontational. From the 1560s the Pope

---

[6] K. Révész, 'Egy érdekes okmány a xvii. század középéről', *PEIL* 39 (1896).

[7] Biró, *Bethlen Gábor és az erdélyi katholicizmus*; Jakab, 'Az erdélyi római katolikus püspöki szék betöltésének vitája a xvii. században', 5–20.

[8] Romanian National Archives (Cluj), Collectia Mike Sándor, no. 762, May 1640.

had been consistently represented in Reformed canons as the Antichrist. Periods of study at Calvinist academies and universities in Germany and the Dutch Republic reinforced such opinions about the Roman hierarchy and offered many student ministers the opportunity to study anti-Catholic polemic theology. As we have seen, many of the public disputations given by Hungarian students defended Reformed theological positions or attacked the doctrine of other confessions. Students abroad also frequently translated catechisms and works of Calvinist dogma, and the increased availability of such works in Hungary and Transylvania extended the reception of standard Calvinist teaching on the Catholic church.[9] In 1629 the eastern Tisza synod at Nagyvárad again rehearsed arguments for a papal Antichrist, discussing the apocalyptic meaning of the seven hills of Rome, papal abuses of ceremony and doctrine, and Catholic opposition to the revelation of the true church during the reformation.[10]

Such antipathy towards Catholic institutions and customs was not confined to Calvinist clergy, and many Reformed communities in Royal Hungary refused to adopt the Gregorian calendar because it was seen as the Pope's idea of time. Rudolf II had accepted the papal bull promulgating reform of the calendar in 1584, but many recalcitrant Calvinist congregations had to be compelled to receive ministers from parishes where the new calendar had reluctantly been accepted. Some sort of uniformity was only finally established when the Hungarian diet intervened in 1599, demanding that the old calendar be abandoned. In January 1600 a northern Tisza synod at Tállya eventually accepted the new calendar, but made it clear that they were acting on the expressed wishes of their temporal lords and in no way thereby accepted any papal claims of authority over them.[11]

From the beginning of the seventeenth century confessional and doctrinal confrontations between the Catholic and Reformed churches in Hungary and Transylvania became inextricably bound up with political and military struggles between the Habsburgs and Transylvania's princes. An

---

9 Szenczi Molnár, *A keresztyéni religióra és igaz hitre való tanitás*; Pál Medgyesi (tr.), *Szent Agoston vallasa* (Debrecen, 1632); Benedek Nagyari (tr.), *Orthodoxus Christianus; azaz, Igaz vallásu keresztyén* (Nagyvárad, 1651); Gyöngyösi (tr.), *A keresztény vallásnak fundamentomi*; Heinrich Diest, *Praxeos sacrae specimen, quo continentur selecta aliquot conciones* ... (Nagyvárad, 1653); Péter Szenczi Csene, *Confessio Helvetica; az az, Az keresztyeni igaz hitröl valo vallás-tétel* (Oppenheim, 1616), repr. as *Confessio et Expositio Fidei Christianae* (Sárospatak, 1654); István Ötvös Szathmári (tr.), *A keresztyén . . . belgiomi ecclésiáknak hitekröl való vallástétele* (Amsterdam, 1650).

10 MOL box 1883, Tiszántúl püspöki jegyzőkönyvek (1629–), ff. 9–42.

11 Pápai Páriz, 'Romlott fal felépítése', 163–4; G. V. Coyne, M. A. Hoskin, and O. Pedersen (eds.), *Gregorian Reform of the Calendar* (Vatican City, 1983), 255–80. Most Protestant states maintained the old calendar until the 18th cent.

Apology for István Bocskai's revolt against the Habsburgs combined political and religious causes, with Bocskai portrayed as both defending Hungary's constitution and protecting Protestant liberties. This *Apology* refuted Catholic propaganda, which claimed that Bocskai was an Arian, and called on all other 'true followers of Christ' in Europe to recognize 'that we, although indeed bodily distant from one another, are one together in Christ'.[12] From Gábor Bethlen's first foray into the Thirty Years War in 1619, political divisions between the two competing Hungarian states were linked with the battles between their supporting confessions. Bethlen's close adviser, Péter Alvinczi, placed the insidious influence of Catholic clergy at the root of all Hungary's problems and as a major cause of the outbreak of war. Péter Pázmány, from 1616 archbishop of Esztergom, responded in kind by asserting that what Protestants in Transylvania apparently meant by Christian freedom was the expulsion of Jesuits from the principality and the denial of places for Catholics to worship.[13]

Clashes between Alvinczi and Pázmány, the two titans of early seventeenth-century Hungarian polemic theology, went to the heart of the conflict between their religious traditions. In 1613 Pázmány, a child convert to Catholicism, had published a work of Catholic dogmatics as *A Guide Leading to the Truth of God* attacking the 'new faiths' as devilish heresies, and claiming that Calvin had made God the author of sin.[14] Alvinczi responded to Pázmány's charge of Calvinist novelty in his 1616 *Guide to Catholic Religion*, aiming to prove the continuous existence throughout history of an unseen church of those holding similar opinions to Luther and Calvin. According to Alvinczi, this included Alfred the Great and a series of medieval Oxford academics. Alvinczi also asserted that the Pope was an irredeemable enemy of Christ, and presented the Protestant churches as

---

[12] Révész, 'Bocskay István apologiája', 304–12.

[13] Péter Alvinczi, *Querela Hungariae. Magyarorszag panasza* (Kassa, 1619); Péter Alvinczi, *Machiavellizatio* (Kassa, 1621); Péter Pázmány, *Falsae originis motuum Hungaricorum succincta refutatio. Az magyarországi támadásoknak hamisan költött eredetének hamisitása* (Vienna, 1620); Thomas Balásfi, *Castigatio libelli Calvinistici, cui titulus est: Machiavellizatio* (Vienna, 1620); E. Zsilinszky, *Polemikus irodalmunk a xvi. és xvii.-ik században* (Budapest, 1891).

[14] Péter Pázmány, *Isteni igazságra vezérlő kalaúz* (Pozsony, 1613); and his *Az mostani támadt új tudományok hamisságának tíz nyilvánvaló bizonysága és rövid intés a török birodalomról és vallásról* (Graz, 1605), 29–63; *Az nagy Calvinus Jánosnak hiszek-egy-istene* (Nagyszombat, 1609); *Alvinczi Péternek sok tétovázó kerengésekkel és cégeres gyalázatokkal felhalmozott feleletinek rövid és keresztyéni szelídséggel való megrostálása* (Pozsony, 1609); *Az kálvinista prédikátorok igyenes erkölcsű tekéletességének tüköre* (Vienna, 1614): all pub. in *Pázmány Péter művei*, ed. Tarnoc; S. Sik, *Pázmány, az ember és az író* (Budapest, 1939); Bitskey, *Pázmány Péter*.

united against Rome.[15] In 1620 Pázmány responded scornfully to Alvinczi's claimed Protestant antecedents and ridiculed the notion of a joint Protestant heritage. Pázmány argued that Lutherans and Calvinists could not agree among themselves and that 'preachers, who row in Calvin's boat, often lie about what they believe, for friendship's sake'.[16] István Melotai Nyilas, the eastern Tisza Reformed superintendent, entered the polemic battle in 1617 with his lengthy examination of Catholic 'errors' of doctrine and ceremony. Meanwhile, János Kecskeméti, Reformed minister at Ungvár, attempted to refute Pázmány's work of guidance on Catholic dogma, by concentrating on perceived Catholic abuses such as the worship of Mary and the saints. Kecskeméti also published a translation of William Perkins's work *Catholicus Reformatus*, which identified Rome as Babylon and challenged certain aspects of Catholic doctrine, particularly purgatory and transubstantiation.[17]

In the early 1620s Gábor Bethlen gave financial support to a Jesuit priest, György Káldi, to publish a translation of the Bible as a reward for his services as an envoy to the Habsburg court. However, even this gesture did not suspend hostilities between the two confessions. In his introduction Káldi warned his readers of the errors and dangers of the 1590 Bible translation by Gáspár Károlyi, which he dubbed a 'Calvinist Bible'. This charge prompted an immediate defence of Károlyi's translation by a Calvinist minister, Péter Dengelegi.[18] In this charged atmosphere the conversion to Catholicism of a Reformed minister, Mihály Veresmárti, caused a predictable storm of controversy. Veresmárti's colleagues at Komját had first tried to combat his doubts about the Reformed church, and in 1609 Veresmárti's objections were sent to Heidelberg University for answers. Veresmárti remained unconvinced by the responses he received and converted to Catholicism in 1611. He stressed that his decision to convert was prompted

---

[15] Péter Alvinczi, *Itinerarium Catholicum; azaz, Nevezetes vetélkedés az felöl: ha az evangelicusok tudományajé uy, vagy az mostani romai valláson valo papistaké?* (Debrecen, 1616), 91–122.

[16] Péter Pázmány, *Rövid felelet két kálvinista könyvecskére* (Pozsony, 1620), 436, 451; Péter Pázmány, *Egy keresztien predikatortul . . . Alvinczi Peter uramhoz iratot eot szep level* (Pozsony, 1609): there are no surviving copies of a published answer to Pázmány by Alvinczi, *Öt levelekre rend szerint való feleleti* (Debrecen, 1609).

[17] István Melotai Nyilas, *A mennyei tudomány szerint való irtovány, melyből az veszedelmes tevelygeseknek, es hamis velekedeseknek kárhozatos, tövisses bokrai* (Debrecen, 1617); János Kecskeméti, *Pázmány Peter kalauzzának, tizenharmadik könyvére való felelet* (Bártfa, 1622); and his (tr.), *Catholicus Reformatus* (Debrecen, 1620); *Fides Jesu et Jesuitarum* (Bártfa, 1619); *Az papistak között es mi közöttünk, vetelkedesre vettetet, harom fő articulusokról* (Bártfa, 1622).

[18] György Káldi, *Szent Biblia* (Vienna, 1626); Péter Dengelegi Biró, *Rövid Anatómia* (Gyulafehérvár, 1630), 231; I. Bitskey, 'Bethlen, Pázmány és a Káldi-Biblia', *Századok*, 115 (1981), 737–43.

by the attractions of the history and universality of the Catholic church, against the views of 'schismatics' and followers of 'new religions'. One Reformed writer still took issue with Veresmárti during the 1640s, arguing that if Catholic arguments were so compelling then why was the violent weight of civil authority needed to make forced conversions in Royal Hungary.[19]

Reformed attacks on Catholic beliefs and institutions continued throughout the early seventeenth century. In 1645 István Geleji Katona wrote of the 'orthodox faith' of the Reformed church as situated squarely 'between the poles of Anabaptism and Catholicism'. Geleji claimed that the Reformed church practised its ceremonies with 'Christian freedom' and without superstition, whilst Catholics remained idolatrous. Pál Medgyesi also published an anti-Catholic tract examining the role of the Pope, the saints, and images in Catholic doctrine and worship, whilst another Calvinist writer enjoined his readers to remain constant in their Reformed faith and not to follow 'the lies of the world' propagated by Catholics.[20] The religious and political battle-lines became ever more firmly drawn between the Reformed church, with its leading role within Transylvanian society, and the Catholic church, whose influence in Royal Hungary was rising with the tide of noble conversions. These divisions were typified by exchanges between the two sides over the education and religion of the Rákóczi family. In 1640 Mátyás Hajnal, Catholic chaplain to Miklós Eszterházy, published a critique of the religious education given to the Rákóczi princes by Pál Keresztúri. Keresztúri had published an examination of the princes' knowledge of the Heidelberg Catechism, but Hajnal asserted that such teaching prepared the princes not for salvation, but for damnation. Keresztúri responded immediately by attacking Hajnal's 'devilish medicine' and restated Reformed teaching on communion and arguments against transubstantiation.[21]

---

[19] Mihály Veresmárti, *Intő s tanító levél* (Pozsony, 1639); and his 'Megtérése históriája', printed in *Magyar Emlékírók 16. -18. század* (Budapest, 1982), 123–84; (tr.), *Tanácskozás, melyiket kelljen az különböző vallások közül választani* (Pozsony, 1611); *Az eretnekeknek adott hitnek megtartásáról* (Pozsony, 1641); A. Ipolyi, *Veresmárti Mihály* (Budapest, 1875); [Anon.], *Pápisták méltatlan üldözése a vallásért* ([n.pl.], 1643).

[20] János Laskai (tr.), *Hittül-szakadasnak tellyes meg orvoslasa, mellyet az' elhatatosoknak és el-eseteknek javokra, három könyvekben leirt* (Nagyvárad, 1644); István Geleji Katona, *Praeconium Evangelicum* (2 vols.; Gyulafehérvár, 1638–40). István Geleji Katona, *Váltság-Titka ... és a' tévelygőnek, ugy mint Sidoknak, Socinianusoknak, Blandristáknak, Pápistáknak, Lutheranus atyafiaknak, és egyebeknek ellenkező vélekedésik meg-czáfoltatnak* (3 vols.; Nagyvárad, 1645–9). For differences over communion, see iii, 825–1,586; Pál Medgyesi, *Egő szövétnek* (Gyulafehérvár, 1645); Anon., *Mennyország kinyittatott egyetlenegy szoros kapuja* (Nagyvárad, 1656).

[21] Keresztúri, *Csecsemő keresztyén; az probában bizonságot tennének*; Mátyás Hajnal, *Kitett cégér* (Pozsony, 1640); Pál Keresztúri, *Felserdült keresztyén* (Nagyvárad, 1641).

This was not the only incident between the two confessions which directly involved members of the Rákóczi family. In December 1638 Zsuzsanna Lórántffy arranged a dinner at Kolozsmonostor and invited both Pál Medgyesi and Dániel Vásárhelyi, a Jesuit priest and former professor at Vienna University. A debate ensued at the dinner over differing interpretations of the Book of Genesis, and whether Jacob had fought with an angel or with Christ. Vásárhelyi argued for an angel, which led Medgyesi to accuse him of Samosatenianism, claiming he had implied that Christ was not eternal and divine. Medgyesi reported that a Catholic noble who sat near Vásárhelyi promised to convert to the Reformed church by Christmas if Vásárhelyi did not improve his arguments. Following this debate a tract was published detailing Vásárhelyi's arguments on the nature of Christ, together with a response from Medgyesi. This episode also provided Zsuzsanna Lórántffy with the impulse to publish a series of connected Bible quotations with assistance from Medgyesi. Lórántffy's work drew sarcastic criticism from an anonymous Catholic author at Pozsony, possibly György Széchényi who later became archbishop of Esztergom. Pál Keresztúri responded to this attack on Lórántffy, and György I Rákóczi too stirred to defend his wife. Rákóczi demanded that the Catholic author be punished by Ferdinand III, but Ferdinand responded that Keresztúri ought to be punished. Neither party offered any satisfactory response, and Rákóczi mentioned this grievance among his reasons for attacking Royal Hungary in his military campaign of 1644.[22]

The relationship between the Reformed and Catholic churches in Hungary and Transylvania in the early seventeenth century was shaped by fierce rivalry between competing clergy hierarchies, ruling dynasties, and nobles, with both sides drawing support from foreign co-religionists. The Reformed church faced persecution from the Catholic establishment and nobility of Royal Hungary, and in Transylvania the Catholic church faced restrictions and disruption from the Reformed establishment. Calvinists in Transylvania were able to take advantage of princely and noble backing in disputes with Catholics over the control of church property. For example, the population of the market town of Székelyudvarhely in eastern Transylvania was evenly divided between Calvinists and Catholics. The town's church had been shared by both communities until 1612, when the

---

[22] Pál Medgyesi, *Szent Atyák Öröme; az az, Daniel Vasarhellyi Jesuita Professorus Paternek tzikkelyinek meg tzikkelyezesére* (Gyulafehérvár, 1640) 11–2, 28–47; Zsuzsanna Lórántffy, *Moses és a prophéták* (Gyulafehérvár, 1641); Anon., *Jesuita páterek titkai, a magok irásiból kiszedegettettek* (Nagyvárad, 1657), 7; J. Heltai, '"Szent Atyák Öröme": Medgyesi Pál és Vásárhelyi Dániel hitvitája', in A. Miskolczy (ed.), *Europa. Balcanica-Danubiana-Carpathica* (Annales, 2A; Budapest, 1995), 224–35.

Reformed church took sole possession of it. From 1614 neither priests nor monks were allowed in the town, and Catholics had to travel to a neighbouring village to worship until 1630, when permission was finally given to build a new Catholic church. However, by an agreement of 1633, once the new church in Székelyudvarhely had been built by local Catholics it had to be handed over to the Reformed congregation, and Catholics were forced to move into the smaller old church. The resolution of the 1568 Torda diet continued to offer all four constitutional churches equal legal freedoms in Transylvania, but by the mid-seventeenth century one church was proving to be more equal than the others.[23]

(II) BEYOND THE PALE: UNITARIANS

Anti-Trinitarianism in Transylvania and in some parts of Hungary reached its greatest extent of support during the years following the Torda settlement, with anti-Trinitarians thickest on the ground in south-eastern Transylvania and in the towns of Kolozsvár and Torda. Support for anti-Trinitarianism declined under the Báthori princes, but the election of Mózes Székely as prince in May 1603 demonstrated that the anti-Trinitarian church remained strong among the Hungarian nobility of the principality. However, Székely's hold on power was short lived, and his defeat in the summer of 1603 at the hands of the Habsburg general, Giorgio Basta, also decimated the ranks of anti-Trinitarian nobles. This traumatic defeat was quickly followed by Bocskai's successful Reformed challenge to Habsburg power and left the anti-Trinitarian community vulnerable to the newly empowered Reformed interest.[24]

During the early seventeenth century Reformed attitudes hardened against anti-Trinitarians, and doubts were raised as to whether their church should be tolerated within a Christian society. Contact between Hungarian Reformed ministers and foreign Calvinists had a major impact upon the position of all the three other constitutional churches but fostered animosity in particular against the Unitarian church, as it was normally called from the 1630s. Hungarian Reformed religion was viewed as distinctive in the rest of Calvinist Europe partly in being strategically positioned between the Habsburgs and Turks, but partly also through its proximity to anti-Trinitarians. That Transylvania's constitution protected a Unitarian

---

[23] F. Zayzon, *A székelyudvarhelyi ev. ref. egyházközség története* (Székelyudvarhely, 1893), 15.

[24] Wilbur, *A History of Unitarianism. Socinianism and Its Antecedents*; Wilbur, *A History of Unitarianism*, 99–126.

church was, however, hardly a matter of pride for Hungarian Calvinists. Exchanges between Transylvanian Reformed clergy and international Calvinism's intellectual élite, both at foreign universities and through domestic academies, engendered an atmosphere in which venomous assaults were directed against Unitarians. Many Reformed student ministers' disputations at Dutch universities detailed arguments against anti-Trinitarian and Socinian theological ideas, as was noted in Chapter 2. Reformed ministers who had studied at western universities later showed little or no respect for the protected legal position of the Unitarian church. This was especially dangerous for the Unitarian community, since the Reformed church could give practical effect to such hostility through collaboration with the princes and Transylvanian state.

The first major salvo in this Reformed campaign against Unitarian beliefs was delivered by István Melotai Nyilas. In 1622 Melotai published *The Image of the Trinity* attacking the ideas of György Enyedi, a late sixteenth-century anti-Trinitarian theologian whose reputation had spread abroad. This book was dedicated to Gábor Bethlen, whom Melotai praised as a destroyer of idolatry. Melotai called upon Bethlen to act against Sabbatarianism, a radical judaizing version of anti-Trinitarianism which had emerged during the latter decades of the sixteenth century. Sabbatarians denied that the New Testament had any divine inspiration and lived by Mosaic law, awaiting the arrival of the Messiah. Sabbatarians never received any formal legal recognition, and the 1610 diet demanded that Sabbatarian ministers be imprisoned. In 1618 the diet again passed a law calling for a search for any remaining Sabbatarians, made difficult because they outwardly conformed to Unitarian churches, or in some localities even to Reformed churches. In the dedication to his book Melotai also reminded Bethlen of a theological colloquium held at the Transylvanian court in 1618. During a discussion on the role of Christ in salvation, Melotai recorded that the prince had been outraged by anti-Trinitarian opinions, but was unable to give such statements their 'true reward'. Melotai, pointedly referring to Unitarians as Arian and Samosatenian heretics, claimed that only political weakness had allowed anti-Trinitarianism to slip into a recognized constitutional position in Transylvania, whilst the rest of the Christian world condemned Unitarians as atheists.[25]

The Unitarian church soon began to feel the impact of Reformed pressure in various regions across the principality. János Keserüi Dajka took

[25] István Melotai Nyilas, *Speculum Trinitatis* (Debrecen, 1622); R. Dán, 'Simon Péchi and Sabbatarianism', in L. Szczucki (ed.), *Socinianism and Its Role in the Culture of the xvi-th to xviii-th Centuries* (Warsaw, 1983), 53–7; J. Káldos, *Ungarländische Antitrinitarier II. György Enyedi* (Bibliotheca Dissidentium, 15; Baden-Baden, 1993), 41–5.

strong action as Reformed superintendent against Unitarian churches in the isolated and mountainous Háromszék region of south-eastern Transylvania. The Unitarian and Reformed churches in the Háromszék counties were joined in a remarkable administrative union, with many Unitarian ministers serving mixed congregations of anti-Trinitarians and Calvinists. In 1619 Keserüi visited the region, accompanied by 300 soldiers, and questioned parishioners on whether they believed in the Trinity. Where Keserüi and his soldiers received the response they wanted, the local minister was then forced to accept Reformed confessions of faith or was replaced by a reliable Trinitarian. By 1622 over sixty Unitarian ministers had been expelled from their parishes in the Háromszék region. Unitarian ministers were henceforth restricted to their remaining parishes in Háromszék, whilst Calvinist clergy could still move freely throughout the three counties. In 1631 the Reformed synod complained to the prince that Unitarian ministers in the Háromszék region should come under the authority of the Reformed hierarchy. From 1647 the Unitarian clergy of this corner of the principality were indeed forced to recognize the Transylvanian Reformed superintendent's jurisdiction over matters of discipline and morality, depending on their own Unitarian bishop only for doctrinal matters.[26] The 1631 Reformed synod also asked the Transylvanian prince to intervene against the Unitarian community in the market town of Székelykeresztúr. Reformed ministers claimed that local Unitarians had occupied their church without providing another building for Reformed worship. At first the Reformed church's pleas went unheeded, with György I Rákóczi suggesting shared use of the church, but by 1646 the local Reformed minister had regained control of the main church in Székelykeresztúr with the active support of János Bethlen, a major Reformed landowner in the area.[27]

The Reformed clergy hierarchy also complained to the prince about the renewed spread of Sabbatarianism in Szekler areas, and especially on the estates of Gábor Bethlen's former chancellor, Simon Péchi. During the 1630s the Transylvanian synod suggested that commissioners be sent to the area, to hear accusations about Jewish-style religious celebrations held on Fridays by Sabbatarians, and deal with this 'condemned and proscribed sect' which the prince 'was not bound to tolerate'.[28] Since Sabbatarians mostly declared themselves to be members of the Unitarian church,

---

[26] Juhász, *A székelyföldi református egyházmegyék*, 49; M. Péter, *A rikánbelöli kommunitás ismertetése és rövid története* (Sepsiszentgyörgy, 1909).

[27] 'Az erdélyi ev. ref. egyház vallássérelmei 1631–ben, beterjesztve I. Rákóczi György fejedelemhez orvoslás végett', ed. J. Koncz, *EPK* (1882), 380–1, 396, 422–3; Juhász, *A székelyföldi református egyházmegyék*, 39.

[28] 'Az erdélyi közzsinatainak végzései', ed. Koncz, 380–1, 396, 422–3.

Reformed ministers could also claim that Unitarians were guilty of breaking the 1572 law against doctrinal innovation. In 1635 the diet again outlawed Sabbatarianism, and in April 1638 the diet demanded a confessional statement from the Unitarian superintendent, Dániel Béke, to prove that the church's doctrine had not in fact been altered by radical infiltrators. In July 1638 the diet was called again at Dés and reached an agreement intended to prevent the spread of Sabbatarianism among Unitarians. This Dés agreement demanded that a new Unitarian catechism be drawn up under the supervision of the Reformed superintendent, which accepted the adoration of Christ as God, allowed for infant baptism and for regular communion services. The diet also required that the Unitarian church in future seek the prince's permission before any anti-Trinitarian books could be published in Transylvania.[29]

The Dés diet then changed into a prosecuting court against hundreds of individuals who would not accept this adorantist anti-Trinitarianism. One death penalty was enforced against János Toroczkai, son of a former Unitarian superintendent. Toroczkai was stoned to death by five gypsies for saying that 'if Jesus would come to earth, I would send him to work in a vineyard'. Others questioned by the court suffered loss of property, and Simon Péchi and his supporters were imprisoned. Evidence was heard concerning Sabbatarian celebrations using unleavened bread and white clothing worn by Sabbatarian women on Péchi's estates. Release from prison was only allowed on the condition of submission to articles of Reformed faith. Pál Medgyesi indeed made fifty-five new Reformed converts on one day alone, including Simon Péchi's chaplain, who remarkably was later ordained as a Reformed minister. These forced conversions also allowed the Reformed church to gain majority control of some congregations in Szekler areas where anti-Trinitarianism had previously been at its strongest.[30]

This Hungarian Reformed offensive against anti-Trinitarianism during the 1630s was warmly supported by foreign Calvinists. There was growing anxiety in the Dutch church about the arrival of Polish Socinian exiles in the Republic, and about an apparent spread of support for anti-Trinitarianism. Hungarian students at Dutch universities were urged to combat their Unitarian variant of the anti-Trinitarian disease widely believed to be lurking in central Europe. There was also concern among Calvinists about

[29] Romanian National Archives (Cluj), Collectia Gr. Kemény József, July 1638; Szilágyi and Orbán, 'Az unitáriusok 1638–diki üldöztetéseinek s a deési complanatiónak történetéhez', 150–62.

[30] Kohn, *A szombatosok*; Bod, *Historia Hungarorum Ecclesiastica*, iii, 303–4 (1638 confession); Bálint Segesvári, 'Krónikája', 157–218.

co-ordination between anti-Trinitarian churches across the Continent. Unitarians in Transylvania certainly had strong connections with Polish Socinians, and a Pole, Valentin Radecki, was superintendent of the Unitarian church in Transylvania from 1616 until 1632. Calvinist fears were heightened in 1638 when Jan Stoiński, formerly a Socinian minister at Raków, wrote from exile in Holland to Adam Franck, minister of the Saxon Unitarian church at Kolozsvár, of his discovery of anti-Trinitarians in the Dutch Republic. Stoiński wrote that 'most of them are Arians or near-Arians, who admit that knowledge of the doctrine [of the Trinity] is not necessary, and that they ought to treat us as brethren.' This letter was intercepted by agents of György I Rákóczi and sent to Johann Heinrich Bisterfeld at Utrecht, where he was on a diplomatic mission for the prince. Bisterfeld interpreted Stoiński's letter as proof of Raków Socinians' intentions to found a colony in Holland, and he forwarded a copy of the letter to Gisbert Voetius, stressing the continuing need to refute anti-Trinitarianism in both Transylvania and the Dutch Republic. Voetius subsequently had this letter translated into Dutch and publicly posted across Utrecht, commenting favourably on the Transylvanians' efforts to weaken the Unitarian church, most recently through the restrictions imposed by the 1638 Dés agreement.[31]

In 1639 Bisterfeld reinforced this international Calvinist collaboration against anti-Trinitarianism by publishing at Leiden a lengthy refutation of the theology of Johannes Krell, rector of the Polish Brethren's academy at Raków. Bisterfeld's work *On One God* aroused great interest in the Dutch Republic, and André Rivet at Leiden University sent part of Bisterfeld's new book to Marin Mersenne in Paris. Bisterfeld visited Mersenne during a visit as Rákóczi's envoy to the French court, and after Bisterfeld met Samuel Hartlib in England, Hartlib also wrote to Mersenne. This episode again demonstrates that correspondence and co-operation among leading Calvinists and others across the Continent was prompted by the anti-Socinian campaign, and is also suggestive of connections between Transylvania's religious and diplomatic contacts with western Europe during the Thirty Years War.[32]

[31] A. Vári, 'Kapcsolatok az erdélyi unitáriusok és a hollandiai remonstránsok között', *Keresztény Magvető*, 67 (1932), 109–20, 167–83; Ö. Miklós, 'Statorius János lengyel socinianus lelkész levele Frank Ádám kolozsvári unitárius lelkészhez, 1638-ből', *Keresztény Magvető*, 52 (1917), 68–85. The letter was published as *Translaet van seckere Latijnsche brief geschreven door eenen Sociniaensch Predicant, waer van het Latijnsche exemplaer (in Transylvanien gheintercipicert zijnde)*.

[32] Johann Bisterfeld, *De Uno Deo. Patre, Filio, ac Spiritu Sancto mysterium pietatis, contra Iohannis Crellii* (Leiden, 1639); Káldos, *Ungarländische Antitrinitarier II. György Enyedi*,

At home an investigation of the reasons behind the dwindling numbers of Szekler soldiers who responded to György I Rákóczi's call to arms against the Habsburgs in 1644 discovered that Sabbatarianism was again spreading in eastern Transylvania.[33] Such a finding was a new call to arms for Reformed polemicists, and János Laskai quickly published a work attempting to persuade Sabbatarians of their errors, offering proofs that the Messiah had already come and that Old Testament prophecy had found complete fulfilment in Jesus. Johann Heinrich Alsted's attack on anti-Trinitarian beliefs was published at Gyulafehérvár in 1644, again directed specifically against the writings of Johannes Krell.[34] In 1645 the Transylvanian superintendent, István Geleji Katona, attacked the 'dangerous sect' of Sabbatarians. Geleji's defence of the 'heavenly secret knowledge of the Trinity' dismissed Transylvanian anti-Trinitarianism as finding its 'perfectly complete' form in such atheism and judaizing. Geleji also argued that use of the name 'Unitarian' was by definition at odds with an adorantist religion and therefore could not fall within the bounds of the anti-Trinitarian religion, or 'binarist' religion as Geleji dubbed it, which had been given constitutional status at Torda in 1568. Geleji reasoned that 'if they are true Unitarians, they should not adore Christ, and for that reason they are not in a received religion, and have no valid rights of free exercise [of their religion]'.[35]

The position of the Unitarian church in Transylvania had certainly significantly weakened during the early seventeenth century. Reformed writers repeatedly attacked anti-Trinitarian beliefs, and in 1638 the Reformed hierarchy worked together with the prince and diet to redefine the doctrinal statements of the Unitarian church and constrain anti-Trinitarian publishing. The Transylvanian prince and Reformed nobles, as patrons and promoters of the Reformed church, also upset delicate inter-confessional balances in various localities across the principality, enabling Calvinists to take possession of some Unitarian churches. The growing impact of this Reformed confessionalism in Transylvania was highlighted by the assault on the Unitarian citadel of Kolozsvár. Kolozsvár's Saxon and

41–5; I. Monok, 'Johannes Henricus Bisterfeld és Enyedi György két levelezés-kiadásban', *Magyar Könyvszemle*, 103 (1987), 317–27; Webster, *The Great Instauration*, 53–5; S. Pumfrey, 'The Hartlib Circle and Magnetic Philosophy', in M. Greengrass, M. Leslie, and T. Raylor (eds.), *Samuel Hartlib and Universal Reformation* (Cambridge, 1994), 259–63.

33 S. Szilágyi, 'Az unitáriusok egyháztörténelméhez a xvii.-ik században', *Keresztény Magvető*, 11 (1876), 62–4.

34 János Laskai, *Jézus Királysága* (Nagyvárad, 1644); Johann Heinrich Alsted, *Prodromus religionis triumphantis* (Gyulafehérvár, 1644).

35 István Geleji Katona, *Titkok Titka*, introd.: 'ha igaz Unitariusok, a' Christust ne imádják, és az okon nem recepto religion vagynak, sem liberum exercitiumjok jure nem lehet.'

Hungarian communities had both largely embraced anti-Trinitarianism under the charismatic influence of Ferenc Dávid. Although in 1581 István Báthori gave the Jesuits possession of the Farkas Street church and supported a Jesuit school, Unitarians continued to dominate the town. In 1603 the town's citizens took advantage of the confusion of war to force the Jesuits to leave, and destroyed the monastery and church which they had occupied. However, when Gábor Bethlen began the work of refurbishing the Farkas Street church, he donated it for the use of the town's small Reformed community. Whilst the Reformed church's attempt to take Kolozsvár's magnificent St Michael's church in the town's central square from the Unitarians was a failure, in 1638 Reformed burghers managed to gain a foothold on the Kolozsvár council, which had previously been exclusively Unitarian. With their congregation growing in size, Reformed representation on the town council increased from one-quarter to a half in 1655. In 1656 György II Rákóczi aided the development of the town's Reformed school and by the end of the seventeenth century there were four Reformed churches in Kolozsvár. Nevertheless, Kolozsvár's Unitarians remained the largest community in the town and retained possession of St Michael's until 1716, when they were finally ousted not by Calvinists but by the Catholic church.[36]

(III) INTERNAL ALLIES? LUTHERANS

The Hungarian Lutheran church was widely supported by the nobility of western Hungarian counties, by German-speakers and some Slavs in Upper Hungary, and in royal free towns. Transylvania's Lutherans were predominantly German-speakers, drawn from the Saxon community of central and southern regions of the principality. Lutherans in Hungary and Transylvania had long-standing connections with German co-religionists, and particularly with Wittenberg University. From the mid-sixteenth century the influence of Melanchthon encouraged support among many Lutherans in Hungary and Transylvania for an intermediate Protestant theology. The Transylvanian superintendent, Matthias Schifbaumer, even sought some form of doctrinal concord with the Reformed church as late as 1601. However, by the end of the sixteenth century Lutheran student ministers were on the whole exposed to more doctrinaire attitudes in Saxony and returned to Hungary and Transylvania committed to strict Lutheran

[36] Bálint 'Krónikája', 157–218; K. Péter, 'Kolozsvár a magyar műveltségben', in *Papok és nemesek. Magyar művelődéstörténeti tanulmányok a reformációval kezdődő másfél évszázadból* (Budapest, 1995), 115–28.

orthodoxy. In western Hungary separate Reformed and Lutheran church structures were nevertheless slow to emerge, but eventually even Protestants there could no longer mask their differences, especially on the critical issue of communion theology. István Pathai was finally elected as a Reformed superintendent in the western Danubian province by a synod at Körmend in 1612. A synod of ministers at Zsolna in 1610 had led to the organization of separate Lutheran church structures in the Danubian province, and the synod also adopted a strictly Lutheran confession. Ministers and teachers could henceforth be asked to swear to uphold this confession, if their loyalty to Lutheran doctrines was doubted.[37] However, in some other areas of Hungary patterns of Protestant co-existence continued longer into the seventeenth century, such as an administrative union of Protestants in Zemplén where a small number of Slav Lutheran congregations accepted the authority of the local Reformed archdeacon.[38]

In Transylvania growing commitment among Lutherans to more orthodox doctrine caused some internal divisions. In 1615 the Lutheran minister at Schässburg in central Transylvania, Simon Paulinus, stopped using the Heidelberg Catechism or any works written by David Pareus at his local school. Paulinus also advocated the doctrine of the real presence of Christ in the communion service, but was then accused of theological innovation by some of his colleagues. Hungarian-speaking Lutherans in south-western Transylvania were particularly enraged by Paulinus and his supporters, and a protest was brought before the Lutheran superintendent. Gábor Bethlen was drawn into the dispute, demanding that the Lutheran superintendent block any attempt to introduce doctrinal innovations. Bethlen also argued that the adoption by Lutherans of an explicitly ubiquitarian understanding of communion was against the interests of Protestantism as a whole, and he prevented the synod from making any changes to their confession.[39]

Bethlen's contribution to this dispute was influenced by the views of Heidelberg's leading professor, David Pareus. As was noted in Chapter 2, Pareus corresponded with the prince in 1617 and 1618. Student ministers returning home from Heidelberg were also greatly affected by Pareus and his irenic teaching. Many Hungarian Reformed clergy thought that the Protestant battle against the Catholic church would have been much aided

37 B. Ila, 'A Thurzó levéltár protestáns egyháztörténeti iratai', in *MPEA* 15 (1934), 44–5, 144.
38 L. Hegedüs, 'A zempléni egyházmegye jegyzőkönyvéből', *Sárospataki Füzetek*, 1 (1857–8), 756–60.
39 Bod, *Historia Hungarorum Ecclesiastica*, iii, 286–301; Révész, 'Bethlen Gábor, a kálvinista fejedelem', 339–58.

if Lutherans could be persuaded to drop remnants of Catholic ceremony from their liturgy and abandon the doctrine of the real presence in communion services. The experience of ministers who had studied at Heidelberg under Pareus reinforced this general impression into a firm shift towards inter-Protestant co-operation. This irenic trend among Hungarian Reformed clergy was evident in discussions held with Lutherans in western Hungary, in unionistic theological works written by Hungarian Reformed ministers, and also in the conciliatory path adopted by Péter Alvinczi towards Lutherans at Kassa in northern Hungary, and each of these elements will now be examined in turn.

In June 1615 ministers from the Lutheran and Reformed churches of the Upper Danubian province of north-western Hungary met to review their theological differences. The Reformed representatives included former Heidelberg students János Samarjai, Imre Pécseli Király, and Pál Czeglédi. Discussions were also held at Komját in September 1615 between western Danubian Protestant superintendents and clergy in an effort to reach a unified position on the problematic issue of communion theology. A form of words was actually agreed by both sides for further debate on how Christ's body and blood were represented in the sacrament, but full agreement was never reached. Debates and correspondence continued after this meeting between István Pathai, the Reformed superintendent, and Mihály Zvonarics, a Lutheran minister from Sárvár. In 1616 and 1617 Pathai invited Zvonarics to the Reformed synod, where he was questioned on his support for the doctrine of the physical ubiquity of Christ. In response Zvonarics stuck by his views and claimed that Calvinists were heretics because of their understanding of communion as merely a commemoration of Christ's death.[40]

Despite this breakdown of dialogue between Lutherans and Calvinists, former Heidelberg students Péter Alvinczi, János Samarjai, and Imre Pécseli Király still tried to promote ideas about union between Hungarian Protestants. On his return home from the Palatinate, Pécseli Király argued against dividing the true church by such labels as 'Lutheran' and 'Calvinist', directly quoting Pareus' works to support his case.[41] In 1628 János

[40] 'Adatok a dunántúl és felsődunamellék kerületekről', ed. E. Thury, 154–6, 189–97.

[41] Imre Pécseli Király, *Consilium Ecclesiae Catholicae Doctorum super ista Quaestione: An homo Christianus possit et debeat se cognominare Lutheranum vel Calvinistam ad Religionem puram ab impura recte discernendam?* (Kassa, 1621). The Lutheran response is by György Zvonarics, *Rövid felelet, melyben Pécseli Imrének . . . tanácsa meghamisittatik . . . e kérdés felől: A keresztyén embernek kellessék-e lutheránusnak avagy kálvinistának neveztetni* (Cseppreg, 1626); J. Heltai, 'Irénikus eszmék és vonások Pécseli Király Imre műveiben', in B. Varjas (ed.), *Irodalom és ideológia a 16–17. században* (Memoria Saeculorum Hungariae, 5; Budapest, 1987), 209–30.

Samarjai, then superintendent of the Upper Danubian province, published a work called *Magyar Harmony* which attempted, again supported by frequent quotations from Pareus' *Irenicum*, to demonstrate that the Helvetic and Augsburg Confessions were fully reconcilable. Samarjai stressed that neither Calvin nor Luther was the source of Protestant faith, which came from Christ and the Apostles, and emphasized that communion was not a mere memorial of Christ's death but a necessity for salvation in which Christ was spiritually present through the elements. Samarjai stood by the need for communion in both kinds and repeated a claim made by Pareus that most Lutherans did not in fact fully subscribe to the doctrine of the real presence as it was set out in the Augsburg Confession.[42]

Hungarian Lutherans responded to these approaches from Calvinist clergy with great scepticism not least since where the Reformed church was in a clear majority, as in the Partium, Reformed polemic attacks tended to outnumber friendly advances. A suspicious Hungarian Lutheran was not long in rejecting Samarjai's proposals in print. István Lethenyei detailed differences across many branches of faith which he saw between the Augsburg and Helvetic Confessions, especially concerning communion theology and the ubiquity of Christ. Lethenyei argued that Calvinism was a 'dangerous science', with 'damnable errors', and suggested that many Calvinists were either Arians or Muslims.[43] János Samarjai, undaunted by this reaction, produced a service-order book for his province in 1636 which made no mention of the Helvetic Confession and even included minor sections of Catholic inspiration. Samarjai suggested that details of sacramental liturgy were open to different interpretations under 'Christian freedom'. On the ceremony of communion services, Samarjai argued that it was of little importance whether a communicant should stand or kneel, or whether the elements should be received in the hands or in the mouth, at an altar or on a table. Samarjai did assume, however, that wafers would not be used in the sacrament, but described the bread as more than 'mere' bread, secretly united for the believer with Christ's body through the sacrament. Imre Pécseli Király supported Samarjai's stance, and in a children's catechism he too stressed that the elements of communion were the seals of the covenant of grace and by faith became Christ's body and blood.[44]

---

[42] János Samarjai, *Magyar Harmónia; azaz, Augustana es az Helvetica confessio articulusinac eggyező értelme* (Pápa, 1628), 47–55, 229; G. Kathona, *Samarjai János gyakorlati theológiája* (Debrecen, 1939).

[43] István Lethenyei, *Az Calvinistac magyar harmonianac; azaz, Az Augustana es Helvetica Confessioc Articulusinac . . . öszve-hasomlétásanac meghamisétása* (Csepreg, 1633).

[44] János Samarjai, *Agenda. Az helvetiai vallason levő ecclesiaknak egyházi ceremoniajokrol es rend tartasokrol valo könyetske* (Lőcse, 1636); Imre Pécseli Király, *Catechismus* (Lőcse, 1635).

Péter Alvinczi tried to put this Protestant irenicism into practice when he became minister of the Hungarian-speaking church in the predominantly German-speaking royal free town of Kassa in Upper Hungary. In 1604 the Catholic bishop of Eger had used imperial troops to occupy St Elizabeth's church in Kassa, expelling Lutheran ministers from the town and forbidding even the private practice of Lutheranism. Lutherans were able to return to Kassa after Bocskai's revolt, and exclusive rights for Lutherans to worship in the town were then fiercely defended by the council against any encroachment by either Catholics or Calvinists.[45] When Alvinczi, ordained a Reformed minister, came to serve the Hungarian community in Kassa, he was pressurized by the town authorities not to attend Reformed church synods, nor accept Reformed discipline, and to sign the Augsburg Confession. István Miskolczi Csulyak, archdeacon in neighbouring Zemplén, wrote in 1607 to David Pareus, informing his former Heidelberg teacher of how Kassa's 'ubiquitarians' had forbidden Alvinczi from visiting his Reformed archdeacon.[46] Although Alvinczi cleared all the images and the organ out of his church at Kassa and did not wear Lutheran vestments during services, he did comply with the council's demands by using wafers instead of bread and wine during communion. Alvinczi's use of the wafer outraged Reformed opinion elsewhere in the region, since it seemed to signal his acceptance of the real presence of Christ in the sacrament. Alvinczi defended his position in a work dedicated to Gábor Bethlen, arguing that the use of wafers was permissible where the community was not yet ready to accept the change to using bread and wine. According to Alvinczi, this variety of practice did not affect the function of the communion service, so long as the ceremony remained free from all superstition. Alvinczi carefully reasoned that although the elements remained unchanged, nevertheless the communicant partook through them of Christ's body and blood.[47]

Alvinczi's lightness of theological touch on some of the complicated issues surrounding communion theology enabled him to outmanoeuvre suspicious German ministers at Kassa, who repeatedly tried and failed to have him barred from preaching on the grounds that he was a Calvinist. In 1623 Alvinczi reported to the Kassa council that Michael Bussaeus, a German

45 O. Paulinyi, 'Iratok Kassa sz. kir. város 1603–1604-ben megkísérelt rekatolizálásának történetéhez', in *MPEA* 14 (1930), 57–61; S. Imre, *Alvinczi Péter* (Marosvásárhely, 1898); Gy. Ráth, 'A felsőmagyarországi kryptokálvinisták hitvitázó irodalmáról', *ITK* 2 (1892), 310–24.

46 *Szenczi Molnár Albert naplója, levelezése és irományai*, ed. L. Dézsi, 213.

47 Péter Alvinczi, *Az Urnak Szent wacsoraiarol valo reovid intes az Szent Pal Apostol tanitasa szerint* (Kassa, 1622).

minister in the town, was refusing to speak to him and had described those attending Alvinczi's communion service as having the reverence of pigs. In June 1625 Alvinczi told the council that he intended to leave Kassa as a result of Bussaeus' continuing insults. Alvinczi had insisted upon the essential unity between Protestants in earlier arguments with Péter Pázmány and now again flatly rejected the label 'Calvinist' as a term of abuse. Alvinczi told the council that 'I am certainly not a Calvinist, neither am I a Lutheran, but a true Christian named after Jesus Christ'. On the understanding that he would receive no more insults from his German colleague, Alvinczi was at length persuaded not to leave Kassa. Bussaeus nevertheless persisted with his attacks, describing the town's Hungarian congregation as Calvinist heretics. Alvinczi appeared again before the council to refute the charge of Calvinism, proclaiming that as 'God is my witness . . . I have held to every point of the Augsburg Confession'.[48]

Following this second dispute, the Kassa council asked Bussaeus to leave the town to prevent further turmoil, but controversy flared up once again in 1627, when an assistant minister at the Hungarian church used bread and wine in a communion service. Alvinczi appealed to the council to support Protestant concord, and warned them that further arguments would give the Catholic church an excuse to press for entry into Kassa if Calvinists were already acknowledged to be present. Alvinczi also had to explain his delicate position at Kassa to a somewhat suspicious György Rákóczi in 1629 and claimed support from Calvin for his stance on communion, stressing the connections between what Calvin and Luther had written on the role of the sacraments.[49] Alvinczi's balancing act at Kassa became increasingly difficult to sustain, with his assistant minister soon forced to leave the town. Some Hungarian residents of Kassa also appeared before the council for having travelled to receive communion in both kinds at churches in neighbouring villages, a mark of their commitment to explicitly Reformed sacramental theology. In 1644 a distinctive Reformed church was finally set up in Kassa by György I Rákóczi during his military campaign in northern Hungary. This breakdown of the Lutheran monopoly in Kassa, which the council had worked so hard to prevent, was confirmed when the 1649 Hungarian diet gave equal rights for Lutherans, Calvinists, and Catholics to worship freely in the town.[50]

[48] L. Kemény, 'Alvinczy Péter életéhez', *ITK* 14 (1904), 112–19, 234–46, 364–7, 490–500; *ITK* 17 (1907), 243–8; *ITK* 20 (1910), 102–6; *ITK* 21 (1911), 366–9.

[49] S. Szilágyi (ed.), 'Rákóczyak levéltárából, 1611–1630', *TT* (1895), 140–1.

[50] K. Révész, *Százéves küzdelem a kassai református egyház megalakulásáért, 1550–1650* (Budapest, 1894).

David Pareus was not the only prominent foreign divine to advance the cause of Protestant union in Hungary and Transylvania during this period. John Dury worked throughout his career to reconcile the various wings of Protestantism across Europe in order to strengthen opposition to the Catholic church. Dury believed in the fundamental unity of Protestantism, and that divisions among Protestants were signs of divine judgement which required immediate repentance.[51] In 1634 Dury framed an irenic address directly to the synod of the Transylvanian Reformed church. Dury wrote to the synod on the need for a conference to sort out key problems between Lutheran and Reformed theologians, and emphasized how Catholics, and particularly Jesuits, wanted to keep divisions between Protestants alive. Dury reported that this approach 'moved them [the Transylvanians] to take the matter into serious consideration, and to make a decree'.[52]

A detailed and supportive response was indeed sent back to Dury in February 1634, signed by the Transylvanian superintendent, István Geleji Katona, and by Johann Heinrich Alsted, Johann Heinrich Bisterfeld, Ludwig Piscator, and all the archdeacons of the Transylvanian province. Alsted also expressed his personal support for Protestant church unity in a letter to Simon Albelius of February 1634. Alsted had studied under Pareus at Heidelberg in 1608 and shared Dury's expectation that rifts between the Protestant churches would be healed as the awaited millennium approached.[53] In the synod's reply to Dury, Geleji stressed that the aim of the Transylvanian church was to find unity and peace among Protestants in order to combat the Antichrist more effectively. Geleji stressed that in Transylvania they were neighbours with barbarians and had to put up with Arians, Anabaptists, Jews, Atheists, and the Orthodox church, so that they had every reason to seek unity with their Saxon Lutheran colleagues. Geleji also expressed a desire to communicate with others in Britain on such matters, and indeed a letter had also been sent to George Abbot, the archbishop of Canterbury, with questions on the possibility of union with Lutherans.[54]

51 John Dury, *A Model of Church-Government; or, The Grounds of the spirituall frame and government of the house of God* (London, 1647), Preface.

52 John Dury, *Motives to Induce the Protestant Princes to Mind the Worke of Peace Ecclesiasticall amongst Themselves* (London, 1641); and his *A Summary Discourse concerning the Work of Peace Ecclesiasticall, How It May Concurre with the Aim of a Civill Confederation amongst Protestants* (Cambridge, 1641); *A Brief Relation of that which Hath Been Lately Attempted to Procure Ecclesiasticall Peace amongst Protestants* (London, 1641).

53 'Drei Briefe an Simon Albelius in Kronstadt', ed. J. Gross, *Korrespondenzblatt des Vereins für Siebenbürgische Landeskunde*, 8 (1885), 1–3, 13–15.

54 House of Lords Record Office, London, MS Braye 1, f. 102, 'István Geleji Katona to George Abbot, the Archbishop of Canterbury, referring to John Durie's mission for the

Dury worked to promote his plans for Protestant union across the Continent throughout this period. In October 1654 Dury wrote that the Transylvanian synod's 1634 statement was going to be printed in England, 'the rather because the Prince of Transylvania is in a reddiness [sic] to come upon the stage for a common Protestant interest'. Dury reported to Samuel Hartlib that 'I sent you the judgment of Transylvania a whole copie at once; so that at severall times you have received now three copies of that judgment'. Hartlib in response cited the 'mutuall safety' and 'edification' from 'a further type of religious communion betwixt the British and their neighbour Protestants beyond the seas'.[55] The want of such a conjunction, Hartlib too believed, gave an advantage to those who wished to impose absolute temporal and spiritual power on the true church. Hartlib wrote: 'nor is it possible to accomplish his [the Pope's] overthrow, except the fault be mended, but by some nearer correspondencie of Protestants among themselves, for their mutuall preservation against his enterprises.'[56]

Despite this enthusiasm for Protestant union from some Calvinists, many Hungarian writers remained only too anxious to identify clear differences between their church and their Lutheran rivals. István Melotai Nyilas published a service-order book in 1621 which stood in marked contrast to that later produced by János Samarjai. Melotai emphasized that communion was a spiritual memorial of Christ's death and concentrated on the importance of striving for accuracy in copying the exact details of the original Last Supper. Melotai argued that 'the wafer is the bread of the Antichrist in communion' which 'infects Christian knowledge', and he accused Lutherans of being indistinguishable from Papists. Melotai illustrated his point by referring to a story he had heard whilst a student in Germany, of a minister in a town near Heidelberg who had wanted to use wafers in communion, but was unable to do so when the wafers flew out of the plate as he prepared for the service.[57]

pacification of Protestant churches'; ff. 104–14, 'Reply of István Geleji Katona with regard to the problem of obtaining ecclesiastical peace among Protestant churches'; Hartl. 59/10, f. 151a, 'Letter of pastors and professors of Transylvania, 7 Feb. Anno 1634'; M. Révész, 'Protestáns unió és az erdélyi reformátusok', *MPEF* 9 (1887), 167–86. Abbot had been forced into virtual retirement by Charles I, and his role by then in public affairs was severely curtailed: P. A. Welsby, *George Abbot. The Unwanted Archbishop, 1562–1633* (London, 1962).

55 Hartl. 4/3, ff. 46, 49a, 50a; Bodleian Library, Oxford, MS Lat Th / c.8 (65–86), John Dury, *Concordiae inter evangelicos quaerendae consilia quae in Transylvania evangelicae pastoribus et scholae Albae Juliacensis professoribus in synodo congregatis probata fuerunt, An. 1634* (London, 1654).

56 Samuel Hartlib, *The Necessity of Some Nearer Conjunction and Correspondency amongst Evangelical Protestants* (London, 1644), 6–7.

57 István Melotai Nyilás, *Agenda; azaz, Anyaszentegyházbeli szolgálat szerint való cselekedet* (Gyulafehérvár, 1621).

Even Geleji, although he had signed the positive response to Dury's irenic appeal in 1634, also attacked Lutheran opinions in his enormous homiletic works. Geleji argued that ubiquitarianism denied the humanity of Christ and remarked that Lutherans did not worship God in a manner which was pleasing to Him. Geleji concluded that the Lutherans were 'half-Papists' and 'neutralists'. This rather indicates that, whilst the Transylvanian superintendent saw the benefits of supporting Protestant union in the context of the international battle against Rome, he remained dedicated to pointing out the errors of Lutherans at home. This indeed typifies the Reformed church's approach to Protestant unionism. Whilst some within the Hungarian Reformed church certainly sought partnership with Lutherans during the early seventeenth century, most were unwilling to compromise over crucial points of doctrinal difference, and Lutherans were quickly derided by Reformed ministers as lukewarm Protestants if their assistance was less obviously helpful, or not forthcoming.[58]

(IV) MISSION: ORTHODOXY AND ISLAM

The privilege granted by princes which extended freedom of worship to the Orthodox church in Transylvania was renewed in 1608, 1615, and again in 1653. The position of the Orthodox community improved during the brief reign in Transylvania of the Wallachian Prince Mihai 'the Brave' during 1600. Mihai supported the foundation of a monastery near Gyulafehérvár as the site of residence for an Orthodox metropolitan. The Orthodox church was then permitted to have this metropolitan consecrated by his Wallachian counterpart, and then confirmed in office by the Transylvanian prince. Mihai also attempted to improve the condition of ordinary Romanian priests, but it was Gábor Báthori who finally released Orthodox priests from previously imposed duties of serfdom in 1609, and they became free to move from village to village.[59] Transylvanian Protestants, both Lutheran and Reformed, had long aimed to reform the Romanian Orthodox church. During the sixteenth century support was given to reform-minded Orthodox priests, and the Psalter and other sections of the Bible were published in Romanian. Indeed, the Romanian communities of the Hátszeg and Karánsebes regions of south-western Transylvania, where a Romanian gentry had been ennobled for their contribution to

58 Geleji Katona, *Váltság-Titka*, i, introd.

59 P. Teodor, 'Mihai Viteazul's Confessional Policy in Transylvania', in P. Teodor (ed.), *Colloquia. Journal of Central European History*, 1 (Cluj, 1994), 87–103; Ş. Andrescu, 'Some Reflections on Michael the Brave's Denominational Policy', in M. Crăciun and O. Ghitta (eds.), *Ethnicity and Religion in Central and Eastern Europe* (Cluj, 1995), 150–6.

defending the principality against the Turks, supported a small number of Romanian Calvinist ministers and schools throughout this period.[60]

Gábor Bethlen continued these previous efforts to sponsor religious reform among Transylvania's Romanians during his reign as prince. In 1616 Bethlen demonstrated personal interest in this project by attending the ordination of Romanian ministers at a synod of the eastern Tisza Reformed church at Nagyvárad. Bethlen also confirmed Ghenadie as Orthodox metropolitan, on condition that he obeyed the Calvinist superintendent and agreed to use Romanian instead of Old Slavonic in Orthodox services. When Ghenadie proved unwilling to implement these changes, Bethlen wrote to Cyril Lukaris, patriarch of Constantinople, hoping to gain his approval for an ambitious plan for the wholesale reformation of Romanian Orthodoxy. Cyril was widely thought to have vaguely Protestant sympathies and was supported by Protestant interests at the Porte through Thomas Roe and the Dutch ambassador, Cornelis Haga. Antoine Léger, chaplain to the Dutch embassy at the Porte, even published Cyril's supposed Protestant catechism, *The Confessions of the Lord Cyril*. Cyril responded to Bethlen's letter by pointing out the many differences between the beliefs of the two churches. Cyril also claimed that the relationship between the Romanian church in Transylvania and sister Orthodox churches in Moldavia and Wallachia was a major stumbling-block to Bethlen's proposed reform of Transylvanian Orthodoxy. Whether or not Cyril was sympathetic to Protestantism, any Calvinist influence over the Orthodox hierarchy was decisively rejected after Cyril's imprisonment in 1635 and death in 1638, with the 1641 Iaşi synod then ratifying a strictly Orthodox confession.[61]

Rather than follow Bethlen's ambitious attempt to instigate a full Orthodox reformation, later princes and Reformed superintendents attempted to revise some Orthodox liturgy and practices, and encouraged Romanians to convert to the Reformed church under a revived Romanian Protestant bishopric. István Geleji Katona wrote that the only major differences between Orthodox and Reformed theology came in the respect shown by the

---

[60] I. Juhász, *A reformáció az erdélyi románok között* (Kolozsvár, 1940); I. Révész, *A reformáció az erdélyi oláhok között* (Budapest, 1938); A. Bitay, *Az erdélyi románok a protestáns fejedelmek alatt* (Dicsőszentmárton, 1925); L. Binder, 'Grundlagen und Formen der Toleranz in Siebenbürgen bis zur Mitte des 17. Jahrhunderts', *Siebenbürgisches Archiv*, 3rd ser., 11 (1976), 123; A. A. Rusu, 'Aspects de la réforme parmi les nobles du Haţeg aux xvi-ème et xvii-ème siècles', *Colloquia. Journal of Central European History*, 1, 61–4.

[61] H. Trevor-Roper, 'The Church of England and the Greek Church in the Time of Charles I', in D. Baker (ed.), *Religious Motivation* (Studies in Church History, 15; Oxford, 1978), 213–40; E. Tappe, 'The Rumanian Orthodox Church and the West', in D. Baker (ed.), *The Orthodox Churches and the West* (Studies in Church History, 13; Oxford, 1976), 277–91.

Orthodox church to saints and icons, and over their doctrine on the Holy Spirit. However, Geleji considered Orthodox ceremonies to be full of superstition and believed that the Reformed church would be harshly judged for any neglect in efforts to assist reform of those abuses.[62] Attempts by the Transylvanian Reformed leadership to foster reform within the Orthodox church needed pliant metropolitans who would agree to enforce reforming measures. In 1640 Geleji wanted the new metropolitan to agree to found Romanian schools, accept a Protestant catechism which had been published that year, provide seating in churches, and only give communion to adults. Geleji also tried without success to link the implementation of these measures with consideration of Romanian priests retaining their non-serf status. Other conditions imposed on the new metropolitan included introducing the Romanian language into services and altering the use of icons and crosses in worship.[63] Orthodox resistance to these Calvinist attempts to stimulate reform was led in the 1640s by Varlaam, the metropolitan of Moldavia. In 1644 Varlaam, backed by the Moldavian prince, Vasile Lupu, presided over a joint synod of the Moldavian and Wallachian churches which formulated grounds for rejecting the new Protestant catechism and assisted the Transylvanian church's defence of Orthodox theology and ceremony.[64]

Despite such opposition, the Reformed church hierarchy and Rákóczi family supported the publication in Romanian of the New Testament in 1648, a Psalter in 1651, and Romanian translations of the Heidelberg Catechism in 1648 and 1656. István Fogarasi, minister at Lugos, complained in his introduction to the 1648 catechism that whilst Jewish children of five and six could already read from the Scriptures, some Christians in their twenties had still hardly touched a copy of the Bible in their lives. Fogarasi acknowledged that Bibles were hardly 'lying scattered in every bush', and so he had produced a catechism or 'little Bible' in Romanian for use in the Protestant schools at Lugos and Karánsebes.[65] There were also attempts during the 1640s and 1650s to monitor the implementation of reform measures among Orthodox priests. In 1647 twenty villages in the Fogaras

---

[62] Ötvös, 'Geleji Katona István élete és levelei I. Rákóczi Györgyhöz', 204, 215.

[63] István Geleji Katona, *Praeconium Evangelicum (Pars hyemalis ac vernalis)* (2 vols.; Gyulafehérvár, 1638–40), i, introd.; P. Hunfalvy, 'Az oláh káté', *Századok*, 20 (1886), 475–90; J. V. Ecsedy, 'Dobre mester erdélyi nyomdaja, 1640–2', *Magyar Könyvszemle*, 109 (1993), 146–66.

[64] Varlaam's *Răspunsuri* of 1645 is printed in J. Lupás, 'Varlaam, Moldova mitropolitája (1632–1653)', *Református Szemle* (1935), 217–25, 348–56.

[65] István Fogarasi, *Catechismus; azaz, A keresztyén vallásnak és hütnek rövid kérdésekben és feleletekben foglaltatott . . . olah nyelvre forditot* (Gyulafehérvár, 1648); A. Mózes, 'A xvi–xvii századbeli protestáns román káték', *Református Szemle*, 29 (1936), 340–5.

region of southern Transylvania were investigated by the Reformed authorities, with local priests examined on their knowledge of Old Slavonic and Romanian. This brought mixed responses on the priests' ability to read, write, and preach in Romanian, but all proved capable of repeating the Lord's Prayer, the Ten Commandments, and Apostle's Creed.[66] Zsuzsanna Lórántffy organized a further visitation of Romanian churches around Fogaras in 1658. This investigation aimed to discover whether Orthodox priests conducted their services in Romanian, and whether they had a copy of the New Testament, Psalter, and catechisms, but again produced mixed results. A school for Romanians was also set up by Lórántffy at Fogaras in the late 1650s to prepare candidates for the priesthood. Romanian teachers instructed pupils in the vernacular, and a common doorway was established to an adjoining Hungarian school.[67]

These policies only made a limited impact on Orthodox religion in Transylvania. In some areas Calvinist clergy could point to successes, such as the sad report of one Orthodox minister in 1655 that the church in his village had been given over to Reformed converts, and that he consequently had nowhere to worship. This Orthodox priest also reported that the Romanian converts to Calvinism were given new names: 'Ioan Boldea was given the Hungarian name Szatmáry János, [and] Dumitru Jelditean after that was called Loszadi Demeter'.[68] Such changes to Transylvanian Romanians' identity have been since regarded with deep suspicion by many Romanian historians, who have seen a lurking agenda of magyarization in the Reformed church's missionary efforts, but there is no evidence that this featured as a significant factor behind the actions of Reformed ministers.

During the 1650s interest was expressed by some within the Transylvanian Reformed hierarchy for irenic *rapprochement* with the Orthodox world, rather than bids to inspire reform or gain converts. This move was led by Isaac Basire, the exiled Anglican priest who from 1655 taught at the Gyulafehérvár Academy. Along with the Transylvanian superintendent, György Csulai, Basire acquired a leading role in Reformed church affairs during the late 1650s, gaining the trust of György II Rákóczi. Basire's interest in dialogue with Orthodox church leaders may indeed have been part of the incentive which had decided his move to Transylvania. Basire had

---

[66] D. Prodan (ed.), *Urbarile Ţarii Făgăraşului* (Bucharest, 1970), i, 831–84; P. Binder, 'Rákóczi György román bibliája', in A. Miskolczy (ed.), *Europa. Balcanica-Danubiana-Carpathica* (Annales, 2A; Budapest, 1995), 194–7.

[67] I. Juhász, 'Az erdélyi egyházak 17. századi együttélésének kérdései a fogarasi vártartományban', *Ráday Gyűjteménye Évkönyve*, 4–5 (1984–5), 9–27.

[68] Zach, *Orthodoxe Kirche und Romänisches Volksbewusstsein im 15. bis 18. Jahrhundert*, 178.

previously travelled around the Near East between 1650 and 1653, attempting to spread knowledge of the Anglican church in the Orthodox world, with a vision of Anglicanism having a unique role to reunite a divided Christendom. Communion with Orthodoxy was particularly attractive to Laudian Protestants such as Basire, because it offered contact with a line of valid descent from the early church untarnished by Rome. Basire had an Anglican catechism translated into Greek, and claimed success in 'spreading among the Greeks the Catholic doctrine of our faith'. Basire later wrote that:

I am not a stranger to the Muscovites' strangeness in point of religion, having observed it, when their ambassadors were entertained by Racozy [sic], whilst I lived at his court: The Greekes . . . are far more moderate . . . [and] when I having removed their stumbling block about the Holy Ghost . . . they readily gave me the right hand of fellowship.[69]

Basire had travelled to Messina, Smyrna, and Morea, where the metropolitan of Achaia allowed him to preach at a meeting of bishops and clergy. Basire also met the Greek patriarch at Jerusalem who apparently expressed the desire 'of communion with our old church of England'. Basire planned further travels to meet with the patriarch of Alexandria and wanted to have the Anglican Catechism translated into Turkish and sent to the bishops of Armenia.[70] In the end Basire instead travelled overland to Aleppo, where he met the patriarch of Antioch, then on to Constantinople, where in 1653 he began ministering to the French Protestant community at Pera near the Ottoman capital. Basire took up correspondence with Antoine Léger, then at Geneva, informing Léger of the positive reception which he claimed Orthodox patriarchs had given an Anglican catechism. Léger in return offered to send Basire copies of the New Testament and Protestant catechisms in Greek.[71]

Whilst the Reformed historicism of Pareus and Dury had inspired their irenic expectation that Lutherans would share with Calvinists the legacy of the reformation in a united Protestant church, Anglicans such as Basire rather looked to the Orthodox church as a potential ally in the battle against Roman claims of historic precedence and continuity. Basire's activities certainly renewed interest in the Orthodox church among exiled Anglican

---

[69] Bodleian Library, Tanner MS 48, f. 76, Dec. 1662. Isaac Basire, *De antiqua Ecclesiae Britannicae* (Bruges, 1656); Durham Cathedral Library, MS Hunter 84, 'An introduction to ye orthodox principles of ye church of England' (1648).

[70] Basire, *Correspondence*, ed. Darnell, 115–20.

[71] Durham University Library, Cosin letter-book, 1A, no. 59; Basire, *Correspondence*, ed. Darnell, 121–7.

royalists during the 1650s. John Cosin corresponded from Paris with a prelate at Trebizond, and Edward Hyde, leading adviser to the exiled Stuart king, also expressed his interest in Basire's exploits.[72] From 1655 Basire was able to find a new stage at Gyulafehérvár to continue his efforts to improve relations between Protestantism and Orthodoxy. Apart from discussions which Basire seems to have held with Orthodox leaders in Transylvania, in 1656 Basire set forward suggestions for improving the Gyulafehérvár Academy, which included support for Romanian scholars to be invited to the academy. This proposal was included in the new 1656 regulations and 'strengthened the custom' that two Romanians and two Germans should attend the academy each year. The places offered to Romanians might have been only intended for those who already belonged to Reformed Romanian communities, but Basire's speech to the academy in January 1657 nevertheless grandly proclaimed that Transylvanians, whether Szekler, Hungarian, Saxon, or 'Wallach', whether noble or peasant, were all now united together in Christ.[73]

The upheavals of the late 1650s in Transylvania curtailed all the various endeavours by the Reformed church to encourage reform within Romanian Orthodoxy. In the long term the Calvinist reforming mission clearly failed, and only a small number of Romanian Calvinist communities survived in south-western Transylvania into the latter decades of the century. The relatively weak constitutional position of the Romanian church had none the less given the Reformed hierarchy the opportunity to interfere in the internal patterns of Orthodox church life. The reluctance of the vast majority of Orthodox priests to change their traditional customs, and the support extended by the churches in Moldavia and Wallachia, enabled the Transylvanian Orthodox community to overcome Reformed intrusions. Transylvanian Orthodoxy was in fact severely disrupted by a completely different institutional reform at the end of the century through the creation of the Greek Catholic or Uniate church. Orthodox priests who recognized the authority of the Pope and accepted key Catholic doctrines were granted Uniate status and permitted to continue to use traditional ritual and liturgy. The Uniate church was offered legal protection by the Habsburgs,

[72] C. J. Cuming, 'Eastern Liturgies and Anglican Divines, 1510–1662', in D. Baker (ed.), *The Orthodox Churches and the West*, 231–8; W. B. Patterson, 'Educating the Greeks: Anglican Scholarships for Greek Orthodox Students in the Early Seventeenth Century', in K. Robbins (ed.), *Religion and Humanism* (Studies in Church History, 17; Oxford, 1981), 227–38; R. Ollard, *Clarendon and His Friends* (London, 1987), 203.

[73] Durham Cathedral Library, MS Hunter 10, pt 33, no. 7. A Romanian student is listed amongst respondents in debates with Bisterfeld in *Beata beatae virginis ars* (Gyulafehérvár, 1651); 'II. Rákóczi György ismeretlen iskolatörvénye', ed. Török, 118–24; Basire, *Schema primum generale sive forma studiorum Albensium*, 21.

and its priests were ennobled as an order. Backed by a majority of Orthodox clergy in Transylvania, the Gyulafehérvár metropolitanate became a bishopric for this new 'received religion' from 1697, and an Orthodox metropolitan did not return to the principality until the mid-nineteenth century.[74]

The Hungarian Reformed church not only bordered the Orthodox world but was also forced to adapt and survive under and near areas of Muslim control. The situation of different Reformed communities in Ottoman-occupied areas of Hungary varied greatly, with some churches confiscated but other congregations left to hold services and choose their own ministers largely undisturbed. Letters of approval were required from the Turkish authorities to guarantee the free practice of religion, and for the right of any church to hold synods. Strict controls were imposed across Ottoman Hungary on renovating Christian church buildings, but records from Hatvan and Gyöngyös show that approval was sometimes given by Ottoman officials for the repair of damaged churches. Rights of visitation by archdeacons also required the agreement of local officials, and the Christian community in occupied Hungary was compelled to recognize Islamic holidays. However, by the 1650s Reformed ministers in Ottoman Hungary were, despite their real grievances, in many respects in a more secure position than were their colleagues in Royal Hungary.[75]

For the most part, fears of Turkish encroachment further north into Hungary and Transylvania dominated Reformed attitudes towards the Muslim world. There was, however, little or no recognition that the Turkish occupation of southern Hungary had become a necessary evil which counterbalanced Habsburg power and allowed Hungarian Protestantism some space in which to flourish. Hungarian Reformed writers showed awareness of the outlines of Muslim theology and included basic information about it in catechisms and children's guides to religion. Reformed canons prevented marriage with Muslims, but allowed for the baptism of converting Muslim children. Steps towards achieving such converts were occasionally considered, often within a wider eschatological context which also included projects for the conversion of Jews. In 1609 Johann Heinrich Alsted encouraged Albert Szenci Molnár to learn Turkish, and in the

---

74 G. Sipos, 'Román református eklézsiák oltalomlevele 1700–ból' in A. Miskolczy (ed.), *Europa. Balcanica-Danubiana-Carpathica* (Annales, 2B; Budapest, 1995), 356–9.

75 Dunamellék Reformed Church Province Archives (Ráday College, Budapest), Gyöngyös református egyh. község levéltárából, nos 19, 26; Pál Thúri, *Idea Christianorum Ungarorum sub Tyrannide Turcica* (Oppenheim, 1616); Földváry, *Adalékok a dunamelléki év. ref. egyházkerület történetéhez*; Földváry, *A magyar református egyház és a török uralom*; Kathona, *Fejezetek a török hódoltsági reformáció történetéből*, 58–70.

1650s Jan Amos Comenius wanted Zsuzsanna Lórántffy to sponsor the translation of the Bible into Turkish. Comenius argued that Christians should not be hostile to Muslims because 'they acknowledge our Christ as a great prophet, and do not allow any blasphemy towards him'. Comenius believed that the conversion of the Turks was impeded by their lack of books other than the Koran, and that under the pretext of teaching languages, books should be provided for them which could act as 'sprinklers of light'. In the 1660s Comenius' attempt to supervise a translation of the Bible into Turkish was backed by his patron Laurence De Geer, but the translator's work proved flawed and remained unpublished. Meanwhile, István Geleji Katona, who had been redeemed from Turkish captivity as a child, also wrote in the 1640s of the possibility of beginning a mission to the Turks, Tartars, Persians, and Jews but there is no evidence that any concrete action was ever undertaken.[76]

By the early seventeenth century Reformed beliefs and ceremonies had become the dominant orthodoxy of the Transylvanian principality. The programme of further reformation to which Reformed ministers were dedicated encouraged the church to work in partnership with Transylvania's princes and Reformed nobles on matters of education and public morality. This project of ongoing reformation was also marked by decreasing tolerance for the presence of alternative religions within Transylvania. Reformed clergy engaged in bitter battles against confessional opponents, with dogmatic positions firmly defended by all sides. Although there were frequent clashes between the churches over doctrine, over control of church property, and over restrictions imposed on the freedoms of the Catholic and Unitarian churches, religious diversity nevertheless persisted in the principality. Even the most ardent confessional absolutist among Reformed ministers could not credibly conceive that the constitutional freedoms of the other received religions would be quickly overturned. Neither could the local results across Transylvania of generations of divided religious authority and political power be easily wiped away. Relations between Transylvania's constitutional religions therefore remained delicately balanced between, on the one hand, acceptance of confessional diversity in law and in many localities and, on the other, strident rivalry between the

---

[76] Geleji Katona, *Váltság Titka*, iii, 420; *Szenczi Molnár Albert*, ed. Dézsi, 332–4; Földváry, *A magyar református egyház és a török uralom*; Kathona, *Fejezetek a török hódoltsági reformáció történetéből*, 58–70; Comenius, *Panorthosia* (*De rerum humanarum emendatione consultationes catholicae*, bk. 6), ed. Dobbie, 119, 246–7; N. I. Matar, 'The Comenian Legacy in England: The Case for the Conversion of the Muslims', *The Seventeenth Century*, 8 (1993), 203–15.

churches, with Transylvania's princes offering partisan support for the Reformed cause. Nevertheless, in comparison with their portrayal of Habsburg rule imposing Catholic tyranny, Calvinist princes could present their preservation of Transylvania's inclusive religious settlement and protection of Christian freedom as an effective element of their appeal to the Hungarian nobility.

5
Reformed Religion:
Public Ceremony and Private Piety

Reformed religion developed in Hungary and Transylvania during the second half of the sixteenth century as reformers collected together insights from a range of theologians including Beza, Bullinger, Melanchthon, Zwingli, and Calvin. Hungarian Reformed religion was distinctive from local confessional rivals primarily through Calvinist sacramental theology, and Calvinists in Hungary were indeed initially described as sacramentarians. A fledgling Reformed church united in 1567 around the *Confessio Catholica*, drawn up by Péter Meliusz Juhász and Gergely Szegedi, and accepted the Second Helvetic Confession. Regional synods of reformminded clergy across Hungary and in Transylvania soon recognized similar confessions of faith and endorsed alterations to the conduct of religious services and ceremonies. The development of the Hungarian Reformed church was heavily influenced by ongoing communication with other Calvinist churches across the Continent. Contact with university teachers and clergy from western Europe tended to buttress the Reformed orthodoxy of the Hungarian church. As we have seen, student ministers returned from periods of study at foreign Calvinist academies determined to publicize in Hungary why they believed Reformed theology was accurate, and why the theology of other churches was disorderly, mistaken, and heretical. Transylvania's princes and Hungarian nobles provided the resources for these students to study at foreign Calvinist academic centres, and also supported the development of local educational facilities. Gradual improvements in the standards of Hungarian colleges and schools aided the ability of Reformed ministers to broaden understanding about changes made to customary beliefs and religious practices.

Preaching and the spoken word remained the most important means by which ministers communicated ideas about religious reform to local communities. However, vernacular printed books also played a significant part in spreading Reformed ideas among the clergy and, to some extent, more broadly within Hungarian and Transylvanian society, and this chapter will consider the developing role of printed books in the religious life of

Reformed Hungary and Transylvania. During the late sixteenth century and early decades of the seventeenth century Reformed students and ministers furnished the church with translations of scripture, creeds, and catechisms. These books were mostly intended to be used by parish clergy to explain religious truth to local communities in public services. From the 1630s piety tracts and books on the everyday problems of religious life also began to be translated and published. Whilst it is very difficult to assess the wider impact on Hungarian society of this so-called 'practical theology', some ministers aimed to direct the private religiosity and personal morality of individual Reformed believers through such printed material.

Hungarian Reformed confessional statements set out the core doctrines of the church, described new administrative church structures, and outlined the function of a reformed ministry. Regulations also established the conduct of public services and the appearance of church buildings, and this model of Reformed religiosity slowly spread into the localities of Hungary and Transylvania. Parish ministers took the lead in reforming the practice of religion in their congregations, introducing Reformed liturgy and ceremonies, and attempting to reform aspects of traditional popular religion. This chapter will attempt to convey something of the emerging character of Hungarian Reformed religion by considering the appearance of church buildings, the format of public services, and conduct of sacraments. Information about the church ceremonies adopted during this period comes partly from canons and the decisions of regional synods, and also from local disputes over detailed points of liturgy and ceremony. The Reformed church claimed to have established Christian freedom in the practice of religion, but the clergy hierarchy demanded that all ministers adhere to a uniform pattern of worship. Disagreements arose during the early seventeenth century between those who feared any unsettling of the established church order and others who argued that further reforms of public ceremony were essential. Ministers who advocated a religion of personal conscience and domestic piety were also often supporters of further ceremonial and liturgical change. Arguments centred particularly on the conduct of the sacraments, on styles of preaching, and on the role of public prayers and music in church services, and this chapter will examine each of these core elements of Reformed religious life in turn.

(1) BOOKS AND BELIEF

The Hungarian Reformed church perceived books and the vernacular written word to be vital sources of truth and authority, able to shape the beliefs of a community and aid individuals' understanding of religion. This enthusiasm for books applied especially to the Bible, and Reformed ministers in the Partium were ordered by their provincial synod to possess a copy of the Bible from the 1570s. The Reformed church was initially reliant on the work of humanists for vernacular versions of the scriptures. János Sylvester had translated the New Testament into Hungarian in 1541, offering the pragmatic explanation for his work that most Hungarians did not speak and could not understand other languages. Leading reformers in turn translated parts of the Bible, with Gáspár Heltai producing a version of the Psalms, and Péter Meliusz Juhász translating parts of the Old Testament during the 1560s. Reformed synods consistently stressed the need for all Christians to understand the fundamentals of their faith and expressed the hope that catechisms would play a primary role in achieving this. In 1567 the Debrecen synod had introduced the requirement for ministers to teach their congregations from catechisms. This move to formalize religious instruction required the production of standard texts, and a number of catechisms and summaries of the main areas of Reformed faith were soon published. These were often directed for ministers to use, as Gáspár Heltai put it, when teaching young people and the 'simple-minded'.[1]

Some service-order books were also published, as were collections of sermons by leading ministers, but the spread of Reformed beliefs through books remained disjointed during the 1570s and 1580s. In 1586 Tamás Félegyházi published a translation of the New Testament, but a translation of the whole Bible into Hungarian was only finally achieved by Gáspár Károlyi at Vizsoly in north-eastern Hungary as late as 1590.[2] Károlyi wrote in the introduction to his translation that, 'God not only desires that priests should read the Holy Scriptures, and that the community hear the scriptures from the mouths of the priests, but He also desires that the books of the Old and New Testaments should be in the languages of every nation.'[3]

---

[1] András Batizi, *Keresztyéni tudományról való rövid könyvecske* (Cracow, 1550); Gáspár Heltai, *Catechismus, melybe a menynyei tudománynak sommája . . . egybe szerzettetett* (Kolozsvár, 1553); Gáspár Heltai, *Catechismus minor* (Kolozsvár, 1550); Péter Méliusz Juhász, *Katekizmus, az egész keresztyéni tudománynak fundamentoma és sommája . . . Calvinus János írása szerint* (Debrecen, 1562), printed in Barth (ed.), *Tánulmányok, 3,* 222–77; Gergély Molnár, *Catechesis scholae Claudiopolitanae* (Kolozsvár, 1564); Bálint Szikszai Hellopoeus, *Az egri keresztyén anyaszentegyháznak . . . rövid catechismus* (Debrecen, 1574); Bálint Szikszai Hellopoeus, *A mi keresztyéni hitünknek és vallásunknak három fő articulusárol . . . való könyvecske* (Debrecen, 1574); Tamás Felegyházi, *Az keresztieni igaz hitnek reszeirol valo tanitas, kerdesekkel es feleletekkel* (Debrecen, 1579).

[2] *Zsinatok végzései,* ed. Kiss, 690–5, no. 6; Péter, 'A bibliaolvasás mindenkinek szóló programja magyarországon a 16. században', *Századok,* 119 (1985), 1,006–28.

[3] 'Nemcsak azt akarja Isten, hogy papok olvassák a Szentírást, és az község azoknak, szájokbál hallja, hanem azt is akarja, hogy az Ó- és Újtestamentum könyvei minden nemzetségnek nyelvén legyenek': Gáspár Károlyi, *Szent Biblia* (Vizsoly, 1590), 4ᵛ–5.

Károlyi commented on the slowness of Hungarians to translate the whole Bible, casting some blame on ministers but more onto magistrates for not having done so earlier. Károlyi declared that his work was intended to be used by rich and poor alike, by men and women, and this Vizsoly Bible indeed became the standard vernacular version of the Bible used within the Reformed church.[4]

In the aftermath of the devastation caused by the Fifteen Years War, the task of rebuilding the Reformed church in Transylvania was led by superintendent Mihály Tasnádi Ruber. Ruber concluded a major revision of the church's canons in 1606, which again emphasized the importance of books in building up the knowledge and abilities of the clergy. Every minister was required to obtain a copy of the Bible, if he did not have one already, as well as possess other unspecified theological works. Revisions and reprints of Károlyi's Bible were published from the first decade of the seventeenth century in Transylvania, Germany, and the Dutch Republic.[5] Reformed ministers also worked on translations of Calvinist catechisms, with synods demanding that regular catechizing be used to teach the 'milk' of the fundamentals of Christian faith so that congregations could then move on to more 'solid foods'. When János Siderius, the Abaújvár archdeacon, published his *Catechism* in 1597 he claimed that there had recently been a decline in the practice of catechizing, and some confusion caused, because different catechisms were being used in different areas. Siderius' *Catechism* did much to rectify this problem, appearing in more than twenty editions during the seventeenth century and becoming a standard text for religious instruction used in schools, churches, and homes across the region.[6]

There appears to have been a revival of interest in catechisms and summaries of faith from the turn of the century, and ever greater familiarity with the 1563 Heidelberg Catechism in particular. The Heidelberg Catechism had been first translated by Dávid Huszár at Pápa in 1577, and a second translation by Ferenc Szárászi appeared at Debrecen in 1604. Albert Szenczi Molnár then published a shorter version of the Heidelberg Catechism in 1607 within his Psalter, and the whole catechism appeared again in 1612 in Molnár's Oppenheim Bible. In 1616 the upper Danubian

---

4 I. Czegle, 'A vizsolyi Biblia elöljáró beszéde', in Barth (ed.), *Tanulmányok, 3*, 517–36.

5 Károlyi's *Szent Biblia* was reprinted by Albert Szenczi Molnár at Hanau (1608) and Oppenheim (1612). Later editions were published at Amsterdam (1645) and Nagyvárad–Kolozsvár (1660–1), and a *Új Testamentoma* at Amsterdam in 1646; 'Az erdélyi közzsinatainak végzései', ed. Szilágyi, 1–9.

6 János Siderius, *Kisded gyermekeknek való katechizmus, azaz a keresztyéni hitnek fő ágazatairúl rövid kérdések és feleletek által való tanitás* (Debrecen, 1597); *Zsinatok végzései*, ed. Kiss, 586–7, 712, 725; J. Barcza, 'Siderius János kátéja', in Barth (ed.), *Tanulmányok, 3*, 849–76.

superintendent Péter Szenczi Csene completed a translation of the 1566 Second Helvetic Confession which was also published by Molnár at Oppenheim. In 1624 Molnár made a further contribution to the range of printed books available to the Hungarian church, when he was supported by Gábor Bethlen and the Rákóczi family to publish his translation of Calvin's *Institutes of the Christian Religion*.7

Without ever entirely displacing home-grown catechisms, the Heidelberg Catechism soon gained official sanction for use across the Hungarian church provinces. In 1619 the upper Danubian church ordered the use of the Heidelberg catechism in its schools. The western Danubian province followed suit in 1630, requiring that congregational catechism classes be held on Sunday afternoons and after weekday morning services. Regular visitations of local parishes were supposed to check that these classes were actually taking place. Johann Heinrich Alsted's Latin–Hungarian shorter version of the Heidelberg Catechism became widely used in Reformed schools in Transylvania, and five editions of Alsted's catechism were published at Gyulafehérvár before 1660. Vernacular schools meanwhile used either wholly Hungarian translations of the Heidelberg Catechism or the catechisms compiled by András Batizi and János Siderius.8 The 1646 national synod at Szatmár instructed ministers to preach explanations of the catechism during Sunday afternoon services before classes were held, and approved both the Heidelberg catechism and Siderius' catechism for general use in the church. The 1649 Transylvanian canons made catechism classes compulsory for all, with boys taught in schools, adults receiving instruction during Sunday afternoon services, and classes for girls and young women held following these services.9

In 1640 the eastern Tisza superintendent, István Keresszegi Herman, published a series of sermons which he had given at Debrecen based on the Heidelberg Catechism. Keresszegi hoped that his book would be used by ministers to build up their congregations' knowledge of Reformed beliefs

---

7 Dávid Huszár, *A keresztyén hitről való tudománynak rövid kérdésekben foglaltatott summája* (Pápa, 1577); Ferenc Szárászi, *Catechesis; azaz, Kérdések és feleletek a kerestyéni tudománynak ágairól* (Debrecen, 1604); Péter Szenczi Csene, *Confessio Helvetica; az az, Az keresztyeni igaz hitröl valo vallás-tétel* (Oppenheim, 1616); Albert Szenczi Molnár, *Kis katekizmus . . . szedetött az heidelbergai öreg Katekizmusból* (Herborn, 1607); Albert Szenczi Molnár, *Szent Biblia . . . az palatinatusi katekizmussal* (Oppenheim, 1612); L. Dézsi, *Szenczi Molnár Albert* (Budapest, 1897); *Szenci Molnár művei*, ed. Vásárhelyi and Tolnai.

8 Johann Heinrich Alsted, *Catechismus religionis Christianae-Catechismus; azaz, A keresztyéni vallásnak és hütnek rövid kerdesekben és feleletekben foglaltatott* (Gyulafehérvár, 1636); B. Nagy, 'A heidelbergi káté jelentkezése, története és kiadásai magyarországon a xvi és xvii században', in Barth (ed.), *Tánulmányok, 2*, 15–92.

9 *Egyházi kánonok*, ed. Kiss, 1646 resolutions, nos. 2, 19; 1649 canons, no. 50.

and would also be widely used in homes. Keresszegi wrote that every householder was a 'prophet and priest in Christ' in their own home and could read the book aloud and search for supporting Bible passages in order to strengthen the faith of the whole household.[10] Later writers stressed the practical role which catechisms could play in developing knowledge about faith in homes as well as in schools and through congregational classes, and also suggested improvements to the ways in which catechisms were being used. Pál Medgyesi wrote in the introduction to his 1645 translation of an English *A-B-C of Salvation* that children should try to learn two or three catechism questions by heart each day, and then repeat on Sunday what they had learned during the previous week. János Apáczai Csere's 1650 *Catechism* criticized the practice of many ministers who, he claimed, stopped holding classes in the winter because of the cold. Apáczai also stressed that answers should not be learned by rote without a full understanding of the words, and Apáczai provided a series of follow-up questions in his catechism to check on progress.[11]

The variety and volume of books in circulation within the Hungarian Reformed community had increased considerably by the mid-seventeenth century, and notable advances had been made to printing facilities at various Reformed centres. A new printing-press was established at Gyulafehérvár in the 1620s and at Sárospatak in 1650, and a press was also set up at Nagyvárad. Stocks of books in the libraries of Reformed colleges and schools were also significantly enhanced during this period, especially at the library of the Gyulafehérvár Academy and the college library founded at Sárospatak in 1641. Other schools also had growing collections of books, which had either been published locally or brought home from western Europe by returning student ministers. Whilst the numbers and range of available books certainly increased, the reception of printed ideas within Hungarian society remained limited to those with access to these books. It is impossible to quantify literacy rates for the region, but there is some sense that during the sixteenth century a greater proportion of the population had begun to acquire some reading skills. There was certainly an increasing number of available cheap books, and a broader range of subject

---

[10] István Herman Keresszegi, *A keresztyén hitnek ágazatiról való prédikációknak tárháza* (Nagyvárad, 1640).

[11] Apáczai Csere, *A keresztyéni vallasra rövid kérdésekben és feleletekben tanito Catechesis*; Pál Medgyesi, *Lelki A-Bé-Cé. A Christus oskolájába az alsó rendben bé állatandó tsetsemökuek közönségessen kiváltképpen; penig a' méltóságos kegyes Fejedelem aszszonynak Lorantfi Susannának, aprobb Tselédgyének hasznokra* (Gyulafehérvár, 1645); János Pósaházi, *Igazság istápja . . . katekizmusi tanítás, melyben a ker. reformáta vallás . . . megmagyaráztatik, és az ellen tusakodó* (Sárospatak, 1669).

matter in printed works. All this, together with the achievements of Reformed schools, suggests that by the early seventeenth century literacy was no longer an exclusive hallmark of social privilege among the clergy, nobility, and urban élites, and that some allowance must also be made for the role of books in the religious life of smaller towns and larger villages. Nevertheless, while many printed books were aimed at ordinary members of Reformed congregations, parish clergy undoubtedly continued to play a vital role in mediating and spreading Calvinist ideas within Hungarian society.[12]

From the 1620s increasing numbers of Hungarian student ministers encountered efforts at Dutch universities and in England to develop a more practical Calvinist theology and to stimulate domestic piety. János Bökényi Filep described a golden, heavenly light shining out from the books of Britain's theologians to illuminate Hungary and stimulate improvements in the lives of ordinary Hungarians.[13] Despite the very different social environment of their homeland, many of those, such as Bökényi, who had studied in the Dutch Republic and visited England, became determined to make similar efforts to stimulate personal religiosity among Hungarian Calvinists. Many translations began to appear in Hungary and Transylvania of practical theological works, piety tracts, children's books, and works about personal morality. This trend was epitomized by the enormously successful translation by Pál Medgyesi in 1636 of Anglican Bishop Lewis Bayly's *The Practice of Piety*. Medgyesi studied at Dutch universities and in England between 1629 and 1631, and his translation of Bayly's work made an immediate impact in Hungary, with Reformed ministers anxious to obtain the new book. Menyhárt Fodorik, the minister at Debrecen where *The Practice of Piety* was first published, received requests in 1637 from his archdeacon and other local ministers quickly to send them copies of Bayly's work.[14] The introduction to *The Practice of Piety* set out its central purpose by admonishing readers not to content themselves with the merely formal religion of the unregenerate, and warned against thinking that good Christians could accept the standards of religious practice followed by

---

[12] Ballági, *A magyar nyomdászat történelmi fejlődése, 1472–1877*; K. Péter, 'A műveltség hordozói', in *Magyarország története*, iii pt 1, 544–8; Naményi, 'A nagyváradi nyomdászat története', 280–91; Irinyi and Benda, *A négyszáz éves debreceni nyomda (1561–1961)*, 7–59, 313–408; Zs. Jakó, *A Bethlen kollégium könyvtárának kezdetei és első korszaka* (Kolozsvár, 1973).

[13] János Bökényi Filep (tr.), *Mennyei Lámpás* (Utrecht, 1652).

[14] Pál Medgyesi (tr.), *Praxis Pietatis* (Debrecen, 1636), repr. 1638, 1640, 1641, 1643. Dunántúl Reformed Church Province Library MS Collection (Pápa), o.1092, Vegyes iratok, 1605–1879, nos. 80.4, 80.6, 80.7, 80.8r; János Siderius, *Kisded gyermekeknec való catechismus* (repr. Nagyvárad, 1642); Medgyesi (tr.), *Lelki A-Be-Ce*.

most people. The main text of the book aimed to give assistance to Bible readers and gave examples of prayers for all occasions from eating, taking medicine, and going to sleep, to walking to church. Medgyesi stated in his introduction that he particularly wanted to encourage understanding of the Bible amongst those of 'our cold nation' who actually bothered to read it, and to stimulate greater personal piety among Reformed congregations.[15]

The two western writers on practical theology most influential in Hungary and Transylvania during the early seventeenth century were William Perkins and William Ames. In 1620 János Kecskeméti translated Perkins's *Catholicus Reformatus*, and in 1637 János Iratosi translated a work by Perkins which set out how individuals ought to behave if they were true Christians. In 1648 a collection of Perkins's tracts, *A Case of Conscience: How a man may know whether he be the child of God, or no*, was translated by Mihály Tsepregi Turkovitz and printed at Amsterdam.[16] Some of Ames's writings were also printed in Hungary, including those published in a collection of tracts at Nagyvárad in 1653. Hungarian student ministers had also been directly exposed to Ames's opinions through his teaching at Franeker University during the 1620s. Returning student ministers brought home many copies of works by Ames and Perkins from the Dutch Republic and England, and both English theologians' ideas were then adapted by some Hungarian ministers in their own books.[17]

Ames and Perkins sought above all to highlight the importance of conscience and individual piety in the practice of religion. They conceived of theology as instruction on how to live properly and believed that pure doctrine and practical divinity were inseparable. Their efforts to bring religion closer to the reality of everyday life forced them to engage with the difficulty of how Calvinists could reconcile the idea of predestination with the requirements of godly living. Perkins and Ames developed the notion of a covenant of grace between God and each individual, through which a

---

[15] Medgyesi, *Praxis Pietatis*, introd.

[16] Kecskeméti (tr.), *Catholicus Reformatus*; János Iratosi (tr.), *Az ember életének boldogul való igazgatásának modgyáról. Patika szerszámos bolt, azaz sokféle haláloknak természetükről* (Lőcse, 1637), repr. 1641; Mihály Tsepregi Turkovitz (tr.), *A lelkiismeretnek akadékiról* (Amsterdam, 1648).

[17] István Telkibányai (tr.), *Angliai Puritanismus avagy kiválkeppen való tudományok azoknak, kik Angliabán a Puritánusok között (a mint közönségesen neveztetnek) legkeményebbeknek tartatnak* (Utrecht, 1654); Peter Ramus, *Dialecticae libri duo* (Nagyvárad, 1653), with Ames's *Technometria* and *Disputatio Theologica adversus metaphysicam*, 98–137, 205–19; Martonfalvi and Komáromi Csipkes, *Ars Concianandi Amesiana*; Koltay, 'Two Hundred Years of English Puritan Books in Hungary', 53–64; Koltay, 'Perkins és Ames recepciója magyarországon 1660-ig', 99–109; Hazagh, 'Amesius és a magyar puritanizmus', 94–112.

believer's conscience offered certainty of pardon from sins. The elect, by this covenant of grace, could only be known to themselves and to God, although Perkins and Ames argued that the effects of election would be reflected in a believer's actions and daily life. Both writers therefore stressed that individuals should strive to attain personal godliness and to improve their standards of personal conduct, in order to provide signs of assurance about their future salvation.[18]

Hungarian Reformed ministers published a range of other practical theological works throughout this period, mostly from English sources. As Gisbert Voetius at Utrecht University commented: 'besides our Dutch scholars, French, Hungarians, Transylvanians, Germans, and Swiss have upheld the standard of this [practical] theology in books translated from English, for which purpose Hungarian, Transylvanian, Dutch, German, and Swiss students, both at home and in England, have studied the English language and examined English books'.[19] Voetius also supported the efforts of Hungarian students at Utrecht to stimulate private prayer and overcome coldness in the practice of religion in Hungary. János Mikolai Hegedüs translated four tracts on practical religion which he was able to have published at Utrecht in 1648. The first of these tracts was a selection of Bible verses on the fundamentals of Protestant faith, whilst the second stressed the importance of the Bible in building up faith. The third tract summarized the chief points of religion for heads of households, so that they could teach others around them, and the last detailed daily steps in the search for holiness in Christian life through private devotions and in struggles for personal sanctification.[20] The metaphor of a road, or path, to represent the life of an individual Christian recurred frequently in this practical theological literature. Imre Pápai Páriz translated *The Narrow Way*, which presented the striking image of a wide road leading down to hell and a narrow winding path up to heaven. János Somosi Petkó presented a 'true and perfect path' leading to happiness in a book of questions

---

[18] Ames, *The Marrow of Sacred Divinity*; [William Perkins], *The Work of William Perkins*, ed. I. Breward (Abingdon, 1970); Sprunger, *The Learned Doctor William Ames*; R. A. Muller, 'Perkins' A Golden Chaine: Predestinarian System or Schematized *ordo salutis*?', *Sixteenth Century Journal*, 9 (1978), 69–82; J. G. Moller, 'The Beginnings of Puritan Covenant Theology', *Journal of Ecclesiastical History*, 14 (1963), 46–67; K. L. Sprunger, 'Ames, Ramus and the Method of Puritan Theology', *Harvard Theological Review* (1966), 133–52; K. L. Sprunger, 'Technometria: A Prologue to Puritan Theology', *Journal of the History of Ideas*, 29 (1968), 115–22.

[19] Gisbert Voetius, 'Selectae Disputationes Theologiae', in J. W. Beardslee (ed.), *Reformed Dogmatics* (New York, 1965), 265–334, esp. 268–9, 282, 331.

[20] János Mikolai Hegedüs (tr.), *Az mennyei igazságnak tüzes oszlopa. Biblia tanui. Az istenes cselédeknek lelki praebendájók. Szentek napi száma* (Utrecht, 1648), quotation at 44; Kristóf Darholcz, *Novissima Tuba, azaz ítéletre serkentő utolsó trombitaszó* (Kassa, 1639).

and answers about true faith. Somosi wrote that as he sat in a church in London, he had noticed that someone in his pew was reading a book before the service. Somosi asked to borrow it and later decided it would be useful for a Hungarian audience, 'since which Christian nation has more need for such translations into its own language? Not one nation more than our own.' Mihály Felsőbányai also translated a work from English on the costs of the Christian path, which contained a selection of biblical quotations as an A to Z of practical things for a believer to remember.[21]

There was also a new emphasis in these books on personal prayer in private worship, and tracts were translated which offered advice about the role of prayer as part of an individual's daily practice of piety. Pál Medgyesi translated prayers by different English authors including William Ames to provide examples and rules for prayer by individuals and congregations. János Mihályko meanwhile compiled a collection of prayers to encourage fear of God, which he wrote believers could use in all conceivable circumstances in their daily lives. István Szokolyai also translated a collection of prayers from Dutch, again intended to assist the everyday needs of individual believers. Practical moralism also featured in the interests of this generation of Hungarian ministers. In 1649, for example, Mátyás Bónis Diószegi translated a work from English on the evils of excessive drinking. Drinking alcohol for any other reason than thirst, according to Diószegi, was a sure and certain path away from God towards immorality and destruction.[22]

Hungarian clergy became sharply divided between ardent supporters and detractors of the growing number of these books on practical theology. As ideas spread about personal piety as a sign of godliness, some Hungarian ministers began to think of their church as divided between a spiritual élite and the spiritually immature. This self-proclaimed élite seemed confident of their own election, thanks to the signs of piety in their daily lives which confirmed the operation of the covenant of grace. The concentration among practical theologians on this covenant of grace was also controversial in affecting attitudes towards the sacraments which, according to

[21] Imre Pápai Páriz (tr.), *Keskény ut* (Gyulafehérvár, 1657); János Somosi Petkó (tr.), *Igaz és tökéletes boldogságra vezérlő ut* (Sárospatak, 1656–8); Mihály Felsőbányai (tr.), *A léleknek uti költsége* (Utrecht, 1651).

[22] Pál Medgyesi, *Doce nos Orare et Praedicare* (Bártfa, 1650); Pál Medgyesi, *Scala Coeli, avagy egynehany bizonyos időkre alkalmasztatot istenes emelkedések es buzgo imadságok*, in *Szent Agoston vallasa* (Debrecen, 1632); János Mihályko (tr.), *Keresztyéni istenes és ájtatos imádságok* (Bártfa, 1640); István Szokolyai (tr.), *A szent Bibliának ótestamentumi könyveiből egybeszedegettetett . . . könyörgések. Sérelmes lelkeket gyógyitó balzsamom* (Leiden, 1648); Mátyás Diószegi Bónis (tr.), *Az részegesnak gyülölséges, utálatos és rettenetes állapota* (Leiden, 1649).

Perkins, were merely 'a prop and stay for faith to lean on'. István Geleji Katona, the Transylvanian superintendent, was extremely concerned by these trends and criticized what he saw as undue attention being paid by some ministers to practical theology and personal piety. Geleji stressed that a balance was needed between 'head knowledge' and 'heart knowledge', with dogmatic theology as important as practical theology. Geleji believed that teaching in schools and by ministers already provided a sensible mixture of these two elements, and that placing a novel emphasis on individual conscience and personal religiosity would prove detrimental to church unity. Some advocates within Hungary and Transylvania of higher standards of personal piety also came to be seen as tarnished by their contacts with English and Dutch advocates of practical theology, and began to be labelled as pharisaical puritans, and the next chapter will return to examine in greater depth debates about clergy puritanism in the Hungarian church.[23]

(II) CHURCH BUILDINGS AND SERVICES

The appearance of Reformed churches in Hungary and Transylvania reinforced a religious culture which was dominated by words and suspicious of the role of visual images. Church buildings were themselves among the first objects to undergo reformation. Reformed synods ordered that all decoration be cleared from churches and directed that ornamental windows, organs, candles, images, and altars should all be removed from church buildings. The 1554 Óvár synod called for the destruction of all images in churches, but was careful to leave the responsibility for carrying out this instruction to local civil authorities. The 1567 Debrecen articles also demanded that pictures be thrown out of churches, since they were 'marks of and opportunities for idolatry', whilst according to the 1570 Csenger synod in Szatmár county, pictures and altars were 'Papist filth' and must be removed immediately.[24]

It seems that the process of reforming church buildings largely proceeded in an orderly fashion, the speed of which was determined by the enthusiasm of local ministers and patrons, and with very little indication of popular iconoclastic zeal. Some sense of what level of decoration was felt appropriate for Reformed churches can be gained from descriptions of the new church completed at Bekecs in 1625. The building had little relief

---

[23] Geleji Katona, *Váltság-Titka*, i, introd.
[24] *Zsinatok végzései*, ed. Kiss, 574. *A szatmármegyében tartott négy első protestáns zsinat végzései*, ed. Á. Kiss (Budapest, 1877), 29, 61.

from its plain appearance with four clear windows and undecorated pillars. The simple services of dedication for the Bekecs church again reflected the character of the new building, with sermons of thanksgiving, songs from the Psalter, a service of communion, and another evening service after a celebratory lunch. Some of the sermons referred proudly to the pristine white walls of the new church, which were said to represent the cleansing power of both Christ's blood and the Holy Spirit to wash away the sins of repentant believers.[25]

If churches on the whole conformed to this austere style of whitewashed walls and spartan decoration, some symbols could still regularly be found in church buildings. These expressions of Hungarian Reformed culture were almost always related to biblical imagery and were often accompanied by Bible verses as forms of decoration. From the late sixteenth century the figure of a lamb, carrying a flag-pole in its front feet raising a banner decorated by a broad cross, was sometimes placed on frontispieces of books and on pulpits. The symbol of a pelican, sacrificially wounding itself in the breast to feed its young, featured on communion jugs and ceiling cassettes. The image of the opened Bible was also common, and the four apostles appeared on an embroidered cover for a communion table donated by Zsuzsanna Lórántffy to the new Reformed church at Kassa. Decoration also often appeared on the spires of churches to identify them as Reformed to the locality, but usually not employing a cross. Cockerels began to appear on Reformed church spires from the early seventeenth century, a reminder to congregations of Peter's denial of Christ. The new church at Bekecs had a cockerel on its spire, but elsewhere some Reformed churches had stars symbolizing the advent of Christ. Other congregations in border areas with Ottoman Hungary even employed crescent moons in an effort to protect their churches from destruction by Turkish raiding parties. The seventeenth-century spire of the church at Csaroda in eastern Hungary managed to cover all the options, combining a star, cockerel, and a crescent moon.[26]

Clergy were obliged by canons and by the decrees of provincial synods to adopt a new standard pattern of services inside their Reformed churches. Two church services were normally held on Sundays, with at least one major weekday service and shorter services of daily prayers. Ministers were instructed to explain the Scriptures clearly during these services, and

---

[25] Nagy Szabó, 'Marosvásárhely Memorial', 71–2; Segesvári, 'Kronika, 1606–1654', 190; Szenczi Molnár, *Consecratio Templi Novi, azaz az újonnan felépített bekecsi templomnak . . . megszentelésekor . . . tett prédikációk.*

[26] B. Takács, *Bibliai jelképek a magyar református egyházművészetben* (Budapest, 1986).

sermons or readings from the Bible in Hungarian became the central focus of acts of worship. The Reformed clergy hierarchy gradually succeeded in establishing a uniform conduct of services and rituals as editions of service order-books were published for each church province. Reformed superintendents and archdeacons proved very determined to prevent ministers either deviating from established patterns of worship or sustaining traditional religious ceremonies and customs. In 1634 the Transylvanian synod warned ministers against participating in any superstitious rituals taking place in or around church buildings, especially during funerals. In 1640 the synod demanded that ministers should take home the bread and wine left over after communion and consume it themselves to avoid any scandalous behaviour. Night services were also condemned as a papal custom, and were forbidden on Christmas Eve or at Easter. Changes to church liturgy and ceremony were sometimes permitted by the authorities. In 1642 the Transylvanian synod adopted 'the custom of other Reformed nations' in resolving that a Bible passage be read during all weekday prayer services, from the Old Testament at morning worship and from the New Testament in the evening.[27]

The church hierarchy remained completely intolerant of any unsanctioned changes to patterns of celebrations and church services. When accusations were raised during the 1640s of attempts to change customary religious holidays, the issue was swiftly taken up by the national church assembly which met at Szatmár in June 1646. Allegations were heard of how some ministers in the northern Tisza province wanted to abandon celebrations which were not on Sundays, including those at Christmas and Easter. Pál Medgyesi supported this change, arguing that the Genevan, French, and Scottish churches only held religious celebrations on Sundays. However, the national synod declared its support for the continued celebration of major Christian festivals. The 1649 canons of the Transylvanian church subsequently forbade any initiatives by individual ministers to alter public ceremonies, and ordered that anyone who wished to raise matters concerning the doctrine or liturgy of the church could only do so through their archdeacons or at a synod, or else they would face suspension from office. These canons compiled by István Geleji Katona also laid out in detail ministers' responsibilities in leading all aspects of public religious life. Clergy were instructed to be active in teaching, preaching, catechizing both boys and girls each week, celebrating festivals without superstition, conducting

[27] Melotai Nyilas, *Agenda*, repub. in 1622, 1634, 1653; Samarjai, *Agenda*; *Zsinatok végzései*, ed. Kiss, 73–285, 563–613; 'Az erdélyi közzsinatainak végzései', ed. Szilágyi, 1–9, 77–84, 473–9; B. Sörös, *A magyar liturgia története* (Budapest, 1904).

marriages, regularly visiting members of their congregation, and administering the sacraments.[28]

(III) BAPTISM AND COMMUNION

The Hungarian Reformed church retained infant baptism as one of its two sacraments, and standards for the administration of baptism were quickly established in articles for each church province. Synods insisted that ordinary water should be used in baptism, and that the sacrament should normally be conducted by a minister in a public place with the local congregation present. Whilst this form of ceremony suggested that baptism was a mark of membership of the visible church, seriously ill children could in fact be baptized at home but only by an ordained minister.[29] Given the somewhat confusing impression about the function of baptism engendered by these articles, it is hardly surprising that the conduct of the sacrament proved to be a source of ongoing controversy within the church. Despite the firm requirements laid down by canons, many nobles absolutely refused to present their healthy children for baptism in churches. Noble patrons frequently required Reformed ministers to perform the sacrament in the greater comfort and security from disease provided by their own homes, and Reformed clergy largely co-operated with these demands. In 1642 the Transylvanian synod gave way to threats from Szekler lords to have their children baptized by Catholic priests rather than abide by Reformed church rules. The synod formally agreed that Szekler church patrons could have their children baptized at home if they did not wish to bring them to church, although the synod ended with a show of defiance stating that 'in Christ there is no difference between servants and lords'.[30]

This convention of allowing sick children and the children of nobles to be baptized at home was challenged by a group of Reformed ministers in northern Hungary during the 1640s. In March 1645 the northern Tisza synod which met at Tállya heard reports that János Tolnai Dali, then Abaújvár archdeacon, was only prepared to conduct baptisms inside church buildings immediately after the Sunday service in the presence of the whole congregation. Tolnai was accused by some of his colleagues of making no allowance for cases of extreme necessity, when the parents of a sick child might want a baptism to be carried out at once in their own home.

---

[28] *Egyházi kánonok*, ed. Kiss, 1649 canons, nos. 34, 85; A. Kiss, 'Szánthay levele a puritánus Tholnay ügyében', *PEIL* 4 (1845), 1,141–3.

[29] *Zsinatok végzései*, ed. Kiss, 709–22, no. 12; *Egyházi kánonok*, ed. Kiss, 1649 canons, nos. 54–8.

[30] Juhász, *A székelyföldi református egyházmegyék*, 100.

Tolnai argued that since baptism marked the entry of a child into the body of the visible church, the congregation therefore needed to be present. Local claims that Tolnai believed some teaching was needed before baptism could take place raised suspicions that his opinions were infected by Anabaptist ideas. Tolnai was also charged with failing to seek the proper authority to alter existing rules governing baptismal services. The northern Tisza synod became more anxious about this situation when parents in Abaújvár county began to take their children to Lutheran ministers for immediate baptism, rather than wait for the next Reformed church service.[31]

News of this dispute in northern Hungary soon spread, and the eastern Tisza superintendent, Mihály Szánthai, wrote to István Bethlen in 1646 explaining that Tolnai refused to recognize emergency cases for baptism, and that many children were dying unbaptized, or their parents were going to Lutheran or Catholic priests. Pál Medgyesi then entered the debate, arguing that the notion of cases of extreme necessity was a Catholic superstition about the nature of baptism which the Reformed church ought not to have retained. Medgyesi quoted support from Johann Heinrich Bisterfeld that everywhere else in the Reformed world baptism was only conducted in public. Medgyesi censured Tolnai for acting without first gaining agreement for change, but argued that the hysterical reaction of the northern Tisza church to Tolnai's actions had made it a laughing-stock.[32]

The northern Tisza archdeacons decided to hold an investigation in order to ascertain exactly what changes Tolnai had made to the conduct of baptisms in Abaújvár. In February 1646 a council at Tállya heard witnesses relate Tolnai's instructions to local ministers that baptism must only be held before an assembled congregation. Tolnai was quoted as replying to objections against this 'new and untried thing', that 'the old decisions of the church wished it to be done thus, and other Christian countries live by this practice'. The minister at Göncruszka claimed that he had tried to defend traditional customs but that Tolnai responded by proclaiming: 'That's fine! If my father was blind, should I too be blind so that I could follow him?'[33] The results of the Tállya investigation were put before an area synod at Tokaj in February 1646, prompted to firm action by a letter

---

[31] 'Acta Synodi Nationalis', ff. 55ᵛ–6ᵛ.

[32] I. Révész, 'Adalék a magyar puritánok történetéhez', *Sárospataki Füzetek*, 2 (1858–9), 717–25; [Magyarországi], 'Adatok a magyarországi puritánus mozgalmak történetéhez', ed. J. Zoványi, in *MPEA* 10 (1911), 21; 'Szánthay levele a puritánus Tholnay ügyében', ed. Kiss, *PEIL* 4 (1845), 1,141–3; K. Császár, *Medgyesi Pál élete és müködése* (Budapest, 1911).

[33] MOL box 1907, ZEP (1638–51), 108–15, 129–33 ('Attestationes, Thállyai tanács' Feb. 1646); 'Adatok a magyarországi puritánus mozgalmak történetéhez', ed. Zoványi, 13–20.

from György I Rákóczi expressing his concern at rumours reaching Transylvania of events in Abaújvár. The Tokaj synod accused Tolnai of causing a great scandal and tumult in the church, and of the violent imposition of his innovatory rules on baptism in Abaújvár. The synod decided to suspend Tolnai from his post as archdeacon until the Szatmár national church assembly to be held in June that year.[34]

When this general assembly met at Szatmár, the delegation from Abaújvár was split between Tolnai and his supporters and defenders of traditional church practices led by János Ványai. Ványai put the case to the national synod that Tolnai had introduced novel restrictions on the procedure for holding baptisms in his district. Tolnai in response argued that any local congregation, as the visible church, needed to be present at all baptism services, whether on Sundays or during a mid-week service. Tolnai denied that he had behaved scandalously or done anything contrary to the canons of the church. Tolnai also claimed that he had sufficient authority as an archdeacon to introduce changes to religious ceremony in his district. A majority at the national synod, however, concluded that Tolnai had disturbed the peace of the church and he was removed from his post as archdeacon. The synod declared that infant baptism was to continue to be normally conducted in public, with exceptions allowed for sick children and respect to be shown for the prerogatives of the nobility.[35]

Calvinist orthodoxy on the sacrament of communion as a spiritual memorial of Christ's death was expressed in the liturgy followed by the Hungarian Reformed church. The normal procedure in communion services began with bread and wine being consecrated by the minister, to recognize the spiritual presence of Christ in the elements. The bread and wine was then distributed to the congregation following the pattern of the original Last Supper as accurately as possible. The canons of the Transylvanian church ordered communion to be held with 'holiness but no superstition' six times a year at Advent, Christmas, on Ash Wednesday, at Easter, on Ascension Day, and at Pentecost. The sacrament had to be announced by the minister at least eight days in advance to give communicants time to prepare for the service by examining their lives and seeking forgiveness for their sins. Those who were unable to judge their own standing before God were prohibited from taking part in the service. Church canons also ordered that the sacrament should only be administered outside the confines

---

34 'Acta Synodi Nationalis', ff. 62ᵛ–7ʳ, 102ᵛ–4ʳ.
35 'Acta Synodi Nationalis', ff. 114ᵛ–8ʳ, 122ᵛ–4ʳ, 137ʳ–8ᵛ, 151ᵛ, 155ʳ–6ʳ, 160ᵛ; 'Szánthay levele a puritánus Tholnay ügyében', ed. Kiss, *PEIL* 4 (1845), 1,141–3; Debreceni Ember, *Historia Ecclesiae Reformatae*, 409.

of church buildings to those who were seriously ill and unable to come to church.[36]

A major debate emerged between Reformed ministers during the 1650s over one liturgical detail of this communion service, on whether the consecrated elements of bread and wine should be raised once or twice in front of the congregation before their distribution. The first raising of the elements was contested by reform-minded ministers because it was thought to be a remnant of Catholic ceremony which held overtones of transubstantiation. Sámuel Lippai, one of the ministers at Sárospatak, argued that the first elevation of the elements was totally unnecessary, idolatrous, and not in line with Christ's example at the Last Supper. Lippai only accepted the second elevation of the bread and wine because this took place during the process of distributing the elements to the congregation. One of Lippai's colleagues at Sárospatak, András Váczi, accused him of doctrinal innovation, of disturbing church peace, and of puritanism. An unapologetic Lippai responded that, 'if I am a puritan, then Christ and Calvin have made me a puritan', and that 'puritans are the true Calvinists, and disciples of the Helvetic Confession'.[37]

A visitation of the church at Sárospatak by the Zemplén district authorities in 1655 revealed just how deep the divisions between the clergy there had become on this issue. Of the town's three ministers, two were committed to reforming the communion service. Both István Keresszeghi and Sámuel Lippai rejected any ceremony during the distribution of the communion elements which lacked direct biblical precedent. When questioned by the Zemplén archdeacon, Keresszeghi revealed that he would resign rather than celebrate communion according to existing church customs. The Zemplén archdeacon then asked Keresszeghi and Lippai why they took part in existing communion services if they objected so strongly to the liturgy, to which Lippai responded that, even if wafers had been served, they could have received them in true faith, since it was the celebrant who was at fault and not the communicants.[38]

The two leading Reformed clergymen of the 1650s were also divided over the exact details of communion ceremony. György Csulai, the Transylvanian superintendent, stoutly defended traditional ceremony against the criticisms of Pál Medgyesi, then chaplain to the dowager princess, Zsuzsanna Lórántffy. In March 1654 Csulai wrote to György II Rákóczi on

---

[36] *Egyházi kánonok*, ed. Kiss, 1649 canons, nos. 59–64.

[37] Sámuel Lippai, *Brevis dissertatio de quaestione an prior elevatio Panis at vini in Sacra Coena, in quibusdam Ecclesiis usitate legitime, observatur?* (Sárospatak, 1654); Sámuel Lippai, *Desperata causa prioris elevationis Panis et Vini in Sacra Coena* (Sárospatak, 1655), 82, 87.

[38] MOL box 1908, ZEP (1653–72), 53–6.

the differences which had arisen over the conduct of communion services, condemning Medgyesi for preaching against conventional liturgy and for introducing a new communion service on his own authority. Csulai wrote that if everyone copied Medgyesi's example, then there would soon be as many different styles of ceremony as there were ministers in the Hungarian church. Csulai considered that Medgyesi had failed to live up to the responsibilities imposed by his position in ignoring the boundary between public and private opinions on such difficult theological questions. Csulai recalled his experience at Heidelberg where, he claimed, David Pareus, Abraham Scultetus, and Hendrik Alting had received communion after the elements were raised during consecration. Csulai also quoted support from Bisterfeld that this form of communion liturgy was not against the instructions of Christ. Four days after receiving this letter Rákóczi forwarded Csulai's opinions to his mother, in an effort to counter Medgyesi's criticisms of the conventional administration of communion. With such strong support from the Transylvanian prince and superintendent, the leaders of the northern and eastern Tisza church provinces called a joint synod at Debrecen in May 1655 to attempt to curtail further debate on communion liturgy. At the synod Pál Medgyesi, János Tolnai Dáli, Sámuel Lippai, and István Keresszeghi were all charged with doctrinal and liturgical innovation and with disturbing church peace, and all four were suspended from their posts.[39]

Despite this bid to establish discipline and liturgical uniformity among the clergy, controversy continued to spread about the proper way to conduct communion services. In 1656 the eastern Tisza synod responded to demands for change by allowing for some local modifications of traditional sacramental ceremonies, albeit only with the consent of the proper regional authorities. Thanks to the intervention of Zsuzsanna Lórántffy, all the ministers suspended in 1655 were soon reinstated to their posts in 1656. The Sárospatak synod then asked Pál Medgyesi, János Tolnai Dali, Ferenc Veréczi, and János Porcsalmi to prepare a new service order for communion in the northern Tisza province. In the mean time Medgyesi also wrote to György II Rákóczi defending himself against the accusation that he had disturbed church peace. Medgyesi claimed that he had been consistent in his attitudes towards raising the communion elements, and that until 1655 he had never been contradicted for his administration of communion

39 [Rákóczi György II], 'Levelek és okiratok II. Rákóczy György fejedelem diplomácziai összeköttetései történetéhez', ed. S. Szilágyi *TT* (1889), 350–2; *A két Rákóczy György fejedelem családi levelezése*, ed. S. Szilágyi (Monumenta Hungariae Historica, 24; Budapest, 1875), 483.

services either by György Csulai, or by his predecessor, István Geleji Katona. Medgyesi also claimed that Csulai himself administered communion without 'the useless first raising' of the bread and wine. Medgyesi appealed to Rákóczi to suffer minor liturgical differences with charity and assured the prince that he was not attempting to construct a dissident church according to separate rites.[40]

When the four ministers completed the revised order for communion in the northern Tisza church, it did not provide a series of minute liturgical regulations but merely presented a pattern for communion services shorn of all possible superstitious overtones. Medgyesi and his colleagues suggested the use of prayers of confession drawn from the Scottish and Palatinate churches, and prayers of thanksgiving used by churches in Scotland, Geneva, the Dutch Republic, and the Palatinate. There was no mention in the service order of the need to elevate the bread and wine, instead describing how the celebrant would simply go to the communion table, uncover the bread, fill the chalice, call the communicants to stand around the table and then distribute the elements. The new service order was agreed for use across the northern Tisza province in 1658 despite the opposition of the Abaújvár archdeacon, János Zebegnyei. The synod, however, conceded that changes were not to be uniformly imposed on every congregation in the region.[41]

The northern Tisza synod tried to defuse the problems surrounding communion services by devolving responsibility onto individual ministers and congregations to find locally acceptable solutions. However, some parishes across the region proved unable to reach agreement and disputes continued. At Bodrogkeresztúr, the town's ministers were split over the conduct of communion, with Márton Dobriczi complaining that his colleague Mihály Rápóti consecrated the communion elements before their distribution, instead of only saying that the bread and wine were a memorial of Christ's death. Rápóti had also been a minister at Tarczal before János Tolnai Dali managed to have him moved on for failing to support liturgical changes there. At Bodrogkerestúr, Dobriczi reported Rápóti to the church's patron, Zsuzsanna Lórántffy, for failing to adopt Medgyesi's new communion liturgy, and Rápóti was subsequently forced to leave the town. At Bereczk, on the other hand, the local noble patron refused to accept communion offered by a reform-minded minister, István Pataki, after he

[40] 'Medgyesi Pál levelei', ed. S. Szilágyi, *EPK* (1877), 3–4, 17–18, 29–30; ZEP (1653–72), 133; MOL box 1883, Tiszántúl egyházkerület levéltára kerületi jegyzőkönyvek (1629–), vol. 1, 93.

[41] Pál Medgyesi, *Liturgia sacra coenae; azaz, Urvacsora kiosztásában való rend* (Sárospatak, 1658); ZEP (1653–72), 177–8; Keserű (ed.), *Adattár 1*, 496–8.

had proposed changes to the communion service.[42] With both ministers
and noble patrons divided on the issue, it proved impossible for the northern Tisza church to arrive at a commonly accepted liturgy for communion
services. Reforming ministers continued to cite their experience of foreign
Calvinist churches as a precedent for change, showing their commitment
to adopt a model of best international Reformed practice in the conduct of
the sacraments and other elements of public worship.

(IV) SERMONS, PRAYER, AND MUSIC

Sermons formed the main focus of Sunday and some weekday church services, and reading and explaining the scriptures were at the heart of the
clergy's efforts to teach their congregations. During the early seventeenth
century leading Hungarian ministers such as Péter Alvinczi, Albert
Szenczi Molnár, and István Geleji Katona followed sixteenth-century reformers in publishing collections of their sermons as examples for other
ministers to copy.[43] Whilst many parish ministers simply read out such sermons, rather than prepare their own material, the rare glimpses available of
the general quality of preaching during this period tend to confirm that
further improvements were sometimes badly needed. During local visitations by senior clergy, congregations sometimes complained about the
lack of sermons, of poor and infrequent preaching, and even on very rare
occasions of ministers preaching whilst drunk.[44] Leading ministers agreed
on the need to improve the quality of preaching, but disagreed over the
most appropriate style, structure, and content for sermons. The combatants in these arguments were broadly divided into two camps, with conservatives and traditionalists led by István Geleji Katona pitched against
innovators and reformers led by Pál Medgyesi.

Geleji set out his views on homiletics in several mammoth collections of
his own sermons and in the canons which he compiled for the Transylvanian church in 1649. According to Geleji, all ministers should give sermons
four times a week, on both Sunday services and during services on Wednesdays and Fridays.[45] Geleji urged clergy in Transylvania to preach from
a rota of texts from the Bible provided by the province, and encouraged

---

[42] ZEP (1653–72), 197–200, 213, 305–7. Tiszántúl Reformed Church Province Library
MS Collection (Debrecen), R. 540: Önéletrajz és lelkészi napló Hajdúnánás, 1627–89;
'Nánási emlékirat', ed. L. Varga, *Sárospataki Füzetek*, 2 (1858–9), 165–75, 689–98, 785–800.

[43] Szenczi Molnár (tr.), *Postilla Scultetica*; Péter Alvinczi, *Postilla* (2 vols.; Kassa, 1633–4);
István Selyei Balog, *Utitárs* (Nagyvárad, 1657).

[44] 'Miskolczi Csulyak jegyzőkönyvei', ed. Zoványi, 375–6, 380–1.

[45] *Egyházi kánonok*, ed. Kiss, 1649 canons, nos. 39–42.

ministers to be brief, which to Geleji meant sermons of not longer than one hour. Geleji described the main aims of preaching as trying to resolve problems of faith and to comfort and improve congregations. The Transylvanian superintendent offered a plan for ministers to follow when composing sermons, beginning with an introduction, followed by a summary of the main argument, a presentation of that week's set Bible passage, cross-analysis with other texts, an examination of the uses of the passage to learn more about God, followed by a conclusion. Geleji stressed the need for a balance in sermons between, on the one hand, presenting orthodox doctrine and its uses in combating confessional opponents and, on the other hand, offering applications of doctrine for believers to put into practice in their daily lives.[46]

Geleji was concerned about the unbalanced stress on individual piety which he perceived in the sermons of clergy who were enthusiastic to promote practical theology. Geleji thought that ministers such as Pál Medgyesi concentrated far too much on matters of conscience and neglected other branches of faith, leading to doubt among weaker members of congregations. Geleji presented Medgyesi as a pharisee, seeking perfect standards of behaviour in others and in the process making salvation seem impossible for many. Geleji suggested that sermons only on morality and the practicalities of personal religion, without any examination of true doctrine, could lead congregations towards Catholicism or atheism. Geleji admitted to preaching in a moralistic way to his sophisticated court audience a few times a year, but claimed that sermons about conscience and piety would prove too subtle for most peasant audiences. Geleji's views were also reflected in the conclusions of the 1646 Szatmár national synod, which commented that preachers' first duty was to offer doctrinal instruction to their congregations, and that sermons should only occasionally dwell on questions related to everyday morality.[47]

Pál Medgyesi responded to this criticism with his own work on homiletics, in which he maintained that knowledge gained through sermons was useless without the ability to apply that knowledge in daily life. Medgyesi used mostly English sources to support his case, including William Perkins's *Cases of Conscience*, William Ames's *Marrow of Sacred Divinity*, and

---

[46] Geleji Katona, *Praeconium Evangelicum*, i, introd.; István Geleji Katona, *Váltság-Titka*, iii, introd.; L. Ravasz, 'A magyar protestáns igehirdetés a xvii. században', *Theológiai Szaklap* (1913), 262–84.

[47] Geleji Katona, *Váltság-Titka*, i, introd.; *Egyházi kánonok*, ed. Kiss, 1649 canons, no. 12; D. Borbáth, 'Medgyesi Pál homiletikája és Geleji Katona Istvánnal folytatott homiletikai vitája', *Református Szemle* (1961), 282–93; L. Gál, *Geleji Katona István igehirdetése* (Debrecen, 1939), 211–17.

the 1644 *Directory of Public Worship* of the Westminster Assembly. Medgyesi argued that ministers should not be forced to follow set weekly readings as the basis for their sermons, rather allowing the 'testimony' of any sermon to be determined by the circumstances and needs of each congregation. Medgyesi described the function of preaching as the presentation, explanation, and revelation of the practical uses of God's word. He also identified problem areas with the current style of preaching employed by many Hungarian ministers. According to Medgyesi, ministers generally preached for too long, failed to introduce their sermons, explained many areas of faith badly or not at all, did not examine cases of personal conscience, and did not use popular stories and examples to aid understanding. Medgyesi argued in favour of a more practical style of preaching about individual piety and the moral life of believers, also warning ministers that their personal conduct should reflect the words which they spoke from the pulpit. Medgyesi also defended himself against Geleji's charges that he constantly nagged his congregation and concentrated on pricking his listeners' consciences. Medgyesi wrote that he could not understand how his preaching style could be thought by Geleji to lead towards a relapse into Catholicism, since at the same time he was accused of puritanism in trying to rid the church of all Catholic survivals in the church's liturgy and ceremony.[48]

Alongside readings from the Bible and sermons based on those texts, the other major element of church services was prayer. Canons from the Transylvanian province ordered that services of prayers should be conducted in each congregation twice daily, at six in the morning and again at two in the afternoon. Collections of prayers were printed for ministers to use at these services, such as Albert Szenczi Molnár's 1621 prayer-book which included prayers written by Calvin and Bullinger.[49] The traditional centrepiece of public prayer in Hungarian church services was the repetition by the whole congregation of the Lord's Prayer, but this practice was to become highly controversial. Pál Medgyesi, who had tried to promote private prayer in *The Practice of Piety*, also questioned the function of public prayer and the place of the Lord's Prayer in church services. Medgyesi suggested that the details of the different requests contained within the Lord's Prayer ought to be completely understood by every member of a congregation before they were allowed to recite the words during public worship.

[48] Pál Medgyesi, *Doce nos Orare et Praedicare* (Bártfa, 1650); I. Bartók, 'Medgyesi Pál: Doce Praedicare', *ITK* 85 (1981), 1–16.

[49] Szenczi Molnár, *Imádságos könyvecske*; *Egyházi kánonok*, ed. Kiss, 1649 canons, no. 46; G. Incze, *A magyar református imádság a xvi. és xvii. században* (Debrecen, 1931), 42–56, 144–58.

Medgyesi was not alone in expressing concern about the dangers of repeating a formula of words which might be perceived by church-goers as having some magical significance. István Komáromi Szvertán also published an examination of the purpose of saying the Lord's Prayer during services, which he translated from William Ames's *Marrow of Sacred Divinity*.[50]

These attempts to consider the role of the Lord's Prayer in church services provoked a storm of debate during the 1650s. In 1653 András Váczi, minister first at Sárospatak and then at Szepsi, published a ferocious attack against Komáromi's translation of Ames's opinions about the Lord's Prayer. Váczi also used this opportunity to lash out against a generation of Hungarian pietists and puritans who, he believed, had been trained at Franeker University and in England. According to Váczi, Ames had taught at Franeker that the church was not bound to use the Lord's Prayer and that too much attention was paid to its words rather than to their meaning. Váczi demanded that Reformed clergy, whilst free to use other prayers in worship, should not abandon the customary recitation of the Lord's Prayer both before and after the sermon. Váczi claimed that innovators already only allowed the Lord's Prayer to be said once after the sermon as a first step towards abandoning its public repetition altogether.[51]

János Tolnai Dali responded to this attack on his former teacher Ames, by arguing that Váczi had falsely represented Ames's opinions, and that Ames only opposed endlessly repeating the Lord's Prayer because of the grave danger of superstition. Tolnai also defended Hungarian ministers who wished to introduce reforms to patterns of church worship against Váczi's accusation of innovation. Tolnai cited a 1652 decision by the archdeacons of the northern Tisza province that innovation in the church should be taken to mean a complete mutation and reformation of doctrine and liturgy, and not to mean any smaller changes which could be described as corrections.[52] Váczi replied to Tolnai in a bad-tempered and personal attack, angrily denouncing Tolnai as trying to destroy the good order of the church. Váczi insisted that whilst congregations were not limited to using the Lord's Prayer and could use a range of prayers, Tolnai and his supporters wanted totally to prevent the use of the Lord's Prayer in all public services. Váczi reported that Márton Tállyai, the minister at Beregszász, had

---

[50] Medgyesi, *Doce nos Orare et Praedicare*; István Komaromi Szvertán, *Mikoron imádkoztok ezt mondgyatok az az: Az uri imadsagnak . . . magyarázattya* (Nagyvárad, 1652).

[51] András Váczi, *A' Mi-Atyanknak avagy minden-napi imadsággal való élésnek állatása és meg-óltalmazása e' mostani időbéli tanetóknak ellenvetések ellen* (Kassa, 1653).

[52] János Tolnai Dali, *Daneus Rácai* (Sárospatak, 1654), 1–123.

told him that Tolnai never used the Lord's Prayer in his own home, and taught that it was a form of a prayer not a real prayer in itself.[53] These arguments about customs of communal prayer in church services, as with disputes about the conduct of the sacraments and styles of preaching, quickly became bound up with fractious clashes between leading clergy. However, such divisions also reflected broader disagreement on the importance of the example set by foreign Calvinist churches, and whether impurity or disorder posed the greater danger to the Reformed cause in Hungary and Transylvania.

Reformed churches across Europe were generally uneasy about using music in church services. Calvin had only allowed the unaccompanied singing of psalms at Geneva, a concession granted because Calvin thought of the psalms as prayers set to music. Calvin wrote in the foreword to the 1543 edition of the Genevan Psalter that singing psalms had a special power which allowed individuals to achieve a form of communion with God and the elect company of heaven. Others within the Reformed camp were even more proscriptive, and singing was not permitted at all in Zurich's churches until the end of the sixteenth century. In the Hungarian church the 1567 Debrecen synod affirmed the place of singing as a corporate activity in church services, but at the same time decried Papist 'howling' because it lacked any sense or meaning. The Debrecen articles therefore stressed the need for congregational singing to be in the vernacular and unaccompanied by any musical instruments. So-called 'graduals' of traditional antiphons, sacred songs, and hymns were collected from Latin sources into books of church music and praises, and were carefully screened to protect against any infiltration of Catholic ideas. The most successful of these hymnals was compiled by György Gönczi Kovács, whose collection was first published at Debrecen in 1592 and reprinted eleven times before 1655.[54]

In 1607 Albert Szenczi Molnár translated the Psalms into Hungarian verses, and this Hungarian Psalter was republished eight times before 1655. In 1608, 1,500 copies of Molnár's Psalter had been printed at Hanau

---

53 András Váczi, *Replica; azaz, Tolnai Dali Janosnak csufos és vádos maga és mások mentésére való valasz-tétel* (Kassa, 1654), 55–194.

54 György Gönczi Kovács, *Keresztyéni énekek* (Debrecen, 1592); *Zsinatok végzései*, ed. Kiss, 545–6, 574; K. Csomasz Tóth, *A református gyülekezeti éneklés* (Budapest, 1950), 127–54. Calvin's foreword to the 1543 *Genevan Psalter* is printed in in C. Garside, 'The Origins of Calvin's Theology of Music: 1536–1543', *Transactions of the American Philosophical Society*, 69 (1979), 31–3; H. Koenigsberger, 'Music and Religion in Early Modern European History', in his *Politicians and Virtuosi. Essays in Early Modern History* (London, 1986), 179–210; H. P. Clive, 'The Calvinist Attitude to Music, and Its Literary Aspects and Sources', *Bibliothèque d'Humanisme et Renaissance*, 19 (1957), 80–102.

with the support of András Asztalos, Molnár's Nagyszombat patron, and the Psalter reappeared in 1612 as an appendix to the Oppenheim reprint of Gáspár Károlyi's Bible. Molnár's translation of the Psalms was based on French verses composed for the Genevan church by Clément Marot and Theodore Beza, but since Molnár could not read French he worked from a 1573 German translation. Molnár composed his verses at the Frankfurt library of Clemens Dubois, minister to French Calvinist refugees there, and he probably gained from Dubois's familiarity with the original French version. Molnár certainly used the original settings for the Genevan Psalter, many of which were written by Louis Bourgeois. These tunes were intentionally simple in order to allow congregations clearly to hear and understand the words, which accorded with the principles behind the use of the Psalms as prayers in Genevan services.[55]

Molnár's attempt to render the messages conveyed by the Psalms of a militant faith, of perseverance in adversity, and of joy in deliverance, was a linguistic triumph. Molnár wrote of his hard work to transform 'the existing verses of little French verbs into verses with long Hungarian verbs'. Initially the French tunes which Molnár employed were poorly received. András Asztalos wrote to Molnár in 1608 that the tunes were too difficult for Hungarians to follow. Asztalos wrote again in 1609 that Hungarians' ignorance of music was a block to the popular reception of the Psalter, and that it would have been better if Molnár had used more familiar Hungarian music. Molnár had in fact also included several dozen 'familiar short hymns' alongside the Psalms from collections of worship songs compiled by Gál Huszár in 1561 and by Péter Bornemisza in 1582, indicating that he did not accept any firm restriction on employing other sorts of music as well as Psalms in church services.[56]

By the early seventeenth century a variety of music was available for use in church services, and divisions quickly arose between ministers over which form of church music was most appropriate for Reformed worship, and over the degree to which Molnár's Psalter should replace traditional songs. This debate intensified after 1636 when István Geleji Katona finished the work of János Keserüi Dajka, his predecessor as Transylvanian superintendent, and completed an Old Gradual of hymns and songs. Geleji's hymnal was more comprehensive than any previous compilation of traditional church music, and two hundred copies of this work were

55 *Szenci Molnár művei*, ed. Vásárhelyi and Tolnai, 49–154; Albert Szenczi Molnár, *Psalterium Ungaricum* (Herborn, 1607).
56 *Szenczi Molnár Albert levelezése*, ed. Dézsi, 297–9, 318–19. *Szenczi Molnár művei*, ed. Vásárhelyi and Tolnai, 592; Szenczi Molnár, *Psalterium Ungaricum*, foreword.

printed and sent out to Transylvanian congregations, each signed by the prince himself. Geleji wrote in the introduction that he had deliberately copied the best practices of foreign Reformed churches' congregational singing, and tried to eliminate all Catholic survivals in his choices of musical praises. The Old Gradual did not include Molnár's translation of the psalms, instead using prose versions from Károlyi's Bible.[57] Geleji's collection of church music was generally not warmly received by Transylvanian congregations, whilst enthusiasm for Molnár's Psalter grew to rival the traditional church music of gradual collections. In 1643 an anxious Transylvanian synod restricted use of the Psalter to just once or twice during weekday services and forbade its use altogether on Sundays. In 1649 the new Transylvanian canons, drawn up by Geleji, dictated that graduals must form the basis of church music with Molnár's Psalter relegated to a merely supplementary role.[58]

Perhaps partly because of Geleji's association with traditional music, singing the verses and French tunes of Molnár's Psalter became linked with those who wished to reform aspects of traditional ceremony in public worship. János Tolnai Dali used Molnár's Psalter extensively when director of the school at Sárospatak, and as archdeacon in Abaújvár. Tolnai was indeed accused of compelling the use of the Psalms to French tunes, and of abandoning traditional church music altogether.[59] András Váczi viewed this as yet another example of Tolnai's liturgical innovations. Váczi also objected to Molnár's Psalter because it diverged from traditional forms of singing and used French tunes instead of Hungarian ones. Váczi wrote that there was much prettier music for the Psalms than the Genevan tunes, and that local music was easier for congregations to learn.[60] Complaints about church music were also raised during the 1660 visitation of Sárospatak, when one of the ministers, Péter Szathmári Baka, was accused of not wanting to sing any paraphrases of the Psalms other than those translated by Molnár to French tunes. Supporters of liturgical reform were strongly influenced by their experience of western Calvinist church life and were no doubt aiming to repeat the popular success of psalm-singing among Calvinists elsewhere. However, singing the Psalms to the signature tunes of the Genevan church also became a badge of identity in Hungary for those, such as Tolnai and Szathmári, who wished to declare their allegiance to the

---

57 István Geleji Katona and János Keserüi Dajka, *A keresztyén hitnek igazságához intéztetett . . . öreg graduál* (Gyulafehérvár, 1636).

58 'Az erdélyi közzsinatainak végzései', ed. Szilágyi, 1–9, 77–84, 473–9; *Egyházi kánonok*, ed. Kiss, 1649 canons, no. 98.

59 ZEP (1638–51), 61.

60 Váczi, *A' Mi-Atyank*, 26–7; Váczi, *Replica*, 114.

cause of further reform of public worship and ceremony in the Reformed church.[61]

Sixteenth-century Hungarian reformers had declared their commitment to Calvinist theology and introduced an avowedly Reformed pattern of worship and ceremony to church services. Increased contact with the rest of the Calvinist world during the early seventeenth century bolstered support for Reformed doctrinal orthodoxy within the Hungarian church, but it also introduced Hungarian and Transylvanian student ministers to differences of emphasis on the importance of personal religiosity and piety in the practice of Reformed religion. Students encountered different styles of public worship across the Calvinist world, and some became committed to a second wave of reformation in the Hungarian church. Senior clergy responded to the unsanctioned reform of aspects of public worship with anxious conservatism. Dark suspicions were expressed about the supposed sectarian intentions of so-called innovators. András Váczi thought that innovators who altered sacramental liturgy, disparaged the Lord's Prayer, massacred the psalms with foreign tunes, and abandoned festivals approved by the Helvetic Confession also wanted to replace the existing authority of superintendents and archdeacons with presbyterian church government.[62] An anonymous tract published at Sárospatak in 1654 accused innovators of being puritans, Independents, Arians, and Anabaptists, who acted with 'pharisaical holiness' merely 'under the pretext of the Helvetic Confession'. Innovators at Sárospatak, it was claimed, did not use traditional church music in their services, did not read the set biblical texts and diocesan prayers, denounced festivals, refused to kneel if Christ was named, approved of adult baptism, and called 'popish' the conventional conduct of communion.[63]

The agenda supported by János Tolnai Dali, Pál Medgyesi, and others to promote personal piety, reform the conduct of the sacraments, and cleanse church services from every possible vestige of Catholic influence, seemed to Hungarian traditionalists to jeopardize the Reformed church's balanced position between the tyranny and idolatry of the Catholic church and the anarchy of Protestant sectarianism. János Tolnai Dali meanwhile opposed the superstition which he saw in many aspects of traditional

---

[61] ZEP (1638–51), 305–7; B. B. Diefendorf, 'The Huguenot Psalter and the Faith of French Protestants in the Sixteenth Century', in B. B. Diefendorf and C. Hesse (eds.), *Culture and Identity in Early Modern Europe (1500–1800)* (Michigan, 1993), 41–63.

[62] Váczi, *A' Mi-Atyank*, 100.

[63] [Rákóczi György II], 'Levelek és okiratok II. Rákóczy György fejedelem diplomácziai összeköttetései történetéhez', ed. Szilágyi, 475–9.

church services, and ridiculed what he described as lukewarm religiosity. Tolnai placed himself within international Calvinist orthodoxy against conservative opponents who, he claimed, were defending Catholic survivals in their customary ceremonies.[64] Party labels were loosely employed in these debates over the value of practical theology and need for reforms of church services. Initially, a connection had been perceived between supporters of ceremonial innovation in Hungary and Dutch Arminianism. Correspondence in August 1638 between István Keresszegi Herman, superintendent of the eastern Tisza province, and István Miskolczi Csulyak, archdeacon in Zemplén, planned measures to obstruct any infiltration of Arminian ideas via student ministers returning from study in the Dutch Republic.[65] Supporters of practical theology and liturgical reform in the Hungarian church were later strongly, and more accurately, associated with English puritanism. Those who were labelled as puritans flatly rejected their opponents' use of the term. Pál Medgyesi wrote that some ministers understood as puritan 'and as bad, those things which they have not learned and did not know, and as good, only those things which come from them', concluding that 'puritanism is therefore a holy heresy'.[66]

During the early seventeenth century serious divisions emerged among Reformed clergy between those whose experience, both at home and abroad, committed them to uphold traditional church authority and customs, and those who wished to carry forward religious reformation by developing personal piety and advancing changes to public worship. Raising the elements once rather than twice during communion, or saying the Lord's Prayer once rather than twice during church services, marked out the boundary between those who wished to push forward with further reform and those who preferred to consolidate what had already been achieved by the Reformed church. This debate became linked with differing views on the correct form of church government, as reformers challenged the church authorities' right to determine the outcome of disputes about public worship. The next chapter will examine this presbyterian challenge to traditional hierarchical authority in the Hungarian church and consider the rise of puritanism among Reformed clergy.

[64] Tolnai Dali, *Daneus Rácai*.
[65] ZEP (1638–51), 309–11. MOL box 1883, Tiszántúl jegyzőkönyvek, vol. 1, 77–80; box 1907, Református . . . levéltárak régebbi könyvanyaga, ff. 474–7.
[66] Medgyesi, *Doce nos Orare et Praedicare*, introd.

6
Hungarian Puritans and Presbyterians

Reformed clergy in Hungary and Transylvania struggled to reconcile different views about the future direction of their church during the early seventeenth century. Whilst many ministers remained entirely satisfied with the achievements of the sixteenth-century reformation, some clergy became dedicated to a further wave of religious reform and wished to adopt the best practices of sister Calvinist churches elsewhere on the Continent. Conservatives meanwhile wanted to silence internal debates which threatened to destabilize the church and undermine its close relationship with Transylvania's princes. These tensions came to the surface at various synods across the region, when accusations were raised that some ministers were importing doctrinal and liturgical innovations and disturbing the peace of the church. Sharp conflicts particularly arose between leading ministers in the northern Tisza province of north-eastern Hungary, where uncertainty and paranoia about the intentions of opponents bred a polemic language of party labelling. The nature of this labelling was closely related to the perception that ideas about reforming the church's doctrine, liturgy, and government had emerged from connections between Hungarian clergy and foreign Calvinists. Contact between student ministers and some Protestants in the Dutch Republic and England therefore brought an anxious and defensive reaction from the church hierarchy at home. Whilst there was no suggestion of completely breaking ties with western co-religionists, there were attempts at the 1631 Nyírbátor synod and 1638 Debrecen synod to restrict student ministers' access to foreign ideas, especially puritanism, and to limit and control connections with western Calvinists.[1]

Despite these regulations, some Reformed ministers in Hungary and Transylvania were accused of being puritans from the late 1630s. This chapter will focus in particular on the troubled career in the northern Tisza church of János Tolnai Dali, who was among the first to be identified as

---

[1] MOL box 1907, ZEP (1629–45), 313; box 1883, Tiszántúl egyházkerületi jegyzőkönyvek, vol. 1, 77, 650.

a puritan on his return from England in 1638. As we have already seen advocates, such as Tolnai, of a practical Calvinist theology which high-lighted personal religiosity and supporters of reforms to the conduct of church services were sometimes dubbed puritans. The term 'puritan' was also often used in the Hungarian church as a term of abuse to denote scandalous attitudes and behaviour, but those clergy who were labelled as puritans came to adopt the term to indicate a sense of their superior commitment to Reformed religion. The charge of puritanism was also related in Hungary and Transylvania to issues concerning church government and to the obedience which ministers owed to their clergy superiors. During this period advocates of an episcopal style of government clashed repeatedly with presbyterians over the scriptural basis for a clergy hierarchy. A campaign led by Pál Medgyesi in the 1650s aimed to supplant the regime of archdeacons and superintendents with largely autonomous lay presbyteries in every parish. Presbyterianism was, however, roundly rejected by the clergy leadership as a dangerous threat to good order in the church. These disputes over ecclesiastical authority in Hungary and Transylvania were contested not only by Reformed ministers but also amongst members of the ruling princely family. The Rákóczi princes consistently opposed any changes to the established pattern of church government, partly motivated by fears of a potential challenge to their own authority by so-called 'Independents'.

(I) JÁNOS TOLNAI DALI AND HUNGARIAN PURITANISM

A 'League of Piety' was signed in London in February 1638 by János Tolnai Dali and nine other Hungarian Reformed student ministers. This League committed its signatories to restore purity to the Hungarian church and to get rid of all hierarchical authority among its clergy. After seven years abroad financed by his home church at Nagyvárad, Tolnai returned to Hungary in 1638 and was appointed to teach at Sárospatak College at the heart of the Rákóczi family's northern Hungarian estates. Fears were almost immediately aroused that he intended to use his position at the college as a 'Trojan horse' for his reforming ideas. Since there was no superintendent in the northern Tisza church, responsibility to control Tolnai's activities fell to the Zemplén archdeacon, István Miskolczi Csulyak. Miskolczi and István Tolnai, chaplain to György I Rákóczi, sought János Tolnai Dali's compliance with their demands for obedience. They required Tolnai to break up the London League and subscribe to conditions agreed by a joint synod of the two Tisza church provinces which had met at Debrecen in September 1638. These included promises to teach only according to the doctrine of the Second Helvetic Confession and the Heidelberg Catechism, and to recognize the authority of the Zemplén archdeacon and the validity of traditional patterns of church government.[2]

The Zemplén church leaders personally confronted János Tolnai Dali with their demands. During this meeting, Miskolczi claimed that Tolnai had been mixing with radical sects in the Dutch Republic and England, and István Tolnai challenged him to agree that he was infected with puritanism. János Tolnai Dali responded that he was indeed a puritan and recognized the authority of clergy superiors only according to human, but not according to divine, laws. János Tolnai Dali's behaviour was viewed by Miskolczi as histrionic and disrespectful, and he accused Tolnai of being a pharasaical libertine. Miskolczi asserted that Tolnai would not be allowed to take up his teaching post at Sárospatak until the London League was broken up, and until he showed himself willing to submit to the established authorities of the church.[3] In December 1638 Miskolczi presented the Zemplén county noble assembly with the local church's concerns over Tolnai's appointment. The Zemplén deputy sheriff, István Bátkai, at first responded that it seemed Tolnai and other puritans only wanted to live pure lives and had dedicated themselves totally to God, whilst men like Miskolczi were caught up in worldly things. Miskolczi nevertheless eventually managed to persuade the noble assembly that Tolnai must be asked to adhere to the conditions of appointment laid down by the Zemplén church.[4]

János Tolnai Dali finally accepted these conditions in April 1639 but, according to Miskolczi, began to break them the very next day. In his opening speech to the Sárospatak College, Tolnai attacked the general standards of his fellow ministers. Tolnai then introduced radical changes to the school syllabus, and his general conduct at Sárospatak also led to growing opposition to his appointment.[5] When István Geleji Katona heard of the disputes surrounding Tolnai, he wrote to György I Rákóczi of his astonishment at the presumption of students returning from England of whom not one who 'had not imbibed some singularity' in religion. According to

---

[2] 'Acta Synodi Nationalis', f. 28. [Magyarországi], 'Adatok a magyarországi puritánus mozgalmak történetéhez', ed. Zoványi, 1–25.

[3] ZEP (1629–45), 228–9, 314–16; Debreceni Ember, *Historia Ecclesiae Reformatae*, 388–9; 'Magyar protestáns egyház történeti kutfők', ed. P. Finkei, *Sárospataki Füzetek*, 1 (1857–8), 335–49.

[4] 'Acta Synodi Nationalis', ff. 28–47.

[5] ZEP (1629–45), 228–9, 313–18, 323–7, 348.

Geleji, those students who had gone to England did not want to be dependent on church superiors, and he advised Rákóczi that Tolnai should be removed altogether from Sárospatak College. Geleji was perhaps particularly embarrassed about Tolnai's behaviour, since his brother Gáspár, a Reformed archdeacon in eastern Hungary, was Tolnai's father-in-law. Geleji also warned the prince that, although Tolnai seemed at that time to be the greatest danger to good order in the church, there were likely to be others watching for encouragement to attempt greater innovatory reforms.[6]

Archdeacon Miskolczi wrote to György I Rákóczi appealing for Tolnai's dismissal, and in December 1640 the prince declared his strong support for the Zemplén church leadership. Rákóczi stated that, unless Tolnai gave an indication that he would obey his superiors in future, he would be dismissed from his post at Sárospatak by the end of the year.[7] Tolnai managed to offer sufficient guarantees on his future conduct to ensure that he stayed at Sárospatak temporarily, but the Zemplén church leadership remained highly suspicious of him. In November 1642 Miskolczi wrote again to György I Rákóczi, asking for Tolnai's immediate dismissal because of his 'new and peculiar opinions', and Tolnai was finally forced to resign in December 1642.[8] Although György I Rákóczi eventually lost confidence in Tolnai, other members of the Rákóczi family continued to support him. In 1644 Tolnai was invited to act as chaplain to Zsigmond Rákóczi, and with Zsigmond's support Tolnai became a minister at Tokaj, and then in 1645 was elevated to become one of the four archdeacons of the northern Tisza province in Abaújvár.

Tolnai's activities as archdeacon, and the instructions which he gave to ministers in Abaújvár on the appropriate liturgy for church services, led to disciplinary procedures being brought against him within a year. A synod at Gönc in January 1646 heard accusations that Tolnai had introduced ceremonial innovations in Abaújvár and taught that each minister was like a bishop in his own parish. These allegations were investigated further by a council held at Tállya in February 1646. At this hearing Tolnai claimed that he had not introduced his reforms in Abaújvár by the authority of his position as archdeacon, but rather with the encouragement and 'warming' of the Holy Spirit. This response only added to charges which

---

[6] MOL box 1907, Liber Reditum Ecclesiasticum Comitatus Zempleniensis 1623, 466–70.

[7] [Rákóczi György I], 'I. Rákóczy György fejedelem levelezése Tolnai István sárospataki pappal', ed. Szilágyi, 1, 388–90.

[8] ZEP (1629–45), 382–5, 388–9, 392–4, 397–9, 424–6; 'Miskolczi István és Görgei János esperesek levelei I. Rákóczy Györgyhez', ed. Szilágyi, 267–9.

were reported against Tolnai to a joint synod of the eastern and northern Tisza church provinces held at Tokaj on 14 February 1646.[9] At this Tokaj synod János Ványai denounced Tolnai, his former colleague, for challenging the authority of clergy superiors, for showing contempt for his fellow ministers in unprovoked attacks, and for having suspicious and heterodox opinions after his contacts with Anabaptists and puritans in England. Tolnai defended himself against the charge of having violated his position as archdeacon in Abaújvár and argued that, if he was doctrinally suspect because of contact with puritans abroad, then the whole Hungarian ministry should also be suspect. The Tokaj synod decided that Tolnai had contravened church articles on baptism and had offended his congregation, and Tolnai and six other ministers were suspended from the Abaújvár ministry pending the Szatmár general church assembly. The Tokaj synod also imposed an oath to be taken by all ministers, who were to swear their innocence in recent plots to introduce innovatory doctrine and liturgy into the Hungarian church and accept that changes to the traditional practices of the church required the approval of the proper authorities. It was also resolved at Tokaj that no one was allowed to describe another minister using the scandalous name of 'puritan', since it implied support for unlawful religious innovation.[10]

A national Reformed synod was held at Szatmár on 10 and 11 June 1646 in the presence of György I Rákóczi. The prince was joined by representatives from western Hungary, twenty-one ministers from the northern Tisza province, sixty-three from eastern Tisza, and twenty-four from Transylvania. The synod debated the need for the church to uphold uniform standards of theological orthodoxy and ceremony, and the assembly formally accepted the Second Helvetic Confession and Heidelberg Catechism as authoritative explanations of doctrine within the church. The synod also decided that the authority of superintendents was crucial in order to uphold standards of orthodoxy, to maintain church unity, and avoid dangerous variations of ceremony in church services. The assembly required anyone wishing to change the government, liturgy, or ceremony of the church to do so through the accepted channels of clergy superiors and synods. All suspected innovators were to be thoroughly investigated, and any proven attempts to introduce innovation were to result in a minister

9 Tiszáninnen Reformed Church Province Archives (Sárospatak), A/II/279/6 (Gönc synod), Zsoldos Benő féle időrendes sorozat, ff. 2ᵛ–3ʳ; 'Acta Synodi Nationalis', ff. 394–8. ZEP (1638–51), 61, 108–15; [Magyarországi], 'Adatok a magyarországi puritánus mozgalmak történetéhez', ed. Zoványi, 13–20.

10 'Acta Synodi Nationalis', ff. 62–104, 398–400; ZEP (1638–51), 129–33; S. Szilágyi, 'A Tolnai-per történetéhez', *MPEIF* 5 (1874), 35–42.

being suspended from office. The synod also roundly condemned what was described as a sinister affectation of religious piety and purity originating in England, and the name 'puritan' was deemed disgraceful, scandalous, and hateful, and the synod ordered that it was not to be used in future within the Hungarian church.[11]

János Tolnai Dali's suspension from the ministry was confirmed by the national synod until improvements were detected in his life and morality. János Borsai Szepsi, a minister at Nagyvárad, was also expelled from the ministry, and other ministers were cited as trouble-makers including Jakab Harsányi, István Kereszturi, István Györi, János Porcsalmi, Márton Tolcsvai, and Péter Kovásznai.[12] In 1648 Tolnai was offered the possibility of returning to the ministry at Déva in Transylvania, on condition that he sign a retraction of his previous opinions. This retraction, drawn up by Geleji and György I Rákóczi, included demands that Tolnai respect and obey the Transylvanian superintendent and not introduce any innovations to church services without the authority of the provincial synod. Tolnai replied to this offer that he was ill, had already recanted once, and for reasons of conscience could not sign the retraction. This drew a furious response from Rákóczi, who accused Tolnai of jesuitical equivocation, and of not truly giving up his plans to conspire with others to create 'a dangerous sect'. Rákóczi concluded by threatening Tolnai that if he broke any of the points agreed by the Szatmár assembly on his lands then the full force of law would be brought against him.[13]

János Tolnai Dali was particularly associated with introducing arguments about puritanism into the Hungarian church. However, ideas commonly held by puritans in England about the importance of personal piety and godliness were also conveyed to the Hungarian church by other student ministers and by works on practical theology translated from English. The authors of such books complained that zeal in religion was frequently called puritanism, and characterized puritanism as the search for a true church. As some Hungarian ministers returned from England to press demands for a renewal of public morality, for further reforms to church ceremony, and for an end to clergy hierarchy to allow individual ministers and congregations greater autonomy, they too found themselves accused of puritanism.[14]

---

[11] 'Acta Synodi Nationalis', ff. 154–60; 'A szatmár-németi zsinat végzései, eddig ösmeretlen eredeti szerkezetökben', ed. I. Révész, *Sárospataki Füzetek*, 4 (1860), 244–7.

[12] Csernák, *A református egyház Nagyváradon, 1557–1660*, 125–263.

[13] 'A Tolnai-per történetéhez', ed. Szilágyi, 35–42, see nos. 7–9.

[14] Medgyesi (tr.), *Praxis Pietatis* (Debrecen, 1636); Debreceni Ember, *Historia Ecclesiae Reformatae*, 383–5; Bod, *Historia Hungarorum Ecclesiastica*, bk. 3, ch. 10, 286–94; Zoványi,

István Szilágyi Benjámin, a minister in the Zemplén church, believed that Hungarian puritans and innovators had been inspired to challenge the liturgy and government of the church as a result of their exposure to London churches, and through contact with foreign theologians such as William Ames at Franeker. Szilágyi also thought that such innovators were influenced by dangerous and fanciful notions of universal reformation, supported in England by Independents and Seekers, as they had been previously in Germany by the 'brothers of the rosy cross'. Szilágyi, concluding that all such expectancy was nonsense, believed that those desiring innovation in Hungary had fallen in with such company, 'promising themselves and others golden hills and golden happiness'.[15] Puritan ministers were also blamed for causing divisions in the Hungarian church. János Tolnai Dali was accused of separating out his students at Sárospatak as either 'pious' or 'impious'. Complaints were also made against Tolnai by some of his Tokaj congregation that he was dismissive of those he thought were not godly enough, and that he attacked them for not being 'proper Christians', with not even 'ten true hypocrites' amongst them.[16]

There were close parallels between the way in which the term 'puritan' was used in the English and Hungarian churches. The charge of puritanism had been initially used in England to abuse those Protestants who were perceived to support a revival of the ancient heresy of perfectionism, whilst those described as puritans knew each other as 'the godly' or 'professors of true religion'. English puritans have perhaps been best described as 'Protestants of the hotter sort', distinctive by the degree of their warmth, or zealous commitment, to a religion of conscience, practical divinity, and personal piety. Although puritanism in England was not inextricably linked with presbyterianism, nor with strident anti-papal attitudes, nor with those with more moral zeal than the norm, nor yet with those with the keenest eschatological vision, many puritans were also presbyterians,

---

Puritánus mozgalmak a magyar református egyházban; Makkai, *A magyar puritánusok harca a feudálizmus ellen*; Makkai, 'Tolnai Dali János harca a haladó magyar kultúráért', 236–49; Makkai, 'The Hungarian Puritans and the English Revolution', 13–45; J. Bodonhelyi, *A puritánizmus lelki élete és magyar hatásai* (Debrecen, 1942); I. Révész, *Társadalmi és politikai eszmék a magyar puritánizmusban* (Budapest, 1948); I. Ágoston, *A magyarországi puritanizmus gyökerei. Magyar puritán törekvések a xvii. század első felében* (Budapest, 1997); L. Makkai, 'A magyar puritánok történetszemlélete', *Theológiai Szemle*, 21 (1978), 342–5; I. Bán, 'The Literary and Cultural Significance of Seventeenth Century Hungarian Puritanism', in P. F. Barton and L. Makkai (eds.), *Rebellion oder Religion? Debrecen Colloquium 1976* (Budapest, 1977); Evans, 'Calvinism in East-Central Europe', 167–97.

[15] 'Acta Synodi Nationalis', ff. 4, 18–23; Tiszántúl Reformed Church Province Archives (Debrecen), Tiszántúl jegyzőkönyvek, 77. [Tiszántúl], *Adalékok a tiszántuli reformált egyházkerület történetéhez*, ed. S. Tóth (Debrecen, 1894), 33–4.

[16] ZEP (1638–51), 108–15; 'Miskolczi Csulyak jegyzőkönyvei', ed. Zoványi, 392–4.

ferociously anti-Catholic, fierce moralists, and apocalyptic enthusiasts.[17] Puritans acted as a self-proclaimed religious élite, with a sense of their own elect status that set them apart from the reprobate and lukewarm in religion. The effects of election were supposed to be noticeable in the daily lives of believers, and puritans' assurance of election needed to be validated by distinctive moral conduct and devotional activities. Puritans therefore adopted strict rules governing behaviour on the Sabbath and proved determined opponents of excesses in public behaviour. When puritans were mocked as sermon-gadders or hair-splitting precisionists, this only acted to confirm both their fragmentation from the rest of society and their impression of themselves as the church's true remnant.[18]

Puritans in England were also attacked by their opponents as hypocrites, as critics identified double standards in their outward show of piety and a reality of hidden sin. Puritans were satirized as loving God with all their souls but hating their neighbours with all their hearts, or ridiculed as excessive and immoderate in life and religion.[19] Accusations of personal misconduct were also raised against Hungarian ministers dubbed puritans, proof to opponents of their double standards and hypocrisy. On his return to Hungary in 1638, János Tolnai Dali travelled from northern Hungary to the Transylvanian court and to Nagyvárad, stopping at noble houses across Transylvania and eastern Hungary to give lengthy devotions, and showing off his distinctively pious manners, dress, and language. He was, however, also reported to his Zemplén superiors by Hendrik Alting for indiscretion with four women at Groningen, and was accused of having 'blood on his hands'. In 1647 János Simándi, the Zemplén archdeacon, heard gossip about impropriety between Tolnai and a woman at a Tokaj fair. To Simándi

[17] P. Collinson, *English Puritanism* (Historical Association pamphlets, 106; London, 1983); P. Collinson, *The Puritan Character. Polemics and Polarities in Early Seventeenth-Century English Culture* (Los Angeles, 1989); K. L. Parker, *The English Sabbath* (Cambridge, 1988); J. C. Brauer, 'Puritanism: A Panel', *Church History*, 23 (1954), 99–118; Moller, 'The Beginnings of Puritan Covenant Theology', 46–67; K. L. Sprunger, *Dutch Puritanism* (Leiden, 1982); K. L. Sprunger, 'English and Dutch Sabbatarianism and the Development of Puritan Social Theology (1600–1660)', *Church History*, 51 (1982), 24–38; M. A. Breslow, *A Mirror of England. English Puritan Views of Foreign Nations, 1618–1640* (Cambridge, Mass., 1970); R. M. Kingdon, *Geneva and the Consolidation of the French Protestant Movement, 1564–1572* (Geneva, 1967).

[18] P. Lake, 'Puritan Identities', *Journal of Ecclesiastical History*, 35 (1984), 112–23; P. Lake, *Moderate Puritans and the Elizabethan Church* (Cambridge, 1982); P. Christianson, 'Reformers and the Church of England under Elizabeth I and the Early Stuarts', *Journal of Ecclesiastical History*, 31 (1980), 463–82; P. Collinson, 'A Comment: Concerning the Name Puritan', *Journal of Ecclesiastical History*, 31 (1980), 483–8.

[19] W. P. Holden, *Anti-Puritan Satire, 1572–1642* (New Haven, Conn., 1954); P. Collinson, *The Elizabethan Puritan Movement* (London, 1967); P. Collinson, *The Religion of Protestants. Church in English Society, 1559–1625* (Oxford, 1982); C. Hill, *Society and Puritanism in Pre-Revolutionary England* (London, 1966).

this was confirmation that Tolnai was a true puritan, a hypocrite whose open passion for morality hid other secret passions, and that he was a 'hideous, infectious person'.[20] The declarations of pious intent in Tolnai's London League of 1638 were similarly interpreted by opponents as a false mask. István Miskolczi Csulyak in a 1639 letter to György I Rákóczi described Tolnai as a 'pharisee in behaviour', humble on the outside but self-willed on the inside. In 1653 András Váczi made similar charges when he identified Tolnai as the leading innovator at Sárospatak:

> But perhaps you have not picked up about whom I am speaking? . . . he speaks with holy simplicity, but his acts show him to be a proud Pharisee . . . Oh ambition, ambition, ambition . . . he plays the priest over others with his pious life, but storing devilish, undying hatred and anger in his heart . . . it is János Tolnai who promises everything, but does nothing, with a holy mouth, but not a holy heart, and who rules on the necks of our youth only with violence.[21]

István Szilágyi Benjámin thought that puritans showed 'affectations of piety' to hide their heterodox opinions and sectarian ambitions and, 'under the pretext of a purer reformation, are introducing anarchy and English Independency into the Hungarian church'. István Geleji Katona wrote in 1640 that puritans caused disturbance to the church in Hungary and Transylvania under the 'pretext of piety and humility'. During a visitation at Sárospatak in 1642 a former colleague of János Tolnai Dali, András Tarczali, claimed that 'he certainly learnt no piety' from Tolnai and reported that Tolnai often displayed his foul temper whilst at Sárospatak College.[22]

Thus, whilst those dubbed puritans in Hungary claimed to represent the vanguard of an ongoing godly reformation, their detractors were mistrustful of their innovatory plans and entirely sceptical of their honest intent. Despite widespread fears to the contrary, puritanism in Hungary did not in fact develop into a schismatic clergy faction, still less into an organized movement with widespread social support. Whilst copies of practical theological works made their way into noble houses and towns, there is only very limited evidence of any success in spreading a puritan culture to lay society in Hungary and Transylvania. Meanwhile, firm action was taken by the ecclesiastical and civil authorities to squash dissident ministers who challenged traditional ceremony and church structures. Attempts to

---

[20] ZEP (1629–45), 229–31; (1638–51), 142; 'Acta Synodi Nationalis', ff. 73ᵛ–4. Keserű (ed.), *Adattár 1*, 412–16; [Magyarországi], 'Adatok a magyarországi puritánus mozgalmak történetéhez', ed. Zoványi, 7.

[21] András Váczi, *A' Mi-Atyank*, 98–100.

[22] ZEP (1629–45), 312, 323; 'Acta synodi nationalis', ff. 19, 24, 58–9; Geleji Katona, *Praeconium Evangelicum*, ii, 496–8.

marginalize reform-minded ministers during the 1640s were largely successful, and reformers became steadily more reliant on the protection of a few sympathetic noble patrons, most notably Zsuzsanna Lórántffy.

(ii) PRESBYTERIANS AND INDEPENDENTS

The system of Reformed church government had evolved, as was outlined in Chapter 1, as powers and responsibilities shifted from regional clergy synods to superintendents and archdeacons. Transylvania's superintendents became particularly powerful, since they were not only elected by the provincial synod but also confirmed in office by the ruling princes. Demands for changes to church government and challenges to the clergy hierarchy of the Reformed church in Hungary and Transylvania were associated with the influence of foreign Protestant radicals. A series of Hungarian ministers, prominent in campaigns to limit the powers of superintendents, or to remove them completely, were also known for having spent time abroad, especially in England. This connection was initially established thanks to Imre Szilvásújfalvi Anderkó, an early visitor to England in 1595. Szilvásújfalvi returned home to support school reform at Debrecen, as was noted in Chapter 2, but he also stridently opposed the powers of the clergy hierarchy in his eastern Tisza province, then led by superintendent Lukács Hodászi. In the face of growing criticism, Hodászi stressed that superintendents acted only with the consent of clergy presbyteries. He also looked for international support, sending a copy of the province's regulations to David Pareus at Heidelberg for his comments. When Pareus' response came, it failed to provide the ringing endorsement which Hodászi had hoped for. Pareus was particularly anxious that the church's powers of excommunication be clearly separated from other civil punishments and opposed the right which Hodászi claimed for superintendents to imprison disobedient ministers.[23]

Hodászi was, however, able to garner sufficient support among local clergy to defend the status quo, and demands for some constraints on the powers of superintendents faded. In 1610 Hodászi was able to have Szilvásújfalvi denounced as a 'pernicious schismatic' at an eastern Tisza synod held at Nagyvárad. Szilvásújfalvi was forced to sign retractions of his previous views on church government, and to resign from his post as archdeacon in Bihar. Szilvásújfalvi was not so easily silenced, and in 1611 accused Hodászi of being on the road to the tyrannical rule of the papal

[23] Lukács Hodászi, *De potestate ecclesiastica* (Debrecen, 1611), surviving copy held by the Teleki Library, Marosvásárhely; Imre Katona Ujfalvi, *Tractatus de patrum, conciliorum, traditionum authoritate* . . . (Frankfurt, 1611); Heltai, 'David Pareus magyar kapcsolatai', 50–5.

Antichrist. As a result of this attack, Szilvásújfalvi was accused of blasphemy and expelled from the ministry in February 1612. He was handed over to the civil authorities, first imprisoned, and then banished from the Transylvanian principality in 1614.[24]

As we have seen, accusations of puritanism during the 1640s were linked to claims that some ministers did not respect the authority of their clergy superiors. A few ministers, indeed, argued that the notion of a clergy hierarchy had no scriptural basis, and that each congregation should appoint its own ruling lay elders. Greater autonomy for congregations certainly offered reform-minded ministers the prospect of being able to alter ceremony and patterns of church services if they could gain local consent for change. Reformers proposed that local presbyteries should at least be set up alongside the existing system of church government. In June 1646 the Transylvanian synod agreed that where it was considered necessary, and with the help of the civil authorities, presbyters and deacons should be appointed throughout the principality.[25] István Geleji Katona's opening letter to the 1646 national assembly made clear that completely replacing existing church structures with a new presbyterian regime was totally impossible, not least because of trenchant opposition from György I Rákóczi. Ministers at the Szatmár assembly confirmed the validity of the offices of superintendent and archdeacon and also concluded that 'difficulties and obstacles' frequently prevented parish presbyteries being set up within the current framework, given the limited abilities of many ordinary parishioners in the countryside.[26]

The resolutions on church government passed by the 1646 national assembly were reinforced by revised Transylvanian canons compiled by István Geleji Katona. These 1649 canons strongly defended the rule of clergy superiors as the right pattern of government for the Transylvanian church. Citing Calvin, Beza, Martin Bucer, and Girolamo Zanchius for support, Geleji expressed the organization of his church province in the following terms:

Although we justly damn and reject [papal] monarchy and anti-Christian hierarchy, nevertheless neither by any means can we bring into our church anarchy, or the polity of Cyclops, in which no one hears anything, and which is far more deadly

---

[24] [Tiszántúl], *Adalékok a tiszántuli reformált egyházkerület történetéhez*, ed. Tóth, 18–20; Debreceni Ember, *Historia Ecclesiae Reformatae*, 337–9, 343–53; Tiszántúl Reformed Church Province Library MS Collection (Debrecen), R. 575, István Szilágyi Benjámin, 'Synodalia', ff. 244, 251–71; S. Kiss, 'Szilvásújfalvi Anderko Imre', *Egyháztörténet*, 5 (1959), 218–41.

[25] 'Az erdélyi közzsinatainak végzései', ed. Szilágyi, 1–9, 77–84, 473–9.

[26] 'A szatmár-németi zsinat végzései', ed. Révész, 244–7; 'Acta Synodi Nationalis', ff. 105–60.

than monarchy but we embrace for the government of our church aristocracy to a certain degree, or rather aristocratic-democracy.[27]

Geleji's canons set out the function of superintendents, including powers to suspend or remove disobedient ministers, and confirmed their right to monitor the flow of student ministers to foreign universities. The role of archdeacons was also strengthened by the 1649 canons to maintain uniform standards of church services in their district and to approve the appointment of new ministers. The canons permitted lay presbyters to be selected to assist parish clergy, but on the prospects for presbyterian church government in Transylvania the canons stated:

> Although this arrangement was certainly, according to its usage, very necessarily and usefully set up in different places and regions of the Christian church elsewhere, and there were those of our people, who, when abroad, grew accustomed to its advantages and wanted to set up the thing here, because of our different political order it has caused difficulties, and is clearly not permissible here.[28]

Supporters of presbyterian government were appalled by the revised canons, and Pál Medgyesi wrote to Zsigmond Rákóczi that the canons offered the church a path to tyranny. Medgyesi believed that the church hierarchy was placing an unhealthy trust upon the value of tradition and suggested that Johann Heinrich Bisterfeld and others should try to persuade the prince not to ratify the new canons. However, after prolonged debate the canons were sanctioned by the Transylvanian synod in 1648, and then confirmed by the new prince, György II Rákóczi, in June 1649.[29]

The Transylvanian clergy hierarchy proved determined to ensure that the church settlement agreed at the Szatmár synod, and restated in their canons, should be strictly adhered to. The personal resolve of György II Rákóczi to oppose presbyterianism was further stiffened when his fears about its political consequences seemed confirmed by news of events in England in 1649. In October 1649 Medgyesi wrote to Zsigmond Rákóczi of a campaign of persecution against ministers who supported presbyterianism conducted that year in Transylvania by Geleji and György Csulai, chaplain to György II Rákóczi. Medgyesi wrote of plots to remove him from the court, and he concluded that 'the church is in reality lying under a great oligarchy, with a few men making all the decisions'.[30] There indeed

---

[27] *Egyházi kánonok*, ed. Kiss, 1649 canons, no. 85.   [28] Ibid. canon no. 99.

[29] S. Szilágyi, 'A kolozsvári egyház történetéhez', *EPK* (1874), 165–6, 172–4; [Rákóczi György II], 'II. Rákóczi György fejedelem, a Geleji Katona féle kánonokat ünnepélyesen megerősíti', ed. I. Révész, *MPEIF* 7 (1876), 91–3; 'Az erdélyi közzsinatainak végzései', ed. Szilágyi, 1–9, 77–84, 473–9.

[30] K. Thály, 'Egykorú tudósítás I. Károly angol király kivégeztetéséről, 1649', *TT* (1879), 396–8; [Rákóczi Zsigmond], 'Herczeg Rákóczy Zsigmond levelezése', ed. Szilágyi,

seems to have been a concerted campaign against any ministers in Transylvania with suspect opinions on church government. Medgyesi and Bisterfeld were forced to appeal to Zsigmond Rákóczi in August 1649 for help to have Benedek Árkosi's appointment at the Gyulafehérvár Academy confirmed. Medgyesi also turned to Zsigmond on behalf of János Gidófalvi, a reform-minded minister at Kolozsvár. Gidófalvi had written to Medgyesi in June 1649 seeking his assistance against the local archdeacon and other colleagues at Kolozsvár, who had accused him of liturgical innovation and were trying to have him replaced. Archdeacon Miklós Váradi described Gidófalvi as an evil-spirited man, and threatened to pull Gidófalvi out of the Kolozsvár pulpit by his beard if he tried to preach there again.[31]

Eventually Pál Medgyesi was forced to give way to his opponents in Transylvania, and he left the Gyulafehérvár court in July 1650. Medgyesi followed Zsigmond Rákóczi and Zsuzsanna Lórántffy to their estates in northern Hungary and became Lórántffy's chaplain. Medgyesi joined János Tolnai Dali, who had been appointed by Lórántffy as director of Sárospatak College in 1649. In 1650 Medgyesi took the opportunity of his new situation to set out a coherent summary of his views on church government as a *Political-Ecclesiastical Dialogue*. Showing understandable caution, Medgyesi asked both Bisterfeld and Zsigmond to read parts of this work before its publication, and Medgyesi dedicated the *Dialogue* to Zsigmond, quoting expressions of his support for the presbyterian cause.[32] Medgyesi's precautions proved insufficient to escape the wrath of an outraged György II Rákóczi. The prince wrote to his mother in May 1650 that Medgyesi had not sought his permission to publish the work, and that the implication of the introduction to the *Dialogue* was offensive in suggesting that his father had been responsible for blocking Medgyesi's presbyterian proposals in the past. This was to prove the first of a number of disagreements over church government which soured the relationship between György II Rákóczi and Zsuzsanna Lórántffy, which was already strained by Lórántffy's evident preference for the prince's younger brother.[33]

TT (1887), 656–8, 671–2; 'Medgyesi Pál levelei', ed. S. Szilágyi, *EPK* (1876), 306–9, 320–2.

[31] 'A kolozsvári egyház történetéhez', ed. Szilágyi, 165–6, 172–4; 'Medgyesi Pál levelei', ed. Szilágyi, *EPK* (1876), 306–9, 320–2.

[32] Pál Medgyesi, *Dialogus Politico-Ecclesiasticus, azaz két keresztyén embereknek eggy mással való beszélgetések: az egyházi igazgató presbyterekről, avagy vénekről, öregekről és a presbyteriumról, eggyházi tanátsról* (Bártfa, 1650); Pál Keresztúri, *Christianus Lactens, quem illustres et magnifici domini, dn. Georgius et dn. Sigismundus Rakoci . . . in solemni examine* (Gyulafehérvár, 1637) 107, 116–18; 'Medgyesi Pál levelei', ed. Szilágyi, *EPK* (1876), 306–9, 320–2.

[33] S. Szilágyi, 'Medgyesy Pál életéhez', *Protestáns Szemle*, 2 (1890), 146–54.

Medgyesi's *Dialogue* recommended that lay presbyteries be set up immediately in the Hungarian church to replace the existing clergy hierarchy. Medgyesi quoted William Ames's opinion that a church could not be rightly ordered without lay presbyteries in every parish. Medgyesi attempted to establish the New Testament basis for presbyterian government from Pauline Letters and argued that inaccurate translation of these texts had led to the belief in Hungary that presbyters ought only to be clergymen. He concluded that church government by clergy hierarchy opened a dangerous path back to Rome, and that the role traditionally given to superintendents and archdeacons lacked any scriptural basis. Medgyesi suggested that in each parish the minister, or teaching presbyter, should be responsible for preaching and the administration of the sacraments, whilst other presbyters should be chosen from the congregation to direct parish life. Presbyters were described in the *Dialogue* as the non-teaching caretakers and directors of each congregation given the duty of monitoring standards of behaviour in each locality.34

Medgyesi suggested that presbyteries were urgently needed to bring moral discipline to Hungarian society and could be started immediately in towns, to be followed in country areas once potential peasant elders had been trained in their duties. Medgyesi later also described the role which synods would play to resolve common problems in his presbyterian system. Medgyesi was concerned that synods should not be conducted as exercises in oligarchic control of the church by the clergy, and he therefore supported the participation at synods of lay elders and leading magistrates alongside the clergy. Medgyesi's *Dialogue* also addressed the political consequences of these proposed changes to church government. Medgyesi denied that presbyteries had affected the authority of princes anywhere in the Reformed world and underlined the fact that the chief magistrate should continue to supervise the external affairs of the church. He also tried to calm noble fears about presbyteries, presenting them as no threat to their traditional rights of patronage.35

Medgyesi gained many of these ideas on the scriptural basis for a synodal-presbyterial model of church government, and on the practical benefits of parish presbyters for social and moral discipline, from his understanding and experience of western Calvinist churches. However, Hungarian ministers' contact with foreign Calvinists by no means uniformly

34 Medgyesi, *Dialogus Politico-Ecclesiasticus*.
35 '. . . az superattendensekhez és esperekhez. Hogy hiszem emberi rendelések ezek: az Presbyterium penig isteni': Medgyesi, *Dialogus Politico-Ecclesiasticus*, 28, 42, 73, 75, 99, 108–9, 126; Pál Medgyesi, *Rövid tanítás a presbyteriumról avagy egyházi tanácsról* (Sárospatak, 1653); Pál Medgyesi, 'Isteni és istenes zsinat', in *Magyar hatodik jajja* (Sárospatak, 1660).

stimulated calls for reform to church government. Many student ministers in fact returned from periods at universities in the Dutch Republic and in England implacably determined to oppose both puritanism and presbyterianism. Some of the most prominent defenders of the authority of superintendents and archdeacons included Ferenc Veréczi, who had studied in England and the Dutch Republic between 1633 and 1635, István Szilágyi Benjámin, who visited Franeker and Utrecht between 1639 and 1641, and András Váczi, who studied in England and the Dutch Republic between 1644 and 1647. On the other hand Péter Szatmári Baka gave a disputation at Franeker in 1649 in which he defended presbyterian church government as divinely inspired. Szatmári's disputation aimed to show that the presbyters described in New Testament texts did not correspond to superintendents in Hungary, and that episcopacy and hierarchy among ministers were human inventions with a propensity to lead to despotic rule. Szatmári also wrote that he agreed with English puritans that presbyterianism did not detract from monarchy in any way, although he was anxious to differentiate his support for puritanism and presbyterianism from congregationalism and Independency.[36]

Szatmári's work was printed at Franeker in 1649, and a response was published the same year by Samuel Maresius, who taught at Groningen University. Maresius chose to hide his intervention into the Hungarian presbyterian debate under a pseudonym, as his text suggested that the author was a Transylvanian ('Petrus Joh. Knollarothzi, Claudiopol.'). Maresius warned that the church in Hungary should beware of 'English simplicity', since sectarian troublemakers such as Independents and Brownists, whilst claiming to aim to improve moral discipline through presbyteries, in reality had the reverse in mind. Maresius also praised the wisdom of György I Rákóczi in trying to prevent this 'English fever' from penetrating into Hungary after the general assembly of 1646. He argued against the necessity of all ministers being equal in rank, citing the examples of inspectors or superintendents in the Swiss and German Reformed churches, and concluded that the presbyters described in the New Testament did in fact correspond to such Reformed superintendents. Maresius was nevertheless concerned at the extent of episcopal authority in the Hungarian church and suggested that synodal power should be strengthened.[37] Szatmári defended his original thesis against this detailed criticism

36 Péter Szatmári Baka, *Defensio Simplicitatis Ecclesiae* (Franeker, 1649), ff. e1–2, f4, ki; J. Herepei, 'Idősebb Szathmári Baka Péterné és fiacskája siratója', *Egyháztörténet*, 2 (1944), 120–3.
37 Samuel Maresius, *Popularis ad Popularem; sive, Irenaei Simplicii Philadelphi epistola . . . ad D. Petrum Bacca Szatthmari* (Groningen, 1649), 5–6, 9–10, 14–15; J. Zoványi, 'Ki volt a

in 1653, restating his argument that the current form of church government in Hungary did not fulfil the requirements on church order set out by Christ and the Apostles. Szatmári also refuted Maresius' insinuation of Independency and stressed that he believed congregational presbyteries should remain linked together through regular synods, where matters of common interest could be discussed.[38]

Despite the best efforts of Medgyesi, Szathmári, and other ministers to promote presbyterianism after 1646, they generated only limited support from either Reformed ministers or noble patrons. In October 1650 Medgyesi was forced to admit to Zsuzsanna Lórántffy that presbyterianism was not widely accepted within the church. In 1651 a synod of the eastern Tisza church held at Piskólt decided to retain the established articles of hierarchical government, reasoning that the essence of presbyteries described in the New Testament was already established in all-clergy church councils. The synod also declared that lay presbyteries were opposed by magistrates and the people, so that their introduction would have had dangerous consequences for the church and nation. Supporters of presbyteries were officially declared a minority party in the eastern Tisza province and could be disciplined in future if they attempted to advance their cause again.[39]

The patronage of presbyterian ministers by Zsuzsanna Lórántffy and Zsigmond Rákóczi in north-eastern Hungary brought some limited success for their cause at synods in the northern Tisza province. In 1650 a synod of the Zemplén church at Újhely supported the development of presbyteries alongside current church structures, whilst in January 1651 a synod at Liszka suggested adapting existing town and village councils to begin local presbyteries. In May 1651 a gathering of Zemplén ministers at Bénye concluded that presbyteries were an important requirement in the drive to improve moral and social discipline. The synod, however, remained very anxious to reach a consensus for any fundamental changes to church government both with local nobles and with other church provinces.[40]

Szathmári Baka Péter irodalmi ellenfele?', *Protestáns Szemle*, 18 (1906), 379–82; [Rákóczi Zsigmond], 'Herczeg Rákóczy Zsigmond levelezése', ed. Szilágyi, *TT* (1888), 298–300.

[38] Péter Szatmári Baka, *Defensio Simplicitatis Ecclesia Christi, . . . adversus Irenaei Simplicii Philadelphi Epistolam. Vindiciae Defensoris Simplicitatis Ecclesiae* (Franeker, 1653), 12.

[39] MOL box 1883, Tiszántúl jegyzőkönyvek, vol. 1, 579; 'A tiszántúl ref. egyházkerület végzése a presbyteriumok ügyében, 1651 Sep. 3', ed. I. Révész, *MPEIF* 4 (1873), 98–9; I. Révész, 'Adalék a magyar puritánok történetéhez', *Sárospataki Füzetek*, 2 (1858–9), 717–25; 'Medgyesi Pál levelei', ed. Szilágyi, *EPK* (1877), 3–4.

[40] 'Medgyesi Pál levelei', ed. Szilágyi, *EPK* (1876), 320–2; ZEP (1638–51), 189–91, 203, 211; [Magyarországi], 'Adatok a magyarországi puritánus mozgalmak történetéhez', ed. Zoványi, 22–4.

These were only very modest advances in the eyes of the most determined presbyterian ministers. In March 1651 Medgyesi complained to Zsigmond Rákóczi of continuing opposition from János Ványai and many of the Zemplén Reformed clergy to presbyteries, although Medgyesi claimed ministers were now giving disingenuous support for presbyteries when speaking before Zsigmond. Medgyesi warned his patron that Ferenc Veréczi, one of the ministers at Sárospatak, was working to stir up trouble against local presbyterians. Medgyesi wrote of a 'terrible and great aversion' to presbyteries, and of the persecution which he had been forced to endure because of his support for presbyterianism. Medgyesi claimed not to be surprised by the great opposition he had encountered, because 'the large part of our nation only holds to the form of religion, and although people think of themselves as knowledgeable, they do not understand the fundamentals of religion, nor do they wish to understand them'.[41]

Feelings evidently ran particularly high at Sárospatak, and the sensitivity of local ministers to any comments about presbyterianism was shown by the frenetic reaction in 1650 to a tract on the issue by Jan Amos Comenius. Just before his arrival to teach at Sárospatak College, Comenius was asked by exiled Moravian Brethren in northern Hungary to write his opinion on the correct form of church government. Comenius proposed that the best path lay through the unification of monarchy, aristocracy, and democracy, but the preface claimed that Comenius opposed those Hungarian ministers who returned from England supporting Independency. Bisterfeld wrote to Zsigmond of his amazement at Comenius' apparent indifference on the issue of church government and warned that Comenius, by trying to please all in Hungary, would end up pleasing none. This tract received a furious response from Medgyesi and Tolnai, who were convinced that Comenius had taken up an anti-presbyterian stance. In March 1651 Medgyesi wrote to Zsigmond that 'no matter how good his [Comenius'] Latin is, we are not going to gain much from him, if it is his wish to cause damage to attempts to make a truly Reformed church'.[42]

Meanwhile, György II Rákóczi continued to be highly suspicious of any suggestion of presbyteries, either to replace the clergy hierarchy or as supplementary disciplinary organs within the church. In January 1653 the Transylvanian diet, with strong backing from Rákóczi, imposed tighter civil controls on the churches of the principality. The diet codified laws

[41] S. Szilágyi, 'Comenius egy ismeretlen munkája', *TT* (1890), 202–4; [Rákóczi Zsigmond], 'Herczeg Rákóczy Zsigmond levelezése', ed. Szilágyi, *TT* (1887), 654–6, 675–6; (1890), 603–4.
[42] Kvacsala, 'Comenius és a Rákóczyak', 113–51; [Rákóczi Zsigmond], 'Herczeg Rákóczy Zsigmond levelezése', ed. Szilágyi, *TT* (1890), 202–4.

which confirmed the rights of superintendents from all four received Transylvanian religions to call synods and undertake visitations. The diet also placed the full weight of the state behind superintendents' efforts to root out any suspected innovation in forms of government or ceremony. Whilst the diet affirmed the right of any of the four religions to conduct internal reform, this was only allowed with the consent of that church's patrons. If unsanctioned doctrinal, liturgical, or administrative innovations were discovered during a visitation, then any clergy involved were ordered by the diet to be dismissed and also face civil charges with the threat of loss of life and property.43

Johann Heinrich Bisterfeld reacted to these proposed laws by writing to the prince, warning him not to harm the interests of the Reformed church nor to put blocks in the way of the development of the church. Bisterfeld reminded the prince that presbyteries were commonplace in other Reformed countries and argued against the threatened punishment of loss of life and property for those supporting the introduction of presbyteries or other innovations. Bisterfeld asked György II Rákóczi to consider the prospect of this law being enacted against his own mother and wrote that conscience required him to defend the 'true Helvetic Reformed religion'. The prince flatly rejected Bisterfeld's suggestions and cursed the impudence of his letter. Rákóczi added that whilst he too recognized the usefulness of presbyteries in disciplining congregations, he feared that the consequences of presbyterianism in Transylvania might be the same as those which he believed had resulted from presbyterianism in England during the 1640s. These new laws also sparked off a series of angry letters between Zsuzsanna Lórántffy and her son, but neither Bisterfeld nor the dowager princess could overcome György's anxiety about the political dangers of any reforms to church government.44

Supporters of presbyterianism therefore failed to gain the backing of any provincial or regional synod in Transylvania or the Partium for a shift from the clergy-dominated hierarchical government to a synodal-presbyterial regime. Despite these defeats, presbyterians persisted in arguing their case throughout the 1650s. The perception began to grow amongst conservatives in the church that presbyterians were in fact aiming

---

43 *Erdélyi országgyűlési emlékek*, ed. Szilágyi, xiii, 444–6. After 1648 the writ of the diet no longer ran over five counties in north-eastern Hungary (Abaújvár, Zemplén, Borsod, Bereg, and Ugocsa), which reverted to Habsburg control on György I Rákóczi's death. Lukinich, *Erdély területi változásai a török hódítás korában, 1541–1711*, 199–335.

44 [Rákóczi György I], *Rákóczy György fejedelem családi levelezése*, ed. Szilágyi, 452, 457, 460–2, 471, 482; see also S. Szilágyi, 'Az 1655-iki pozsonyi országgyűlés történetéhez', *Történeti Lapok* (1874), 117.

for congregationalism and Independency, and the complete breakdown of a unified Reformed church. These fears were not entirely without foundation, since some presbyterians suggested that single congregations rather than any general institution formed visible, true churches. Others clearly wanted to introduce presbyteries and remove congregations from the control of archdeacons in order to introduce local changes to the conduct of church services. This allegation of Independency was particularly serious in the light of the 1653 Transylvanian laws and György II Rákóczi's view that presbyterianism and Independency carried an implicit threat to princely authority. Despite this mounting opposition, János Tolnai Dali and Pál Medgyesi among others continued to advocate reform, but they became entirely reliant on the protection and support of Zsuzsanna Lórántffy, especially after Zsigmond Rákóczi's death in February 1652.

The Zemplén synod at Liszka had first heard reports in January 1651 of moves towards Independency at Sárospatak, allegedly orchestrated by János Tolnai Dali. At an informal meeting held at István Szilágyi Benjámin's house in Sárospatak, leading conservatives in the Zemplén church agreed that Tolnai wanted to introduce congregationalist Independency in the Hungarian church by ending archdeacons' powers of spiritual supervision and by breaking all existing ties, through visitations and synods, between Reformed congregations. The meeting in Szilágyi's house was also persuaded that Tolnai was planning to introduce imported doctrinal and liturgical innovations at Sárospatak which would lead to anarchy in the church. Szilágyi and his friends concluded that Independency was a devilish discovery, and that where it ruled no church could stand. At a synod at the end of February 1651 in Sárospatak, archdeacon János Simandi claimed publicly that Tolnai opposed inspections of local congregations by church superiors. Simandi quoted Tolnai as saying that 'a diocesan church is anti-Christian and diabolical' and accused him of teaching Independency at Sárospatak College. Whilst a majority of Zemplén's clergy remained ready to consider a supplementary role for presbyteries at the Bénye synod of May 1651, suspicions steadily grew about presbyterians' real intentions.[45]

In 1654 András Váczi again attacked János Tolnai Dali, this time for trying to force the formation of a presbytery at Sárospatak in order to introduce liturgical and ceremonial innovations. Váczi wrote that whilst he approved of presbyteries in principle, their introduction had proved completely impossible because of great opposition to any changes from within the church. Váczi reasoned that since believers could gain salvation

45 ZEP (1638–51), 188, 192, 211–13, 221–5.

without introducing a presbyterian regime, the harmful practical consequences to church harmony of any changes to its government were not worth the trouble.[46] Tolnai responded by ridiculing the claims of Váczi and others about so-called 'innovators' in the church. Tolnai scorned suggestions that he did not pray or preach from the Bible and mocked rumours that reformers were supposed to think that every man should have three wives, that the ecclesiastical regime had to be destroyed and Independency introduced in its place, and that higher civil powers would not be necessary in a future republic. Tolnai argued that in reality he was only an innovator to the extent that he desired to change certain 'uncommon' practices within the church.[47]

Complaints about the nest of presbyterians at Sárospatak continued unabated. In February 1654 an anonymous tract reached György II Rákóczi which claimed that presbyterians at Sárospatak in fact aspired to Independency, did not respect the authority of the church hierarchy, and failed to attend local synods. These Sárospatak Independents were accused of introducing new ideas on their own authority, of abandoning traditional ceremonies, and of wanting to differentiate themselves like Pharisees from the rest of the church: 'There are such amongst them, who are attached to puritanism, giddy Independency, the anarchy of "feet without a head (*fejetlenlábság*)", Arminianism, Anabaptism, and more such sects'.[48] In March 1654 György Csulai also wrote to the prince condemning Pál Medgyesi for his activities at Sárospatak. Csulai claimed that Medgyesi wanted to bridle the authority of magistrates, which would inevitably lead Transylvania down a path towards 'hideous English disturbances'. Csulai considered that trouble had begun in England when a window was opened to error and false religion, and soon '180 sects' began attacking the Anglican church. Csulai concluded by warning Rákóczi that he should act at once to eradicate similar dissent in Hungary.[49]

Gáspár Miskolczi Csulyak, son of the former Zemplén archdeacon István Miskolczi Csulyak, published a work on *English Independency* at Utrecht in 1654. Miskolczi claimed that presbyterians and Independents in England had developed from 'new puritans' of the early seventeenth century. Miskolczi believed that Independents had deformed the church in England and opened the door to sectarian anarchy there. Miskolczi warned that similar innovation could quickly spread to Hungary because some ministers thought that 'a bald crow, if it is foreign, is dearer than a

---

[46] Váczi, *Replica*, 85, 187–9.   [47] Tolnai Dali, *Daneus Rácai*, 122–3, 159–60.
[48] [Rákóczi György II], 'Okiratok II. Rákóczy György diplomácziai összeköttetései történetéhez', ed. Szilágyi, 475–9.   [49] Ibid. 479–81.

home-bred fattened calf'. Miskolczi sought to ridicule such groups, by comparing them with fanatics in England waiting for the Apostle John to return either in Suffolk or in Transylvania! At the same time Miskolczi played on the dangers of anarchic radicalism, which he too dubbed 'feet without a head'. Under the cover of Christian freedom, Miskolczi believed that Independents had introduced all sorts of poisons into the English church. Miskolczi blamed Independents for the downfall of Anglican episcopacy and the execution of Charles I, arguing that Independents equated the seven monarchies described in Revelation to seven kings in Europe and wanted to cut down six more dynasties to follow the Stuarts.[50]

István Telkibányai responded to Miskolczi's book by translating William Bradshaw's work *English Puritanism, containing the main opinions of the rigidest sort of those that are called Puritans*, which was also published at Utrecht in 1654. Bradshaw's work had been translated into Latin in 1605 by William Ames, and when reprinted in English in 1640 was ascribed to Ames. This tract defended the views of puritans, and suggested that hierarchical church government would lead to the return of papal tyranny. Bradshaw denied that there was any New Testament justification for a clergy hierarchy, and concluded that 'either the order of bishops, filled with lies, has to be completely abolished, or the Pope must be brought back from hell'. Since Bradshaw argued that a single congregation constituted a visible church, he suggested that parish elders should not be subject to any superior ecclesiastical jurisdiction, but at the same time carefully defended the role of magistrates as holding supreme power over all the churches within their dominions.[51]

Much of the concern about Independency in the Hungarian church continued to arise from events in Sárospatak, where Zsuzsanna Lórántffy seemed determined to introduce a presbytery which could act independently of the Zemplén archdeacon's authority. In 1652 Lórántffy had tried and failed to get Sárospatak council to install her castle chaplains, Medgyesi and Tolnai, as town preachers. In 1653 Lórántffy called upon the council to introduce a presbytery, and this time the council accepted nominations for elders which were announced in the town's church. Some parishioners complained that they did not want the new presbytery which had been imposed upon them, and started to go to churches in neighbouring villages rather than accept the rule of the appointed elders. In January

1655 the Zemplén archdeacon, Pál Tarczali, led a visitation to Sárospatak and met the congregation's new elders. This was, however, the last visitation at Sárospatak until two months after Lórántffy's death in 1660, when the visitors recorded that:

Since the reformation the church at Sárospatak, has been dependent on, and visited by, the archdeacons of the diocese of Zemplén county; through the advice of some, for a presbytery, or under the cover of some other thing, for the past five or six years it has been taken from under the direction of the archdeacons of the diocese; but now thanks to the grace of God, we have regained the direction of this church.[52]

The 1655 visitation had sparked a concerted campaign by the Zemplén authorities to combat reformers, despite the protection which they could call upon from Lórántffy. At the beginning of 1655 Lórántffy heard reports that archdeacon Pál Tarczali had secretly gathered together leading Zemplén clergy who opposed presbyterianism and 'fermented something against us'. Lórántffy accused some Zemplén ministers of treating her with disrespect, particularly Ferenc Veréczi, who on one occasion had refused to serve her communion and condemned her for spreading a new faith.[53] In April 1655 a Zemplén district synod was held at Liszka, and the archdeacon castigated János Tolnai Dali for disrespecting his authority and claimed Tolnai believed that a 'pig's priest' was more honourable than an archdeacon. The synod issued stern warnings to Tolnai, Medgyesi, Sámuel Lippai, and István Keresszeghi for disturbing the church's good order.[54]

In May 1655 leading conservatives called a joint synod of the northern and eastern Tisza provinces at Debrecen, presided over by superintendent Miklós Szathmári Lázár. At this synod Medgyesi, Tolnai, Lippai, and Keresszeghi were all suspended from their posts and János Belényesi, an archdeacon in the eastern Tisza province, was also suspended from the ministry for one year. Lórántffy directed the overseer of her Transylvanian estates to appeal to the diet to have this decision reversed. The Transylvanian diet replied with a noncommittal letter of March 1656, claiming that the church in north-eastern Hungary had complete independence from them and that they could not interfere. Lórántffy was only able to get the four suspended clergy reinstated in September 1656 after the Gálszécs meeting of the northern Tisza synod, over which she could exert greater influence.[55]

[52] ZEP (1653–72), 53–6, 305–7; 'Magyar protestáns egyház történeti kuftők', ed. Finkei, 361–2; Péter, *Papok és nemesek*, 197–8.

[53] 'Két levél Lórantfy [*sic*] Zsuzsannától', ed. S. Szilágyi, *EPK* (1875), 141.

[54] 'Egyháztörténelmi adatok', ed. Szilágyi, 313–14, 329–30, 344–5, 360–1.

[55] ZEP (1653–72), 133.

The 1655 Debrecen synod decided that other ministers who had resisted the authority of superintendents were also to be removed from their posts. It was agreed that if these ministers attacked the synod's decisions they were to be given over to the civil powers for severe punishment. The synod also received some individuals, including Péter Szathmári Baka, back into the ministry after a period of suspension. Szathmári was forced to retract his previously stated support for presbyterianism, and the synod warned that any future offence would lead to his dismissal from the ministry.[56] All four ministers from Nagyvárad, István Szikra, Benedek Nagyari, Péter Kovásznai, and Ferenc Szatmári, were also suspended from their posts by the Debrecen synod. Tensions affecting Nagyvárad and the surrounding Bihar region in the Partium were highlighted by an anonymous author at the Nagyvárad School, 'Pasquillus', who wrote comic verses attacking the innovatory opinions of twenty ministers and two teachers in the area. 'Pasquillus' chastised Szikra, Kovásznai, and Nagyari in particular, and berated the divisions which they were seen to be causing in the local church. István Telkibányai, who had translated *English Puritanism* in 1654, was also ridiculed for supporting presbyteries, whilst another minister was rebuked for advancing innovation at Nagyvárad after having been thrown out of the school at Kolozsvár because of his 'new learning'.[57]

The arrival of Isaac Basire at the Transylvanian court in 1655 only acted to heighten György II Rákóczi's fears still further about the possible impact of presbyterianism and Independency on princely authority. In September 1655 Basire clashed with János Apáczai Csere, a supporter of presbyteries at Kolozsvár, in a public debate about church government held in Rákóczi's presence. Basire spoke about his experience of Independency in England and linked it with Charles I's execution. Apáczai in response tried to differentiate presbyterianism from Independency, but the prince retorted that the one led to the other, and by the end of the debate Rákóczi was so angry with Apáczai that he threatened to throw him from the tower in Marosvásárhely where the debate was being held.[58] Basire later presided over the 1656 Transylvanian synod, defending the existing clergy hierarchy of what he described as a 'Catholic-Reformed' church. Basire claimed that episcopacy was divinely established and that magistrates held authority to protect and champion the church by divine right. Basire identified 'covenanters' as the chief opponents of true religion, who at first favoured

---

[56] MOL box 1883, Tiszántúl jegyzőkönyvek, vol. 1, 578.
[57] [Váradi], 'Egy gúnyirat a váradi ref. esperesség presbyterianus papjai ellen 1655-ből', ed. K. Szabó, *MPEIF* 1 (1870), 590–8.
[58] *Apáczai Csere János*, ed. Orosz, 163–6; [Rákóczi György I], *Rákóczy családi levelezése*, ed. Szilágyi, 490–1.

presbyterian government but then later became Independents, and in a letter of April 1656 Basire recounted to Charles II his battles in Transylvania against 'Independency and presbytery (flown over here from England)'.[59] In 1656 an anonymous Sárospatak author responded to what Basire had been saying about the church in Transylvania. The author, probably Pál Medgyesi, claimed that the Hungarian church was not episcopal but presbyterian in government, with clergy presbyteries meeting under each archdeacon, and that no one before Basire had ever equated the rank of superintendent with episcopacy.[60]

The continuing unhappy divide between György II Rákóczi and Zsuzsanna Lórántffy over the issue of church government was revealed in a number of letters reacting to events in the church in 1655. In November 1655 Lórántffy criticized Rákóczi's approval of the Debrecen synod, which she characterized as 'without justice'. Lórántffy wrote again in January 1656 to her son, accusing him of making her suffer.

> I have already written many times of this to you, and I do not see any point in it . . . it pleased you to humiliate my chaplains, with the agreement of the bishop; you did not say 'my mother is an innovator', but when you said such [things] about my chaplains, you have already done this; . . . I only see from you harsh deeds against me.

In February 1656 Rákóczi responded that he had only acted to uphold his obligations under the law. The prince also claimed that the clergy in Transylvania and eastern Hungary had now largely accepted the continuation of traditional structures of church government, and he insisted that this peace should not be disturbed.[61]

In fact, the ramifications of the 1655 Debrecen synod continued to be felt, as two suspended ministers from Nagyvárad, Benedek Nagyari and Péter Kovásznai, still refused to endorse hierarchical church government. In June 1656 a synod at Szatmár received two other ministers back into their posts, after they signed formulas of repentance promising not to cause any more trouble. Nagyari and Kovásznai were imprisoned in Szatmár castle in June 1656 for three weeks, until they too gave way and agreed to abide by the church's canons and accept Transylvanian laws on church

---

59 Isaac Basire, *Pro Unitate Verae Ecclesiae* (Gyulafehérvár, 1656); Basire, *History of the English and Scotch Presbytery* ([n.pl.], 1659), 129, 220–8; *Domestic Calendar of State Papers (1655–1656)*, nos. 38–9, 258.

60 Isaac Basire, 'Triumviratus sive Calvini, Bezae et Zanchii testimoniae luculente pro Episcopatus', in *Trecentumviratus et ultra* (Sárospatak, 1656); Durham Cathedral Library, MS Hunter 85, 88, 140/12; Ö. Miklós, 'Ki a 'Trecentumviratus' szerzője?', *Magyar Könyvszemle*, 31 (1916), 256–8.

61 [Rákóczi György I], *Rákóczy családi levelezése*, ed. Szilágyi, 497–500, 502–3.

government. Retractions offered by Kovásznai and Nagyari promised that in future they would be 'obedient sons' of the church.[62] In July 1656 György II Rákóczi wrote to Lórántffy with news of these retractions from the two Nagyvárad ministers. Rákóczi also wrote that prison had not improved Nagyari and Kovásznai, and that their local superiors wanted them to sign another retraction since 'a dog which has swum across the Danube once, can swim over a second time'.[63] At the eastern Tisza synod at Böszörmény in September 1656, Nagyari and Kovásznai defended themselves once again from allegations of innovation. However, they were eventually, and very unwillingly, forced to sign yet another retraction before being formally received back into the ministry of the church.[64]

In early seventeenth-century disputes over church government, conservative ministers were primarily concerned to prevent any disturbances to church peace, fearing the disruptive results of any imported innovations. Reformers, on the other hand, believed that if Christian liberty in the Hungarian church was constrained by human institutions then they would inexorably be led back towards papal tyranny. Reform-minded ministers had been encouraged by first-hand experience of foreign Calvinist churches to challenge the established pattern of church government in Hungary and Transylvania, arguing that the existing clergy hierarchy was incompatible with a truly Reformed church. Their agenda for renewal in the church centred on removing the powers of clergy superiors and replacing some traditional ceremonies. Despite all the fears expressed about the implications of presbyterianism and Independency, there is little evidence from the 1650s of any sectarian enthusiasm to undermine the unity of the Hungarian Reformed church, and no evidence at all of any real radical challenge to the rule of Transylvania's princes.

Ministers of the Reformed church who supported presbyterianism were continually harried by the church authorities, especially at Sárospatak and Nagyvárad. After the disastrous venture into Poland by György II Rákóczi in 1657, there was some prospect of relief for presbyterians when Ákos Barcsai became Transylvanian prince. Barcsai's sympathy for presbyterianism caused a split at the 1658 Transylvanian synod which assembled at Marosvásárhely. The Rákóczi family meanwhile pulled together against their common opponents during this crisis. Zsuzsanna Lórántffy

[62] MOL box 1883, Tiszántúl jegyzőkönyvek, vol. 1, 93, 624, 630, 632; Csernák, *A református egyház Nagyváradon*, 200–17.
[63] J. Koncz, 'Egyháztörténeti adalékok', *Protestáns Közlöny* (1891), 5–6; [Rákóczi György I], *Rákóczy családi levelezése*, ed. Szilágyi, 508–9.
[64] MOL box 1883, Tiszántúl jegyzőkönyvek, vol. 1, 580.

reproached Pál Medgyesi in an emotionally charged letter for harsh things which he had evidently been saying about György II Rákóczi. She accused Medgyesi of supporting Barcsai as prince, not because of his presbyterianism, but out of his own 'private affections', presumably meaning revenge against Rákóczi.[65]

Even after Barcsai was replaced as prince, some support continued to be expressed for outright presbyterianism. A 1662 disputation given under György Mártonfalvi Tóth at Debrecen College argued that presbyteries should be introduced immediately to replace the current form of church government. Individual ministers were also on occasion accused of innovatory opinions about church government. In 1667 Pál Tarczali and the Zemplén synod still felt the need to denounce Independency and renewed warnings to local patrons of its dangerous consequences, again particularly mentioning the fate of Charles I.[66] Local fears of challenges to traditional religion remained strong in Transylvania as well, and in 1659 the town council of Marosvásárhely became nervous of the opinions of a new minister and sought the town guilds' reaction to the threat of possible innovations. In July 1659 the Marosvásárhely guilds responded with a chorus of disapproval. The saddlers and barbers did not want 'puritan religion' to be introduced, and the barbers replied that they did not want a presbytery either but instead to follow the Ten Commandments and the laws of God! The hat-makers guild, meanwhile, commented on 'presbyterian religion' that 'we do not know what it is, do not understand it, and therefore do not want to have it brought in', instead sticking with 'the true Christian confession'.[67]

The loss of Nagyvárad to the Turks, and the deaths of Zsuzsanna Lórántffy and János Tolnai Dali in 1660, shortly followed by Pál Medgyesi, marked the end of a serious presbyterian challenge to the established order of the Hungarian church. Most noble patrons remained more concerned to uphold their own role within local church life than support presbyterianism and, with the exception of Ákos Barcsai, Transylvania's princes continued to support the authority of superintendents in the Reformed church. The 1664 Transylvanian synod decided that the accustomed form of church government must remain in place, but allowed for discussion on the merits of presbyteries as long as 'this gives no cause for hatred or scandal'. The more immediate external threats to the survival of the Reformed

---

[65] Szilágyi, 'Medgyesy Pál életéhez', 146–54.

[66] ZEP (1653–72), 273–8, 305–7. *Disputatio theologica de presbyterio . . . sub praesidio Georgii Martonfalvi* (Debrecen, 1662); Ágoston, *A magyarországi puritanizmus gyökerei*, 136–7.

[67] Maros Reformed Church District Archives (Marosvásárhely), no. 65/B.

church during the second half of the seventeenth century increased the pressure for existing hierarchical authority to be strengthened. By the 1670s clerical dominance of church government was being eroded not by congregational presbyteries but by meetings of the Transylvanian consistory under Prince Mihály Apafi. This ecclesiastical council of invited lay and clergy leaders met regularly in parallel with the Transylvanian synod from 1671 and slowly gained authority at the expense of the provincial synod. As the prince and leading Reformed nobles in Transylvania became more involved in all important decisions about the church, the tendency to abide by established precedents steadily rose, confirming the place of traditional structures of hierarchical government and forms of public worship in the life of the Reformed church.[68]

---

[68] Nagy, *Fejezetek a magyar református egyház 17. századi történetéből*, 201–37; Révész (ed.), *A magyar református egyház története*, 132–42; Pokoly, *Az erdélyi református egyház története*, iv, 179–213.

7

The Reformation of Hungarian Life: Religious, Moral, and Social Discipline

Reformed Protestantism was partly distinctive from its confessional rivals through strident commitment to supervise religious observance, to regulate social order, and to reform morality in public and private life, all through the exercise of congregational discipline. Calvinist attacks on the perceived disorder and irrationality of Catholic theology and popular religion were matched by an assault on disorderly conduct and immoral behaviour in newly Reformed communities. Indeed, the confessions of the Scottish and Dutch Reformed churches included the enforcement of discipline, alongside sound preaching and the proper administration of the sacraments, as signs of a true church. The disciplinary campaigns launched by Reformed churches across the Continent were therefore essential to Calvinist beliefs, derived from Reformed theological understanding of the relationship between divine providence and human action, rather than a free-standing mission of social control. In their efforts to instil a renewed sense of discipline and order in society, Calvinist ministers generally made no obvious distinction between what might be characterized as religious sins and social crimes, rather attacking those who offended against the moral norms and codes of right conduct established by scriptural precept and civil law. Policing deviancy was conventional during the early modern period, and yet also a mark of Calvinist communities and a vital part of the reformation of life to which Calvinists felt committed and to which rivals often offered only muted echoes. In a society where Calvinist discipline reigned, conscientious attempts were made scrupulously to monitor and supervise all aspects of morality in the public and private spheres, with the misdemeanours of an individual, or of a family, perceived to be capable of bringing judgement against any community which, by connivance or neglect, allowed offences against divine law to go unpunished.[1]

[1] H. Schilling, '"History of crime" or "history of sin"?', in E. I. Kouri and T. Scott (eds.), *Politics and Society in Reformation Europe* (London, 1987), 289–310; H. Schilling,

This chapter will examine the preoccupation among Hungarian Reformed ministers to constrain disorder of all kinds, and to raise standards of public conduct and private behaviour within their communities. The Hungarian Reformed church shared the fundamental disciplinary ambitions of sister Calvinist churches elsewhere, dedicated to ongoing reformation of the spiritual and daily life of Reformed congregations. By the early seventeenth century Hungarian Reformed clergy had embarked upon a campaign to set tighter limits on acceptable moral conduct, and to enforce punishments against those who offended against the standards which they required to be maintained. The nature of Reformed church discipline in Hungary and Transylvania emerged from the convergence of three key components. First, from the nature of the institutions through which controls over behaviour was exercised; secondly, through the methods which were used to punish offenders; and thirdly, through the offences which ministers highlighted as especially significant. The international contacts between Hungarian Reformed clergy and western Calvinists, which have already been surveyed, were influential in shaping the attitudes of ministers to disciplinary issues, particularly on the slowly emerging role of the laity in Hungarian church administration. This chapter will concentrate on establishing in turn these three central elements of the disciplinary regime of the Hungarian church to form a pattern directly comparable with the rest of the international Calvinist community.

(I) THE INSTITUTIONS OF REFORMED DISCIPLINE

Across the Reformed churches of the Continent different balances were struck between ecclesiastical power and secular authority in the administration of religious, moral, and social discipline. While Zurich's moral courts were directed by magistrates, at Geneva an autonomous consistory of pastors and elders met weekly to deal with church administration and congregational discipline. This pattern of consistories or presbyteries, independent of secular authority, was followed at Emden and in France. Where Calvinist churches dominated territorial states, such as in Scotland or parts of the Empire, representatives of the state directly influenced the

'Confessional Europe', in J. D. Tracey, T. A. Brady, and H. A. Oberman (eds.), *Handbook of European History, 1400–1600. Late Middle Ages, Renaissance and Reformation, 2, Visions, Programs and Outcomes* (Leiden, 1995), 641–81. On the 'intrinsic sacrality' for Calvinists of discipline and order, see B. J. Kaplan, *Calvinists and Libertines. Confession and Community in Utrecht, 1578–1620* (Oxford, 1995), 28–67. M. Spufford, 'Puritanism and Social Control?', in A. Fletcher and J. Stevenson (eds.), *Order and Disorder in Early Modern England* (Cambridge, 1985), 41–57.

selection and endeavours of presbyteries. Princely edicts rather than synodal decisions provided the authority for local disciplinary bodies in Reformed Germany, and indeed in the Palatinate and Hesse powers to prosecute religious and moral offenders lay with ecclesiastical officials from the central bureaucracy. While participation in regional synods remained exclusively in the hands of the clergy, members of Calvinist congregations across the Continent commonly acted as elders alongside ministers and state officials to enforce standards of discipline in their localities, as well as acting in other areas of church life such as the administration of poor relief.[2] These lay elders, typical of Calvinist church life elsewhere, as we have seen were only slowly introduced in a piecemeal fashion in Hungary and Transylvania. Since congregational presbyteries only gradually affected the imposition of discipline in the Hungarian church, success was more dependent upon the efforts of parish clergy and local judicial officers, supported by senior ministers and noble patrons. The concerted efforts by ministers to curb popular immorality were marked by the application of spiritual correction, and by demands on civil authorities to prosecute and severely punish a wide range of moral and criminal offences.

Turning to examine the legal framework for the exercise of Reformed discipline, in Royal Hungary the palatine was the final appellate jurisdiction for legal cases, as was the prince in Transylvania through powers inherited from the medieval voivode, or crown governor. István Werbőczi's 1514 codification of laws and noble privileges (*Codex Tripartitum*) was still accepted by the Hungarian kings, Transylvanian princes, and by the two diets as authoritative. The diets indeed mostly confined themselves during this period to producing interpretations of the law which were basically in conformity with Werbőczi's *Codex*. Authority to uphold the law, establish good order, and punish wrongdoing in Hungary and Transylvania mostly lay with local landowners and their noble county assemblies. These assemblies had the right to adopt their own ordinances and to shape the local administration of justice. Each Hungarian county had four judges led by a crown nominee, the high sheriff (*főispán*), and by the deputy sheriff (*alispán*), who was chosen by the county assembly. In Transylvania, the prince had the right to select county sheriffs, except in the Saxon lands, and acted himself as sheriff to the Szeklers. Twelve jurors worked as officials of each county court, which had broad jurisdiction over both criminal and civil law, only restricted by the varying exemptions allowed to royal free towns, royal towns, mining, and market towns each with differing degrees

---

[2] E. W. Monter, 'The Consistory of Geneva, 1559–1569', *Bibliothèque d'Humanisme et Renaissance*, 38 (1976), 467–84; Hsia, *Social Discipline in the Reformation*.

of self-government. Towns appointed a judge along with usually twelve sworn burghers as jurymen to form the town court, whose competence was frequently resisted by any resident nobles.

Meanwhile in the countryside, manorial courts were chaired by an official of the local landowner, with appeals possible to the county court. Landowners routinely delegated authority to a village justice or judge (*bíró*), chosen by the community usually from three nominated candidates. This village justice was in charge of local funds and generally held a book which set out local customs and regulations. Assisted by a council of jurymen, village justices were also charged to decide the punishment of offenders in their locality. The relationship between this communal self-government and seigneurial authority was variable and is difficult to ascertain. Serious legal cases were reported back to manorial officials, and over time nobles increasingly encroached on village councils' control over communal property. Councils, meanwhile, gained responsibility over parish administration and the payment of clergy income in Reformed areas and played some role in the selection of Reformed clergy, although this was more often the case in Transylvania than in Royal Hungary.[3]

There is some evidence about how local communes were organized from records of the Hegyalja region in Zemplén county. Three villages at the centre of local wine-production, Tokaj, Bodrogkeresztúr, and Tarczal, lost their village books of laws and regulations in the destruction following General Basta's invasion of the region in 1604. These villages first consulted one another over what their traditional ordinances were believed to have been, and by 1610 all three had renewed their village books. This no doubt aimed to obstruct any noble ambitions to erode customary village rights over the production and sale of wine. All three new books of regulations contained similar instructions on the election of a village justice, who was exempt from the tithe whilst in office. According to the ordinances, each justice was to be chosen by the council, and this choice was then sanctified in a public church service. The minister was to offer a suitable sermon approving of the new justice and twenty-one-man council, who all stood in front of the pulpit facing the whole community in a public demonstration of close co-operation between the local church and village authorities.[4]

---

3 P. Angyal and A. Degré (eds.), *A xvi. és xvii. századi erdélyi büntetőjog vázlata* (Budapest, 1943); Kann and David, *The Peoples of the Eastern Habsburg Lands, 1526–1918*, 55–71; Szabó, *Tanulmányok a magyar parasztság történetéből*, 265–310.

4 G. Németh (ed.), *Hegyaljai mezővárosok 'törvényei' a xvii–xviii. századból* (Budapest, 1990), 29–59.

This was the structure of civil authority with which the Reformed church sought to co-operate to implement its agenda of moral and social renewal. The church charged each Reformed minister with the responsibility to bring cases of religious or moral offences to light in his own parish, and with the duty to ensure that appropriate spiritual sanctions were enforced against wrong-doers. The Reformed church also sought the agreement of secular authorities in both towns and countryside to have appropriate punishments meted out against offenders. Individual ministers indeed relied heavily on collaboration with local noble patrons and village officials to establish tight discipline in their congregations. This was complicated by local rights to select and retain parish ministers, and northern Hungarian canons at the turn of the seventeenth century expressed concern as to whether this process might be influenced by a desire to escape the injunctions of Reformed discipline.[5] This power of patrons and parishioners was mitigated to some degree by the right of Reformed superintendents and archdeacons to inspect local congregations, which allowed the disciplinary performance of each minister to be monitored. These visitations became semi-inquisitions into local life, and the occasions on which major disciplinary cases were aired and settled.[6] Church canons ordered regular examinations of the behaviour of ministers and parishioners, with two or three visitations each year ordered by the 1567 Debrecen Confession. The accompanying church articles agreed at Debrecen only required an annual visitation of every parish, whilst the 1649 revised canons for the Transylvanian province specified an annual visitation by archdeacons of all local churches, with an investigation of archdeacons by the Transylvanian superintendent also to take place each year.[7]

There is only very limited surviving evidence about the operation of Reformed church discipline in Hungary and Transylvania, but the pattern laid down by canons seems, from what records do remain, to have been broadly established throughout the region by the early seventeenth century. Senior clergy embarked upon regular rounds of visitations, and their work was supported by regional synods. Rare glimpses into parish life within Transylvania during this period show visitations in progress, and in the eastern Tisza province district synods were prominent in concerted

---

5 '. . . [a gyülekezet] a maga kedve szerint való pásztort választ magának, hogy minden rendre utasítás nélkül szabadabban élhessen', from Borsod-Gömör-Kishont church articles in *Zsinatok végzései*, ed. Kiss, 729.

6 Illyés, *Egyházfegyelem a magyar református egyházban*; Nagy, *Fejezetek a magyar református egyház 17. századi történetéből*.

7 *Zsinatok végzései*, ed. Kiss, 263, 563–613; *Egyházi kánonok*, ed. Kiss, 1649 canons, nos. 88, 92.

efforts to tighten public morality, particularly through decisions which attempted to restrain excessive behaviour at religious festivals.[8]

Detailed information about how this system of visitation worked is only provided by the surviving records for the Zemplén district of the northern Tisza province. Zemplén county, which straddles the modern border between Hungary and Slovakia, contained part of the huge Rákóczi estates centred on their castle at Sárospatak. Zemplén is a mountainous county, but with southern regions prone to spring floods from the Rivers Tisza and Bodrog. It was this territory of settled and largely Hungarian-speaking villages stretching to the north and east of Sárospatak, rather than the predominantly Slav villages of northern Zemplén, which formed the Reformed heartland of the county. Church visitors travelled around the villages of southern and central Zemplén throughout the year, with letters sent out by the archdeacon warning parishes that he was about to arrive. In 1647 a register of the number of churches in the Zemplén district listed seventy-six parishes served by sixty-four clergy, whilst in 1653, sixty-five churches were recorded with, in addition, nine 'Slav' congregations which accepted Reformed visitation. Conscientious dedication to the task of supervising local standards was provided by archdeacons István Miskolczi Csulyak from 1629, János Simándi from 1646, and Pál Tarczali from 1653 until 1669. Whilst the survival of detailed records of the visitations undertaken by Zemplén's archdeacons is extraordinary, this should not be taken to mean that archdeacons elsewhere were not equally meticulous in performing their disciplinary functions. The treatment of disciplinary issues in Zemplén in fact followed the normal pattern set out in church canons of infrequent examinations of each locality and commune by the Reformed church hierarchy, with their attempts to enforce uniform standards supported by discussions at regular meetings of the region's clergy synod. Zemplén's archdeacons looked to their synod for support, especially when called upon to intervene in difficult local disputes in the face of competing claims from ministers, noble patrons, and local parishioners.[9]

8 Tiszántúl Reformed Church Province Archives (Debrecen), I. 31b, Debrecen egyházmegye; igazgatási iratok, I. 35a 1, Nagykárolyi (Középszolnok) egyházmegye iratai; G. Rákosi, 'Erdély református egyházközségi élet a xvii. században', in *MPEA* 1 (1902), 31–49. For Unitarian discipline in Transylvania, see *Torda város tanácsi jegyzőkönyvek, 1603–1678*, ed. R. Wolf (Kolozsvár, 1993).

9 Tiszáninnen Reformed Church Province Library MS Collection (Sárospatak), vols. 16–18, and also MOL boxes 1907–8, ZEP (1629–45) (1638–51) (1653–72) and Liber Reditum Ecclesiasticum Comitatus Zempleniensis 1623. ZEP (1638–51), 127–9 (Catalogus Eccles. in dioecesi Zempleniensi et Ministri Anno 1647); (1653–72), 2–7. 'Miskolczi Csulyak jegyzőkönyvei', ed. Zoványi, 48–102, 266–313, 368–407; 'Miskolczi Csulyak István esperesi

Instructions from the beginning of the seventeenth century on the conduct of visitations in Zemplén required an annual appraisal of the maintenance of each church building, graveyard, minister's house, and sacramental plate. A check also had to be made on any church land in the parish, and on the income paid to ministers. During a visitation the archdeacon and other senior clergy who normally accompanied him gathered together the local congregation to enquire about the minister's soundness of doctrine, diligence in teaching and catechizing, conduct of the sacraments and marriages, about care of church property, and about the minister's personal conduct. This, on occasions, proved to be a delicate task as István Miskolczi Csulyak reflected in his diary during a dispute between the minister and congregation at Szilvásujfalu in 1629: 'I am a judge, and I hold one ear to the accuser, and one ear to the defendant, and I have to judge the accusation.' These annual visitations by Zemplén's archdeacons were also the prime means of investigating standards in local communities. Parish ministers were questioned about their congregations' attendance at services and communion, and about their general behaviour. Visitation parties were also required to ask questions about the conduct of schoolmasters, and about the punishments being handed down by village justices for different offences.[10]

In Royal Hungary the progress of Reformed discipline through church visitations was obstructed both by Catholic nobles and by Reformed archdeacons' fear of the Turks in border areas. This weakness of Reformed hierarchical organization forced congregations and communities to become more self-reliant in maintaining satisfactory order and discipline. In 1616 the minister at Pápa, János Kanizsai Pálfi, gained local support to follow the model which he had experienced as a student at Heidelberg of a congregational presbytery. Elders appointed at Pápa were made responsible for order and discipline in the town, as well as for ensuring the efficient conduct of all church services. The Pápa presbytery was also empowered to decide whether to retain their minister at the end of each year, and was to call the minister to account if complaints were raised about his preaching or

naplója és leveleskönyve', ed. J. Zoványi, in *MPEA* 10 (1911), 26–142; 11 (1927), 168–91; 12 (1928), 186–219; 13 (1929), 142–8; Felső-magyarországi 1595 church articles, no. 52, and Borsod–Gömör–Kishont church articles, no. 35, in *Zsinatok végzései*, ed. Kiss, 709–22, 723–33.

[10] 'A zempléni ref. dioecesis egyházlátogatási kerdőpontjai', ed. J. Zoványi, *Protestáns Szemle*, 18 (1906), 40–1: 'Biró vagyok, és egyik fülemet az vádosnak, másiknak az maga mentőnek tartom, meg kell itílnem az vádolást.' 'Miskolczi Csulyak István esperesi naplója es leveleskönyve', ed. Zoványi, in *MPEA* 10 (1911), 33, 113. A similar procedure was used in Udvarhely in Transylvania: Pokoly, *Erdélyi református egyház története*, iv, 159–60.

behaviour.[11] In 1630, one year after Kanizsai was appointed as superintendent of the western Danubian province, a synod held at Pápa supported the organization of presbyteries in all of the province's congregations. After he was thrown out of Pápa and Némétujvár in 1633 by local Catholic nobles, Kanizsai moved on to Kiskomárom and began a *senatus ecclesiasticus* there in 1634, with eleven elders initially selected to look after moral discipline and to maintain peace and harmony in the town. As this presbytery developed, there were between fourteen and sixteen elders, whose role was compared in the statutes to those who held up Moses' arms as the Israelites fought the Amalekites.[12] The continuing work of elders at Kiskomárom and of active presbyteries throughout western Hungarian counties was confirmed in 1650 by Balázs Nagymaráczi, then minister at Kiskomárom. According to Nagymaráczi, elders at Körmend and Pápa were largely drawn from resident nobles and from the middle ranks of townsmen, whilst at Kiskomárom he listed the Somogy county deputy sheriff, the county assessor, nobles, and 'honourable' tradesmen amongst twenty-four elders. Nagymaráczi claimed that 'in every town and in every village there are presbyters who, in a proper and godly manner, watch over both the outer orders and the minister'.[13]

As was discussed in the previous chapter, some Reformed ministers in Transylvania and the Partium, as well as in the very different environment of western Hungary, supported the formation of presbyteries in conjunction with, or even replacing, the established clergy hierarchy. Presbyterians were convinced that the selection of lay elders offered a better prospect of tightly controlling the behaviour of parishioners than regular visitations by even the most conscientious archdeacon. Pál Medgyesi proposed that elders would aid discipline by bolstering ministers' determination and ability to punish wrong-doing, and argued that the want of presbyteries was the cause of good order being such a 'rare bird' in Hungary.[14] Medgyesi, indeed, had bitter personal experience of the difficulties for a minister

[11] Dunántúl Reformed Church Province Archives (Pápa), A pápai református egyh. levéltára Liszkay-féle besorolás, no. 29 (Anno 1650 3 Julii Consules Ecclesiastici ad Regimen Ecclae Papensis Constituti); Thury, *A dunántúli református története*, 179–87; Pokoly, 'Az első magyar ref. presbyterium keletkezése és szervezete', 202–20; Tóth, *A pápai református egyház története*, 40–80; J. Makár, *Kanizsai Pálfi János élete és munkássága* (New Brunswick, NJ, 1961).
[12] Dunántúl Reformed Church Province Archives (Pápa), no. 131, A kiskomáromi ref. egyházközség legrégébbi anyakönyve 1624–1732.
[13] [Rákóczi György II], 'Okiratok II. Rákóczy György diplomácziai összeköttetései történetéhez', ed. Szilágyi, *TT* (1889), 350–2.
[14] Medgyesi was aware presbyters would have to learn the skills of disciplining a congregation. See his *Rövid tanítás a presbyteriumról avagy egyházi tanácsról*; Medgyesi, *Dialogus Politico-Ecclesiasticus*, 73, 86, 90–1, 93, 99, 177, 198.

acting alone to impose standards of behaviour which were opposed by his congregation. Whilst minister at Váralja, Medgyesi had alienated his congregation by preaching against what he described as a godless market held outside the church immediately after each Sunday service and which, he claimed, led to 'terrible carousing, shrieking, horrible blasphemies, and fights'. Medgyesi had the market moved to Saturdays but, in the face of local discontent and noble connivance, the market started again on Sundays. Also battling in vain to stop traditional Whitsun celebrations, Medgyesi soon left Váralja in disgust.[15]

In the 1650s the Zemplén area synod supported the principle of developing congregational presbyteries alongside existing church structures, suggesting that communal councils and villages justices be incorporated as elders to begin local presbyteries. In May 1651 the synod concluded that presbyteries were an essential instrument in achieving stricter church discipline, and that the current regime was in some places excessive whilst elsewhere defective.[16] Only limited progress was made in introducing presbyteries, mainly because of strident opposition from Transylvania's princes and many ministers who were deeply anxious about the consequences of making any changes to the established pattern of church government. A presbytery was nevertheless set up at Sárospatak, with the support of Zsuzsanna Lórántffy. Selected elders were led by Pál Medgyesi in a discussion of a recent 'apocalyptic star', perhaps seen as a portent of the need for stronger discipline in the town. In February 1654 an anonymous complaint reached György II Rákóczi that the Sárospatak presbytery had excommunicated some nobles and publicly denounced the lifestyles and marriages of other nobles as immoral. The author also accused the Sárospatak presbytery of grasping power from local magistrates and ruling 'on the necks of the congregation', and of 'prohibiting every Christian conversation, youthful pleasure, and honourable enjoyment' with 'pharisaical holiness'.[17]

Other presbyteries were set up during this period only in a few congregations in Transylvania and eastern Hungary at Fogaras, Ung, Nagyvárad, and in the Küküllő region of central Transylvania.[18] This is not to say that

[15] 'Medgyesi Pál levelei', ed. Szilágyi, *EPK* (1876), 306–9.
[16] Ibid. 320–2; ZEP (1638–51), 189–91, 203, 211; [Magyarországi], 'Adatok a magyarországi puritánus mozgalmak történetéhez', ed. Zoványi, 22–4.
[17] [Rákóczi György II], 'Okiratok II. Rákóczy György diplomácziai összeköttetései történetéhez', ed. Szilágyi, 476–9, no. xxxvii. Tiszáninnen Reformed Church Province Archives (Sárospatak), Protocollum Judicis Primarii et Senatus Oppidi Sáros Nagy Patak iii, 427, 435.
[18] 'A fogarasi egyházközség levéltárából', ed. Pokoly, 106–7, 120–5, 129–130; Juhász, 'Az erdélyi egyházak 17. századi együttélésének kérdései a fogarasi vártartományban', 9–27;

there was little lay enthusiasm for becoming more involved in thwarting and punishing disorderly conduct and immoral behaviour. In some localities traditional communal institutions for the administration of justice were strengthened and directed to the task of combating immorality with the encouragement and active participation of local ministers. The Szekler lands of eastern Transylvania had strong traditions of local self-government, and many villages there had the right to draw up regulations for the smooth running of their own communities and to decide how to punish miscreants. This tradition was built upon at Berekeresztur in 1602 when the local minister, the Maros archdeacon, the deputy sheriff of Maros county, and representatives from Berekeresztur and six satellite hamlets agreed to select a number of churchwardens to restore good order in their district.

Since building a Christian people has been impossible without pious and true teachers of good conduct, the minister shall receive certain such persons, whose judgement and recognition of knowledge and morality is like that of the clergy. They shall be received at all times by the informed will of the whole parish.[19]

New regulations for the seven villages were drawn up, which threatened anyone found working on the Sabbath with hefty fines, and brought an end to wine-trading in the churchyard. Church-goers were admonished in the new ordinances for their past behaviour at services, especially for sitting outside the church, and they were encouraged to hurry inside to hear the minister or face a day in the stocks. The burden of responsibility for upholding these standards of discipline, and for assisting the practical running of the Berekeresztur church, was placed upon the new churchwardens. Whilst unfortunately no records of the operation of these statutes survive, the arrangements apparently proved satisfactory to both the minister and the community, with fourteen churchwardens along with twenty-one jurymen confirmed in their offices in the presence of Reformed church visitors in 1624.[20]

The preamble to the 1606 village book of regulations drawn up at Tarczal in Zemplén claimed that villagers had decided to renew their book of

G. Kúr, *A komáromi református egyházmegye* (Pozsony, 1993), 158–69; 'A kecskeméti reform. egyház jegyzőkönyvéből', ed. L. Fördös, *MPEF* 2 (1880), 35–7; Illyés, 'Az Apafiak szerepe a küküllői református egyházmegye történetében', 468–72, 482–6; Komjáthy, *Adalékok az ungvári ev. ref. egyház történetéhez*, 12.

[19] J. Kolozsvári, 'Egyházi fegyelemre, rendtartásra vonatkozó határozatok a berekeresztúri ref. egyházközségben az 1602 évben', *Református Szemle* (1933), 469–75, art. 1: 'Annak okáért a Praedikátor fogadása forogjon olly bizonyos Személyeken, kik a Tanító rendet mind tudományokban, mind erköltsökben meg tudják itélni és ismerni'.

[20] Kolozsvári, 'Határozatok a berekeresztúri ref. egyházközségben az 1602 évben', 469–75; I. Imreh, *A törvényhozó székely falu* (Bucharest, 1983), 99–120, 279–85.

ordinances in order to ensure that local people lived in a manner which honoured God. This introduction demonstrated the strong influence on the locality of its Reformed minister István Szentandrási, then also Zemplén's archdeacon. The introduction declared that the sins of the Hungarian nation were almost as bad as those of Sodom, and were responsible for the cruel invasions, hunger, and disease which had reduced the region to a pathetic condition, and which required immediate remedial action.[21] Some villages in eastern Hungary also attempted to provide a more effective local regime of moral and social discipline. At Tecső in 1639 a new book of regulations for village officials opened with a prayer that the community might be obedient to God's laws. A justice was to be chosen by the town to ensure good order and to punish those who disturbed it, supported by a council of jurymen. When offenders such as 'marriage-breakers, thieves, and the devil-possessed' were caught, the jurymen and others were to pursue them in a hue and cry through the village. After the chase, offenders were to be placed in the stocks or pay a fine of one forint to the justice.[22] At Misztótfalu the village council aimed to enhance control over behaviour through the annual selection of a justice to promote order and prevent public disturbances, and to reconcile warring parties in preparation for communion. The local council subsequently stoutly defended its administration of justice against outside interference from Szatmár county's deputy sheriff.[23]

From the beginning of the seventeenth century the Hungarian Reformed church had clear procedures in place to oversee local clergy in their task of imposing discipline on Reformed communities. In some places parish clergy shared this responsibility for disciplinary matters with elders in formally organized presbyteries, although the formation of presbyteries in the Transylvanian principality became mired in bitter arguments about authority in church government. Most clergy therefore continued to charge and punish offenders in partnership with traditional local authorities, which in some places had introduced tightened mechanisms to deter and punish immorality and disorder.

(II) THE PUNISHMENT OF OFFENDERS

The second component of Reformed church discipline was the manner in which Calvinist authorities sought to punish offenders by demanding that

[21] Németh (ed.), *Hegyaljai mezővárosok törvényei*, 29–42.

[22] Tiszántúl Reformed Church Province Library Manuscript Collection (Debrecen), R. 111/2769, Tecső protocolluma 1639–1805.

[23] Tiszántúl Reformed Church Province Library Manuscript Collection (Debrecen), R. 3289, Misztótfalu mezőváros jegyzőkönyve, 1596–1803, esp. 84–5, 100–1.

they perform public acts of penance, or ultimately by excommunicating offenders from Christian society. Calvinist discipliners did not aim primarily
to impose a regime of draconian and fearful retributive justice for its own
sake, but instead aspired to encourage genuine repentance from offenders
for their misconduct. Presbyteries and consistories across the continent
had powers to reprimand and rebuke offenders who appeared before them
on various charges. Worse still for those charged with wrong-doing was the
ordeal of public penance and confession before the whole congregation,
usually involving a reserved seat in the church and requiring special clothes
to be worn. Penance as demanded by Anglican church courts could require
the confessor to make a public admission of fault dressed in a white sheet
and carrying a white rod, or to go barelegged for greater shame. In Scotland, kirk-sessions could demand that penitents wore a black gown and left
their heads uncovered, or went barefoot in sackcloth.[24]

Whilst Calvinists did not invent such ceremonies, nor had a monopoly
over their use, these rituals were central to Reformed notions of exemplary
spiritual punishment and meaningful contrition, rather than an ongoing
cycle of frequent sin and only notional remorse. Punishments were in fact
graded by Calvinist church authorities so that re-offenders were more
harshly dealt with in an effort to cleanse communities of certain proscribed
forms of behaviour. The ultimate spiritual weapon available to Reformed
churches remained excommunication and subsequent complete social exclusion from a local community. Again excommunication was generally intended to be an exemplary punishment for serious offences, although at
Geneva the regular use of excommunication led to those found quarrelling
at home being routinely excommunicated in the 1560s. Once someone was
excommunicated the only route back into the community was to undergo
repentance in church and receive a public rebuke from the minister. The
exercise of Calvinist discipline was not a purely spiritual battle against
wrongdoing. The institutional co-operation between the church and local
civil authorities over disciplinary matters was complemented by a mixture
of penitential and punitive elements in the treatment of offenders. Impeni-
tent sinners and those who had committed serious offences were particularly likely to suffer punishment at the hands of the civil authorities as well
as the church. Church discipliners also often supported the imposition of
punishments by secular officials for a range of lesser misdemeanours.

[24] M. Ingram, 'Puritans and the Church Courts, 1560–1640', in C. Durston and J. Eales
(eds.), *The Culture of English Puritanism, 1560–1700* (London, 1996), 65; G. Parker, 'The
"Kirk by Law Established" and the Origins of "The Taming of Scotland": St Andrews
1559–1600', in L. Leneman (ed.), *Perspectives in Scottish Social History: Essays in Honour of
Rosalind Mitchison* (Aberdeen, 1988), 1–33.

Established town or local regulations were routinely used to impose fines, terms of imprisonment, or subject offenders to corporal punishment as supplements to acts of penance.[25]

The Hungarian church had a range of spiritual sanctions at its disposal in the battle against sin, as well as influence over the policies of the civil authorities towards particular offences. The central aim of Reformed ministers was to use publicity to shame the weak into repentance, and to encourage a spiritual response to any accusation of wrongdoing. The most potent weapon in the disciplinary arsenal of the church was the right to excommunicate its members. According to the Debrecen articles of 1567 and the Herczegszőllős canons of 1576, those who did not want to hear the word of God or who refused to accept communion would be excommunicated as apostates. The Debrecen articles warned ministers to refuse access to the sacraments to any who would spoil their purity and 'not to give what is holy to dogs'. Canons detailed that after repeated warnings from a minister, unreformed thieves, adulterers, blasphemers, makers of false oaths, and drunkards were also to be excommunicated from their congregations. The 1649 Transylvanian canons concluded that temporary exclusion from the church should be imposed if reprimands from a minister were having no obvious effect on open sinners. Those who continued with their sinful actions despite such warnings could then be excommunicated on the approval of the local synod, with the minister damning the offender in a public service and abandoning him or her to the power of Satan.[26]

Sinners could be accepted back into the church community after exclusion if they showed a willingness to repent. The 1567 Debrecen Confession stressed that 'the truly repentant are not to be left outside the church in misery for long in the land of Satan, but when they have mended their ways we will call them back'. Repentance of sin required a public admission of guilt and a renunciation of the offence which had been committed. This was marked in church services by the penitent wearing dark clothing and either sitting on a special stool of repentance or standing at the church door.[27] Ministers in the upper Danubian province were first required to

---

[25] During the 1560s 1 in 25 Genevan citizens was excommunicated each year: Monter, 'The Consistory of Geneva, 1559–1569', 467–84. M. F. Graham, 'Equality before the Kirk? Church Discipline and the Elite in Reformation-Era Scotland', *Archiv für Reformationsgeschichte*, 84 (1993), 289–310.

[26] *Zsinatok végzései*, ed. Kiss, 584–5, 686: 'ne adjátok azt a mi szent az ebeknek'; *Egyházi kánonok*, ed. Kiss, 1649 canons, no. 44.

[27] 'nem is hagyjuk a valódi bünbánókat kivül az egyházon soká nyomorogni a sátán országában, hanem mihelyt megjavultak, visszahivjuk': *Zsinatok végzései*, ed. Kiss, 241, 723–33, no. 27. J. Zoványi, 'Egyházi fegyelem és szeretetmunkásság a régi magyar protestánsokkal', *Szeretetszövetség* (1935), 2–3, nos. 1–2.

preach against a particular sin and then to expel any consistent offenders from the congregation. Formal reconciliation with the church in this province required kneeling penitence in 'mourning clothes' before absolution could be granted. The penitent was even then kept out of church for some more weeks, before being ceremonially received back into the congregation with a further public confession of the sin and another rebuke by the minister. If repentance was seen to be genuine, and admission back into the church community permitted, then the civil authorities were often not called upon to punish the original offence.[28]

Records from Zemplén county offer some detail on how this system of punishment worked in practice. Zemplén's archdeacons consistently attempted to establish public shaming as the central element of correction for offences. There were, however, frequent occasions when parishioners balked at the standards of punishment and public humiliation which the visitors were encouraging the clergy to apply, with many trying to evade making public repentance for their sins in church. Grumbling amongst congregations at such punishments was occasionally reported back by ministers to archdeacons on visitation. At the village of Terebes in 1648 an 'abominable sinner' was so angry with his local minister that he refused to come to church, whilst at Rozvágy and Zsadány in 1654 several parishioners refused to take part in communion services after disputes over public repentance. Those who stubbornly resisted the church authorities invited the application of more severe sanctions against them. Whilst excommunication was very sparingly used by the Zemplén church, at Izsép in 1648 when János Simándi was faced with a man who refused to follow the public penance set for him, Simándi decided that he could not be absolved from his sins and must be excommunicated until he reformed his attitudes. Similarly at Cigánd in 1656 Pál Tarczali advised the local minister that if an old woman who had refused to take communion did not change her ways then she was to be excommunicated, whilst at Rozvágy the minister was instructed that excommunication could fall on any unregenerate 'abominable blasphemers' as he felt it was deserved.[29]

The church also reserved the right to refuse a Christian burial to those who never regained admittance to a congregation, and who were therefore considered to have died in sin. A village justice in Zétény was required by his minister to repent publicly of his sin, but repeatedly refused to do so.

[28] Samarjai, *Agenda*; Kathona, *Samarjai János gyakorlati theológiája*; Borsod–Gömör–Kishont church articles in *Zsinatok végzései*, ed. Kiss, 723–33, no. 28; Dunántúl Reformed Church Province Archives (Pápa), no. 7 (Egyházkerületi jegyzőkönyvek mutatója), 1654 Farkasd synod.

[29] ZEP (1638–51), 148; (1653–72), 31–2, 53–6, 112–13, 115.

István Miskolczi Csulyak advised the local minister that if the justice died without making public confession of his faults, then he should not be given an honourable funeral and was not to be buried in the church graveyard. Resistance was also offered to church discipliners by a certain Ambrus Vajda, who refused to go to church, saying that even if they killed him he did not want to go. The visitors instructed his local council that the church bell should not be rung at his death and that he was not to be buried in the graveyard, the hallmarks of a so-called 'ass's funeral' (*szamár módon temettessék el*). The 1606 Tarczal village book offers some more detail on these shaming rituals at funerals. One of the Tarczal regulations required that anyone found guilty of attempting to heal the sick using magic was to be cursed by the minister and given an ass's funeral. Church bells were not to be rung at such a funeral, pupils from the local school were not to follow the coffin, and the graveyard was not to be used, with the body instead deposited at the foot of the gallows.[30]

Zemplén's archdeacons attempted to impose clear and uniform standards of active and public repentance for sins, but found that standards of punishment ranged enormously from village to village. In some congregations the archdeacon and other visitors were delighted by the fearless application of ministers to the task of disciplining offenders. At Olaszi in 1629 the minister was reported to burden offending sinners with harsh rebukes, without regard for their social status. On 15 September 1629 at five in the morning Miskolczi visited the village of Agárd, where the minister was able to report no outstanding difficulties with his congregation, but by nine the same morning Miskolczi had moved on to the neighbouring village of Perbenyik, where he found uncontrolled swearing and fighting, and concluded that all sense of law had collapsed there with no effort either to stop offences being committed or to punish them.[31]

The archdeacons in Zemplén believed that such a variety of standards pointed towards inconsistency among ministers in demanding public penance from offenders, as well as different attitudes among village justices and councils to imposing punishments through fines or by placing offenders in the stocks. The first year of visitations completed by Miskolczi in 1629 revealed widespread abuses in the disciplining of offenders by village justices and a lack of standardized punishment, or no punishment at all, for many offences targeted by the church. In response, Miskolczi recommended that local village councils become more involved in the process of

---

[30] Németh (ed.), *Hegyaljai mezővárosok törvényei*, 29–42. 'Miskolczi Csulyak jegyzőkönyvei', ed. Zoványi, 58–9, 300, 304, 312.
[31] 'Miskolczi Csulyak jegyzőkönyvei', ed. Zoványi, 94–5.

enforcing spiritual discipline. Miskolczi suggested that local councils should be able to judge if someone was required to repent for having committed an offence, and also share the burden with the clergy by deciding on the circumstances for repentance, such as how many times penitents should appear in church and whether they should stand hooded or not.[32]

Miskolczi's vision of local ministers and councils working together in harmony to form a mixed regime of penitential and punitive discipline seems often to have been far from reality. It proved very difficult to persuade councils to disrupt traditional norms of community justice with the more exacting punishments now demanded by the church. The minister at Kápolna reported to his archdeacon in 1639 that the justice and village council there were still not punishing swearing or fornication at all, and that convictions for theft only resulted in a fine of wine or other alcoholic drink to be donated by an offender for the rest of the village to enjoy. Fines of wine, or sometimes of money, were in fact the normal punishment handed down by local authorities for many offences. The 1606 Tarczal regulations detailed fines for a range of offences, including for those who tried to sell the famous sweet wines of the region before the Sunday morning service.[33]

Zemplén's archdeacons repeatedly admonished communal authorities for their perceived laxity of punishments, preferring to see corporal punishment for certain offences rather than fines, and calling for the death penalty to be enforced against unrepentant blasphemers and adulterers. Whilst on visitation at Vitány and Kajata in 1641, Miskolczi recommended that the customary punishment for blasphemous swearing and minor acts of theft of a 1-forint fine should not be drunk in wine, but the money set aside for the common use of the village. Miskolczi and the other archdeacons were also anxious to prevent any variation of punishment according to the social status of the transgressor. Such a distinction was uncovered at Szilvásujfalu between ordinary people, who were put in the stocks and beaten for swearing, and jurymen, who could pay off punishment through a fine of wine. At Zalkod the minister reported that those living with the local noble patron went unpunished despite being guilty of swearing, and at Sárospatak the minister related that punishment for cursing was normally enforced in the town except against Hajduck soldiers and those who lived at the Rákóczi's castle.[34]

[32] Ibid. 48–9.
[33] Németh (ed.), *Hegyaljai mezővárosok törvényei*, 29–42; 'Miskolczi Csulyak jegyzőkönyvei', ed. Zoványi, 274, 371.
[34] 'Miskolczi Csulyak jegyzőkönyvei', ed. Zoványi, 54, 76, 82, 97–9, 296, 372, 383.

This evidence from Zemplén county suggests that resistance to the regime of strict punishments demanded by the Reformed church came not only from the poor and lowly in society. Sometimes not only ordinary church members refused to participate in rituals of public contrition for their sins, so too did local law enforcers. Village justices and councils also only partially adopted and implemented the punishments recommended by the Reformed church for a range of offences. Reformed archdeacons and parish clergy nevertheless persisted in their attempts to extract formal acts of repentance from offenders, insisted that the punishment of a range of highlighted problems be made more rigorous, and demanded that offences such as swearing, drunkenness, and sexual immorality be taken more seriously by local authorities.

(III) REFORMED MORALITY

Calvinist discipliners across the Continent were initially mostly engaged in prosecuting errors of dogma and in correcting heterodox religious beliefs. At Geneva, concern about poor knowledge of prayers and creeds, especially amongst women, dominated early consistory meetings. Once a better grip had been established on theological orthodoxy, the focus of Calvinist discipliners progressively shifted towards maintaining high standards of religious observance and addressing moral offences. Variations emerged between the proportion of religious and moral offences considered by Calvinist disciplinary bodies in different churches, largely determined by how long the congregation had been established and on the degree of contact with those of other religions. Poor attendance at church services remained a major problem for many Calvinist authorities, especially for presbyteries in the Palatinate where roll-calls revealed widespread absenteeism at weekday and Sunday evening services. Long battles were also fought by ministers and elders against traditional forms of behaviour no longer deemed acceptable, particularly against swearing and certain forms of recreation, especially dancing. Calvinist discipliners equally laboured to uphold general standards of social order against sexual scandals, public disputes, violent quarrelling, drunkenness, lying, and theft.[35]

Different consistories and congregations across the Continent displayed distinct moral preoccupations. Although making direct comparisons

35 J. R. Watt, 'Women and the Consistory in Calvin's Geneva', *Sixteenth Century Journal*, 24 (1993), 429–39; B. Vogler and J. Estèbe, 'La genèse d'une société protestante: Étude comparée de quelques registres consistoriaux Languedociens et Palatins vers 1600', *Annales*, 31 (1976), 362–88.

between churches is problematic, some sense of the disciplinary issues which were highlighted helps to provide a context for conclusions about the crusade to impose Reformed standards of behaviour in Hungary and Transylvania. In the Languedoc the greatest number of cases to appear before consistories by the late sixteenth century involved arguments, fighting, and violent disputes. There was also a notable campaign against traditional games and festivities, with more people brought before the Nîmes consistory accused of dancing than for sexual misconduct. In the Palatinate there was a concentrated attack against cursing and swearing in the wake of a 1592 law proscribing blasphemous oaths. In the Palatinate and at Emden in East Friesland there was also a relatively high number of cases involving drunkenness, which was seen as endangering family life and causing public scandals. At St Andrews in Scotland, meanwhile, a majority of cases brought before the kirk session in the last quarter of the sixteenth century dealt with fornication and adultery, with another third concerning disorderly conduct. A study of cases before sessions in lowland Scotland between 1560 and 1610 has revealed that about half of all hearings there involved some sort of sexual offence. English Puritans complained about the lack of a concerted campaign by Anglican church court officials on issues of Sabbath observance, drinking, and traditional sports, although there is some evidence of increased attention during the late sixteenth century to prosecute cases of fornication and bridal pregnancy. This would only rather seem to confirm that British Protestants were singular in their obsession with matters of sexual propriety.[36]

Insufficient records have survived in Hungary to allow any precise quantification of the extent to which discipline was applied against Reformed congregations, or to indicate how this might have changed over time, nor can the proportion of religious offences be accurately measured against various moral offences. It is only from visitation records for Zemplén county and minutes of the meetings of the Kiskomárom presbytery

---

[36] R. A. Mentzer, '*Disciplina nervus ecclesiae*: The Calvinist Reform of Morals at Nîmes', *Sixteenth Century Journal*, 18 (1987), 89–115; A. Somas and E. Labrousse, 'Le registre consistorial de Coutras, 1582–1584', *Bulletin de la Société de l'histoire du Protestantisme Français*, 126 (1980), 193–228; R. A. Mentzer, 'Le consistoire et la pacification du monde rural', *Bulletin de la Société de l'histoire du Protestantisme Français*, 135 (1989), 373–89; H. R. Schmidt, 'Moral Courts in Rural Berne during the Early Modern Period', in K. Maag (ed.), *The Reformation in Eastern and Central Europe* (Aldershot, 1997), 155–81; H. Schilling, *Civic Calvinism in Northwestern Germany and the Netherlands. Sixteenth to Nineteenth Centuries* (Kirksville, Mo., 1991), 44, 58. Watt, 'Women and the Consistory', 429–39; Vogler and Estèbe, 'La genèse d'une société protestante', 362–88; Ingram, 'Puritans and the Church Courts', 65; Parker, 'The "Kirk by Law Established"', 1–33; Graham, 'Equality before the Kirk?', 289–310; Monter, 'The Consistory of Geneva', 467–84.

that any assessment can be made of the developing impact of the formal process of church discipline on rural and urban life in Hungary, and some impression gained about the concerns which dominated the attention of archdeacons, ministers, elders, and village justices. The remainder of this chapter will firstly consider cases in Zemplén involving both religious offences and such moral offences as swearing, drinking, immorality associated with festivals, sexual misconduct, theft, quarrels, and violent arguments, and then assess the offences which featured in the work of the Kiskomárom presbytery.

Most reports by Zemplén's parish ministers to their superiors on visitation dealt with cases of immoral behaviour and disorderly conduct, but there were also some occasional instances of religious offences. At Hotyka in 1629 András Batka, who had been married by a Catholic priest, was charged with refusing to listen to church services inside the church building, a case which was put by the visitors to the Zemplén synod for further consideration. At Visnyó a piper called István Bárány was punished for crouching down after saying the Lord's Prayer, whilst at Tolcsva in 1643 Miskolczi recorded that a certain layman, György Bónis, had attempted to baptize a child only to die instantly on doing so. At Szécskeresztur in 1629 Miskolczi found pieces of an altar remaining in place in the church, and ordered them to be removed immediately. Complaints about such incidences of religious heterodoxy and malpractice were very infrequent, since the Reformed church was already well ensconced in a dominant position in Zemplén by the 1620s. There were, however, frequent complaints about the state in which churches were being kept. At Polyánka the church in 1629 was described as disgustingly smelly with cured pork hanging from the beams and rafters. Meanwhile at Vámosujfalu mice were found in wheat kept in the church making it smelly, and meat was found to have been stored on church benches at Újlak in 1629.[37]

Individuals were often reprimanded for non-attendance at church services and at communion, and there were several general accusations against Zemplén congregations for poor church attendance. The minister at Bénye in 1635 noted that there were sometimes only three people present for some of his services, and that local men did not attend church on the slightest pretext. Nobles were not immune from criticism for poor attendance at church, and there were also particular problems in persuading congregations to attend weekday services, with occasional comments on low turn-out at communion services as well. In the 1650s congregations at Zsadány and Rozvágy were still being reprimanded for not attending

37 'Miskolczi Csulyak jegyzőkönyvei', ed. Zoványi, 75, 80, 270.

weekday services or catechizing classes, and even at Sárospatak the ministers complained of absenteeism from the Sunday evening service in 1660. Ministers in Zemplén also raised objections about the behaviour of their congregations during church services. At Ricse in 1639 the minister complained that there was always shouting or noise near the church during prayers, and he wanted the congregation to depart quietly after services rather than stand around 'contending with one another'.[38]

Zemplén's archdeacons and clergy saw plenty of room for improvement in the religious observance of the county's Reformed community. However, their attention was mostly taken up in consideration of moral offences. In particular, a striking campaign was conducted by Reformed ministers in Zemplén during this period against foul language, cursing, swearing, and blasphemy. Laws passed in Geneva from 1551, the Palatinate in 1592, and in England in 1650 confirm that attempts to reform language were an important aspect of Calvinist efforts to reshape popular behaviour and pre-reformation forms of religiosity. Customs of cursing and swearing were deemed a significant problem across all the church provinces of Hungary and Transylvania. The Küküllő area synod of Transylvania intoned in 1619 that through obscene talk and oaths people were allowing their mouths to become instruments of the devil. Pál Medgyesi too was appalled by the common usage of phrases such as 'devil-spirited', and at sayings which showed a lack of honour for God's name such as 'God preserve you', 'God help you', and 'God overcome you'.[39]

Popular usage of the name of God in curses, or invoking the devil in oaths, or swearing by the power of holy things was viewed with the utmost seriousness by Reformed visitors in Zemplén. Particular concern was expressed by the archdeacons in Zemplén's visitation records about incidences when individuals invoked the power of their spirit and their status as baptized Christians in blasphemous oaths (*lelkével szitkozódik, kereszteltével szitkozódik*). Cursing was more likely to be used by the weak in society against the strong, and in the Zemplén records women were frequently

---

[38] ZEP (1638–51), 187; (1653–72), 115, 307. 'Miskolczi Csulyak jegyzőkönyvei', ed. Zoványi, 56–8, 71, 78, 82, 85, 285, 301, 376, 402.

[39] Pál Medgyesi, *Igaz magyar nép negyedik jajja s-siralma* (Sárospatak, 1657), 17–18; A. Montagu, *The Anatomy of Swearing* (London, 1968); G. Hughes, *Swearing. A Social History of Foul Language, Oaths and Profanity in English* (Oxford, 1991), 91–100; H. R. Schmidt, 'Die Ächtung des Fluchens durch reformierte Sittengericht', in P. Blickle (ed.), *Der Fluch und der Eid. Die metaphysische Begründung gesellschaftlichen Zusammenlebens und politischer Ordnung in der ständischen Gesellschaft* (Zeitschrift für Historische Forschung 15; Berlin, 1993), 65–120; K. Thomas, *Religion and the Decline of Magic* (London, 1978), 599–611; C. Durston, 'Puritan Rule and the Failure of Cultural Revolution', in C. Durston and J. Eales (eds.), *The Culture of English Puritanism, 1560–1700* (London, 1996), 217–21.

those reported making oaths and blasphemous curses, lacking the same re-
course as men to violent action to redress their grievances. Ministers expressed outrage at customary oath-making, both because of the irreverence
with which God's name was being treated and because making oaths was
perceived to claim power mechanically to manipulate divine authority
through uttering sacred words. The clergy however retained their power to
damn in services of excommunication, and their campaign to curtail cursing implied tacit acceptance that oaths could form a potential challenge to
the operation of providence. Common swearing and foul language was
hardly viewed with any more sympathy by Zemplén's ministers, even
though it was often the result of immediate anger at the tensions and
rivalries of everyday life rather than the result of preconceived malice.[40]

Efforts to eradicate prevailing customs of blasphemous cursing, profane
swearing, and the use of foul and sexually explicit language were at the
heart of the Zemplén Reformed church's attempt to cleanse local society of
offences which might provoke divine retribution. At Tarczal the importance of cursing and swearing was stressed above all other offences in the
1606 village regulations. The ordinances committed the Tarczal justice
and council to punish anyone found guilty of uttering disgusting or blasphemous curses, or of using obscene or abominable language. Those who
cursed by the power of their spirit or baptism were to be fined 12 forints, or
to spend Sunday in the stocks. Any second instance of such cursing was to
be punished by being beaten, and for a third case the offender's tongue or
head was to be cut off. Anyone caught uttering what were described as 'disgraceful oaths' was to be fined 3 forints, or 6 forints if the offender was a
member of the local council. The money raised by these fines was supposed
to go towards the upkeep of the Tarczal church and school and to support
the poor. Parents were to be punished for their children's swearing, and the
council issued a particular warning for women and girls to be careful about
their language. Further evidence on how the minister and leading figures at
Tarczal understood the challenge posed to their community by cursing
comes from regulations which proscribed reading passages from the Bible
in efforts to cure a sick person or animal. The power of words invoking divine power was accepted as real by the minister and the council, but its unsanctioned use for evil intent or profane purposes was strictly forbidden.

[40] For a list of blasphemies and curses cited at a 1653 synod in central Hungary, see MOL
box 1890, Simandianum Protocollum (kerületi jegyzőkönyvek, 1629–1731), 20–1. See also
[Küküllővári], 'Az 1619. évi küküllővári zsinat felterjesztése Bethlen Gábor fejedelemhez',
ed. G. Illyés, *Református Szemle* (1934), 501–5; 'Protocollum primum seu Gyarmatianum
Tractus Beregiensis (1593–1631)', printed in Illyés, *Egyházfegyelem a magyar református egyházban*.

Anyone caught in Tarczal reading from the Bible to try to heal was to be first beaten, at a second offence to have his or her tongue cut out, and on the third occasion to be burned.[41] Zemplén's Reformed clergy identified cursing as a widespread disease afflicting their community, and at Kisazar in 1648 the minister accused his whole congregation of 'devilish and abominable blasphemies'. A list of foul names which the son of János Horvát had used at Szilvásujfalu in 1651 included 'son of the devil, son of the devil's wife, son of a devil-given whore, and son of a thieving whore'. There was particular anxiety about anyone who invoked the devil in curses, and at Bári such offenders were immediately excluded from the congregation in 1648.[42] It often proved very difficult for ministers to gain general acceptance in Zemplén for the standards of language which they wished to impose. When the minister at Viss tried to reprimand a girl guilty of cursing and blaspheming he was castigated for doing so by the girl's mother. At Szentes in 1629 when the sexually explicit swearing of the wife of Miklós Thót was overheard, she was reported to the minister, who then publicly rebuked her in church, but both the offender and the informant were so angered with the minister that they refused thereafter to come to church.[43]

The Zemplén visitation records detail a long struggle by the archdeacons to enforce appropriate punishments for cursing and swearing. At Horvát in 1629 Miskolczi found that 'spirit blaspheming' was not being punished at all, whilst the local justice at Szőlőske punished cursing by having offenders' hands placed in the stocks. The minister at Toronya reported that whilst the local custom was for swearing to be punished by a place in the stocks, 'when they want to punish somebody lightly, they gather together and make him pay for drink, and if there is little to drink, they upbraid the offender, and then drink till they are drunk'. Miskolczi thought that all these sanctions were insufficient, and found blasphemy equally weakly punished at Olaszi, Pelejte, Zsadány, Újlak, Jesztreb, Szőlőske, Rozvágy, Imreg, and Redmecz. Miskolczi ordered that one blasphemous oath should be punished by the offender's neck being placed in the stocks for the duration of a sermon, for two offences the guilty party

---

[41] 'undok és istenkáromló gyalázatos szitok', 'trágárság és fertelmes beszéd': Németh (ed.), *Hegyaljai mezővárosok törvényei*, 29–42.

[42] ZEP (1638–51), 100–1, 147, 150–1, 219. 'Miskolczi Csulyak jegyzőkönyvei', ed. Zoványi, 387; G. Klaniczay, 'Hungary: The Accusations and the Universe of Popular Magic', in B. Ankarloo and G. Henningsen (eds.), *Early Modern European Witchcraft* (Oxford, 1990), 219–57; L. Makkai, 'Puritánok és boszorkányok Debrecenben', *A Hajdú-Bihar Megyei Levéltár Évkönyve*, 8 (1981), 113–30.

[43] 'Miskolczi Csulyak jegyzőkönyvei', ed. Zoványi, 60, 89.

should remain in the stocks until the evening, and on the third occasion those who cursed should be beaten as well.[44]

Stricter punishments were beginning to be enforced for cursing in some villages, such as at Kazsu in 1639 where offenders stood in the stocks and were publicly rebuked by their minister. At Kozma in 1641 a blasphemous oath resulted in the offender's head being put in the stocks and a beating, but Miskolczi found that cursing was still not punished at all at Szerdahely and Kápolna in 1639. At Pelejte the minister and local gentry came to an agreement in June 1641 on how to punish cursing and swearing. Anyone who offended would have their necks placed in the stocks, and if they made any difficulty then they would also have to pay 1 forint to be used by the village. However, in the two neighbouring villages of Izsép and Lasztócz swearing was still not even recognized as a serious offence by the local justices and went completely unpunished. After Pál Tarczali became archdeacon in the 1650s, reports still continued of the lax punishment of blasphemous curses and oaths. The archdeacons and clergy in Zemplén appear none the less to have had some success in establishing that cursing and swearing were important sins, and in encouraging the enforcement of more consistent and severe penalties against offenders.[45]

Drunkenness had long been highlighted by Hungarian Reformed clergy as a significant source of disorder and immorality. Ministers worked together with local authorities in towns and the countryside to regulate access to alcohol. In most areas taverns were closed during church services, and local regulations typically prevented the sale of wine after eight in the evening, as at Kolozsvár in Transylvania. Music was also commonly forbidden in taverns during the evening, and local officials were vigilant in the battle to maintain good order and avoid fighting and scandals which might occur after late night drinking and music. Reformed ministers demanded that people control their level of drinking, and individuals were sometimes cited during visitations in Zemplén for habitual drunkenness. At Olaszi in 1650 the minister complained about the drunkenness of Gergely Bolyko, who was known to frequent the local pub on Sunday afternoons. The minister was particularly annoyed since he thought Bolyko, as a juryman, should have been setting an example for others in the village to follow.[46]

---

44 'Miskolczi Csulyak jegyzőkönyvei', ed. Zoványi, 51, 53–4, 59, 77, 269, 273, 277–9, 285–90, 300, 305, 309, 370–1, 384.

45 ZEP (1653–72), 77, 79, 81, 111; 'Miskolczi Csulyak jegyzőkönyvei', ed. Zoványi, 388, 396, 406.

46 ZEP (1638–51), 187; Gáspár Heltai, *A részegségnek és tobzódásnak veszedelmes voltáról való dialogus*, ed. B. Stoll (Budapest, 1951; orig. pub. Kolozsvár, 1552); Diószegi Bónis, *Az részegesnek gyülölséges, utálatos és rettenetes állapota*.

There were also a significant number of cases recorded in the Zemplén visitation reports of ministers being encouraged to change customary patterns of drinking at taverns, particularly during festivals when temporary taverns were set up in many villages. In 1629 Miskolczi found that there had been a tavern in Vily at Easter, and on the second day of Whitsun at Izsép and Toronya. Heavy drinking at Christmas and Easter was reported against the youth of Hotyka, and at Lasztócz the local minister complained that drinking on the second day of major religious festivals meant that parishioners were not attending evening church services on those days. There was popular resistance to the church's attack on holiday taverns at Terebes, where resentment was expressed against the local minister who had preached against traditional drinking customs.[47] Resistance to the demands of the archdeacons and clergy to limit drinking at festivals continued into the 1630s. The Újváros minister complained in 1632 of a festival tavern with beer-drinking, dancing, and whistling. At Szécs, servants of a local noble continued to organize holiday taverns, and the minister claimed that the village justice had been prevented from punishing anyone for it. Reformed visitors sought to limit or eradicate such taverns because they were perceived, with some justification, to be sources of all sorts of immoral behaviour. At Nagyazar in 1635 there was fighting at Christmas in a tavern, and a certain Jancsi Kotnyeles had apparently demonstrated his reputed magical skills. Dancing was reported at the Újlak tavern after church services on festival days in 1636, and ministers remained concerned about the impact on moral standards of taverns at Radvány in 1641 and at Kajata in 1648.[48]

Reformed ministers in Zemplén also sought to end other sorts of traditional recreation and celebrations which they associated with drunkenness and immorality. Church canons specified that 'idolatrous games' and dancing were strictly prohibited as completely inappropriate for decent people, especially for ministers and their families. Most towns and counties banned music and dancing at fairs or on festivals, with Debrecen banning dancing altogether in 1610 and again on Gábor Bethlen's death in 1629. Dancing was customary at wedding and baptism celebrations, but preachers were vituperative against music-makers and dancers alike. János Debreczeni Kalocsa described dancing as the devil's invention so that he could spread sin, and in 1649 the Marosvásárhely town council ordered that anyone caught making music on Sundays with a violin, cimbalom, lute, or pipe was

---

47 'Miskolczi Csulyak jegyzőkönyvei', ed. Zoványi, 56, 59, 63–5, 71, 78–9.
48 ZEP (1638–51), 145. 'Miskolczi Csulyak jegyzőkönyvei', ed. Zoványi, 275–7, 282, 287.

to be placed in the stocks and to have their instrument confiscated. The Transylvanian superintendent István Geleji Katona complained bitterly about other popular festival customs, including traditions of electing kings and holding masked carnivals at Whitsun. In Zemplén the Tarczal village book demanded that unmarried men abandon the customary practice of celebrating Shrove Tuesday by chasing after women and showering them with water, a tradition which, to the chagrin of most Hungarian women, continues to the present day. Masked carnival celebrations were forbidden during visitations of Újlak and Csarnahó in 1629. At Bénye local youths were reported to the visitors in 1655 for holding some sort of scandalous carnival celebrations, whilst at Kövesd locals were finally persuaded by their minister in the 1650s to abandon their custom of building a St John's fire in the middle of the village at midsummer, which marked another occasion for music-making and dancing around bonfires.[49]

Senior clergy in Zemplén also paid close attention to cases of sexual misconduct, to the behaviour of the unmarried, and to problems concerning marriage. The archdeacons of this period were particularly concerned to uphold sexual probity in villages by preventing women from gathering together in communal spinning-rooms during the winter months. Parish ministers were encouraged to stop this practice altogether, or at least to have it controlled, since according to István Miskolczi Csulyak it was 'nothing other than a cover for roguery'. The practice was apparently commonplace in Zemplén's villages, and the archdeacon received news of spinning-rooms in operation at Kajata, Szilvásujfalu, and Szécskeresztur in 1629, at Pelejte, Nagyrozvágy, and Kozma in 1632, at Újlak in 1636, and at Imreg in 1639. Miskolczi warned the congregation at Szentes in 1629 that 'spinning-rooms are forbidden among Christians. They give opportunities for wrongdoing.' However, at Zétény in 1639 he conceded that if locals were determined to continue to spin together, then it should at least take place in an honourable home and men should not be admitted under any circumstances. This gives some indication that Miskolczi and Zemplén's ministers were prepared to show some flexibility in their demands, but perhaps only when they could not in any case hope for complete compliance from local communities.[50]

---

49 *Zsinatok végzései*, ed. Kiss, 173, 228–31, 251, 598–99; Geleji Katona, *Váltság Titka*, ii, 414; Németh (ed.), *Hegyaljai mezővárosok törvényei*, 29–42; ZEP (1653–72), 111; 'Miskolczi Csulyak jegyzőkönyvei', ed. Zoványi, 81, 83, 87; S. Takáts, *Művelődéstörténeti tanulmányok a xvi–xvii századból*, ed. K. Benda (Budapest, 1961), 296–316; T. Dömötör, *Naptári ünnepeknépi színjátszás* (Budapest, 1964).

50 'Miskolczi Csulyak jegyzőkönyvei', ed. Zoványi, 66, 68, 70, 89, 96, 275, 277, 287, 304, 309.

The Zemplén visitation records also show a consistent drive to create a harsher climate of discipline against fornication and other sexual misconduct. Village authorities were responsible for punishing fornication before offenders were allowed to offer public repentance at church for their wrongdoing. The clergy were determined that this initial punishment should be severe, and István Miskolczi Csulyak criticized justices for weak punishments imposed in response to cases of fornication at Nagygéres, Rad, Battyán, and Szentes in 1629. At Szerdahely Miskolczi ordered that the hands of fornicators be beaten until they cried out in pain. During his visitations Miskolczi also uncovered many instances in which fornication was not properly punished by some ministers, who failed to impose public repentance on offenders or did not require penitents to wear the required hood over their heads as a sign of shame. There was also popular resistance to the church's demands, and a woman accused of fornication at Lasztócz in 1651 refused to make public repentance. However, when young men at Jesztreb who had been found guilty of fornication declared themselves unwilling to undergo public repentance, Miskolczi ordered that if any of them died they were not to receive a proper Christian burial.[51]

Apart from regularly issuing injunctions on the need for harsher punishments for fornication and sexual immorality, Zemplén's archdeacons also heard difficult cases of sexual misconduct to decide on appropriate punishment. A reported case of incest at Újlak in 1629 led to a punishment of two days in the stocks, followed by public repentance whilst hooded. Miskolczi recorded a case of sodomy in Erdőbénye in 1632 between two students, only one of whom was imprisoned for a short time. Miskolczi ordered that in future such cases should be dealt with much more severely with longer gaol sentences. At Toronya suspicion of a woman whose house was known to be frequented by local students sparked an immediate investigation. An extraordinary example of bigamy came to light during the visitation of Sárospatak in 1641, in which the wife of Tamás Magyar was found to have another husband in Tarczal, whilst Magyar himself had two other wives in neighbouring villages.[52]

Appeals for divorce or requests to have marriages annulled were usually reported to regional synods, where appeals were normally only granted in cases of bigamy, impotence, adultery, or abandonment. Some supplicants for divorce clearly felt that other grounds should also be permitted. Simon

---

[51] 'az paráznáknak büntetésében nagyobb disciplinának kell lenni': ZEP (1638–51), 231. 'Miskolczi Csulyak jegyzőkönyvei', ed. Zoványi, 59, 81, 86–90, 96.

[52] ZEP (1629–45), 147–63, 197–207, 348–51; (1653–72), 57–69. 'Miskolczi Csulyak jegyzőkönyvei', ed. Zoványi, 71, 80, 267, 273, 372, 380.

Magyar unsuccessfully appealed to an area synod in Transylvania in 1657 for a divorce merely on the grounds that his wife was 'smelly and bad-tempered'. Much of the Zemplén synod's time was taken up with the consideration of divorce cases and hearing appeals for the annulment of engagements. Many couples were disciplined for the secret exchange of tokens as signs of engagement. The synod usually required that the gifts exchanged between an engaged couple be returned in the presence of their local minister, and for a public reconciliation to take place in front of their families and community. The Zemplén synod was also presented with some extraordinary appeals, such as that in 1641 when György Békési was freed from his engagement to be married on the grounds that his partner had bound his will by diabolic possession.[53]

Cases of theft, public quarrelling, and violent arguments form a much smaller proportion of the offences reported in Zemplén's visitation records. Convicted thieves were subject to a mixture of civil and ecclesiastical punishments, such as thieves at Viss who were first fined and then required to make public repentance of their sins. Zemplén's archdeacons were again active in seeking out any abuses of this system, and at Zétény in 1639 Miskolczi noted that there were thieves who had made public repentance three times, yet still continued in their activities. A more satisfactory case was recorded at Zsadány where a pig thief, György Kovács, having been punished by the civil authorities then lived such a godly life that the Zemplén visitors released him from the necessity of public repentance and confession.[54]

Some local disputes were also investigated by the archdeacons during visitations ranging from petty quarrels and arguments, especially recorded between women, to more serious cases involving violence. Some incidences of the kind of local quarrels and squabbles that led to defamation and sexual slander also appear in the archdeacons' records. In 1629 Miskolczi wanted 'women of bad repute' in Nagyrozvágy to be punished for fear that they would bring sin into the village. At Bacska in 1639 some women who had scolded their husbands as rogues and thieves had gone unpunished to Miskolczi's annoyance. Young unmarried men also sometimes came under scrutiny during visitations, such as the 'violin-playing, drinking cobblers' living in a house at Szőlőske in 1635. Miskolczi again intervened when he

53 'A zempléni ref. diocesis zsinatai, 1629–1645', ed. J. Zoványi, *TT* 10 (1909), 184–211, 406–38, divorce petitions at 205, 411–2, 416, 426–7; *Zsinatok végzései*, ed. Kiss, 169; Erdély (Transylvania) Reformed Church Province Archives (Kolozsvár), Protocollum Matricula Székiensis (Szolnok-Doboka), ff. 73, 77, 83; R. M. Kingdon, *Adultery and Divorce in Calvin's Geneva* (Cambridge, Mass., 1995).

54 'Miskolczi Csulyak jegyzőkönyvei', ed. Zoványi, 60, 304, 313.

discovered that young men who had been causing trouble at Nagyrozvágy had neither been asked to make penance in church nor been punished by the civil authorities, since it was seen locally as unsuitable for the sons of prominent village families to endure such humiliating punishment in public. Cases involving violent deaths and threats of violence were very occasionally passed on to the visitors for their deliberation. An investigation of claims that a local man had been murdered was recorded during a visitation to Kisfalud in 1638, and reports taken of a family row which led to a death in 1639 at Karcsa. These matters clearly could not be dealt with by the minister and village justices alone, and the details of such cases were passed on to local manorial officials.[55]

The disciplinary regime of the Reformed church at Kiskomárom in Royal Hungary offers some contrast to this pattern of offences and punishments in rural Zemplén. Kiskomárom was a small garrison town in Zala county, one of a number of fortified towns defending the border with Ottoman-occupied Hungary. Kiskomárom in fact was to fall to Ottoman attack in 1664, before the Habsburg victory at the battle of Szentgotthárd recovered lost ground. The first meeting of the Kiskomárom presbytery was held at the church in August 1634 with the deputy commander of the town's garrison in attendance. The selected elders were thereafter normally consulted about disciplinary matters brought to the attention of the minister, János Kanizsai Pálfi, although on occasions he continued to act alone. The Kiskomárom elders were immediately concerned with absenteeism from church services, and numbers were kept of those who received communion. These records show that attendance at communion was very patchy indeed, with a list of twelve communion services held in 1635 showing sixty-two communicants present at Christmas but only eleven present for communion in July and again in August. The Kiskomárom minister and elders were also active in protecting the purity of their communion. At Whitsun in 1637 Lőrinc Busani approached the Lord's Table for communion but, because Kanizsai suspected him to be guilty of impropriety with a servant, he was sent away without receiving the sacrament.[56]

Kanizsai received the support of his presbytery and the civil authorities of Kiskomárom to engage in a sustained campaign against immorality and public disorder, and to ensure that wrongdoers received appropriate and corrective punishment. In July 1635 the Kiskomárom justice consulted the presbytery on the need to tighten local regulations over general behaviour

---

55 Ibid. 63, 96, 63, 77, 96, 271, 291, 299, 303, 369.
56 Dunántúl Reformed Church Province Library Manuscript Collection (Pápa), no. 131, A kiskomáromi ref. egyházközség legrégébbi anyakönyve 1624–1732.

in the town. Kanizsai and his elders suggested harsher punishment of blasphemy and better protection of the Sabbath by prohibiting the passage of carts into the town on Sundays. The presbytery also requested that taverns be forced to close until evening church services were finished, and a ban was suggested on the sale of wine after eight in the evening. The presbytery spent much of its time reconciling minor disputes and petty arguments between family members and neighbours in Kiskomárom. Some offenders were asked to make public repentance for their sins in church, but many were rebuked only in front of the assembled elders. In December 1634 an unmarried woman was reprimanded by the elders for being short-tempered, whilst in April 1635 a mother and son were brought before the presbytery in order that the son should apologize for dishonouring his mother. In August 1635 János Szabó was warned by the elders to live peaceably with his wife in future, or face further and more public disciplinary action.

Cases of sexual scandal and theft were also brought before the Kiskomárom presbytery. The elders co-operated with the town's civil authorities in such cases to enforce a mixture of penitential and punitive discipline. In March 1635 the wife of Gergely Szakos, who had been caught with a young man at night, appeared before the presbytery. It was noted that the woman had been sentenced to death by the civil authorities for her actions, but the presbytery enforced three Sundays of public penance to be followed by a full public confession in place of the death penalty. The woman was required to stand alone at the outer door of the church and to wear sober clothing. She was specifically warned that this repentance must be shown to be deeply heart-felt, corresponding to the seriousness of her offence. Similarly a thief was sentenced to be hanged in June 1635, but instead faced three weeks of public penance in church followed by a public confession of his sins over a further four weeks. In October 1636 a married woman found guilty of adultery was forced to undergo three weeks of public penance, but a convicted thief was executed in the same month, and another woman caught by her own husband with another man in April 1635 was put in the stocks and beaten.[57]

The significance of the formal procedure of public penance as a punishment was shown by the strenuous efforts which some offenders made to avoid it. Mihály Csizma risked everything to avoid public penance, and when he died in November 1635 without showing contrition for his offences he was given a dishonourable burial. György Csabai and his wife repeatedly went to the minister's house pleading for the opportunity to make private repentance for their behaviour in front of the minister. Despite

57 Dunántúl Manuscript Collection (Pápa), no. 131, 198–208.

their efforts to avoid publicity, the problems between Csabai and his wife were first aired at a regional synod and the couple then reconciled in Kiskomárom church on Good Friday in full view of the whole community. This case also indicates that a history of informal discipline and warnings often preceded a formal investigation and reprimand by the presbytery. The elders of Kiskomárom's church had quickly acquired a pivotal role in maintaining discipline and upholding order in the town, able to enforce spiritual sanctions of real consequence against wrongdoers. Kanizsai and his elders acted in close co-operation with the council to tighten controls on daily life in the town, and dealt particularly with cases of sexual immorality and public quarrelling.[58]

The imposition and tightening of discipline over the religious, moral, and social life of the Reformed community in Hungary and Transylvania during the early seventeenth century followed a pattern similar to the rest of the Calvinist world. Hungarian Reformed ministers seem to have applied the range of spiritual punishments at their disposal with ever greater determination during this period, treating certain offences more severely and working in co-operation with the civil authorities to provide stiff punishments for offenders against their moral and behavioural code. Sinning offenders faced exclusion from the church and its sacraments, or a shaming ritual of public repentance, which was seen by the church as key to engendering meaningful repentance. This response to wrong-doing and disorder was supplemented by the imposition of fines, physical punishment, and terms of imprisonment by local justices and councils. Reformed ministers in Hungary and Transylvania tried to impose apparently novel standards of discipline against cursing, drunkenness, and sexual immorality, and on issues of church attendance and Sabbath observance. The mixed success of these efforts was a result of real difficulties in applying rigorous scrutiny through visitations in many inaccessible areas, and of considerable resistance from ordinary people and some law officers to the demands of parish clergy.

Even with the painstaking application of rights of visitation by senior clergy in Zemplén county, where offenders could not easily escape the disciplinary tentacles of the church, progress towards controlling behaviour was very patchy. However, by the 1650s reports from many Zemplén parishes contain praise from both the community about their minister and from the minister about his congregation. In the light of the outspoken

[58] Dunántúl Manuscript Collection (Pápa), no. 131, 198–208; Révész, 'A presbyterium legelső nyomai hazai református egyházunkban', 419–46.

reports of previous years, this change can hardly be attributed to any reticence on the part of the Zemplén Reformed community to criticize one another. Visitations by Pál Tarczali in 1655 and 1656 seem to have gone particularly well, with comparatively few scandals reported and many congregations even complimented on their diligent attendance at church services.59 The progress signalled by these visitations, supported by local nobles and village officials, was not matched elsewhere. In Ungvár county, visitations during the 1650s to some of the more remote areas of Slav villages still revealed hair-raising situations. In one village the archdeacon discovered the church 'quite destroyed, with Ruthene [Orthodox?] flags and idols piled against it'. The parochial house was also in a bad state, and thieves had stolen cattle which belonged to the minister. The villagers had burned the school, and apparently told the visitors that they had 'no problems that needed a priest to be brought', leaving the archdeacon to write that they honoured a dog more than a spiritual teacher.60

The minister and elders at Kiskomárom, meanwhile, seemingly made considerable progress towards curbing disorder and immorality, becoming involved with problems arising from petty family disputes. Controls over everyday life were undoubtedly much more easy to establish in a small town such as Kiskomárom, where the minister could work in close co-operation with the council, than in the scattered villages of Zemplén. The relative success of such initiatives nevertheless only acted to increase the frustration of presbyterian clergy with the slow progress being made towards achieving a reformation of life in other Hungarian towns and in the countryside. The Reformed church's disciplinary efforts continued to rely heavily on diligent archdeacons, on the commitment of ordinary parish clergy, and on the support of noble patrons. Success in the drive to reform the lifestyle of Reformed communities was therefore immediately connected with the provision of a well-educated ministry and with the emergence of godly Hungarian magistrates and gentlemen. The Reformed clergy hierarchy called upon the nobility and ultimately upon Transylvania's princes to act against external confessional opponents and against internal dissidents. The church also sought the assistance of the secular authorities to impose its standards of social and moral discipline, and the next chapter will examine further this crucial relationship for the Reformed church between Transylvania's princes, Hungarian nobles, and the clergy.

59 ZEP (1653–72), 75–81, 126–30.
60 MOL box 1912, Tiszáninneni ref. egyházkerület: Ungi egyházmegye egyházlátogatási jegyzőkönyve, 1618–1774 (Liber Ecclae seu Matricula diocese Ungensis). For the village of Budzka Dluha [*sic*], see K. Haraszy (ed.), *Az ungi református egyházmegye* (Nagykapos, 1931), 42–3.

8

Building a Reformed Church and Society: Clergy, Princes, and Nobles

By the late sixteenth century the lines of demarcation between Europe's three major confessions had hardened to form rival blocs straddling the Continent. The Calvinist, Lutheran, and Catholic churches consolidated their hold over mostly discrete areas through reforms which aimed to tighten the enforcement of regulations on doctrine and moral discipline. Each of the three major confessions looked for state support in their intense competition with one another, and the process of church-building proceeded in parallel with the centralizing tendencies of early modern states. Churches, through clergy hierarchies and parish ministers, and states, through princes and nobles, largely co-operated to exert religious and social controls over territories under their domination. This symbiotic relationship between churches and states encouraged the integration of ecclesiastical and secular authority, and strengthened both confessional and territorial identities. Calvinist leaders sought, with no less enthusiasm than their rivals, to ally with kings, princes, and nobles to build up Reformed churches. Calvinist church-building was driven by an ideology which highlighted the need to conduct further and ongoing reformation of the church and society. Where Calvinists gained initial support for their statements of faith, they then tried to establish high standards of theological orthodoxy and moral discipline. This proved most successful where the commitment of individual new adherents was complemented by the approval and active encouragement of ruling dynasties, local nobles, or urban magistrates.[1]

By the early seventeenth century the different churches in Hungary and Transylvania had become more polarized, with traditional patterns of confessional co-existence increasingly challenged by the force of denominational loyalty. Calvinists, Unitarians, Lutherans, and Catholics drew further apart from one another into confrontation, each developing their own

---

[1] Schilling, 'Die Konfessionalisierung im Reich', 1–45; W. Reinhard, 'Reformation, Counter-Reformation, and the Early Modern State. A Reassessment', *Catholic Historical Review*, 75 (1989), 383–404; J. F. Harrington and H. W. Smith, 'Confessionalization, Community, and State Building in Germany, 1555–1870', *Journal of Modern History*, 69 (1997), 77–101; Kaplan, *Calvinists and Libertines*; Schilling, 'Confessional Europe', 641–81; Hsia, *Social Discipline in the Reformation*.

centres of education and institutional hierarchies. Each of the Hungarian churches sought to bolster its position by building or maintaining close relationships with co-religionists abroad, and by gaining the support of the Hungarian king, Transylvanian prince, and a native nobility whose patronage was crucial both on their estates and in most towns. For the Reformed church, princely governance and noble support was primarily responsible for making the Transylvanian principality and north-eastern Hungarian counties, under the influence and periodic control of Transylvania's princes, more closely attached to Reformed religion. During the period from the accession of István Bocskai to the death of György II Rákóczi, the Reformed church came to be described as the orthodox religion of this region, and was the major beneficiary of princely patronage. Whilst the letter of the Transylvanian constitution on four 'received religions' remained in place, the balance of power shifted decisively towards a leading role for the Reformed church within the Transylvanian state and society.[2]

   This chapter will consider this process of Reformed church-building in Hungary and Transylvania and examine the nature of co-operation between the clergy, princes, magnates, and gentry who supported the Calvinist cause. The limitations of surviving sources make it difficult to survey the place of the clergy within Hungarian parish life, but the degree to which local ministers lived up to the expectations placed upon them by their own hierarchy will be discussed here. Reformed ministers worked to win over princes and nobles not only to accept Reformed confessions of faith, but also to adopt high standards of personal morality and to sponsor the imposition of social and moral discipline. This chapter will assess, again as far as sources permit, the performance of Transylvania's Reformed princes and nobles in assisting the reform of popular religion and behaviour and chart tensions between the clergy and noble patrons in directing parish life across the region.

(1) THE REFORMATION OF THE CLERGY

Hungarian clergy had a tarnished image at the time of the reformation, but by the early seventeenth century the place of ministers in Hungarian society had been entirely remodelled. Reformed clergy emerged, if not as a separate social caste, then certainly as a well-trained group of professional

---

[2] Pokoly, 'Az erdélyi fejedelmek viszonya a protestáns egyházakhoz', 608–124: 'Bocskay Istvánnak fejedelemmé választásával új korszak kezdődik az erdélyi protestáns egyházakra nézve, melynek egyik legfőbb jellemvonása az, hogy a fejedelmek reformátusok lévén, a négy recepta religio egyensúlyát a reformátusok javára felbillentik.'

preachers. Ministers were no longer set apart from the rest of society because of their capacity to perform magical rituals, but the status of Reformed clergy was instead partly based upon improving standards of education. There were also deliberate attempts to mould Reformed ministers into a well-disciplined élite, perceptibly different from other orders in their dress and behaviour. Reformed ministers were rigorously regulated in their duties by their own hierarchy, and internal disciplining of the clergy was more severe than that of the rest of Hungarian society during this period.

These efforts to achieve some degree of distinct social status for ministers were greatly enhanced in 1629 when Reformed clergy in Transylvania were ennobled as an order. The ministry had in fact already become a family profession to some extent. Ministers who were from clergy families registered at foreign universities and appear in church records with 'Pastoris' or 'Pap' in their name. Some clergy simply adopted the middle initial 'P', although this initial could also stand for a family's place of origin. István Miskolczi Csulyak registered at Heidelberg University in 1603 as 'Stephanus Pastoris Miskolcinus', and Pál Medgyesi at Frankfurt an der Oder in 1628 as 'Paulus P. Medgiesi'. Of registrations at foreign universities during the early seventeenth century, up to one-tenth have some indication that student ministers came from clergy families, whilst there were only very few ministers from traditional noble families. Many of the leading clergy of the period came from clergy families, including István Miskolczi Csulyak, whose son Gáspár in turn became a minister, and István Geleji Katona, whose brother Gáspár was an archdeacon in eastern Hungary, whilst Gáspár was János Tolnai Dali's father-in-law. In the Tiszabecsi family the father, Tamás, and two sons were all ministers, and three generations of ministers from the Csuzi Cseh family visited Franeker University during the seventeenth century. Other leading ministers from clergy families included Lukács Hodászi, Sámuel Pathai, István Tolnai, András Váczi, and István Telkibányai, and there were generations of prominent Reformed clergy during this period from the Nógrádi, Jászberényi, Harsányi, Köleséri, Czeglédi, and Pápai Páriz families.[3]

The education given to students at higher level Reformed academies and schools at Gyulafehérvár, Sárospatak, Debrecen, Nagyvárad, and Pápa was the first stage of formally shaping future generations of Reformed clergy. As we have seen, the content of the syllabus followed at these schools was closely monitored by superintendents and patrons. A number

3 Zoványi, *Magyarországi protestáns egyháztörténeti lexikon*; Pettegree, 'The Clergy and the Reformation', 1–22.

of school regulations were introduced during the early seventeenth century setting out details on teaching, administrative structure, finance, and expected standards of behaviour for both staff and students. Regulations on student conduct are particularly revealing of a determined effort to fashion future generations of ministers. At Gyulafehérvár, Gábor Bethlen issued instructions on the running of his new academy in 1612, which were later supplemented by the three German professors in 1630. Student officers were charged with disciplining the student body and given powers to punish offenders with fines, which increased if any misdemeanour was repeated. Wine was not allowed to be bought or sold in the academy, and students were expected to abstain from excessive drinking. Other offences listed in the regulations included 'being rowdy and turbulent, picking quarrels, bickering, fighting, aimlessly roaming around at night, hunting, bird catching, fishing, and playing games of chance'. Serious offences were punished severely, and any student found drunk in church faced being ceremonially thrown out of the college in front of all the other students, to the accompaniment of the funereal ringing of the school bells.[4]

At Sárospatak, school orders were compiled in 1618, 1621, and 1648, which were originally partly based on Wittenberg University regulations. A compulsory pattern of religious life and worship was specified for students, with stipulations for regular attendance at church, prayer at meals, and reading the Bible every morning and evening. There was also a proscription on older students from speaking Hungarian at the college, and detailed rules on behaviour including a ban on playing cards or other games of chance.[5] Regulations for the school at Debrecen were framed partly in response to repeated violent student disturbances there in 1627, 1644, 1648, 1650, and 1657, and rules from the 1650s forbade shooting, smoking, fighting, dancing, and music-making. Fines for misbehaviour at Debrecen ranged from 5 denar for not attending church to 20 denar for playing cards, 25 denar for not paying attention in church, and 50 denar for leaving the college at night. Meanwhile the behavioural code for the school at Nagyvárad offered a stern warning against writing love poems and verses, whilst 'cavorting about' and dancing were also both strictly prohibited.[6]

---

4 Juhász and Jakó (eds.), *Nagyenyedi diákok 1662–1848*, 5–46; Váró, *Bethlen Gábor kollégiuma*.

5 'Leges de moribus', in 'A sárospataki ev. ref. főiskola 1621-iki törvényei', ed. R. Békefi, in *ÉTTK* 18/3 (Budapest, 1899), 54–61; Makkai, 'A kollégium története alapitásától 1650-ig', 17–59; Gulyás, *A sárospataki ref. főiskola rövid története*, 1–20; Marton, *A sárospataki református főiskola története, 1621-ig*, 129–56.

6 'De moribus scholarium', in *A debreczeni ev. ref. főiskola xvii. és xviii. századi törvényei*, ed. R. Békefi, (Budapest, 1899), 87–97; Nagy, *A debreceni kollégium*, 21–108; Zsigmond,

Orders at the Pápa School also established student officers in charge of discipline, and strict rules were drawn up governing general behaviour. Students were expected to attend daily prayers without fail, and had to wake at four in the morning to begin the round of worship and classes. Regulations at Pápa also demanded that students steer clear of bad company, drunkenness, dances, cursing, and games. Their behaviour was to be respectable and honourable whenever they walked in the town, and they were not allowed to carry weapons at any time.[7]

These regulations for Reformed colleges and schools were also preoccupied with appropriate and morally proper clothing for students and were concerned that student ministers should be easily distinguishable from the rest of urban youth. In 1624 the school orders at Debrecen set out a uniform for its students to observe of a long ankle length cloak, a green toga strikingly highlighted with yellow cord, and a high fur cap with green trimming. Students were strictly warned against being seen bare-headed 'like Turks', wearing Tartar-style hats, or any clothing associated with soldiers, and they were to avoid wearing wide belts, and any colour of gloves except black or white. The regulations demanded that any student failing to comply with these rules on dress was to be thrown out of the college at once. Rules for students' dress at Pápa also indicated that any clothing associated with soldiers was not permitted; older students had to wear a long black toga and were not allowed to have long hair or to wear gloves. Students at the Reformed school at Nagyvárad also had to comply with requirements in their school regulations to wear proper academic dress, and in the 1650s the eastern Tisza synod threatened expulsion from the school for anyone who disobeyed.[8]

After leaving school, student ministers generally served first for at least a year as teachers in parish schools, then perhaps studied for a period at foreign universities. Once ordained and resident as an assistant minister in a town or as a village priest, all clergy became subject to their hierarchical superiors. As has already been shown, superintendents and archdeacons were anxious to establish theological orthodoxy amongst the clergy, and punished any lack of respect or obedience due to church superiors. Superintendents and archdeacons could warn, suspend, or sack erring ministers

A debreceni református kollégium története 1538–1938, 31–73; Barcza (ed.), *A debreceni református kollégium története*, 5–43; Mészáros, *Az iskolaügy története Magyarországon, 996–1777 között*, 368–406; 'A marosvásárhelyi ev. ref. iskola xvii. századi törvényei', ed. Békefi, 29–32.

7 Lampérth, *A pápai református főiskola története*, 21–35; E. Kis, *A dunántuli ev. ref. egyházkerület pápai főiskolájának története, 1531–1895* (Pápa, 1896), 9–48.

8 *A debreczeni főiskola törvényei*, ed. Békefi, 87–97; Lampérth, *A pápai református főiskola története*, 21–35; 'A böszörményi . . . zsinat végzései', *MPEIF* 1 (1870), 612–13.

under their jurisdictions, and ministers with rogue opinions on church government or liturgy could be forced to recant before being allowed to continue in office. Some of the cases against ministers discussed in depth in Chapter 6 demonstrated this disciplinary regime in practice, from Imre Szilvásujfalvi Anderkó, who was locked up in a bishop's prison as a schismatic in 1612, to János Tolnai Dali, who was suspended from office in 1646 on suspicion of innovatory opinions, to Benedek Nagyari and Péter Kovásznai, who were imprisoned in 1656 until they swore retractions of previously held opinions. The church authorities were equally intolerant of any variation in the conduct of church services, and monitored by means of regular visitations whether ministers were strictly following canons.[9]

The Reformed church hierarchy was also anxious to control the public appearance and conduct of parish clergy. Just as school regulations established a dress code for Reformed students, so synods acted to regulate the clothing of ministers, making frequent pronouncements on approved dress for clergymen, clergy wives, and schoolmasters. The 1567 Debrecen Confession and articles encouraged decent dress for all church officers and forbade ministers from copying the clothes of courtiers and appearing like 'fops, buffoons, or palace guards'. Superintendents were instructed not to 'sparkle in gold, silver, or expensive clothing', and schoolteachers were forbidden from having excessively short hair, and clothing like that of soldiers. Early Reformed synods maintained that separate clothing for a priestly caste was both nonsensical and superstitious. The 1570 Csenger synod in Szatmár declared that there were no regulations in the Bible about everyday clothing for clergy, and proclaimed 'Christian freedom' for ministers over matters of dress as well as over what to eat and drink. Rather, synods restricted their pronouncements to advising ministers to adopt honourable and appropriate moderation in dress. The 1577 Nagyvárad church articles warned clergymen to avoid all forms of luxurious dress and prohibited ministers from adopting military or other styles of clothing deemed inappropriate, with soldiers' clothing especially to be avoided because of the licence associated with soldiers' lifestyles.[10]

9 MOL box 1883, Tiszántúl egyházkerület levéltára kerületi jegyzőkönyvek, vol. I (1629–) 93, 624, 630–2; Kiss, 'Szilvásújfalvi Anderko Imre', 218–41; 'Adatok a magyarországi puritánus mozgalmak történetéhez', ed. Zoványi, 13–20; 'A szatmárnémeti zsinat végzései', ed. Révész, 244–7.

10 *Zsinatok végzései*, ed. Kiss, 33–44, 181, 583, 690–5; *A szatmármegyében tartott négy első protestáns zsinat végzései*, ed. Kiss, 44–50, 61; S. Payr, *A Magyar protestáns papi öltöny története* (Sopron, 1935); D. Roche, *The Culture of Clothing. Dress and Fashion in the 'ancien régime'* (Cambridge, 1994), 44–63. For comparison with Scotland, see I. B. Cowan, *The Scottish Reformation. Church and Society in Sixteenth-Century Scotland* (London, 1982), 204; Dawson, 'Calvinism and the Gaidhealtachd in Scotland', 231–2.

Under the banner of Christian freedom, some Hungarian clergy apparently began to assume the right to dress in finery. A collection of popular proverbs at the end of the sixteenth century included such sayings as 'a gown doesn't make a minister', 'a monkey is still a monkey, even if dressed up in golden clothes', and 'who likes the minister, and who likes his gown?'[11] Upper Hungarian articles from 1595 again stressed the need for ministers and their families to avoid luxurious, expensive, or foreign clothes. Transylvanian canons from 1606 advised that the dress of all ministers must be suitable to their office and lacking in luxury. Archdeacons in the eastern Tisza province were empowered by a 1624 synod at Nagyvárad to admonish those who failed to abide by expected standards of dress. Teachers and students were reminded that they were only allowed to wear short-heeled boots in winter, or when it was muddy, but were not to wear fur under any circumstances. In 1630 a synod at Debrecen ordered ministers to wear clothes 'appropriate to their order', and strictly outlawed wearing boots, shorter decorated fur-lined coats, or golden collars. In 1632 by order of the Zemplén area synod, iron-shod boots and fur-lined coats were forbidden for ministers, 'so that people go about in clothes appropriate to their office'.[12]

In 1638 a Transylvanian synod at Nagyenyed resolved that ministers should not wear boots, and could be fined for doing so, and after a third offence could even be removed from office. The synod also forbade schoolteachers and students from wearing high hats, or collared, fur-lined coats. In 1642 another synod at Nagyenyed threatened expulsion from the ministry for those who wore unbecoming clothing, particularly velvet, and coloured or decorated clothes, although exceptions were made for the Transylvanian superintendent, court chaplains, and senior archdeacons. The Szatmár national synod of 1646 required ministers to obey dress codes laid down by provincial synods, commenting that it was 'a foul disturbance and laughable thing if teachers of decent knowledge by their clothes are transformed into boorish soldiers'. The synod also mentioned that foreign clothing was prohibited, perhaps referring to the dress worn by student ministers returning from western universities. Certainly on János Tolnai

---

[11] 'Nem a köntös teszi a papot', 'Az majom ugyan majom, ha aranyos ruhába öltöztetik is', 'Ki szereti a papját, ki a palástját': János Baranyai Decsi, *Adagiorum* [1592], printed in J. Jankovics, G. Galavics, and Á. R. Várkonyi (eds.), *Régi erdélyi viseletek* (Budapest, 1990), 16; from 'The true and exact dresses and fashions of all the nations in Transylvania', British Library, Additional MS 5256.

[12] [Várad], 'Constitutiones in generali synodo Varadina anno 1624, 1 die Julii', ed. J. Lugossy, *PEIL* 6 (1847), 235–6; MOL boxes 1907–8, Zempléni Egyházmegye Protocolluma (1629–45), 147–63; *Zsinatok végzései*, ed. Kiss, 720.

Dali's return from England in the autumn of 1638 his distinctive clothing was commented upon by opponents as one sign of his affectation of piety and humility. In 1649 the revised Transylvanian canons again did not stipulate any specific form of dress for clergy but declared that ministers' dress ought to be appropriate to their order and office, neither as wretched in appearance as Anabaptists, nor as laughable as friars, nor yet gleaming like that of the leading orders of the Roman hierarchy, but moderate and decent. The canons expected students and teachers not to have Turkish-style haircuts, and wear neither fur caps, nor red or yellow boots.[13]

This proliferation of regulations on dress not only attempted to control the clothing of ministers, teachers, and students, as the outward appearance of ministers' wives was also subjected to detailed scrutiny. The 1567 Debrecen articles prohibited clergy wives from any immoderation in dress, and warnings were issued against copying the dress of noblewomen or affecting decoration in their appearance with 'promiscuous' beads and styled hair. In 1624 the eastern Tisza synod ordered clergy wives to avoid wearing golden shirts, rings, red or yellow boots, wide fur belts or straps, short sheepskin coats, or multi-layered skirts. In 1642 the Transylvanian synod ordered ministers' wives to avoid golden robes, luxurious clasps, pearls, any neck decoration, and boots that diverged from normal styles. The 1649 canons required that the wives of ministers should not wear expensively decorated clothes or any jewellery, and that their hair be styled moderately.[14]

The clothing of Reformed clergy remained a significant issue throughout this period, and an eastern Tisza synod in 1680 warned ministers against wearing their hair long, then suspected to be a mark of attachment to Cocceian opinions. Synods in Transylvania during the early eighteenth century still argued about the official attitude to ministers having beards and outlawed the wearing of wigs by ministers.[15] The church's enthusiasm for regulating ministers' dress and appearance was part of a more general concern about immoral abuses in clothing, which were seen to have potentially disastrous consequences. István Magyari wrote in 1605 of how excessive pride in clothing and attention to dress was one of the sinful causes which had brought destruction upon the country in recent wars. István

---

[13] 'Az erdélyi közzsinatainak végzései', ed. Szilágyi, 1–9, 77–84, 473–9; *Egyházi kánonok*, ed. Kiss, 1646 resolutions, no. 28; 1649 canons, nos. 83, 94, 96; Keserű (ed.), *Adattár 1*, 412–16; 'Adatok a magyarországi puritánus mozgalmak történetéhez', ed. Zoványi, 7.

[14] *Zsinatok végzései*, ed. Kiss, 583; [Várad], 'Constitutiones in generali synodo Varadina', ed. Lugossy, 235–6. *Egyházi kánonok*, ed. Kiss, 1649 canons, no. 84; 'Az erdélyi közzsinatainak végzései', ed. Szilágyi, 1–9, 77–84, 473–9.

[15] Zoványi, *A tiszántúli református egyházkerület története*, 40; Bod, *Smirnai szent polikárpus . . . erdélyi református püspököknek historiájok*, 85; Evans, 'Calvinism in East Central Europe', 189.

Czeglédi also included abuses of dress codes among the causes of God's anger falling upon Transylvania in the military disasters of 1657.[16]

The question of appropriate clergy dress was treated so seriously because clothing was both a significant element in the public presentation of Reformed religious values, and also an important marker of ethnic, social, and occupational difference in Hungarian and Transylvanian society. Laws in the principality which protected the distinctive appearance of nobles were reflected in Reformed church articles. If, as seems likely, some ministers were aping aspects of noble dress, then, as travellers to Hungary noted, they had adopted striking, multi-coloured clothing. On his travels through Hungary in the 1670s Edward Brown remarked that nobles favoured blues, yellows, and reds, and commented that it was rare to see any noble wearing black.[17] The more sober, and less expensive, clothing required of Reformed ministers established their distinct social status and functions as teachers and moral discipliners. Early seventeenth-century northern Hungarian articles declared that the modesty of ministers' clothes should reflect the honour of their office and be a sign of humility, while the 1612 Köveskút synod ordered ministers to be discernibly different from traders, soldiers, and cobblers and recommended that long gowns and cloaks of 'an appropriate colour for the office' be worn at all times.[18]

It was not only in dress that ministers, teachers, and student ministers were encouraged to be distinct within local society, but also in their language and behaviour. Eastern Tisza church articles from 1577 forbade ministers from going into taverns, since they were supposed to provide an example of sobriety for the community. These articles permitted ministers to attend decent wedding celebrations, but if dancing began they were to get up and leave the room immediately.[19] The 1642 Transylvanian synod at Nagyenyed detailed fines for ministers and their wives for dancing, playing the violin, taking part in markets on Sundays or holidays, or any involvement in superstitious healing. Transylvanian canons from 1649 detailed how ministers' lives were to be exemplary, temperate, and completely beyond reproach. Good company was advised, and conversations only to be engaged in to build up neighbours and friends, with swearing and arguing

---

[16] István Czeglédi, *Az országok romlásáról irott könyvnek első része* (Kassa, 1659), 23: 'Hat te cifra öltözet mint vagy? Mert te vonod eggyik le az éghbül az haragos Istent!' Jankovics, Galavics, and Várkonyi (eds.), *Régi erdélyi viseletek*, 7.

[17] Edward Brown, *A Brief Account of Some Travels in Hungaria, Severia . . . with the Figures of Some Habits and Remarkable Places* (London, 1673), 22–3.

[18] [Dunántúl], '1550–1617 adatok a dunántúl és felsődunamellék egyházkerületekről', ed. Thury 127–40; *Zsinatok végzései*, ed. Kiss, 726–7.

[19] *Zsinatok végzései*, ed. Kiss, 1576 Hercegszőllős articles, no. 30; 1577 Várad articles, no. 15; Upper Hungarian articles, no. 44.

with other ministers completely forbidden. The canons also insisted that all usury and business trading must be avoided, since ministers were not to 'sink into the problems of life'. Clergy were neither to keep weapons, hawks, nor hunting dogs, since instead they were to be 'fishers of men'. Sobriety was ordered, with ministers not slaves to their stomachs but 'the light of the world, and the salt of the earth'. For those whose attitudes and actions fell short of these ideals, warnings could be given by senior clergy to be followed ultimately by dismissal from office.[20]

The Reformed church in Hungary and Transylvania set high standards of doctrinal orthodoxy, personal piety, and public behaviour and appearance which its ministers were expected to uphold. Superintendents and archdeacons investigated clergy standards during regular visitations of parishes, when congregations were asked to comment on ministers' general conduct, their preaching ability, and on their application to other duties and responsibilities.[21] Individual ministers therefore had the difficult task of trying to please several different constituencies, needing to satisfy church superiors, local noble patrons who held annual rights of presentment over them, and members of their congregation who had an open channel of complaint against them. Ministers indeed found themselves set at a certain distance from the surrounding community, not least through their leading role in applying the church's demands for moral discipline. Records from the Zemplén church reveal many examples of anti-clerical attitudes and verbal assaults on ministers in the process of their disciplinary activities. Local justices were repeatedly reminded by the archdeacons that they should punish those who verbally abused ministers when such cases came to their attention. When István Miskolczi Csulyak learned in 1629 that the wife of István Szász had called the minister at Olaszi a hangman, he immediately demanded appropriate punishment. In 1651 a village justice stood accused of describing his minister as a 'priest for pigs' and 'the son of a whore', whilst at Kisfalud in 1654 János Nagy was accused of telling the minister that he had given himself to the devil.[22]

Although Zemplén's archdeacons were often met with praise from congregations about the conduct of the clergy, some communities proved more than willing to break local loyalties and criticize their minister in front of outside visitors if they believed that his standards of private

---

[20] Kiss, *Zsinatok végzései*, 1577 articles, no. 15; *Egyházi kánonok*, ed. Kiss, 1646 resolutions, nos. 14–22; 1649 canons, nos. 78–82. 'Az erdélyi közzsinatainak végzései', ed. Szilágyi, 1–9, 77–84, 473–9.

[21] 'A zempléni ref. dioecesis egyházlátogatási kerdőpontjai', ed. Zoványi, 40–1.

[22] ZEP (1638–51), 215; (1653–72), 39. 'Miskolczi Csulyak jegyzőkönyvei', ed. Zoványi, 54, 87, 311.

conduct or professional behaviour had fallen below what was expected. Many ordinary parishioners in Zemplén's villages seemingly felt little inhibition about forwarding information to visitation parties about ministers' perceived weaknesses, and visitations frequently led to a remarkably frank expression of popular resentment against some ministers. The surviving Zemplén records do not allow for any precise estimate of the proportion of ministers under fire from their own congregations, but much more critical opinions were voiced in Reformed Zemplén compared with the bland mutual praise recorded in visitations of Lutheran congregations in western Hungary.[23] Occasionally, accusations were raised in Zemplén that ministers were generally neglectful of their duties, or complaints made about ministers' preaching. Criticisms about ministers' overall poor performance of their duties were levelled by congregations at Bereczk and Helmecz in 1629, at Erdőbénye in 1632, at Hotyka and Újhely in 1641, at Saava in 1647, and Bári in 1648. At Helmecz in 1629 the congregation informed István Miskolczi Csulyak that the local minister did not hold a service on Sunday evenings. The minister, however, responded that he would gladly have held a service if he had seen a desire for one in the village. At Hotyka in 1641 the congregation complained of infrequent preaching, but again the minister maintained that when he had held mid-week services only two people came.[24]

Zemplén congregations in some instances cited drunkenness as the cause of ministers' neglect of duties, and in a very few extreme cases there were claims that a minister had preached whilst drunk. Accusations of drunkenness were made against the minister at Nagygéres in 1629, at Zétény in 1634, at Hotyka in 1639, and Újváros in 1641. At Sára in 1641 the minister was reported to have got so drunk one Sunday lunch that he was unable to conduct the evening service. Drunkenness during church services was reported against the minister at Jesztreb in 1639, and the visitors were informed that he also argued with and regularly hit his wife, and had been neglecting his catechizing duties for the past six months. Accusations were also made against some ministers for swearing, and both the minister at Zsadány and his wife were accused by their congregation of cursing in 1654, as was the minister at Lasztócz in 1655 and the minister's wife at Fűzér in 1639.[25] Complaints were also raised against some schoolteachers

[23] [Dunántúl], 'Kis Bertalan és Musay György dunántúli ág. hitv. ev. püspökök egyházlátogatási jegyzőkönyve, 1631–1654', ed. E. Thury, in *MPEA* 6 (1907), 11–193.
[24] ZEP (1638–51), 100–1, 150, 215; (1653–72), 21, 42, 75–8, 123; 'Miskolczi Csulyak jegyzőkönyvei', ed. Zoványi, 84–5, 91, 375–6, 380–3.
[25] ZEP (1653–72), 42. 'Miskolczi Csulyak jegyzőkönyvei', ed. Zoványi, 89–90, 199, 295, 308–9, 312, 371, 377–9, 385.

during visitations. At Terebes in 1629 the schoolteacher was reported to the archdeacon for swearing, singing love songs, and for hitting his pupils, whilst the teacher at Csörgő was reported as rowdy when drunk in 1643. The teacher at Bénye was reported by the local congregation in 1638 for laziness, cruelty, and for chasing a young married woman. He was warned by the visitors to teach diligently in future or face removal from the school.[26]

Such serious charges against any minister or schoolmaster initiated disciplinary action from his district superiors. Cases could be referred by archdeacons to the regional synod for resolution, or the archdeacon could decide on an appropriate remedy himself during his visitation of the parish. In 1631 the case of a minister who had been reported by his congregation for drunkenness, and for threatening to kill the schoolmaster, was referred back to the synod for consideration when it met at Újhely. In 1634 Miskolczi found on visitation that the congregation at Olaszi was unhappy with their minister, János Rozgonyi. The congregation had first reported that Rozgonyi preached whilst drunk in 1629 and stated that they would prefer him not to preach at all than have him preach scandalously. In 1634 Rozgonyi was again accused of drunkenness, swearing, defamation, and of hitting a parishioner, Imre Kelőczi, with a Bible. Miskolczi, after hearing from many local witnesses about Rozgonyi's behaviour, decided that the minister must leave Olaszi and find a vacant parish elsewhere. Miskolczi warned Rozgonyi that if he heard the slightest complaint about his behaviour in the future, then he would be dismissed from the ministry altogether. Miskolczi also demanded that Rozgonyi never get drunk again, since he believed that alcohol was at the root of all his problems.[27] On occasion the church authorities encountered difficulties in imposing punishment on a minister, if he was supported by his local noble patron. In 1634 the archdeacon decided that the minister at Zétény ought to be removed from his post for swearing, drunkenness, and generally inappropriate behaviour. There were also complaints from the congregation that he preached for too long and did not even bother to wake those who fell asleep during his sermons. However, the local patron, András Thót, resisted the removal of his minister. The Zemplén archdeacon countered this defiance by placing the church at Zétény under an exclusion order, and no Reformed minister was allowed to go to Zétény until obedience was assured from both Thót and his minister.[28]

---

[26] 'Miskolczi Csulyak jegyzőkönyvei', ed. Zoványi, 79, 291–2, 406–7.
[27] Ibid. 279–82; 'A zempléni ref. diocesis zsinatai', ed. Zoványi, 419.
[28] 'Miskolczi Csulyak István esperesi naplója és leveleskönyve', ed. Zoványi, in *MPEA* 12 (1928), 199–200.

The relationship between Reformed clergymen and their congregations was also affected by disputes arising from the financial demands which ministers could make on their parishioners. Reformed church administration of the tithe adapted the pre-reformation system in which instructions on the level of payments were issued by the royal chamber of finance. Area collectors then met with village justices to decide how the burden should be distributed in each locality. Under the Reformed church system, archdeacons and gentry patrons supervised the payment of ministers, but in practice village justices and councils largely became responsible for settling the income due to parish clergy, schoolmasters, sextons, and bell-ringers. Each minister was generally entitled to payments in cash and kind from rights to the tithe and could use land or other resources owned by the church in the parish. Local records revealed exactly what every parishioner was expected to pay the minister each year either in money, or in wheat, wine, or wood. Reformed archdeacons were careful during visitations to monitor the income which ministers and schoolmasters could rightfully claim, to check whether payments were being made quickly and in full by all parishioners, as well as to investigate the state of local church property.[29]

In Bodrogkeresztúr in Zemplén, for example, the archdeacon and village council agreed that the church owned four vineyards, some plough-land, and pasture in the parish. The minister could claim either labour or cash from the congregation towards the upkeep of church land, as well as dues in wine from all in the parish who held vineyards and money from the rest. The minister could also claim two-thirds of the fish drawn from a nearby lake. The assistant minister and schoolmaster at Bodrogkeresztúr also held vineyards and had the right to dues in either wine or money from every householder each year. In addition, the schoolmaster could ask for payments from the families of his pupils and had the right to eat at the minister's house. Smaller payments, often in wine, were also set down in the Bodrogkeresztúr village book of regulations for the sexton, bell-ringer, and also, perhaps surprisingly, for a clock-keeper. Additional charges were made by clergy for particular services across Zemplén and elsewhere, with a chicken commonly paid for conducting baptisms, wine or

---

[29] Erdély (Transylvania) Reformed Church Province Archives (Kolozsvár), Matricula Ecclesiarum Reformatorum in Sede Siculicali Maros; Tiszántúl Reformed Church Province Archives (Debrecen), Nagykárolyi (Középszolnok) egyházmegye iratai, I. 35a. 1; 'A marosi traktus 17. századbeli történetéből', ed. Gy. Dávid, *Református Szemle* (1930), 151–4, 165–8, 210–12, 232–4, 246–8, 263–6, 311–16, 487–490; I. Szilágyi, 'A máramarosi helv. hitvallású egyházmegye és egyházközségek rendezete a 17. század elején', *Sárospataki Füzetek*, 2 (1858–9), 382–91, 678–89, 984–6; Magyarósi, *A zilahi ev. ref. anyaszentegyház története*.

money given for marriage ceremonies, and money charged for funeral sermons.[30]

Visitations of Zemplén's congregations often revealed disputes over the extent of local church property and heard complaints from ministers of income due to them not being handed over quickly enough. Miskolczi ordered the re-measurement of a disputed field at Újváros in 1629, whilst at Perbenyik the minister complained that there were some people who had not handed over payment in wood for three years. Problems were also reported by the minister at Cigánd in obtaining his income from parishioners because of their pretence of poverty. At Bacska the minister claimed that the delivery of his income was late in 1639, whilst at Tárkány, István Istenes (ironically, his name means 'godly') was reported to the archdeacon for threatening the minister and swearing at him when he was asked for an overdue payment of grain.[31]

As far as it is possible to judge from the reports of their superiors and congregations, the performance of Reformed clergy in the countryside of Zemplén seems to have been rather uneven. The process of disciplining ministers who were perceived to be failing in their posts was apparently slow, and whilst the clergy hierarchy could rebuke ministers, removing them from parish office required at least the passive agreement of local noble patrons. The Reformed clergy nevertheless emerges on the whole as an order devoted to discipline, and mostly enthusiastic to support the cause of curbing immoral behaviour, even though this could give rise to resentment against them in their locality. The rules which governed behaviour at schools and detailed regulations passed at synods shaped the lives of most Reformed students and ministers. Whilst the social status of the clergy was undoubtedly enhanced by such strict regulation, by better education, and by ennoblement as an order, Reformed ministers thereby became more isolated from their congregations. Distinctive in appearance, sometimes from clergy families, and moving from one parish to another on a regular basis, Reformed ministers were frequently the targets of resentful criticism from below over the payment of their incomes as well as over the exercise of their disciplinary responsibilities. These sources of tension in the relationship between Reformed ministers and their congregations, between

---

[30] J. Zoványi, 'Protestáns lelkészek nyugtatványai régi tizedjegyzékek mellett', in *MPEA* 13 (1929), 5–142; MOL box 1907, Liber Reditum Ecclesiasticum Comitatus Zempleniensis 1623, 7–11, 29, 83; box 1884, Tiszántúli ref. egyházkerület; debreceni egyházmegye jegyzőkönyvei, vol. 1 (1615–55), 414–29, 433; Németh (ed.), *Hegyaljai mezővárosok törvényei*, 72–5. For the practice of working for the church as serfs (*egyház jobbágyság*) amongst Szeklers, see Transylvania Reformed Church Province Archives (Kolozsvár), Matricula Ecclesiarum Reformatorum in Sede Siculicali Maros, 10–13, 57.

[31] 'Miskolczi Csulyak jegyzőkönyvei', ed. Zoványi, 69, 88, 90, 94–7, 302–3.

discipliners and the disciplined, increased the separation of Reformed clergy from their communities. This was, however, essential to the moderate advances made during this period in the crusade against popular immorality and towards implementing the church's agenda of reforming everyday life in Hungary and Transylvania.

(II) GODLY PRINCES

The Reformed church tried very hard to shape the religiosity of Transylvania's princes, encouraging them to set high standards of personal morality and piety. During the late sixteenth century Transylvania's provincial synod had urged princes to be 'the images and mirrors of the virtues of God', to act according to the laws of the land, take care that God's word was preached effectively, fight for the defence of their homeland, build up schools and academies, punish wrong-doers, and stop idolatrous worship. Reformed princes who were seen to act in this way during the early seventeenth century were portrayed as liberators of the people from tyranny and as guarantors of true faith and justice. From the reign of István Bocskai, Calvinist princes in Transylvania were elevated by the Reformed clergy to an idealized role as defenders of a godly citadel, and parallels were frequently drawn between the princes and Old Testament kings. Reformed ministers used these comparisons with biblical history to stress how princes should fulfil their divinely appointed role of creating the conditions for faith and morality pleasing to God upon which the entire survival of the state was seen to be dependent. Whilst such parallels were on the whole positive, the church also offered stark predictions that any failure on the part of princes to offer the people godly rule would lead to 'a hideous death because of indulgence and drunkenness like Belshazzar, Darius, Alexander the Great, and Attila'. The typology of Transylvania's princes as Old Testament kings was part of a Europe-wide pattern, and was far from unique to Calvinists. However, Transylvania's position as a lone Reformed outpost in east-central Europe during the early seventeenth century led to a particularly powerful concentration on the motif of biblical Israel. The history of God's relationship with ancient Israel became a model through which the Hungarian Reformed community sought to understand their current circumstances. There was an eschatological tone to much of this literature and rhetoric about Transylvania as a new Israel, especially during the 1650s, and this will be examined further in Chapter 9.[32]

---

[32] *Zsinatok végzései*, ed. Kiss, 175–80, 589, 607–11. Cf. Lutheran Sweden, in I. Montgomery, 'The Institutionalisation of Lutheranism in Sweden and Finland', in O. P. Grell (ed.), *The Scandinavian Reformation* (Cambridge, 1995), 144–79.

In the aftermath of his 1604 anti-Habsburg rebellion, István Bocskai was depicted as acting with divine sanction to take revenge on the sinful higher authorities at the Habsburg court. Members of the Hungarian diet acclaimed Bocskai as 'Moses of the Hungarians' as they elected him prince protector, and Péter Alvinczi, then minister at Kassa, recorded fantastic signs, strange animal portents, loud noises, and fire in the sky at that time around Kalló. Suitably encouraged, Bocskai sent a message to Emperor Rudolf II claiming, 'God has been with me in this. Account for my position through my acting on God's secret counsel; just like Moses from his shepherding, David from the sheep-pen, like the fleeing Jehoshaphat, [all of] whom God made prince and king over His people.'[33] Subsequent successes by Transylvania's princes in conflicts against the Habsburgs during the Thirty Years War reinforced the impression among Reformed ministers that the Transylvanian principality formed a resting place of divine favour, thanks primarily to its godly rulers. Gábor Bethlen inherited Bocskai's mantle and was described in a speech to the Transylvanian diet given by János Mikola as not chosen by the diet alone.

Your Grace is given to us today by God, as He gave David after Saul, or Hezekiah after Ahaz, and we ask that as of old God blessed holy kings from amongst His people; David, Solomon, and Hezekiah, He will bless and sanctify Your Grace with wisdom, truth, and bravery.[34]

Gábor Bethlen was repeatedly depicted by Reformed ministers during his reign as a new King David. This image was particularly important in allowing Bethlen to be compared favourably with his murdered predecessor, Gábor Báthori, who was described after his death as a new Saul. There had been accusations at the time of Bethlen's accession that he was directly responsible for Báthori's death. By becoming identified with David, Bethlen was portrayed by his supporters as divinely appointed to inherit the princely title. When Báthori's remains were finally interred in 1628, the sermon at this service was given by Péter Alvinczi. Alvinczi's homily outlined the relationship between David and Saul, describing how David's love and compassion for Saul was shown by punishing those who murdered him and by praising those who had given Saul a decent burial. Alvinczi paralleled this with Bethlen's generosity towards Báthori, his execution of

---

33 *Magyar Országgyűlési Emlékek*, ed. Fraknoi, xi, 152–4; Benda, 'A kálvini tanok hatása a magyar rendi ellenállás ideológiájára', 322–30; *Szalárdi János krónikája* ed. Szakály, 85; Makkai, 'Nemesi köztársaság és kálvinista teokrácia a 16. századi Lengyelországban és Magyarországon', 17–29; K. Benda, 'Alvinczi Péter kassai prédikátor történeti följegyzései, 1598–1622', *Radáy Gyüjtemény Évkönyve*, 1 (1955), 14.

34 *Erdélyi Országgyűlési Emlékek*, ed. Szilágyi, vi, 355.

Báthori's murderers, and Alvinczi praised Bethlen for the respect which he continued to show for Báthori by arranging his funeral.[35]

Bethlen proved successful not only in attracting these positive portrayals of himself as a godly prince, but also in demonizing his opponents among the surviving family of Gábor Báthori. In 1618 Bethlen brought a prosecution against Báthori's sister, Anna, under witchcraft legislation passed by the Transylvanian diet in 1614. Anna was the cousin of the infamous Erzsébet Báthori, imprisoned in her own castle in 1609 after charges of mass murder and involvement in witchcraft were initiated by her own relatives. This further attack on the Báthori family saw Anna accused of infanticide, of causing the illness of Bethlen's wife, Zsuzsanna Károlyi, and of involvement in witchcraft. Death sentences were passed against Báthori and others for witchcraft in 1621, but the sentence was delayed because Bethlen seems to have believed in the power of these witches to reverse their magic and cure his wife. When Zsuzsanna Károlyi died in 1622, Bethlen ensured that she was buried with great honour and ceremony. A collection of speeches, verses, and nineteen sermons given by Reformed clergy during the ceremonies leading up to Károlyi's final burial was published on Bethlen's orders in 1624.[36] Despite Károlyi's death, Anna Báthori still escaped the death penalty, but her estates in Transylvania were confiscated, and she was banished from the principality along with two other aristocratic widows related to the Báthoris, Kata Török and Kata Iffju. Whether or not Bethlen believed that some truth lay behind his accusations against Anna Báthori, the interpretation which was placed upon the death of his first wife reinforced his claims to be a godly prince under attack from diabolic forces. This episode also bolstered Bethlen's power in a more practical way, since he acquired substantial new lands in the principality which had previously been held by the Báthori family.[37]

---

35 Péter Alvinczi, *Az néhai felséges Báthori Gábor . . . testének eltakarításakor tett intések* (Gyulafehérvár, 1628); J. Heltai, 'Bethlen Gábor és Báthori Gábor viszonya a kortársak szemében', *Irodalomtörténet* 65 (1983), 685–708; Rácz, 'Főhatalom a xvi.–xvii. századi erdélyben', 857–64; Biró, *Az erdélyi fejedelmi hatalom fejlődése*; Kovács (ed.), *Bethlen Gábor állama és kora*; L. Makkai, 'Bethlen Gábor és az európai művelődés', *Századok*, 115 (1981), 673–97.

36 János Keserüi Dajka et al., *Exequiae principales; azaz, Halotti pompa, mellyel Károlyi Susannának, Bethlen Gábor házastársának utolsó tisztesség tétetett 1622 esztendőben* (Gyulafehérvár, 1624).

37 Hungarian witch-trials often dealt with accusations of *maleficium* rather than claims of diabolism. There were few trials before 1650 and the greatest number of accusations came only in the first decades of the 18th cent. G. Klaniczay, 'Witch-Hunting in Hungary: Social or Cultural Tensions?', in G. Klaniczay, *The Uses of Supernatural Power. The Transformation of Popular Religion in Medieval and Early-Modern Europe* (Cambridge, 1990), 151–67; Makkai, 'Puritánok és boszorkányok Debrecenben', 113–30; Evans, *The Making of the Habsburg Monarchy*, 404–10; *Magyarországi boszorkányperek, 1529–1768*, ed. F. Schram (2 vols.; Budapest, 1970).

Reformed ministers produced a stream of elegiac propaganda about Bethlen throughout his reign, including poetry praising his true faith and his battles against tyranny. Bethlen's character and actions were idealized in heroic form using mainly, but not exclusively, Old Testament imagery. István Melotai Nyilas wrote of Bethlen during the war of 1619 as like David when he faced the Philistines. Péter Alvinczi portrayed Bethlen rather as a new Jehoshaphat, struggling against the wiles of Catholic clergy, and a poem written by András Prágai compared Bethlen to both Gideon and Joseph.[38] In 1626 János Pataki Füsüs described Bethlen as Hungary's 'brilliant star', a new Gideon coming like a comet 'as a heavenly sign, leading Your Majesty in the last times to be King Josiah of Hungary, father to your people'.[39] A great comet, often interpreted as a portent of impending doom, had been seen in Transylvania in 1618. The records of one congregation at Kecskemét in Hungary also described months of 'heavenly wonders' with 'flashing flames and shining clouds . . . stretching north from Constantinople like an executioner's sword'.[40] Responding to the anxiety raised by this comet, the 1619 Küküllő district synod in Transylvania petitioned Bethlen to offer the country moral leadership by setting high standards of behaviour at court and asked the prince to instigate a period of national repentance. The Küküllő synod specifically requested that Transylvanians be encouraged to adopt a more modest lifestyle, humbler dress, and to keep weekly fasts on Sundays. The synod demanded the severe punishment of sinners, especially fornicators, without regard for their social status, and the punishment of adulterers and blasphemers according to

[38] 'It lova reank tekinte az nagy Syonből, Uj Fejedelemmel bodoghita kedveből, Aegyptusböl zabadita, S az kis Bethlenből, Silöt haza. Mint Iosephet nagy Aegyptöböl. Gabriel küldetek, s, nekünk öröm hirdetek, Meniböl Istentöl adatek s-ki muttatek, Bethlen Gabor kegyes Urunk zekben ültetek, Romlot orzagban, Rex Salem, be zenteltetek': András Prágai, 'Sebes agynak késő sisak', in B. Stoll and T. Komlovszki (eds.), *Bethlen Gábor korának költészete* (Régi Magyar Költők Tára. XVII század, 8; Budapest, 1976), 58–61; István Melotai Nyilas, *A szent Dávid XX. zsoltárának magyarázatja* (Kassa, 1620); István Vásárhelyi Kerekes, *Epitaphion katastrophikon; azaz, Szomoruságról örömre váltózó versek Bethlen Gábor erdélyi fejedelem tisztességére* (Nagyszeben, 1618); Gáspár Bojti Veres, *Panegyris . . . Gabrielis Bethlen* (Heidelberg, 1617); Redmeczi, *Az felséges Bethlen Gábornak öt rendbeli Isten anyaszentegyházával cselekedett jótéteményéről*; Gáspár Bojti Veres, *A nagy Bethlen Gábor viselt dolgairól*, in *Bethlen Gábor emlékezete*, ed. L. Makkai (Budapest, 1980), 19–66.

[39] János Pataki Füsüs, *Királyoknak Tüköre* (Bártfa, 1626), 22: 'Felségedet választotta Isten újonnan mostan Magyarország tündöklő csillagává, kit az égen feltetsző üstökös csillag ez utolsó időnek 1618 esztendejében napkeleti Gedeonként eljönni utolsó napján karácson havának nyilván mutatott. Ez mennyei jel vezérelte Felségedet, hogy ez utolsó időben lenne Magyarországnak Jósiás királya, hazájának atyja'; Péter Alvinczi, *Querela Hungariae* as *A nemes magyarország panaszainak megoltalmazása*, ed. J. Heltai (Budapest, 1989), 40; E. Hargittay, 'A fejedelmi tükör mű faja a 17. századi magyarországon és erdélyben', *ITK* 99 (1995), 441–84.

[40] 'Kecskeméti ref. anyakönyvi följegyzések', ed. S. Szilágyi, *Sárospataki Füzetek*, 1 (1857–8), 652–9; 2 (1858–9), 65–78.

God's law. Bethlen was also asked to defend the Sabbath from all activities and trade, and the Küküllő synod wanted anyone who was discovered playing musical instruments at weddings or festivities severely punished.[41]

In 1619 Gábor Bethlen responded to this series of requests, and introduced stringent new laws at the Transylvanian diet on morality and public behaviour. These *Articuli Bethleniani* encouraged people to pray, fast, and show greater enthusiasm in God's service. The articles prohibited work and travel on Sundays, blasphemous swearing and cursing, and imposed restrictions on the sale of alcohol. Harsh punishments were set for a variety of offences, including fines of 6 forints for nobles and 2 forints for peasants who broke rules on observing the Sabbath. Swearing was punishable by a 1-forint fine for nobles and by a morning in the stocks for peasants. Bethlen also accepted the Küküllő synod's complaint that punishments for wrongdoing were not being enforced according to God's law against thieves, murderers, or adulterers, and his articles ordered that these crimes be punished in future with the death penalty. These 1619 articles were later renewed by Bethlen in 1629, this time at the request of Péter Margitai, the eastern Tisza superintendent.[42]

Partly thanks to these laws, Gábor Bethlen was perceived by the Reformed clergy leadership as an outstanding advocate of further reformation in Transylvania. Reformed ministers responded not only by eulogizing their prince's character, but also by producing works which aimed to raise the imagery of kingship and the status of princes in Transylvania. James I's vision of kingly responsibility in *Basilikon Doron* had already been translated into Hungarian in 1612 by György Szepsi Korocz.[43] In 1626 the cult of the Protestant prince was further extended in *The Mirror of Kings* by János Pataki Füsüs, which he dedicated to Bethlen. Pataki's book represented the qualities of a godly king through twelve precious stones (jasper, for example, represented strength, topaz stood for intelligence, and emerald for mercy), together with a staff of law, a crown of true religion, and a golden orb of truth. Pataki described the ideal Christian ruler as active in

---

[41] 'Az 1619. évi küküllővári zsinat felterjesztése Bethlen Gábor fejedelemhez', ed. Illyés, 501–5.

[42] 'Articuli Bethleniani, Illustrissimi Gabrielis Bethlen, ad ecclesiam Dei pertinenti', in Illyés, *Egyházfegyelem a magyar református egyházban*, 95; MOL box 2177, Tiszántúli református tus egyházkerület levéltárának . . . válogatott iratok, no. 6, July 1629.

[43] György Szepsi Korocz (tr.), *Basilikon Doron. Az angliai . . . első Jakab királynak . . . fia tanitásáért irt királyi ajándéka* (Oppenheim, 1612); I. Bitskey, 'Irodalompolitika Bethlen Gábor és a két Rákóczi György udvarában', *Magyar Könyvszemle*, 96 (1980), 1–14; *Bethlen Gábor krónikásai, krónikák, emlékiratok, naplók a nagy fejedelemről*, ed. L. Makkai (Budapest, 1980); T. Toth Somlyói, 'Erdélyi királytükör', in B. Varjas (ed.), *Irodalom és ideológia a 16–17. században* (Memoria Saeculorum Hungariae, 5; Budapest, 1987), 275–93.

building churches and schools, punishing criminals, and bringing justice to his people, and these were all qualities which Pataki wrote were exhibited by Bethlen.[44]

Pataki's description of the role of princes in working for the common good and disciplining society was in part influenced by the writings of Justus Lipsius. Lipsius' ideas on politics proved influential in Transylvania and some of his works discussing Christian stoicism, providence, and the value of steady, benevolent princely rule were translated into Hungarian during the 1640s.[45] Another study on godly authority was dedicated by András Prágai to György Rákóczi in 1628, two years before Rákóczi succeeded Bethlen as prince. Prágai translated a work by Antonio Guevara, court preacher to Emperor Charles V, on the life of Marcus Aurelius, which explained the virtues of a godly prince through a description of twelve gems on a clock-face. Rákóczi was also personally lauded by Reformed writers, culminating in the funeral oration given for the prince by Pál Medgyesi in 1649. Medgyesi recounted Rákóczi's modest life, personal piety, his renowned devotion to reading the Bible, and all his work on behalf of the church. According to Medgyesi, this had made Rákóczi 'our sweet David, the shining light of our eyes . . . the ornate crown of our head'.[46]

The relationship between the Reformed church and Transylvania's princes was decisive in shaping commitment to further reformation in the Transylvanian principality. The princes were the political guarantors of Reformed church liberties, supported the church against its domestic rivals, developed local schools, and gave vital backing for the implementation of the church's programme of moral reform. Reformed ministers also benefited from tax exemptions for their families after the Fifteen Years War, and the ennoblement of the clergy as an order in 1629. Reformed clergy responded by depicting Transylvania's princes as the legitimate and absolute masters of their own land and supported their challenge to Habsburg power in Royal Hungary. The clergy employed potent imagery,

44 Pataki Füsüs (tr.), *Királyoknak Tüköre*; Hargittay, 'A fejedelmi tükör műfaja a 17. századi magyarországon és erdélyben', 441–84.

45 János Laskai (tr.), *Iustus Lipsiusnak az alhatatossagrol irt ket könyvei* (Debrecen, 1641); note also *Justus Lipsius könyvei* (Nagyvárad, 1644) and *Epistolica Institutio* (Nagyvárad, 1656); I. Bán, 'Fejedelemeknek serkentő órája', *Irodalomtörténet*, 40 (1958), 360–73; T. Komlovszki, 'Egy manierista "theatrum europaeum" és szerzője', *ITK* 70 (1966), 85–105; A. Vargha, *Iustus Lipsius és a magyar szellemi élet* (Budapest, 1942); G. Oestreich, *Neostoicism and the Early Modern State* (Cambridge, 1982); T. Wittman, 'A magyarországi államelméleti tudományosság xvii. század eleji alapvetésének németalföldi forrásaihoz: Justus Lipsius', *Filológiai Közlöny*, 3 (1957), 53–66.

46 András Prágai (tr.), *Fejedelmeknek serkentő órája; azaz, Marcus Aurelius . . . életéről* (Bártfa, 1628); Pál Medgyesi, *Erdély s egész magyar nép . . . hármas . . . jajja* (Nagyvárad, 1653).

mostly based on representations of Old Testament kings, to present Transylvania's princes as paragons of godly virtues. This imagery of native princes leading their people under divine inspiration proved to be an important source of a distinct cultural and political identity for the Transylvanian state. The representation of godly princes at Gyulafehérvár was also crucial for the Reformed church in providing a clear example for nobles to follow in their patronage of local clergy and leading role in parish life.

The consolidation of Hungarian Calvinists' administrative and disciplinary mechanisms was buttressed by a degree of informal integration with the Transylvanian state. A dominant Calvinist confession offered Transylvania's princes the prospect of shaping a disciplined society in which popular religiosity and behaviour was being tamed and ordered, and a society in which their authority was being sanctified by Reformed clergy across their territory. The Transylvanian constitution continued to reflect the older sixteenth-century tradition of integrating a multiplicity of confessions to hold together the variety of ethnic and political groups within the then fledgling state. Whilst the confidence of the Reformed community within Transylvania proper, supported by the strongly Calvinist counties of the Partium, never grew so great that this previous policy was entirely abandoned, for rivals of the Reformed church the trend towards Calvinist confessional absolutism was clear enough.

(III) THE CHURCH AND THE NOBILITY

The important role of the Hungarian nobility as patrons of Reformed churches was readily acknowledged by the clergy hierarchy. However, leading ministers also aspired to greater autonomy in directing most aspects of local church life. The respect which was shown for noble rights of patronage was therefore often finely balanced against the authority which superintendents and archdeacons claimed over church affairs. As we have already seen, conflicts arose when nobles demanded the right to have their children baptized at home. There were also arguments about rights of presentment to parishes and over prerogatives about disciplining. Whilst many of the nobility and gentry were certainly committed to orthodox Calvinist doctrine, there is only very limited available evidence about the success of Reformed ministers in inspiring nobles to abide by high standards of moral discipline. The delicate equilibrium between clergy and their noble patrons was thrown into sharpest relief on occasions when disciplinary charges were brought against individual nobles. When arguments arose in a locality between nobles and the clergy, both sides tended to appeal for aid to the prince, as the ultimate authority over the Reformed church and in the Transylvanian principality.

The Reformed clergy leadership attempted to assert greater control over the movement of ministers between parishes during the early seventeenth century, even against the expressed wishes of noble patrons. This interfered with the traditional custom in many areas of annually re-selecting ministers (*papmarasztás*). After a minister had worked in a parish for one year, the church patron, and in some places also the congregation, could choose not to retain the minister's services. Ministers also had the right every year to decide to leave for a new parish if they could find a vacant post. The Debrecen Confession had placed limits on these powers by stating that a congregation could not introduce a minister against the wishes of the local archdeacon, and that if a priest believed that he was doing a good job in a parish then he could not be arbitrarily removed. The church nevertheless conceded that archdeacons could not simply impose their selections for a parish over the heads of the congregation, or without reference to the local noble patron.[47]

The whole system of annually re-selecting ministers was seen by many within the clergy hierarchy as a stumbling-block to the effective imposition of moral discipline by ministers in their local communities, since it was thought that many ministers would not wish to upset those with powers to remove them. In the western Danubian province the Köveskút canons of 1612 forbade noble patrons to remove a minister without the agreement of the church authorities. In 1623 the Komját canons of the upper Danubian church claimed the right to move ministers in cases where the church hierarchy deemed it necessary.[48] In 1633 the Transylvanian synod also decided that ministers could be moved to parishes where the church hierarchy judged they were most needed, even against the minister's own will, and in 1639 the synod laid down a requirement that no minister could be moved from a parish without the prior knowledge and permission of the church authorities.[49]

The increased disciplinary zeal of the Reformed ministry profoundly affected the relationship between clergymen and noble patrons, as well as with their congregations. In one sense Reformed discipline could appear to challenge noble privilege, since the church wanted all its members to be

---

47 *Egyházi kánonok*, ed. Kiss, 81–98.
48 [Dunántúl], 'Adatok a dunántúl és felsődunamellék kerületekről', ed. Thury, 127–40; *Canones Ecclesiastici in Quinque Classes Distributi* (Pápa, 1625).
49 'Az erdélyi közzsinatainak végzései', ed. Szilágyi, 1–9, 77–84, 473–9.

equally subject to spiritual punishments, but inevitably social status and influence could not be ignored. There were also great differences within the ranks of the nobility between the position of powerful magnates, whose authority few ministers would dare to challenge, and that of petty nobles and minor gentry, whose opposition could more easily be overcome.[50] Hungarian Reformed canons from the late sixteenth century stressed the role which nobles played as partners in the process of leading and disciplining congregations. However, ministers were also instructed to rebuke nobles whenever necessary, particularly over issues such as Sabbath observance, failing to partake regularly in communion, living opulently, drunkenness, or for failing in their duties as magistrates and administrators of local justice.[51]

Serious divisions on occasions arose in Zemplén county between Reformed nobles and ministers over disciplinary cases. The area synod at Újlak heard a case in 1632 from Izsép of a noble, Pál Petróczi, who had argued with his local minister and threatened to hit the minister's hat into his head. The synod was satisfied that this matter deserved to be taken seriously, but placed their evidence before the next gathering of the Zemplén county assembly with the expectation that Petróczi would be punished by them. The Zemplén synod again proceeded with caution when it received a letter in 1632 from the county deputy sheriff, intervening in a disciplinary case brought against a noblewoman, Kata Egri. The sheriff had decided not to proceed with any civil punishment against Egri and asked that, if the synod was still determined to enforce public repentance on her, for the circumstances to be mild, not requiring special clothes, nor using the special seat reserved for penitents during a Sunday service. The synod struggled to find some sort of compromise with noble opinion on this case and finally decided to allow Egri to make public repentance in her own clothes, so long as they were dark, but still required her to sit in the penitents' chair.[52]

The 1651 Zemplén synod at Újhely considered a different sort of conflict between a noble and the minister at Lasztócz. An escaped peasant had claimed sanctuary in the Lasztócz church but was dragged out by his master, Ferenc Balog. The synod appealed to the Zemplén county assembly for redress against Balog in this case, and for the assembly to support

---

[50] Cf. the 'titanic struggle of aristocratic pride and clerical pretension' in France after the wife of Philippe de Mornay was excluded from communion for wearing a wig to church. M. Walzer, *The Revolution of the Saints. A Study in the Origins of Radical Politics* (London, 1966), 50–1. See also K. M. Brown, 'In Search of the Godly Magistrate in Reformation Scotland', *Journal of Ecclesiastical History*, 40 (1989), 553–81; Graham, 'Equality before the Kirk?', 289–310.

[51] *Zsinatok végzései*, ed. Kiss, 610–11.   [52] ZEP (1629–45), 147–54.

the freedom of churches from violence and respect rights of sanctuary in church buildings.[53] Disciplinary issues also arose from the consideration by area synods of noble appeals for divorce and the annulment of engagement promises. In one appeal brought before the Szolnok-Doboka synod in Transylvania by Mihály Kovács, his stepdaughter, Ilona Szentmártoni, was absolved from engagement oaths which she had made with a servant named Simon. The grounds given by the synod for this decision were that Szentmártoni was from a noble family, whilst the man was a servant and Romanian, but a condition was imposed that Szentmártoni should publicly confess her sin of making such a secret engagement.[54]

Alongside many examples of collaboration between Reformed ministers and nobles over church discipline, there was also clearly potential for competition between the increasingly assertive claims of the clergy as discipliners and the established authority of nobles over the administration of local justice. Nobles were also accustomed to holding decisive sway in church affairs generally, for example, undertaking the responsibility to restore many church buildings in the aftermath of the devastation of the Fifteen Years War. In a meeting at Petneháza in January 1636 the Szabolcs county assembly stressed their view that nobles should continue to play a leading role in the life of the Reformed church in the Partium. The assembly highlighted the need for noble patrons to continue to rebuild damaged churches, and to provide decent homes for ministers. The assembly also instructed landowners that each village should be compelled to select a justice, jurymen, and sextons, of the kind depicted in Chapter 7 in Zemplén county, to enforce discipline and the punishment of offenders. The Szabolcs nobility ordered that stocks and gallows be built in every town and village and agreed that, in disputes between the nobility and clergy, nobles should complain to their deputy sheriff, whilst ministers could report to their archdeacons.[55]

Despite this attempt to settle the relationship between nobles and clergy in eastern Hungary, unresolved tensions came to the surface during the early 1640s. The noble assembly of Szatmár county forwarded an eleven-point memorandum to the Szatmár area synod of November 1641, expressing concern that the church's drive for discipline was infringing upon nobles' traditional rights and privileges. The Szatmár nobles demanded

53 ZEP (1638–51), 225, 231.

54 Erdély (Transylvania) Reformed Church Province Archives (Kolozsvár), Protocollum Matricula Székiensis (Szolnok-Doboka), 73, 77, 83.

55 Tiszántúl Reformed Church Province Archives (Debrecen), Szabolcs egyházmegye iratai; I. 37.a, A tiszteletes szabóltsi tractus mátriculája . . . 1597-dik esztendőtől fogva, 9–11.

confirmation of their rights of patronage over the selection and dismissal of parish ministers and complained about the presumptuous behaviour of the local archdeacon, István Medgyesi. The Szatmár assembly declared its opposition to the use of excommunication 'without good cause' and demanded that public repentance not be required for minor offences, nor even if a noble killed someone in self-defence. The assembly also complained about the announcement of noble marriages in church and demanded the right for nobles to have their children baptized at home.[56]

The noble assemblies of Szabolcs, Bereg, and Ugocsa supported their colleagues in Szatmár, adding a further complaint that the church should not try to prohibit traditional wedding celebrations. The assemblies then jointly forwarded their demands to the 1642 Nagyvárad synod of the eastern Tisza church province. The synod, led by superintendent Mihály Szánthai, responded by arguing that public repentance must be made for all sins, regardless of the rank of the offender, but conceded that public repentance would not be necessary for nobles found to have committed acts of minor theft. The synod refused to sanction the principle that baptisms could be held outside church buildings, but allowed for noble marriages to go unannounced in churches if there was clearly no obstacle between the proposed partners. On rights of noble patronage, the synod argued that if a congregation was generally satisfied with their minister's performance then the local patron could not summarily dismiss him. The church in the eastern Tisza province called for support for its stance from the four archdeacons of the northern Tisza province. Meeting at Újhely in April 1642, the four archdeacons responded cautiously, uncertain as to what had provoked the noble attack on Reformed church discipline in the first place, and concerned that any outspoken response might bring the wrath of their own nobility upon them. The archdeacons eventually wrote back to the leaders of the church at Szatmár, asserting that there were many who sometimes disregarded the authority of the church and others who tried to destroy it completely. The archdeacons confirmed the scriptural and historic basis of the church's power to excommunicate its members, free from any intervention by 'kings, landowners, nobles, or royal constitutions'. The archdeacons also stressed the continuing need for the exercise of such powers against the unrepentant, because without the right to expel people from the church its sacraments would become corrupted. The archdeacons

---

[56] MOL box 1884, Debrecen egyházmegye jegyzőkönyvei, vol. 1 (1615–55), 442–5; Zoványi, *A tiszántúli református egyházkerület története*, 31–2. Nagy, *Fejezetek a magyar református egyház 17. századi történetéből*, 213, overstated the co-operation of church and secular authorities.

concluded that the proposals of the noble assemblies in eastern Hungary were in their view 'ill considered'.[57]

The tightening of Reformed discipline was clearly beginning to put some degree of pressure on noble lifestyles, an impression reinforced by the tensions exhibited between the clergy and nobility of the Szekler lands in eastern Transylvania. In 1643 a list of recommendations was submitted by Szekler lords to the Maros district church, including requests for the maintenance of traditional church practices concerning baptisms, marriages, and funerals. Ministers were asked not to exclude people from church services on the smallest of pretexts. The Szekler lords also opposed excommunications from the church until a clear sentence had been arrived at for any disciplinary offence. In response the Maros synod asserted that individual ministers could not be criticized for their use of powers to excommunicate church members, since ultimately the district synod had to confirm any exclusions. Otherwise the synod felt confident enough of its own position to offer little substantive satisfaction to any of the Szeklers' main grievances.[58]

One way in which nobles could weaken clerical control over disciplinary matters was to support the greater involvement of local laity in the administration of the church through congregational presbyteries. Presbyterian clergy, indeed, tried their best to attract noble support and to allay noble fears that the privileges of their rank would not be respected by elders. Pál Medgyesi argued that in practice peasants would not rule over their social superiors in a presbytery, since nobles mostly attended their own court chapels or worshipped in towns. With continuing strains between the increasingly assertive disciplinary force of the clergy and a nobility who generally accepted the need for discipline but on occasion remained defensive of their rights in the face of clerical power, some nobles began to see the potential advantages of presbyteries. In 1646 Zsigmond Lónyai, a county high sheriff in the Partium, wrote to György I Rákóczi that even he had been disciplined by his own minister for failing to punish local miscreants quickly enough. Lónyai then wrote that:

Although I do not favour the other opinions of [János] Tolnai [Dali], in so far as in other Reformed churches there is a secular presbytery to bridle ministers, I cannot disapprove of it, with relation to the way in which they [the clergy] are beginning to dominate over us, which has never been the case before, but only since God

---

57 MOL box 1884, Debrecen egyházmegye jegyzőkönyvei (1615–55), 442–5; ZEP (1629–45), 380, 384–6.

58 [Marosi], 'Az 1643. évi [marosi] zsinat válasza a székely urak felterjesztésére', ed. G. Illyés, *Református Szemle* (1936), 261–5.

encouraged Your Grace the prince to their side, by which I know that Your Grace did not pay heed to the abuses of this growth. I do not disagree with this in religion, but on morality I think that, if Your Grace does not take care over the lords and nobility, some of the clergy will gladly dominate . . . and I do not know what to do with them, if Your merciful Grace does not assist us.[59]

The impression given by Lónyai that the gentry and even leading nobles needed support from György I Rákóczi against the disciplinary powers of the clergy was exactly contrary to that given to the prince in a 1648 letter from the four archdeacons of the northern Tisza province. The archdeacons cited the demands made by the noble assemblies of eastern Hungary in 1642 as a sorrowful example of how the nobility 'want to take for themselves a free life, and using all their ability want to pull themselves from under every discipline of the church'. The archdeacons argued that neither the authority of archdeacons nor superintendents was sufficient to counter such recalcitrance, and that the nobility could only be brought completely under Reformed church discipline with the support of the prince.[60]

When György II Rákóczi became prince in 1648 he continued the policies favouring strict moral discipline of his predecessors, enacting similar laws to Gábor Bethlen's 1619 articles. A new Transylvanian law code of 1653 described how Sundays and major festivals should be filled with 'more worthy things' than travelling, work, fairs, or drinking. The death penalty was renewed for adultery, with a beating followed by public repentance as punishment for those found guilty of fornication.[61] The Szabolcs noble assembly also proposed their own new punishment code for the county in 1653. This code set out a series of measures aiming to eradicate blasphemous cursing and foul language, citing outlawed phrases including 'devil-given, devil-spirited, devil-created, dog-spirited, and dog-faith'. The nobles ordered that a first offence of cursing should result in punishment of time in the stocks and a beating, whilst after a second offence local landowners were to have offenders put in irons, beaten with a cane, and then forced to undergo public repentance. The nobles placed onto local justices the responsibility of handing over offenders to landowners, under pain of punishment themselves if they failed to comply.[62]

59 S. Szilágyi, 'Lónyay Zsigmond pere saját papjaival', *MPEF* 8 (1886), 147–9; Medgyesi, *Dialogus Politico-Ecclesiasticus.*

60 L. Hegedüs, 'A zempléni egyházmegye jegyzőkönyvéből', *Sárospataki Füzetek,* 1 (1857–8), 472–3.

61 'Approbatae Constitutiones', 5/51, in *Magyar Törvénytár. 1540–1848 évi erdélyi törvények,* ed. D. Márkus, S. Kolozsvári, and K. Óvári (Budapest, 1900).

62 'Liber Protocolaris Venerabilis Districtus Szatmariensis ab anno 1670 inchoatus', in Kiss, *A szatmári reform. egyházmegye története,* 156.

Pressure was increasingly being placed on other noble assemblies by the Transylvanian prince and the clergy hierarchy to tighten the punishment of immorality, and to compile and put into effect regulations of this kind. In October 1654 the prince wrote to the Szatmár county nobility, expressing his concern at the daily growth in swearing and immoral behaviour. Rákóczi also demanded that nobles in Szatmár should not impede the work of the clergy nor prevent the prosecution of sin and evil-doing. In response the noble assembly denied that they had in any way restricted the activities of the church in Szatmár, but their reply indicated that the problems of the 1640s had still not been resolved.

In those things which affect the direction of the church and discipline, we are the servants of the true church, of which we are members, but we are not aware by which privilege the clergy, of whatever rank, can impose things on us by themselves, without our knowledge and will, and set every direction of the church by themselves. About which matters we could have made our complaints; but we do not wish to burden Your Grace with an enumeration of them.[63]

The Reformed church's attempts to fashion the religiosity and morality of nobles, in the image of idealized pious princes, achieved certain successes. Many nobles supported local schools, rebuilt churches following the Fifteen Years War, and sponsored student ministers to study at foreign universities. Reformed nobles also mostly co-operated with parish clergy over the exercise of moral discipline, and the combination of princes and senior clergy certainly encouraged at least some nobles towards the Reformed model of godly magistrates and gentlemen. The enthusiasm of some nobles to abide by the demands of the Reformed clergy during this period should not, however, obscure the reluctance of others. Co-operation between Reformed noble patrons and an increasingly assertive clergy hierarchy could break down, especially when the disciplinary role of ministers was seen to pose something of a challenge to traditional noble jurisdictions and prerogatives. If there was some unease among the nobility about clergy determination to impose strict moral discipline, then there was also disquiet among ministers about the extent of some noble patrons' commitment to the Reformed cause of further reformation.

Support from powerful magnates, significant landowners, and to a lesser extent from petty nobles and gentry, had been crucial in Hungary and Transylvania, as elsewhere in central and eastern Europe, in deciding the outcome of the reformation. Hungarian nobles who converted to Protestantism had done so partly as a badge of opposition to the state-building

---

[63] 'Liber Protocolaris Szatmariensis', in Kiss, *A szatmári egyházmegye története*, 119–20.

pretensions of the Catholic Habsburgs. By the mid-seventeenth century some nobles found themselves once again opposing the centralizing impact of confessionalization in their localities, but this time resisting the pretensions of the Transylvanian state and Reformed church. In Royal Hungary and in Transylvania, when Protestant princely power withered from the latter decades of the seventeenth century, noble protection proved vital for the Reformed church's survival through to the nineteenth century. However, during the early seventeenth century the church benefited greatly from princely endorsement of its disciplinary ambitions, and princely power was enhanced by Reformed ministers' portrayal of their authority as divinely inspired. This combination of Reformed clergy and princes attempted to order and discipline local communities in the interests of the church and the state. On occasions this met with stubborn resistance from some nobles and from local communities and was also tempered by the need not to alienate other confessional groups from political loyalty to the principality. The final chapter will examine further the relationship between Transylvania's princes and Reformed clergy and assess the role of the church in shaping Transylvania's relations with the rest of Protestant Europe.

9

A Militant and Expectant Faith

Calvinist churches across Europe were bound together by shared doctrine, mutual recognition of confessional statements, common forms of organization, and by expressions of solidarity for persecuted and exiled co-religionists. The unity of the Calvinist cause of further reformation was strengthened and sustained by an extensive network of clergy, students, and exiles at cosmopolitan educational facilities, along trading routes, and through printing centres. The passage of Reformed student ministers from east-central Europe to study at western European universities was particularly important in cementing links between distant Calvinist communities. This international Reformed network of godly professors, ministers, churches, and communities, extended to include princes as well. Calvinist rulers across the Continent were encouraged by their clergy to support the international Protestant cause through diplomatic and military co-operation. This cause was directed against Rome and her allies, especially the Habsburgs, who were commonly portrayed as the prime secular agents of papal tyranny and persecution. Protestant historicism and prophetic revelation confirmed that the Pope was the Antichrist in a Romish Babylon, and discussion of Protestant diplomatic alliances was often tinged with a spiritual enthusiasm which inclined towards millenarianism.

The presentation of an ideology of the Protestant cause in international politics was sustained from the French Wars of religion and the Dutch revolt to the Thirty Years War. Widespread belief in papal inspiration of a conspiracy to subvert Protestantism led on occasions to concerted diplomatic and military action. However, the Calvinist states of western Europe had a mixed track record of matching rhetoric with reality. So whilst Johann VI of Nassau, among others, favoured 'correspondence' between Protestant princes, Nassau-Dillenburg offered contributions to the Dutch rebels, and William of Orange and Johann Casimir, son of Frederick III of the Palatinate, made expeditions to aid the Huguenots, there was also much prevarication and internal wrangling, especially over unpaid debts. Elizabeth in England also often posed as a sincere Protestant in her diplomatic dealings with co-religionists but usually proved unwilling to match such sentiment with money or troops.[1]

There was some revival in the influence of Calvinist ideology among Reformed princes and their advisers from the 1590s. The providential and apocalyptic perspective of Reformed politics certainly needs to be taken into account with regard to Palatine activists such as Christian of Anhalt, regent of the Upper Palatinate, who aided Henri IV and worked to establish the Evangelical Union. In the 1610s Johann Sigismund's conversion strengthened Calvinist expectations in the Rhineland, where the 1609 Cleves–Jülich crisis had already revealed a willingness among German Protestant princes to resort to force. However, diplomatic and military plans for a Protestant union before the Thirty Years War were repeatedly thwarted by divisions between Calvinists and Lutherans, by the withdrawals of some German princes, and by the failure of the English, French, or Dutch to live up to expectations since without their support any plans to combat the Habsburgs in the Empire were completely impractical. There were some efforts again in the 1650s to resuscitate the Protestant cause in England under Cromwell, but by then thoughts of aggressive confessional diplomacy had largely gone out of fashion elsewhere.[2]

Reformed princes therefore proved capable on occasions of successfully combining the demands made on their pious consciences with the furtherance of their own personal and dynastic interests. Many historians, however, remain justifiably sceptical about the extent to which confessional rhetoric was connected with political reality and doubt whether religious commitment was decisive in the diplomatic counsels of Protestant princes. Some historians have even suggested that the standard of religious solidarity frequently provided merely a convenient cover for *raisons d'état* and have argued that Reformed rulers' ambitions were in fact often acted out under the guise of religious and ideological concerns, which princes utilized to vindicate their actions.[3]

This chapter will examine how far a network of international Calvinist connections across Europe informed the development of diplomatic policy

[1] Schilling, *Civic Calvinism in Northwestern Germany and the Netherlands*, 6; Pettegree, Duke, and Lewis (eds.), *Calvinism in Europe, 1540–1610. A Collection of Documents*, 230–2; E. I. Kouri, 'For True Faith or National Interest? Queen Elizabeth I and the Protestant Powers' in E. I. Kouri and T. Scott (eds.), *Politics and Society in Reformation Europe* (London, 1987), 411–37.

[2] Adams, 'The Union, the League and the Politics of Europe', 25–38.

[3] G. Parker, *Europe in Crisis, 1598–1648* (Glasgow, 1979), 161–4; M. Hughes, *Early Modern Germany* (London, 1992), 61–113; S. L. Adams, 'Spain or the Netherlands? The Dilemmas of Early Stuart Foreign Policy', in H. Tomlinson (ed.), *Before the English Civil War* (London, 1983), 86–8.

at the Transylvanian court during the early seventeenth century. As contact grew between western Calvinists and the Reformed church in Hungary and Transylvania there were various attempts to include the Transylvanian principality in Calvinist and Protestant alliances. As the discussion in Chapter 4 revealed, Calvinists were often willing to include Lutherans in an international, pan-Protestant front against Rome, whilst at the same time maintaining a strident rivalry with Lutherans at home. A broadly defined Protestant foreign policy was advocated at the Transylvanian court by prominent figures within the local Reformed church hierarchy, and by Johann Heinrich Bisterfeld and Jan Amos Comenius. Contemporary propaganda also consistently emphasized the confessional motivation behind the actions of Transylvania's princes. This chapter will assess the degree to which Transylvanian military action against the Habsburgs before 1645, and the catastrophic decision to join the Second Northern War in 1657, were in fact motivated by a desire within the principality to further the international Protestant cause, even though there were few remaining advocates of this cause in European politics and diplomacy by the 1650s.

Attempts by the Reformed church to influence diplomatic and military affairs were underpinned to a large degree in Hungary and Transylvania by eschatological expectancy. Calvinists could present a dour face to the world as harsh disciplinarians and austere theologians, sternly defending strict orthodoxy. Calvinist systems of belief certainly valued highly uniformity, order, and discipline, but renewal and regeneration were equally at the heart of early modern Calvinism. This aspiration for religious, moral, and social renewal fostered and sustained beliefs in Reformed communities about the possible imminence of the end times. Calvinist eschatology tended to look for gradual improvements towards the end of history with increasing revelations of knowledge, and potential victories over satanic powers in the world which required immediate political and military activism. Reformed communities living in fear of invasion or persecution, or in exile, found particular hope in their expectation of a final judgement to which the godly could look forward. A minority of Calvinist theologians were not content with this general apocalyptic expectation and tried to work out the exact date of the end of the world, despite the explicit biblical proscription against doing so.[4]

This chapter will outline ideas within the Hungarian Reformed church about divine judgement and an imminent end of the world. Important

[4] N. Cohn, *The Pursuit of the Millennium* (London, 1957); Ball, *A Great Expectation*; Firth, *The Apocalyptic Tradition in Reformation Britain*; M. Bull (ed.), *Apocalypse Theory and the Ends of the World* (Oxford, 1995).

parallels were drawn between the fate of Hungary and Israel which informed notions about a special and predestined role for Hungary and the Transylvanian principality in the apocalypse to come. Much attention was paid to prophetic scripture and also to signs and portents in nature and in the sky, which linked élite and popular apocalyptic traditions. Hungarian Reformed beliefs about the apocalypse stressed the urgent need for further reformation at home to combat immorality, and further reformation abroad to fight satanic powers in the world. This chapter will examine how far not only confessional interests but also such apocalyptic beliefs came to feature in diplomatic decision-making at the Transylvanian court.

(I) HEBRAIC PATRIOTISM AND APOCALYPTIC BELIEF

Calvinists across Europe drew many parallels between the history of Old Testament Israel and their own experiences, which at first had focused on Geneva, a new Jerusalem, and then spread as far as Ireland and Hungary on Europe's peripheries. Whilst Calvinist concern to learn lessons from God's relationship with ancient Israel was by no means unique, Reformed clergy across the Continent pursued Hebraic patriotism with extraordinary zeal, offering thoroughgoing applications of comparisons with Israel to their congregations. Calvinists looked to the history of Israel to understand their own past, present circumstances, and future expectations. The moral implications of a new covenanted relationship with God were successfully highlighted and applied to settled Calvinist communities, whilst the image of wandering Israel also provided hope of future deliverance to Calvinist refugees 'under the cross'. Israel was at first mostly identified by Calvinists as the true church throughout the world. Whilst an exclusive understanding was on the whole retained about who could come under the new covenant, ideas about building a new Israel slowly changed from an embattled holy remnant within any nation to embrace the possibility of elect nationhood by the early seventeenth century.[5]

Transylvania's unique position as a lone eastern Reformed outpost, on narrow ground between Habsburg and Turkish powers which were both identified as demonic, led to a powerful concentration among Transylvanian Calvinists on the motif of biblical Israel. Comparisons spread beyond the typology of Transylvanian princes as biblical kings of Israel, examined

---

5 G. Groenhuis, 'Calvinism and National Consciousness: The Dutch Republic as the New Israel', in A. C. Duke and C. A. Tamse (eds.), *Britain and the Netherlands, 7. Church and State since the Reformation* (The Hague, 1981), 118–34; P. Regan, 'Calvinism and the Dutch Israel Thesis', in B. Gordon (ed.), *Protestant History and Identity in Sixteenth-Century Europe, 2. The Later Reformation* (Aldershot, 1996), 91–107.

in the previous chapter, into parallels between the history and language of Israel and Hungary. Hungarians' strong sense of particularity and myths concerning their Asian origins were adapted by Calvinists to reconstruct the Hungarian Reformed community's perception of their history and contemporary circumstances.[6] Hungarian Calvinists did not have a monopoly on Hebraic patriotism in the region, and the anti-Trinitarian theologian Jacob Palaeologus compared Prince János Zsigmond to the Old Testament King Josiah in a 1574 tract. However, by the early seventeenth century the Reformed community had developed notions that Hungarians were a new chosen people, living under divinely inspired princes, and worshipping in a true church with a reformed and pure communion.[7]

A tradition of using Old Testament records of God's relationship with Israel to understand contemporary events in Hungary and Transylvania extended back to the collapse of the Hungarian kingdom. The catastrophic defeat at the battle of Mohács in 1526 was widely regarded as a divine punishment, and the Hungarian reformation owed much to a reactive desire to purify religion in order to avoid any further judgements. Protestant writers made connections between the nations of Hungary and Israel from the earliest stirring of reform preaching during the 1530s. In 1538 András Farkas wrote a poem entitled 'A Chronicle of the Movement of Scythians to Hungary and of the Jews from Egypt', which paralleled the arrival of Hungarians in Pannonia and Dacia with the Jewish exodus to their promised land. Farkas described how God had wondrously 'brought the ancient Hungarians out of Scythia as of old he brought the Jewish people from their misery under the Egyptian Pharaoh'. Farkas portrayed his ancestors as coming in a single movement of people under God's guidance from Asia, a drastically simplified version of the Hungarian tribes' long migration from the Urals to the Black Sea steppe around the fifth century, with waves of Huns and Magyar tribes advancing westwards until the Danubian Basin was finally conquered at the end of the ninth century. Farkas suggested that just as the tribes of Israel were led into a promised land made fertile by the River Canaan, so the Magyar tribes' new chosen lands of Pannonia and Dacia were made fertile thanks to the Rivers Danube, Drava, Szamos, and Maros.

According to Farkas's 'Chronicle', the Hungarians were at first blessed in their Canaan by the rule of good and faithful kings but later punished for sin and faithlessness by that of bad kings, whose wickedness had ultimately led to the Ottoman invasion. Farkas compared the Israelites' loss of the

[6] Cf. S. Schama, *The Embarrassment of Riches* (London, 1987), 93–124.
[7] Williams, *The Radical Reformation*, 372–8, 742.

temple at Jerusalem and their exile in Babylon with the Ottoman sultan's destruction of Hungary's monasteries and imprisonment of the Hungarians. Farkas's 'Chronicle' certainly had a clear reforming message, stressing that God's grace alone was the author of Hungary's migration to Europe and subsequent conversion, and suggesting that Catholic idolatry had caused defeat at the hands of the Turks. Hungarians, Farkas argued, must now accept those teachers who were proclaiming the message of the Gospel and hope that their response to true preaching would soon be rewarded by pious kings who could lead them out of their present captivity.[8]

Drawing parallels between Israel's exodus from Egypt to their Promised Land and the Hungarians' migration from Asia to their holy land in the Danubian Basin proved to be significant in cementing commitment to the Reformed cause in Hungary. It constructed a credible and coherent historical narrative which explained Hungary's past and contemporary position, and gave reasons as to why religious reform was necessary. This narrative of Hungary's history, moving from initial blessing at the time of migration to Europe into judgement under the Ottoman invasion, had become firmly established among Reformed writers by the early seventeenth century. Albert Szenczi Molnár wrote that as Israel had been directed by God across the Sinai Desert through signs of cloud by day and fire by night towards the Promised Land, so the Hungarians were led by God out of the Scythian steppe. Molnár claimed that the Hungarians had travelled across the Maeotian swamps around the Sea of Azov under the miraculous guidance of a stag and then onwards to the most beautiful part of Europe. Another Reformed minister, János Iratosi, wrote that Hungarians had been brought to enjoy their land of plenty by God. Iratosi argued that although their ancestors had come from Scythia as pagans, they had understood through nature that there was one true God who was drawing them from Asia to Pannonia. Iratosi believed that God had been dealing, and would continue to deal, with the Hungarians through providence and judgements as he had done with the people of Israel in the past.[9]

[8] 'Oe ymmár hagyuk el ah szydo nepeket vegyük elö az reg magyarokat ingyen mayd értyuk hogy as Isten öket illy, bő földre magyarrá el ky hozza, mind regen ky hozza a zsydó nepeket Egyptom országból ah meg igért bő földre.' András Farkas, 'Cronica de introductione Scyttarum in Ungariam et Judaeorum de Aegypto' (1538), preserved in a 19th-cent. manuscript copy at the Hungarian Academy of Science, Manuscript Collection (Budapest), sign. Történl. 4rét, 38[(Q) volume], ff. 55–60. There has been a long tradition of identifying Hungarians with Scythians: N. Ascherson, *Black Sea. The Birthplace of Civilisation and Barbarism* (London, 1996), 54–5, 76–81.

[9] *Szenci Molnár művei*, ed. Vásárhelyi and Tolnai, 177–8; Iratosi, *Az ember életének boldogul való igazgatásának módjáról. Patika szerszámos bolt, azaz sokféle haláloknak természetükről.*

Interest also increased during the early seventeenth century among Reformed students in matters concerning the Jews and the Hebrew language. Attention was given to prophecy that the Jews would be converted to Christianity before the end of the world. Transylvanian ministers certainly showed concern to convert radical Sabbatarians who had adopted Jewish law, and István Geleji Katona quoted the Talmud and the works of Jewish scholars in arguments against Sabbatarian beliefs.[10] Works were also produced about Hebrew grammar, and many clergy wrote verses and dedications in Hebrew. One Reformed minister even attempted to compose Hebrew poetry at Sárospatak in the early 1650s, and Johann Heinrich Alsted wrote an elegiac poem for Gábor Bethlen's funeral in Hebrew.[11]

This increased study of Hebrew by Reformed ministers led to striking claims of linguistic links between Hebrew and Hungarian. A now lost sixteenth-century work by János Sylvester had first suggested links between the languages, and the publication by Albert Szenczi Molnár of his *Latin–Hungarian Dictionary* at Nuremberg in 1604 aroused renewed discussion in Protestant circles about the origins of Hungarian. Among German Protestants, Bartholomaeus Keckermann at Danzig called on Molnár to show how close Hungarian really was to Hebrew, whilst Georg Rem at Nuremberg was much more sceptical and thought that Hungarian must be linked to Scythian tongues. In the 1640s Jan Amos Comenius was also certain that Hungarian was related to 'the languages of Asia, whence it came'. Comenius thought that some aspects of Hungarian grammar, particularly the lack of gender in nouns and adjectives, deserved to be adopted in the new perfect language which he was working to develop in order to facilitate universal intellectual communication. Molnár had written cautiously on the issue of the origins of Hungarian that he was not aware of connections to any other languages. István Geleji Katona on the other hand made the straightforward assertion that Hungarian was not related to any language except Hebrew in his 1645 *Hungarian Grammar*. György Komáromi

---

[10] István Komaromi Szvertán, *Disputationes Anti-Judaicae . . . de conversione iudaeorum* (Utrecht, 1646), 210–11; András Horvath, *De Judaeorum, ante novissimum diem conversione futura* (Kassa, 1658); Gáspár Tiszabecsi, *Disputatio Theologica de plenitudine temporis contra Judaeos* (Franeker, 1651): this last tract was amongst volumes taken from Hungarian libraries by the Soviet army and is now probably in Nyiznij Novgorod. Laskai, *Jézus királysága*, 152; István Geleji Katona, *Titkok Titka* (Gyulafehérvár, 1645); Kohn, *A szombatosok*; R. Dán, 'Eőssi András és az erdélyi szombatosság genezise', *ITK* 78 (1974), 572–7; C. Hill, 'Till the Conversion of the Jews', in R. H. Popkin (ed.), *Millenarianism and Messianism in English Literature and Thought, 1650–1800* (Leiden, 1988), 12–37.

[11] György Komáromi Csipkés, *Oratio Hebraea, continens elogium Linguae Hebraeae* (Utrecht, 1651); György Komáromi Csipkés, *Schola Hebraica* (Utrecht, 1654); G. Szinyei, 'Adalék Komáromi Csipkés György életéhez és irodalmi működéséhez', *MPEIF* 6 (1875), 72–82; R. Dán, 'Héber hungaricák a xvi.-xvii. században', *Magyar Könyvszemle*, 81 (1965), 352–8.

Csipkés agreed in his 1655 *Hungaria Illustrata* that 'of all the languages under the sky none has more affinity to Hebrew than Hungarian'.[12] Parallels with Israel proved to be a powerful means of connecting the history and language of Hungarian communities with the Reformed project of re-establishing a covenantal relationship with God through further reformation. However, by the late 1640s the tone of parallels between Old Testament Israel and Hungarian Calvinists had grown perceptibly more anxious. Pál Medgyesi was especially concerned at the slow pace of progress towards a reformation of morality in Reformed congregations, and in a series of sermons published as *Three Woes of Transylvania and the Whole Hungarian People* predicted impending judgement as a result. When Gábor Bethlen's younger brother István died in January 1648, the princely branch of the Bethlen family died out with him. At his funeral service in March 1648, Medgyesi delivered the first of his sermons of lament, arguing that Bethlen's death marked the removal of a major column of support from the Transylvanian principality. Medgyesi preached from a text on the death of Josiah, the seventh-century king of Judah, urging his audience of leading nobles to repent of their sins if they wanted to remove the threat of imminent divine judgement. Medgyesi gave a warning that 'when I think of the state of the nations of Israel and Judah, before their captivity in Assyria and Babylonia, I see as if in a mirror the frightening position of our own nation. Oh Lord, favour Your people!'[13] Medgyesi's second and third 'Woes' were heard at the funerals of György I Rákóczi in 1649 and of his younger son Zsigmond Rákóczi, who died aged only 29 in February 1652. At Zsigmond's funeral, Medgyesi preached again on Josiah's death, reminding his audience of the prophecy that Josiah would be killed so that he did not have to witness the destruction of the temple at Jerusalem. Medgyesi concluded that the deaths of such godly men as György and Zsigmond Rákóczi meant that the future would prove very dark for Transylvania and argued that, more than ever before, the time was ripe for Hungarians to turn towards God and away from their sins.[14]

Pál Medgyesi's depiction of the deaths of István Bethlen, György I Rákóczi, and Zsigmond Rákóczi as gathering woes to afflict Transylvania,

---

[12] *Szenczi Molnár Albert naplója, levelezése és irományai*, ed. Dézsi, 159–62; J. Hegedűs, 'Megjegyzések Szenczi Molnár Albert nyelvészeti munkásságához', *ITK* 62 (1958), 45–52; György Komáromi Csipkés, *Hungaria Illustrata* (Utrecht, 1655), 23; Comenius, *Panglottia*, ed. Dobbie, 51–2; Sadler, *Comenius and the Concept of Universal Education*, 152–3.

[13] Medgyesi, *Erdély s egész magyar nép . . . hármas jajja* 58–9. For some earlier fears, see the funerals of Gábor Bethlen and the younger István Bethlen: Mihály Váradi, 'Prodromus Funestus', printed in L. Dézsi, 'Váradi Mihály verse Bethlen Gábor haláláról', *Magyar Könyvszemle*, 6 (1898), 372–84; see also I. Acsády, 'Halotti búcsuztató 1633-ból', *ITK* 1 (1891), 131–6. [14] Medgyesi, *Erdélyi s egész magyar nép . . . hármas jajja*, 25, 36, 41.

linked contemporary events with Isaiah's Old Testament prophecy of six laments which would deliver judgement upon a sinful Israel. Isaiah predicted that the deaths of political and military leaders would leave Israel vulnerable to external attack. Medgyesi similarly used the testimony of the deaths of godly nobles in Transylvania as signs of imminent judgement against the ungodly living of the principality. Medgyesi preached again on this message at a funeral in 1656 at Szerdahely for Zsuzsanna Lónyai, wife of Zemplén's high sheriff. This sermon was later published under the title 'The Fate of the Just in the World' and was filled with dark warnings that all God-fearing people in Transylvania should prepare for a menacing battle ahead.[15]

Ideas about divine punishment and judgement had been consistently prominent in the writings of Hungarian Reformed clergy. Hungarian minds were no doubt concentrated on this subject by the proximity of the non-Christian world, seen as a likely instrument of divine retribution for sin. In 1563 Gáspár Károlyi published *Two Books, on the Causes of Good- and Ill-Fortune for All Countries and Kings, from which to understand the cause of Hungary's destruction and to recognize the symptoms showing that God's judgement is at hand*. Károlyi explained the causes of the destruction of the Hungarian kingdom by detailing how in Hungary, as in Israel, God's covenant had been destroyed by idolatry. Károlyi concluded that 'the Turkish emperor is a servant of God for the punishment of the Hungarian nation' and argued that only a profound spiritual and moral renewal in Hungary would force the Ottomans to withdraw. Another prominent reformer, Mihály Sztárai, used the Old Testament history of the wicked King Ahab to warn contemporary kings and princes of the dangers of invoking God's wrath through their sin.[16]

Gáspár Károlyi was persuaded that there were clear signs that final judgement was at hand in wars and rumours of wars, in the spread of evil among the people, and in the growing power of Antichrists in Constantinople and Rome. Károlyi followed Melanchthon in dividing history into six ages and four world empires. Of the last 2,000 years of the sixth age he calculated that 1,505 had already passed, and he expected the remaining time to pass more quickly leading to the end of the world.[17] Apocalyptic

[15] Pál Medgyesi, *Igazak sorsa a világon. Gyászbeszéd Bocskai István felesége Lónyai Zsuzsanna felett* (Sárospatak, 1657).

[16] '. . . bizony az török császár Isten szólgája az magyar nemzetségnek büntetésére': Gáspár Károlyi, *Két könyv minden országoknak és királyoknak jó és gonosz szerencséjeknek okairól, melyből megérthetni, mi az oka a magyarországnak is romlásának és miczoda ielensegekből esmerhettiuc meg, hogy az istennec iteleti közel vagion* (Debrecen, 1563), pp. f6, 77. Mihály Sztárai, *História a zsidó Ákháb királynak bálványozásáról* (Debrecen, 1619).

[17] G. Kathona, *Károlyi Gáspár történelmi világképe* (Debrecen, 1943).

enthusiasm in sixteenth-century Hungary reached a peak after the prediction by Ferenc Dávid that 1570 would bring the destruction of the Antichrist. Expectations reached fever pitch in 1569 after heavenly signs were detected, and especially after the discovery of a 'black man', a popular prophet called to lead a holy army and defeat the Turks. This prophet, called György Karácsony, encamped with his supporters around Debrecen in 1569 and 1570. The captain of the Hungarian frontier fortress at Eger, Simon Forgách, wrote that his garrison had to be dissuaded from joining Karácsony, since 'religion had gripped them as if thunder-struck, they broke no law, did not curse or swear, and reprimanded one another for such offences'. In expectation of a miraculous victory Karácsony led a band of 600 men to the frontier at Törökszentmiklós, only to be crushed by the Turks and scattered in confusion.[18]

During the early seventeenth century contact between Hungarian student ministers and western Calvinist theologians stimulated a further wave of interest in apocalyptic ideas. The influential Heidelberg teacher, David Pareus, wrote of the Papacy as the source of the true church's spiritual afflictions, whilst the Ottoman empire provided physical torments. Pareus also believed that the period following the reformation would lead quickly to the end of the world, seeing prophecies from the Book of Revelation reflected in contemporary events across Europe. In April 1618 Pareus wrote to Gábor Bethlen explaining that he was preparing a new exegesis on Revelation. Pareus praised Bethlen for understanding the need to combat the adulterous Rome and recommended that Bethlen spend time reading the 'deep secrets' of Revelation.[19] Johann Heinrich Alsted was a confirmed millenarian, and apocalyptic reasoning may well have drawn Alsted eastwards to Transylvania, which he believed was a vital station in the dramas of regeneration which he foresaw. Alsted believed that the millennium was yet to come, but denied that he was a chiliast on the grounds that he awaited spiritual and not earthly joys. Alsted believed that the 'thousand years of the Revelation' would end in 2694, basing his calculations on the movements of the planets and the appearance of a new star in 1604. He also predicted a revival in Protestant fortunes from 1625 and maintained that a conjunction of Saturn and Jupiter in 1642 suggested that a major revolution should be expected among Europe's governments.[20]

[18] Révész, 'Debreceni lelki válsága, 1561–1571', 76.

[19] David Pareus, *A Commentary upon the Divine Revelation of the Apostle and Evangelist John* (Amsterdam, 1644); Páriz Pápai, 'Romlott fal felépítése', 129–81, no. 4.

[20] Johann Heinrich Alsted, 'Diatribe de mille annis apocalypticis' [1630], and 'The Beloved City; or, The saints reign on earth a thousand years' [1643] tr. William Burton, in B. Griesing, J. Klein, and J. Kramer (eds.), *J. H. Alsted, Herborns calvinistische Theologie und*

Despite Alsted's influence in Transylvania, Reformed ministers who were interested in apocalyptic ideas, such as István Geleji Katona, rejected attempts to set a definite date for the return of Christ.[21] Alexis János Kecskeméti, a former student at Heidelberg, also argued that the end of the world was near without suggesting exactly when this might occur. Kecskeméti rebuked those, such as Pareus, who tried to predict the future decline of the Habsburg and Ottoman empires from Old Testament prophecies, and condemned predictions based on astronomy as erratic. Kecskeméti's examination of prophetic scripture nevertheless led him to suggest that a Hungarian prince was needed in the end times who would protect the true church, establish high moral standards, and lead the recovery of national independence. Expectation in Hungary and Transylvania about impending judgement and the imminent end of the world flared up during periodic crises or after unusual natural events, commonly interpreted as signs of God's anger. Péter Alvinczi recorded that when a strong earthquake hit Nagyvárad in May 1603, causing two church towers to lean towards each other, local people believed that their final hour had come. Even Alexis János Kecskeméti drew attention to comets and earthquakes as signs of wars, and as indicators of the need for people to repent of their sins.[22] The way in which God dealt with Israel in the Old Testament remained the reference point from which it was taught that natural disasters, fire, and military defeats all resulted from sin. In 1634 Máté Csanaki dedicated a work to György I Rákóczi which examined connections between sin and the appearance of the plague. Csanaki, who had studied extensively in the west, presented stars and angels as the agents of the arrival and departure of plague. Csanaki stressed, however, that it was not stars themselves which were to be feared, but God who directed them and whose anger could only be assuaged by penitence.[23]

Wissenschaft im Spiegel der englischen Kulturreform des frühen 17. Jahrhunderts (Studien zu englisch-deutschen Geistesbeziehungen der frühen Neuzeit, 16; Frankfurt, 1988), 20–73; Alsted, *The World's Proceeding Woes and Succeeding Joys* (London, 1642); István Geleji Katona, *Váltság-Titka*, i, 94; H. Hotson, 'Johann Heinrich Alsted', D.Phil thesis (Oxford, 1994).

[21] Geleji, *Váltság-Titka*, i, 1,026; G. Nagy, *Geleji Katona István eschatologiája* (Budapest, 1941).

[22] *Kecskeméti Alexis János prédikációs könyve*, ed. L. O. Gombáné (Budapest, 1987), 200, 413, 591; István Magyari, *Az országokban való sok romlásoknak okairól és azokból való megszabadulásnak jó módjáról* (Sárvár, 1602); István Szathmári Ötvös (tr.), *Titkos jelenése* (Nagyszeben, 1668); Benda, 'Alvinczi Péter kassai prédikátor történeti följegyzései, 1598–1622', 5–26.

[23] Máté Csanaki, *A döghalálról való rövid elmélkedés* (Kolozsvár, 1634); Anon., *Lelki tömjénező, melyben a . . . könyörgésnek kedves illatu füstöletivel az Istennek . . . haragja engeszteltetik* (Gyulafehérvár, 1646).

The predilection for prophecy within the Hungarian Reformed community extended from the elaborate and convoluted calculations based on planetary movements made by theologians such as Alsted to the sections of 'Astronomical Prognoses' published in Hungarian calendars, as they were elsewhere in Europe, which advanced predictions about harvests, disease, and wars based on the movements of heavenly bodies and stars. A calendar for 1620 predicted that a November eclipse would mean grave dissension in religion in Hungary and the death of a leading churchman. Another calendar, dedicated to Gábor Bethlen, predicted three eclipses for 1625, and the author advised Hungarians to seek protection from a spiritual eclipse through the light of the Gospel. Gáspár Debreczeni believed that a solar eclipse in 1636 would 'cause changes for the worse in religion, and the oppression of good old customs and just laws'. In 1644 David Fröhlich studied the movements of Jupiter and Mars to find the most dangerous days in the year, on which wars could be expected to start, and described how conjunctions of the planets would bring wonderfully beneficial changes for the church and in politics.[24]

There was some resistance within the Reformed church to such attempts to predict the future. In a 1660s tract György Komáromi Csipkés argued that Christians should not believe lying astronomers and that the sun, moon, and stars were merely natural bodies. Komáromi also denied that comets were signs of impending evil, or of God's anger, or of the end times. Komáromi suggested that comets had no particular significance for any one country, and he reviewed previous comets which had no perceptible effect on events in Hungary and Transylvania. However, causal connections between natural omens and human affairs continued, as Komáromi himself conceded, to be widely accepted by Reformed writers throughout this period.[25]

The mid-1650s were years of particularly high eschatological excitement across Protestant Europe, and eclipses in 1652 and a comet in 1653 raised expectations about the apocalyptic results of a solar eclipse in August 1654. Verses written by a minister at Nagyvárad in 1655 talked of the passing and changing times, and of the sun and moon prophesying in 'mourning clothes'. These verses also referred to the 1654 eclipse as evidence that the final days were at hand, requiring repentance and church

---

[24] Bálint Hancken, *Kalendárium* (Debrecen, 1620); Dávid Herlicius, *Kalendárium* (Gyulafehérvár, 1625); Gáspár Debreczeni, *Kalendárium* (Debrecen, 1635); Dávid Fröhlich, *Kalendárium . . . Prognosis Astrologica* (Nagyvárad, 1644).
[25] György Komáromi Csipkés, *A Judiciaria astrologiáról és üstökös csillagokról való judicium* (Debrecen, 1665), 36–7, 49–50.

unity.[26] Predictions were published suggesting 1655 as the final dawn of the Messiah, and if not 1655 then possibly 1656, the supposed number of years between the creation of the world and Noah's flood. In 1662 János Szalárdi's *Miserable Hungarian Chronicle* recorded bad omens from the year of György II Rákóczi's election as Transylvanian prince, with two lightning strikes on the castle at Nagyvárad and the accidental death of a man when a church bell fell on him. Szalárdi wrote that such 'sad signs of the imminent general great evil were seen as if shown by a finger'. Szalárdi also recalled that Imre Szilvásújfalvi Anderkó had prophesied that 1657 would be the year of destiny. He pointed out that György II Rákóczi had embarked upon an invasion of Poland in 1657 which ended in disastrous defeat and destructive invasions of Transylvania, seeming to confirm the validity of these omens and Szilvásújfalvi's prophecy.[27] The remainder of this chapter will assess the degree to which ideas about the Protestant cause in international politics, and about Hungary's future in an unfolding divine plan, were in fact influential in shaping the direction of Transylvanian diplomatic policy up to Rákóczi's decision to invade Poland.

(II) THE PROTESTANT INTEREST AND TRANSYLVANIAN DIPLOMACY

Early seventeenth-century politics and diplomacy in Hungary and Transylvania were transformed by the Fifteen Years War, by the bloody Habsburg occupation of Transylvania in 1603, and by the revolt of the Hungarian nobility in 1604 under István Bocskai. Peace treaties at the end of the Fifteen Years War recognized the integrity of Transylvania's borders, but Transylvania henceforth maintained a hostile relationship with Royal Hungary, which periodically sparked into open conflict. Transylvania's princes built ever-closer links with western Protestant powers, and from cautious and pragmatic beginnings under Gábor Bethlen in the 1610s a path of Protestant diplomatic and military co-operation was established

---

[26] 'Az üdők el multak, mindenek változnak, /Még az csillagok, is egekben bujdosnak, /Nap és hold egy más közt gyász ruhát hordoznak, /Azok is minékünk ugyan praedicálnak. /Másodszor jelenti az világnak végét, /Amaz rettenetes napnak el jövését, /Az Chrisztus szinének hamar jelenését, /Mind az egész főldnek az ő vétkes terhét.' [Váradi], 'Egy gúnyirat a váradi ref. esperesség presbyterianus papjai ellen, 1655-ből', ed. K. Szabó, *MPEIF* 1 (1870), 590–8.

[27] *Szalárdi János krónikája*, ed. Szakály, 197–8, 342–3. 'Ezerhatszázötvenhétben, Mikor ember, jutsz ennyiben, Rezzen világ minden részben, mert a nagy év percen ebben. Avagy jegy kezd ködben lenni, vagy az Halys visszafolyni, Az nagy Taurus elolvadni, kis Halycon adattatni. Azért kérlek így igyedben, jobbitsd magad életben, Ne félj semmit, ha Istenben, hited vagyon, ki úr ebben.' (Ibid. 349–50.) See also Hill, 'Till the Conversion of the Jews', 14–15.

which was followed by the Rákóczi princes. As outlined in Chapter 1, Protestants in Transylvania and Hungary, as well as in Poland, Bohemia, and Austria, tied their challenge to Habsburg and Catholic domination in the 1610s with similar efforts by co-religionists in Germany and the Netherlands. In 1618 the estates of Bohemia and Upper Austria rebelled, inspiring the refusal of Lower Austria, Silesia, and Moravia to accept the rule of Ferdinand II. The Bohemians found in Frederick V a leader for their cause, and Frederick's move to claim the Bohemian throne was not only the result of Wittelsbach ambition, as his purification of St Vitus' cathedral in Prague demonstrated.

By August 1619 Gábor Bethlen felt that Habsburg difficulties had become Transylvania's opportunity. Bethlen led his army towards Vienna in alliance with the Bohemian confederates and maintained contact with their newly elected king, Frederick. Within four weeks Bethlen had taken almost all of Royal Hungary, and in August 1620 the Transylvanian prince was elected king of Hungary.[28] Propagandists from both sides were not slow to put their confessional gloss on the unfolding conflict. Péter Alvinczi laid the blame for the war at the door of Catholic priests, and particularly the Jesuits, for instigating attacks on Protestants in Royal Hungary. Alvinczi argued that Bethlen was duty-bound to defend Hungarian constitutional liberties and Protestant rights. Péter Pázmány, the archbishop of Esztergom, responded with a ringing denunciation of Bethlen's rebellion against Ferdinand's lawful authority and accused Protestants of interfering with the free practice of Catholicism in Transylvania.[29]

The events of 1620 revealed the lack of real coherence among Protestants in central Europe, who failed first to rescue Bohemia and then the Palatinate. By 1621, apart from Bethlen, only the dukes of Saxe-Weimar and Christian of Brunswick-Wolfenbüttel remained loyal to Frederick. Although Bethlen had a successful campaign in the spring of 1621, abandoned by his coalition partners, and fearful of being seen by the Turks as too independent, he made peace with Ferdinand at Nikolsburg in December 1621. Whilst Bethlen renounced his claim to the Hungarian throne, he persisted with his active anti-Habsburg policy and embarked upon a

---

[28] S. Szilágyi, 'Bethlen Gábor fejedelem uralkodása történetéhez', *TT* (1879), 242–3; 'Bethlen Gábor levelei', ed. S. Szilágyi, *TT* (1885), 655–6, 659–65.

[29] Alvinczi, *Querela Hungariae*, tr. in French as *Manifeste complaincte du Royaume de Hongrie, addressée a toute la Chrestienté, et specialement a ses alliés* (Heidelberg, 1620); in German as *Copia eines Sendschreibens . . . von Bethlehem Gabor Fürsten in Sibenbürgen* (Prague, 1619); in Dutch as *Articulen Vande Confederatie der Hungarische, Bohemische Ende gheincorporeerte Provintien* (Hague, 1620). See also Pázmány, *Falsae originis motuum Hungaricorum succincta refutatio*, I, 11, 32–3.

further campaign in Hungary in August 1623. This time Bethlen had only Brunswick and Count Mansfeld for support, and the Hungarian estates, suitably cowed by Bohemia's fate, denied Bethlen the support which they had given during his first campaign. Bethlen fought on until April 1624 but then made peace again with Ferdinand on similar terms to the 1621 Nikolsburg treaty.[30]

Despite his undoubted contribution to the anti-Habsburg cause, some western diplomats remained suspicious of Bethlen's motivation for taking the field. Thomas Roe wrote to Bethlen from Constantinople in 1624, encouraging him to ally again with Protestant powers for the 'publique benefit of Christendome'.[31] Roe perhaps knew something of Bethlen's offer that year to marry the 13-year-old Habsburg princess, Cecilia Renata. Secret instructions given to Bethlen's representative at negotiations in Vienna included the suggestion that the Habsburgs could regain Transylvania from Turkish suzerainty through this marriage.[32] When Bethlen's marriage proposal was rejected, he returned to his previous anti-Habsburg policies. During a visit to England in 1624, Albert Szenczi Molnár organized meetings with George Abbot, archbishop of Canterbury, and with the Palatinate's ambassador to London. Both sent messages encouraging the Transylvanians to contact Charles I with the aim of forging a Protestant alliance.[33] Towards the end of 1625 Bethlen's envoy, Matthias Quadt, met Christian IV of Denmark, and Christian despatched an agent to Transylvania. Bethlen's return to the Protestant party was sealed by his marriage to Catherine of Brandenburg in March 1626, the same month in which an anti-Habsburg alliance was ratified at The Hague between England, Denmark, and the Dutch Republic. In April 1626 Bethlen wrote to Charles I and began protracted negotiations through Quadt to join the anti-Habsburg allies. Negotiations stalled over the 40,000-thaler monthly subsidy which Bethlen requested in return for embarking upon a new campaign against the Habsburgs. Bethlen's rigid demands in these negotiations received a bad press in England, and he was satirized in verse:

---

[30] K. Péter, 'A fejedelmség virágkora (1606–1660)', in *Erdély története*, ii, 656–87; K. Péter, 'Two Aspects of War and Society in the Age of Prince Gábor Bethlen of Transylvania', in J. M. Bak and B. K. Király (eds.), *War and Society in Eastern Central Europe, 3. From Hunyadi to Rákóczi: War and Society in Late Medieval and Early Modern Hungary* (New York, 1982), 297–313.

[31] *The Negotiations of Sir Thomas Roe*, ed. Richardson, 350.

[32] [Bethlen Gábor], 'Adalékok Bethlen Gábor szövetkezéseinek történetéhez', ed. S. Szilágyi, in *ÉTTK*, 2/8 (Budapest, 1873), 44–56.

[33] Vásárhelyi, *Eszmei áramlatok és politika Szenci Molnár Albert életművében*, 86; Welsby, *George Abbot*.

... We heare he [Bethlen] has ...
A Drumme, to fill all Christendome with the sound,
But he cannot drawe his forces neere it,
To march yet, for the violence of the noise.
And therefore he is faine by a designe,
To carry 'hem in the ayre, and at some distance,
Till he be married, then they shall appeare.
Lick-finger: Or never; well, God b'wi'you.[34]

Negotiations finally reached a successful conclusion with the Westminster treaty of 30 November 1626, by which Bethlen gained diplomatic recognition for Transylvania from England. Denmark and the Dutch Republic later ratified the Westminster agreement in separate accords of February 1627. Thomas Roe sent his congratulations to the Transylvanian prince, claiming that 'you have now begunne to enter into a more honorable and secure way, by a confederacy with those princes, who by the common bond of one Christian faith, will nor forsake their allyes, nor bee wanting to their owne honours'. Bethlen had launched a new attack against the Habsburgs in August 1626, but concluded a peace treaty at Pozsony in December 1626 along the lines established at Nikolsburg in 1621. A letter of March 1627 from his prospective Danish ally, Christian IV, indicated that Bethlen had concealed the progress of these negotiations from his allies, and Roe too became embittered against Bethlen.[35]

Western historians have been largely unimpressed by Bethlen's trustworthiness and unconvinced about the significance of his military contribution to the anti-Habsburg coalition.[36] Bethlen's interventions in the Thirty Years War had at least drawn attention in the west towards Transylvania as a potential ally against the Habsburgs. The precedent was also clearly established within Transylvania that the principality could and should intervene militarily in the interest of European Protestantism, as

---

[34] A discussion between Lick-Finger and Thomas Barberi from Ben Jonson, 'The Staple of News 14–24 Apr. 1626'. G. Gömöri, 'Bethlen Gábor a korabeli angol nyomtatványokban és szépirodalomban', *ITK* 98 (1994), 60; Gál, 'Maksai Péter angol nyelvű Bethlen Gábor életrajza, 1629-ből', 223–38; M. Sebestyén, 'Maksai Őse Péter; gyulafehérvári rector', *Magyar Könyvszemle*, 110 (1994), 203–7; V. Fraknói, 'Bethlen Gábor és IV. Keresztély dán király', *TT* (1881), 102–3.

[35] [Bethlen Gábor], *Adalékok Bethlen Gábor szövetkezéseinek történetéhez*, ed. Szilágyi, in *ÉTTK*, 2/8 (Budapest, 1873), 78–93; *The Negotiations of Sir Thomas Roe*, ed. Richardson, 539, 716–17, 809; Fraknói, 'Bethlen Gábor és IV. Keresztély dán király', 98–102; H. Marczali (ed.), 'Regesták a külföldi levéltárakból', *TT* (1879), 546, 550; *Bethlen Gábor fejedelem levelezése*, ed. S. Szilágyi (Budapest, 1886), 341–2.

[36] See e.g. M. Roberts, *Gustavus Adolphus. A History of Sweden, 1611–1632* (2 vols.; London, 1953–8), ii, 309–11.

well as to defend Hungarian constitutional freedoms. Bethlen's success in the 1620s against the Habsburgs certainly reinforced the impression among Reformed clergy at home that Transylvania was a resting-place of divine favour, mainly thanks to its godly ruler.

During the 1630s lengthy negotiations continued between György I Rákóczi and the Swedes to forge a new anti-Habsburg coalition. Paul Strassburg was sent to the Transylvanian court, opening a channel for negotiations between Rákóczi and the Swedes from 1631 until 1633, and in May 1632 Gustav Adolf wrote to the Transylvanian prince calling upon him to join his coalition.[37] Although this phase of negotiations remained unfruitful, Transylvania continued to be courted as a potential ally by the Swedes and French. The level of trust in György I Rákóczi was enhanced by the reputation of his prime negotiator and diplomatic envoy, Johann Heinrich Bisterfeld. Bisterfeld travelled to western Europe on foreign policy missions between 1637 and 1639, sometimes under the assumed name of Henrik Meerbolt, with proposals for an alliance between Transylvania, France, and Sweden. Bisterfeld also contacted others interested in Transylvanian affairs on these trips, including John Dury and Samuel Hartlib, who reported rumours that Habsburg agents intended to assassinate Bisterfeld because they felt that he was stirring up Rákóczi for war.[38] After Bisterfeld's second mission to Paris, proposals were made for an alliance between France and Transylvania. Negotiations reached a final stage in Germany in 1638, but Bisterfeld had not been empowered to conclude an agreement prior to leaving Transylvania, and the opportunity slipped away. In December 1638 the Swedish council gave Johann Salvius the task of forming an alliance with Transylvania, but whether through caution on Rákóczi's part, or because of disagreements over subsidies, this also came to nothing.[39]

In June 1641 the French and Swedes renewed their partnership and from 1642 began once again the tortuous task of encompassing Transylvania within their alliance. In August 1642 Bisterfeld presented a draft plan to Rákóczi for a treaty with the Swedes, but negotiations dragged on into 1643 over subsidy payments and the need for Rákóczi to secure Turkish approval for any external military action. In September 1643 Rákóczi received

37 [Rákóczi György I], *I. Rákóczi György elsö diplomacziai összeköttetései történetéhez*, ed. Szilágyi, 16–24, 51–2.

38 Hartl. 2/6, f. 6a; 9/1, f. 95b; 43, f. 21a. On Bisterfeld: Hartl. 2/6, f. 4a; 37, f. 90a; 1/33, f. 39a. See also Keserű (ed.), *Adattár 1*, 401–6.

39 *I. Rákóczi György elsö diplomacziai összeköttetései történetéhez*, ed. Szilágyi, 130–1; Gergely, 'I. Rákóczi György összeköttetése francziaországgal', *TT* (1889), 686–7, 692–4; 'Magyarország történetét érdeklő okiratok a svédországi levéltárakból', ed. K. Wibling, *TT* (1892), 440–73, 593–634.

encouragement from István Geleji Katona to the effect that co-religionists in England, Scotland, Germany, Bohemia, and the Dutch Republic placed high hopes in a positive intervention by Rákóczi in the current conflict.[40] Rákóczi finally signed a treaty with the Swedes in November 1643 and with the French in April 1644, agreeing to continue fighting against Ferdinand III until a general peace was concluded. The prince also gained the consent of the Ottomans for his attack on Royal Hungary, and there were plans for a Turkish army to join Rákóczi's advance from Buda. The alliance with the French caused some problems on both sides, and János Kemény insisted that the Swedes, although Lutherans, deserved prior mention in all treaties since the French were not fighting for the sake of religion.[41] The French meanwhile expressed concern over Rákóczi's plans to advance Protestantism in Hungary, and *The Manifesto of George Racokzkie* published in 1644 certainly contained the unequivocal claim that Rákóczi's rising showed his love for God, the Protestant religion, and the liberty of his country.[42]

French and Swedish diplomats wrote to Bisterfeld, encouraging him to sustain Rákóczi's resolve and remain faithful to their agreements. Bisterfeld had very high expectations of the results of the alliance which he had worked so hard to create, after prolonged struggles at court to win the prince over to an active policy against more conservative advisers. In a letter to Rákóczi in January 1645 Bisterfeld enthused on the expected arrival of Lennart Torstensson and the Swedish army in Moravia and predicted that the long-awaited days of the fall of the Antichrist were now finally at hand.[43] Rákóczi started out to meet Torstensson, but the Swedes were soon forced out of Moravia to face an attack from the Danes. Rákóczi fought on until March 1645, but resigned from the coalition in August 1645, and the Transylvanian principality did not therefore participate in

---

[40] [Rákóczi György I], *I. Rákóczi György svéd és franczia szövetkezéseinek történetéhez*, ed. Szilágyi, nos. xviii, xxiii, xliv; 'I. Rákóczi György fejedelem és Geleji Katona István püspök levelezéséből', ed. S. Szilágyi, *EPK* (1874), 21–3.

[41] Gergely (ed.), 'I. Rákóczi György összeköttetése francziaországgal', *TT* (1890), 61–72.

[42] *The Declaration or Manifesto of George Racokzkie, Prince of Transylvania, to the States and Peeres of Hungarie; together with the reasons added thereunto of his modern taking up of armes* (London, 1644); *A Declaration or Manifesto, wherein the Roman Imperiall Majesty makes known to the States and Peeres of Hungarie, what reasons and motives have compelled him to proceed in open warre against the Prince of Transylvania* (London, 1644); Miklós Esterházy, *Rákóczi György erdélyi fejedelemnek irt egynéhány intő leveleinek igaz pariája* (Pozsony, 1644).

[43] 'Naplókönyv, 1632-ból', ed. L. Abafi, *TT* (1883), 519–42, 645–55; *Erdély és az északkeleti háború. Levelek és okiratok*, ed. S. Szilágyi (2 vols.; Budapest, 1890–1), ii, 210; [Rákóczi György I], *Rákóczy családi levelezése*, ed. Szilágyi, 510; [Rákóczi György I], *I. Rákóczi György svéd és franczia szövetkezéseinek történetéhez*, ed. Szilágyi, 155–6, 180–1, 229–30; [Rákóczi György I], *I. Rákóczi György első diplomacziai összeköttetései történetéhez*, ed. Szilágyi, 144–5.

the Westphalia peace negotiations. A separate peace was instead finalized between Transylvania and the Habsburgs at Linz in December 1645, confirming the freedoms of Hungarian Protestants and returning the seven north-eastern counties of Hungary previously held by Bethlen back to direct Transylvanian control. In February 1646 Bisterfeld wrote to French diplomats of his huge disappointment at the sudden end to hostilities, but stated his firm belief that the peace could not be permanent. Bisterfeld also defiantly proclaimed in a letter to the prince's younger son, Zsigmond, that there would never be real peace in Europe until Rome had been completely destroyed.[44]

Diplomatic and military co-operation to advance the Protestant cause had been a significant rallying cry in Transylvania throughout the period of the Thirty Years War, but the principality seemed most ready to act on that confessional call after the outbreak of the general European peace. The convention of support for a confessional foreign policy was by then firmly established at the Transylvanian court. The decade from 1648 had constant speculation about a resumption of conflict either against Catholic Poland or directly against the Habsburgs. During the 1650s Protestant alliances were strongly advocated at court, often within a context of apocalyptic and millenarian enthusiasm. Bisterfeld continued with his attempts to engage Transylvania in alliances with western Protestant powers and solidify an anti-Habsburg partnership. Meanwhile, clerics made connections between Hungary's constitutional grievances, the Rákóczi family's dynastic ambitions, and the promotion of true religion. Some prominent Reformed figures, both within Transylvania and elsewhere, advocated that György II Rákóczi take positive action to support the Protestant cause, although others feared that, without national repentance of sin, divine judgement and military disaster would result.

Protestants exiled from their homes in Austria, Bohemia, and Moravia, who had seen the Westphalia peace confirm the Habsburg drive for spiritual absolutism in their monarchy, were particularly enthusiastic for the Transylvanians to renew military activity on behalf of the Protestant cause in east-central Europe. Jan Amos Comenius, working at Sárospatak from 1650, encouraged Rákóczi to take immediate military action on the basis of the prophetic skills of his fellow Moravian exile, Mikuláš Drabík. Drabík had made initial contact with the Rákóczi family in 1636, and records from Kecskemét noted that Drabík's early prophecies for the Rákóczi house were 'of great encouragement' but also brought 'grave dangers'. In 1644

---

44 Gergely (ed.), 'I. Rákóczi György összeköttetése francziaországgal', *TT* (1890), 72–6; Kvacsala, 'Bisterfeld János Henrik élete', 548.

Drabík again approached György I Rákóczi promising he would gain the Hungarian crown, and whilst at Sárospatak in September 1652 Drabík prophesied that the Rákóczis would ally with the Swedes and the Palatinate, and join with the Turks and Tartars to overthrow the Habsburgs and defeat the Papacy. Drabík claimed that by the end of 1653 György II Rákóczi would be crowned king of Hungary at Pozsony, and that the Turks would hand Buda back to him.[45]

To Bisterfeld's horror, Comenius addressed an appeal to Zsigmond Rákóczi in support of Drabík's prophecies as a 'Secret sermon of Nathan to David'. Comenius laid out the role which he foresaw for Zsigmond as the liberator of central Europe, who would spread light from Hungary into Moravia, Bohemia, and Poland. Zsigmond was depicted as a new King David who would free his people from the yoke of the Antichrist and Turkish oppression, and then move on to free neighbouring peoples from Austria to Poland from the same fate. According to Comenius, Zsigmond would then achieve the liberation of Europe and the conversion of the Turks. This tract could be dismissed as the vacuous and deluding bleatings of a far-gone millenarian, except that Comenius was so well regarded by the Rákóczi family and had strong contacts with prominent Transylvanian diplomats and courtiers. Comenius' appeal to Zsigmond was also couched in language already current at Gyulafehérvár and Sárospatak, thanks partly to Bisterfeld. Comenius' expectation was further encouraged when he was asked to conduct the marriage service in June 1651 between Zsigmond and Maria Henrietta, daughter of Frederick V of the Palatinate. However, Comenius' extravagant plans for Zsigmond quickly began to unravel, when Maria Henrietta died in September 1651 after only three months of marriage. In December 1651 Henrietta was buried at Sárospatak 'leaving her pious husband in unspeakably bitter and sad mourning'. Zsigmond was reportedly convinced by Comenius' explanation that Henrietta's sudden and unexpected death had been caused by his failure to act quickly enough upon Drabík's prophecies.[46]

---

45 [Comenius], *Korrespondence*, ed. Kvacsala, no. cxviii; 'Kecskeméti ref. anyakönyvi följegyzések', ed. Szilágyi; Kvacsala, 'Egy álpróféta a xvii-ik században', 745–66; Kvacsala 'A xvii. századbeli chiliasmus történetéhez', 428–50; Mout, 'Chiliastic Prophecy and Revolt in the Habsburg monarchy', 93–109.

46 'Comenius irata Rákóczi Zsigmondhoz', ed. Kvacsala, 128–43; *Szalárdi János krónikája*, ed. Szakály, 312. Comenius had Drabík's prophecies published in *Lux in Tenebris* (1657) alongside those of Christoph Kotter and Christina Poniatowska, with further publications of Drabík's *Revelations* in 1659 and 1663 and a complete edition in 1664 as *Lux e Tenebris*. See also J. C. Davis, 'Formal Utopia/Informal Millennium: The Struggle between Form and Substance as a Context for Seventeenth-Century Utopianism', in K. Kumar and S. Bann (eds.), *Utopias and the Millennium* (London, 1993), 17–31.

From the late 1640s the attention of the Transylvanian court had turned to Poland. Before his death in 1648, György I Rákóczi tried to promote Zsigmond as a potential candidate for the Polish throne. Zsigmond Rákóczi's status was enhanced when he inherited a large swathe of the family estates in north-eastern Hungary, but in 1648 Jan Casimir was elected to succeed his brother Władysław IV. Zsigmond then told a Swedish envoy, Berndt Skytte, that the Swedes, despite being Lutherans, would not find better partners than the Transylvanians in any war against the Poles and the Emperor. Skytte reported back to the Swedish chancellor, Axel Oxenstierna, that the Transylvanians would readily attack Royal Hungary, on condition that they received permission to do so from the Porte.[47] György II Rákóczi certainly tried to co-ordinate anti-Habsburg resentment among Catholic nobles in Royal Hungary, who were disgruntled about the lack of any positive action against the Ottomans at the end of the Thirty Years War. When the Hungarian diet was asked to elect a new palatine in 1649, supporters of the Rákóczi family backed one such noble, Pál Pálffy. In 1651 Pálffy sent a message to György II Rákóczi indicating his willingness to co-operate with Zsigmond in northern Hungary. However, in January 1652 Zsigmond wrote to his brother, expressing his own doubts about whether Transylvania's immediate neighbours could in fact be relied upon as allies. Zsigmond concluded that they had to think mainly in terms of distant Protestant allies, even though they might not always be able to help Transylvania with force of arms in a crisis.[48]

All these speculative plans and manoeuvres came to an abrupt halt following Zsigmond's death in 1652. Comenius' faith in Drabík's prophecies was badly undermined by Zsigmond's death, but his doubts vanished again after Drabík correctly predicted when György II Rákóczi would name his son Ferenc to succeed him as prince. Comenius then tried to bring Drabík's other prophecies to Rákóczi's attention at the Transylvanian court through János Kemény and András Klobusiczky. The focus of Comenius' attention and expectation now fell upon György II Rákóczi alone. In 1654 Comenius suggested in 'The Happiness of the People' that it was György who was a political messiah, blessed with a heroic spirit passed down from Moses, which would enable György to liberate his country and its neighbours, and to reform religion as a new Gideon.

47 *Erdély és az északkeleti háború*, ed. Szilágyi, i, 200–2; [Rákóczi György II], *Okmánytár II. Rákóczi György diplomacziai összeköttetéseihez*, ed. S. Szilágyi, (Monumenta Hungariae Historica, 23; Budapest, 1874), 64–73.
48 'Herczeg Rákóczy Zsigmond levelezése', ed. Szilágyi, (1891), 232–3; *Erdély története* ii, 715.

And who will it be, if not you György Rákóczi, most noble Transylvanian prince? You are the one, you alone, you at last, at last the hope of your own! Of your home, land, people, the only holy anchor. Do you not hear God searching for the man . . . Oh, be open to discovery! Your Israel, all your people, tremble before the Turks, groan before the Jebusites! They cry aloud with the perpetual oppression of the Antichrist approaching, that God himself should send a messiah. Do you not hear? Oh may God uncover your ears, and your heart, that you may hear!49

Rákóczi's response to this appeal was somewhat uncertain. In a letter to Jonás Mednyánszky, Rákóczi wrote that he, like Bisterfeld, did not believe Drabík's prophecies to be divinely inspired. However, Rákóczi also wrote that if some God-given opportunity opened for action abroad he was ready to seize it, especially if he could work with other allies to advance the international Protestant cause.50

In 1654 Rákóczi sent Constantin Schaum as an envoy to the Protestant powers of northern and western Europe, galvanizing Transylvania's friends abroad into activity. These included Comenius, who left Hungary in 1654 for Leszno in Poland, frustrated with the lack of prompt action in response to his proposals. Comenius put Schaum in touch with a series of his friends and contacts in Sweden and the Dutch Republic and wrote to Hartlib in London in January 1655 recommending the 'Transylvanian agent' to him. In November 1654 Schaum sent news back from London to Rákóczi on the progress of his diplomatic mission, which again demonstrated intimate connections between diplomatic activity and confessional interests. Schaum's report included the prophecies of an 'astronomical doctor' which had been given to him by Comenius. These predictions threatened the imminent destruction of central Europe in war, to be followed by a return to true religion, and offered Rákóczi the prospect of becoming the next Hungarian king.51

---

49 'Quis autem ille erit, si non Tu Georgi Racoci, Celsissime Transylvaniae Princeps? Tu unus, Tu solus, Tu ultimus, ultima Tuorum spes! Tuae inquam Domus, Tuae Terrae, Tuae Gentis, solus unus Anchora sacra. Audis Deum quaerere Virum . . . Ah patere Te inveniri! Israel Tuus, tota Gens Tua, trepidat a Turcis, gemit a Jebusitis! clamant oppressi anti-Christiano jugo vicini etiam, ut sibi Deus mittet Salvatorem. Non audis? . . . O aperiat Deus aures Tuas, et cor Tuam, ut audias!' 'Gentis Felicitas', in 'Comenius irata II. Rákóczy Györgyhöz', ed. Kvacsala, 144–68. See also Hartl. 114/1, f. 19a; 7/72; [Comenius], *Korrespondence*, ed. Kvacsala, 187.
50 '. . . az cseh ember látási, hogy revelationes divinae sint, nem hihetjük, holott sokakban, többire mindenekben ellenkező dolgok találtattak . . . higyje el azt kld jó Menanszki uram, valamiben istenes út, mód adatik, ad omnes occasiones készen találtatunk.' *Erdély és az északkeleti háború*, ed. Szilágyi, i, 334–5.
51 Ibid. i, 340–3.

In March 1655 Schaum travelled to Sweden and met twice with Charles X, who asked the envoy about Transylvania's relationship with the Ottomans. Schaum then returned to England in May 1655 through Denmark and the Dutch Republic, and John Dury promised that for his part he would endeavour to satisfy the expectation of 'the Transylvanian gentleman'. Samuel Hartlib was sufficiently encouraged by Schaum's return to London for him to write in a memorandum to Oliver Cromwell that the Transylvanian prince was now 'to give a proofe of his zealous activity and devoted services, as in bearing witness of the uprightness and zeale of your Highn[ess's] intentions towards the whole Protestant interest'.[52] Schaum, probably aided by Hartlib's good offices, was able to address Cromwell on 4 May 1655. Schaum conveyed a proposal to Cromwell that England and Transylvania should work together towards building up an alliance of Protestant countries. Cromwell's response to this initiative was a letter to Rákóczi, agreeing with the principle of a brotherhood between Protestant princes and highlighting his own project to relieve the plight of Alpine Protestants as an example of how such co-operation might work.[53]

Apocalyptic expectations were raised among Protestants in Transylvania during the mid-1650s, and visionaries in the principality received widespread credence for their claims of an imminent turning-point in Transylvania's destiny. Peter Figulus, Comenius' travelling secretary and former assistant to John Dury, brought news to Hartlib in 1654 of 'Jesuits . . . forced to entertain themselves with the tragical objects which God hath set before them: of the vanishing of their hopes . . . of the Transylvanian army which is on foot; of some terrible signs from heaven such as is an earthquake'.[54] In 1655 Comenius wrote to Hartlib of the imminent destruction of Babylon and the reconstruction of Zion, and by late 1655 Comenius became convinced that Rákóczi was about to act for the Protestant cause. Figulus informed Hartlib that at this time 'Mr. Comenius hath every month his owne cursor into Hungarie to his Brethren', and that Comenius was in correspondence with some of Rákóczi's officials. In September 1655 Comenius certainly wrote to one of Rákóczi's advisers, András Klobusiczky, expressing his conviction that the destruction of the Papacy was at hand. Comenius enquired about the state of negotiations with Sweden, and about opinions at the Transylvanian court of Drabík's talents as a prophet, and asked whether Drabík's prophecies had been

[52] Hartl. 4/3, ff. 97a–106a; 34/4, f. 15a; 54, f. 72a.

[53] Bodleian Library, Oxford, MS Rawlinson A. 261, f. 46; A. 26, f. 81. *Okmánytár II. Rákóczi György diplomacziai összeköttetéseihez*, ed. Szilágyi, 182–3; E. Simonyi, *Londoni Magyar okmánytár, 1521–1717* (Pest, 1859), 216–17, 219–21.

[54] Hartl. 43, f. 45a.

translated yet into Hungarian. Comenius even offered to act as an honest broker in negotiations between Transylvania and Sweden in 1656, a message which was passed on to the prince by another of his contacts, Jonás Mednyánszky.[55] Such expectations followed the events of the summer of 1655, when Charles X led 18,000 troops in a Swedish deluge over Polish Prussia. Charles aimed to secure control of the Baltic coast but also had an ill-defined imperial design to extend his authority into south-eastern Europe, with thoughts of a Swedish protectorate over the Ukraine as a bar to Russian expansion. It was clear that Rákóczi was anxious to join Charles in Poland, and the prince had already shown his determination to pursue an active foreign policy. In 1653 Rákóczi replaced the Moldavian voivode, Vasile Lupu, with the more pliant Gheorghe Ştefan, and in 1655 ensured that his protégé Constantin Şerban survived a domestic revolt in Wallachia. Contacts to co-ordinate anti-Habsburg sentiment also continued between the Transylvanian court and some nobles in Royal Hungary, including the new palatine, Ferenc Wesselényi, and Miklós Zrínyi. Frustration abounded at the Transylvanian court when Charles X sent Gothard Welling to the principality only to ensure Rákóczi's favourable neutrality during the invasion of Poland. Bisterfeld's death in 1655 was keenly felt in such delicate circumstances, and Zsuzsanna Lórántffy wrote to Rákóczi in 1656 of how much Bisterfeld's advice and loyalty had been missed during this crucial period.[56]

Faced with Sweden's successful invasion, malcontents among leading Polish nobles sought foreign aid. Janusz Radziwiłł, the Protestant Lithuanian grand hetman, had written to Rákóczi claiming that some Polish senators favoured a new election for the crown. Radziwiłł also suggested a cautious correspondence among Protestants in east-central Europe, but stressed that advertising such manoeuvres would be politically disastrous within Poland. Jerzy Lubomirski then advanced Rákóczi as a candidate to replace Jan Casimir, conditional on the vain hope that Rákóczi would convert to Catholicism. Discussions continued until the end of 1655, when Casimir made it clear that Lubomirski was negotiating independently of the court. Although Casimir was very reluctant to consider Rákóczi as a candidate for succession, in the spring of 1656 he sent grand secretary

55 [Comenius], *Korrespondence*, ed. Kvacsala, nos. cliv, clv, clx; *Erdély és az északkeleti háború*, ed. Szilágyi, i, 384–5; ii, 95–6.

56 [Rákóczi György I], *Rákóczy családi levelezése*, ed. Szilágyi, 510. *Erdély és az északkeleti háború*, ed. Szilágyi, i, 518–19; ii, 73; M. Roberts, *From Oxenstierna to Charles XII. Four Studies* (Cambridge, 1991), 100–43.

Mikołaj Prażmowski as an envoy to Transylvania. Negotiations began over the suggestion that Rákóczi's son could succeed in Poland if he was brought up as a Catholic, but this plan was also stymied by the question of religion.[57]

In September 1656 Rákóczi concluded an alliance with the anti-Ottoman voivodes he had established in Wallachia and Moldavia, and also with the Cossack leader Bogdan Chmielnicki. Negotiations with the Swedes then finally led to a formal alliance at Radnot in December 1656. This extraordinary agreement envisaged the future promotion of Protestantism in a conquered Poland. By the terms of the alliance the Polish commonwealth was to be divided between Rákóczi, who was to acquire much of Little Poland, lands in Lithuania, and the titles of king of Poland and grand duke of Lithuania, whilst the Cossacks were to be granted control of the Ukraine, with Sweden taking Prussia and Brandenburg acquiring part of Great Poland.[58]

In spite of opposition from Rákóczi's mother, wife, and some leading councillors, the Radnot treaty was approved by the Transylvanian council and ratified by the diet. Rákóczi embarked for Poland in January 1657 before spring floods could slow his progress, and without seeking prior consent from the Sultan for his external military action. This unprecedented move went against normal Transylvanian diplomatic practice and ignored a direct demand from an Ottoman emissary for Rákóczi to return immediately to Transylvania. Rákóczi's foolhardy determination to proceed into Poland was at least partly based on a miscalculation of the situation at Constantinople. Rákóczi's representative at the Porte was Jakab Harsányi, who had trained as a Reformed minister and studied in the Dutch Republic in the 1640s. In 1646 Harsányi had been charged with misconduct at the Szatmár national synod, probably because of presbyterian sympathies, and Harsányi was at first only sent to Constantinople as an interpreter until he gained Rákóczi's trust. In April 1656 Harsányi reported that chaos reigned within the Ottoman administration, but then in late 1656 wrote to Rákóczi informing him of a take-over by the new Albanian grand vizier, Mehmed Köprülü. Harsányi confirmed that the Ottomans definitely wanted Rákóczi

---

57 R. I. Frost, *After the Deluge: Poland-Lithuania and the Second Northern War, 1655–1660* (Cambridge, 1993), 34–7, 59–67; R. I. Frost, '"*Initium calamitatis regni*"? John Casimir and Monarchical Power in Poland-Lithuania, 1648–1668', *European History Quarterly*, 16 (1986), 181–209.

58 [Rákóczi György II], *Okmánytár II. Rákóczi György diplomacziai összeköttetéseihez*, ed. Szilágyi, 315–19, 368–9; *Erdély és az északkeleti háború*, ed. Szilágyi, ii, 190–6; [Rákóczi György II], 'Diplomácziai okmányok II. Rákóczy György uralkodása történetéhez', ed. K. Wibling, *TT* (1893), 421–3.

to stay out of the Polish war. Despite acknowledging the revival of policy direction under Köprülü, Harsányi wrote that if the campaign in Poland was successful then the Turks were unlikely to intervene, but warned of revenge if Rákóczi should fail.[59]

Commanded by János Kemény, the Transylvanian army of 10,000 cavalry and 3,000–4,000 infantry left for Poland, joined first by 6,000 Moldavian and Wallachian troops and then by 20,000 Cossacks. In April 1657 the combined army took Cracow, then met with Charles X's army before attacking Brest in May. It was left to the Habsburgs to attempt to resuscitate the Polish cause. After Ferdinand III died in April 1657, his young son Leopold, although not yet elected as Emperor, renewed Habsburg support for Casimir and encouraged Frederick III of Denmark to attack Holstein. In May 1657 Charles was compelled to send back part of his army to face the Danes, and then to withdraw completely from Poland in June. Meanwhile, Rákóczi made for the Ukraine to consider his position, but in late June his Romanian and Cossack allies abandoned the campaign under threats from the Ottomans and their Tartar allies. This left Rákóczi with no alternative but to sign a humiliating capitulation to Casimir on 22 July. Rákóczi agreed to hand back all occupied territory, break off all his anti-Polish agreements, apologize to Casimir, and pay compensation of some 1.2 million florins.

Rákóczi then retreated back to northern Hungary with 300 cavalry ahead of the main body of the army. The bulk of his remaining forces under János Kemény were surprised by an attack from the Tartars, and those who survived were taken prisoner back to the Crimea. The Tartar khan demanded a ransom for the release of the Transylvanian army, which Rákóczi was slow to pay. Even if the ransom had been paid immediately, perhaps only 3,000–4,000 troops were still in any condition to fight for Transylvania's survival, with the remainder dead or injured. The Poles were the first to take advantage of this weakness. Lubomirski attacked north-eastern Hungary as far as Szatmár, and then in August 1657 the Tartar khan was sanctioned by the Porte to sweep into the Szekler lands of eastern Transylvania. In October 1657 Köprülü sent a message to the Transylvanian diet that Rákóczi's attack on Poland, his interference in Wallachian affairs in 1655, and his alliance with the Cossacks meant that he must be replaced as prince. The diet was initially uncertain on how to proceed, but Rákóczi put forward conditions for his resignation from office, and Ferenc Rhédei,

---

59 *Okmánytár II. Rákóczi György diplomacziai összeköttetéseihez*, ed. Szilágyi, 483–4; B. Keserű (ed.), *Adattár 2. Apáczai és kortársai* (Budapest–Szeged, 1966), 52–63. In the late 1660s Harsányi moved to Brandenburg to work for Frederick William.

Gábor Bethlen's nephew, was then elected as the new prince in November 1657.[60]

The wave of optimism which had propelled Rákóczi into action in Poland quickly dissolved. Arguments about the reasons behind the unfolding diplomatic and military catastrophe began almost immediately, and some nobles claimed that the initial attack on Poland had been ill considered and badly prepared. For Pál Medgyesi, who had long predicted doom and disaster, the failure of Rákóczi's Polish adventure appeared to be the calamity which he had been prophesying. Medgyesi argued that the lack of honour given to the name of God, and failures to adopt moral and religious reforms in Transylvania, had caused the military defeats. Medgyesi compared the situation in Transylvania with the state of Israel at the time of Hosea the prophet. Medgyesi quoted from Hosea, but substituted Hungarians for Israelites: 'Hear the word of the Lord, you Hungarians [sons of Israel], because the Lord has a charge to bring against you who live in the land . . . the Hungarians [Israelites] are stubborn, like a stubborn heifer'.[61] In another sermon Medgyesi compared Transylvania under György II Rákóczi to Judah under Josiah, who reigned just before the Babylonian invasion, and warned, 'Oh, Magyar Judah! Will you not learn from the example of old Judah, in whose path you are walking, and believe that your payment will be the same'.[62]

In September 1657 Medgyesi again hammered away at this message of the sins of 'Magyar Judah' as the root cause of military defeat and invasion. Medgyesi intoned in his *Fifth Woe and Lament of the Hungarians* that 'glory has left our Israel', so 'woe, woe, unto us for we have sinned!'.[63] Medgyesi became fearful that the recent deaths of godly individuals would soon now be followed by the universal death of the apocalypse.

Verily, verily if we do not repent, it is to be feared, yes to be feared, that with the passing of that thousand years, and because furious pagans are upon us, that the period of final judgement should not be drawn onto our heads. There are three great woes in the apocalypse, the next more troublesome than the last: then the final stage of the seventh trumpet. Oh, thus will our woes begin to flow over us!

---

[60] K. Benda (ed.), *Magyarországi történeti kronológiája*, 2, 474–86; *Erdély története*, ii, 716–26; Á. R. Várkonyi, 'Országegyesítő kísérletek (1648–64)' in *Magyarország története*, iii pt 1, 1,043–91.

[61] Pál Medgyesi, *Igaz magyar nép negyedik jajja s-siralma* (Sárospatak, 1657), 17–18, 20–1.

[62] Pál Medgyesi, *Istenhez való igaz magtérés* (Sárospatak, 1658), 35–6.

[63] Pál Medgyesi, *Ötödik jaj és siralom* (Sárospatak, 1657), in G. Szigethy (ed.), *Erdély romlásának okairól* (Budapest, 1984), 21: 'elment, elköltözött a dicsőség a mi Izraelünkből, megszünék és nagy hirtelen elvágódék a mi szívünknek s állapotunknak koronája. Jaj, jaj! (méltán felvehetjük e szókat, sirathatjuk vele magunkat) jaj, jaj nekünk, mert vétkeztünk!'

Medgyesi preached in his *Sixth Woe of the Hungarians* of 'fatal periods' in history every 350, 500, 700, and 1,000 years. Medgyesi claimed that 1,000 years had elapsed since Hungarians had first settled in Pannonia and Dacia, and concluded that the fate of Judah and Israel was paralleled in their own current position. Medgyesi offered his audience meagre comfort, merely repeating the message which Jeremiah had given to Israel of the need to turn back to God for deliverance.[64]

Comenius also reacted with despair to the news of Rákóczi's disastrous retreat from Poland: 'Alas! We hoped for alleviation from the never-failing tyranny of the Antichrist, and behold we have fallen deep into a trap'.[65] Comenius wrote to the Transylvanian prince of attempts to secure assistance from England and Switzerland, and to achieve peace between the Danes and Swedes. Protestant activists continued to try to assist Rákóczi, and some hope remained into 1658 that the situation could still be saved from total defeat. In February 1658 peace was reached at Roeskilde between Sweden and Denmark, and Constantin Schaum was sent back to Sweden, attempting to persuade Charles to take up arms again in Poland. However, an offensive treaty was concluded at Berlin against Sweden by Jan Casimir, Leopold, and Frederick William of Brandenburg, who had been won over by the concession of sovereignty over Ducal Prussia. In March 1658 Schaum passed messages from Comenius to Rákóczi detailing contacts which Hartlib had made with Cromwell, and on Cromwell's efforts to assist Rákóczi through the Porte, and the extent of Rákóczi's desperation can be gauged by an approach which he made to Leopold for help in Transylvania's hour of greatest need.[66]

The years between 1658 and 1660 were chaotic in the principality. A bitter battle was waged by Rákóczi to retain control of Transylvania against domestic rivals and against Turkish armies. That Rákóczi was re-elected prince in place of Rhédei in January 1658, and continued to receive so much backing at home through three years of conflict, was almost as remarkable as the support for his original decision to invade Poland. With the army still in Crimea, and only some Hajduck forces left to defend the principality,

---

[64] Pál Medgyesi, *Magyarok hatodik jajja* (Sárospatak, 1660), Foreword, with sermons *Kétség torkából kihatló lélek, Bünön buskodó lélek kénszergése, Joseph romlasa avagy magyar nemzet 1658 esztendőbéli nagy pusztulása, Felgerjedt s pokol fenekeig hatalmazott rohogo tüz, Rabszabadító isteni szent mesterség, Külön ülő keresztyén,* and *Serva domine.* M. Tarnóc, 'Szalárdi János történetszemlélete', *ITK* 74 (1970), 689–96.

[65] [Comenius], *Korrespondence*, ed. Kvacsala, 224: 'Levamen sperabamus a juga antiChristianae tyrannidis et ecce profundius in laqueos incidimus! eheu!'

[66] Hartl. 7/100, f. 1*a*; 9/17, ff. 28*b*, 31*a*; 54/14; 52, ff. 14*a*, 29*a*; J. V. Kvacsala, 'II. Rákóczy György fejedelemsége történetéhez', *TT* (1893), 673–7; *Erdély és az északkeleti háború,* ed. Szilágyi, ii, 498, 506.

grand vizier Köprülu headed an invasion army in May 1658 which quickly overran border fortresses, whilst the undefended Transylvanian capital was destroyed by Tartars. Ákos Barcsai, former president of Rákóczi's council, negotiated with the Turks to gain the princely title, promising higher tribute payments and the hand-over of fortresses at Lugos and Karánsebes. In October 1658 the diet accepted Barcsai as prince, and the Ottoman army then left the principality. Rákóczi launched an immediate offensive against Barcsai and his supporters, and, once János Kemény returned from the Crimea, a three-way struggle broke out for power. None of the combatants attended to the provision of the annual tribute demanded by the Sultan's representatives. When Rákóczi was recalled as prince by the diet in September 1659, he therefore faced the prospect of a second invasion force sent from Constantinople in 1660 to secure the agreed tribute payments.[67]

Peace treaties between the other major powers of the Second Northern War in May 1660 came too late to save Rákóczi. The treaty of Copenhagen confirmed the terms agreed at Roeskilde between Denmark and Sweden, and a settlement was reached at Oliva between Sweden, Poland, and Brandenburg. The main Ottoman army arrived in Transylvania in the summer of 1660, but Rákóczi had already been injured in a battle at Gyalu against Ahmed Sidi, the Buda pasha, and died of his wounds at Nagyvárad in June 1660. Rákóczi's death at least meant that he was spared from witnessing the final Ottoman attack on Transylvania, when a 50,000-strong army besieged and captured the crucial border fortress of Nagyvárad. The garrison at Nagyvárad was severely depleted by the time of the siege. Remaining soldiers and a few hundred citizens came under the direction of Máté Balogh, assisted by János Szalárdi and János Rácz, deputy sheriff of Bihar county. Szalárdi survived the siege to complete his *Miserable Hungarian Chronicle*, which highlighted 'worthy comparisons' between Transylvania and Israel and argued that the sins of his 'stiff-necked nation' were the root cause of God's wrath and punishment. When Szalárdi dealt with the painful subject of the loss of Nagyvárad, which had appeared a godly citadel during the 1650s, he sadly pointed out that divine judgement always had a just cause.[68] János Rácz died of wounds sustained during the siege of Nagyvárad, and György Komáromi Csipkés gave the funeral oration for Rácz at Debrecen in November 1660, later published as *A Mirror of Mournful Things*. Csipkés

---

[67] *Erdély és az északkeleti háború*, ed. Szilágyi, ii, 320–2; Á. R. Várkonyi, 'Az önálló fejedelemség utolsó évtizedei (1660–1711)', in *Erdély története*, ii, 784–805; János Bethlen, *Innocentia Transylvaniae* (Kolozsvár, 1659).

[68] *Szalárdi János krónikája*, 322, 630–3: 'Méltán hasonlíttatik, és igen méltán, e mi szegény hazánknak, Erdélyországnak és ahhoz tartozó részeknek állapota az Izrael és Judá nemzetének azon Istentől rendeltetett fejedelemségi igazgatás alattvaló boldog állapotához' (ibid. 72).

compared Rácz's death with that of Josiah, brought back wounded from the plain of Megiddo (or Armageddon) to die in Jerusalem, as Rácz had been brought back from Nagyvárad to die at Debrecen.[69] The Rákóczi family was only finally able to conduct György's funeral at Sárospatak in April 1661. Zsuzsanna Lórántffy had suffered a fatal stroke in April 1660, ending Pál Medgyesi's connections with the Rákóczi family, and so it fell to István Czeglédi to give Rákóczi's funeral oration. An audience of magnates from Hungary and Transylvania heard Czeglédi claim that their inability to adhere to moral standards of behaviour had brought divine judgement against the country. Czeglédi argued that sinfulness had destroyed 'our Israel's glory' and caused God's blessing to be withdrawn from the Transylvanian army. Czeglédi excluded Rákóczi from all responsibility for the military disaster. For Czeglédi, Rákóczi's glorious death in battle against a heathen army revealed that he had been 'Israel's illuminating candle', and Czeglédi sadly wondered 'are we looking at the closed eyes of you, who was the sweet light of our eyes?'[70]

Comenius' belief that Transylvania would spark a revival of the Protestant interest in central Europe was crushed by the failure of Rákóczi's Polish campaign. The weight of criticism from Hungarian ministers tended not to blame Rákóczi, rather concentrating on the sins of the nation. Comenius meanwhile firmly attached responsibility to the Rákóczi family, charging that Zsuzsanna Lórántffy had first held back Zsigmond and then György from taking positive action in the Protestant interest. Comenius cited as a specific example of Lórántffy's lack of commitment to religion her refusal to pay for the translation of the Bible into Turkish. Comenius recalled that one of Drabík's prophecies had promised that if Lórántffy supplied funds for such a translation, the Turks would co-operate with Protestant powers against the Catholic church. Comenius concluded his judgement on the Rákóczi family in damning terms:

the Crown of Hungary was promis'd to them, it is true; but the condition often iterated, that they would purge this land from idolatry; deliberating and consulting upon this matter, with the Eastern and the Northern: but what did it profit to be admonish'd? When neither they, nor the King of Swede, would do any of those things; they drew themselves by their disobedience headlong into destruction.[71]

---

[69] György Komáromi Csipkés, *Szomoru esetek tüköre. Gyászbeszéd Rácz János fölött* (Sárospatak, 1661).

[70] 'Tégedet, tégedet szemünk szép világa szem bé-hunyva nézzünké?': István Czeglédi, *Ama ritka példájú . . . II. Rákóczi György . . . testének földben tétele felett predikáció* (Kassa, 1661), b3; Czeglédi, *Az országok romlásáról irott könyv; Szalárdi János krónikája*, 648–9.

[71] J. A. Comenius, *A Generall Table of Europe Representing the Present and Future state thereof* (Amsterdam, 1669), 202; *Didactica Magna*, ed. Keatinge, 84.

Comenius believed that György II Rákóczi had acted out of personal ambition to gain the Polish crown rather than to advance the interests of his faith. Comenius even gave some credence to a story that Rákóczi had followed the false prophecy of a dying soldier and not listened to Drabík's instructions. The soldier had urged the prince to attack the Ottomans directly, promising that God would raise an army up from Russia to save him. Comenius concluded that 'it may be well thought, that this was a satanical mockery ... seeing nothing fell out accordingly, but rather the ruin of the prince, who was seduced, like Ahab by Zedekiah and his companions. God giving them up to believe a lie, who will not believe the truth.'[72]

Ákos Barcsai resigned as prince in December 1660 to be replaced by János Kemény in January 1661. Kemény was backed by imperial troops under Raimondo Montecuccoli, and the Transylvanian diet declared that the principality had broken with the Sultan and placed itself under the protection of Emperor Leopold. Mehmed Köprülü launched a new attack on the south and east of Transylvania, and by September 1661 the diet was forced, in the presence of the Buda pasha, to elect Mihály Apafi as prince. Montecuccoli withdrew from Transylvania, abandoning Kemény to struggle on alone until he was killed in 1662. Transylvania was then left to recover from the devastation of these years of conflict, whilst trying to pay annual tribute to the Porte which had increased from 15,000 to 40,000 florins. After his unsuccessful intervention in Transylvania, Leopold was anxious to limit any further confrontation with the Ottomans, but a Turkish army began an offensive against Royal Hungary in the spring of 1664. The peace of Vasvár swiftly ended this conflict in August 1664, a shock to Hungarian opinion since it followed so quickly after a promising victory over the Turks at Szentgotthárd. In the Vasvár treaty the Emperor and the Sultan declared their peaceful intentions towards one another and agreed a twenty years' truce which dashed Hungarian hopes of a new anti-Turkish alliance. Leopold also recognized Ottoman suzerainty over Transylvania, with Apafi as prince, and acknowledged the loss of Nagyvárad. From being an active agent in European diplomacy, the 1664 treaty condemned the Transylvanian principality to become a passive object in the late seventeenth-century battle for supremacy in the northern Balkans between the Habsburgs and Ottomans.[73]

[72] Comenius, *A Generall Table of Europe*, 279; Jan Comenius, *History of the Bohemian Persecution* (London, 1650). Drabík was executed by the Habsburgs at Pozsony in 1671.

[73] J. P. Spielman, *Leopold I of Austria* (London, 1977), 1–60; J. Bérenger, *A History of the Habsburg Empire, 1273–1700* (London, 1990), 320.

György II Rákóczi's foreign political designs, and in particular his decision to invade Poland without seeking prior consent from the Porte, have been seen by historians ever since as very difficult to understand. Some have concluded that it demonstrated Rákóczi's immaturity and obstinacy, or his political incompetence, but others, even if mostly unwilling to consider the significance of religion in Hungarian society, have suggested that the prince was swayed by apocalyptic visionaries.[74] Dynastic interests clearly played an important role in Rákóczi's policy, and his multi-confessional council and contacts with Catholic nobles in Royal Hungary demonstrated that he was not confined to think only in confessional terms. Demands for action to free Ottoman-occupied Hungarian territory indeed proved increasingly capable of overcoming confessional differences between Hungarian nobles during the latter decades of the seventeenth century. However, the influence exerted over Rákóczi by Bisterfeld, Comenius, Reformed superintendents, court chaplains, and preachers meant that Protestant interests featured prominently in discussions during the 1650s about diplomatic affairs at Gyulafehérvár.

Thoughts of the Calvinist international and the Protestant cause, tinged with apocalyptic expectancy, seem to have at least encouraged the consideration of aggressive policies at the Transylvanian court in the decade after 1648. Transylvania's alliance with Sweden and invasion of Poland in 1657 came against a background of widespread expectations that an eschatological revolution and final judgement were at hand. Interest in prophecy about the apocalypse in Transylvania added to pressure for military action, since godly princes were supposed to lead a spiritual renewal, to bring freedom from the Turks, and defeat the Antichrist. The precedent of good and faithful princes who had gone into battle against the Emperor also weighed heavily upon the shoulders of György II Rákóczi. It may therefore have seemed a short step for Rákóczi from being a prince standing as it seemed in divine favour, in a tradition of parallels with biblical kings, and encouraged

---

74 'Pour comprendre le sort tragique de Georges II Rákóczi, il ne suffit pas de tenir compte du tempérament et de la mentalité du jeune prince. Il faut aussi prendre en considération l'atmosphère spirituelle dans laquelle il se trouvait.' Makkai, *Histoire de Transylvanie*, 238–9. See Szekfű and Hóman, *Magyar történet*, iv, 82; Evans, *The Making of the Habsburg Monarchy, 1550–1700*, 237, on Rákóczi's 'wild ambitions'; K. Péter 'The Later Ottoman Period and Royal Hungary, 1606–1711', on his 'senseless behaviour', in P. F. Sugar et al (eds.), *A History of Hungary* (London, 1990), 115, and P. F. Sugar, 'The Principality of Transylvania', on the role of 'religious convictions' and his 'boundless personal ambition', ibid. 135. Bérenger, *A History of the Habsburg Empire*, 320, describes Rákóczi's 'passion and personal ambition', whilst T. M. Barker, *Double Eagle and Crescent. Vienna's second Turkish siege and Its Historical Setting* (Albany, New York, 1967), 22, has Rákóczi 'imagining himself a crusader for Protestantism at a time when such sentiments were already passé'.

by Reformed leaders to play the role of leading a chosen people, to combine dynastic and religious interests in 1657 and accept a messianic part in an apocalyptic struggle to be directed first against Catholic Poland.

International Calvinist contacts had greatly assisted the efforts of Transylvania's princes to become engaged in alliances with western powers, but in 1657 this relationship proved to be a destabilizing force for the principality. György II Rákóczi was in the end encouraged to aspire to grander European designs than the principality's limited resources could support, and the Transylvanian state and Reformed religion in central Europe emerged greatly weakened by the Polish crisis of the late 1650s. Reformed writers easily found explanations for the disastrous results of Rákóczi's venture into Poland. The moral imperatives provided by apocalyptic reasoning, which had done much to inspire religious reformation in Hungary during the mid-sixteenth century, continued to hold sway within the Reformed church. Belief in an all-powerful and transcendent deity had initially bred a confident church with universalist ambitions, but Reformed clergy also remained apprehensive of judgement if their efforts fully to reform the church and society began to falter. An undercurrent of criticism during the 1650s had identified failures truly to reform public morality and wipe out idolatry as likely causes of divine displeasure, and the worst fears of such pessimists seemed to be justified in the years of devastating conflict which followed in the wake of György II Rákóczi's campaign in Poland.

Conclusions

The Calvinist reformation was not a western European event, nor was the community it produced overwhelmingly a western European one. The Reformed congregations of Hungary and Transylvania formed by far the largest Calvinist church in central Europe, and constituted a fundamental component of the international Calvinist world. The late reformation in central and eastern Europe has too often been presented as a process which merely mediated and modified 'western' patterns of religious and cultural change. The Hungarian church certainly did not provide any home-grown theologians of great distinction, but the direction of reform was not ultimately determined by western influences. Whilst maintaining broad and deep contacts with western co-religionists, the Hungarian Reformed church adhered to home-grown confessional statements, maintained a hierarchical church structure, and became closely allied with a series of sovereign princes in Transylvania. The church also remained distinctive within the international Calvinist community, not least because of its close proximity to the Ottoman world and immediate contact with a large anti-Trinitarian church.[1]

During the early seventeenth century the political support of Transylvanian princes from István Bocskai to György II Rákóczi brought the Hungarian Reformed church a golden age of stability unparalleled in east-central Europe, or indeed in much of the Empire. From the relative security of the Transylvanian principality the Hungarian Calvinist church was able to develop under princely protection and noble patronage. Domestic education flourished with ambitious plans for local colleges, whilst student ministers were in addition financed to travel to academies and universities in Germany, the Dutch Republic, and England. These student ministers returned home to form an emerging professional clergy élite, many of

---

[1] K. Maag (ed.), *The Reformation in Eastern and Central Europe* (Aldershot, 1997). There are many difficulties of terminology in attempting to describe a zone between east and west, since usage of 'central Europe' generally has suggested affinity with the 'west'. See T. G. Ash, *The Uses of Adversity. Essays on the Fate of Central Europe* (London, 1983); Milan Kundera, 'The Tragedy of Central Europe', *The New York Review of Books*, 31/7 (Apr. 1984), 33–8; G. Schöpflin and N. Wood (eds.), *In Search of Central Europe* (Oxford, 1989); N. Davies, *Europe: A History* (Oxford, 1996), 1–46. For Transylvania as a meeting-point of west and east, see Károly Kós, *Erdély* (Kolozsvár, 1934), 7; L. Wolff, *Inventing Eastern Europe. The Map of Civilization on the Mind of the Enlightenment* (Stanford, Calif., 1994), 1–16.

whom proved anxious to apply lessons learned abroad and lead the church towards some sort of second wave of reformation. Whilst Reformed clergy remained conscious of Hungarian political and social conditions, princes, nobles, and ordinary parishioners were increasingly expected not only to show personal commitment to strictly ordered doctrine and worship, but also to meet demanding standards of individual piety and morality.

Some Hungarian ministers' enthusiasm to adopt the best practices of foreign Calvinist churches led to strident clashes about the need for further reform, which were sharpest over ecclesiological issues, particularly over lay participation in the administration of congregations. Such debates focused on a perceived puritan infection of some clergy, who advocated reforms to traditional ceremonies and to the established pattern of church government. Transylvania's ruling princes feared that any plans to replace the existing clergy hierarchy with presbyteries might well also undermine princely authority, as presbyterians seemed to have done elsewhere. It fell to senior clergy during the 1640s—often, but not always, from an older generation than the reformers and to whom the reality of English religion was largely unknown—to caution younger enthusiasts about the dangers of foreign radicalism and warn of the need to continue to work in partnership with Transylvania's princes and Hungarian nobility. Despite causing such divisions, the engagement of student ministers with foreign Calvinist universities and churches on the whole bolstered the spread of Reformed religion in Hungary and Transylvania. The Hungarian church benefited from improved standards of clergy education, from an influx of western theological literature, and from the influence over local colleges of leading foreign Calvinists resident in the region.

Transylvania's political élite, as well as its Reformed clergy, came into ever-closer contact with foreign Calvinists during this period. Some nobles were sent abroad to foreign universities, and Johann Heinrich Alsted, Johann Heinrich Bisterfeld, and Jan Amos Comenius were prominent as advisers and envoys to the princes and their families. Transylvania's growing attachment to Reformed religion was accompanied by greater diplomatic co-operation with other Protestant powers during the Thirty Years War. Calvinist ideas about the eschatological meaning of contemporary warfare and diplomacy made some impact on decision-making at the Gyulafehérvár court. The heightened expectancy during the 1650s of many within the Reformed church that providence had placed them on the verge of an age of renewal was only finally crushed by the military defeats suffered by György II Rákóczi in 1657. Reformed preachers laid the blame for these disasters not on any faults of their godly princes but, rather, on the wider failure of the church to complete a true reformation of Hungarian life. Some at home and abroad were less charitable, and Paul Rycaut, secretary to the English ambassador at the Porte, offered a damning verdict on Rákóczi after his death.

> This was the end of that vain leerus [sic], who attempted to fly with feigned wings and borrowed feathers; this is the fate of ambitious spirits, whom pride elevates and exhales like a vapour, unto that height, until it dissolves them into showers, or precipitates them into the abyss of all confusions.[2]

The Hungarian Reformed church emerged gravely weakened from the aftermath of György II Rákóczi's Polish adventure. The waning political power of Transylvania's princes severely limited the Reformed church's ability to challenge the increasing dominance of the Catholic church in Royal Hungary during the second half of the seventeenth century. In 1661 John Dury wrote to Samuel Hartlib of the fate to which the Hungarians were now abandoned.

> The Protestants in Hungarie and Transylvania will bee a prey on the one side to the Turck on the other to the Jesuits, and that of the Turck will be the less burdensome by how much the conscience is left free without constraint which the Jesuits put in practice. The Lord in his owne time will send relief and breake the power of all that will establish religion by violence.[3]

The Reformed church crucially soon lost the patronage of the Rákóczi family, when György II Rákóczi's widow, Zsófia Báthori, reconverted to Catholicism. Báthori invited Jesuits into Sárospatak in 1663, and imperial troops then occupied the town's church and college. In 1672 the commander of the garrison handed Sárospatak's church over to the Jesuits. Reformed residents of the town were left to attend services in the neighbouring village of Hotyka until they managed to find a new building for worship in Sárospatak.[4] Bálint Kocsi Csergő, an exiled teacher from Pápa living in Zurich, completed a history of the Reformed church in 1677 which recounted the persecution suffered by Reformed communities across western Hungarian counties during the 1660s and 1670s. Kocsi related how Protestants were constantly harassed, threatened with punishment if they failed to attend mass, and how Reformed churches at

---

[2] Paul Rycaut, *The History of the Turkish Empire from the Year 1623 to the Year 1677* (London, 1680), 69–82.
[3] Hartl. 4/4, letter from John Dury, Dec. 1661.
[4] K. Péter, 'A jezsuiták működésének első szakasza Sárospatakon', in *Papok és nemesek*, 186–99.

Körmend and Komárom were destroyed altogether by Catholic nobles in the 1660s. Kocsi blamed Pál Eszterházy for the armed occupation of the Reformed church at Pápa in 1660, for the arrest of members of the presbytery, and for throwing one pious widow out of the town to be dumped in a nearby marsh. Kocsi wrote that when Eszterházy grew bored of his atrocities against the Pápa Reformed community, the town was handed over to an Austrian army captain who then organized further arrests and threw the minister's family out of the manse.[5]

From being active partners in the international Calvinist community, Protestants in Royal Hungary were reduced to little more than supplicants to foreign Protestants for external intervention against the worse excesses of Catholic oppression during the latter decades of the seventeenth century. The Habsburg court used the failed Wesselényi conspiracy as a pretext for the centralization of government and violent persecution of Protestants after 1670. In fact, of the aristocratic malcontents who had gathered around the palatine Ferenc Wesselényi, Péter Zrínyi and Ferenc Nádasdy were Catholic, although Wesselényi was also supported by some Protestant gentry led by István Vitnyédy. Noble plotting was largely directed against the passivity of court policy towards the Ottomans during the 1660s, but Leopold feared that it amounted to a threat to his rule and had the leading conspirators executed. Charges of *lèse-majesté* were then brought against over seven hundred Protestant ministers and teachers at a special court assembled at Pozsony by archbishop Szelepcsényi in January 1674. Found guilty of preaching against Mary and the saints, and of being in alliance with the Ottomans, the ministers were sentenced to death. Many converted, renounced their offices, or went into exile in the ensuing months, but over forty ministers who had refused to recant were sent on a forced march through Italy in 1675. Thirty survivors were then sold to the Spanish fleet as galley-slaves. This incident caused an international scandal, and western Protestant powers led by Sweden and the Dutch Republic tried to gain the ministers' release. Eventually a Dutch fleet under Admiral Michael de Ruyter intervened in February 1676 off Naples to release twenty-three Hungarian Protestant ministers from their slavery. Some of the ministers were former students at Dutch universities and could thank their liberators in their own language.[6]

---

5 Bálint Kocsi Csergő, 'Brevis delineatio ecclesiarum reformatarum in Hungaria et Transylvania' [1677], in *Az első rendszeres magyar református egyháztörténet*, ed. D. Miklós (Budapest, 1994). See also his 'Kősziklán épült ház ostroma' [1676], in *A magyarországi gályarab prédikátorok emlékezete. Galleria omnium sanctorum*, ed. L. Makkai (Budapest, 1976), 31–109.

6 *A Short Memorial of the Most Grievous Sufferings of the Ministers of the Protestant Churches in Hungary by the Instigation of the Popish Clergy there*, tr. from Dutch (London, 1676);

This repression of Protestants in Royal Hungary heightened the sense of the Reformed community in the Transylvanian principality of being an embattled Israel. Catholic obstruction denied Calvinists access to the same extent and range of international contacts of earlier decades. The numbers of Hungarian student ministers who arrived at western universities fell sharply after 1660. The number of Hungarian students at Franeker halved between the 1650s and 1660s, and had halved again by the 1670s. Taking Leiden, Utrecht, and Franeker Universities together, the total of Hungarian students fell from 259 in the 1650s to only 107 in the 1660s. However, even links with distant England were not completely severed, and when Edmund Chishull travelled through Transylvania on his way back to England from Constantinople in 1702 he still found that the teacher at Gyulafehérvár School, Sámuel Kaposi, had many English books in his library and taught his students English once a week. At Nagyenyed College, Chishull discovered another teacher, István Kolozsvári, who had also studied in England, whilst at Debrecen College he met with a local minister, Pál Gyöngyösi, who had studied at Oxford.7

In the face of persecution encroaching from the west, Reformed ministers in Transylvania and the Partium renewed their dedication to reforming the public morality and private behaviour of their congregations. Ministers remained watchful against traditional vices which could bring divine punishment upon their communities. Pál Szenci warned in *The Drunkards' Cup of Laments* of how the devil puts people on the road to drunkenness. István Szentpéteri, meanwhile, declared in his *Devil's Harpoon* that his spirit was in bitter pain against the continuing common swearing of the 'hell-tongued Hungarian world'. Miklós Tótfalusi Kis blamed a major fire in Kolozsvár in the 1690s on persistent theft, fornication, and the wearing of luxurious clothing in the town.8 Ministers also found new

L. Makkai (ed.), *Studia et Acta Ecclesiastica, n.s. 1. In Memoriam Eliberationis Verbi Divini Ministrorum Hungaricorum ad Triremes Condemnatorum 1676* (Budapest, 1976); M. Dezső, 'L'histoire des galériens Hongrois', *Bulletin de la Société de l'histoire du Protestantisme Français*, 122 (1976), 54–65.

7 [Leiden], 'Die Studierenden aus Ungarn und Siebenbürgen an der Universität Leiden 1575–1875', ed. F. Teutsch, *Archiv des Vereins für Siebenbürgische Landeskunde*, 16 (1881), 204–26; 'Az utrechti és leideni egyetemeken járt magyar ifjak névjegyzéke', ed. Antal, 278–9, 409–12, 437–41; 'Verzeichnis der Studenten aus Ungarn und Siebenbürgen an der Universität Utrecht in den Jahren 1643–1885', *Archiv des Vereins für Siebenbürgische Landeskunde*, 22 (1889), 79–92; L. Segesváry, *Magyar református ifjak az utrechti egyetemen 1636–1686* (Debrecen, 1935); 'A franekeri egyetemén tanúlt magyarok', ed. Á. Hellebrant, *TT* (1886), 599–608, 792–800; Edmund Chishull, *Travels in Turkey and back to England* (London, 1747), 94–111.

8 Miklós Tótfalusi Kis, *Siralmas panasz Istennek Kolozsváron fekvő nagy haragjáról* (Kolozsvár, 1697); István Szentpéteri, *Ördög szigonnya, avagy ama' káromkodásnak lelkétől*

targets for their attacks, including the growing habit of smoking. The eastern Tisza synod met at Avasújváros in 1686 to forbid ministers and teachers from smoking, a habit with which the synod claimed they were idly filling their time. Some Hungarian towns and counties banned smoking for fear of causing fire, whilst elsewhere the 'drink for heathens' was outlawed on moral grounds. Legislation against smoking was also passed in the Transylvanian diet after Mihály Apafi became ill from smoking 'strong Turkish tobacco' in 1663. Apafi moved the diet to ban the import or use of tobacco, and diets in 1670, 1683, 1686, 1688, and 1689 tried to combat the growing fashion for smoking. The diet recorded that threats of heavy fines and bans on the local production of tobacco made a negligible impact. Eventually the battle against smoking was given up as a lost cause, and the diet instead offered monopolies to Greek merchants on the external trade in tobacco.[9]

There was also a notable series of attacks by Reformed clergy against dancing from the 1670s. Anonymous verses written in the western Danubian province described dancing as a foul, devilish obscenity. The English traveller Edward Brown certainly remarked upon extraordinary Hajduck dances which he had witnessed, 'with naked swords in their hands, advancing, brandishing, and clashing the same; turning, winding, elevating, and depressing their bodies with strong and active motions'.[10] In the eastern Tisza province Mihály Gyulai argued that the *Reward of Infectious and Promiscuous Dancing* would be divine displeasure and punishment of the Reformed community. Gyulai attacked dancing for the many sins which he argued accompanied it, including swearing and lecherous glances between the dancers, and concluded that dancing was 'the work of the devil'. Gyulai encouraged ministers to excommunicate offenders and argued that when violins were discovered they should be cut up immediately for firewood. István Szentpéteri added his voice to the denunciation of dancing and music-making in 1697, explaining that the constant dangers of *The Plague of Dancing* raised such evil desires that husbands and wives could not safely join in dances, and that even watching dances brought indecency into people's hearts.[11]

---

eredett ... való bányattyában 's búsúlásában (Debrecen, 1699); Pál Szenci, *Reszegesek jajos pohara* (Debrecen, 1681).

9 Zoványi, *A tiszántúli református egyházkerület története*, 40; Takáts, *Művelődéstörténeti tanulmányok a xvi–xvii századból*, ed. Benda, 256–67.

10 Brown, *A Brief Account of Some Travels in Hungaria*, 17–18.

11 Mihály Gyulai, *Fertelmeskedő, s' bujálkodó tancz jutalma* (Debrecen, 1681); 'Görcsös bot', in K. Révész, 'Egy régi vers a táncz ellen', *ITK* 3 (1893), 449–56; István Szentpéteri, *Tancz Pestise* (Debrecen, 1697); Péter Apor, *Metamorphosis Transylvaniae; azaz, Erdélynek*

Whilst Reformed ministers remained vigilant to uphold high standards of discipline and morality within their communities throughout the latter decades of the seventeenth century, external violent repression of the Reformed church in Royal Hungary was curtailed to some degree from the early 1680s. A combination of native resistance through *kuruc* raiding parties loosely led by Imre Thököly, and the international diplomatic situation after the French seizure of the imperial city of Strasburg, convinced Leopold of the need to establish terms with the Hungarian estates. Leopold recalled the diet at Sopron and, in return for receiving a general levy, appointed a palatine and affirmed the terms on religious freedom laid down by the 1606 Vienna treaty. However, rights of Catholic noble patronage continued to circumscribe Protestant freedoms severely, and the diet specified only two sites for Protestant worship in each of the western counties in Royal Hungary. Confiscated Lutheran and Reformed churches were ordered by the diet to be returned, but this decision was rendered virtually meaningless because no churches already sanctified for Catholic use were to be handed over to Protestants. Thököly's *kuruc* forces renewed their revolt in Upper Hungary in 1682, initially supported by many Catholic nobles and by Mihály Apafi from Transylvania. Most nobles, however, soon reverted to support the Habsburgs when a Turkish army marched on Vienna in 1683. The subsequent demise of Ottoman power in the northern Balkans after the failure of their siege of Vienna further augmented Catholic strength in the region. Liberated southern Hungarian counties were largely repopulated by the Habsburgs with Catholic communities, although some Orthodox Slav refugees were also allowed to settle on reconquered lands.

The changing balance of military power between the Habsburgs and Ottomans fundamentally affected the position of the Transylvanian principality. In 1686 the Transylvanian diet turned to Leopold for protection, and by the terms of the 1688 treaty of Hermannstadt the Transylvanians accepted imperial troops within the principality. In 1691 the Transylvanian diet agreed to the *Diploma Leopoldinum*, which brought the principality under Habsburg sovereignty while retaining a separate chancellor and treasury. The privileges of the four received religions in Transylvania were also confirmed by this agreement. After the Habsburg triumph at the battle of Zenta in 1697, Leopold was finally able to confirm Transylvania's place within his monarchy through the 1699 Karlowitz treaty, by which the Sultan relinquished all previous claims over the principality. Whilst in law

régi együgyű alázatos idejében való gazdaságából e mostani kevély, cifra, felfordult állapotjában koldusságra való változása, ed. Gy. Tóth (Budapest, 1972).

the position of Protestants in Transylvania seemed secure under Habsburg rule, Edmund Chishull wrote that:

the whole reformed people of Transylvania, especially the Calvinists, begin to be under great apprehensions, and from the governor to the meanest gentleman, earnestly embraced this occasion of recommending their cause . . . after which they implored the prayers and good wishes of the church of England, and in many places took a solemn melancholy leave of us, as if they were just entering upon a martyrdom.[12]

The Catholic church nevertheless remained in a weaker position in Transylvania and the Partium than in western Hungarian counties. The new Habsburg regime in Transylvania was, however, able to establish a Greek Catholic church from within the Orthodox community and promoted Catholic bids to gain control over Protestant church buildings.

The final challenge to Habsburg domination of Hungarian politics and society was raised during the Rákóczi rebellion from 1703, when Ferenc II Rákóczi became the focus of both Catholic noble discontent directed against the court and Protestant gentry hatred of the Habsburgs. This new *kuruc* rising aimed to take advantage of the War of Spanish Succession to win Transylvanian independence and secure Hungarian noble rights and religious freedoms. The rebellion ended in 1711 with the peace agreed at Szatmár by Rákóczi's deputy, whilst Rákóczi himself went into exile. The terms of the Szatmár peace recognized the Habsburgs as rulers over Hungary by hereditary right, but acknowledged the autonomy of the Hungarian diet and county administration. The treaty also further enshrined Catholic dominance of Hungarian public life. No Protestant could henceforth hold a state office, and Protestants were compelled to pay tithes to support Catholic ministers. During the eighteenth century more Reformed schools and churches in Hungary were closed, synods could only meet with royal approval, Protestant books were confiscated, and restrictions were placed on the conduct of Protestant marriages. In the 1760s the authorities even demanded the removal from the Heidelberg Catechism of certain questions which were deemed offensive to the Catholic church and prevented the full publication of the catechism. This systematic discrimination against Protestants continued even after 1781, when a patent of toleration was finally promulgated by Joseph II.[13]

---

[12] Chishull, *Travels in Turkey*, 94–111.

[13] Révész (ed.), *A magyar református egyház története*, 107–19; Pokoly, *Erdély református egyház története*, iii, 111–12, 127; *Erdély története*, ii, 881–9; Spielman, *Leopold I of Austria*.

The proportion of Protestants within Hungarian society reached its peak during the latter decades of the sixteenth century, and the early seventeenth century proved to be the high point of Calvinist influence within Hungarian and Transylvanian society. At the end of the sixteenth century about half of those living in Hungary and Transylvania were Calvinists, but by the beginning of the nineteenth century slightly over half the population were Catholic, with only around one in six still belonging to the Reformed church.[14] The enduring influence of the Reformed church on Hungarian political and cultural identity nevertheless remained profound. This influence can be traced back to István Bocskai's revolt in 1604, when Hungarian nobles and Hajduck commoners rallied to the standard of rebellion to protect Protestant religious liberties and defend the national community. While tensions between nobles and Hajducks remained strong, both were at least temporarily united under the flag of national resistance after September 1604. Bocskai rewarded his Hajduck supporters by collective ennoblement and grants of land as a new warrior estate. This suggests that Hajduck support for Bocskai's appeal to national sentiment was both grounded in confessional solidarity and also to some degree motivated by hopes for liberation from servitude and inclusion in the political nation of the privileged élite. Protestant ministers, vocal in calls to defend 'our dear nation' in sermons and poems during Bocskai's revolt, also later received collective ennoblement from Gábor Bethlen in 1629.[15]

Bocskai's revolt against Habsburg claims of sovereignty and efforts to impose a counter-reformation united most of the noble *natio hungarica* with other Hungarian-speakers who were Calvinists, and also with other non-Magyar Protestants. This coalition challenged the Habsburgs and their mostly Catholic supporters over competing claims to the political legacy of the medieval Hungarian kingdom. Memory of Bocskai's rising and triumph offered a sense of mission to the Calvinist-dominated Transylvanian principality during the early seventeenth century. A coalition of Reformed princes, nobles, and clergy supplied the state with a Protestant and anti-Habsburg identity. Transylvanian princes were idealized as new biblical kings, and ordinary supporters of true religion were depicted as a new Israel. The bonds between the Reformed church and the Hungarian political nation during the early seventeenth century were represented through frequent parallels drawn between the history, language, and

---

[14] Benda, 'La réforme en Hongrie', 30–53.
[15] Makkai, 'István Bocskai's Insurrectionary Army', 275–97, quotation at 284; Daniel, 'The Fifteen Years War and the Protestant Response to Habsburg Absolutism in Hungary', 38–51.

destiny of Hungary and biblical Israel. This conjunction of ethnic and religious identity among Calvinists in Hungary and Transylvania buttressed a sense of distinctiveness, which might be described as some sort of patriotic sentiment, if a patriotism perhaps on the whole restricted to the social élite.

According to István Werbőczi's 1514 codification of customary Hungarian law and noble privileges, the 'gens Hungarica' or 'natio Pannonica' was 'una eademque nobilitas'. Nobles alone were 'members' of the holy crown of St Stephen, the symbol of the kingdom, and it was the noble estates who crowned Hungary's kings. However, this depiction of a self-contained and discrete social élite who formed the Hungarian nation was to a large extent a gentry fiction. While the early modern Hungarian *natio* was mostly identified with the nobility, it also could, as during Bocskai's revolt or under the motif of tribal Israel, prove capable of wider extension and popularization. Although many in Hungarian society were multi-lingual, this broader sense of patriotism was also partly founded upon a linguistic community. Hungarian was so clearly different from other local languages that it was commonly believed to be linked with ancient Hebrew. Popular cultural identification with the Hungarian language also extended to embrace an awareness of ethnic difference, among those who knew, or were told, that they had once migrated as a people from another continent. There was certainly also a strong awareness of the memory of the historic Hungarian kingdom, with pain at its loss to Ottoman advances and anger at subsequent Habsburg failures to regain it which focused around the Transylvanian court. No clear notion of a separate Transylvanian nation emerged at the Gyulafehérvár court, although this is not to deny Transylvania's undoubted distinct political status within the medieval Hungarian kingdom, nor to neglect its important links with the Romanian principalities. The Transylvanian principality rather represented, for those dissatisfied with life under the Habsburgs, 'the conscience of Hungary as a whole'.[16]

What then of the place of religion within Hungarian identity during this period? Hungarian enthusiasm to become involved in the international Calvinist community did not preclude the view of Reformed religion as a distinguishing badge in east-central Europe. The Hungarian Reformed community's sense of exclusivity was certainly augmented as other Protestants in the region fell victim to Habsburg confessional absolutism. Hungarian Calvinists' development of a vernacular culture also helped to reinforce some perception of a wider national community, at least among

---

[16] Evans, *The Making of the Habsburg Monarchy*, 267; S. Pascu (ed.), *The Dangerous Game of Falsifying History* (Bucharest, 1987); K. Péter, 'A haza és a nemzet az ország három részre hullott állapota idején', in *Papok és nemesek*, 211–32.

the literate. Nevertheless, it would be certainly wrong to overstate any degree of 'semi-conscious deepening of communal values through confessional solidarity', given that ethnicity had at no stage been the single determining factor in deciding religious allegiance in Hungary or Transylvania.[17]

During the post-reformation period Hungarian cultural and linguistic cohesion, strengthened by confessional solidarity among Calvinists, was expressed in a patriotism of more substance than mere anti-German prejudice. This Hungarian identity, based around Transylvania's princes and Calvinism, withered after 1660 in the face of Habsburg power and the counter-reformation. This might suggest that this early modern Protestant Hungarian patriotism should have few, if any, modern resonances. After all, it was not only Transylvanian political weakness that lost the Calvinist church the support of so many Hungarian nobles. Whilst sixteenth-century Protestants had successfully explained the need for religious reform in order to repel the Ottoman advance, seventeenth-century Protestant polemicists had few answers as to why religious reform had not been followed by a reversal of Hungarian fortunes. The attractions of royal service and counter-reformation culture simply proved too strong for most nobles to resist, and the handful of families who dominated the administration of Royal Hungary were already lost to Catholicism long before 1660.

During the late seventeenth century Catholic and Protestant nobles on occasions joined forces against Habsburg failures to repel the Ottomans, for example in the horrified response of Hungarian opinion to the Vasvár peace in 1664. Such 'country' party resentment against the Habsburgs endured among some nobles and gentry into the eighteenth century. Traditions of resistance were sustained by Imre Thököly's defiance of Leopold, and from 1703 by Thököly's stepson, Ferenc II Rákóczi. These *kuruc* risings emerged from Ottoman Hungary and eastern Hungarian counties where Calvinists, who retained an especially strong sense of grievance against their Habsburg rulers, had never been wholly subdued. Protestants were generally heavily implicated in these anti-Habsburg revolts, so that when Louis XIV considered ridding himself of Huguenot Camisard rebels from the Cévennes, a plan was promoted in 1704 to transport them via the Adriatic to fight in Rákóczi's rebellion. Thököly indeed was a Protestant, and one of Ferenc II Rákóczi's lieutenants had even studied Mikuláš

---

[17] Evans, 'Calvinism in East-Central Europe', 192–3; G. Murdock, 'International Calvinism, Ethnic Allegiance, and the Reformed church of Transylvania in the Early Seventeenth Century', in M. Crăciun and O. Ghitta (eds.), *Ethnicity and Religion in Central and Eastern Europe* (Cluj, 1995), 92–100.

Drabík's prophetic utterances. However, Rákóczi was educated by Jesuits
in Bohemia, and in any case Catholic noble discontent with court officials
and administrators was absolutely critical to all the conspiracies and rebel-
lions of this period against Habsburg rule.[18]

Whatever the reality around the turn of the eighteenth century, by the
nineteenth century an impression had widely formed of Hungarian Calvinism as the religion of anti-Habsburg rebellion. The Reformed church's
increased isolation from western Protestants from the latter decades of the
seventeenth century had encouraged the earlier perception of cultural cohesion among Calvinists in Hungary to tighten into a common identification of Calvinism as the 'Magyar religion'. This sense of Magyar
exclusivity did little justice to previous generations' strong commitment to
the international Calvinist community. However, combined with Calvinism's heritage of anti-Habsburg sentiment, this notion of a 'Magyar religion' had clear potential in the hands of nineteenth-century nationalist
nobles and intellectuals. Although by the mid-nineteenth century only
three-tenths of the country's Magyars were Calvinists, their significance in
Hungary's political and cultural life in fact still far outweighed their numbers. Such popular perceptions were only strengthened by the declaration
of the Habsburgs' dethronement and Hungarian independence from a
Calvinist church at Debrecen in April 1849.

The construction of a modern Hungarian national community occurred
within the specific context of nineteenth-century politics, with a native
noble élite sponsoring a national project based upon ethnic, linguistic, and
in part upon religious affinity. This enterprise aimed to overcome class divisions within Hungarian society, much as Bocskai had tried to overcome
feudal divisions, with a political language of national community.[19] The

---

[18] P. Serisier, 'Le projet de transférer des Camisards en Hongrie: Échec en 1704 d'un dessein royal', *Bulletin de la Société de l'histoire du Protestantisme Français*, 138 (1992), 119–34;
Evans, *The Making of the Habsburg Monarchy*, 263–6, 399. Cf. T. Barnard, 'Scotland and Ireland in the Later Stewart Monarchy', in S. G. Ellis and S. Barber (eds.), *Conquest and Union.
Fashioning a British State, 1485–1725* (London, 1995), 221: 'Despite some halting steps towards congruence, integration and Anglicisation, a feeble trickle of cash and a noisy stream of
soldiers, Ireland still played Bohemia to England's Austria and Scotland's Hungary in the
composite monarchy of the later seventeenth century.'

[19] J. G. Hoensch, *A History of Modern Hungary, 1867–1994* (London, 1996); E. J. Hobs-
bawm, *Nations and Nationalism since 1780* (Cambridge, 1993); E. Gellner, *Nations and Nationalism* (Oxford, 1983); B. Anderson, *Imagined Communities. Reflections on the Origin and
Spread of Nationalism* (London, 1991), 81–2, 101–18. A. D. Smith, *The Ethnic Origins of Nations* (Oxford, 1986), 88: 'Given favourable military, social and cultural conditions, aristocratic
ethnie like the Hungarian nobility (or the Ottoman Turks), can perpetuate their ethnic identities into the modern era of nationalism, even if it requires a measure of transformation . . . to
turn this identity into a modern nation.'

new meanings offered in the nineteenth century in the unfolding narrative of what the word 'magyar' represents took many of their origins from the Protestant Hungarian identity which had emerged after the reformation. Then, the invigoration of vernacular Hungarian culture and religious distinctiveness found in Calvinism increased awareness of supposed ethnic uniqueness and raised the possibility of a non-Habsburg, Hungarian identity of relevance not only to the nobility. Despite later partisan impressions of the role of the Reformed church within Hungarian society, some sort of patriotism sprang from the relationship between ethnicity, language, and Protestantism in post-reformation Hungary, a patriotism from which Hungarian nationalism was later to emerge.[20]

[20] 'The fatal gap between a theory, according to which the Protestant heritage was anathematized, and a practice, where it could not be altogether eliminated, left a potent focus for opposition: both Hungarian and Czech nationalism grow directly out of it.' Evans, *The Making of the Habsburg Monarchy*, 448. See also D. Sayer, 'The Language of Nationality and the Nationality of Language: Prague, 1780–1920', *Past and Present*, 153 (1986), 164–210.

BIBLIOGRAPHY

(I) MANUSCRIPT SOURCES

Bodleian Library, Oxford
Rawlinson MSS A26, 81; A261, 46.
Tanner MSS 48, 76; 66, 18.

Dunamellék Reformed Church Province Manuscript Collection (Ráday College, Budapest)
Körmendi Péter peregrinációs albuma 1662–1663, K-1. 461.

Dunamellék Reformed Church Province Archives (Ráday College, Budapest)
Gyöngyös református egyházközség levéltárából.

Dunántúl Reformed Church Province Archives (Pápa)
Egyházkerületi jegyzőkönyvek mutatója, no. 7.
A pápai református egyházközség levéltára Liskay-féle besorolás, no. 29.
A kiskomáromi református egyházközség legrégébbi anyakönyve 1624–1732, no. 131.

Dunántúl Reformed Church Province Library Manuscript Collection (Pápa)
Vegyes iratok, 1605–1879, o. 1092.
Veszprémi ref. egyházmegye protokolluma, o. 969, ff. 114–22.

Durham Cathedral Library
Hunter MS (partly published in *Codices Manuscriptae Ecclesiae Cathedralis Dunelmensis* ed. T. Rud).

Durham University Library
Cosin letter-book.

Erdély (Transylvania) Reformed Church Province Archives (Kolozsvár)
Matricula Ecclesiarum Reformatorum in Sede Siculicali Maros.
Protocollum Matricula Székiensis (Szolnok-Doboka).

House of Lords Record Office, London
Braye MSS 1, 102, 104–14.

Hungarian National Archives (Budapest)
A kiskomáromi református egyházközség legrégébbi anyakönyve, 1624–1732, boxes 1882, A.1525.
Tiszántúl egyházkerület levéltára kerületi jegyzőkönyvek (püspöki), vol. 1, (1629–), box 1883.
Tiszántúli református egyházkerület; debreceni egyházmegye jegyzőkönyvei, vol. 1, 1615–1655, box 1884.

Simandianum (Mihály Simándi) Protocollum (kerületi (Danubian) jegyző-könyvek, 1629–1731), box 1890.
Nomina Studiosorum Illustris Scholae Saros Patachinae, box 1903.
Liber Reditum Ecclesiasticum Comitatus Zempleniensis 1623, box 1907.
Református egyházkerületi levéltárak régebbi könyvanyaga, box 1907.
Zempléni Egyházmegye Protocolluma, 1629–1645, box 1907.
Zempléni Egyházmegye Protocolluma, 1638–1651, box 1908.
Zempléni Egyházmegye Protocolluma, 1653–1672, box 1908.
Liber Ecclae seu Matricula dioecese Ungensis, box 1912.
Tiszántúli református egyházkerület levéltárának . . . válogatott iratai, box 2177.
Protocollum Judicis Primarii et Senatus Oppidi Sáros Nagy Patak, (3 vols.), boxes 20493–4.

Hungarian Academy of Science (Budapest)
Farkas, András, *Cronica de Introductione Scyttarum in Ungariam et Judaeorum de Aegypto* (1538) (manuscript copy), Történl. 4rét, 38 [(Q) volume].

Maros Reformed Church District Archives (Marosvásárhely, Transylvania)
65/B, July 1659.

Romanian National Archives (Transylvania, Cluj/Kolozsvár)
Collectia Gr. Kemény József.
Collectia Mike Sándor.

Sheffield University Library
Hartlib Papers (H50).

Tiszáninnen Reformed Church Province Archives (Sárospatak)
Zsoldos Benő féle időrendes sorozat.

Tiszáninnen Reformed Church Province Library Manuscript Collection (Sárospatak)
Szilágyi Benjámin, István, 'Acta Synodi Nationalis Hungaricae . . . 1646', vol. 21.
Rakocziana, vol. 1113.

Tiszántúl Reformed Church Province Library Manuscript Collection (Debrecen)
Lugossy József oklevél gyűjtemény 1281–1854, R. 111.
Tecső protocolluma, 1639–1805, R. 111/2769.
Series Studiosorum in Schola Debrecina, R. 495.
Önéletrajz és lelkészi napló Hajdúnánás, 1627–89, R. 540.
Synodalia of István Szilágyi Benjámin, R. 575.
Kismarjai Veszelin Pál peregrinációs albuma 1653–1654, R. 692.
Misztótfalu mezőváros jegyzőkönyve, 1596–1803, R. 3289.

Tiszántúl Reformed Church Province Archives (Debrecen)
Debrecen egyházmegye; igazgatási iratok, I. 31b.
Nagykárolyi (Középszolnok) egyházmegye iratai, I. 35a.1.
Egyházkerületi iratai, 1/J.
Szabolcs egyházmegye iratai, I. 37.a.

(2) PRINTED SOURCES

(i) Primary Sources

Adattár 13. Magyarországi magánkönyvtárak, 1533–1657, 1, ed. A. Varga (Szeged–Budapest, 1986).

Adattár 14. Partiumi könyvesházak, 1623–1730, ed. B. Keserű (Szeged, 1988).

Adattár 15. Kassa város olvasmányai, 1562–1731, ed. B. Keserű and I. Monok (Szeged, 1990).

Adattár 16. Erdélyi könyvesházak, ed. B. Keserű (Szeged, 1991).

Alsted, Johann Heinrich, *Rudimenta Linguae Graecae* (Gyulafehérvár, 1634).

—— *Rudimenta Linguae Latinae* (Gyulafehérvár, 1634).

—— *Rudimenta Linguae Hebraicae* (Gyulafehérvár, 1635).

—— *Latinum in nuce* (Gyulafehérvár, 1635).

—— *Grammatica Latina* (Gyulafehérvár, 1635).

—— *Catechismus religionis Christianae- Catechismus; azaz, A keresztyéni vallásnak és hütnek rövid kerdesekben és feleletekben foglaltatott* (Gyulafehérvár, 1636).

—— *The World's Proceeding Woes and Succeeding Joys* (London, 1642).

—— *Prodromus religionis* (Gyulafehérvár, 1644).

—— 'Diatribe de mille annis apocalypticis' (1630) and 'The Beloved City; or, The saints reign on earth a thousand years' (1643), in B. Griesing, J. Klein, and J. Kramer (eds.), *J. H. Alsted, Herborns calvinistische Theologie und Wissenschaft im Spiegel der englischen Kulturreform des frühen 17. Jahrhunderts* (Studien zu englisch-deutschen Geistesbeziehungen der frühen Neuzeit, 16; Frankfurt, 1988), 20–73.

Alvinczi, Péter, *Itinerarium Catholicum; azaz, Nevezetes vetélkedés az felöl: Ha az evangelicusok tudományajé uy, vagy az mostani romai valláson valo papistaké?* (Debrecen, 1616).

—— *Querela Hungariae. Magyarorszag panasza* (Kassa, 1619).

—— *Macchiavellizatio* (Kassa, 1621).

—— *Az Urnak Szent wacsoraiarol valo reovid intes az Szent Pal Apostol tanitasa szerint* (Kassa, 1622).

—— *Az néhai felséges Báthori Gábor ... testének eltakarításakor tett intések* (Gyulafehérvár, 1628).

—— *Postilla* (2 vols; Kassa, 1633–4).

Ames, William, *Bellarminus Ennervatus; vel, Disputationes anti-Bellarminae in illustri Frisiorum academia, quae est Franekerae, publice habitae, A Guilielmo Amesio, theologiae doctore* (Franeker, 1625).

—— *The Marrow of Sacred Divinity* (London, 1643).

—— and Bradshaw, William, *English Puritanism* (London, 1605).

Anon., *Az keresztyéni vallásnak rövid tudománya* (Kolozsvár, 1632).

Anon., *Pápisták méltatlan üldözése a vallásért* ([n.pl.] 1643).

Anon., *Lelki tömjénező, melyben a ... könyörgésnek kedves illatu füstöletivel az Istennek ... haragja engeszteltetik* (Gyulafehérvár, 1646).

Bibliography 307

Anon., *Mennyország kinyittatott egyetlenegy szoros kapuja* (Nagyvárad, 1656).

Anon., *Jesuita páterek titkai, a magok irásiból kiszedegettettek* (Nagyvárad, 1657).

Apáczai Csere, János, *A keresztyéni vallasra rövid kérdésekben és feleletekben tanito Catechesis* (Amsterdam, 1650).

—— *Magyar Encyclopaedia; az az, Minden igaz es hasznos böltségnek szep rendbe foglalása és magyar nyelven világra botsátása* (Utrecht, 1653).

—— *Tanács, mellyet Joachymus Fortius ad Apáczai János által egy tanulásba élesüggedt ifjúnak* (Gyulafehérvár, 1654).

—— *Magyar Logikácska* (Gyulafehérvár, 1654).

—— 'Apáczai Jánosnak egy eddig ismeretlen levele Barcsai Ákos fejedelemhez', ed. G. Herepei, *EPK* (1879), 492–3.

Apáczai Csere János beszéde 'a bölcsesség tanulásáról', ed. I. Bán (Debrecen, 1955).

Apáczai Csere János válogatott pedagógiai művei, ed. L. Orosz (Budapest, 1956).

Apáczai Csere János. Magyar encyclopaedia, ed. I. Bán (Budapest, 1959).

Apor, Péter, *Metamorphosis Transylvaniae; azaz, Erdélynek régi együgyű alázatos idejében való gazdaságából e mostani kevély, cifra, felfordult állapotjában koldusságra való változása*, ed. Gy. Tóth (Budapest, 1972).

Arnold, Nicholas, *Heinrici Echardi, Lutherani, scopae dissolutae seu fasciculus ejus controversiarum succincte refutatus et quadraginta publicis disputationibus in Academia Franekerana dissolutus a Nicolao Arnoldo* (Franeker, 1654).

Balásfi, Thomas, *Castigatio libello Calvinistici, cui titulus est: Machiavellizatio* (Vienna, 1620).

Basire, Isaac, *De antiqua ecclesiae Britannicae* (Bruges, 1656).

—— *Pro unitate verae ecclesiae* (Gyulafehérvár, 1656).

—— *Schema primum generale sive forma studiorum Albensium* (Gyulafehérvár, 1657).

—— *History of the English and Scotch Presbytery* ([n.pl.], 1659).

—— *Correspondence*, ed. W. N. Darnell (London, 1831).

—— 'Basire védirata válasz az "Innocentia Transylvaniae" czimű röpiratra', ed. L. Kropf, *TT* (1888), 509–65, 667–706.

Batizi, András, *Keresztyéni tudományról való rövid könyvecske* (Cracow, 1550).

[Bázel], 'A bázeli egyetem anyakönyvéből', ed. I. Zsindely, *Sárospataki Füzetek* 4 (1860), 161–5.

[Bethlen, Gabór], *Adalékok Bethlen Gábor szövetkezéseinek történetéhez*, ed. S. Szilágyi, in *ÉTTK* 2 pt 8 (Budapest, 1873).

Bethlen Gábor fejedelem kiadatlan politikai levelei, ed. S. Szilágyi (Budapest, 1879).

'Bethlen Gábor levele Alvinczi Péterhez', ed. S. Szilágyi, *EPK* (1879), 26–7.

'Bethlen Gábor levelei', ed. S. Szilágyi, *TT* (1885), 209–56, 431–80, 623–73.

Bethlen Gábor fejedelem levelezése, ed. S. Szilágyi (Budapest, 1886).

Bethlen Gábor krónikásai, krónikák, emlékiratok, naplók a nagy fejedelemről, ed. L. Makkai (Budapest, 1980).

Bethlen, János, *Innocentia Transylvaniae* (Kolozsvár, 1659).

Bethlen Miklós önéletirásai, ed. E. Windisch (Budapest, 1955).

Beza, Theodore, *Correspondance de Théodore de Bèze*, ed. H. Meylan et al., 16 vols. (Geneva, 1978–93).

Bisterfeld, Johann Heinrich, *Elementa Logica* (Gyulafehérvár, 1635).

—— *De uno Deo. Patre, Filio, ac Spiritu Sancto mysterium pietatis, contra Iohannis Crellii* (Leiden, 1639).

—— *Medulla Priscae Puraque Latinatis* (Gyulafehérvár, 1646).

—— *Beata Beatae Virginis Ars* (Gyulafehérvár, 1651).

—— *Gladii Spiritus Ignei, vivi, et ancipitis; seu, Scripturae Sacrae divina eminentia et efficientia* (Gyulafehérvár, 1653).

—— 'Bisterfeld végrendelete', ed. F. Zimmermann, *TT* (1893), 171–5.

Bocskai István levelek, ed. K. Benda (Budapest, 1992).

Bod, Péter, *Smirnai szent polikárpus . . . erdélyi református püspököknek historiájok* (Nagyenyed, 1766).

—— *Magyar Athenas avagy az erdélyben és magyarországon élt tudós emberek* [1766], in *Bod Péter válogatott művei*, ed. I. Torda (Budapest, 1982), 237–459.

—— *Historia Hungarorum Ecclesiastica* (Leiden, 1888/9).

Bojti Veres, Gáspár, *A nagy Bethlen Gábor viselt dolgairól*, in *Bethlen Gábor emlékezete*, ed. L. Makkai (Budapest, 1980), 19–66.

Bökényi Filep, János (tr.), *Mennyei Lámpás* (Utrecht, 1652).

[Bottka, Ferenc], 'Ferenc Bottka kéri Klobusiczky Andrást . . . pápai iskola számára', ed. B. Szilágyi, *MPEIF* 7 (1876), 43–4.

'A brémai főiskola magyar diákjai (1618–1750)', ed. I. Czegle, *ITK* 87 (Budapest, 1974).

Brown, Edward, *A Brief Account of Some Travels in Hungaria, Severia . . . with the Figures of Some Habits and Remarkable Places* (London, 1673).

Bullinger, Heinrich, *Libellus epistolaris . . . pressis et afflictiss[imis] ecclesiis in Hungaria, earu[n]demq[ue] pastoribus et ministris transmissus* (Kolozsvár, 1559).

Calamy Revised. Being a Revision of Edmund Calamy's Account of the Ministers and Others Ejected and Silenced, 1660–2, ed. A. G. Matthews (Oxford, 1934).

A Calendar of the Letter Books of the French Church of London from the Civil War to the Restoration, 1643–1659, ed. R. D. Gwynn (Huguenot Society of London, 54; 1979).

Canones Ecclesiastici in quinque classes distributi [1623 Komját canons] (Pápa, 1625).

Chishull, Edmund, *Travels in Turkey and back to England* (London, 1747).

Comenius, Jan Amos, *A Reformation of Schooles* (London, 1642).

—— *A History of the Bohemian Persecution* (London, 1650).

—— *A Patterne of Universall Knowledge* (London, 1651).

—— *Fortius Redivivus* (Sárospatak, 1652).

—— *Eruditionis scholasticae pars prima, Vestibulum; Pars secunda, Janua; Pars tertia, Atrium* (Sárospatak, 1652).

—— *Primitiae laborum scholasticorum in illustri Patakino gymnasio* (Sárospatak, 1652).

—— *Schola Ludus; seu, Encyclopaedia vive* . . . *janua linguarum praxis comica* (Sárospatak, 1656).

—— *Praecepta morum in usum juventutis collecta* (Nagyvárad, 1658).

—— *A General Table of Europe Representing the Present and Future State Thereof* (Amsterdam, 1669).

—— *Korrespondence Jana Amose Komenského*, ed. J. V. Kvacsala (Prague, 1897).

—— 'Comenius sárospataki beköszöntője', ed. L. Stromp, *Protestáns Szemle*, 12 (1900), 560–83.

—— 'Comenius irata Rákóczi Zsigmondhoz', ed. J. V. Kvacsala, in *MPEA* 4 (1905), 128–43.

—— 'Comenius irata II. Rákóczy Györgyhöz', ed. J. V. Kvacsala, in *MPEA* 4 (1905), 144–68.

—— *Didactica Magna*, ed. M. W. Keatinge (New York, 1910).

—— *Opera Didactica Omnia* (3 vols.; Prague, 1957), vol. 2, book 3.

—— *Comenius magyarországon. Comenius sárospatakon írt műveiből*, ed. E. Kovács (Budapest, 1962).

—— *Panglottia; or, Universal language*, ed. A. M. O. Dobbie (Warwick, 1989).

—— *Panorthosia; or, Universal reform*, ed. A. M. O. Dobbie (Sheffield, 1995).

Csanaki, Máté, *A döghalálról való rövid elmélkedés* (Kolozsvár, 1634).

Czeglédi, István, *Az országok romlásáról irott könyvnek első része* (Kassa, 1659).

—— *Ama ritka példájú* . . . *II. Rákóczi György* . . . *testének földben tétele felett predikáció* (Kassa, 1661).

Darholcz, Kristóf, *Novissima Tuba, azaz ítiletre serkentő utolsó trombitaszó* (Kassa, 1639).

Dávid, Ferenc, and Blandrata, Georgio, *Catechismus Ecclesiaru[m] Dei* (Kolozsvár, 1566).

Debreceni Ember, Pál, *Historia ecclesiae reformatae, in Hungaria et Transylvania* (Utrecht, 1728).

A debreczeni ev. ref. főiskola xvii. és xviii. századi törvényei, ed. R. Békefi (Budapest, 1899), 79–117.

Debreczeni, Gáspár, *Kalendárium* (Debrecen, 1635).

A Declaration or Manifesto, wherein the Roman Imperiall Majesty makes known to the States and Peeres of Hungarie, what reasons and motives have compelled him to proceed in open warre against the Prince of Transylvania (London, 1644).

The Declaration or Manifesto of George Racokzkie, Prince of Transylvania, to the States and Peeres of Hungarie; together with the reasons added thereunto of his modern taking up of armes (London, 1644).

Dengelegi Biró, Péter, *Rövid Anatómia* (Gyulafehérvár, 1630).

'A deventeri athenaeumon tanult magyarok 1644–9', ed. L. Segesváry, *Századok*, 71 (1937), 506–8.

Diószegi Bónis, Mátyás (tr.), *Az részegesnek gyülölséges, utálatos és rettenetes állapota* (Leiden, 1649).

'Drei Briefe an Simon Albelius in Kronstadt', ed. J. Gross, *Korrespondenzblatt des Vereins für Siebenbürgische Landeskunde*, 8 (1885), 1–3, 13–15.

[Dunántúl], 'Kis Bertalan és Musay György dunántúli ág. hitv. püspökök egyházlátogatási jegyzőkönyve, 1631–1654', ed. E. Thury, in *MPEA* 6 (1907), 11–193.

—— 'Adatok a dunántúl és felső dunamellék kerületekről', ed. E. Thury, in *MPEA* 7 (1908), 127–40, 154–6, 189–92, 196–7.

—— 'Adatok a dunántúli ref. egyházkerület történetéhez', ed. E. Thury, in *MPEA* 8 (1909), 1–101; 9 (1910), 1–113.

Dury, John, *Motives to Induce the Protestant Princes to Mind the Worke of Peace Ecclesiasticall amongst Themselves* (London, 1641).

—— *A Summary Discourse concerning the Work of Peace Ecclesiasticall, How It May Concurre with the Aim of a Civil Confederation amongst Protestants* (Cambridge, 1641).

—— *A Brief Relation of that which Hath Been Lately Attempted to Procure Ecclesiasticall Peace amongst Protestants* (London, 1641).

—— *A Model of Church-Government; or, The grounds of the spirituall frame and government of the House of God* (London, 1647).

—— *The Earnest Breathings of Foreign Protestants for a Compleat Body of Practicall Divinity* (London, 1658).

—— *An Information, concerning the Present State of the Jewish Nation in Europe and Judea* (London, 1658).

Ecclesiae Londino-Batavae archivum epistulae et tractatae formationis historiam illustrantos, 3, ed. J. Hessels (Cambridge, 1897).

Egyházi kánonok. Geleji Katona István 1649 és a Szatmárnémetiben 1646 évben tartott zsinat végzései, ed. Á. Kiss (Kecskemét, 1875).

'Egyháztörténelmi adatok', ed. S. Szilágyi, *EPK* (1880), 313–14, 329–30, 344–5, 360–1.

Enyedi Fazekas, János, *Mennyei szó a lelki álomból* (Nagyvárad, 1652).

Erdély és az északkeleti háború. Levelek és okiratok, ed. S. Szilágyi, 2 vols. (Budapest, 1890–1).

'Az erdélyi anyaszentegyház közzsinatainak végzései kivonatban', ed. I. Szilágyi, *MPEIF* 3 (1872), 1–9, 77–84, 473–9.

'Az erdélyi ev. ref. egyház vallássérelmei 1631-ben, beterjesztve I. Rákóczi György fejedelemhez orvoslás végett', ed. J. Koncz, *EPK* (1882), 380–1, 396, 422–3.

Erdélyi országgyűlési emlékek. Monumenta comitialia regni Transylvaniae, ed. S. Szilágyi (21 vols.; Budapest, 1875–98).

Esterházy, Miklós, *Rákóczi György erdélyi fejedelemnek irt egynéhány intő leveleinek igaz pariája* (Pozsony, 1644).

Felegyházi, Tamás, *Az keresztieni igaz hitnek reszeirol valo tanitas, kerdesekkel es feleletekkel* (Debrecen, 1579).

Felsőbányai, Mihály, *A léleknek uti költsége* (Utrecht, 1651).

'A fogarasi egyházközség levéltárából', ed. J. Pokoly, in *MPEA* 8 (1909), 106–7, 120–5, 129–30.

Fogarasi, István, *Catechismus; azaz, A keresztyén vallásnak és hütnek rövid kérdésekben és feleletekben foglaltatott . . . olah nyelvre forditot* (Gyulafehérvár, 1648).

'A franekeri egyetemén tanúlt magyarok', ed. Á. Hellebrant, *TT* (1886), 599–608, 792–800.

[Frankfurt an der Oder], 'A magyarországi ifjak az odera melleti Frankfurt egyetemében', ed. J. Zoványi, *Protestáns Szemle*, 1 (1889), 178–202.

Fröhlich, Dávid, *Kalendárium . . . Prognosis Astrologica* (Nagyvárad, 1644).

Geleji Katona, István, *Magyar Grammatikatska* (Gyulafehérvár, 1636).

—— *Praeconium Evangelicum* (2 vols.; Gyulafehérvár, 1638–40).

—— *Titkok Titka* (Gyulafehérvár, 1645)

—— *Váltság-Titka . . . és a' tévelygőnek, ugy mint Sidoknak, Socinianusoknak, Blandristáknak, Pápistáknak, Lutheranus atyafiaknak, és egyebeknek ellenkező vélekedésik megczáfoltatnak* (3 vols.; Nagyvárad, 1645–9).

—— 'Geleji István levele', ed. J. Erdélyi, in *Sárospataki Füzetek*, 1 (1857–8), 177–80.

—— 'Geleji Katona István levelei Rákóczyhoz', ed. A. Beke, *ITK* 4 (1894), 336–46.

Geleji Katona, István and Keserüi Dajka, János, *A keresztyén hitnek igazságához intéztetett . . . öreg graduál* (Gyulafehérvár, 1636).

'A genfi akadémia magyar diákjai (1566–1772)', ed. B. S. Nagy, *ITK* 87 (1983), 388.

[Genfi], 'A magyarhoni egyházra vonatkozó egyes adatok a genfi papi testület jegyzőkönyvéből', ed. K. Szél, *Sárospataki Füzetek* 6 (1862), 922–9.

Gönci, György, *De disciplina ecclesiastica; seu, Gubernationis ecclesiasticae legitima forma, in Ungarica natione Cis Tibiscum* (Debrecen, 1613).

Gönczi Kovács, György, *Keresztyéni énekek* (Debrecen, 1592).

'A groningeni egyetem tanult magyarok névsora', ed. Ö. Miklós, *Dunántuli Protestáns Lap* (1917), 194–7, 202–7.

Gyöngyösi, László, *A keresztyéni vallásnak fundamentomi* (Utrecht, 1657).

A gyulafehérvári főiskola 1657-iki szabályzata, ed. Z. Varga (Budapest, 1907).

Gyulai, Mihály, *Fertelmeskedő, s' bujálkodó tancz jutalma* (Debrecen, 1681).

Hajnal, Mátyás, *Kitett cégér* (Pozsony, 1640).

Haller, Gábor, 'Napló, 1629–1644', in *ETA 4* (Kolozsvár, 1862), 1–103.

Hancken, Bálint, *Kalendárium* (Debrecen, 1620).

'A harderwijki egyetem magyarországi hallgatói', ed. J. Zoványi, *ITK* 1 (1891), 433–6.

Hartlib, Samuel, *The Necessity of Some Nearer Conjunction and Correspondency amongst Evangelical Protestants* (London, 1644).

'A heidelbergben tanult magyarok névsora', ed. J. Szeremlei, *Sárospataki Füzetek*, 5 (1861), 452–71, 556–67; 6 (1862), 559–67.

[Heidelberg], 'Adatok a heidelbergi egyetem magyarországi hallgatóinak névsorához', ed. J. Zoványi, *Protestáns Szemle* 16 (1904), 111–14.

Heltai, Gáspár, *Catechismus Minor* (Kolozsvár, 1550).

—— *A részegségnek és tobzódásnak veszedelmes voltáról való dialogus* ed. B. Stoll (Budapest, 1951: orig. pub. Kolozsvár, 1552).

Heltai, Gáspár, *Catechismus, melybe a menynyei tudománynak sommája . . . egybe szerzettetett* (Kolozsvár, 1553).

—— *Két könyv minden országoknak és királyoknak jó és gonosz szerencséjeknek okairól* (Debrecen, 1563).

A herczegszöllösi kánonok más egyházi kánonokkal egybevétve, ed. Gy. Mokos (Budapest, 1901).

Herlicius, Dávid, *Kalendárium* (Gyulafehérvár, 1625).

C. J. Hiltebrandt's *dreifache schwedische Gesandtschaftsreise nach Siebenbürgen, der Ukraine und Constantinopel (1656–1658)*, ed. F. Babinger (Leiden, 1937).

Hodászi, Lukács, *De potestate ecclesiastica* (Debrecen, 1611).

Horváth, András, *De Judaeorum ante novissimum diem conversione Futura* (Kassa, 1658).

Huszár, Dávid, *A keresztyén hitről való tudománynak rövid kérdésekben foglaltatott summája* (Pápa, 1577).

Iratosi, János, *Az ember életének boldogul való igazgatásának modgyáról. Patika szerszámos bolt, azaz sokféle haláloknak természetükről* (Lőcse, 1637).

[Kanizsai Pálfi, János], 'Kanizsai Pálfi János levele a gyulafehérvári prófesszorokhóz', ed. Gy. Mokos, *ITK* 15 (1905), 489–90.

—— 'Pathai István és Kanizsai Pálfi János levelezése (1607–1636)', ed. E. Thury, in *MPEA* 4 (1905), 49–92.

Károlyi, Gáspár, *Szent Biblia* (Vizsoly, 1590).

—— *Két könyv minden országoknak és királyoknak jó és gonosz szerencséjeknek okairól, melyből megérthetni, mi az oka a magyarországnak is romlásának és miczoda ielensegekből esmerhettiuc meg, hogy az istennec iteleti közel vagion* (Debrecen, 1563).

—— *A mi Urunk Jésus Christusnak Uy Testamentoma* (Amsterdam, 1646).

'Kecskeméti ref. anyakönyvi följegyzések', ed. S. Szilágyi, *Sárospataki Füzetek*, 1 (1857–8), 652–9; 2(1858–9), 65–78.

'A kecskeméti reform. egyház jegyzőkönyvéből', ed. L. Fördös, *MPEF* 2 (1880), 35–7.

Kecskeméti Alexis János prédikációs könyve, ed. L. O. Gombáné (Budapest, 1987).

Kecskeméti, János, *Fides Jesu et Jesuitarum* (Bártfa, 1619).

—— (tr.) *Catholicus Reformatus* (Debrecen, 1620).

—— *Pázmány Peter kalauzzának, tizenharmadik könyvére való felelet* (Bártfa, 1622).

—— *Az papistak között es mi közöttünk, vetelkedesre vettetet, harom fő articulusokról* (Bártfa, 1622).

Kemény, János, *Gilead Balsamuma, azaz Sz. Dávid 150 Soltárinak* (Sárospatak, 1659).

—— *Kemény János önéletírása és válogatott levelei*, ed. E. Windisch (Budapest, 1959).

Keresszegi Herman, István, *A keresztyén hitnek ágazatiról való prédikációknak tárháza* (Nagyvárad, 1640).

Keresztúri, Pál, *Christianus Lactens, quem illustres et magnifici domini, dn. Georgius et dn. Sigismundus Rakoci . . . in solemni examine* (Gyulafehérvár, 1637).

—— *Csecsemő keresztyén, mellyet . . . Rakoczi György és Sigmond . . . igaz vallások-ban való szép épületekröl abban az probában bizonságot tennének* (Gyulafehérvár, 1638).

—— *Felserdült keresztyén* (Nagyvárad, 1641).

Keserüi Dajka, János, et al., *Exequiae principales; azaz, Halotti pompa, mellyel Károlyi Susannának, Bethlen Gábor házastársának utolsó tisztesség tétetett 1622 esztendőben* (Gyulafehérvár, 1624).

Kinner, Cyprian, *A Continuation of Mr. John-Amos-Comenius School-Endeavours; or, A summary delineation of Dr Cyprian Kinner Silesian his thoughts concerning education* (London, 1648).

Kocsi Csergő, Bálint, 'Kősziklán épült ház ostroma' [1676], in *A magyarországi gályarab prédikátorok emlékezete. Galleria omnium sanctorum*, ed. L. Makkai (Budapest, 1976), 31–109.

—— 'Brevis delineatio ecclesiarum reformatarum in Hungaria et Transylvania' [1677], in *Az első rendszeres magyar református egyháztörténet*, ed. D. Miklós (Budapest, 1994).

Komáromi Csipkés, György, *Oratio Hebraea, continens elogium linguae Hebraeae* (Utrecht, 1651).

—— *Az keresztyén isteni tudománynak . . . rövid summája* (Utrecht, 1653).

—— *Schola Hebraica* (Utrecht, 1654).

—— *Hungaria Illustrata* (Utrecht, 1655).

—— *Szomoru esetek tüköre. Gyászbeszéd Rácz János fölött* (Sárospatak, 1661).

—— *A Judiciaria astrologiáról és üstökös csillagokról való judicium* (Debrecen, 1665).

Komaromi Szvertán, István, *Mikoron imádkoztok ezt mondgyatok az az: Az uri imadsagnak . . . magyarázattya* (Nagyvárad, 1652).

[Königsberg], *Die Matrikel der Albertus-Universität zu Königsberg, 1544–1829*, ed. G. Erler (3 vols.; Leipzig, 1910–17).

[Küküllővári], 'Az 1619. évi küküllővári zsinat felterjesztése Bethlen Gábor fejedelemhez', ed. G. Illyés, *Református Szemle* (1934), 501–5.

Laskai, János, *Iustus Lipsiusnak az alhatatossagrol irt ket könyvei* (Debrecen, 1641).

—— *Jézus királysága* (Nagyvárad, 1644).

—— *Hittül-szakadasnak tellyes meg orvoslasa, mellyet az' elhatatosoknak és el-eseteknek javokra, három könyvekben leirt* (Nagyvárad, 1644).

[Leiden], 'Die Studierenden aus Ungarn und Siebenbürgen an der Universität Leiden 1575–1875', ed. F. Teutsch, *Archiv des Vereins für Siebenbürgische Landeskunde*, 16 (1881), 204–26.

Lethenyei, István, *Az Calvinistac magyar harmonianac; azaz, Az Augustana es Helvetica confessioc articulusinac . . . öszvehasomlétásanac meghamisétása* (Csepreg, 1633).

Lippai, Sámuel, *Brevis dissertatio de quaestione an prior elevatio panis at vini in sacra coena, in quibusdam Ecclesiis usitate legitime, observatur?* (Sárospatak, 1654).

Lippai, Sámuel, _Desperata causa prioris elevationis panis et vini in sacra coena_ (Sárospatak, 1655).

Lórántffy, Zsuzsanna, _Moses és a prophéták_ (Gyulafehérvár, 1641).

A magyar országgyűlések vallásügyi tárgyalásai a reformátiotól kezdve, ed. M. Zsilinszky (Budapest, 1880).

Magyar országgyűlési emlékek. Monumenta comitialia regni Hungariae, ed. V. Fraknói et al. (Budapest, 1874–1917).

'Magyar protestáns egyház történeti kutfők', ed. P. Finkei, _Sárospataki Füzetek_ 1 (1857–8), 161–77, 335–49, 467–74, 753–60, 957–62, 972–81.

Magyar törvénytár. 1540–1848 évi erdélyi törvények, ed. D. Márkus, S. Kolozsvári, and K. Ovári (Budapest, 1900), 5–243.

Magyar utazási irodalom 15–18. században, ed. I. S. Kovács and I. Monok (Budapest, 1990).

[Magyar], _A xvi. században tartott magyar református zsinatok végzései_, ed. Á. Kiss (Budapest, 1881).

Magyari, István, _Az országokban való sok romlásoknak okairól és azokból való megszabadulásnak jó módjáról_ (Sárvár, 1602).

'Magyarország történetét érdeklö okiratok a svédországi levéltárakból', ed. K. Wibling, _TT_ (1892), 440–73, 593–634.

Magyarországi boszorkányperek oklevéltára, ed. A. Komáromy (Budapest, 1910).

Magyarországi boszorkányperek, 1529–1786, ed. F. Schram (2 vols.) (Budapest, 1970).

[Magyarországi], 'Adatok a magyarországi puritánus mozgalmak történetéhez', ed. J. Zoványi, in _MPEA_ 10 (1911), 1–25.

Maresius, Samuel, _Popularis ad Popularem; sive Irenaei Simplicii Philadelphi epistola . . . ad Petrum Bacca Szatthmari_ (Groningen, 1649).

—— _Xenia Academica; sive, Disputatio theologica de personalitate adeoque divinitate Spiritus Sancti contra Socinianos_ (Groningen, 1650).

'A marosi traktus 17. századbeli történetéből', ed. Gy. Dávid, _Református Szemle_ (1930), 151–4, 165–8, 210–12, 232–4, 246–8, 263–6, 311–16, 487–90.

[Marosi], 'Az 1643. évi zsinat [marosi] válasza a székely urak felterjesztésére', ed. G. Illyés, _Református Szemle_ (1936), 261–5.

'A marosvásárhelyi ev. ref. iskola xvii. századi törvényei', ed. R. Békefi, in _ÉTTK_ 18/8 (Budapest, 1899), 26–37.

Mártonfalvi, György, and Komáromi Csipkes, György, _Ars concianandi Amesiana_ (Debrecen, 1666).

Medgyesi, Pál (tr.), _Szent Agoston vallasa_ (Debrecen, 1632).

—— _Praxis Pietatis_ (Debrecen, 1636).

—— _Het napoki edgyüt beszelgetesek, ket öszvetalalkozott embereknek tudnia-illik edgy Keresztyen es mas edgy papista Catholicusnak_ (Debrecen, 1637).

—— _Szent Atyák öröme; az az, Daniel Vasarhellyi Jesuita Professorus Paternek tzikkelyinek meg tzikkelyezésére_ (Gyulafehérvár, 1640).

—— *Lelki A-Bé-Cé. A Christus oskolájába az alsó rendben bé állatandó tsetsemökuek közönségessen kiváltképpen; penig a' méltóságos kegyes Fejedelem aszszonynak Lorantfi Susannának, aprobb Tselédgyének hasznokra* (Gyulafehérvár, 1645).

—— *Egő szövétnek* (Gyulafehérvár, 1645).

—— *Doce nos Orare et Praedicare* (Bártfa, 1650).

—— *Dialogus Politico-Ecclesiasticus, azaz két keresztyén embereknek eggy mással való beszélgetések: az egyházi igazgató presbyterekről, avagy vénekről, öregekről és a presbyteriumról, eggyházi tanátsról* (Bártfa, 1650).

—— *Rövid tanítás a presbyteriumról avagy egyházi tanácsról* (Sárospatak, 1653).

—— *Erdély s egész magyar nép . . . hármas . . . jajja* (Nagyvárad, 1653).

—— *Igaz magyar nép negyedik jajja s-siralma* (Sárospatak, 1657).

—— *Ötödik jaj és siralom* (Sárospatak, 1657).

—— *Igazak sorsa a világon. Gyászbeszéd Bocskai István felesége Lónyai Zsuzsanna felett* (Sárospatak, 1657).

—— *Liturgia sacra coenae; azaz, Urvacsora kiosztásában való rend* (Sárospatak, 1658).

—— *Istenhez való igaz magtérés* (Sárospatak, 1658).

—— *Magyarok hatodik jajja. Kétség torkából kihatló lélek; Bünön buskodó lélek kénszergése; Joseph romlasa avagy magyar nemzet 1658 esztendőbéli nagy pusztulása; Felgerjedt, s pokol fenekeig hatalmazott rohogo tüz; Rabszabaditó isteni szent mesterség; Külön ülő keresztyén; Serva domine* (Sárospatak, 1660).

——'Medgyesi Pál levelei', ed. S. Szilágyi, *EPK* (1876), 306–9, 320–2; (1877), 3–4, 17–18, 29–30.

Melotai Nyilas, István, *A mennyei tudomány szerint való irtovány, melyből az veszedelmes tevelygéseknek, es hamis velekedéseknek kárhozatos, tövisses bokrai* (Debrecen, 1617).

—— *A szent Dávid XX. zsoltárának magyarázatja* (Kassa, 1620).

—— *Agenda; az az, Anya szent egyház beli szolgálat szerint való cselekedet* (Gyulafehérvár, 1621).

—— *Speculum Trinitatis* (Debrecen, 1622).

Mihályko, János (tr.), *Keresztyéni istenes és ájtatos imádságok* (Bártfa, 1640).

Mikolai Hegedüs, János, *Az mennyei igazságnak tüzes oszlopa; Biblia tanui; Az istenes cselédeknek lelki praebendájók; Szentek napi száma* (Utrecht, 1648).

Milton, John, *Areopagitica*, ed. J. W. Hales (Oxford, 1898).

'Miskolczi Csulyak István zempléni ref. esperes (1625–1645) egyházlátogatási jegyzőkönyvei', ed. J. Zoványi, *TT* 7 (1906), 48–102, 266–313, 368–407.

—— 'Miskolczi Csulyak István esperesi naplója és leveleskönyve', ed. J. Zoványi, in *MPEA* 10 (1911), 26–142; 11 (1927), 168–91; 12 (1928), 186–219; 13 (1929), 142–8.

—— 'Miskolczi Csulyak István diarium-ából', ed. F. Zsinka, in *MPEA* 11 (1927), 119–67; 12 (1928), 89–122.

—— 'Miskolczi István és Görgei János esperesek levelei I. Rákóczi Györgyhez', ed. S. Szilágyi, *EPK* (1875), 267–9.

316   *Bibliography*

Miskolczi, Gáspár, *Angliai Independentismus vagy az ecclésiai fenyitékben, és a külső isteni tiszteletre tartozó jó rendtártasokban, minden reformata ecclesiakról különöző fejetlen lábság* (Utrecht, 1654).

Molnár, Gergély, *Catechesis scholae Claudiopolitanae* (Kolozsvár, 1564).

Nagy Szabó, Ferenc, 'Marosvásárhely Memorial', (*ETA* 1; Kolozsvár, 1855).

Nagyari, Benedek, *Orthodoxus Christianus; azaz, Igaz vallásu keresztyén* (Nagyvárad, 1651).

'Nánási emlékirat', ed. L. Varga, *Sárospataki Füzetek*, 2 (1858–9), 165–75, 689–98, 785–800.

'Naplókönyv, 1632-ból', ed. L. Abafi, *TT* (1883), 519–42, 645–55.

Pápai Páriz, Ferenc, 'Romlott fal felépítése (Rudus Redivivum) [1685]', in *MPEA* 5 (1906), 129–73.

Pápai Páriz, Imre (tr.), *Keskény ut* (Gyulafehérvár, 1657).

Pareus, David, *Collegiorum . . . theologicorum pars prima* (Heidelberg, 1611).

—— *Collegiorum theologicorum quibus universa theologica orthodoxa, et omnes prope theologorum huius temporis controversae perspicue et varie explicantur pars altera postremum est anti-Bellarminianum succinctum in omnes Rob. Bellarmini Card. controversias* (Heidelberg, 1620).

—— *A Commentary upon the Divine Revelation of the Apostle and Evangelist John* (Amsterdam, 1644).

Pataki Füsüs, János, *Királyoknak Tüköre* (Bártfa, 1626).

Pathai, István, *A sakramentumokról közönséges és kiváltképpen az Ur vacsorájáról való könyvecske* (Gyulafehérvár, 1643).

Pázmány, Péter, *Az mostani támadt új tudományok hamisságának tíz nyilvánvalo bizonysága és rövid intés a török birodalomról és vallásról* (Graz, 1605).

—— *Egy keresztien predikatortul . . . Alvinczi Peter uramhoz iratot eot szep level* (Pozsony, 1609).

—— *Isteni igazságra vezérlő kalaúz* (Pozsony, 1613).

—— *Falsae originis motuum Hungaricorum succincta refutatio. Az magyarországi támadásoknak hamisan költött eredetének hamisitása* (Vienna, 1620).

—— *Rövid felelet két kálvinista könyvecskére* (Pozsony, 1620).

—— *Pázmány Péter művei*, ed. M. Tarnoc (Budapest, 1983).

Pécseli Király, Imre, *Consilium Ecclesiae Catholicae doctorum super ista quaestione: An homo Christianus possit et debeat se cognominare Lutheranum vel Calvinistam ad religionem puram ab impura recte discernendam?* (Kassa, 1621).

—— *Catechismus* (Lőcse, 1635).

[Perkins, William], *The Work of William Perkins*, ed. I. Breward (Abingdon, 1970).

Piscator, Ludwig, *Rudimenta Rhetorica* (Gyulafehérvár, 1635).

—— *Ars Poetica* (Gyulafehérvár, 1642).

—— *Rudimenta Oratorica* (Gyulafehérvár, 1645).

Polyander, Johannes, *Prima concertatio anti-Sociniana disputationibus XLVIII in Leydensi* (Amsterdam, 1640).

Pósaházi, János, *Igazság istápja . . . katekizmusi tanítás, melyben a ker. reformáta vallás . . . megmagyaráztatik, és az ellen tusakodó* (Sárospatak, 1669).

'Pozsony városának elöljárói evang. főiskola épitéséhez fogván, kérnek Lórántfi Zsuzsanna fejedelemnőtől', ed. S. Szilágyi, *MPEIF* 6 (1875), 153–4.

Prágai, András, *An Calviniani, quos vocant, Fundamentum Fidei Sartum, Tectum retineant?* (Heidelberg, 1617).

—— (tr.), *Fejedelmeknek serkentő oraja; azaz, Marcus Aurelius . . . életeről* (Bártfa, 1628).

—— 'Sebes agynak késő sisak', in B. Stoll and T. Komlovszki (eds.), *Régi Magyar Költők Tára. XVII század, 8. Bethlen Gábor korának költészete* (Budapest, 1976), 58–61.

Rákóczi, György I, *Instructio, quam tradidit Georgio Rakoci, filio suo* (Gyulafehérvár, 1638).

—— *Instructio, quam tradidit Sigismundo, filio suo* (Gyulafehérvár, 1640).

[Rákóczi György I], *Okmánytár I. Rákóczi György svéd és franczia szövetkezéseinek történetéhez*, ed. S. Szilágyi (Budapest, 1873).

—— *A két Rákóczy György fejedelem családi levelezése*, ed. S. Szilágyi (Monumenta Hungariae Historica, 24; Budapest, 1875).

—— 'I. Rákóczy György fejedelem levelezése Tolnai István sárospataki pappal', ed. S. Szilágyi, *PEIL* 18 (1875).

—— *Okirattár Strassburg Pál 1631–1633-iki követsége és I. Rákóczi György elsö diplomacziai összeköttetései történetéhez*, ed. S. Szilágyi (Budapest, 1882).

[Rákóczi György II], *Okmánytár II. Rákóczi György diplomacziai összeköttetéseihez*, ed. S. Szilágyi (Monumenta Hungariae Historica, 23; Budapest, 1874).

—— 'II. Rákóczi György fejedelem, a Geleji Katona féle kánonokat ünnepélyesen megerősiti', ed. I. Révész, *MPEIF* 7 (1876), 91–3.

—— 'Okiratok II. Rákóczy György diplomácziai összeköttetései történetéhez', ed. S. Szilágyi, *TT* (1889), 350–2, 476–9.

—— 'Diplomácziai okmányok II. Rákóczy György uralkodása történetéhez', ed. K. Wibling, *TT* (1893), 421–3.

—— 'II. Rákóczi György ismeretlen iskolatörvénye', ed. P. Török, *Erdélyi Irodalmi Szemle*, 4 (1927), 118–24.

[Rákóczi, Zsigmond], 'Herczeg Rákóczy Zsigmond levelezése', ed. S. Szilágyi, *TT* (1887), 417–62, 653–84; (1888), 104–19, 285–300; (1890), 229–60, 424–55, 597–636; (1891), 75–108, 209–36.

[Ramus, Petrus], *Petri Rami dialecticae libri duo . . . ungarico idiomate resoluti et illustrati*, ed. György Mártonfalvi (Utrecht, 1658).

Redmeczi, János, *Az felséges Bethlen Gábornak öt rendbeli Isten anyaszentegyházával cselekedett jótéteményéről* (Kassa, 1622; ed. L. Makkai, in *Erdélyi öröksége, 4* (Budapest, 1994), 24–46).

The Reformed Confessions of the 16th Century, ed. A. C. Cochrane (London, 1966).

[Roe, Thomas], *The Negotiations of Sir Thomas Roe in His Embassy to the Ottoman Porte from 1621–1628*, ed. S. Richardson (London, 1740).

Rycaut, Paul, *The History of the Turkish Empire from the Year 1623 to the Year 1677* (London, 1680).

Samarjai, János, *Magyar Harmónia; azaz, Augustana es az Helvetica confessio articulusinac eggyező értelme* (Pápa, 1628).

—— *Agenda. Az helvetiai vallason levő ecclesiaknak egyházi ceremoniajokrol es rend tartasokrol valo könyvetske* (Lőcse, 1636).

'A sárospataki ev. ref. főiskola 1621-iki törvényei', ed. R. Békefi, in *ÉTTK* 18/3 (Budapest, 1899), 44–73.

Segesvári, Bálint, 'Kronika, 1606–1654', in *ETA* 4 (Kolozsvár, 1862).

Selyei Balog, István, *Utitárs* (Nagyvárad, 1657).

Sepsi Laczkó, Máté, 'Krónika, 1521–1624', in *ETA* 3 (Kolozsvár, 1858), 119–246.

A Short Memorial of the Most Grievous Sufferings of the Ministers of the Protestant Churches in Hungary by the Instigation of the Popish Clergy there (London, 1676).

Siderius, János, *Kisded gyermekeknek való katechizmus, azaz a keresztyéni hitnek fő ágazatairúl rövid kérdések és feleletek által való tanitás* (Debrecen, 1597).

Somosi Petkó, János (tr.), *Igaz és tökéletes boldogságra vezérlő ut* (Sárospatak, 1656–8 [sic]).

Spanheim, Frederick, *Disputationum theologicarum syntagma (Miscellanearum pars prima) (pars secunda . . . Anti-Anabaptisticas controversias complectitur)* (Geneva, 1652).

Stoughton, John, *Felicitas ultimi saeculi* (London, 1640).

Szalárdi János és siralmas magyar krónikája, ed. F. Szakály (Budapest, 1980).

Szamosközy, István, *Erdély története (1598–9, 1603)* (Budapest, 1981).

Szárászi, Ferenc, *Catechesis; azaz, Kérdések és feleletek a kerestyéni tudománynak ágairól* (Debrecen, 1604).

Szathmári, Ötvös István (tr.), *A keresztyén . . . belgiomi ecclésiáknak hitekről való vallástétele* (Amsterdam, 1650).

Szatmári Baka, Péter, *Defensio Simplicitatis Ecclesiae* (Franeker, 1649).

—— *Defensio simplicitatis ecclesias Christi, . . . adversus Irenaei Simplicii Philadelphi Epistolam. Vindiciae Defensoris Simplicitatis Ecclesiae* (Franeker, 1653).

A szatmármegyében tartott négy első protestáns zsinat végzései, ed. Á. Kiss (Budapest, 1877).

'A szatmár-németi zsinat végzései, eddig ösmeretlen eredeti szerkezetökben', ed. I. Révész, *Sárospataki Füzetek*, 4 (1860), 244–7.

Széki, Ferenc, *De Orthodoxa Antiquitate et Heterodoxa Novitate* (Utrecht, 1656).

Szenci, Pál, *Reszegesek jajos pohara* (Debrecen, 1681).

Szenci Csene, Péter, *Confessio Helvetica; az az, Az keresztyeni igaz hitröl valo vallás-tétel* (Oppenheim, 1616).

—— *Confessio et expositio fidei Christianae, azaz, Az keresztyeni igaz hitről vallástétel, melyet . . . Helvetiában irtanak* (Sárospatak, 1654).

Szenczi Molnár, Albert, *Kis katekizmus . . . szedetött az heidelbergai öreg Katekizmusból* (Herborn, 1607).

—— *Psalterium Ungaricum* (Herborn, 1607).

—— *Szent Biblia* (Hanau, 1608).

—— *Szent Biblia . . . az palatinatusi katekizmussal* (Oppenheim, 1612).

—— (tr.), *Postilla Scultetica: az egész esztendő által való vasárnapokra és fő innepekre rendeltetett evangeliomi textusoknak magyarázatja* (Oppenheim, 1617).

—— *Secularis concio evangelica, azaz: Jubileus esztendei prédikáció Abraham Scultetus után* (Oppenheim, 1618).

—— *Syllecta Scholastica. Lexicon Latino-Graeco-Ungaricum* (Heidelberg, 1621).

—— *Imádságos könyvecske . . . az igaz religión való tanítóknak és mártíroknak az szentírás szerint szerzett új és ó könyveikből szedettek* (Heidelberg, 1621).

—— *A keresztyéni religióra és igaz hitre való tanitás* (Hanau, 1624).

—— *Consecratio templi novi, azaz az újonnan felépített bekecsi templomnak . . . megszentelésekor . . . tett prédikációk* (Kassa, 1625).

Szenczi Molnár Albert naplója, levelezése és irományai, ed. L. Dézsi (Budapest, 1898).

Szenci Molnár Albert válogatott művei, ed. J. Vásárhelyi and G. Tolnai (Budapest, 1976).

Szentpéteri, István, *Tancz Pestise* (Debrecen, 1697).

—— *Ördög szigonnya, avagy ama' káromkodásnak lelkétől eredett . . . való bányattyában 's búsúlásában* (Debrecen, 1699).

Szepsi Csombor, Márton, *Europica varietas* (1620), ed. S. Kovács and P. Kulcsár (Budapest, 1979).

—— *Udvari Schola, melyben . . . minden szép erkölcsökre . . . oktatja* (Bártfa, 1623).

Szepsi Korocz, György, *Basilikon Doron. Az Angliai, Scotiai, Franciai, es Hiberniai elsö Jacob kiralynac . . . fia tanitásáért irtt királyi ajándéka* (Oppenheim, 1612).

Szikszai Hellopoeus, Bálint, *Az egri keresztyén anyaszentegyháznak . . . rövid catechismus* (Debrecen, 1574).

—— *A mi keresztyéni hitünknek és vallásunknak három fő articulusárol . . . való könyvecske* (Debrecen, 1574).

Szilvásújfalvi Anderkó, Imre, *Admonitiones de ratione discendi, atque docendi* (Debrecen, 1597).

Szokolyai, István, *A szent Bibliának ótestamentumi könyveiből egybeszedegettetett . . . könyörgések. Sérelmes lelkeket gyógyitó balzsamom* (Leiden, 1648).

Sztárai, Mihály, *História a zsidó Ákháb királynak bálványozásáról* (Debrecen, 1619).

Telkibányai, István, *Angliai Puritanismus avagy kiválképpen való tudományok azoknak, kik Angliában a Puritánusok között (a mint közönségesen neveztetnek) legkeményebbeknek tartatnak* (Utrecht, 1654).

'Thállyai János Cambridge-i tanuló levele', ed. L. Kemény, *ITK* 19 (1909), 482–5.

Thúri, Pál, *Idea Christianorum ungarorum sub tyrannide Turcica* (Oppenheim, 1616).

'A tiszántúl ref. egyházkerület végzése a presbyteriumok ügyében, 1651 Sep. 3', ed. I. Révész, *MPEIF* 4 (1873), 98–9.

[Tiszántúl], *Adalékok a tiszántuli reformált egyházkerület történetéhez*, ed. S. Tóth (Debrecen, 1894).

Tolnai Dali, János, *Daneus Rácai* (Sárospatak, 1654).

Torda város tanácsai jegyzőkönyve, 1603–1678, ed. R. Wolf (Kolozsvár, 1993).

Tótfalusi Kis, Miklós, *Siralmas panasz Istennek kolozsváron fekvő nagy haragjáról* (Kolozsvár, 1697).

Tsepregi Turkovitz, Mihály, *A lelkiismeretnek akadékiról* (Amsterdam, 1648).

Úriszék xvi.–xvii. századi perszövegek, ed. E. Varga (Budapest, 1958).

'Az utrechti és leideni egyetemeken járt magyar ifjak névjegyzéke', ed. G. Antal, *PEIL* 31 (1888), 278–9, 409–12, 437–41.

Váczi, András, *A' Mi-Atyanknak avagy minden-napi imadsaggal való élésnek állatása és meg-óltalmazása e' mostani idöbéli tanetóknak ellenvetések ellen* (Kassa, 1653).

—— *Replica; azaz, Tolnai Dali Janosnak csufos és vados maga és mások mentésére való valasz-tetel* (Kassa, 1654).

[Várad], 'Constitutiones in generali synodo Varadina anno 1624, 1 die Julii', ed. J. Lugossy, *PEIL* 6 (1847), 235–6.

[Váradi], 'Egy gúnyirat a váradi ref. esperesség presbyterianus papjai ellen 1655-ből', ed. K. Szabó, *MPEIF* 1 (1870), 590–8.

[Váradi, Mihály], 'Váradi Mihály verse Bethlen Gábor haláláról', ed. L. Dézsi, *Magyar Könyvszemle*, 6 (1898), 372–84.

Vásárhelyi Kerekes, István, *Epitaphion katastrophikon; azaz, Szomoruságról örömre váltózó versek Bethlen Gábor erdélyi fejedelem tisztességére* (Nagyszeben, 1618).

Vedelius, Nicholas, *Opuscula theologica nova Nicolai Vedelii theologiae doctoris ac professoris in academia Franecquerana* (Franeker, 1651).

Veresmárti, Mihály, *Intő s tanitó levél* (Pozsony, 1639).

—— *Az eretnekeknek adott hitnek megtartásáról* (Pozsony, 1641).

—— 'Megtérése históriája' in *Magyar Emlékírók 16.–18. század* (Budapest, 1982), 123–84.

Voetius, Gisbert, *Selectarum disputationum theologicarum pars prima* (Utrecht, 1648).

—— *Theologiae in acad. Ultrajectina professoris, selectarum disputationum theologicarum pars secunda* (Utrecht, 1655).

—— 'Selectae Disputationes Theologiae', in J. W. Beardslee (ed.), *Reformed Dogmatics* (New York, 1965), 265–334.

'A wittenbergi egyetem magyarországi hallgatóinak névsora, 1601–1812', ed. M. Asztalos, in *MPEA* 14 (1930), 111–74.

Wollebius, Johann, *Christianae theologiae compendium* (Debrecen, 1634).

'A zempléni egyházmegye jegyzőkönyvéből', ed. L. Hegedüs, *Sárospataki Füzetek*, 1 (1857–8), 753–60, 972–81; 3 (1859), 338–58.

'A zempléni ref. dioecesis egyházlátogatási kerdőpontjai', ed. J. Zoványi, *Protestáns Szemle*, 18 (1906), 40–1.

'A zempléni ref. diocesis zsinatai, 1629–1645', ed. J. Zoványi, *TT* 10 (1909), 184–211, 406–38.

Zvonarics, György, *Rövid felelet, melyben Pécseli Imrének* ... *tanácsa meghamisittatik* ... *e kérdés felől: A keresztyén embernek kellesék-e lutheránusnak avagy kálvinistának nevezteni* (Csepreg, 1626).

(ii) Secondary sources

Acsády, I., 'Halotti búcsuztató 1633-ból', *ITK* 1 (1891), 131–6.

Adams, S. L., 'The Protestant Cause: Religious Alliance with the West European Calvinist Communities as a Political Issue in England, 1585–1630', D.Phil. thesis (Oxford, 1973).

—— 'Foreign Policy and the Parliaments of 1621 and 1624', in K. Sharpe (ed.), *Faction and Parliament: Essays on Early Stuart History* (Oxford, 1978), 139–72.

Ágoston, I., *A magyarországi puritanizmus gyökerei. Magyar puritánus törekvések a xvii. század első felében* (Budapest, 1997).

Akerman, S., 'Queen Christina of Sweden and Messianic Thought' in D. S. Katz, and J. Israel (eds.), *Sceptics, Millenarians and Jews* (Leiden, 1990), 142–61.

Angyal, D., 'Erdély politikai érintkezése angliával', *Századok*, 34 (1900), 309–25, 398–420, 495–508, 702–11, 873–904.

Angyal, P., and Degré, A. (eds.), *A xvi. és xvii. századi erdélyi büntetőjog vázlata* (Budapest, 1943).

Antal, G., *A magyar protestáns egyház külföldi érintkezései* (Pápa, 1908).

Ash, T. G., *The Uses of adversity. Essays on the fate of central Europe* (London, 1983).

Bahlcke, J., 'Calvinism and Estate Liberation Movements in Bohemia and Hungary (1570–1620)', in K. Maag (ed.), *The Reformation in Eastern and Central Europe* (Aldershot, 1997), 72–91.

Bák, J. M. and Király B. K. (eds.), *War and Society in Eastern Central Europe, 3. From Hunyadi to Rákóczi. War and Society in Late Medieval and Early Modern Hungary* (Brooklyn, Mass., 1982).

Bakos, J., 'Comenius az anyanyelvről és az anyanyelvi oktatás jelentőségéről', *Pedagógiai Szemle*, 20 (1970), 998–1,007.

Balázs, M., *Az erdélyi antitrinitarizmus az 1560-as évek végén* (Budapest, 1988).

—— *Ungarländische Antitrinitarier. Bibliotheca Dissidentium, 12. Répertoire des nonconformistes religieux des seizième et dix-septième siècles* (Baden-Baden, 1990).

Ball, B. W., *A Great Expectation: Eschatological Thought in English Protestantism to 1660* (Leiden, 1975).

Ballági, A., *A magyar nyomdászat történelmi fejlődése, 1472–1877* (Budapest, 1878).

Bán, I., 'Apáczai Csere János magyar enciklopediája', *Irodalomtörténet*, 35 (1953), 146–66.

—— *Apáczai Csere János* (Budapest, 1958).

—— 'Fejedelemeknek serkentő órája', *Irodalomtörténet*, 40 (1958), 360–73.

—— 'Comenius és a magyar szellemi élet', *Pedagógiai Szemle*, 8 (1958), 928–36.

—— 'The Literary and Cultural Significance of Seventeenth Century Hungarian Puritanism', in P. F. Barton and L. Makkai (eds.), *Rebellion oder Religion? Debrecen Colloquium 1976* (Budapest, 1977).

Barcsa, J., *A debreceni kollégium és partikulai* (Debrecen, 1905).

—— *A tiszántuli ev. ref. egyházkerület történelme* (Debrecen, 1906), 1–110.

Barcza, J., 'Siderius János kátéja', in T. Barth (ed.), *Tanulmányok és szövegek a magyarországi református egyház xvi. századi történetéből. Studia et acta ecclesiastica, 3* (Budapest, 1973), 849–76.

—— 'A puritanizmus kutatásának ujább eredményei', in *Theologiai Szemle*, 19 (1976), 333–6.

—— 'A vallási türelem elvi alapjai a xvii. század magyar protestáns teológiájában', *Theológiai Szemle*, 21 (1978), 282–91.

—— *Bethlen Gábor, a református fejedelem* (Budapest, 1980).

—— (ed.), *A debreceni református kollégium története* (Budapest, 1988).

Barnes, T. G., *Somerset, 1625–1640. A County's Government during the 'Personal Rule'* (Oxford, 1961).

Barta, G., 'A tolerancia társadalmi gyökerei: erdély a 16. században', in A. Miskolczy (ed.), *Europa. Balcanica-Danubiana-Carpathica* (Annales 2A; Budapest, 1995), 102–11.

Barth, T. (ed.), *Der Heidelberger Katechismus in Ungarn* (Budapest, 1967).

—— (ed.), *Tánulmányok és okmányok a magyarországi református egyház történetéből. Studia et acta ecclesiastica, 2. A második helvét hitvallás magyarországon és Méliusz életművei* (Budapest, 1967).

—— (ed.), *Tanulmányok és szövegek a magyarországi református egyház xvi. századi történetéből. Studia et acta ecclesiastica, 3* (Budapest, 1973).

Bartók, I., 'Medgyesi Pál: Doce Praedicare', *ITK* 85 (1981), 1–16.

Batten, J. M., *John Dury: Advocate of Christian Reunion* (Chicago, 1944).

Benda, K., 'Alvinczi Péter kassai prédikátor történeti följegyzései, 1598–1622', *Radáy Gyüjtemény Évkönyve*, 1 (1955), 5–26.

—— 'A kálvini tanok hatása a magyar rendi ellenállás ideológiájára', *Helikon*, 17 (1971), 322–30.

—— 'Le calvinisme et le droit de résistance des ordres hongrois au commencement du xviie siècle', in *Études Européennes. Mélanges offerts à Victor-Lucien Tapié* (Publications de la Sorbonne 6; Paris, 1973), 235–43.

—— 'La réforme en Hongrie', *Bulletin de la Société de l'histoire du Protestantisme Français*, 122 (1976), 30–53.

—— 'Le droit de résistance de la Bulle d'Or hongroise et le calvinisme', in B. Köpeczi and É. Balázs (eds.), *Noblesse Française, noblesse Hongroise xvie-xixe siècles* (Budapest–Paris, 1981), 155–63.

—— (ed.), *Magyarország történeti kronológiája, 2 (1526–1848)* (Budapest, 1989).

—— 'Habsburg Absolutism and the Resistance of the Hungarian Estates in the Sixteenth and Seventeenth Centuries', in R. J. W. Evans and T. V. Thomas (eds.), *Crown, Church and Estates. Central European Politics in the Sixteenth and Seventeenth Centuries* (London, 1991), 123–8.

Benrath, G. A., 'Die Theologische Fakultät der Hohen Schule Herborn im

Zeitalter der Reformierten Orthodoxie', *Jahrbuch der Hessischen Kirchengeschichtlichen Vereinigung*, 36 (1985), 1–17.

Bérenger, J., *A History of the Habsburg empire, 1273–1700* (London, 1990).

Berg, P., *Angol hatások tizenhetedik századi irodalmunkban* (Budapest, 1946).

Betts, R. R., 'Poland, Hungary and Bohemia: The Reformation in Difficulties' in G. R. Elton (ed.), *The New Cambridge Modern History, 2. The Reformation, 1520–59* (7th edn.) (Cambridge, 1987), 186–209.

Binder, L., 'Grundlagen und Formen der Toleranz in Siebenbürgen bis zur Mitte des 17. Jahrhunderts', *Siebenbürgisches Archiv*, 3rd ser. 11 (1976).

—— *Die Kirche der Siebenbürger Sachsen* (Erlangen, 1982).

Bireley, R., *Religion and Politics in the Age of the Counterreformation. Emperor Ferdinand II, William Lamormaini S.J., and the Formation of Imperial Policy* (Chapel Hill, NC, 1981).

Biró, V., *Az erdélyi fejedelmi hatalom fejlődése* (Kolozsvár, 1917).

—— *Bethlen Gábor és az erdélyi katholicizmus* (Kolozsvár, 1929).

Bitay, A., *Az erdélyi románok a protestáns fejedelemek alatt* (Dicsőszentmárton, 1925).

Bitskey, I., 'Irodalompolitika Bethlen Gábor és a két Rákóczi György udvarában', *Magyar Könyvszemle*, 96 (1980), 1–14.

—— 'Bethlen, Pázmány és a Káldi-Biblia', *Századok*, 115 (1981), 737–43.

—— *Pázmány Péter* (Budapest, 1986).

—— 'The Collegium Germanicum Hungaricum in Rome and the Beginning of Counter-Reformation in Hungary', in R. J. W. Evans and T. V. Thomas (eds.), *Crown, Church and Estates. Central European Politics in the Sixteenth and Seventeenth Centuries* (London, 1991), 110–22.

Blekastad, M., *Comenius. Versuch eines Umrisses von Leben, Werk, und Schicksal des Jan Amos Komensky* (Oslo, 1969).

Bodonhelyi, J., *A puritánizmus lelki élete és magyar hatásai* (Debrecen, 1942).

Borbáth, D., 'Medgyesi Pál homiletikája és Geleji Katona Istvánnal folytatott homiletikai vitája', *Református Szemle* (1961), 282–93.

Brauer, J. C., 'Puritanism: A Panel', *Church History*, 23 (1954), 99–118.

Brennen, C., 'The Life and Times of Isaac Basire', Ph.D. thesis (Durham, 1987).

Breslow, M. A., *A Mirror of England. English Puritan Views of Foreign Nations, 1618–1640* (Cambridge, Mass., 1970).

Brown, K. M., 'In Search of the Godly Magistrate in Reformation Scotland', *Journal of Ecclesiastical History*, 40 (1989), 553–81.

Bucsay, M., *Der Protestantismus in Ungarn, 1521–1798. Ungarns Reformationskirchen in Geschichte und Gegenwart, 1. Im Zeitalter der Reformation, Gegenreformation und katholischen Reform* (Vienna, 1977).

Bull, M. (ed.), *Apocalypse Theory and the Ends of the World* (Oxford, 1995).

Christianson, P., 'Reformers and the Church of England under Elizabeth I and the Early Stuarts', *Journal of Ecclesiastical History*, 31 (1980), 463–82.

Clasen, C. P., *The Palatinate in European History, 1559–1660* (Oxford, 1963).

Clive, H. P., 'The Calvinist Attitude to Music, and its Literary Aspects and Sources', *Bibliothèque d'Humanisme et Renaissance*, 19 (1957), 80–102.

Cohn, H. J., 'The Territorial Princes in Germany's Second Reformation, 1559–1622', in M. Prestwich (ed.), *International Calvinism, 1541–1715* (Oxford, 1985), 135–65.

Cohn, N., *The Pursuit of the Millennium* (London, 1957).

Cole, P., *A Neglected Educator: Johann Heinrich Alsted* (Sydney, 1910).

Collinson, P., 'The Elizabethan Puritans and the Foreign Reformed Churches in London', *Proceedings of the Huguenot Society*, 20/5 (1962–3), 528–55.

—— *The Elizabethan Puritan Movement* (London, 1967).

—— *The Religion of Protestants. Church in English Society, 1559–1625* (Oxford, 1982).

—— *English Puritanism* (Historical Association pamphlets, 106; London, 1983).

—— 'English and International Calvinism, 1558–1640', in M. Prestwich (ed.), *International Calvinism* (Oxford, 1985), 198–216.

—— *The Puritan Character. Polemics and Polarities in Early Seventeenth-Century English Culture* (Los Angeles, 1989).

Cottret, B., *The Huguenots in London. Immigration and Settlement, c. 1550–1700* (Cambridge, 1991).

Crăciun, M., and Ghitta, O. (eds.), *Ethnicity and Religion in Central and Eastern Europe* (Cluj, 1995).

Császár, K., *Medgyesi Pál élete és müködése* (Budapest, 1911).

Csernák, B., *A református egyház Nagyváradon, 1557–1660* (Nagyvárad, 1934).

Csipkay, S., *Magyar-holland irodalmi kapcsolatok kezdetei* (Budapest, 1935).

Csomasz Tóth, K., *A református gyülekezeti éneklés* (Budapest, 1950).

Csorba, C., Földy, F., and Ködöböcz, J. (eds.), *Comenius és Magyarország* (Sárospatak, 1990).

Cuming, C. J., 'Eastern Liturgies and Anglican Divines, 1510–1662', in D. Baker (ed.), *The Orthodox Churches and the West* (Studies in Church History, 13; Oxford, 1976), 231–8.

Cuno, F. W., 'Bisterfeld János Henrik', *MPEF* 4 (1882), 295–304.

Czegle, I., 'Amesius korai magyar tanítványai', in *Acta Historiae Litterarum Hungaricorum, 10–11*, ed. B. Keserű (Szeged, 1971).

—— 'A vizsolyi Biblia elöljáró beszéde', in T. Barth (ed.), *Tanulmányok és szövegek a magyarországi református egyház xvi. századi történetéből. Studia et acta ecclesiastica, 3* (Budapest, 1973), 517–36.

Dán, R., 'Héber hungaricák a xvi.–xvii. században', *Magyar Könyvszemle*, 81 (1965), 352–8.

—— 'Eőssi András és az erdélyi szombatosság genezise', *ITK* 78 (1974), 572–7.

—— 'Szenci Molnár Albert Angliában', *ITK* 83 (1979), 278–80.

—— 'Erdélyi könyvek és John Dee', *Magyar Könyvszemle*, 95 (1979), 225–30.

—— (ed.), *Antitrinitarianism in the Second Half of the Sixteenth Century* (Budapest, 1982).

—— 'Simon Péchi and Sabbatarianism', in L. Szczucki (ed.), *Socinianism and its Role in the Culture of the xvi-th to xviii-th Centuries* (Warsaw, 1983), 53–7.

Daniel, D. P., 'Ecumenicity or Orthodoxy: The Dilemma of the Protestants in the Lands of the Austrian Habsburgs', *Church History*, 49 (1980), 387–400.

—— 'The Fifteen Years War and the Protestant Response to Habsburg Absolutism in Hungary', *East Central Europe*, 8 (1981), 38–51.

—— 'Hungary', in A. Pettegree (ed.), *The Early Reformation in Europe* (Cambridge, 1992), 49–69.

—— 'Calvinism in Hungary: The Theological and Ecclesiastical Transition to the Reformed Faith', in A. Duke, A. Pettegree, and G. Lewis (eds.), *Calvinism in Europe, 1540–1620* (Cambridge, 1994), 205–30.

Davis, J. C., 'Formal Utopia/Informal Millennium: The Struggle between Form and Substance as a Context for Seventeenth-Century Utopianism', in K. Kumar and S. Bann (eds.), *Utopias and the Millennium* (London, 1993), 17–31.

Dawson, J., 'Calvinism and the Gaidhealtachd in Scotland', in A. Pettergree, A. C. Duke, and G. Lewis (eds.), *Calvinism in Europe, 1540–1620* (Cambridge, 1994), 231–53.

Demény, L., *Bethlen Gábor és kora* (Bucharest, 1982).

Dézsi, L., *Szenczi Molnár Albert* (Budapest, 1897).

Dezső, M., 'L'histoire des galériens Hongrois', *Bulletin de la Sociéte de l'histoire du Protestantisme Français*, 122 (1976), 54–65.

Diefendorf, B. B., 'The Huguenot Psalter and the Faith of French Protestants in the Sixteenth Century', in B. B. Diefendorf and C. Hesse (eds.), *Culture and Identity in Early Modern Europe (1500–1800)* (Michigan, 1993), 41–63.

Domján, I., 'A gyulafehérvári akadémia 1657 tanrendje', *Erdélyi Múzeum*, 13 (1896), 481–4.

Dömötör, T., *Naptári ünnepek-népi színjátszás* (Budapest, 1964).

Dósa, D., *A szászvárosi év. ref. Kún-kollégium története* (Szászváros, 1897).

Duke, A. C., 'Perspectives on European Calvinism' in A. Pettegree, A. C. Duke, and G. Lewis (eds.), *Calvinism in Europe, 1540–1620*, 1–20.

Durston, C., 'Puritan Rule and the Failure of Cultural Revolution', in C. Durston and J. Eales (eds.), *The Culture of English Puritanism, 1560–1700* (London, 1996), 210–33.

Eberhard, W., 'Bohemia, Moravia and Austria', in A. Pettegree (ed.), *The Early Reformation in Europe* (Cambridge, 1992), 23–48.

—— 'Reformation and Counterreformation in East Central Europe' in J. D. Tracey, T. A. Brady, and H. A. Oberman (eds.), *Handbook of European History, 1400–1600. Late Middle Ages, Renaissance and Reformation, 2. Visions, Programs and Outcomes* (Leiden, 1995), 552–84.

Ecsedy, J. V., 'A gyulafehérvári fejedelemi nyomda második korszaka (1637–58) és utóélete', *Országos Széchényi Könyvtár Évkönyve* (1978), 291–341.

—— 'Dobre mester erdélyi nyomdaja, 1640–1642', *Magyar Könyvszemle*, 109 (1993), 146–66.

Eszlary, C. d', 'Jean Calvin, Théodore de Bèze et leurs amis hongrois', *Bulletin de la Société de l'histoire du Protestantisme Français*, 110 (1964), 74–99.

Evans, R. J. W., 'Alsted és Erdély', *Korunk*, 32 (1973).

—— *The Making of the Habsburg Monarchy, 1550–1700* (Oxford, 1979).

—— *Rudolf II and His World: A Study in Intellectual History, 1576–1612* (Oxford, 1984).

—— 'Calvinism in East Central Europe: Hungary and Her Neighbours', in M. Prestwich (ed.), *International Calvinism, 1541–1715* (Oxford, 1985), 167–97.

—— and Thomas, T. V. (eds.), *Crown, Church and Estates. Central European Politics in the Sixteenth and Seventeenth centuries* (London, 1991).

Fábién, M., *A dunamelléki ref. egyházkerület története* (Sárospatak, 1867).

Fekete, C., and Király, L. (eds.), *Apáczai Csere János, 1625–1659* (Budapest, 1975).

Firth, K. R., *The Apocalyptic Tradition in Reformation Britain, 1565–1645* (Oxford, 1979).

Földes, E., and Mészáros, I. (eds.), *Comenius and Hungary* (Budapest, 1973).

Földváry, A., *Adalékok a dunamelléki év. ref. egyházkerület történetéhez* (Budapest, 1898).

—— *A magyar református egyház és a török uralom* (Budapest, 1940).

Fraknói, V., 'Bethlen Gábor és IV. Keresztély dán király', *TT* (1881), 98–113.

Frost, R. I., '"*Initium calamitatis regni*"? John Casimir and Monarchical Power in Poland-Lithuania, 1648–1668', *European History Quarterly*, 16 (1986), 181–209.

—— *After the Deluge. Poland-Lithuania and the Second Northern War, 1655–1660* (Cambridge, 1993).

Gál, I., 'Maksai Péter angol nyelvű Bethlen Gábor életrajza, 1629-ből', *ITK* 36 (1926), 223–38.

Gál, L., *Geleji Katona István igehirdetése* (Debrecen, 1939), 211–17.

Garside, C., 'The Origins of Calvin's Theology of Music: 1536–1543', *Transactions of the American Philosophical Society*, 69 (1979), 31–3.

Gelderen, M. van, *The Political Thought of the Dutch Revolt, 1555–1590* (Cambridge, 1992).

Gergely, S., 'I. Rákóczi György összeköttetése francziaországgal', *TT* (1889), 686–707; (1890), 59–76.

Gömöri, G., 'Szenci Molnár Albert művei és bibliakiadásai cambridgei könyvtárakban', in *Acta Historiae Litterarum Hungaricarum, 10–11* (Szeged, 1971), 297–301.

—— 'Some Hungarian *alba amicorum* from the Seventeenth Century', in J. Fechner (ed.), *Stammbücher als kulturhistorische Quellen* (Wolfenbütteler Forschungen, 2; Munich, 1981), 97–109.

—— 'Magyar peregrinusok a xvii. században Cambridge-ben', *ITK* 89 (1985), 194–202.

—— 'A fiatal Coccejus magyar barátai és tanítványai', in *Acta Historiae Litteraum Hungaricarum, 25* (Szeged, 1988), 189–96.

—— *Angol-Magyar kapcsolatok a xvi.–xvii. században. Irodalomtörténeti Füzetek* (Budapest, 1989).

—— 'Két levél a xvii. századból Tolnai Dali János levelezéséből', in B. Keserű (ed.), *Adattár 10. Collectanea Tibortiana* (Szeged, 1990), 331–7.

—— *Erdélyiek és angolok* (Budapest, 1991).

Gordon, B. (ed.), *Protestant History and Identity in Sixteenth-Century Europe, 2. The Later Reformation* (Aldershot, 1996), 91–107.

Graham, M. F., 'Equality before the Kirk? Church Discipline and the Elite in Reformation-Era Scotland', *Archiv für Reformationsgeschichte*, 84 (1993), 289–310.

Green, I. M., *The Re-Establishment of the Church of England, 1660–1663* (Oxford, 1978).

Greengrass, M., 'Samuel Hartlib and International Calvinism', *Proceedings of the Huguenot Society*, 25/5 (1993), 464–75.

—— Leslie, M., and Raylor, T. (eds.), *Samuel Hartlib and Universal Reformation. Studies in Intellectual Communication* (Cambridge, 1994).

Grell, O. P., 'The French and Dutch Congregations in London in the Early Seventeenth Century', *Proceedings of the Huguenot Society*, 24/5 (1987), 362–77.

—— *Dutch Calvinists in Early Stuart London* (Leiden, 1989).

—— 'Merchants and Ministers: The Foundations of International Calvinism', in A. Pettegree, A. C. Duke, and G. Lewis (eds.), *Calvinism in Europe, 1540–1620* (Cambridge, 1994), 254–73.

—— *Dutch Exiles in Tudor and Stuart England* (Aldershot, 1996).

—— and Scribner, R. (eds.), *Tolerance and Intolerance in the European Reformation* (Cambridge, 1996).

Griffiths, D. N., 'Isaac Basire, 1607–1676', *Proceedings of the Huguenot Society of London*, 17 (1986), 303–16.

Groenhuis, G., 'Calvinism and National Consciousness: The Dutch Republic as the New Israel', in A. C. Duke and C. A. Tamse (eds.), *Britain and the Netherlands, 7. Church and State since the Reformation* (The Hague, 1981), 118–34.

Gulyás, J., *A sárospataki ref. főiskola rövid története* (Sárospatak, 1931).

Hangay, Z., *Erdély választott fejedelme* (Budapest, 1987).

Haraszy, K. (ed.), *Az ungi református egyházmegye* (Nagykapos, 1931).

Hargittay, E., 'A fejedelmi tükör műfaja a 17. századi magyarországon és erdélyben', *ITK* 99 (1995), 441–84.

Harrington, J. F., and Smith, H. W., 'Confessionalization, Community, and State Building in Germany, 1555–1870', *Journal of Modern History*, 69 (1997), 77–101.

Harsányi, I., 'A Rákóczi könyvtár és katalógusa', *Magyar Könyvszemle*, 38 (1913), 17–28, 136–47, 232–40, 341–4.

—— 'Miskolczi Csulyak István élete és munkái, 1575–1645', *Theológiai Szemle*, 2 (1926), 562–86.

Hazagh, M., 'Amesius és a magyar puritanizmus', *Angol Filológiai Tanulmányok*, 4 (1942), 94–112.

Hegedűs, J., 'Megjegyzések Szenczi Molnár Albert nyelvészeti munkásságához', *ITK* 62 (1958), 45–52.

Hegedüs, L., 'A tiszáninneni helv. hitv. egyházmegyék kormányzata a Carolina resolutio kiadatása elött', *Sárospataki Füzetek*, 3 (1859), 475–83.

Hellebrant, Á., 'Adalék a külföldi iskolázás történetéhez a xvii. században', *Századok*, 17 (1883), 154–5.

Heltai, J., 'Adattár a heidelbergi egyetemen 1595–1621 között tanult magyarországi diákokról és pártfogóikról', *Országos Széchenyi Könyvtár Évkönyve* (1980), 243–345.

—— 'Bethlen Gábor és Báthori Gábor viszonya a kortársak szemében', *Irodalomtörténet*, 65 (1983), 685–708.

—— 'Irénikus eszmék és vonások Pécseli Király Imre mű veiben', in B. Varjas (ed.), *Irodalom és ideológia a 16–17. században. Memoria Saeculorum Hungariae, 5* (Budapest, 1987), 209–30.

—— 'David Pareus magyar kapcsolatai', in J. Herner (ed.), *Adattár 23. Tudóslevelek; Mű velő désünk külföldi kapcsolataihoz, 1577–1797* (Szeged, 1989), 13–77.

—— *Alvinczi Péter és a heidelbergi peregrinusok* (Budapest, 1994).

—— '"Szent Atyák Öröme": Medgyesi Pál és Vásárhelyi Dániel hitvitája', in A. Miskolczy (ed.), *Europa. Balcanica-Danubiana-Carpathica. Annales 2A* (Budapest, 1995), 224–35.

Herepei, J., 'Szenci Molnár Albert tragédiája', *ITK* 70 (1966), 160–5.

Herner, J. (ed.), *Adattár 23. Tudóslevelek; Mű velő désünk külföldi kapcsolataihoz, 1577–1797* (Szeged, 1989).

Hill, C., *Society and Puritanism in Pre-Revolutionary England* (London, 1966).

—— *Antichrist in Seventeenth Century England* (London, 1971).

—— 'Till the Conversion of the Jews', in R. H. Popkin (ed.), *Millenarianism and Messianism in English Literature and Thought, 1650–1800* (Leiden, 1988), 12–37.

Hintze, O., 'Calvinism and raison d'état in Early Seventeenth Century Brandenburg', in F. Gilbert (ed.), *The Historical Essays of Otto Hintze* (New York, 1975), 88–156.

Holden, W. P., *Anti-Puritan Satire, 1572–1642* (New Haven, Conn., 1954).

Hóman, B., and Szekfű, Gy., *Magyar történet* (5 vols.; Budapest, 1935), vols. 3–4.

Hotson, H., 'Johann Heinrich Alsted', D.Phil. thesis (Oxford, 1994).

—— 'Philosophical Pedagogy in Reformed Central Europe between Ramus and Comenius: A Survey of the Continental Background of the "Three foreigners"', in M. Greengrass, M. Leslie, and T. Raylor (eds.), *Samuel Hartlib and Universal Reformation. Studies in Intellectual Communication* (Cambridge, 1994), 29–50.

—— 'Irenicism and Dogmatics in the Confessional Age: Pareus and Comenius in Heidelberg, 1614', *Journal of Ecclesiastical History*, 46 (1995), 432–53.

—— 'Johann Heinrich Alsted's Relations with Silesia, Bohemia and Moravia: Patronage, Piety and Pansophia', *Acta Comeniana*, 12 (1997), 13–35.

Hsia, R. Po-Chia, *Social Discipline in the Reformation: Central Europe, 1550–1750* (London, 1989).

Hughes, G., *Swearing. A Social History of Foul Language, Oaths and Profanity in English* (Oxford, 1991).

Hunfalvy, P., 'Az oláh káté', *Századok*, 20 (1886), 475–90.

Illyés, E., *Egyházfegyelem a magyar református egyházban* (Debrecen, 1941).

Illyés, G., 'Az Apafiak szerepe a küküllői református egyházmegye történetében', *Református Szemle* (1930), 468–72, 482–6.

—— 'A református esperes és az egyházmegyei kormányzás a 17. és 18. században', *Református Szemle* (1932), 179–83, 213–18.

—— 'A papmarasztás az erdélyi református egyházban', *Református Szemle* (1936), 110–6.

Imre, S., *Alvinczi Péter* (Marosvásárhely, 1898).

Imreh, I., *A törvényhozó székely falu* (Bucharest, 1983).

—— *Székelyek a múló időben* (Budapest, 1987).

Incze, G., *A magyar református imádság a xvi. és xvii. században* (Debrecen, 1931).

Ingram, M., *Church Courts, Sex and Marriage, 1570–1640* (Cambridge, 1987).

—— 'Puritans and the Church Courts, 1560–1640', in C. Durston and J. Eales (eds.), *The Culture of English Puritanism, 1560–1700* (London, 1996), 58–91.

Ipolyi, A., *Veresmárti Mihály* (Budapest, 1875).

Irinyi, K., and Benda, K. (eds.), *A négyszáz éves debreceni nyomda (1561–1961)* (Budapest, 1961), 7–59, 313–408.

Israel, J., *The Dutch Republic. Its Rise, Greatness, and Fall, 1477–1806* (Oxford, 1995).

Jakab, A., 'Az erdélyi római katolikus püspöki szék betöltésének vitája a xvii. században', *Erdélyi Múzeum*, 49 (1944), 5–20.

Jakab, B., *Opitz Márton a gyulafehérvári Bethlen-iskolánál* (Pécs, 1909).

Jakab, E., 'Erdély és az anabaptisták a xvii.–xviii. században', *Keresztény Magvető*, 11 (1876), 1–14.

Jakó, Zs., 'Miskolci Csulyak István peregrinációs albuma', in Keserű, B. (ed.), *Acta Historiae Litterarum Hungaricarum, 10–11* (Szeged, 1971), 59–71.

—— *A Bethlen kollégium könyvtárának kezdetei és első korszaka* (Kolozsvár, 1973).

Jankovics, J., Galavics, G., and Várkonyi, Á. R. (eds.), *Régi erdélyi viseletek* (Budapest, 1990).

Jensma, G. T., Smit F. R. H., and Westra, F. (eds.), *Universiteit te Franeker 1585–1811* (Leeuwarden, 1985).

Josten, C. H., and Sherwood Taylor, F., 'Johannes Banfi Hunyades, 1576–1650', *Ambix* (1953–5).

Juhász, I., *A reformáció az erdélyi románok között* (Kolozsvár, 1940).

—— *A székelyföldi református egyházmegyék* (Kolozsvár, 1947).

Juhász, I., 'Az erdélyi egyházak 17. századi együttélésének kérdései a fogarasi vártartományban', *Ráday Gyűjteménye Évkönyve*, 4–5 (1984–5), 9–27.

—— and Jakó, Zs. (eds.), *Nagyenyedi diákok, 1662–1848* (Bucharest, 1979).

Káldos, J., *Ungarländische Antitrinitarier II. György Enyedi* (Bibliotheca Dissidentium, 15; Baden-Baden, 1993), 41–5.

Kann, R., and David, Z., *The Peoples of the Eastern Habsburg Lands, 1526–1918* (A History of East Central Europe, 6; London, 1984).

Kaplan, B. J., 'Dutch Particularism and the Calvinist Quest for "Holy Uniformity"', *Archiv für Reformationsgeschichte*, 82 (1991), 239–56.

—— *Calvinists and Libertines. Confession and Community in Utrecht, 1578–1620* (Oxford, 1995).

Kathona, G., *Samarjai János gyakorlati theológiája* (Debrecen, 1939).

—— *Károlyi Gáspár történelmi világképe* (Debrecen, 1943).

Kathona, G., *Fejezetek a török hódoltsági reformáció történetéből* (Budapest, 1974).

—— 'Pótlások az 1711-ig angliában tanult magyar diákoknévsorához', *ITK* 80 (1976), 92–8.

—— 'A debreceni és sárospataki tanulók részvétele a hollandiai és angliai peregrinációban 1623-tól 1711-ig', *Theológiai Szemle*, 22 (1979), 89–94.

Kavka, F., 'Bohemia', in B. Scribner, R. Porter, and M. Teich (eds.), *The Reformation in National Context* (Cambridge, 1994), 131–54.

Kelemen, B., 'Ioan Zoba és a puritanizmus', in E. Csetri, Zs. Jakó, and S. Tonk (eds.), *Művelődéstörténeti tanulmányok* (Budapest, 1979), 116–20.

Kemény, L., 'Alvinczy Péter életéhez', *ITK* 14 (1904), 112–19, 234–46, 364–7, 490–500; 17 (1907), 243–8; 20 (1910), 102–6; 21 (1911), 366–9.

Kendall, R. T., *Calvin and English Calvinism to 1649* (Oxford, 1979).

Keserű, B., (ed.) *Adattár 1. Polgári irodalmi és kulturális törekvések a tizenhetedik század első felében* (Budapest–Szeged, 1965).

—— (ed.) *Adattár 2. Apáczai és kortársai* (Budapest–Szeged, 1966).

—— 'Újfalvi Imre és a magyar későreneszánsz', in *Acta Historiae Litterarum Hungaricarum*, viii, 3–16; ix 3–47 (Szeged, 1968).

—— (ed.) *Adattár 3. Művelődési törekvések a század második felében* (Szeged, 1971).

—— (ed.) *Adattár 4. Szenci Molnár Albert és a magyar késő reneszánsz* (Szeged, 1978).

Kingdon, R. M., *Geneva and the Consolidation of the French Protestant Movement, 1564–1572* (Geneva, 1967).

—— 'Calvinism and Resistance Theory, 1550–1580', in J. H. Burns (ed.), *The Cambridge History of Political Thought, 1450–1700* (Cambridge, 1991), 193–219.

—— 'International Calvinism', in J. D. Tracey, T. A. Brady, and H. A. Oberman (eds.), *Handbook of European History, 1400–1600. Late Middle Ages, Renaissance and Reformation, 2: Visions, Programs and Outcomes* (2 vols.; Leiden, 1995), 229–47.

—— *Adultery and Divorce in Calvin's Geneva* (Cambridge, Mass., 1995).

Kis, E., *A dunántuli ev. ref. egyházkerület pápai főiskolájának története, 1531–1895* (Pápa, 1896).

Kiss, É. S., 'Diákzendülések a debreceni kollégiumban', in I. Mészáros (ed.), *Tanulmányok a magyar nevelésügy xvii.–xx. századi történetéből* (Budapest, 1980), 31–9.

Kiss, K., *A szatmári reform. egyházmegye története* (Kecskemét, 1878).

Kiss Rugonfalvi, I., *Az egyházi rend közjogi helyzete Erdélyben és Bethlen Gábor armalisa* (Debrecen, 1936).

Kiss, S., 'Szilvásújfalvi Anderko Imre', *Egyháztörténet*, 5 (1959), 218–41.

Kittelson, J. M., 'The Confessional Age: The Late Reformation in Germany', in S. Ozment (ed.), *Reformation Europe: A Guide to Research* (St Louis, Mo., 1982), 361–81.

Klaniczay, G., 'Hungary: The Accusations and the Universe of Popular Magic', in B. Ankarloo and G. Henningsen (eds.), *Early Modern European Witchcraft* (Oxford, 1990), 219–57.

—— 'Witch-Hunting in Hungary: Social or Cultural Tensions?', in G. Klaniczay, *The Uses of Supernatural Power. The Transformation of Popular Religion in Medieval and Early-Modern Europe* (Cambridge, 1990), 151–67.

Koenigsberger, H. G., *The Habsburgs and Europe, 1516–1660* (Cornell, NY, 1971).

Kohn, S., *A szombatosok: történetük, dogmatikájuk és irodalmuk* (Budapest, 1890).

Kolozsvári, J., 'Egyházi fegyelemre, rendtartásra vonatkozó határozatok a berekereszturi ref. egyházközségben az 1602 évben', *Református Szemle*, (1933), 469–75.

Koltay, K., 'Two Hundred Years of English Puritan Books in Hungary', *Angol Filológiai Tanulmányok*, 20 (1989), 53–64.

—— 'Perkins és Ames recepciója Magyarországon 1660-ig', in A. Tamás and I. Bitskey (eds.), *Studia Litteraria. Tanulmányok a xvi.–xvii. századi magyar irodalomból* (Budapest, 1991), 99–109.

Koltay-Kastner, J., 'Tótfalusi Kis Miklós coccejánizmusa', *ITK* 58 (1954), 284–99.

Komjáthy, G., *Adalékok az ungvári ev. ref. egyház történetéhez* (Ungvár, 1906).

Komlovszki, T., 'Egy manierista *"theatrum europaeum"* és szerzője', *ITK* 70 (1966), 85–105.

Komor, I., 'Tanulmányok a xvii. századi magyar-német kulturális érintkezések köréből. Martin Opitz gyulafehérvári tanársága', *Filológiai Közlöny*, 1 (1955), 534–44.

—— 'Schola ludus', *Pedagógiai Szemle*, 8 (1958), 975–90.

—— 'Comenius a pataki ifjúság iskolánkivüli neveléséről', *Pedagógiai Szemle*, 10 (1960), 888–98.

—— 'Comenius in Sárospatak; Apáczai in Gyulafehérvár', *Acta Litteraria Academiae Scientiarum Hungaricae* (1960), 191–204.

Komor, I., 'A Comenius utópia alkotmánya', *Pedagógiai Szemle*, 20 (1970), 916–22.

Koncz, A., *Debreczen város régi büntető joga* (Debrecen, 1913).

Koncz, J., *A marosvásárhelyi evang. reform. kollégium története* (Marosvásárhely, 1896).

—— 'Geleji Katona István könyveinek lajstroma', *Magyar Könyvszemle*, 24 (1899), 270–6.

Köpeczi, B. (ed.), 'Bethlen Gábor és állama', *Századok*, 115 (1981), 659–750.

—— (gen. ed.), *Erdély története* (3 vols.; Budapest, 1988); i, L. Makkai and A. Mócsy (eds.); ii, L. Makkai and Z. Szász (eds.).

—— (gen. ed.), *History of Transylvania* (Budapest, 1994).

Kós, K. *Erdély* (Kolozsvár, 1934).

Kovács, K. (ed.), *Bethlen Gábor állama és kora. Bethlen-bibliográfia, 1613–1980* (Budapest, 1980).

Kristóf, Gy., 'Zsidó, görög és latin gyászversek Bethlen Gábor temetésére', *Erdélyi Múzeum*, 36 (1931), 90–7.

Kropf, L., 'Basirius Izsák életrajzához', *TT* (1889), 491–502.

Kundera, M., 'The Tragedy of Central Europe', *The New York Review of Books*, 31/7 (April 1984), 33–8.

Kúr, G., *A komáromi református egyházmegye* (Pozsony, 1993).

Kvacsala, J. V., 'Comenius és a Rákóczyak', *Budapesti Szemle* (1889), 113–51.

—— 'Egy álpróféta a xvii-ik században', *Századok*, 23 (1889), 745–66.

—— 'Johann Heinrich Alstedt', *Ungarische Revue*, 9 (1889), 628–42.

—— 'A xvii. századbeli chiliasmus történetéhez', *Protestáns Szemle*, 2 (1890), 428–50.

—— 'Bisterfeld János Henrik élete', *Századok*, 25 (1891), 447–78, 545–77.

—— 'Az angol-magyar érintkezések történetéhez, 1620–1670', *Századok*, 26 (1892), 709–19, 793–810.

—— 'II. Rákóczy György fejedelemsége történetéhez', *TT* (1893), 673–7.

Lake, P., *Moderate Puritans and the Elizabethan Church* (Cambridge, 1982).

—— 'Puritan Identities', *Journal of Ecclesiastical History*, 35 (1984), 112–23.

—— 'Calvinism and the English Church, 1570–1635', *Past and Present*, 114 (1987), 32–76.

Lamperth, G., *A pápai református főiskola története, 1531–1931* (Pápa, 1931).

Laurentzy, V., 'Apáczai Csere János calendarium perpetuuma', *Debreceni Szemle*, 7 (1933), 257–66.

Lecler, J., *Toleration and Reformation* (2 vols.; London, 1960).

Lewis, G., 'The Genevan Academy', in A. Pettegree, A. C. Duke, and G. Lewis (eds.), *Calvinism in Europe, 1540–1620* (Cambridge, 1994), 35–63.

Lindeboom, J., *Austin Friars. History of the Dutch Reformed Church in London, 1550–1950* (The Hague, 1950).

Liu, T., *Puritan London. A Study of Religion and Society in the City Parishes* (Newark, NJ., 1986).

Loemker, L. E., 'Leibniz and the Herborn Encyclopedists', *Journal of the History of Ideas*, 22 (1961), 323–38.

—— *Struggle for Synthesis: The Seventeenth Century Background of Leibniz's Synthesis* (Cambridge, Mass., 1972).

Lugossy, J., 'Máramarosi egyházmegye a xvii. században', *PEIL* 6 (1847), 1418–20.

—— 'Nagybányai, máskép aranyasmeggyesi egyházvidék személyzete a xvii. században', *Protestáns Szemle*, 6 (1847), 186–91.

Lukinich, I., *Erdély területi változásai a török hódítás korában, 1541–1711* (Budapest, 1918).

—— *A Bethlen-fiúk külföldi iskoláztatása, 1619–1628* (Budapest, 1926).

Lunsingh Scheurleer, T. H. and Posthumus Meyjes, G. H. M. (eds.), *Leiden University in the Seventeenth Century. An Exchange of Learning* (Leiden, 1975).

Lupás, J., 'Varlaam, Moldova mitropolitája (1632–1653)', *Református Szemle* (1935), 217–25, 348–56.

Lynch, M., 'Calvinism in Scotland, 1559–1638', in M. Prestwich (ed.), *International Calvinism, 1541–1715* (Oxford, 1985), 225–55.

Maag, K., *Seminary or University? The Genevan Academy and Reformed Higher Education, 1560–1620* (Aldershot, 1995).

—— (ed.), *The Reformation in Eastern and Central Europe* (Aldershot, 1997).

—— and Pettegree, A., 'The Reformation in Eastern and Central Europe', in K. Maag (ed.), *The Reformation in Eastern and Central Europe* (Aldershot, 1997), 1–18.

MacHardy, K. J., 'The Rise of Absolutism and Noble Rebellion in Early Modern Habsburg Austria, 1570–1620', *Comparative Studies in Society and History*, 34 (1992), 407–38.

McNeill, J. T., *The History and Character of Calvinism* (New York, 1954).

Magyarósi, I., *A zilahi ev. ref. anyaszentegyház története* (Kolozsvár, 1880).

Makár, J., *Kanizsai Pálfi János élete és munkássága* (New Brunswick, N. Y., 1961).

Makkai, L., *Histoire de Transylvanie* (Paris, 1946).

—— *A magyar puritánusok harca a feudálizmus ellen* (Budapest, 1952).

—— 'Tolnai Dali János harca a haladó magyar kultúráért', *ITK* 57 (1953), 236–49.

—— *A felsőtiszavidéki parasztfelkelés, 1631–1632* (Budapest, 1954).

—— 'The Hungarian Puritans and the English Revolution', *Acta Historica*, 5 (1958), 13–45.

—— 'Gentis Felicitas', *Pedagógiai Szemle*, 8 (1958), 964–72.

—— *Studia et Acta Ecclesiastica, n.s. 1. In Memoriam Eliberationis Verbi Divini Ministrorum Hungaricorum ad Triremes Condemnatorum 1676* (Budapest, 1976).

—— 'A magyar puritánok történetszemlélete', *Theológiai Szemle*, 21 (1978), 342–5.

—— 'Puritánok és boszorkányok Debrecenben', *A Hajdú-Bihar Megyei Levéltár Évkönyve*, 8 (1981), 113–30.

—— 'A kollégium története alapitásától 1650-ig', in *A sárospataki református kollégium* (Budapest, 1981), 17–59.

Makkai, L., 'Bethlen Gábor és az európai művelődés', *Századok*, 115 (1981), 673–97.

—— 'István Bocskai's Insurrectionary Army', in J. M. Bák and B. K. Király (eds.), *From Hunyadi to Rákóczi. War and Society in Late Medieval and Early Modern Hungary* (Brooklyn, Mass., 1982), 275–97.

—— 'Nemesi köztársaság és kálvinista teokrácia a 16. századi Lengyelországban és Magyarországon', *Ráday Gyűjtemény Évkönyve*, 3 (1983), 17–29.

—— 'The Crown and the Diets of Hungary and Transylvania in the Sixteenth Century', in R. J. W. Evans and T. V. Thomas (eds.), *Crown, Church and Estates. Central European Politics in the Sixteenth and Seventeenth Centuries* (London, 1991), 80–91.

Mandelbrote, S., 'John Dury and the Practice of Irenicism', in N. Aston (ed.), *Religious Change in Europe, 1650–1914. Essays for John McManners* (Oxford, 1997), 41–59.

Marczali, H. (ed.), 'Regesták a külföldi levéltárakból', *TT* (1879), 539–57.

Márki, S., 'Cromwell és Erdély', *Erdélyi Múzeum*, 18 (1901), 16–37.

Marton, J., *A sárospataki református főiskola története, 1621-ig* (Sárospatak, 1931).

Matar, N. I., 'The Comenian Legacy in England: The Case for the Conversion of the Muslims', *The Seventeenth Century*, 8 (1993), 203–15.

Menk, G., 'Das Restitutionsedikt und kalvinistische Wissenschaft. Die Berufung Johann Heinrich Alsteds, Philipp Ludwig Piscators und Johann Heinrich Bisterfelds nach Siebenbürgen', *Jahrbuch der Hessischen Kirchengeschichtlichen Vereinigung*, 31 (1980), 29–63.

Mentzer, R. A., '*Disciplina nervus ecclesiae*: The Calvinist Reform of Morals at Nîmes', *Sixteenth Century Journal*, 18 (1987), 89–115.

—— 'Le consistoire et la pacification du monde rural', *Bulletin de la Société de l'histoire du Protestantisme Français*, 135 (1989), 373–89.

Mészáros, I., *Az iskolaügy története Magyarországon, 996–1777 között* (Budapest, 1981).

—— 'Comenius és a sárospataki kollégium anyanyelvi osztálya', *Magyar Pedagógia*, 72 (1972), 185–97.

Meszlényi, A., *A magyar jezsuiták a xvi. században* (Budapest, 1931).

Miklós, Ö., 'Ki a Trecentumviratus szerzője?', *Magyar Könyvszemle*, 31 (1916), 256–8.

—— 'Statorius János lengyel socinianus lelkész levele Frank Ádám kolozsvári unitárius lelkészhez, 1638-ből', *Keresztény Magvető*, 52 (1917), 68–85.

—— 'Apáczai Cseri János utrechtbe történt meghivásáról', *Dunántuli Protestáns Lap* (1917), 178–81, 186–9.

—— *Magyar diákok a leideni staten collegeben* (Debrecen, 1928).

—— 'Presbiteriális elemek a magyar protestáns egyház ősi szervezetében', *Protestáns Szemle*, 47 (1935), 457–64.

—— *A magyar protestáns egyházalkotmány kialakulása a reformáció században* (Pápa, 1942).

Milton, A., *Catholic and Reformed. The Roman and Protestant Churches in English Protestant Thought, 1600–1640* (Cambridge, 1995).

Moens, W. J. C. (ed.), *The Walloons and Their Church at Norwich: Their History and Registers* (Huguenot Society of London, 1; 1887–8).

Mokos, Gy., *Adalékok a dunamelléki reform. püspökök életéhez* (Pápa, 1892).

Moller, J. G., 'The Beginnings of Puritan Covenant Theology', *Journal of Ecclesiastical History*, 14 (1963), 46–67.

Monok, I, 'Johannes Henricus Bisterfeld és Enyedi György két levelezés-kiadásban', *Magyar Könyvszemle*, 103 (1987), 317–27.

—— 'Johannes Polyander magyar kapcsolataihoz', in J. Herner (ed.), *Adattár 23. Tudóslevelek; Művelődésünk külföldi kapcsolataihoz, 1577–1797* (Szeged, 1989), 89–115.

Monter, E. W., *Calvin's Geneva* (New York, 1967).

—— 'The Consistory of Geneva, 1559–1569', *Bibliothèque d'Humanisme et Renaissance*, 38 (1976), 467–84.

Mout, N., 'Chiliastic Prophecy and Revolt in the Habsburg Monarchy during the Seventeenth Century', in M. Wilks (ed.), *Prophecy and Eschatology* (Studies in Church History, Subsidia, 10; Oxford, 1994), 93–109.

Mózes, A., 'A xvi.–xvii. századbeli protestáns román káték', *Református Szemle*, 29 (1936), 340–5.

Müller, M. G., 'Protestant Confessionalization in the Towns of Royal Prussia and the Practice of Religious Toleration in Poland–Lithuania', in O. P. Grell and R. Scribner (eds.), *Tolerance and Intolerance in the European Reformation* (Cambridge, 1996), 231–49.

Muller, R. A., 'Perkins' A Golden Chaine: Predestinarian System or Schematized *ordo salutis?*', *Sixteenth Century Journal*, 9 (1978), 69–82.

Murdock, G., 'International Calvinism, Ethnic Allegiance, and the Reformed Church of Transylvania in the Early Seventeenth Century', in M. Crăciun and O. Ghitta (eds.), *Ethnicity and Religion in Central and Eastern Europe* (Cluj, 1995), 92–100.

—— 'The Experience of Péter Körmendi. Foreign Calvinist Students' Contact with Presbyterians and Puritans in England', in M. Balázs et al (eds.), *Adattár 35. Művelődési törekvések a korai újkorban. Tanulmányok Keserű Bálint tiszteletére* (Szeged, 1997), 433–52.

—— 'The Importance of Being Josiah: An Image of Calvinist Identity', *Sixteenth Century Journal*, 29 (1998), 1,043–59.

Murphy, D., *Comenius. A Critical Reassessment of His Life and Work* (Dublin, 1995).

Nagy, B. K., 'Szilvásújfalvi Imre pedagógiai intelmei', in *Studia et Acta Ecclesiastica*, 3 (Budapest, 1955), 879–87.

—— 'A heidelbergi káté jelentkezése, története és kiadásai magyarországon a xvi és xvii században', in T. Barth (ed.), *Tánulmányok és okmányok a magyarországi református egyház történetéből. Studia et acta ecclesiastica*, 2 (Budapest, 1967), 15–92.

Nagy, G., 'Geleji Katona István személyisége levelei alapján', *Erdélyi Múzeum*, 47 (1940), 35–52.

—— *Geleji Katona István eschatologiája* (Budapest, 1941).

—— *Fejezetek a magyar református egyház 17. századi történetéből* (Budapest, 1985).

Nagy, B. S., and Szentimray, M., 'Szikszai Hellopoeus Bálint kátéja', in T. Barth (ed.), *Tanulmányok és szövegek a magyarországi református egyház xvi. századi történetéből. Studia et acta ecclesiastica, 3* (Budapest, 1973), 929–1,001.

Nagy, S., *A debreceni kollégium* (Debrecen, 1940).

Náhlik, Z., 'Lórántffy Zsuzsanna fogarasi román iskolája', in I. Mészáros (ed.), *Tanulmányok a magyar nevelésügy xvii.–xx. századi történetéből* (Budapest, 1980), 17–29.

Naményi, L., 'A nagyváradi nyomdászat története', *Magyar Könyvszemle*, 16 (1901), 280–91.

Naphy, W. G., *Calvin and the Consolidation of the Genevan Reformation* (Manchester, 1994).

Németh, G. (ed.), *Hegyaljai mezővárosok 'törvényei' a xvii–xviii. századból* (Budapest, 1990).

Nischan, B., 'The Second Reformation in Brandenburg: Aims and Goals', *Sixteenth Century Journal*, 14 (1983), 173–87.

—— 'The Schools of Brandenburg and the "Second Reformation": Centers of Calvinist Learning and Propaganda', in R. V. Schnucker (ed.), *Calviniana. Ideas and Influence of Jean Calvin* (Sixteenth Century Essays and Studies, 10; Kirksville, Mo., 1988), 215–33.

—— *Prince, People and Confession. The Second Reformation in Brandenburg* (Philadelphia, Pa., 1994).

—— 'Confessionalism and Absolutism: The Case of Brandenburg', in A. Pettegree, A. Duke, and G. Lewis (eds.), *Calvinism in Europe, 1540–1620* (Cambridge, 1994), 181–204.

Oberman, H. A., '*Europa afflicta*: The Reformation of the Refugees', *Archiv für Reformationsgeschichte*, 85 (1992), 91–111.

Odlozilík, O., 'A Church in a Hostile State: The Unity of Czech Brethren', *Central European History*, 6 (1973), 111–27.

Oestreich, G., *Neostoicism and the Early Modern State* (Cambridge, 1982).

Ong, W. J., *Ramus: Method and the Decay of Dialogue* (Cambridge, Mass., 1958).

Opalinski, E., 'The Local Diets and Religious Tolerance in the Polish Commonwealth (1587–1648)', *Acta Poloniae Historica*, 68 (1993), 43–57.

Orient, Gy., *Erdélyi alchimisták. Bethlen Gábor fejedelem alchimiája* (Kolozsvár, 1927).

Orosz, L., 'Apáczai kolozsvári helyezése és az 1656-i erdélyi iskolatörvény', *Pedagógiai Szemle*, 10 (1960), 162–9.

Ötvös, A., 'Geleji Katona István élete és levelei I. Rákóczi Györgyhöz', *Új Magyar Múzeum*, 10 (1859), 199–233.

Pánek, J., 'The Question of Toleration in Bohemia and Moravia in the Age of the Reformation', in O. P. Grell and R. Scribner (eds.), *Tolerance and Intolerance in the European Reformation* (Cambridge, 1996), 262–81.

Parker, G., *The Thirty Years War* (London, 1984).

—— 'The "Kirk by Law Established" and the Origins of "The Taming of Scotland"*: St Andrews, 1559–1600', in L. Leneman (ed.), *Perspectives in Scottish Social History: Essays in Honour of Rosalind Mitchison* (Aberdeen, 1988), 1–33.

Parker, K. L., *The English Sabbath* (Cambridge, 1988).

Patterson, W. B., 'James I and the Huguenot Synod of Tonneins of 1614', *Harvard Theological Review*, 65 (1972), 241–70.

Paulinyi, O., 'Iratok Kassa szabad király város 1603–1604 ben megkisérelt rekatolizálásának történetéhez', in *MPEA* 14 (1930), 57–61.

Payr, S., *A Magyar protestáns papi öltöny története* (Sopron, 1935).

Péter, K., 'Az 1608 évi vallásügyi törvény és a jobbágyok vallásszabadsága', *Századok*, 111 (1977), 93–113.

—— 'Drabík Miklós, a lehoktai próféta', *Világosság*, 18 (1977), 36–41.

—— 'Two Aspects of War and Society in the Age of Prince Gabor Bethlen of Transylvania', in J. M. Bak and B. K. Király (eds.), *War and Society in Eastern Central Europe, 3. From Hunyadi to Rákóczi: War and Society in Late Medieval and Early Modern Hungary* (New York, 1982), 297–313.

—— 'A bibliaolvasás mindenkinek szóló programja magyarországon a 16. században', *Századok*, 119 (1985), 1,006–28.

—— 'The Struggle for Protestant Religious Liberty at the 1646–47 Diet in Hungary', in R. J. W. Evans and T. V. Thomas (eds.), *Crown, Church and Estates. Central European Politics in the Sixteenth and Seventeenth Centuries* (London, 1991), 261–8.

—— 'Hungary', in R. Scribner, R. Porter, and M. Teich (eds.), *The Reformation in National Context* (Cambridge, 1994), 155–68.

—— *Papok és nemesek. Magyar művelődéstörténeti tanulmányok a reformációval kezdődő másfél évszázadból* (Budapest, 1995).

—— 'Tolerance and Intolerance in Sixteenth-Century Hungary', in O. P. Grell and R. Scribner (eds.), *Tolerance and Intolerance in the European Reformation* (Cambridge, 1996), 249–61.

Péter, M., *A rikánbelőli kommunitás ismertetése és rövid története* (Sepsiszentgyörgy, 1909).

Pettegree, A., 'The Clergy and the Reformation: From "Devilish Priesthood" to New Professional Elite', in A. Pettegree (ed.), *The Reformation of the Parishes* (Manchester, 1993), 1–22.

—— Duke, A. C., and Lewis, G. (eds.), *Calvinism in Europe, 1540–1610. A Collection of Documents* (Manchester, 1992).

——, ——, and —— (eds.) *Calvinism in Europe, 1540–1620* (Cambridge, 1994).

Pettkó, B., 'Külföldi alumnusok levelei', *TT* (1885), 179–84.

338 Bibliography

Pirnát, A., *Die Ideologie der Siebenbürger Antitrinitarier in den 1570er Jahren* (Budapest, 1961).

Pócsi, K., 'Pataki Füsüs János királytükrének jelképrendszeréről', *Irodalomtörténet*, 74 (1992), 99–114.

Pokoly, J., 'Az első magyar ref. presbyterium keletkezése és szervezete', *Protestáns Szemle*, 2 (1890), 202–20.

——— 'Az erdélyi fejedelemek viszonya a protestáns egyházakhoz', *Protestáns Szemle*, 8 (1896), 546–61, 608–24.

——— *Az erdélyi református egyház története* (5 vols.; Budapest, 1904).

Polišenský, J. V., 'Comenius, magyarország és az európai politika a xvii. században', *Magyar Pedagógia*, 72 (1972), 179–84.

——— 'Comenius, Hungary, and European Politics in the Seventeenth Century', in E. Földes and I. Mészáros (eds.), *Comenius and Hungary* (Budapest, 1973).

Pongrácz, J., *Magyar diákok angliában* (Pápa, 1914).

Ponting, K. G., *The Woollen Industry of South-West England* (Bath, 1971).

Postma, F., *Disputationes Exercitii Gratia: Een inventarisatie van disputaties verdedigd onder Sibrandus Lubbertus Prof. Theol. te Franeker, 1585–1625* (Amsterdam, 1985).

Prestwich, M. (ed.), *International Calvinism, 1541–1715* (Oxford, 1985).

Rácz, I., *A hajdúk a xvii. században* (Debrecen, 1969).

——— *Tanulmányok erdély történetéről* (Debrecen, 1988).

Rácz, L., *Comenius Sárospatakon* (Budapest, 1931).

——— 'Vallási türelem erdély- és magyarországon', *Protestáns Szemle*, 46 (1934), 198–204.

Rácz, L., 'I. Rákóczi György erdélyi állama', *Jogtudományi Közlöny* (1981), 495–502.

——— 'Főhatalom a xvi.–xvii. századi erdélyben', *Jogtudományi Közlöny* (1981), 857–64.

Rady, M., 'A Transylvanian Alchemist in Seventeenth-Century London', *Slavonic and Eastern European Review*, 72 (1994), 140–51.

Raitt, J., 'Elizabeth of England, John Casimir, and the Protestant League', in D. Visser (ed.), *Controversy and Conciliation. The Reformation and the Palatinate, 1559–1583* (Allison Park, Pa., 1984), 117–45.

Rákosi, G., 'Erdély református egyházközségi élet a xvii. században', in *MPEA* 1 (1902), 31–49.

Ráth, Gy., 'A felsőmagyarországi kryptokálvinisták hitvitázó irodalmáról', *ITK* 2 (1892), 310–24.

——— 'Bullinger Henrik és a magyar reformáczió', *ITK* 6 (1896), 42–58.

Ravasz, L., 'A magyar protestáns igehirdetés a xvii. században', *Theológiai Szaklap* (1913), 262–84.

Regan, P., 'Calvinism in the Dutch Israel Thesis', in B. Gordon (ed.), *Protestant History and Identity in Sixteenth-Century Europe, 2. The Later Reformation* (Aldershot, 1996), 91–107.

Reinhard, W., 'Reformation, Counter-Reformation, and the Early Modern State. A Reassessment', *Catholic Historical Review*, 75 (1989), 383–404.

Révész, I., 'Adalék a magyar puritánok történetéhez', *Sárospataki Füzetek*, 2 (1858–9), 717–25.

—— 'A debreceni főiskoláról', *MPEIF* 1 (1870), 275–90, 391–427.

Révész, I., 'Bethlen Gábor, a kálvinista fejedelem', *Protestáns Szemle*, 26 (1914), 339–58.

—— 'Szempontok a magyar kalvinizmus eredetéhez', *Századok*, 68 (1934), 257–75.

—— 'Debrecen lelki válsága 1561–1571', in *ÉTTK* 25/6 (Budapest, 1936).

—— *A reformáció az erdélyi oláhok között* (Budapest, 1938).

—— *A szatmárnémeti nemzeti zsinat és az első magyar református ébredés* (Budapest, 1947).

—— *Társadalmi és politikai eszmék a magyar puritánizmusban* (Budapest, 1948).

—— (ed.) *A magyar református egyház története* (Budapest, 1949).

—— *A History of the Hungarian Reformed Church* (Budapest, 1956).

Révész, K., 'A presbyterium legelső nyomai hazai református egyházunkban', *Protestáns Szemle*, 4 (1892), 419–46.

—— 'Egy régi vers a táncz ellen', *ITK* 3 (1893), 449–56.

—— *Százéves küzdelem a kassai református egyház megalakulásáért, 1550–1650* (Budapest, 1894).

—— 'Bocskay István apologiája', *Protestáns Szemle*, 18 (1906), 304–12.

Révész, M., 'Protestáns unió és az erdélyi reformátusok', *MPEF* 9 (1887), 167–86.

Roberts, M., *From Oxenstierna to Charles XII. Four Studies* (Cambridge, 1991).

Román, J., *A sárospataki kollégium* (Budapest, 1956).

Rood, W., *Comenius and the Low Countries* (Prague, 1970).

Ruzsás, L., *A pápai kollégium története* (Budapest, 1981).

Sadler, J. E., *J. A. Comenius and the Concept of Universal Education* (London, 1966).

Schama, S., *The Embarrassment of riches* (London, 1987).

Schilling, H. (ed.), *Die Reformierte Konfessionalisierung in Deutschland. Das Problem der 'Zweiten Reformation'* (Gütersloh, 1985).

—— ' "History of Crime" or "History of Sin"?', in E. I. Kouri and T. Scott (eds.), *Politics and Society in Reformation Europe* (London, 1987), 289–310.

—— 'Die Konfessionalisierung im Reich. Religiöser und gesellschaftlicher Wandel in Deutschland zwischen 1555 und 1620', *Historische Zeitschrift*, 246 (1988), 1–45.

—— *Civic Calvinism in Northwestern Germany and the Netherlands. Sixteenth to Nineteenth centuries* (Sixteenth Century Essays and Studies, 16; (Kirksville, Mo., 1991).

—— 'The Second Reformation: Problems and Issues', in H. Schilling, *Religion, Political Culture and the Emergence of Early Modern Society. Essays in German and Dutch history* (Leiden, 1992), 205–301.

Schilling, H., 'Confessional Europe', in J. D. Tracey, T. A. Brady, and H. A. Oberman (eds.), *Handbook of European History, 1400–1600. Late Middle Ages, Renaissance and Reformation, 2: Visions, Programs and Outcomes* (2 vols.; Leiden, 1995), 641–81.

Schlegl, I., 'Die Beziehungen Heinrich Bullinger zu Ungarn', *Zwingliana. Beiträge zur Geschichte Zwinglis, der Reformation und des Protestantismus in der Schweiz*, 12 (1966), 330–70.

Schmidt, H. R., 'Die Ächtung des Fluchens durch reformierte Sittengericht', in P. Blickle (ed.), *Der Fluch und der Eid. Die metaphysische Begründung gesellschaftlichen Zusammenlebens und politischer Ordnung in der ständischen Gesellschaft*. (Zeitschrift für Historische Forschung, 15; Berlin, 1993), 65–120.

—— 'Moral Courts in Rural Berne during the Early Modern Period', in K. Maag (ed.), *The Reformation in Eastern and Central Europe* (Aldershot, 1997), 155–81.

Schneller, I., 'Comenius és Apáczai', *Protestáns Szemle*, 30 (1918), 27–39.

Schwarz, I., 'Magyar alchimisták', *Természettudományi Közlöny*, 23 (1891), 57–70.

Scribner, R., Porter, R., and Teich, M. (eds.), *The Reformation in National Context* (Cambridge, 1994).

Sebestyén, K., 'A kolozs-kalotai (kalotaszegi) református egyházmegye népoktatásának adattára a xv. századtól 1900-ig', *MPEA* 17 (Budapest, 1993).

Sebestyén, M., 'Maksai Őse Péter; gyulafehérvári rector', *Magyar Könyvszemle*, 110 (1994), 203–7.

Segesváry, L., *Magyar református ifjak az utrechti egyetemen 1636–1686* (Debrecen, 1935).

Serisier, P., 'Le projet de transférer des Camisards en Hongrie: Échec en 1704 d'un dessein royal', *Bulletin de la Société de l'histoire du Protestantisme Français*, 138 (1992), 119–34.

Setton, K. M., *Venice, Austria and the Turks in the Seventeenth Century* (Philadelphia, 1991).

Shaw, W. A., *A History of the English Church during the Civil Wars and under the Commonwealth, 1640–1660* (2 vols.; London, 1900).

Sík, S., *Pázmány, az ember és az író* (Budapest, 1939).

Simonyi, E., *Londoni magyar okmánytár, 1521–1717* (Pest, 1859).

Sipos, G., *Olvasmánytörténeti dolgozatok 1. A kolozsvári református kollégium könyvtára a xvii. században* (Szeged, 1991).

Smith, A. D., *The Ethnic Origins of Nations* (Oxford, 1986).

Soltész, J., *A nagybányai reformált egyházmegye története* (Nagybánya, 1902).

Somas, A., and Labrousse, E., 'Le registre consistorial de Coutras, 1582–1584', *Bulletin de la Société de l'histoire du Protestantisme Français*, 126 (1980), 193–228.

Sörös, B., *A magyar liturgia története* (Budapest, 1904).

Spielman, J. P., *Leopold I of Austria* (London, 1977).

Spinka, M., *John Amos Comenius. That Incomparable Moravian* (Chicago, 1943).

—— 'Comenian Pansophic Principles', *Church History*, 22 (1953), 155–65.

Sprunger, K. L., 'Ames, Ramus and the Method of Puritan Theology', *Harvard Theological Review* (1966), 133–52.

—— 'Technometria: A Prologue to Puritan Theology', *Journal of the History of Ideas*, 29 (1968), 115–22.

—— *The Learned Doctor William Ames* (Chicago, 1972).

—— *Dutch Puritanism* (Leiden, 1982).

—— 'English and Dutch Sabbatarianism and the Development of Puritan Social Theology (1600–1660)', *Church History*, 51 (1982), 24–38.

Spufford, M., 'Puritanism and Social Control?', in A. Fletcher and J. Stevenson (eds.), *Order and Disorder in Early Modern England* (Cambridge, 1985), 41–57.

Stieg, M., *Laud's Laboratory. The Diocese of Bath and Wells in the Early Seventeenth Century* (London, 1982).

Subtelny, O., *Domination of Eastern Europe. Native Nobilities and Foreign Absolutism* (Gloucester, 1986).

Sugar, P. F., *Southeastern Europe under Ottoman Rule, 1354–1804* (A History of East Central Europe, 5; London, 1977).

—— et al. (eds.), *A History of Hungary* (London, 1990).

Szabó, G., *Geschichte des Ungarischen Coetus an der Universität Wittenberg, 1555–1613* (Halle, 1941).

—— *A magyar református orthodoxia a xvii. század theológiai irodalma* (Budapest, 1943).

Szabó, I., *Tanulmányok a magyar parasztság történetéből* (Budapest, 1948).

Szabó, K., 'A gyulafehérvári Bethlen féle főtanoda szervezeti szabályzata', *TT* (1879), 797–805.

Szabó, M., 'Erdélyi diákok külföldi egyetemjárása a xvi.-xviii. században', in Zs. Jakó, S. Tonk, and E. Csetri (eds.), *Művelődéstörténeti tanulmányok* (Bucharest, 1980), 152–68.

Szathmáry, K. P., *A gyulafehérvári-nagyenyedi Bethlen-főtanoda története* (Nagyenyed, 1868).

Szathmáry, L., *Magyar alkémisták* (Budapest, 1986).

Szekfű, Gy., *Bethlen Gábor* (Budapest, 1929).

Szilágyi, I., 'A máramarossziget református tanoda történeteinek rövid vázlata', *Sárospataki Füzetek*, 1 (1857–8), 957–71.

—— 'A máramarosi helv. hitvallású egyházmegye és egyházközségek rendezete a 17. század elején', *Sárospataki Füzetek*, 2 (1858–9), 382–91, 678–89, 984–6.

Szilágyi, S., 'A kolozsvári egyház történetéhez', *EPK* (1874), 165–6, 172–4.

—— 'A Tolnai-per történetéhez', *MPEIF* 5 (1874), 35–42.

—— 'Az unitáriusok egyháztörténelméhez a xvii.-ik században', *Keresztény Magvető*, 11 (1876), 62–4.

—— 'Bethlen Gábor fejedelem uralkodása történetéhez', *TT* (1879), 219–61, 429–65, 742–86.

—— 'A sárospataki egyház és iskolai történetéhez', *MPEF* 7 (1885), 497–501.

—— 'Lónyay Zsigmond pere saját papjaival', *MPEF* 8 (1886), 147–9.

Szilágyi, S., 'Medgyesy Pál életéhez', *Protestáns Szemle*, 2 (1890), 146–54.

—— 'Comenius egy ismeretlen munkája', *TT* (1890), 202–4.

Szilágyi, S. and Orbán, B., 'Az unitáriusok 1638-diki üldöztetéseinek s a deési complanatiónak történetéhez', *Keresztény Magvető*, 9 (1874), 150–62.

Szimonidesz, L., 'A sárospataki ref. főiskolában és sárospatak környéke iskoláiban használt, ismert és ismeretlen tankönyvek', *Magyar Könyvszemle*, 58 (1942), 410–13.

Szinyei, G., 'Adalék Komáromi Csipkés György életéhez és irodalmi működéséhez', *MPEIF* 6 (1875), 72–82.

—— 'A sárospataki főiskola Comenius előtt és Comenius idejében', *Sárospataki Lapok* (1898), 294–7, 325–7, 359–63, 385–8, 454–60.

Szombathi, J., *A sárospataki főiskola története*, ed. J. Gulyás and G. Szinyei (Sárospatak, 1919).

Tappe, E., 'The Rumanian Orthodox Church and the West', in D. Baker (ed.), *The Orthodox Churches and the West*, (Studies in Church History, 13; Oxford, 1976), 277–91.

Takács, B., *Bibliai jelképek a magyar református egyházművészetben* (Budapest, 1986).

Takáts, S., *Művelődéstörténeti tanulmányok a xvi–xvii századból*, ed. K. Benda (Budapest, 1961).

Tanka, E., 'Rudabányai A. Mátyás levele tuniszból 1678 Dec. 1', *Lymbus Füzetei*, 6 (1989).

Tarnóc, M., 'Szalárdi János történetszemlélete', *ITK* 74 (1970), 689–96.

—— *Erdély művelődése Bethlen Gábor és a két Rákóczi György korában* (Budapest, 1978).

Teodor, P., 'Mihai Viteazul's Confessional Policy in Transylvania', in P. Teodor (ed.), *Colloquia. Journal of Central European History*, 1 (Cluj, 1994), 87–103.

Thály, K., 'Egykorú tudósítás I. Károly angol király kivégeztetéséről, 1649', *TT* (1879), 396–8.

Thomas, K., *Religion and the Decline of Magic* (London, 1978).

Thury, E., *A dunántúli református egyházkerület története* (Pápa, 1908).

Thurzó, F., *A nagybányai ev. ref. főiskola (schola Rivulina) története, 1547–1755* (Nagybánya, 1905).

Toon, P. (ed.), *Puritan Eschatology* (Cambridge, 1970).

Török, I., *A kolozsvári ev. ref. collégium története* (Kolozsvár, 1905).

Tóth, B., 'Ramus hatása Debrecenben', *Könyv és Könyvtár*, 17 (1979), 85–107.

Tóth, E., *A pápai református egyház története* (Pápa, 1941).

—— 'A második helvét hitvallás története magyarországon', in T. Barth (ed.), *Tánulmányok és okmányok a magyarországi reformatús egyház történetéből. Studia et acta ecclesiastica, 2. A második helvét hitvallás magyarországon és Méliusz életművei* (Budapest, 1967), 11–53.

Toth Somlyói, T., 'Erdélyi királytükör', in B. Varjas (ed.), *Irodalom és ideológia a 16–17. században* (Memoria Saeculorum Hungariae, 5; Budapest, 1987), 275–93.

Toth, W., 'Highlights of the Hungarian Reformation', *Church History*, 9 (1940), 141–56.

Trevor-Roper, H., *Archbishop Laud, 1573–1645* (London, 1962).

——— 'Three Foreigners: The Philosophers of the Puritan Revolution', in H. Trevor-Roper (ed.), *Religion, the Reformation and Social Change* (London, 1967).

——— 'The Church of England and the Greek Church in the Time of Charles I', in D. Baker (ed.), *Religious Motivation* (Studies in Church History, 15; Oxford, 1978), 213–40.

Trócsányi, B., 'Református theológusok Angliában a xvi. és xvii. században', *Angol Filológiai Tanulmányok*, 6 (1944), 115–46.

Trócsányi, Zs., *Az erdélyi fejedelemség korának országgyűlései* (Budapest, 1976).

——— 'Bethlen Gábor erdélyi állama', *Jogtudományi Közlöny* (1980), 617–22.

——— *Erdélyi központi kormányzata, 1540–1690* (Budapest, 1980).

——— 'I. Rákóczi György erdélyi állama', *Jogtudományi Közlöny* (1981), 495–502.

Turnbull, G. H., *Samuel Hartlib: A Sketch of His Life and His Relations to J. A. Comenius* (Oxford, 1920).

——— 'An Incomplete *Orbis Pictus* of Comenius Printed in 1653', *Acta Comeniana*, 16 (1957), 35–40.

——— *Hartlib, Dury and Comenius* (London, 1947).

Underdown, D., *Somerset in the Civil War and Interregnum* (Newton Abbot, 1973).

Uray, P., 'Az irénizmus magyarországon a 16–17. század fordulóján', in B. Varjas (ed.), *Irodalom és ideológia a 16–17. században* (Memoria Saeculorum Hungariae, 5; Budapest, 1987), 187–207.

Vane, C. M., 'The Walloon Community in Norwich: The First Hundred Years', *Proceedings of the Huguenot Society*, 24/2 (1984), 129–40.

Varga, A., 'Az altdorfi egyetem magyar diákjai (1583–1718)', *Lymbus. Művelődéstörténeti Tár*, 5 (Szeged, 1994).

Varga, B., *Szenci Molnár Albert. A magyar zsoltáréneksszerző élete és írói működése* (Budapest, 1932).

Vargha, A., *Iustus Lipsius és a magyar szellemi élet* (Budapest, 1942).

Vári, A., 'Kapcsolatok az erdélyi unitáriusok és a hollandiai remonstránsok között', *Keresztény Magvető*, 67 (1932), 109–20, 167–83.

Várkonyi, Á. R. (ed.), *Magyarország története* [gen. ed. P. Zs. Pach, 10 vols.], *iii pts 1–2 (1526–1686)* (Budapest, 1987).

——— 'Comenius éjszakái', *Liget* (1993), 46–57.

——— 'Pro quite regni; az ország nyugalmáért', *Protestáns Szemle* (1993), 260–77.

Várkonyi, G., *II. Rákóczy György esküvője* (Budapest, 1990).

Varó, F., *Bethlen Gábor kollégiuma* (Nagyenyed, 1903).

Vásárhelyi, J., *Eszmei áramlatok és politika Szenci Molnár Albert életművében* (Budapest, 1985).

Veress, E., *Olasz egyetemeken járt magyarországi tanulók anyakönyvei és iratai* (Budapest, 1941).

Vogler, B., 'Europe as Seen through the Correspondence of Theodore Beza', in E. I. Kouri and T. Scott (eds.), *Politics and Society in Reformation Europe* (London, 1987), 252–66.

—— and Estèbe, J., 'La genèse d'une société protestante: Étude comparée de quelques registres consistoriaux Languedociens et Palatins vers 1600', *Annales*, 31 (1976), 362–88.

Walzer, M., *The Revolution of the Saints: A Study in the Origins of Radical Politics* (London, 1966).

Watt, J. R., 'Women and the Consistory in Calvin's Geneva', *Sixteenth Century Journal*, 24 (1993), 429–39.

Webster, C., *Samuel Hartlib and the Advancement of Learning* (Cambridge, 1970).

—— *The Great Instauration. Science, Medicine and Reform, 1626–1660* (London, 1975).

Welsby, P. A., *George Abbot. The Unwanted Archbishop, 1562–1633* (London, 1962).

Whitebrook, J. C., 'Dr J. Stoughton the Elder', *Transactions of the Congregational Historical Society*, 6 (1913–15), 89–107, 177–84.

Wilbur, E. M., *A History of Unitarianism. Socinianism and Its Antecedents* (Cambridge, Mass., 1946).

—— *A History of Unitarianism in Transylvania, England and America* (Cambridge, Mass., 1952).

Williams, G. H., *The Radical Reformation* (Philadelphia, Pa., 1962).

Wittman, T., 'A magyarországi államelméleti tudományosság xvii. század eleji alapvetésének németalföldi forrásaihoz: Justus Lipsius', *Filológiai Közlöny*, 3 (1957), 53–66.

Wolff, L., *Inventing Eastern Europe. The Map of Civilization on the Mind of the Enlightenment* (Stanford, Calif., 1994).

Yates, F. A., *Lull and Bruno. Collected Essays, 1* (London, 1982).

Zach, K., *Orthodoxe Kirche und Romänisches Volksbewusstsein im 15. bis 18. Jahrhundert* (Wiesbaden, 1977).

Zayzon, F., *A székelyudvarhelyi evang. reform. egyházközség története* (Székelyudvarhely, 1893).

Zoványi, J., 'Coccejus és theológiai rendszere', *Protestáns Szemle*, 2 (1890), 78–104, 241–66.

—— 'Ki volt a Szathmári Baka Péter irodalmi ellenfele?', *Protestáns Szemle*, 18 (1906), 379–82.

—— *Kisebb dolgozatok a magyar protestantizmus történetének köréből* (Sárospatak, 1910).

—— *Puritánus mozgalmak a magyar református egyházban* (Budapest, 1911).

—— *A reformáczió magyarországon 1565-ig* (Budapest, 1921).

—— (ed.), 'Protestáns lelkészek nyugtatványai régi tizedjegyzékek mellett' in *MPEA* 13 (1929), 5–142.

—— *A tiszántúli református egyházkerület története* (Debrecen, 1939).

—— *A magyarországi protestántizmus 1565-től* (Budapest, 1977).

—— (ed.) *Magyarországi protestáns egyháztörténeti lexikon*, (3rd edn., ed. S. Ladányi; Budapest, 1977).

Zsigmond, F., *A debreceni református kollégium története 1538–1938* (Debrecen, 1938).

Zsilinszky, E., *Polemikus irodalmunk a xvi. és xvii.-ik században* (Budapest, 1891).

Zsilinszky, M., *A magyar országgyűlések vallásügyi tárgyalásai a reformátiotól kezdve* (Budapest, 1880).

—— *A linczi békekötés és az 1647-ki vallásügyi törvényczikkek története* (Budapest, 1890).

Zsindely, E., 'Bullinger Henrik magyar kapcsolatai', in T. Barth (ed.), *Tánulmányok és okmányok a magyarországi református egyház törtétenéből. Studia et acta ecclesiastica, 2. A második helvét hitvallás magyarországon és Méliusz életművei* (Budapest, 1967), 55–86.

—— 'Svájci levelesláda a reformáció korából', in T. Barth (ed.), *Tánulmányok és szövegek a magyarországi református egyház xvi. századi történetéből. Studia et acta ecclesiastica, 3* (Budapest, 1973), 929–1,001.

INDEX